RAF Bomber Command Profiles

408 (Goose) Squadron RCAF

RAF Bomber Command Profiles

408 (Goose) Squadron RCAF

Chris Ward

www.aviationbooks.org

This edition first published 2024 by Aviation Books Ltd., 25 Cromwell Street, Merthyr Tydfil, CF47 8RY.

Copyright 2024 © Chris Ward.

The right of Chris Ward to be identified as Author of this work is asserted by him in accordance with the Copyright, Designs and Patents Act 1988.

The original Operational Record Book of 408 Squadron RCAF and the Bomber Command Night Raid Reports are Crown Copyright and stored in microfiche and digital format by the National Archives. Material is reproduced under Open Licence v. 3.0.

All rights reserved. No part of this publication may be reproduced, stored in a retrieval system, transmitted in any form or by any means, electronic, mechanical, or photocopied, recorded or otherwise, without the written permission of the copyright owners.

This squadron profile has been researched, compiled and written by its author, who has made every effort to ensure the accuracy of the information contained in it. The author will not be liable for any damages caused, or alleged to be caused, by any information contained in this book. E. & O.E.

Every effort is made to trace the copyright holders of photographs and we apologise in advance for any unintentional omissions. These and other errors brought to our attention will be corrected in subsequent editions of this Profile.

Cover design: Topics - The Creative Partnership www.topicsdesign.co.uk

Photos and captions: Clare Bennett

A CIP catalogue reference for this book is available from the British Library.

ISBN 9781915335357

Also by Chris Ward from Bomber Command Books:

Casualty of War: Letters Home from Flight Lieutenant Bill Astell DFC

Dambuster Deering: The Life and Death of an Unsung Hero

Dambusters : The Complete WWII History of 617 Squadron
(with Andy Lee and Andreas Wachtel)

Other RAF Bomber Command Profiles:

IX Squadron
10 Squadron (with Ian MacMillan)
35 (Madras Presidency) Squadron
44 (Rhodesia) Squadron
49 Squadron
50 Squadron
57 Squadron
75(NZ) Squadron (with Chris Newey)
83 Squadron
101 Squadron
102 (Ceylon) Squadron
103 Squadron (with David Fell)
106 Squadron (with Herman Bijlard)
115 Squadron
138 Squadron (with Piotr Hodyra)
207 Squadron (with Raymond Glynne-Owen)
300 Squadron (with Grzegorz Korcz)
301, 304 and 305 Squadrons (with Grzegorz Korcz)
460 Squadron RAAF
467 Squadron RAAF
514 Squadron (with Simon Hepworth)
617 Squadron
619 Squadron

Table of Contents

Introduction 9
Dedication 11
Narrative History 12
June and July 1941 12
August 1941 13
September 1941 19
October 1941 22
November 1941 28
December 1941 33
January 1942 39
February 1942 45
March 1942 51
April 1942 58
May 1942 66
June 1942 73
July 1942 80
August 1942 87
September 1942 94
October to December 1942 98
January 1943 128
February 1943 132
March 1943 139
April 1943 147
May 1943 156
June 1943 161
July 1943 167
August 1943 175
September 1943 181
October 1943 185
November 1943 191
December 1943 197

January 1944	233
February 1944	240
March 1944	244
April 1944	252
May 1944	258
June 1944	263
July 1944	271
August 1944	279
September 1944	287
October 1944	294
November 1944	301
December 1944	306
January 1945	311
February 1945	315
March 1945	323
April 1945	331
May 1945	336
Roll of Honour	337
STATIONS	352
GROUPS	352
COMMANDING OFFICERS	352
AIRCRAFT	352
OPERATIONAL RECORD	353
Aircraft Histories	355

Introduction

RAF Bomber Command Squadron Profiles first appeared in the late nineties and proved to be very popular with enthusiasts of RAF Bomber Command during the Second World War. They became a useful research tool, particularly for those whose family members had served and were no longer around. The original purpose was to provide a point of reference for all of the gallant men and women who had fought the war, either in the air, or on the ground in a support capacity, and for whom no written history of their unit or station existed. I wanted to provide them with something they could hold up, point to and say, "this was my unit, this is what I did in the war". Many veterans were reticent to talk about their time on bombers, partly because of modesty, but perhaps mostly because the majority of those with whom they came into contact had no notion of what it was to be a "Bomber Boy", to face the prospect of death every time they took to the air, whether during training or on operations. Only those who shared the experience really understood what it was to go to war in bombers, which is why reunions were so important. As they approached the end of their lives, many veterans began to speak openly for the first time about their life in wartime Bomber Command, and most were hurt by the callous treatment they received at the hands of successive governments with regard to the lack of recognition of their contribution to victory. It is sad that this recognition in the form of a national memorial and the granting of a campaign medal came too late for the majority. Now this inspirational, noble generation, the like of which will probably never grace this earth again, has all but departed from us, and the world will be a poorer place as a result.

RAF Bomber Command Squadron Profiles are back. The basic format remains, but, where needed, additional information has been provided. Squadron Profiles do not claim to be comprehensive histories, but rather detailed overviews of the activities of the squadron. There is insufficient space to mention as many names as one would like, but all aircraft losses are accompanied by the name of the pilot. Fundamentally, the narrative section is an account of Bomber Command's war from the perspective of the bomber group under which the individual squadron served, and the deeds of the squadron are interwoven into this story. Information has been drawn from official records, such as group, squadron and station ORBs, and from the many, like myself amateur enthusiasts, who dedicate much of their time to researching individual units, and become unrivalled authorities on them. I am grateful for their generous contributions, and their names will appear in the appropriate Profiles. The statistics quoted in this series are taken from The Bomber Command War Diaries, that indispensable tome written by Martin Middlebrook and Chris Everitt, and I am indebted to Martin for his kind permission to use them.

Finally, let me apologise in advance for the inevitable errors, for no matter how hard I and other authors try to write "nothing but the truth", there is no such thing as a definitive account of history, and there will always be room for disagreement and debate. Official records are notoriously unreliable tools, and yet we have little choice but to put our faith in them. It is not my intention to misrepresent any person or Bomber Command unit, and I ask my readers to understand the enormity of the task I have undertaken. It is relatively easy to become an authority on single units or even a bomber group, but I chose to write about them all, idiot that I am, which means 128 squadrons serving operationally in Bomber Command at some time between the 3rd of September 1939 and the 8th of May 1945. I am dealing with eight bomber groups, in which some 120,000 airmen served, and I am juggling around 28,000 aircraft serial numbers, code letters and details of provenance and fate. I ask not for your sympathy, it was, after all, my choice, but rather your understanding if you should find something with which you disagree. My thanks to you, my readers, for making the original series of RAF Bomber Command Squadron Profiles so popular, and I hope you receive this new incarnation equally enthusiastically.

Particular thanks are due to Dave Birrell at the Bomber Command Museum of Canada and also to Major Sylvain Lapierre and Capt Barry Austreicher of the 408 (Goose) Squadron Association for their help with photographs. My thanks, as always, to my gang members, Andreas Wachtel in Germany, photo editor, Clare Bennett, Steve Smith and Greg Korcz for their unstinting support, without which my Profiles would be the poorer. Finally, my appreciation to my publisher, Simon Hepworth of Aviation Books Ltd for his belief in my work, untiring efforts to promote it, and for the stress I put him through to bring my books to publication.

Chris Ward. Skegness, Lincolnshire. March 2024.

Dedication

This history of 408 (Goose) Squadron in the Second World War is dedicated to the memory of

Air Commodore Nelles Woods Timmerman DSO DFC MiD CD,

who in the rank of Wing Commander became the squadron's first commanding officer in June 1941 and its "founding father", forging a legacy and inspiring an esprit de corps as a platform for his successors to build upon.

He stands as the representative of all who served this great squadron during its four years of wartime action, whether officer or other rank, in the air on the ground.

Narrative History

June and July 1941

On the 31st of October 1939 negotiations began between representatives of the British and Canadian governments on the subject of the British Commonwealth Air Training Plan (BCATP). Both sides approached the talks with entirely different perceptions and goals, and this would lead to protracted discussions and acrimonious relations over the following three years. The "Canadianisation" of Royal Canadian Air Force personnel serving with the Royal Air Force was enshrined in Article XV of the BCATP agreement, which originally called for the formation of twenty-five RCAF squadrons overseas. These were to be financed by Canada's contribution to the Plan, still known to this day in the UK as the Empire Air Training Scheme, which was agreed at $350 million. From the outset the talks were dogged by the questions of control of the RCAF contingent and finance, and the Canadian negotiators found themselves being constantly outmanoeuvred by their British counterparts.

Canada envisaged an independent air force operating alongside the RAF, much as the American 8th Air Force would from 1942. Britain, however, saw Canada as a source of manpower, and intended to integrate Canadian personnel into existing RAF Squadrons, or at least, to place the RCAF squadrons within RAF Groups. Canada expressed itself unwilling to finance RCAF personnel over whom it had no control, and after much wrangling, a compromise was eventually reached, which would allow all RCAF squadrons to operate from stations within close proximity to one-another, and under the same RAF Group. Once sufficient squadrons had been formed, a RCAF Group would come into existence. By the time that negotiations had reached this stage, it was already 1942, and only four RCAF squadrons had thus far been formed, all in 1941. In the event, outside influences caused the programme to be cut back, allowing for just seven new squadrons in 1942, making a total of eleven. However, the number was considered acceptable to constitute an effective Group, and this compromise became a cherished dream in itself, achieving realization on the 1st of January 1943. This was the best that Canada could achieve, having been backed into a corner by its own negotiators, and thus the RAF acquired the manpower and the control, while Canada footed the bill.

The first commanding officer was W/C Nelles Timmerman, a Canadian who had joined the RAF in 1936, and who had undertaken at least fifty operations with 49 and 83 Squadrons at Scampton on Hampdens by the time of his appointment, during which period he gained the award of the DFC for shooting down an Arado 196 seaplane during a mining operation on the night of the 1/2nd of May. He had flown his first operational sortie with 49 Squadron on the 17th of April 1940, and having completed his tour in July, was posted as an instructor to Cottesmore in Rutland. He returned to Scampton in March 1941 to join 83 Squadron as a flight commander, stepping into the shoes of the newly-promoted W/C Learoyd VC. He was joined at 408 (Goose) Squadron on the 12th of July by the newly promoted S/L Clayton, also from 83 Squadron, who was appointed as one of two flight commanders, the other post filled by S/L Burnett DFC, who was posted in from the OTU at Finningley, and like their commanding officer, both were Canadians serving in the RAF.

At the time, 5 Group was operating the twin-engine Handley Page Hampden, a sturdy and excellent medium bomber that was in the process of being phased out in favour of the new Avro Manchester, a heavy bomber with a sound airframe but, as events were to prove, unreliable Rolls Royce Vulture engines, which failed frequently and caused the type to be grounded for extended periods. As a consequence, the spread of Manchesters across 5 Group was protracted during 1941 and it was the trusty Hampden that continued to be the workhorse throughout the year. The first three Hampdens, AE190, AE196 and AE197 had arrived on the 10th and were soon joined by AE244, AE245 and AD972, and working up to operational status began in earnest once the squadron had changed address with a transfer from Lindholme to Syerston, which nestled then as now alongside the A46 Leicester to Lincoln road in Nottinghamshire. The station had been occupied previously by Polish units and was one of a number of former 1 Group stations to transfer to 5 Group around this time. The move took place on the 20th of July, and shortly afterwards crews began to arrive from OTUs, and the first contingent of Canadian ground crews was on station by early August.

August 1941

It was not long after this, during the second week of August, that the squadron was declared operational and four crews were called to briefing on the 11th to learn that they were to be part of a 5 Group force of thirty-one freshmen to target the docks at Rotterdam, while twenty others from North Luffenham operated against marshalling yards in the Ruhr city of Krefeld. New Zealander, Sgt Bradley and his crew departed Syerston at 00.59 and were followed into the air over the ensuing three minutes by three other crews, each sitting on four 500lb bombs. The Bradley crew reached the Dutch coast at 02.30 to encounter cloud at 12,000 feet and circled for twenty minutes before bombing through a gap from 13,000 feet on a north-westerly heading and observing bursts but no detail. Two other crews were unable to locate the target, while F/L Dunlop-Mackenzie and crew descended to 3,500 feet to deliver their attack from north to south at 02.48 and reported fires in the approximate area of their bomb bursts.

The crews of Bomber Command were unaware that June and July had been significant months as their performance was monitored in order to provide an assessment of its effectiveness for the War Cabinet. The project was initiated by Churchill's chief scientific advisor, Lord Cherwell, who handed the responsibility to David M Bensusan-Butt, a civil-servant assistant to Cherwell working in the War Cabinet Secretariat. The main focus of the Command's attention during this period was the morale of Germany's civilian population and the country's transportation system, which had been alluded to in a new Air Ministry directive on the 9th of July as areas of weakness. From this point, the C-in-C, Sir Richard Peirse, was to concentrate his efforts accordingly, which meant that during the moon period, his brief was to attack the major railway centres ringing the industrial Ruhr, to hamper movement in of raw materials and the export of finished goods. On dark nights, the Rhine cities of Cologne, Düsseldorf and Duisburg would be easier to locate, while on nights with unfavourable weather conditions more distant urban targets were to be attacked in northern, eastern and southern Germany. Already during the month, raids had been laid on to, amongst other destinations, Hamburg, Berlin, Frankfurt, Mannheim, Karlsruhe, Hannover and Essen, all by small to medium size forces. This was in keeping with the policy of the day, which was to divide the available strength and hit a number of targets simultaneously. The result was to dilute the effectiveness of the operations, and as the Butt Report was about to demonstrate in spectacular fashion, despite the propaganda to the contrary, few bombs were falling within five miles of their intended objectives.

The night of the 12/13th was to be a busy one for the Command, and throughout the day aircraft were made ready for operations to Berlin, Hannover, Magdeburg and Essen. 5 Group detailed thirteen Hampdens to join sixty-five Wellingtons for Hannover, and thirty-six to operate on their own at Magdeburg, while a force of seventy aircraft assigned to the capital included nine Manchesters. Together with minor operations, the night's activities involved a total of 234 aircraft. Hannover lay in northern Germany on the route to both Magdeburg and Berlin, and the three forces would fly out together until reaching it, at which point the Berlin element would continue straight on for the 150 additional miles, while the Magdeburg element peeled off to the south-east with eighty miles still ahead of them. The 408 (Goose) Squadron crews of S/Ls Burnett and Clayton and Sgt Hall departed Syerston between 22.05 and 22.10 bound for Hannover, the flight commanders carrying a 1,000-pounder and two 500-pounders each and the Hall crew four 500-pounders and two small bomb containers (SBCs) of 4lb incendiaries. The last-mentioned experienced engine problems shortly after crossing the German frontier and dropped their bombs on Lingen from 8,000 feet at 23.45, before returning home. The remaining two pressed on towards their destination, a major centre of war production and home among others to the Accumulatoren-Fabrik AG factory which manufactured lead acid batteries for U-Boots and torpedoes, the Continental tyre and rubber factory at Limmer, the Deurag-Nerag synthetic oil refinery at Misburg, the VLW (Volkswagen) metalworks, and the Maschinenfabrik Niedersachsen Hannover and Hanomag factories, which were producing guns and tracked vehicles. Conditions in the target area were largely favourable and the attacks by the 408 (Goose) Squadron pair were carried out from 13,000 feet at around 00.45 and bomb bursts were observed but no detail. Many crews failed to reach their designated target areas on this night and all of the operations were inconclusive.

Orders were received across the Command on the 14th to prepare for operations that night against railway targets in three major cities in northern Germany to the north of the Harz mountains, Hannover the most westerly, Magdeburg the most easterly and Braunschweig (Brunswick) in-between. 5 Group detailed eighty-one Hampdens to operate alone against the main railway station in Braunschweig, while seven Manchester crews were briefed for Magdeburg as part of an overall force of fifty-two aircraft. No report came out of Braunschweig to provide details of damage, and the likelihood is that very little occurred. The city would prove to be elusive, and it would be a further three years before it succumbed to a devastating Bomber Command attack.

Railway objectives featured again on the 16th, when orders went out to stations across the Command to prepare for attacks on installations in the Ruhr cities of Düsseldorf and Duisburg and nearby Cologne. Düsseldorf was to be a 5 Group show involving fifty-two Hampdens and six Manchesters, and the bombing took place through cloud and industrial haze in the face of a spirited searchlight and flak defence. Despite the fact that many fires were reported, no detail was gleaned, and no report came out of the target city.

Having not been invited to participate in the above operations, 408 (Goose) Squadron answered the call on the 17th to make ready four Hampdens to contribute to the 5 Group force of thirty-nine assigned to the main goods railway station in Bremen, while twenty 4 Group Whitleys targeted the city's Focke-Wulf aircraft factory in the south-eastern Hemelingen district. They departed Syerston between 23.02 and 23.27, and as Sgt Hall and crew climbed away, a seven-foot-long flame issued from the starboard engine and persuaded them to abort their sortie, leaving the crews of P/Os Biggane, Pim and Caldwell to continue on and benefit from generally favourable conditions as they made their way via the Frisians to the target area, where cloud, haze and extreme darkness obscured ground detail. Some crews followed the course of the River Weser into the city, where haze compromised the vertical visibility and most ultimately bombed the built-up area guided by evidence of searchlights and flak. Two of the 408 (Goose) Squadron element delivered their four 500 and two 250-pounders each from around 14,000 feet shortly after 02.00, while the Caldwell crew failed to identify the primary target and bombed an alternative also from 14,000 feet. It was another inconclusive attack, and no results were observed by the 5 Group crews, while a number of those from 4 Group claimed hits on the aircraft factory.

While the above operation was in progress, other 5 Group crews were engaged in mining at various locations in the North Sea and the Baltic and among them was the crew of P/O Campbell, who departed Syerston at 23.33 bound for one of the Nectarine gardens off the Frisians, laded with a single 1,500lb parachute mine and two wing-mounted 250-pounders. 5 Group had carried out the first mine-laying operation of the war on the night of the 13/14th of April 1940, and it was a task to which the Hampden would prove itself eminently suited. This represented the initial tentative steps in a new type of operation for Bomber Command, which would prove to be hugely successful, and by war's end, would have sunk or damaged more enemy vessels than the Royal Navy. The laying of parachute mines by air was given the code-name "gardening" and the entire enemy-held coastline from the Pyrenees in the south-west to the Baltic port of Königsberg in the north-east, and even the northern Italian coast, was divided into gardens, each with a horticultural or marine biological name. The process of delivery was known as planting and the mines themselves were referred to as vegetables, and it would not be long before the other groups joined in to create a spiders' web of mines in chains across all of the sea-lanes employed by the enemy. Ten months after it had begun, an assessment of the efficacy of mining operations revealed that seventeen enemy vessels had been sunk in the Baltic's Great and Little Belts and eighteen damaged. It was believed that a further eighteen had probably been sunk and it was considered safe to estimate that for every known case of a sinking or damage, another would have occurred without news of it reaching England. Among the known sinkings was that of a troopship carrying three thousand men, of whom fewer than four hundred survived.

The Frisian Island chain followed the line of the Dutch and German coasts from Den Helder to Jade Bay and was split into three gardens, Nectarine I from Texel to the eastern tip of Ameland, Nectarine II, from east of Ameland to Memmert, and Nectarine III, Juist to Wangerooge, and ORBs frequently failed to identify which was the target on a particular night. On this night the route took the Campbell crew out over Skegness to the target, where the vegetable was delivered from below 1,000 feet after conducting a timed run from a specific but unrecorded pinpoint. They then climbed as they flew on to northern Holland to drop the two 250-pounders onto Leeuwarden aerodrome from 10,000 feet and observed bursts but no detail. Leeuwarden was known to the Germans as "Wespennest" or Wasps Nest, because of the crack fighter units based there, but the nearby town was also famous as the birthplace of the ill-fated Great War spy, Mata Hari.

On the 18th, the Butt Report on the Command's operational effectiveness was released, and it sent shock waves reverberating around the War Cabinet and the Air Ministry. Having taken into account around four thousand bombing photos produced during night operations in June and July, it concluded that only a fraction of bombs had fallen within miles of their intended targets, and the poorest performances had been over the Ruhr, the region most important to Germany's war production. It was a massive blow to morale and demonstrated that thus far the efforts of the crews had been almost totally ineffective in reducing Germany's capacity to wage war. The claims of the crews were shown to be wildly optimistic, as were those of the Command, and Sir Richard Peirse's tenure as Commander-in-Chief would forever be blighted by the report's revelations, which also provided ammunition for the detractors, who believed that bomber aircraft could be more gainfully employed in other theatres of operation.

While the report was being digested that evening, an example of the Command's ineffectiveness was being enacted by forty-two 5 Group Hampdens from North Luffenham and Coningsby in company with twenty Whitleys and Wellingtons attempting to bomb the West Station in Cologne. Returning crews reported many fires on the western side of the Rhine, but local reports of nothing more than damage to a single building suggested that a decoy fire site had attracted the main weight of bombs. 408 (Goose) Squadron had not been invited to take part and remained on the ground also on the 19th, when Scampton and Waddington dispatched twenty-six and sixteen Hampdens respectively to join sixty-seven other aircraft for an operation against a railway junction at Kiel. The frustrations that the C-in-C would experience over the ensuing three months were typified by this night's events, beginning with extremely poor weather conditions for the outward flight with severe icing and thunderstorms over the Danish coast extending as high as 18,000 feet. All ground features were obscured to leave crews struggling to establish their positions and a number turned back at this stage or when over the Schleswig-Holstein peninsula and attacked alternative targets at Sylt, Hamburg and Cuxhaven. Any reaching Kiel encountered nine to ten-tenths cloud with tops at around 8,000 feet and a base below 5,000 feet in places and bombed on the flashes from flak batteries.

A series of three operations against Mannheim began on the night of the 22/23rd, for which 5 Group provided forty-one Hampdens from Coningsby, Syerston and Waddington, which were to join forces with fifty-six Wellingtons. 408 (Goose) Squadron made ready six Hampdens, loading each with either a 1,000-pounder and two of 500lbs or four 500-pounders and sent them on their way from Syerston between 21.25 and 21.45 with S/L Burnett the senior pilot on duty. P/O Campbell and crew turned back within the hour after the wireless equipment failed, leaving the others to press on to the target, where they encountered extreme darkness and haze that obscured the railway yards aiming point and reduced them to bombing the general area from 10,000 to 14,500 feet between 00.35 and 00.56. At debriefing, the 408 (Goose) Squadron crews reported that searchlight glare had prevented them from observing bomb bursts, while others reported fires and local sources claimed that only one house had been destroyed and five others lightly damaged.

It was left to Scampton to provide a dozen Hampdens to represent 5 Group at Düsseldorf on the 24th, when 4 Group Whitleys and Halifaxes completed the force of forty-four aircraft. Six additional Hampdens were assigned to searchlight suppression duties in the Wesel defensive belt, north of the Ruhr, their task to attack with 40lb bombs and guns any battery holding a bomber in its beams. The intruder activity turned out to be more effective than the raid on Düsseldorf and caused the beams either to become erratic or to be extinguished altogether.

A 5 Group attack on Mannheim by thirty-eight Hampdens and seven Manchesters was briefed out on all stations on the 25th, when the main post office was specified as the aiming point for what was, in reality, an assault on the city centre at a time when it was still not admitted publicly that population centres were being targeted. 408 (Goose) Squadron loaded each of five of its Hampdens with two 500 and two 250-pounders and 120 x 4lb incendiaries and dispatched them from Syerston between 20.39 and 20.45 with F/L Dunlop-Mackenzie the senior pilot on duty. He and his crew were just ten minutes from the Dutch coast when they were let down by the wireless equipment and oxygen supply system and were forced to turn back. The outward flight was undertaken in conditions of cloud and icing, but gaps appeared over the target to enable crews to identify the city if not the briefed aiming point. P/O Pim and crew spotted a gap through which they observed a built-up area and released their bombs from 14,000 feet at 00.15 and did not realise until landing that one SBC of incendiaries had hung-up and was still on board. The names on the Form 541 of the ORB are difficult to decipher and it looks like a Sgt Beck and crew withheld their bombs in the target area because of uncertainty about their location and turned back with the intention of finding a more suitable target not obscured by cloud. It was an endeavour in which they were unsuccessful and brought their load home, while the crews of Sgt Hall and Sgt Rea, also thwarted by the ten-tenths cloud, had delivered their attacks on estimated positions from 11,000 and 14,000 feet at 23.20 and 23.35 respectively guided by evidence of searchlights and flak. Returning crews generally claimed a moderate success, but it was, in reality, another inconclusive affair.

Cologne was posted as the target on the 26th, and a force of ninety-nine aircraft made ready, which included twenty-nine Hampdens and a single Manchester drawn from Coningsby, Scampton and Syerston, while six other Hampdens were to carry out flak suppression sorties to the west of the city. 408 (Goose) Squadron briefed five crews for the main event and one for mining duties in the Nectarine II garden off the central Frisians, loading those for the main event with four 500 and two 250-pounders. They departed Syerston between 23.38 and 23.50 with W/C Timmerman and F/L Dunlop-Mackenzie the senior pilots on duty and set course via corridor G to make landfall over the Scheldt estuary. This left Sgt Bradley and crew to follow in their wake at 00.15 to fly out over Skegness on their way to their garden area to deliver a single 1,500lb mine. They enjoyed favourable weather conditions and pinpointed on the eastern end of Ameland, before conducting a timed run to the north-west to plant their vegetable according to brief from 600 feet at 02.08.

Meanwhile, at Cologne, W/C Timmerman and crew had picked up a bend in the Rhine south of the city and had run up on a heading of 145° to drop their bombs from 11,000 feet at 02.05, observing bursts and a fire between the planned aiming point and a set of marshalling yards. The crews of F/L Dunlop-Mackenzie, P/Os Campbell and Caldwell and Sgt Sanderson also failed to identify the specific railway aiming point and attacked the general target area from 11,500 to 14,500 feet between 01.30 and 02.10, observing bursts but no detail through the searchlight glare. This was another occasion on which good results were claimed by returning crews, when in fact, only a small proportion of bombs had fallen within the city boundaries.

Orders arriving on 5 Group stations on the 27th revealed a return to Mannheim for ninety-one aircraft, including thirty-five Hampdens from North Luffenham, Waddington and Swinderby.

They were to attack the main railway station, while elements of 1, 3 and 4 Groups focused on other aiming points within the city and seventeen Hampdens from the same stations mined the waters of the Nectarine gardens around the Frisians. The benefits of clear skies over Mannheim were nullified by extreme darkness and haze, and many crews were prevented by searchlight glare from identifying the aiming point, forcing them to bomb the built-up area generally. No aircraft were lost, but seven Wellingtons and a Whitley crashed in England on return. There was some optimism at debriefing concerning the effectiveness of the raid, but local sources reported no significant damage.

Marshalling yards in Duisburg were posted as the target for a force of 118 aircraft on the 28th, thirty Hampdens and six Manchesters contributed by 5 Group along with six further Hampdens for searchlight suppression duties. 408 (Goose) Squadron briefed six crews for the main even and the crew of Sgt Farrow to join a freshman raid on the docks and shipping at Ostend. The last-mentioned departed Syerston first at 21.30 and followed the briefed route to the target, only to find it obscured by ten-tenths cloud, which persuaded them to head south-west to Dunkerque, where they delivered their four 500-pounders from 10,000 feet at 23.40. At the same time back at Syerston, the others were trundling towards the threshold, where between midnight and 00.15 they launched themselves skyward with F/L Dunlop-Mackenzie the senior pilot on duty and four 500-pounders in each bomb bay and two wing-mounted 250-pounders. They all arrived in the target area to be greeted by heavy flak and none was able to identify the marshalling yards, all but one bombing the general built-up area from 12,000 to 17,000 feet between 02.05 and 02.50. One crew, whose names cannot be deciphered, sought out an alternative target in the form of an aerodrome, the name of which is also too corrupted to read, which they attacked from 12,000 feet at 03.00 and caused the lights to be extinguished. Returning crews claimed a successful raid, but, again, this was disputed by local reports, which suggested that only around a dozen bomb loads had hit the city.

The final raid of the Mannheim series was posted on Wellington stations on the 29th, while Frankfurt was notified as the destination for a 4 and 5 Group force of 143 aircraft. This would be the first time that this city had faced an attack by a hundred-plus aircraft, the crews of which had been briefed to use the inland River Main docks as the aiming point. 5 Group would be contributing seventy-three Hampdens and three 207 Squadron Manchesters, 408 (Goose) Squadron providing five Hampdens for the crews of P/O Campbell and Sgts Beck, Bradley, Farrow and Hall, which departed Syerston between 21.55 and 22.07, carrying either four 500 and two 250-pounders or two 500-pounders plus 120 x 4lb incendiaries. Some crews adopted the briefed route from Orfordness to make landfall south of Ostend and bypass Namur, while others opted to fly directly to the target from the English coast, which meant landfall over the Scheldt estuary and skirting northern Belgium to pass south of Cologne. Cloud lay over most of the route and icing became a problem, and those reaching the target area encountered seven to nine-tenths cloud topping out at 10,000 feet, which prevented many from identifying the planned aiming point. However, some were able to pick out the river and docks by running in from below 10,000 feet, and bombing was carried out on largely estimated positions. Four of the 408 (Goose) Squadron crews carried out their attacks from 10,000 to 14,500 feet between 00.32 and 01.02, while Sgt Hall and crew had been ensnared by searchlights when some fifty miles north-west of Frankfurt and had spent twenty minutes vainly attempting to break free. Forced down to 2,000 feet, they let the bomb go "live" but observed nothing of the impact through the searchlight glare. At debriefing, some crews reported bursts in the built-up area but no detail, and local sources described scattered and insignificant damage, and certainly nothing commensurate with the size of the force and the effort expended.

During the course of its first month in the front line, the squadron took part in eleven operations, including two of the gardening variety, and dispatched forty-one sorties without loss.

September 1941

There would be no activity for 408 (Goose) Squadron for more than two weeks in September, despite being on stand-by for a daylight "circus" operation on a number of occasions, for which the underside of each Hampden had been painted sky blue. "Circus" was a predominantly 2 Group type of operation, for which the target was of secondary importance to the main purpose of drawing up the Luftwaffe for a battle of attrition with escorting Spitfires. In a similar type of operation, "Ramrod", the target was of primary importance and the drawing up of enemy fighters secondary. Operations began for 5 Group with a raid on Cologne on the 1st involving twenty Hampdens in company with thirty Wellingtons from other groups, in what turned out to be favourable weather conditions. Despite this, few bombs found the mark, and the fires reported by returning crews were probably from decoy sites.

Briefings took place across the Command on the 2nd for two operations to be carried out that night, both supported by the 5 Group stations of North Luffenham, Scampton, Swinderby and Waddington. The main operation was to be conducted by 126 aircraft, including eleven Hampdens, against the inland docks at Frankfurt, while a force of forty-nine aircraft targeted the Schlesischer railway station in Berlin, some 260 miles to the north-east. The bulk of the latter force, thirty-two Hampdens and four Manchesters, was provided by 5 Group with a handful of 3 Group Stirlings and 4 Group Halifaxes in attendance. Berlin was at the limit of the type's range, and by the time that returning crews reached England, many were flying on fumes and in desperate need of somewhere to land, lobbed down at the first airfields to present themselves or on any tract of level ground. Both operations were ineffective and wasteful and heaped further pressure on the beleaguered C-in-C.

The arrival at Brest at the end of March of the German heavy cruisers Scharnhorst and Gneisenau, and the occasional residency there also of the Hipper class Prinz Eugen, had required the Command to commit a sizeable effort against the port ever since. This would continue until early in the following year, when the Kriegsmarine resolved the situation once and for all. In the meantime, operations continued against the warships, and thirty Hampdens were included in a raid on the 3/4th, only to be recalled through worsening weather conditions. This was to be a recurring theme for the remainder of the year and would frustrate Peirse's attempts to improve the Command's image after the damning Butt Report. A return to Berlin on the night of the 7/8th by 197 aircraft included a Hampden contingent of forty-three, and the 137 crews reaching the target area claimed good results, which were modestly confirmed by local sources.

Other operations during the month involving a sizeable Hampden element included Kassel on the 8/9th, the first time that this city was attacked in numbers, Rostock on the 11/12th, Frankfurt on the

12/13th, Brest on the 13/14th and Hamburg on the 15/16th. Only the first and last mentioned were conducted in clear conditions and the latter, particularly, produced some useful damage.

Finally, on the 17th, the 408 (Goose) Squadron crews of S/L Burnett, F/L Clayton, P/Os Caldwell, Campbell and Constance and Sgt Hall were briefed for a "circus" operation, for which the target was a shell (munitions) factory at Marquise in the Hauts-de-France region some five miles south of the coastal town of Wissant, while a simultaneous operation by 2 Group Blenheims would target the Mazingarbe power station further inland. They departed Syerston at 13.35 and flew out over Reading to rendezvous with the Spitfire escort over Dungeness at 17.26, before crossing the Channel to make landfall near Hardelot-Plage and run in on the target from the south. They were met at the French coast by accurate heavy and light flak, which caused damage to all but one of the Hampdens, including to S/L Burnett's hydraulics system, which prevented the bomb doors from opening. Four separate attacks were carried out by BF109s, one of which was observed to dive towards the sea issuing smoke to be claimed as destroyed. In the event, the lead navigator failed to pick up the target and all of the ordnance was returned to the Syerston bomb dump.

The six Hampdens were made ready again on the following day for a "circus" operation against the marshalling yards at Abbeville and departed Syerston at 13.05 with W/C Timmerman and S/L Reginald Otto Altmann the senior pilots on duty. Altmann was of German ancestry and a highly experienced pilot who had served with 61 and 144 Squadrons and had attained deputy flight commander status at 106 Squadron before his posting to Syerston and elevation to flight commander in early September. They arrived at the rendezvous point at Rye a few minutes early and circled for an hour and twenty-three minutes waiting for the Spitfire escort to turn up, until a recall signal at 15.55 sent them home. They could see the French coast under clear skies and learned frustratingly that the escort had been put off by a thin band of nine-tenths cloud over the English coast thirty miles wide at 7,000 feet. The operation was rescheduled for the 20th, when each Hampden received a bomb load of a single 1,900-pounder and departed Syerston at 13.46 with W/C Timmerman and S/L Altmann once more the senior pilots on duty. This time the escort joined the bombers at Rye and no opposition was encountered as the target was bombed from 14,000 feet at 15.34, and although the bombing photos caught the bombs during their fall, just five bursts were observed in the yards.

S/L Burnett and F/L Clayton were the senior pilots on duty on the 21st, when briefings took place for a raid on a railway repair shop at Lille in north-western France, for which five of six Hampdens were loaded with a 1,900-pounder and one with four 500-pounders. They departed Syerston at 13.25 and met the Spitfire escort over Manston at the appointed time in excellent conditions, which persisted as they made landfall between Dunkerque and Calais and ran into heavy flak as they passed over Bailleul and Armentieres. The flak was equally intense at Lille as the attack was carried out from 15,000 feet, one 1,900-pounder falling out of an unidentified Hampden when the bomb doors opened and by good fortune hitting a large factory on the western side of Lille. All sustained flak damage over the target and on their way to the coast, and only one BF109 was observed, which sheered away when fired upon.

Briefing at Syerston on the 22nd revealed the Mazingarbe power station to be the target, located between Bethune and Lens some fifty miles south-east of Calais. They took off at 13.35 with S/L Altmann and F/L Dunlop-Mackenzie the senior pilots on duty, only to be recalled ninety minutes later for an undisclosed reason. This proved to be the last daylight operation for the squadron and its aircraft were duly repainted for night duties. There were no operations for 5 Group for a week thereafter because of adverse weather conditions, and 408 (Goose) Squadron was not called into action as operations resumed on the 28th when 5 Group detailed forty-eight Hampdens from Coningsby, Scampton, Swinderby and Waddington for an attack that night on the main railway station at Frankfurt. However, continuing bad weather caused the withdrawal of the less experienced crews, and, together with accidents and incidents, this reduced the numbers to thirty Hampdens from Scampton, Coningsby and Waddington.

On the 29th, the 408 (Goose) Squadron crews of S/L Burnett, F/O Caldwell, P/O Biggane and Sgts Bradley and Hall were called to briefing to be told that a force of eighty-nine aircraft was being assembled to attack the Hamburger Flugzeugbau aircraft factory, a subsidiary of the Blohm & Voss company, situated in Hamburg's Finkenwerde district on the southern bank of the Elbe to the west of the city centre. 5 Group's contribution would be thirty-eight Hampdens and four Manchesters, while ten others, including Sgts Bradley and Hall and their crews, attempted to hit the Blohm & Voss shipyards and the Deutschland class Admiral Scheer pocket battleship moored nearby. They departed Syerston between 17.58 and 18.05 and had to negotiate a ten-tenths band of ice-bearing cloud at up to 14,000 feet over the North Sea, which forced the Hall crew progressively lower until abandoning their sortie at 2,000 feet. The others arrived over Germany's second city under clear skies, but the Bradley crew was unable to identify the target vessel and attacked the docks area with their 2,000-pounder in the face of a spirited flak defence. Those assigned to the shipyards carried out their attacks with a 1,000-pounder and two of 500lbs from 13,600 to 15,000 feet between 20.40 and 21.04 and some bursts were observed through the searchlight dazzle, while a large fire could be seen from as far away as the Frisian Island of Ameland.

Hamburg was posted as the destination again on the following night, this time for eighty-two aircraft again targeting the Blohm & Voss aircraft factory and shipyards after the previous night's failure. 5 Group put up forty-eight Hampdens from Coningsby, Scampton, North Luffenham, Syerston and Swinderby, while sixteen freshman crews were briefed to bomb the docks and shipping at Cherbourg. 408 (Goose) Squadron briefed a record nine crews, which departed Syerston between 18.10 and 18.27 with F/Ls Clayton and Dunlop-Mackenzie the senior pilots on duty and flew out over Skegness on course for the southern end of the Island of Sylt. They had to contend with the frequently-met weather fronts harbouring icing conditions to reach their objective and Sgt Beaver's engines were overheating to the point where he jettisoned the wing-mounted 250-pounders to ease the strain. This proved to be ineffective, and the rest of the bomb load was jettisoned "live" into the sea some ninety miles short of Sylt. The others were hampered over the target by varying amounts of cloud and intense searchlight and flak activity, through which some ground references were established. The remaining 408 (Goose) Squadron crews bombed the general area of Hamburg with their loads of either two 500, two 250-pounders and 120 x 4lb incendiaries or single 1,000-pounder and two 500-pounders, and some observed bursts while others saw nothing. It was another unsatisfactory endeavour which caused fourteen fires and some housing damage, but nothing commensurate with the effort expended.

During the course of the month, the squadron took part in six operations and dispatched thirty-eight sorties without loss.

October 1941

The adverse weather conditions would continue to disrupt operations at the start of the new month, and the forty-four Hampdens dispatched to Karlsruhe on the night of the 1/2nd were recalled because of the risk of fog at the time of their return. Among these were four representing 408 (Goose) Squadron, three of which had departed Syerston at 19.30 leaving Sgt Fraser and crew to catch up five minutes later after being delayed by an engine issue. They were crossing The Wash when the port engine failed, and landed at Newton before returning the few miles to Syerston by road. Meanwhile, F/O Caldwell and crew received the recall signal at 21.00 when they were around thirty-five miles south-east of Brussels and dropped their 1,000 and two 500-pounders on Dunkerque docks from 14,000 feet on the way home at 21.24. Sgt Bradley and crew did not pick up the recall until 22.00, when close to the city of Saarbrücken, upon which they deposited their two 500-pounders, two 250-pounders and two SBCs of incendiaries from 12,000 feet ten minutes later. P/O Biggane and crew were totally unaware that the operation had been aborted and found their way to the target to bomb from 8,000 feet before returning to land at North Luffenham shortly after 03.00, having been airborne for seven-and-a-half-hours.

There were no operations for 5 Group and most other elements of the Command between the 2nd and 9th as the weather took a hand, and this would pave the way for a busy and record-breaking night of operations on the 12th. In the meantime, on the 10th, an overall force of seventy-eight aircraft was assembled for an operation against the Krupp organisation the home of which was in the city of Essen in the central Ruhr. Sixty-nine others were assigned to attack Cologne, thirty-five miles away to the south, while eighty mostly freshman crews cut their teeth on occupied ports from Rotterdam to Bordeaux. 5 Group detailed forty-six Hampdens and ten Manchesters for Essen, six Hampdens for searchlight suppression duties in the Bocholt-Borken area on the northern approaches to the Ruhr and twenty-three freshmen for Dunkerque.

The name Krupp conjures up a vision of a massive factory, but this is far from what actually existed. The Krupp organisation had been the largest manufacturer of weapons in Europe since before the Great War and had a hand in all aspects of German war production from tanks to artillery and ship and U-Boot construction and was given a controlling share in all major heavy engineering companies in Germany and the Occupied Countries. It also built manufacturing sites in other parts of Germany, many situated close to concentration camps, and employed vast numbers of forced workers in all of its factories. Once known as "Die Waffenschmiede des Reichs", the weapons-forge of the realm, its manufacturing sites in Essen included among others the Friedrich Krupp steelworks, the Friedrich Krupp locomotive and general engineering works, six coal mines and ten coke-oven plants, the Altenberg zinc works, the Presswerk plastics factory and the Goldschmidt non-ferrous metals smelting plant, all situated either within or close to the four Borbeck districts in a segment radiating out from near the city centre to the Rhine-Herne Canal on the north-western boundary on the banks of the Emscher River. The steel and engineering works alone employed in the region of eighty thousand workers, and the company's sites covered an area of more than two thousand acres, of which three hundred acres were occupied by factories and workshops. All of that required massive rail and canal access in the form of marshalling yards and its own harbour, and energy from at least four nearby power stations.

The ten-strong 408 (Goose) Squadron element departed Syerston between 23.49 and 00.30 with F/L Dunlop-Mackenzie the senior pilot on duty and each Hampden carrying either a high-explosive and incendiary mix or a 1.900-pounder and two 250-pounders. They flew out over Skegness on course for a point twenty-five miles north-east of the Dutch town of Zwolle for a southerly final leg to the target, and immediately lost the services of Sgt Farrow and crew to intercom failure and P/O Campbell and crew to engine trouble at the Dutch coast. Cloud and industrial haze prevented all but thirteen crews from positively identifying Essen as the built-up area beneath them and the attack was spread across many miles with no point of concentration and, therefore, no significant damage. The 408 (Goose) Squadron crews bombed largely on estimated positions on e.t.a. and dead-reckoning (DR) from 11,000 to 16,000 feet and had nothing of value to pass on to the intelligence section at debriefing.

The first major night of operations in the month was notified across the Command on the 12th, when a number of targets were posted in northern and southern Germany and the Ruhr in-between, which would require the highest number of sorties yet in a single night. The largest effort, for which 152 aircraft were detailed from 1, 3 and 4 Groups, was the first major assault of the war on the southern city of Nuremberg, the site of massive Nazi rallies during Hitlers rise to power in the thirties. The other targets were the shipbuilding yards at Bremen, for which ninety-nine aircraft were detailed, including twenty-two Hampdens, and the "Buna" works at Marl-Hüls on the northern rim of the Ruhr, which was to be a 5 Group show involving seventy-nine Hampdens and eleven Manchesters. The total number of sorties for the night was a record 373, which included eight Hampdens to carry out an intruder role in the searchlight belt in the Bocholt area to the north of the Ruhr.

F/Sgt Titcomb and crew departed Syerston at 19.00 as the sole 408 (Goose) Squadron representatives at Bremen, where the Deutsche Schiff und Maschinenbau A G shipyards had been formed in the mid-twenties under the abbreviated name Deschimag, as a co-operation of eight shipyards to compete with the Blohm & Voss and Bremer Vulkan yards. The largest was the A G Weser company, which, after six of the others had fallen by the wayside before the outbreak of war, was partnered only by the Seebeckwerft, now as part of the Krupp empire, after that organisation had been handed a controlling interest earlier in 1941. They flew from Skegness to Heligoland, before turning to the south-east and encountering heavy flak from the southern bank of the Elbe as they bypassed Hamburg. After searching in vain for the target for thirty minutes over ten-tenths cloud, they eventually aimed their 1,000-pounder and two 500-pounders at a flarepath from 14,000 feet and were on their way home by the time that the crews of P/O Biggane and Sgts Beaver and Beck took off between 00.40 and 00.43 to join the others engaged in searchlight suppression north of the Ruhr.

Finally, the eight crews bound for the Chemische Werke-Hüls GmbH set off between 00.55 and 01.10 with S/L Pitt Clayton and F/L Dunlop-Mackenzie the senior pilots on duty. The "Buna" works had been so christened by the work force and local population because of the chemicals butadiene and natrium employed in the manufacturing process of synthetic rubber for tyres. It had been formed in 1938 after its acquisition by the I G Farben company in association with the Bergwerkgesellschaft Hibernia A G and was almost certainly using slave workers at this time. The I G Farben chemicals and pharmaceuticals company, or to give it its full name, Interessen-Gemeinschaft Farbenindustrie, in English, Common Interest Conglomerate of chemical dye-making corporations, was formed in 1925 as a merger between BASF, Bayer, Hoechst, Agfa, Chemische Fabrik Griesheim-Elektron and Chemische Fabrik vormals Weiler Ter Meer and was heavily involved in the development and production of synthetic oil, employing slave labour at all of its factories across Germany, including 30,000 from the Auschwitz concentration camp, where it had built a plant. One of the company's subsidiaries manufactured the Zyklon B gas used during the Holocaust to murder millions of Jewish victims. *(In some of my previous books I have mistakenly located the Buna works in the Hüls district of Krefeld in the western Ruhr).*

The Ruhr-bound element flew out over Skegness and set course in ideal conditions under a half-moon for Enkhuizen on the eastern side of the Den Helder peninsula, before crossing the Ijsselmeer to encounter a build-up of nine-tenths cloud at 8,000 feet which obscured the target area. Not one of the 408 (Goose) Squadron crews was able to identify the primary target, and all roamed far and wide across the Ruhr in search of alternatives, eventually delivering their loads of either a 1,900-pounder and two of 250lbs or a 1,000-pounder and two of 500lbs from 8,500 to 15,000 feet on the estimated position of the target or on flak concentrations from Essen to Dortmund. P/O Campbell and crew brought their bombs home after water in the hydraulics system froze and prevented the bomb doors from opening. Meanwhile, the intruder trio had reached their patrol beat, also to run into cloud at 8,000 feet, and dropped eight 250-pounders each in salvoes onto searchlight concentrations from 6,000 to 10,000 feet, succeeding in temporarily extinguishing some, only for them to reactivate once the danger was past. The Nuremberg raid was equally disappointing and the loss of thirteen aircraft, a high price to pay for little or no return, deepened further the gloom and frustration at Bomber Command HQ.

Thirty Hampdens and nine Manchesters eventually made their way to take-off from 5 Group stations in the early hours of the 14th, after a number had been withdrawn for technical reasons. The target for this 5 Group operation was the main railway station in Cologne, situated in the shadow of the cathedral on the West Bank of the Rhine, while twenty miles to the north, elements of 1 and 3 Groups would be seeking out aiming points in Düsseldorf. The close proximity of the two operations would guarantee an intense searchlight and flak response. The sole 408 (Goose) Squadron representative was the crew of Sgt Bradley, who departed Syerston at 00.50 carrying a 1,000-pounder and two 500-pounders and flew out over Orfordness to make landfall on the Belgian coast, before passing to the south of Liege to begin the final leg to the target. Severe icing conditions from the Belgian coast to twenty miles inland persuaded some crews to turn back, while those reaching the target encountered haze and searchlight glare along with accurate flak that rendered identification of the aiming point almost impossible. Most were reduced to bombing the built-up area generally or a last resort objective, the Bradley crew going for the former from 17,500 feet, observing bursts but no detail. On return to base, they handed AE360 back to the ground crew to have a dozen flak holes patched up.

A force of eighty aircraft was assembled from 1, 3 and 4 Groups for a return to Nuremberg on the 14th for what turned out to be another disappointing effort, which was compromised largely by adverse weather conditions during the outward flight, and only a single 78 Squadron Whitley crew managed to identify and hit the Siemens factory and destroy a workshop. 3 Group sent thirty-four Wellingtons and Stirlings to Cologne on the 15/16th, and returning crews claimed large fires, while local sources reported only a few bombs and no damage.

On the 16th, 5 Group contributed twenty-six Hampdens from Scampton and Syerston to a force of eighty-one aircraft assembled to attack railway yards at Duisburg, for which 408 (Goose) Squadron contributed nine Hampdens and another for the freshman crew of Sgt Fraser to employ in company with twenty-one others against the docks and shipping at Dunkerque. The latter departed Syerston first at 19.15 and set course via Orfordness for the target, where slight haze proved to be no impediment to target identification, and three of the four 500-pounders fell away from 13,000 feet, leaving the fourth hung-up in the bomb bay. The intercom failed on the way home and they landed at Balderton, a future residence for the squadron on the outskirts of Newark, and at debriefing reported a few fires in the docks area and some dummies to the east.

Those involved in the main event were still on the ground at Syerston, and eventually took off between 00.23 and 00.55 with P/Os Biggane, Constance and Pim the only commissioned pilots on duty. They flew out over Skegness on their way to Enkhuizen and Borken, and Sgt Titcomb and crew had just set course at 6,000 feet when AE197 became uncontrollable. Over the ensuing harrowing minutes, the Hampden stalled and ended up on its back heading for the sea at 300 mph, before control was regained at 1,000 feet and the bombs were jettisoned. On return to base it was found that half of the port bomb door was missing and the rest was wrapped around the wing leading edge. The others, meanwhile, enjoyed ideal conditions until encountering cloud at around 6,000 feet over the Ijsselmeer and then had to run the gauntlet of accurate heavy flak during the final leg. Sgt Rea and crew had been contending with a worsening intercom problem since take-off and turned back with their load after reaching the Ijsselmeer, while Sgt Bradley and crew were struggling to gain height and speed with overheating engines and unloaded the contents of their bomb bay onto a searchlight concentration south of Den Helder. The others delivered their loads of either two 500-pounders and 240 x 4lb incendiaries or 1,000-pounder and two of 500lbs on estimated positions from 12,000 to 15,000 feet and could report only an impression of bursts on the ground.

The weather intervened to keep the bomber force on the ground on the following three nights, until orders came through on the 20th to prepare for operations against the ports of Bremen, Wilhelmshaven and Emden in north-western Germany and Antwerp in Belgium for freshman crews. A force of 153 aircraft assembled to target marshalling yards in Bremen included a 5 Group contribution of eighty-two Hampdens and eight Manchesters, eleven of the former representing 408 (Goose) Squadron, which provided another for the freshman crew of Sgt Fraser to take mining in the Nectarine II garden off the central Frisians. They departed Syerston together between 18.05 and 18.45 with S/L Burnett the senior pilot on duty carrying one or the other of the two standard bomb loads, and lost the crew of P/O Campbell almost immediately to intercom failure, leaving the others to make their way via Skegness under relatively clear skies and, in the absence of a moon, extreme darkness to a point fifteen miles south-west of Heligoland, from where they were to head for landfall between Cuxhaven and Bremerhaven. Sgt Titcomb and crew were an hour out when engine issues ended their interest in proceedings, while the rest arrived at the enemy coast to find themselves constantly harassed by searchlights, which blinded them to ground features and combined with the six to seven-tenths cloud to prevent them from establishing their precise positions. They also had to contend with tracer reaching 10,000 feet, while the heavier calibre shells were exploding above them at 17,000 feet. Some picked up the River Weser to the north and south of the city or caught a glimpse of the ground by the light of flares, but the briefed railway junction aiming point remained elusive and bombing was carried out by the Syerston crews on estimated positions from 12,000 to 16,500 feet, and Wilhelmshaven, Oldenburg and Rotenburg were among other targets under the bombs either by design or by accident. The gardeners, meanwhile, experienced no difficulty in pinpointing on Schiermonnikoog, from where the Fraser crew conducted a timed run towards Borkum and planted their vegetable according to brief from 600 feet.

The night ended badly for 408 (Goose) Squadron with its inevitable first fatalities, after P1212 crashed at 00.45 at Haltham, some four miles south-south-west of Horncastle while on final approach to Coningsby, and according to the squadron ORB, Sgt Bradley RNZAF and two others lost their lives, while Sgt Cole survived with bruises and concussion. He was apparently able to report that the engines cut and the Hampden span into the ground. It will be recalled that Sgt Bradley had captained the first aircraft to take off on the occasion of the squadron's first operation in August, since which time he had completed eight further sorties. *(According to Bill Chorley's Bomber Command Losses for 1941, there were no survivors.)*

Bremen was posted as the destination again on the 21st for a force of 136 aircraft, including eighteen Hampdens and two Manchesters, whose crews were briefed to attack shipyards. Conditions were similar to those of twenty-four hours earlier and local sources reported another scattered attack which hit largely housing but landed one bomb in the Vulkan shipyard.

Mannheim was selected as the target for 123 aircraft on the 22nd, for which 5 Group put up forty-five Hampdens, eleven of them belonging to 408 (Goose) Squadron, which departed Syerston between 18.02 and 18.45 with S/L Clayton and F/L Dunlop-Mackenzie the senior pilots on duty. They crossed the English coast outbound at Orfordness and made landfall on the other side of the Channel in the Dunkerque region, before heading across Belgium to enter Germany north of Luxembourg. Sgt Beck and crew had been contending with an intermittently functioning intercom since crossing the English coast and decided to bomb one of the Channel ports before turning back. Ten-tenths cloud rendered the intention more difficult than expected and two 500 and two 250-pounders were eventually aimed at a searchlight concentration in the Dunkerque area from 12,000 feet. Thick cloud, electrical storms and icing conditions up to 15,000 feet made life difficult also for the others during the outward flight, and Sgt Sanderson and crew found themselves unable to climb out of it. When the static caused the intercom to fail, they opted to turn back and drop their 1,000-pounder and two 500-pounders on the docks at Dunkerque and were pounded by accurate flak stirred up by the Beck crew. One burst threw the wireless operator backwards and damaged his eardrums, leaving him temporarily deaf, and when they touched down at Martlesham Heath, the port undercarriage collapsed. The others pressed on to arrive at the target on e.t.a. and deliver their bomb loads on estimated positions through six to seven-tenths cloud from 11,000 to 14,000 feet. Some were aided by flares, which highlighted built-up areas below, but fewer than half of the crews would claim at debriefing to have reached the primary target and local sources reported a light raid. 408 (Goose) Squadron posted missing F/Sgt Titcomb and crew in P1218, which came down in the general target area with fatal consequences for the pilot and two others, among which was F/Sgt Walker, who was on his forty-first sortie. The sole survivor, Sgt Gifford RCAF, was taken into captivity on what was his eleventh sortie, one fewer than his captain.

The squadron would not operate again in numbers for a further week, and in the meantime the main operation on the night of the 23/24th was a two-wave attack on the shipyards in Kiel involving

114 aircraft, including thirty-eight Hampdens from Swinderby and Coningsby and six Manchesters from 97 (Straits Settlement) Squadron. The two waves were widely separated, and it was the second one that gained some success by hitting the Deutsche Werke U-Boot yards. Sgt Dadson and crew were among thirteen freshman crews sent to bomb the docks and shipping at Le Havre and took off from Syerston at 03.53 only to be thwarted by ten-tenths cloud over the target, which prevented them from delivering an attack. Orders were received across the Command on the 24th to prepare for that night's operation against railway workshops and marshalling yards in Frankfurt-am-Main, which would involve a force of seventy aircraft. They ran into ten-tenths cloud at around 8,000 feet shortly after crossing the enemy coast, and this persisted all the way to the target, which was located by just a fraction of the crews taking part. The dismal failure of the operation was typical for the period, and the situation continued to heap frustration on C-in-C, Sir Richard Peirse.

Hamburg was posted as the target for 115 aircraft on the 26th, for which 5 Group contributed an unknown number of Hampdens and six Manchesters, briefing the crews of the former to aim for the Blohm & Voss shipyards and the latter the main railway station. Those reaching the target area found good bombing conditions under moonlight and delivered a sharp and effective attack. The destination for Sgt Dadson and crew on this night was Cherbourg, for which, with Syerston not operating, they departed Swinderby at 18.40 and flew out over Chesil Beach to find the target covered by ten-tenths cloud with tops at 7,000 to 8,000 feet. They were unable to establish a pinpoint, and having stooged around for forty-five minutes, returned with their bombs to Swinderby.

Orders were received at Coningsby, Swinderby and Syerston on the 29th to prepare forty-one Hampdens and five Manchesters to attack Schiphol aerodrome, 408 (Goose) Squadron responding with nine Hampdens, which took off between 21.53 and 22.11 with W/C Timmerman the senior pilot on duty, four 500-pounders in each bomb bay and two wing-mounted 250-pounders. They flew out over Skegness on a direct course for the target located to the south-west of Amsterdam and lost the services of P/O Constance and crew to an engine issue after twenty minutes. The others experienced turbulent conditions in snow and ice-bearing cloud, which over the Dutch mainland bottomed out below 1,000 feet and it proved impossible to establish a pinpoint to put them on track for the target. Most abandoned their sorties after failing to find some kind of navigational reference and brought their bombs home, while P/O Campbell and crew spent an hour in a vain search for the Ijmuiden docks from which to conduct a timed run and eventually came upon an aerodrome, which they believed was at Alkmaar. They circled it eight times at 1,000 feet before dropping their entire load in a stick along the flarepath, which resulted in a plume of white smoke rising into the air. The percussion from the bomb blasts at such a low altitude caused consternation in the Hampden as it threatened to disintegrate, but it held together, and a safe return was completed after five hours aloft.

The month ended with a return to the Blohm & Voss shipyards at Hamburg on the 31st, for which a force of 123 aircraft was assembled. 5 Group called upon the services of Syerston, Coningsby and Swinderby to prepare forty-two Hampdens and five Manchesters, while a further eighteen Hampdens and a single Manchester were assigned to gardening duties in northern waters in the Forget-me-not garden in Kiel Harbour and Nectarine II off the central Frisians. 408 (Goose) Squadron made ready ten Hampdens for the main event and another to take Sgt Dadson and crew to Nectarine II, and they took off together between 17.36 and 18.27 with F/O Caldwell the senior pilot on duty and a bomb load of either a 1,000-pounder and two 500-pounders or two 500 and two 250-pounders with two SBCs of incendiaries. They flew out over Skegness on course for Husum on the western coast of Schleswig-Holstein and climbed to 7,000 feet to clear the cloud that extended all the way to the enemy coast. There it dissipated to some extent, enabling crews to map-read to an extent the rest of the way to the target aided by moonlight. There were gaps in the cloud over the city, and the 408 (Goose) Squadron crews were able to identify the built-up area if not the precise aiming point, and delivered their attacks from 11,500 to 15,000 feet, some after searching for a considerable time. Again, fewer than half of the force claimed to have reached and bombed the city area, and seven of the fourteen fires reported by local sources were classed as large, but no concentration was achieved, and no significant damage inflicted.

During the course of the month, the squadron took part in sixteen operations, including seven by single aircraft, and dispatched eighty-two sorties for the loss of two Hampdens and crews.

November 1941

On the 1st, preparations were put in hand to send a force of 132 aircraft to attack the Deutsche Werke shipyard and harbour installations at Kiel, for which 5 Group detailed thirty-two Hampdens from Scampton, North Luffenham and Waddington. They found the target area to be completely obscured and bombs were delivered largely on e.t.a. The weather kept most aircraft on the ground on the 2nd, and only minor operations were mounted on the 3rd, among them an anti-shipping patrol by six Hampdens off the Frisians. The anti-shipping activity was repeated on the 4th, while Coningsby, Swinderby and Syerston made ready twenty-four Hampdens and four 97 (Straits Settlement) Squadron Manchesters for mining duties in the Forget-me-not garden in Kiel Bay. Ten 408 (Goose) Squadron Hampdens departed Syerston between 23.57 and 00.14 with F/L Dunlop-Mackenzie the senior pilot on duty and flew out over Skegness on course for the western coast of Jutland. Sgt Sanderson and crew turned back after an hour because of an engine issue, while the others pressed on to complete the entire outward flight in bright moonlight but over ten-tenths cloud, which prevented all from establishing their positions. Those that descended into the cloud in the hope of breaking into clear air experienced icing conditions and all but one decided to turn back, some dropping their wing-mounted 250-pounders on flak positions. Believing themselves to be over the Baltic, P/O Biggane and crew circled and chanced upon a gap in the cloud through which their belief was confirmed by a glimpse of water. They descended to 1,000 feet and found themselves over Flensburg Fjord, from where they followed the coastline south to the head of Kiel Fjord and carried out a timed run to the release point, all the time under the glare of a searchlight and fire from two flak positions. The mine was released from 600 feet and the 250-pounders jettisoned to enable a swift climb into the safety of cloud for the return journey, which ended with a diversion to Swanton Morley. AE267 was found to be severely holed by shrapnel and would remain where it landed for repairs, while the crew was ferried home in other 408 (Goose) Squadron Hampdens. P/O Biggane's dogged determination would be rewarded ten days hence with a DFC, the first award to be made to a member of the squadron.

While the rest of the bomber force remained on the ground, a busy night awaited 5 Group on the 5th, the programme of operations involving six Hampden "sneakers" to target towns and cities in north-western Germany, five on anti-shipping sorties, twenty-four gardeners and twenty-two freshmen to bomb the docks and shipping at Cherbourg. The 408 (Goose) Squadron crews of P/Os Brackenbury, Brown, Hull and Wilson were briefed for Cherbourg and departed Syerston between 02.55 and 03.11, each with four 500-pounders beneath their feet, and set course for Bognor Regis to begin the Channel crossing. P/O Brown and crew abandoned their sortie almost immediately because of the failure of their intercom, while the others continued on to encounter dense cloud over the target with tops at around 10,000 feet. Some gaps appeared, which enabled the crews of P/Os Wilson and Brackenbury to identify the docks, the former descending initially to 2,000 feet before climbing to 5,000 feet to deliver an attack. The Wilson crew remained at 9,000 feet to release their load and observed bursts but no detail. The Hull crew was unable to establish a pinpoint and returned their load to the bomb dump.

The 408 (Goose) Squadron crews of F/O Caldwell, P/Os Constance and Pim and Sgts Beaver and Dadson were summoned to briefing on the 6th to learn that they would be engaged in further "sneaker" operations that night, the purpose of which was to cause maximum alarm in the target areas with the fewest number of aircraft. They were allowed free rein to attack any built-up area in north-western Germany and departed Syerston between 00.31 and 00.43, each carrying a 1,000 and two 500-pounders. They set course for an area encompassing Osnabrück in the south to Wilhelmshaven and Emden in the coastal region, but F/O Caldwell and crew were led astray by an unexpected weather front and buffeted by 80 mph winds, which pushed them further east than planned. They found themselves over Hamburg, where they dropped the 1,000-pounder from 14,000 feet, before heading south to Osnabrück to divest themselves of the 500-pounders. P/O Constance and crew were also driven by the wind over Hamburg, where they identified the docks and dropped all three bombs from 11,000 feet and continued north thereafter to exit the Schleswig-Holstein coast via Sylt, having descended to get beneath the conditions. The Dadson crew attacked Osnabrück from 15,000 feet and were then engaged by a BF110, which opened fire at 250 yards range. As his gunners returned fire, Sgt Dadson pointed the Hampden's nose towards the ground and evaded the night-fighter, but the smell from the guns suggested something burning and he warned the crew to prepare to bale out if necessary. It soon became clear that the aircraft was not damaged, but on checking round the crew, it was discovered that the navigator, Sgt Palastanga, was absent, and all of his charts and flimsies had followed him out of the aircraft. In the absence of their navigator, they flew west until clear of enemy territory and then a series of QDMs guided them home. P/O Pim and crew attacked a town from 11,000 feet, which has not been traced but could have been Rendsburg, while the Beaver crew, intending to bomb Emden, came first upon Wilhelmshaven and dropped their bombs there from 12,000 feet, observing bursts but no detail.

Unquestionably still frustrated by his inability to deliver a telling blow on Germany during the extended period of unfavourable weather, and conscious of the besmirched reputation of the Command after the damning Butt Report, Peirse planned a major night of operations on the 7th. The original intention had been to send over two hundred aircraft to Berlin, but continuing doubts about the weather prompted the 5 Group A-O-C, AVM Slessor, to question the wisdom of going ahead with that plan, and he was allowed to withdraw his force and send it instead to Cologne. A third operation, involving fifty-three Wellingtons and two Stirlings from 1 and 3 Groups, was also to take place with Mannheim as the target, and together with the extensive minor operations, including a freshman raid on the docks and shipping at Ostend, the total number of 392 sorties represented a new record. Sadly, this huge effort was not to be blessed with success as the night degenerated into a disaster.

A force of 169 aircraft eventually took off for Berlin, while sixty-one Hampdens and fourteen Manchesters set off for the Rhineland capital, among them two of the former from 408 (Goose) Squadron bearing aloft the crews of F/L Dunlop-Mackenzie and Sgt Farrow at 18.46 and 19.14 respectively. They had been preceded into the air between 18.10 and 18.15 by the crews of P/O Biggane and Sgts Beck and Sanderson, who were bound for the Maastricht region of south-eastern Holland to carry out searchlight suppression duties. The Beck crew had travelled just sixty miles on course for Orfordness when the intercom failed and forced them to abandon their sortie. The last to depart Syerston, between 19.19 and 19.30, were the freshman crews of P/Os Brackenbury, Brown and Dowie and Sgt Fraser, who had Ostend as their destination and set course via Orfordness following in the wake of the Cologne-bound duo. They flew directly to the target along corridor G, making landfall over the Scheldt estuary, before reaching the target to find up to nine-tenths cloud at between 6,000 and 11,000 feet and haze obscuring the main railway station aiming point situated in the shadow of the Cathedral. However, F/L Dunlop-Mackenzie's bomb-aimer found the River Rhine to be clearly visible and employed it to establish a position over the city, releasing the two 500 and two 250-pounders and 120 x 4lb incendiaries from 12,500 feet and observing fires to spread as they turned for home. On return, the Farrow crew told a similar story and reported bombing from 12,000 feet.

Meanwhile, on their way to Ostend, P/O Brown and crew had been contending with an intermittent intercom connection between the pilot and bomb-aimer, which would prevent them from delivering an attack, and having spent forty-five minutes in a vain attempt to fix the problem, they were forced to take their bombs home. The others were able to identify the target in the moonlight filtering through gaps in the cloud and P/O Dowie and crew glided down from 15,000 to 8,000 feet to drop their four 500-pounders, observing them to burst in the docks. The Brackenbury crew carried out their attack from 11,000 feet, while Sgt Fraser and crew were prevented from releasing their load after the bomb doors were damaged by a flak burst and refused to open. Shortly after turning for home, the starboard engine began to overheat, and it was decided to pump the bomb doors down to allow the bombs to be jettisoned to ease the pressure on the engine. On reaching the English coast the ailing engine cut altogether, followed soon after by the port engine, upon which Sgt Fraser carried out a crash-landing near Coltishall in Norfolk. The crew walked away from what appeared to be a terminally-damaged Hampden, but it was repaired, and the cause of the starboard engine issue was found to be the same flak burst that had caused the bomb door problem.

The German searchlight crews were becoming accustomed to the suppression patrols and doused the lights as soon as an approaching aircraft was heard. As a result, P/O Biggane and crew found difficulty in establishing the positions of searchlight batteries in their beat between Maastricht and Aachen and dropped their eight 250-pounders at intervals from 12,000 feet before returning home. Sgt Sanderson and crew dropped their bombs on the larger concentrations from between 10,500 and 13,000 feet and also returned safely from a largely uneventful six-hour round trip.

Once every aircraft from the night's endeavours had landed, it became clear that a record thirty-seven were missing, more than twice the previous highest loss in a single night. An analysis revealed that fewer than half of the Berlin force had managed to reach their objective, and twenty-one had failed to return. The Mannheim contingent missed its target altogether and suffered the loss of seven Wellingtons in the process, and despite the claims of returning 5 Group crews of flashes as their bombs hit home and many fires, local sources mentioned just eight high-explosive bombs and sixty incendiaries falling into the city, causing minor housing and no industrial damage. The only positive on a disastrous night for Peirse and the Command was the absence of casualties from the 5 Group raid, and the debacle proved to be the final straw for the War Cabinet, the Air Ministry and the Prime Minister, who summoned Sir Richard Peirse to an uncomfortable meeting at Chequers on the 8th to make his explanations.

That night, 5 Group detailed twenty Hampdens for an attack on the Krupp complex at Essen in company with thirty-four other aircraft, ten Hampdens and five Manchesters for freshman sorties against the docks and shipping at Dunkerque and six for searchlight suppression duties in support of the Essen force. 408 (Goose) Squadron briefed the crews of F/O Caldwell, P/Os Constance, Houghton and Pim and Sgt Beck for Essen and sent them on their way from Syerston between 17.17 and 17.24, each sitting on a 1,000-pounder and two 500-pounders. They flew out over Orfordness on course for Enkhuizen, losing the services of the Pim crew at the Dutch coast when the wireless receiver failed, preventing them from picking up any recall signal, which had been mentioned at briefing as a possibility because of the likelihood of fog descending upon the stations. The others ran into extensive searchlight activity, including what seemed to be a new concentration south-east of the Ijsselmeer, which was well supported by flak batteries, but survived to reach the target and deliver their attacks from 8,500 to 14,000 feet in the face of a hostile defence. It was not possible to observe the outcome in the glare of searchlights and flashes from the flak, but returning crews reported large fires. Absent from debriefing and one of six missing crews was that of P/O Houghton RNZAF in AE433, which had been brought down by the night-fighter of Oblt Willi Dimter of III./NJG1 to crash homebound at 22.30 at Maasbree on the Dutch side of the frontier with Germany. The pilot and two others had been with the squadron since the start and were on their sixteenth sortie, while the fourth member of the crew was on his first, but all survived in enemy hands, a fact announced to the world by German radio.

This was the start of a period of sustained losses up to the end of the year, and sadly, there would be only one more survivor among the missing crews. Hamburg was posted as the main target on the 9th, the aiming point for which was the Blohm & Voss shipyards on Kühwerder Island in the Finkenwerder district. A force of 103 aircraft was assembled, thirty Hampdens and six Manchesters provided by 5 Group, while 408 (Goose) Squadron made ready four Hampdens to take the crews of P/Os Brown, Dowie, Hull and Wilson to Ostend to attack the docks and shipping. They departed Syerston between 17.52 and 17.55, each loaded with four 500 and two 250-pounders and adopted the usual route to the Belgian coast via Orfordness. Haze in the target area proved to be no impediment to accurate bombing, which took place from 10,000 to 14,000 feet and bursts were observed in various parts of the docks. AE438 failed to return with the crew of P/O Wilson, having crashed at Westkerke, some six miles south-east of Ostend, and there were no survivors from the crew of P/O Wilson, three of whom were on their maiden operation.

On the 13th, Peirse was informed by the Air Ministry that he was to restrict future operations, while the future of the Command was considered at the highest level. It was also on this day, that His Majesty King George VI paid the first of his two visits to 408 (Goose) Squadron, accompanied on this occasion by the beleaguered commander-in-chief and the 5 Group air-officer-commanding.

His majesty was introduced to the crews by W/C Timmerman and the station commander, G/C Taafe, during a brief stay lasting just twenty-five minutes.

Adverse weather conditions would keep the bulk of 5 Group on the ground for the ensuing two weeks, the group's only operational activity during the period coming on the 15th and involving eleven Hampdens and six Manchesters in a raid on the port of Emden. The 408 (Goose) Squadron crews of P/Os Brackenbury, Brown, Dowie and Hull departed Syerston between 17.17 and 17.33, each with four 500-pounders beneath their feet and set course via Skegness for a map reference over the North Sea to the north of the target. Sgt Hull and crew had progressed some ninety miles before engine trouble ended their interest in proceedings, leaving the others to arrive over the target to find it concealed beneath ten-tenths cloud. P/O Brackenbury and crew bombed from 13,000 feet, aiming for the flashes from flak batteries, while P/O Brown and crew attempted to do so from a thousand feet lower, only to be thwarted by bomb doors that refused to open. P/O Dowie and crew homed in also on evidence of flak, and were rewarded by a gap in the clouds that revealed the entire docks area illuminated by a flare from another aircraft, upon which they released their hardware from 9,500 feet and observed two bursts and a fire.

The first phase of a massive construction project on Lorient's Keroman peninsula had begun in March 1941 and would continue until January 1942, by which time the K1, K2 and K3 bunkers would be completed and capable of sheltering thirty vessels and their crews under cover. The complex boasted a revolutionary lift system, which could raise U-Boots from the water and transport them across the facility to repair and servicing bays. The thickness of the concrete rendered the structure impervious to the bombs available to Bomber Command at the time, and attacks were directed predominantly at the town and its approaches to prevent access by road and rail, while extensive minelaying compromised access by sea. 5 Group assembled a force of fifty-one Hampdens and two Manchesters to send against the port on the 23rd, a dozen of the former provided by 408 (Goose) Squadron, which departed Syerston between 15.57 and 16.35 with S/L Burnett the senior pilot on duty and four 500-pounder SAP bombs and two 250-pounders to cause the damage. They flew south to exit England over Chesil Beach, where, as it was still broad daylight, they circled for half an hour to kill time. Shortly after beginning the Channel crossing, P/O Dowie and crew misinterpreted a recall signal and turned back, and P/O Constance experienced difficulty in breathing at 10,000 feet and also aborted the sortie. Sgt Fraser and crew lost an engine at the French coast and limped back home after jettisoning the bomb load, while the others made landfall between Saint-Brieuc and St-Malo on the Brittany coast, before arriving at the target under favourable conditions that allowed a visual identification of the town. The bombing was carried out from 11,000 to 14,000 feet on a variety of headings including from north to south, north-east to south-west and south-west to north-east from Groix Island, fortunately without collision. Returning crews reported bomb bursts and fires, but no report emerged from local sources to provide details of damage.

W/C Timmerman attended an investiture at Buckingham Palace on the 25th and received his DSO from the hand of His Majesty, King George VI. Operations for the remainder of the month continued to employ only small forces, the Wellingtons and twenty Hampdens despatched to Emden on the 26/27th representing one of the larger ones, but it, too, failed to produce any noteworthy damage. Most 5 Group stations were alerted on the 27th to prepare for a raid that night on marshalling yards in Düsseldorf in company with elements of 3 Group in an overall force of eighty-six aircraft. Thirty-four Hampdens and six Manchesters were made ready, 408 (Goose) Squadron contributing eight, which departed Syerston between 16.39 and 17.02 with S/L Clayton the senior pilot on duty and a 1,000-pounder and two 500-pounders in each bomb bay. The route was not recorded but was almost certainly via corridor G to the Scheldt estuary and on to the southern Ruhr, which was found to be largely cloud-free, although some crews would report up to eight-tenths of the white stuff and the usual blanket of industrial haze creating poor vertical visibility. Attacks were carried out by the 408 (Goose) Squadron crews from 11,500 to 14,500 feet and despite claims of large fires in the railway yards, local reports detailed only light damage, while nearby Cologne attracted plenty of attention and recorded damage to 119 houses.

A request for a fix was received at Heston direction-finding station at 22.29 from F/O Caldwell and crew, and a bearing of 221 degrees was sent to the Hampden. It seems that the crew believed themselves to be over the North Sea and headed in a south-westerly direction and then west, expecting to hit the Norfolk coast, when in reality, they were way out over the Atlantic to the west of Brest. A "running short of fuel" message was received at 00.59 and "coming down in the sea" six minutes later, and despite a search by 19 Group when daylight arrived, no trace of AE437 and its crew was found. F/O Caldwell was another who had been with the squadron from the start and had twenty-three sorties to his credit.

Syerston was not called into action when a force of 181 aircraft was assembled on the 30th, which included forty-eight Hampdens and four Manchesters, whose crews had been briefed to aim for the Blohm & Voss shipyards in Hamburg. Most crews located the target under clear skies and in good visibility provided by bright moonlight, and attacked either the shipyards or the city, while Wilhelmshaven and Cuxhaven provided alternatives. Local sources confirmed twenty-two fires but only two classed as large, and there was sufficient housing damage to deprive 2,500 people of their homes.

During the course of the month the squadron took part in eleven operations and dispatched sixty-one sorties for the loss of two experienced crews.

December 1941

The dominant theme during December would be the continuing presence at Brest of Scharnhorst, Gneisenau and, sometimes, Prinz Eugen, and no fewer than fifteen operations of varying sizes would be mounted against the port and its guests during the month, some by daylight. The weather kept the entire Command on the ground for the first six nights of the new month, and it was not until the 7th that a posted operation actually went ahead. Syerston was about to be closed for the laying of concrete runways and an advance party set off that morning on the six-mile journey to Balderton, located on the south-eastern edge of Newark on the other side of the A46. It was a grass aerodrome that had opened in June as a satellite for 25 O.T.U at Finningley and would be employed by the squadron for operational and training purposes, while administration and billeting remained at Syerston, and personnel were bussed in each day. Meanwhile, preparations went ahead for that night's operation to Aachen, Germany's most westerly city, perched on the frontiers with both Holland and Belgium for which a force of 130 aircraft was assembled. A second operation on this night involved 3 Group Wellingtons and Stirlings against the enemy warships at Brest, during which the Stirling element would conduct the first operational trials of the Oboe blind bombing device, a game-changing system not destined to enter service for almost thirteen months.

The briefed aiming point at Aachen was the Nazi Party HQ, which had no special significance other than the fact that it was situated in the city centre, at a time when it was still not admitted publicly that population centres were being bombed. 5 Group detailed fifty Hampdens and a dozen Manchesters, six of the former provided by 408 (Goose) Squadron and dispatched from Syerston between 02.10 and 02.22 with W/C Timmerman the senior pilot on duty and a variety of bomb loads. They flew out over Orfordness in initially fair weather conditions with isolated clouds, and having negotiated a flak welcome at the Belgian coast, W/C Timmerman and crew map-read their way over the snow-covered landscape below to arrive at what they described as an easily identifiable target. Other crews were less certain about their positions over nine to ten-tenths thin cloud with tops at up to 15,000 feet, interpreted by some crews as dense ground haze, upon which the bright moonlight reflected to create an equally impenetrable visual barrier. Flares were dropped, in the light of which built-up areas were observed but not necessarily identified, and the squadron scribe recorded only one bombing height of 7,000 feet. The crews of Sgts Beaver and Rea were unable to identify the primary target and brought their bombs home after seeking out but failing to find an alternative. It became clear at debriefings that barely half of the force had attacked the city, and local sources estimated a raid by sixteen aircraft, reporting just five high explosive bombs falling and causing minimal damage with no casualties.

Later, on the 8th, a few Hampdens were flown over to Balderton to be followed on the 9th by the main party and remaining aircraft, and a stand-down from operations for the rest of the day enabled all sections to settle in.

The previously mentioned escorted daylight "circus" operations undertaken by 2 Group had the purpose of tempting enemy fighters into the air to face RAF Spitfires in a war of attrition. These were, however, very different from the unescorted daylight operations known as "moling", conducted by the other groups, which relied on cloud cover and surprise to protect the crews. It was utter madness to put crews' lives at risk for a very small potential gain, but 5 Group ordered six crews into the air on the 10th to target ports and aerodromes in Germany and Holland. The 408 (Goose) Squadron crews of P/Os Biggane and Pim drew the short straws and were assigned respectively to the Luftwaffe aerodrome at Leeuwarden in northern Holland and the port of Emden some sixty miles further to the east, for which they departed Balderton at 12.06, each carrying four 500-pounders with an eleven-second delay fuse. P/O Biggane remained below the cloud base for as long as possible until it sank almost to sea level and crossed the enemy coast in cloud at 2,000 feet, before soon, thereafter, recognising the futility of continuing in such poor visibility. P/O Pim and crew were in cloud for most of the outwards flight and found the base over Germany to be at 200 feet, far too low to offer a chance of identifying the target. While flying over the River Ems at 14.13 they chanced upon a tanker and attacked it with three bombs, one of which was believed to be a direct hit, and the gunners strafed the decks and wheel house. The fourth bomb was dropped on an active flak position on the eastern bank of the Ems at 14.22 and the gunners strafed it as the Hampden escaped into cloud to begin the homeward journey.

A busy programme of day and night operations awaited fifteen 408 (Goose) Squadron crews on the 11th, beginning in the morning with the briefing of the crews of Sgts Beaver and Sanderson to repeat the previous day's moling sorties to Leeuwarden and Emden, while four other 5 Group crews attended to other targets. The Beaver crew departed Balderton at 12.10 bound for "Wespennest" Leeuwarden and flew out over the North Sea in cloud with a base at 3,000 feet, crossing the Dutch coast at Harlingen, from where cloud broke occasionally to enable them to establish position. By this means they came upon the target and dived onto it on a north-westerly heading, before turning sharply and bombing and strafing hangars and buildings from 50 feet, observing a large explosion that sent debris flying into the air and smoke issuing from a hangar. Meanwhile, the Sanderson crew had run out of cloud as they approached Emden and were left with no choice but to take their bombs home.

A flurry of activity in the late afternoon brought the departure of five Hampdens from Balderton between 16.36 and 17.15 bound for the Forget-me-not garden in Kiel Bay, and five freshman crews between 17.36 and 18.21 to join ten others from the group in attacking the docks and shipping at Le Havre. Finally, the crews of P/Os Pim and Rea got away at 18.20 to join a dozen others from the group to bomb the main railway station in Cologne. P/O Dowie and crew crossed the North Sea at 7,000 feet but having been unable to establish their position on the Danish coast, backtracked and recognising the mouth of the Elbe estuary, planted their vegetable there in the Eglantine garden. P/O Brown and crew experienced similar difficulties at the Danish coast and turned around to seek out the Rosemary garden in Heligoland Bight, where the mine was dropped and observed to enter the water with its parachute deployed. Sgt Beck and crew reached the western Baltic but failed to break cloud at 300 feet and brought their store home. Sgt Fraser and crew descended to 400 feet and established a pinpoint, from which they carried out a timed run and were the only 408 (Goose) Squadron crew known to have planted their vegetable according to brief. It is possible that P/O Hull RCAF and crew were also successful, but AE148 failed to return after crashing near Odense on Denmark's Fyn Island north of the target area and there were no survivors.

Meanwhile, the freshman crew of Sgt Sterling had taken off thirty minutes behind the others heading for the French coast and was recalled by a signal that the wireless operator in P/O Coulter's crew mistakenly took as a general order. They turned back also and were only some thirty miles from base when the error was realised, far too late to be able to complete their sortie. Sgt Vaughan and crew also aborted their sortie because of a technical issue, leaving the crews of P/Os Priest and Clarke to soldier on to the target, where ten-tenths cloud prevented them from establishing their position and they, too, returned their six 250-pounders to the bomb dump. A thoroughly wretched night's activities concluded at Cologne, where dense cloud thwarted the efforts of P/O Pim and crew, who, while circling in the hope of finding a gap, spotted an aerodrome near the city and dropped a 2,000-pounder on it, observing the lights to be extinguished. P/O Rea and crew had identified Liege and Charleroi in Belgium through gaps on the way out, and guided to the general target area by flak, dropped their 2,000-pounder on e.t.a. and observed a yellow flash.

On the morning of the 13th, six 408 (Goose) Squadron Hampdens took off between 12.50 and 13.01 on a "moling" trip to Brest, with P/O Pim the senior pilot on duty and each crew sitting on a 1,900-pounder. One unidentified crew turned back at the English coast because of engine trouble and the others were within twenty miles of the French coast when the absence of cloud persuaded them also to return to base. On the 14th, Scampton, Syerston (Balderton) and Waddington made ready twenty-two Hampdens to attack Scharnhorst and Gneisenau at Brest on a night of extremely unfavourable weather conditions including ten-tenths ice-bearing cloud at between 1,500 and

3,500 feet over the sea, which persuaded most to turn back after reaching a position west of the Channel Islands. The nine-strong 408 (Goose) Squadron element departed Balderton between 23.46 and 00.15 with S/L Burnett the senior pilot on duty, and they were followed into the air between 00.20 and 00.32 by the freshman crews of P/O Priest and Sgts Vaughan and Sterling, whose targets were the docks and shipping at Cherbourg. The Brest-bound crews of Sgts Dadson, Fraser and Sanderson and S/L Burnett were defeated by the appalling conditions, leaving the others to battle on to reach the target area, where the crews of Sgt Rea and P/O Brown dropped four and twelve bundles of leaflets (nickels) from 15,000 and 16,000 feet respectively, but withheld their bombs after failing to identify the aiming point. The crews of Sgts Beaver and Farrow and P/O Dowie soon realised the futility of trying to locate the enemy vessels in the conditions and returned their bombs to the dump.

Meanwhile, the freshmen crews were faring equally badly, and P/O Priest and crew having failed to locate the primary target through the ten-tenths cloud, headed east to Le Havre and then on to Ostend in a vain search for better pickings. Conditions, if possible, were even worse and the eight 250-pounders found their way back to the bomb dump. P5392 had crossed the Hampshire coast homebound when it crashed at 03.27 at New Farm, near Lyndhurst and burst into flames killing Sgt Sterling and his crew, who had only recently been recalled while on their maiden operation. Three horribly charred bodies were recovered and eventually identified, but at the time of the ORB entry, there was no trace of the fourth member of the crew. To compound this tragedy, AT133 disappeared without trace with the crew of Sgt Vaughan, who, with the exception of one crew member with ten sorties to his credit, were on their first operation together.

Among small-scale operations involving 5 Group on the 16th was a raid on the docks and shipping at Dunkerque, for which 408 (Goose) Squadron provided three of five Hampdens containing the freshman crews of P/Os Clarke, Coulter and Priest. They departed Balderton between 16.58 and 17.02, each carrying eight 250-pounders, and arrived at the target to encounter eight-tenths cloud, which prevented the Clarke and Coulter crews from identifying the town despite extensive searches lasting up to fifty minutes. They delivered bundles of reading matter to the local populace and brought their bombs home, while P/O Priest and crew chanced upon a gap in the clouds and dropped their load from 14,500 feet at 18.45 and saw nothing of the impact.

Another major assault on Brest was notified across the Command on the 17th, for which a force of 121 aircraft was assembled, among them twenty-five Hampdens from Waddington, Scampton and Syerston (Balderton). Nine 408 (Goose) Squadron Hampdens received a bomb load of four 500 and two 250-pounders and took off between 18.36 and 19.15 with all pilots either of pilot officer or sergeant rank and headed for the Dorset coast to begin the Channel crossing. Three crews were unable to identify the target through cloud and brought their bombs home, while the remaining six found little difficulty in picking out first the coastline, and then, guided to an extent by flak, the town, and in the light of flares delivered their attacks from 9,000 to 10,000 feet between 20.35 and 21.18, observing nothing of the impact as the flashes from flak and bomb bursts merged.

Eleven Manchesters took part in the next attempt on Brest, by daylight on the 18th, when claims were made of at least one hit on Gneisenau. W/C Bradshaw RCAF joined the squadron on this day to understudy W/C Timmerman before taking command of 5 Group's newest addition to the frontline, 420 (Snowy-Owl) Squadron RCAF, which would be formed officially at Waddington on the 19th under the temporary stewardship of W/C Collier DFC & Bar, a well-known figure in 5 Group after serving with distinction with 83 and 44 Squadrons.

The main operation on the 23rd was to be directed at Cologne for which a force of sixty-six aircraft included a 5 Group contribution of twenty Hampdens, six belonging to 408 (Goose) Squadron, while eighteen others were assigned to mining duties. 408 (Goose) Squadron provided the crews of P/Os Priest and Clarke among thirteen briefed for one of the Nectarine gardens off the Frisians, and they departed Balderton first at 16.20 and 16.22. Seven minutes later, Sgt Farrow and crew took off for the Forget-me-not garden in Kiel Bay and were followed into the air over the ensuing eleven minutes by the crews of Sgts Rea and Beaver and P/Os Pim and Constance. Finally, the Cologne-bound element consisting of the crews of P/Os Biggane, Brackenbury and Dowie, F/Sgt Sanderson and Sgts Beck and Fraser lifted off between 16.44 and 16.57, carrying either a 1,000-pounder and two 500-pounders or two each of 500 and 250-pounders and 120 x 4lb incendiaries.

P/O Clarke was unable to lock his cockpit hood and returned to base before even reaching the English coast, leaving the Priest crew to go on alone to the Frisians target area, where the cloud base down almost at sea-level thwarted their attempts to establish a pinpoint and persuaded them to go home. P/O Constance and crew were two hundred miles out on the way to making landfall on the Jutland coast, when excessive engine vibration convinced them to abandon their sortie also. P/O Pim and crew crossed the Danish coast in cloud at 5,000 feet and descended in stages to 1,400 feet until well past e.t.a. at the Baltic coast, at which point it was decided to turn back. Flying at 6,000 feet, at one minute past e.t.a., flak forced the Beaver crew to take evasive action and a shell burst threw the Hampden on its back. The pilot regained control after a spin, and the bombs were dropped on a flak position at Kiel, before minutes later, the port engine cut, probably because of icing and the mine had to be jettisoned to maintain altitude. This left just the crews of Sgts Farrow and Rea of the Forget-me-not element, neither of them able to establish a pinpoint in the conditions, and they returned their vegetables to store having jettisoned the 250-pounders, one "live" onto a flak position and the other "safe". Those reaching Cologne were confronted by up to ten-tenths cloud and unable to establish any kind of reference other than evidence of flak, all delivered their bombs indiscriminately from 12,000 to 14,000 feet between 19.28 and 19.40, before returning with nothing of value to pass on at debriefing.

W/C Bradshaw elected to spend his Christmas Day at nearby Digby, the home of 409 Squadron RCAF, a night-fighter unit, and proceeded there on the 24th. The third wartime Christmas passed peacefully, W/C Bradshaw returned to Syerston/Balderton on Boxing Day and operations resumed on the 27th, when 50 Squadron Hampdens supported the epic and successful Vaagso raid by Royal Marines off the Norwegian coast. Düsseldorf was posted as the target for 132 aircraft later that night and 5 Group contributed thirty Hampdens and seven Manchesters, a dozen of the former representing 408 (Goose) Squadron, whose crews were briefed to aim for the main Derendorf marshalling yards. They departed Balderton between 17.06 and 17.18 with the newly promoted F/Ls Constance and Pim the senior pilots on duty and either of the standard bomb loads on board and were followed into the air immediately by the Boulogne-bound crews of F/L Price RCAF and P/O Clarke, the former having recently been posted in as a flight commander elect. It was the last-mention pair that arrived first at their destination, easily identifying the river mouth and docks through six-tenths cloud and facing little opposition as they delivered their eight 250-pounders each from 12,000 and 14,000 feet at 19.05 and 19.10, without observing bursts.

Sgt Beaver and crew ran into icing conditions, which froze the pitot head and various instruments and left them with little choice but to turn back, and they were joined on the ground a little later by F/L Pim and crew, who complained of excessive vibration in the port engine. Those arriving in the Düsseldorf area expressed mixed views as to the conditions, some reporting that they were able to map-read along the Rhine and found the city and its marshalling yards to be easily identifiable. Others reported up to eight-tenths cloud with large clear patches but were unable to identify the briefed aiming point and bombed the general target area or alternatives. The bombing was carried out from 12,000 to 15,000 feet between 19.20 and 20.00 in the face of a spirited searchlight and flak defence, and most of the bomb bursts were lost in the glare. Local sources reported little damage and no casualties from a raid that cost seven aircraft and crews. At debriefing, the crews of P/O priest and F/L Constance reported attacking alternative targets at Duisburg and Roermond in Holland respectively.

The two main operations on the 28th involved eighty-six Wellingtons at Wilhelmshaven, while eighty-one Hampdens returned to the "Buna" synthetic rubber factory at Marl-Hüls on the northern edge of the Ruhr. 408 (Goose) Squadron made ready a dozen Hampdens and dispatched them from Balderton between 18.05 and 18.55 with S/L Clayton and F/Ls Constance and Pim the senior pilots on duty. Sgt Fraser and crew lost their intercom when fifty miles out over the North Sea and aborted their sortie, and F/L Constance had to contend with rising engine temperatures until finally deciding also that they should turn back. Perfect conditions enabled the others to map-read their way from the Dutch coast and pinpoint on Haltern Lake before reaching the target area to find clear skies and bright moonlight glinting off the snow-covered landscape. The 408 (Goose) Squadron contingent delivered their attacks from 12,500 to 15,500 feet between 20.30 and 21.00, and many bursts were observed in and around the factory along with fires. Returning crews were confident of a successful outcome, although no local report emerged to confirm or deny. Four Hampdens failed to return, and among them was P1165, which fell victim over Holland to the night-fighter of Oblt Emil Woltersdorf of III./NJG1 and crashed near Winterswijk, killing three members of the crew and delivering the pilot, P/O Brackenbury, into enemy hands. This was the squadron's final casualty of the year, and five months of operations had so far cost it nine crews from 343 sorties.

During the course of December, the squadron undertook seventeen operations and dispatched ninety-one sorties for the loss of three Hampdens and crews.

It had been a disappointing year for the Command, and despite the best efforts of the crews, one of under-achievement, with little advance on the performance of 1940. The new aircraft types, the Stirling, Halifax and Manchester, introduced into operational service early in the year, had each failed to meet the requirements expected of them and had undergone long periods of grounding while essential modifications were carried out. 1942 would bring changes, however, chief among which were the arrival on the operational scene of the war-winning Lancaster, and a new Commander-in-Chief, who would know how to exploit it.

January 1942

As far as most crews were concerned, the incoming year would look and feel exactly like the outgoing one, and still under the restrictions of the November directive, the Command's activities reflected the continuing obsession with the German raiders at Brest, against which a further eleven operations would take place during January, eight during the first two weeks. 5 Group would be without 44 (Rhodesia) Squadron until early March as it worked towards operational status on the Lancaster.

408 (Goose) Squadron began the year with a complement of twenty-three aircrew officers and 112 NCOs and was not involved in 5 Group's first operational activity of the year, which involved four Hampdens each from 49, 106 and 144 Squadrons conducting daylight "moling" duties over Holland and north-western Germany on the 2nd. Later, that day, eight 408 (Goose) Squadron crews were called to briefing to learn that they would be spending a large part of the evening engaged in mining activities at three locations off the Biscay coast, three in the Cinnamon garden off La Rochelle, two in the Beech garden off St-Nazaire and three in the Deodar garden in the Gironde estuary that led to the port of Bordeaux. All three ports contained U-Boot fleets protected by concrete bunkers, while the Gironde estuary was also the gateway to the Atlantic for tankers servicing a number of oil production and storage plants located along its length at Pauillac, Blaye and Bec-d'Ambes. The 408 (Goose) squadron elements departed Balderton together between 16.50 and 17.38 with F/Ls Priest and Constance bound for Beech, F/Sgt Sanderson and Sgts Beck and Rea for Cinnamon and Sgts Beaver, Farrow and Fraser for Deodar. They flew out over the Dorset coast to make landfall between St-Malo and Saint-Brieuc, and F/L Priest and crew dropped their two wing-mounted 250-pounders on the aerodrome at Vannes-Meucon from 9,000 feet at 19.30, observing bursts at the intersection of the runways, before continuing on to reach the Biscay coast and pinpoint on Pointe-de-Croisic. From there they carried out a timed run in a north-westerly direction to release their mine from 600 feet at 19.55. F/L Constance and crew, meanwhile, had run into conditions of poor visibility and inexplicably had spent more than two hours searching for the first beacon at Upper Heyford to establish their position before setting course for the next leg to the coast. By the time that Upper Heyford was located it was too late to continue and the sortie was abandoned.

The Deodar-bound Sgt Farrow had been unable to lock his cockpit canopy and on returning to base to have the problem rectified could not land because of poor visibility and ended up at North Luffenham, too late to complete the sortie. Sgt Fraser and crew lost the use of their intercom shortly after crossing the French coast and turned back, leaving Sgt Beaver and crew to carry on alone to the Gironde estuary, where they arrived at 2,000 feet contending with a severe engine problem. The vegetable was released "live" at 20.53 in an approximate position some four miles off the western bank of the estuary, and a tense return flight ended at Moreton-in-Marsh after five minutes short of eight hours aloft.

F/Sgt Sanderson and crew reached their target area off La Rochelle, but the navigator was unable to find a pinpoint by which to establish their position. After flying around for thirty minutes the vegetable was dropped "live" from 4,000 feet into an estimated position, which was plotted later to be to the north-east of the Ile-de-Re, fairly close to the briefed drop zone. Sgt Rea and crew were also defeated by poor visibility and after a fruitless search lasting fifty minutes, jettisoned their mine and wing-mounted 250-pounders off the Biscay coast. On the way home they reported some kind of naval activity involving a fast-moving vessel off the Channel Island of Guernsey, heading for the French coast and firing its guns and receiving return fire from the shore. Sgt Beck and crew had experienced the same ten-tenths cloud until arriving at the French coast, where it began to break up to leave excellent visibility. In the target area it had built again to seven-tenths at 2,000 feet, but after descending to beneath the cloud base the navigator was able to establish a pinpoint on the northern-most tip of the Ile-de-Oleron and a timed run was completed to deliver the mine into the briefed location.

The 5th of January brought a change in structure for 408 (Goose) Squadron, with the addition of a C Flight, which was to be commanded by S/L Burnett, while the newly promoted S/L Price assumed command of A Flight and S/L Clayton remained in post as B Flight commander. The main operation that night involved a force of 154 aircraft targeting the Scharnhorst and Gneisenau and the naval dockyard at Brest, for which 5 Group provided twenty-seven Hampdens and twelve Manchesters. Many crews were thwarted by an effective smoke screen and eight to ten-tenths cloud at around 10,000 feet, and despite claims of large fires by some returning crews, no accurate assessment of results could be made. At 05.15 on the following morning, S/L Price and crew set off to attack the docks and shipping at Cherbourg with eight 250-pounders and flew out over Portland Bill to cross the Channel in excellent conditions. Halfway across, they encountered eight-tenths cloud, and the coast could only be glimpsed through occasional gaps, which persuaded them to withhold their bombs but release bundles of nickels over the area from 14,000 feet at 06.55. On the way home a BF110 was spotted dead astern and below with an intermittently-flashing white headlight in the nose, but it was evaded as was a BF109 a little later.

The crews of Sgts Beaver, Beck, Farrow and F/Sgt Sanderson were briefed for "Scuttle A", a roving commission raid in which they were authorised to attack any built-up area in north-western Germany in company with fifteen others from the group. They departed Balderton between 03.30 and 03.30, each carrying a 1,900-pounder and two 250-pounders and flew out over Skegness bound for landfall on the enemy coast via the Frisians. The Beck crew found the outward route to be cloud-covered as far as Baltrum Island, where breaks revealed the ground and the navigator reported vessels, which they decided to investigate. They turned back, and then made a second run, the report of which is confusing and suggests that a town was attacked from 13,000 feet at 06.23 after a four-minute timed run. We must assume this to be Westdorf, the larger of two villages on the island, which also received propaganda leaflets. The cloud prevented the other crews from positively identifying any landmark until heading home, when the Beaver crew bombed the aerodrome on Norderney from 13,000 feet at 06.35 and the Farrow crew a flak concentration believed to be at Emden from 13,000 feet at 06.16. F/Sgt Sanderson and crew flew into Germany for thirty minutes and dropped their bombs from 13,800 feet at 06.37 with no clue as to their precise location and the flash of the 1,900-pounder's detonation was observed. As they regained the Waddensee homebound, they identified the uninhabited Islands of Scharhörn and Neuwerk off Cuxhaven.

AM Sir Richard Peirse left his post as C-in-C Bomber Command on the 8th to be succeeded temporarily by AVM Baldwin, the A-O-C 3 Group. In February, Peirse would take up a new appointment as C-in-C Allied Air Forces in India and South-East Asia, but the sense that he had been "sacked" from Bomber Command would linger, and perhaps unjustly tarnish his legacy. Brest was posted as the target for a force of 151 aircraft that night, reconnaissance having revealed that Scharnhorst and Gneisenau had been joined once more by Prinz Eugen. 5 Group contributed thirty-seven Hampdens and ten Manchesters to the main event, including nine of the former belonging to 408 (Goose) Squadron, and six Hampdens and seven Manchesters for freshman crews to employ against the docks and shipping at Cherbourg. The Balderton crews, including that of the Cherbourg-bound S/L Price, took off in bright moonlight between 03.40 and 04.15 with S/L Burnett the senior pilot on duty and each Hampden assigned to Brest carrying four 500 and two 250-pounders, while S/L Price's was loaded with eight 250-pounders. S/L price and crew reached their target area with overheating engines, which prevented them from spending any time lining up an attack and dispensed nickels before bringing their bombs home.

Brest was concealed by up to ten-tenths cloud, and despite the deployment of many flares, it proved impossible for most crews to identify the target and they dispensed nickels before turning back with their bombs. Sgt Beaver and crew searched for fifty-five minutes before catching a glimpse of the docks area and bombing it from 14,000 feet at 05.35, the rear gunner reporting two bursts. Twenty-five minutes later, F/L Constance and crew identified the northern shore of the Rade-du-Brest and attacked it from 11,000 feet at 06.00 and saw nothing to report to the intelligence section at debriefing. A force of eighty-two aircraft was assembled for a return to Brest on the following night, for which 5 Group put up twenty-seven Hampdens and six Manchesters from Bottesford, Coningsby, North Luffenham and Scampton, and five Hampdens from 49 Squadron for mining duties in the Jellyfish garden on the approaches to the port. The weather in the target area continued to be unhelpful with eight to ten-tenths cloud and poor visibility, and many crews returned home with their bombs.

Thirty-four Hampdens and nine Manchesters from Bottesford, Coningsby, Scampton, Swinderby and Syerston/Balderton were detailed by 5 Group on the 10th to contribute to an overall force of 124 aircraft bound for Wilhelmshaven that night to attack the main railway station. The 408 (Goose) Squadron contingent of ten Hampdens took off between 16.28 and 16.53 with W/C Timmerman and S/L Price the senior pilots on duty and two of the deputy flight commanders, F/Ls Constance and Priest also on the order of battle. Each crew had either a 1,900lb bomb beneath their feet and two wing-mounted 250-pounders or a 1,000-pounder and two 500-pounders, while P/O Coulter and crew, who followed immediately afterwards, carried four 500 and two 250-pounders to drop on the docks at Emden. They flew out together over Skegness on course for pinpoints on the western Frisians and benefitted from excellent conditions, those bound for Wilhelmshaven arriving in their target area to find clear skies and good visibility.

By this time, P/O Coulter and crew had lost their port engine and had turned back from a position eighty-six miles out over the North Sea, landing at Donnanook some two hours after taking off. F/Sgt Sanderson and crew also turned back because of an engine issue, leaving the others to complete the 320-mile outward flight, at which point F/L Constance and crew located the north-western coast of Jade Bay and began their bombing run, only to find that the bomb doors refused to open, even when hand pumped. Some time was spent circling while attempts were made to rectify the problem, but to no avail and they set off home, losing the use of their wireless on the way and descending to 1,000 feet, where they managed to jettison the 1,900-pounder. They were given permission to land at Leconfield and the pilot discovered that the undercarriage would not lock but approached anyway with the alarm sounding and on touchdown the undercarriage held, and the alarm stopped. Meanwhile, five crews delivered their attacks from 12,000 to 15,000 feet between 19.30 and 19.50, while Sgt Fraser and crew were unable to positively identify the port and bombed a flak position to the north.

P/O Brown and crew were another to suffer the frustration of initially reluctant-to-open bomb doors, and when they did finally function, the bombs were dropped onto the uninhabited Alte Mellum Island at the mouth of the bay. The port engine had been emitting flames up to that point and cut out abruptly as soon as the bombs fell away, leaving them unable to maintain their height at 14,000 feet and forced to jettison guns and ammunition to save weight. They continued to sink and were at 500 feet by the time they reached Terschelling, from where they were fired upon by light flak, but were not hit and managed to claw back 2,500 feet. Their ordeal was not yet over, however, as the instruments either failed due to icing or the excessive vibration and the wireless broke down thirty minutes from the English coast. They received no response from the Coltishall beacon to their W/T "Darky" call, but Horsham-St-Faith lit up its flare path and they lobbed in, happy to be back on Mother Earth. The wireless operator received praise for sticking by his morse key to secure a succession of navigational fixes and the navigator also deserved credit. Sadly, F/L Priest and crew failed to return in AE286 and were lost without trace on what was the pilot's eighth sortie and the second pilot's eleventh.

Adverse weather conditions kept 5 Group on the ground for the next three nights, and when the faithful were called to prayer at Bottesford, North Luffenham, Scampton and Swinderby on the 14th, it was to reveal Hamburg as the destination for an overall force of ninety-five aircraft. The targets were the Blohm & Voss shipyards situated on the Kuhwerder Island opposite the Sankt Pauli district to the west of the city centre and the nearby Hamburger Flugzeugbau airframe factory located on Finkenwerder Island. 5 Group was to have supported the operation with thirty-five Hampdens and fifteen Manchesters, but four of the former from 61 Squadron could not be made ready in time and three from 49 Squadron were cancelled after one crashed on take-off and prevented the other two from getting away. Severe icing conditions over the North Sea persuaded some crews to dump bombs in order to maintain height, and those reaching the target were challenged by extreme darkness and thick ground haze, which created difficult conditions for aiming point identification. That said, crews could always rely on the searchlight and flak batteries to guide them into the heart of the city, where large ground features like the Binnen and Aussen-Alster Lakes on the north-western edge of the centre were a good guide for non-precision bombing. It became clear at debriefings that only half of the force had attacked the Hamburg area and local sources confirmed seven large fires and hits on the Altona railway station but no significant damage.

Hamburg was "on" again twenty-four hours later, for which a force of ninety-six aircraft was assembled with a 5 Group contribution of twenty-seven Hampdens and ten Manchesters. Seven 408 (Goose) Squadron crews were called to briefing to learn that they were to attack the city centre and departed Balderton between 16.48 and 17.18 with S/Ls Burnett and Price the senior pilots on duty and a bomb load each of two 500-pounders and four SBCs of 4lb incendiaries. Cloud over the North Sea had dissipated by the time that Heligoland and Friedrichskoog provided a pinpoint to follow the course of the River Elbe into the heart of the city, where extreme darkness and poor visibility hampered attempts to establish a position, despite the blanket of snow on the ground.

Three 408 (Goose) Squadron crews bombed from 9,000 to 14,000 feet between 20.05 and 20.14, while the others attacked flak positions and an aerodrome in the general target area with their 500-pounders and brought the incendiaries home. On return at 03.00, after fifteen minutes short of ten hours aloft, AE393 crashed at Dalefoot, West Burton, thirteen miles south-west of Catterick, killing three members of the crew and seriously injuring S/L Wilf Burnett RCAF, whose broken leg, ankle and jaw would require a lengthy stay in hospital. It became clear at debriefing that, again, only a little over a half of the force had bombed the primary target and the raid proved to be another in the long line of disappointments since the start of the autumn. According to local sources, the emergency services dealt with thirty-six fires, only three of them classed as large, and there had been no major incidents.

F/L Constance was promoted to acting squadron leader rank in order to be installed as the new C Flight commander, while over at Bottesford, 207 Squadron set up a Conversion Flight on the 16th in preparation for the arrival of its first example of the Lancaster, having been selected as the third unit to receive it after 44 and 97 Squadrons. The flight would be equipped, initially, with two Manchesters, the type it had introduced into squadron service and had struggled with for more than a year. Once the first Lancaster arrived on the 25th, the conversion programme would begin with selected second pilots and crews from the squadron.

Attention remained on north-western Germany on the 17th, when Bremen was posted as the target for eighty-three aircraft, including twenty Hampdens and six Manchesters from Coningsby, North Luffenham and Scampton. 408 (Goose) Squadron was not involved in the main event and dispatched the lone crew of P/O Clarke at 18.03 to attack the docks and shipping at Dunkerque with eight 250-pounders. Ten-tenths cloud in the target area concealed the target completely and eight bundles of nickels were dispensed, while the bombs were returned to the dump.

Emden had been a regular destination for small forces since the 10th, sometimes with a contribution from 5 Group, and five 49 Squadron Hampdens were detailed to join twenty Wellingtons to attack it on the 20th, after snow and severe frost had kept aircraft on the ground for two nights. Bremen and Emden shared the Command's attention on the night of the 21/22nd, when eleven Hampdens joined in a raid by fifty aircraft on the former, while twelve Hampdens and three Manchesters attended to the latter in an overall force of thirty-eight aircraft. 408 (Goose) Squadron supported both endeavours with the crews of P/Os Clarke and Dowie, F/Sgt Sanderson and Sgts Farrow and Rea for Bremen and P/O Coulter for Emden, and it was the last-mentioned that departed Balderton first at 16.50, to be followed into the air by the others between 17.08 and 17.50. Each was carrying a 1,000-pounder and two 500-pounders as they climbed over the station intending to fly out over Skegness, but F/Sgt Sanderson and crew were back on the ground within forty minutes after the rear gunner's door blew open and could not be closed. Nine minutes later Sgt Rea and crew returned with engine trouble and P/O Coulter and crew lost their port engine having reached operational altitude and returned after being airborne for two-and-a-half hours. P/O Dowie and crew crossed the German coast close enough to Emden to be troubled by searchlights, but pressed on to Bremen, where haze concealed the marshalling yards aiming point and the bombs were dropped over the city from 10,500 feet.

Sgt Farrow and crew had selected a route across Holland and had reached Haselünne, twenty miles inside Germany, when they were surprised by a nest of around thirty searchlight beams, which they attempted to evade by weaving violently and shedding half of their altitude. The bomb doors had frozen shut and had to be pumped down in order to jettison the bombs, but once relieved of the weight, they were able to sneak away and were heading home when set upon from the port quarter by two BF110s. Sgt Farrow turned into the attack and the wireless operator claimed to have shot down one of the assailants before five bursts of fire hit the Hampden and knocked out the intercom. The enemy aircraft were evaded, leaving the Hampden with a coughing engine at 6,000 feet and little prospect of getting home, whereupon the order was given to abandon the aircraft. Unaware that the message had not been heard and assuming that the crew had baled out, Sgt Farrow decided to attempt a return and found the aircraft handled better at 1,500 feet. Once over England and uncertain of his whereabouts, Sgt Farrow flashed SOS with his identification light and was directed by searchlights to West Malling in Kent, where he carried out a belly-landing and only then discovered that the others were still on board. All were badly injured, and the navigator and lower rear gunner succumbed within forty-eight hours, while the wireless operator would require a lengthy stay in hospital to repair a cannon shell wound in a leg. The Hampden, AD754, was returned to flying condition, and Sgt Farrow would receive an immediate award of a DFM.

P/O Clarke RCAF and crew had taken off some twenty minutes late because of an engine issue and their return in X3051 was awaited in vain. No trace of the Hampden and crew ever surfaced, and it must be assumed that they had gone down in the North Sea during what for the pilot and two others was their fifth sortie.

An excess of snow and surface water rendered Balderton unsuitable for flying and all serviceable Hampdens were flown to North Luffenham on the 25th along with sixty ground crew, all under the command of S/L Clayton. According to the squadron and 5 Group ORBs, seven of the eight crews were called to briefing during the afternoon to learn of their part in that night's assault on Brest and its lodging enemy warships, for which a force of sixty-one aircraft was made ready, 5 Group contributing thirty-five Hampdens and fifteen Manchesters from North Luffenham and Scampton. However, the squadron ORB lists only the crews of S/L Price, P/Os Brown and Dowie, F/Sgt Sanderson and Sgt Dadson, which took off between 17.34 and 17.40, each sitting on four 500lb semi-armour-piercing (SAP) bombs with two wing-mounted 250-pounders. AD782 had reached 1,500 feet when it stalled and dived nose-first into the ground, killing Sgt Victor Dadson RCAF, who was on his seventh sortie, and the other three occupants. The others began the Channel crossing at Chesil Beach and despite perfect weather conditions all the way, a smoke screen caused poor visibility over the target and prevented all but one crew from establishing their position. In the face of a hostile flak defence, three jettisoned their bombs and turned for home, while P/O Dowie and crew chanced upon a gap in the smoke through which the docks were clearly visible and bombed from 12,000 feet, observing bursts in the docks area in close proximity to the torpedo-boat station. What had been a successful sortie was marred somewhat when levelling out too late from the glide path and undershooting the threshold, ripping off a wheel and causing damage to the fuselage.

50 Squadron represented 5 Group at Hannover on the 26th in a force of seventy-one aircraft, fewer than half of which attacked the primary target. The next assault on Brest was posted on the 27th and involved thirty-two Hampdens and three Manchesters from Scampton, North Luffenham and Bottesford. *(The Bomber Command War Diaries does not record any operations taking place on this night)*. It was reported that Prinz Eugen was also "still in town" as an added attraction for the

force, which included six Hampdens representing 408 (Goose) Squadron and taking off between 00.27 and 00.46 with S/L Price and F/L Pim the senior pilots on duty. They received the same bomb loads and adopted the same route as for two nights earlier and lost the services of S/L Price at Upper Heyford because of overheating engines, leaving the others to arrive in the target area under a bright half-moon and two to ten-tenths cloud with a base at 3,000 feet. Haze or a smoke-screen further obscured the docks area creating challenging conditions for target identification, but four of the 408 (Goose) Squadron crews delivered their bomb loads from 11,500 to 16,000 feet in the face of an intense flak defence and observed bursts but no detail. F/Sgt Sanderson and crew had been contending with icing and had jettisoned the 250-pounders, and on failing to identify the docks, returned their 500-pounders to the dump. F/L Pim and crew returned with a badly flak-damaged AE190, which had lost its automatic pilot and heating and oxygen systems but would be returned to service.

Orders were received at Coningsby and Swinderby on the 28th to prepare for an attack on Münster, for which a force of fifty-five Wellingtons and twenty-nine Hampdens was prepared, while a second force consisting of four Hampdens, seven Manchesters from Bottesford, Coningsby, North Luffenham and Scampton and thirty-seven aircraft from other groups was assembled for a freshman operation against the docks and shipping at Boulogne. 408 (Goose) Squadron remained on the ground until the last night of the month, when a force of seventy-one aircraft took off for another tilt at Brest, among them forty-one Hampdens and eleven Manchesters representing 5 Group. The seven-strong 408 (Goose) Squadron element departed North Luffenham between 17.50 and 18.02 with S/L Price and F/L Pim the senior pilots on duty and each Hampden carrying the usual load of four 500-pounders and two of 250lbs. They lost the services of P/O Brown and crew over the south coast when the wireless operator's microphone failed, the oxygen system froze and the port engine overheated, while the rest pressed on to find the target area bathed in bright moonlight that provided excellent visibility. As usual, there were varying opinions as to the cloud conditions ranging from clear skies to eight-tenths, but what was not in doubt was the smoke screen, which prevented many crews from establishing a pinpoint and carrying out an attack. Others had fixed their positions by coastal features including the Rade-de-Brest, and intense flak and searchlights pointed the way to the docks area for what would be an uncomfortable bombing run. Five of the 408 (Goose) Squadron element delivered an attack from 12,000 to 14,000 feet, while Sgt Fraser and crew abandoned their attempt after searching for thirty minutes and took their bombs home. Returning crews reported bursts and fires near the Port Militaire, but no hits were claimed on the cruisers, and this inconclusive operation cost two Hampdens and three out of nine 61 Squadron Manchesters.

During the course of the month, the squadron took part in fourteen operations and dispatched sixty-seven sorties for the loss of four Hampdens, three complete crews and three members of another.

February 1942

There were no operations for 5 Group during the first few days of the new month, and all available personnel were press-ganged into snow-clearing duties. Although the impending breakout from Brest by the three enemy warships would take the Royal Navy and the RAF by complete surprise in what would be a most humiliating episode for the government and the nation, which became known as "The Channel Dash", there was clearly some advance warning. At 17.00 on the 3rd, 5 Group called for nine experienced 408 (Goose) Squadron crews to be ready to attend briefing at 06.30 on the 4th and for S/L Constance and crew to be called over from Balderton to take part. The aircraft were fuelled and bombed up in readiness, and the briefing revealed that S/Ls Clayton, Price and Constance was each to lead a section of three to intercept the cruisers as they made their way up the English Channel. The crews remained on stand-by all day along with three Manchesters at Bottesford, but the weather conditions over Brittany prevented any reconnaissance from taking place to ascertain whether or not the ships had weighed anchor. At 16.00 six crews were requested for mining duties, which was changed at 16.45, before being cancelled altogether at 20.30. It was a similar story on the 5th, when six Manchesters were put on stand-by and six 408 (Goose) Squadron crews were requested for bombing and mining operations, which were cancelled at 17.45. Earlier, His Royal Highness Air Commodore The Duke of Kent had arrived at North Luffenham for lunch and left shortly afterwards.

5 Group notified its stations on the 6th to prepare for daylight mining operations in the Nectarine I and II gardens off the southern and central Frisians, and between them they raised a force of thirty-three Hampdens and thirteen Manchesters. The 408 (Goose) Squadron crews of Sgt Rea and the newly promoted F/Sgts Beaver and Beck departed North Luffenham between 10.51 and 10.56, Sgt Rea and crew bound for Nectarine I and flying in good visibility below the cloud base at 1,000 feet to locate Terschelling and plant their vegetable in the briefed location from 600 feet at 13.07. Further north, the Beaver and Beck crews pinpointed respectively on Ameland and Schiermonnikoog before delivering their mines according to brief from 700 and 600 feet at 12.41 and 13.05. That night, Brest was targeted by Wellingtons and Stirlings, and the daylight gardening operation in the Frisians was repeated on the following day employing thirty-two Hampdens, when the target area on this occasion was further north in the Nectarine III garden off the island of Wangerooge in the Waddenzee. *(The Waddenzee/Waddensee extends along the Dutch and German coasts as far as Schleswig-Holstein, the Dutch spelling with z and the German with s.)*

5 Group was not called into action again until the 10th, when a dozen 49 Squadron Hampdens were made ready to attack the main railway station in Bremen. The entire operation had descended into a shambles even before take-off, when the contributions from North Luffenham and Syerston were cancelled because of dangerous ice and water conditions on the aerodromes and a similar situation at Scampton delayed the preparation of six of the original eighteen Hampdens and led to them also being scrubbed. A further raid on Brest was also mounted on this night by a dozen Wellington and six Stirlings of 3 Group, which found the target area completely concealed beneath cloud.

Orders were received at Bottesford, Coningsby and Swinderby on the 11th to prepare a dozen Hampdens and six Manchesters between them for an operation that night against a railway station at Mannheim. They were part of an overall force of forty-nine aircraft, which enjoyed favourable conditions, that enabled them to identify the target and release their bombs unopposed by flak in the vicinity of the briefed aiming point. Among other small-scale operations on this night was one against Brest by eighteen Wellingtons, the crews of which would have been unaware that they were the last to engage in this seemingly endless saga. As the sound of their engines receded into the eastern cloud-filled skies, Vice-Admiral Otto Cilliax, the Brest Group commander, whose flag was on Scharnhorst, put Operation Cerberus into action at 21.14, and Scharnhorst, Gneisenau and Prinz Eugen slipping anchor, before heading into the English Channel under an escort of destroyers and E-Boats. It was an audacious bid for freedom, covered by bad weather, widespread jamming and meticulously planned support by the Kriegsmarine and the Luftwaffe, all of which had been rehearsed extensively during January. The planning, and a little good fortune, allowed the fleet to make undetected progress until spotted off Le Touquet by two Spitfires piloted by G/C Victor Beamish, the commanding officer of Kenley, and W/C Finlay Boyd, both of whom maintained radio silence and did not report their find until landing at 10.42 on the morning of the 12th.

The British authorities had prepared a plan in advance for precisely this eventuality, under the Codename, Operation Fuller, but so secret was it, that few, it seemed, either knew of its full requirements or even of its existence. Once the enemy fleet was spotted in the late morning, frantic efforts were made to get Coastal and Bomber Command aircraft away, and it was after 13.00 before the first sorties were launched. The 5 Group stations worked frantically to get sixty-four Hampdens and fifteen Manchesters into the air, 408 (Goose) Squadron sending eight Hampdens away between 14.42 and 14.52 with S/Ls Clayton and Constance the senior pilots on duty and orders to make for a search position off The Hague and the Hoek of Holland. They were part of the largest commitment of aircraft by daylight in the war to date, amounting to 242 sorties, and arrived to find rainstorms, squally conditions and a cloud base down in places to 100 feet that compounded the difficulties of locating a fleet at sea. Most crews would fail in that regard, and Sgt Brown and crew were forced to drop out at Southwold when their starboard engine failed. S/L Constance's section did manage to locate the ships, and they released their bombs from eight hundred feet at 15.58 but scored no hits. AT154 was hit by flak and the port aileron shot away and, for a time, S/L Constance doubted that he would make it home but landed safely after less than three hours aloft. S/L Clayton and crew broke cloud at 15.42 right over the battle fleet, which was some sixteen miles off the Hoek of Holland, but because of the low cloud base were unable to get into a favourable position for an attack and after circling in and out of cloud dodging intense flak, they brought their four 500-pounders back. Fifteen aircraft failed to return, 5 Group alone posting missing nine Hampdens and crews, all lost in the North Sea, six of them without trace. They could be added to all of the others sacrificed to this endeavour over the past eleven months.

Despite the heroic effort and sacrifice of the Bomber Command, Coastal Command and Fleet Air Arm crews, the enemy fleet made good its escape into open sea, although, its own trials and tribulations were not yet over. Scharnhorst struck a mine in the late afternoon and began to fall back, and at 19.55, a magnetic mine detonated close enough to Gneisenau, when off Terschelling, to open a small hole in the starboard side, and temporarily slow her progress also. Later still, at 21.34, when passing through the same stretch of water, Scharnhorst hit another mine which stopped both engines and damaged steering and fire control. The vessel got under way again at 22.23 using its starboard engines and making twelve knots, while carrying an additional one thousand tons of seawater. The day's activities were not yet over for 5 Group, and the crews of fourteen Hampdens and nine Manchesters were briefed to lay mines in the Nectarines garden off the Frisians through which the enemy fleet would have to pass to reach safety.

Gneisenau and Prinz Eugen reached the Elbe Estuary at 07.00 on the 13th, and tied up at Brunsbüttel North Locks at 09.30, while Scharnhorst arrived at Wilhelmshaven at 10.00 with three months-worth of damage to repair. The mines had been laid almost certainly by 5 Group Hampdens over the preceding nights and demonstrated the remarkable effectiveness of this war-long campaign. The entire episode was a major embarrassment to the government and the nation, but on a positive note, this annoying and distracting itch had been scratched for the last time and the Command could now concentrate its forces against the strategic targets for which it was best suited.

A new Air Ministry directive, issued on the 14th, was to change the emphasis of bomber operations from that point until the end of the war. Lengthy consideration having been given to the Butt Report and the future of an independent bomber force, the new policy authorised the blatant area bombing of Germany's industrial towns and cities in a direct assault on the morale of the civilian population, particularly its workers. This had, of course, been going on since the summer of 1940, but no longer would there be the pretence of claiming to be attacking industrial and military targets. Waiting in the wings, in fact, at this very moment, four days into his voyage from the United States in the armed merchantman, Alcantara, was a new leader, a man well-known to 5 Group, who not only would pursue this policy with a will, but also possessed the self-belief, arrogance and stubbornness to fight his corner against all-comers on behalf of his beleaguered Bomber Command.

That night, a force of ninety-eight aircraft took off to employ the main post office and railway station as the aiming points for an area attack on Mannheim, to which 5 Group contributed twenty-five Hampdens and nine Manchesters. 408 (Goose) Squadron dispatched the crews of F/Ls Brown and Dowie and F/Sgt Beaver and Beck from North Luffenham between 18.01 and 18.08, each with a 1,000-pounder and two 500-pounders beneath their feet and lost the services of the crews of F/L Brown and F/Sgt Beaver to the failure of their heating systems very soon thereafter. F/Sgt beck and crew reached the target area by homing in on the searchlight and flak activity and River Rhine and encountered four to ten-tenths cloud at between 2,000 and 12,000 feet, with fair visibility above and ground haze below. Such weather conditions proved to be unhelpful, and they were unable to identify the briefed aiming point, bombing instead the general built-up area from 13,500 feet at 21.06. F/L Dowie and crew could not positively establish a position and sought out last resort SEMO and MOPA targets, respectively, "self-evident military objective" and "military objective previously attacked". They came upon a built-up area to the south-west of Mannheim and north-west of Karlsruhe, where the navigator dropped the bombs in a stick from 10,500 feet at 21.10 without observing the results. Despite the claims of sixty-seven crews to have bombed the city, local sources reported two buildings destroyed and fifteen damaged.

5 Group detailed thirty-seven Hampdens and twelve Manchesters on the 16th to carry out mining duties in three areas, the Nectarine I garden off Terschelling, the Nectarine III garden, encompassing the east Frisian islands of Wangerooge, Juist and Borkum, and Rosemary in the Heligoland Bight. 408 (Goose) Squadron briefed the crew of W/C Bradshaw, the 420 Squadron commanding officer, for Nectarine I along with the crew of P/O Coulter, and the crews of S/L Price, F/Ls Brown and Dowie and F/Sgts Beaver and Beck for Rosemary and sent them on their

way from North Luffenham between 17.30 and 17.40. S/L Price and F/Sgt Beaver and their crews turned back early, the former after the rear gunner's door jammed open and the latter because of a failed heating system. W/C Bradshaw and crew were unable to establish a position in conditions of extreme darkness and poor visibility and abandoned the sortie, while the remaining four crews managed to locate a pinpoint and plant their vegetables according to brief from 700 feet between 20.29 and 20.50.

The night of the 18/19th was devoted to mining and nickelling operations, the former undertaken by twenty-five Hampdens off the Frisians in all three Nectarine gardens, the Rosemary garden in the Heligoland Bight and the Yam garden in the Schillig Roads approaches to Jade Bay and the Weser estuary. S/L Price and F/L Brown and their crews took off at 17.12 and 17.20 respectively to return to the Rosemary garden, where the former broke cloud in extreme darkness at 800 feet, before pinpointing on Heligoland and planting their vegetable from 700 feet at 20.16. The latter struggled to establish a pinpoint on a Frisian island, but the pilot spotted Trischen Island off the mouth of the Elbe, and this was employed as the starting point for a timed run that culminated with the dropping of the mine from 800 feet at 20.47. Meanwhile, F/L Dowie and crew had taken off at 17.24 bound for Nectarine II and pinpointed on Schiermonnikoog before planting their vegetable from 700 feet at 19.53.

Air Chief Marshal Sir Arthur Harris took up his post as the new Commander-in-Chief of Bomber Command on the 22nd. He was a man well-known to 5 Group, having served as its A-O-C until November 1940, when he became second deputy to Sir Charles Portal, the Chief-of-the-Air-Staff. Harris arrived at the helm with firm ideas already in place on how to win the war by bombing alone, a pre-war theory, which no commander had yet had an opportunity to put into practice. It was obvious to him, that the small-scale raids on multiple targets favoured by his predecessor served only to dilute the effort, and that such pin-prick attacks could not hurt Germany's war effort. He recognized the need to overwhelm the defences and emergency services by pushing the maximum number of aircraft across the aiming point in the shortest possible time, and this would signal the birth of the bomber stream and an end to the former practice, whereby squadrons or even crews determined for themselves the details of their sorties. He knew also that urban areas are most efficiently destroyed by fire rather than blast, and it would not be long before the bomb loads carried in his aircraft reflected this thinking.

In the meantime, while he developed his ideas, he would continue with the fairly small-scale attacks on German ports favoured by his predecessor, and later on the evening of his appointment, he sent thirty-one Wellingtons and nineteen Hampdens to Wilhelmshaven to attack the floating dock likely to be employed during repairs to Scharnhorst and Gneisenau. 408 (Goose) Squadron briefed the crews of the newly promoted F/Sgts Fraser and Rea and dispatched them from North Luffenham at 18.12 and 18.15 with four 500lb and two 250lb SAP bombs on board, but neither would carry out an attack. The Fraser crew turned back after around two hours when the carburettors iced up and the Rea crew failed to identify the target and both bomb loads ended up on the bed of the North Sea. The rest of the force encountered ten-tenths cloud that concealed the target area, and many gave up, while those carrying out an attack on estimated positions guided by searchlight and flak activity produced such scant results that their efforts were insufficient even to gain them a mention in the town diary.

On the night of the 23/24th, 5 Group detailed twenty-three Hampdens for mining duties in the Rosemary and Yam gardens in the Heligoland Bight and Schillig Roads respectively, and forty-two Hampdens and nine Manchesters on the 24/25th to return to the same gardens and Nectarine I and II. 408 (Goose) Squadron assigned three crews each to Yam, Rosemary and Nectarine II and the freshman crew of Sgt Meech to Nectarine I and dispatched them from North Luffenham between 18.24 and 19.15 with the senior pilot on duty, S/L Price, bound for Rosemary and the now commissioned P/O Beaver and crew heading for Yam. Instructions had been issued at briefings to "not fight the weather", which in the North Sea and Waddenzee areas was unhelpful with six to ten-tenths cloud spewing out severe snow squalls from a base that in places was as low as 300 feet. The crews of S/L Price and Sgt Hunter returned before reaching the Rosemary garden because of engine and compass issues respectively, while freshmen, Sgts Fern and Dillon and their crews and P/O Beaver and crew went the distance but were defeated by the conditions. F/Sgt Fraser and crew suffered the frustration of a hang-up and had to return their mine to store, leaving the freshman Meech crew to find visibility at five miles and a cloud base at 1,000 feet as they pinpointed on Texel and Terschelling and delivered their mine into the allotted location from 600 feet at 21.08.

On the 25th, 5 Group detailed a dozen Manchesters to target the Gneisenau, now believed to be at Kiel, while eighteen Hampdens and a Manchester took care of gardening duties in the Nectarines I and II, Yams and Rosemary gardens. W/C Bradshaw again guested for 408 (Goose) Squadron and took off with his crew at 18.27 bound for Nectarine I and P/O Coulter and crew followed in their wake at 18.30 on their way to nectarine II. Both returned early, the former because of ten-tenths cloud with a base as low as 200 feet and the latter because of technical issues including an unserviceable heating system and broken navigator's seat.

The main event on the 26th was a raid on the floating dock at Kiel for which 49 and 144 Squadrons detailed four and six Hampdens respectively to join Wellingtons and Halifaxes in an overall force of forty-nine aircraft. A further twenty-seven Hampdens were made ready for mining duties in the Yam, Rosemary, Nectarine I and Hawthorn gardens, the last mentioned located in the Waddensee off southern Jutland. 408 (Goose) Squadron briefed four crews for Rosemary, three for Yam, two, including S/L Price, for Hawthorn and one for Nectarine I, and sent them on their way from North Luffenham between 18.25 and 18.35. The crews of S/L Price and Sgts Fern, Meech and Norton returned early, either as the result of technical issues or the towering ice-bearing cloud, while the others enjoyed favourable conditions in their respective target areas, including bright moonlight, and planted their vegetables in five allotted gardens and one alternative from 700 to 1,000 feet between 20.42 and 21.34. The bombing element, meanwhile, had encountered thin ice-bearing cloud topping out at around 19,000 feet as it approached the target area, and some crews were unable to climb through it to reach clear air. Kiel stood out against the snow-covered background as bombs were delivered into the docks area, and returning crew claimed good results.

The Kiel operation threw up one of the war's great ironies, after a high explosive bomb struck the bows of Gneisenau, now supposedly in a safe haven after enduring eleven months of constant bombardment at Brest, and not only did it kill 116 of her crew, it also ended her sea-going career for good. Her main armament was removed for use in coastal defence, and she was towed to Gdynia, where she remained unrepaired for the remainder of the war. The British authorities were unaware of the success, however, and sent another raid of sixty-eight aircraft on the 27th, which included a 5 Group contribution of eighteen Hampdens and seventeen Manchesters from Bottesford, North Luffenham, Scampton and Swinderby. They encountered bright moonlight above the ten-tenths cloud in the target area, but poor visibility below, which offered no chance of identifying the floating dock, and most bombed the general area of the town guided by the flashes of searchlights and flak. 408 (Goose) Squadron was not involved but dispatched the crews of W/C Bradshaw and P/O Coulter at 18.29 and 18.32 to conduct mining sorties in the Nectarine I Garden. Benefitting from excellent conditions and the light of a three-quarter moon, the vegetables were planted from 600 and 700 feet at 20.03 and 20.12 and this concluded the month's operations.

During the course of the month, the squadron took part in ten operations and dispatched fifty-one sorties without loss.

March 1942

Adverse weather conditions welcomed in the new month and kept the bomber force on the ground on the 1st. It was the same on the 2nd, and it was the 3rd before orders were received across the Command to prepare for an operation, which, in its bold conception, was a clear indication of what was to come. Bomber Command's evolution to war-winning capability was to be long, arduous and gradual, but the first signs of a new hand on the tiller came early on in Harris's reign with this meticulously planned attack on the Renault lorry factory, which was located in a loop of the River Seine in the district of Billancourt to the south-west of central Paris. The plant was capable of producing 18,000 lorries per year, which was a massive boon to the German war effort, and the attempt to destroy it came in response to an Air Ministry request. The operation would be conducted in three waves, led by experienced crews, and would involve extensive use of flares to provide illumination. In the face of what was expected to be scant defence, crews were also encouraged to attack from as low a level as practicable, both for the sake of accuracy and in an attempt to avoid civilian casualties. In time, such operations would be led by Gee-equipped aircraft, but the 3 Group squadrons already employing the device were forbidden from taking part on this occasion, lest one be lost over enemy territory and its secrets revealed.

A force of 235 aircraft was assembled, a new record for a single target, and among them were forty-eight Hampdens and twenty-six Manchesters representing 5 Group, six of the former provided by 408 (Goose) Squadron. They departed North Luffenham between 18.08 and 18.23 with S/L Clayton the senior pilot on duty and soon lost the services of P/O Beaver and crew when a propeller fell off and they had to jettison their 1,900-pounder and two 250-pounders and make an emergency landing at Grafton Underwood. The others reached the target area, where bright moonlight filtered through four-tenths cloud at 16,000 feet to aid target location and most crews picked up the River Seine in good time to enable them to plan their bombing runs. The 408 (Goose) Squadron crews delivered their bomb loads from 1,500 to 4,000 feet between 21.00 and 21.25 and many bursts and explosions were observed. 223 crews reported successful sorties, many describing the factory buildings as well alight as they turned away, and post-raid reconnaissance confirmed the operation to have been an outstanding success for the loss of just one aircraft. 40% of the factory's buildings had been destroyed, and production was halted for four weeks, costing the Germans around 2,300 lorries, although, sadly, not all of the bombs had fallen precisely where intended. Inevitably, adjacent workers' housing had been hit by stray bombs, killing 367 French civilians, and severely injuring 341 others, some of whom would die. At the time, this was more than twice the heaviest death toll inflicted on a German target. It was somewhat paradoxical, that, as a champion of area bombing, Harris should gain his first major victory against a precision target.

While the above was in progress, some 330 miles to the north, four Lancasters taxied to the runway under the approving eyes of the 5 Group A-O-C, AVM Slessor, each carrying four mines for delivery to the Yams and Rosemary gardens in the Schillig Roads and Heligoland Bight in what would be the type's maiden operation.

It rained all day on the 4th, the day on which the recently commissioned P/O Beck was declared tour expired after two hundred hours of operational flying, and he was posted to 25 O.T.U at Finningley. It snowed all day on the 5th and it was the 7th before orders came through from 5 Group to make ready seventeen Hampdens for gardening duties in the Artichoke garden on the approaches to the port of Lorient, an operation not recorded in the 5 Group ORB.

Despite the fact that Essen, as home to the Krupp organisation, was the beating heart of the Ruhr Valley's war production, it had not been paid particular attention thus far in the war. This was about to change as Harris fixed his attention upon it, and, like a dog with a bone, would not abandon his quest to destroy it until that aim had been achieved. It was a fight he would win, but the first twelve months would be frustrating, unrewarding and expensive, and began with the first of three raids on consecutive nights on the 8th. A force of 211 aircraft was assembled, of which thirty-seven Hampdens and twenty-two Manchesters were provided by 5 Group, while the leading aircraft, which belonged to 3 Group, would be those equipped with the new Gee navigation device. This carried the great hope that it could solve the problem of blind target locating. The five-strong 408 (Goose) Squadron element consisting of the crews of F/L Dowie, P/Os Beaver and Farrow and F/Sgts Fraser and Rea departed North Luffenham between 00.51 and 01.29 and were followed into the air at 01.43 and 01.47 by the freshman crews of Sgt Hunter RCAF and Sgt Fern, who had been assigned to mining duties in the Nectarine I garden. Four minutes later, AD842 crashed on the flare path just beyond the airfield boundary and burst into flames, presumably having turned back. Two members of the crew were killed, while the pilot, Sgt Hunter, and navigator were taken to Stamford Infirmary with serious injuries including third degree burns.

Those participating in the main event arrived over the Ruhr after following the course of the Rhine from Emmerich and Wesel and identified the autobahns leading into Essen, where they found clear skies and good visibility provided by a half-moon. They also encountered the ever-present industrial haze, which obscured ground detail including the assigned aiming point "B", the Krupp complex. Few crews were able to make a positive identification and most bombed the general city area, those from 408 (Goose) Squadron from 9,000 to 13,000 feet between 02.40 and 02.59, while P/O Beaver and crew did pick out the primary aiming point and dropped their 1,900-pounder and two 250-pounders from 11,000 feet at 03.21. Some crews observed bursts and others not, and local sources reported a light raid with a little housing damage in southern districts. Meanwhile, Sgt Fern and crew fulfilled their brief by pinpointing on Terschelling and planting their vegetable from 700 feet at 03.17. Navigator, Sgt Ball, passed away in hospital on the following afternoon, leaving Sgt Hunter as the sole survivor from what had been his second sortie.

The Krupp complex was back on twenty-four hours later as one of two aiming points at Essen, and a force of 187 aircraft made ready, which included a 5 Group contribution of fifteen Hampdens and ten Manchesters. This figure had originally been higher, but adverse weather conditions, technical difficulties and one unidentified Manchester becoming bogged down on the way to take-off at Bottesford reduced the numbers significantly. 408 (Goose) Squadron made ready four Hampdens for mining duties and briefed the crews of W/C Bradshaw, who was still guesting, and P/O Coulter for the Nectarine II garden and the crews of Sgts Meech and Norton for Nectarine I, before sending them on their way from North Luffenham between 18.49 and 18.55. A little over two hours later, the Coulter and Meech crews returned to Wittering and Waddington respectively, the former because of engine trouble and the latter having been defeated by the conditions, leaving the Norton crew to pinpoint on Texel lighthouse and Vlieland and deliver their mine into the briefed location from 800 feet at 20.45, while further north, W/C Bradshaw and crew pinpointed on a sandbank to the east of Ameland and planted their vegetable from the same height at 21.39.

Meanwhile, some Essen-bound crews claimed to be able to see the flares over the city even before reaching the Dutch coast, which confirmed that the horizontal visibility was reasonable, while vertical visibility at the target was again compromised by industrial haze. Major landmarks were identified through the five-tenths cloud with tops at around 8,000 feet, but not the Krupp districts in the western and north-western region of the city and the bombing was scattered over twenty-four other Ruhr towns and cities, with Hamborn and Duisburg the chief beneficiaries. The Essen authorities reported the destruction of two buildings, with seventy-two others damaged, which was another major disappointment for Harris.

Essen was posted as the primary target again on the 10th, for which a force of 126 aircraft was made ready to attack two aiming points, the Krupp sector and the city centre. 5 Group provided almost half of the force in the form of forty-three Hampdens, thirteen Manchesters and, for the first time over Germany, two 44 (Rhodesia) Squadron Lancasters, which would be employing TR1335 (Gee) for the first time. 408 (Goose) Squadron made ready five Hampdens for the main event and briefed the crews of S/L Price, P/Os Beaver and Farrow and F/Sgts Fraser and Rea to attack aiming point B, the "old town", before sending them on their way between 19.19 and 20.02. They had been preceded into the air at 19.13 by Sgt Fern and crew, who were to join twenty-two other freshmen for an attack on the docks and shipping at Boulogne but turned back with overheating engines when some thirty miles out over the Channel. The crews of F/Sgt Fraser and P/O Farrow were also thwarted by engine issues and returned their 1,900-pounder and two 250-pounders to the bomb dump, while the remaining three pressed on to reach the target area and find two to eight-tenths cloud at between 3,000 and 8,000 feet. They were also confronted by extreme darkness and poor visibility, made worse by the glare from searchlights and flares and the attentions of intense and accurate flak. Unable to identify either the Krupp sector or the main square, most bombed the built-up area generally, the crews of F/Sgt Rea and S/L Price from 14,000 feet at 21.56 and 22.00 respectively, while P/O Beaver and crew bombed the town of Dorsten on the northern rim of the Ruhr from 12,000 feet at 21.50. Returning crews reported some bursts and fires but no detail, and an analysis revealed that fewer than half of the crews had reached the primary target. Thirty-five others had bombed alternatives, and according to local sources, the nearest any bombs fell to the Krupp complex was on a railway line serving the area and one house had been destroyed.

The Deutsche Werke and Germania Werft U-Boot construction yards at Kiel were the targets for a force of sixty-eight Wellingtons on the night of the 12/13th, while forty Wellingtons and Whitleys, probably crewed by freshmen, attended to Emden. 5 Group, meanwhile, committed twenty-six Hampdens and a lone Manchester to mining duties in the Yam, Hawthorn and Rosemary gardens off Germany's North Sea coast. 408 (Goose) Squadron was not called into action and responded to a request from group on the 13th to provide six Hampdens for that night's main event at Cologne and four for mining duties in the Nectarine I garden. A force of 135 aircraft of six different types was assembled to attack the Rhineland capital, which included a contribution from 5 Group of twenty-two Hampdens, sixteen Manchesters and a single Lancaster. The gardening crews of Sgts Fern, Meech and Norton and P/O Coulter departed North Luffenham first between 18.36 and 18.42, and they were followed into the air by the bombing brigade between 18.59 and 19.06 led by W/Cs Timmerman and Bradshaw, the former operating with the squadron for the final time. Those reaching the target found the visibility to be good through the partial cover of three to five-tenths cloud at between 8,000 and 12,000 feet and had to run the gauntlet of intense searchlight and flak to arrive at the aiming point. Flares provided effective illumination, which assisted the 408 (Goose) Squadron crews to deliver their attacks from 8,500 to 15,000 feet between 21.50 and 22.19 and contribute to an unusually effective raid that inflicted substantial damage on a number of war industry factories in the Nippes district located to the north of the city centre, west of the Rhine, where a major marshalling yard was also located. In addition to this, 1,500 houses were hit in what proved to be the first genuinely successful Gee-led raid.

The gardening gang, meanwhile, found visibility of up to five miles and experienced no difficulty in establishing pinpoints on Texel, Vlieland and Terschelling from which to carry out timed runs and deliver their mines according to brief from 700 and 800 feet between 20.46 and 20.56.

On the 17th, Balderton was declared fit once more for operational flying, and the squadron returned there from North Luffenham. On the following day, the aircrew vacated the accommodation at Syerston to take up residence for the first time at Balderton, while 242 members of groundcrew moved into Winthorpe, a satellite of Swinderby situated five miles away on the north-eastern edge of Newark.

5 Group would spend the next ten nights on the ground as the weather largely closed down all but small-scale bomber operations. Crews were put on stand-by daily for the possibility of an operation, only for them to be stood-down when the inevitable cancellation came through. A daylight mining operation by thirteen Manchesters and six Lancasters went ahead in the Nectarine region on the 20th, and on return, one of the Lancasters grazed a house roof with a wingtip and was crash-landed on a beach near Boston, where it was written off by the incoming tide to become the first Lancaster to be lost as a result of operations.

It was the 23rd before the next night operation was announced, which was to involve a dozen Hampdens, two Manchesters and three 3 Group Stirlings mining in the Artichoke garden off Lorient. 408 (Goose) Squadron briefed the crews of Sgts Norton and Dillon, who departed Balderton at 18.21 and 18.23 respectively before heading for the Dorset coast to begin the Channel crossing. Both reached the target area to find clear skies and good visibility, but neither was able to deliver their mine, the former as a result of starboard engine failure, which force them to jettison, and the latter after searching in vain for an hour and forty-five minutes for a pinpoint on the Ile-de-Groix.

Briefings on the 24th revealed a return to the Artichoke garden that night, for which 5 Group provided a dozen Hampdens and two Manchesters, which would be joined by three 3 Group Stirlings on the occasion of the type's mining debut. The six 408 (Goose) Squadron participants departed Balderton between 18.25 and 18.37 with S/Ls Constance and Price the senior pilots on duty and began the Channel crossing in the region of Portland Bill on a heading for landfall over the Ile-de-Brehat off the north Brittany coast. They skirted Brest and pinpointed on the Ile-de-Groix under clear skies and in bright moonlight, before conducting timed runs and planting their vegetables from 600 to 900 feet between 21.15 and 22.01.

Harris resumed his campaign against Essen on the night of the 25/26th, when sending the largest force yet to a single target of 254 aircraft. 5 Group played its part by contributing twenty Manchesters, nine Hampdens and seven Lancasters, and despite clear skies and good visibility, thick industrial haze thwarted the attempts of all crews to identify the target. On return, crews commented that some of the Wellington-laid flares were burning at 18,000 feet, which was of no benefit in terms of illuminating ground features and the promise of Gee, demonstrated in the recent attack on Cologne, was not repeated as much of the effort was wasted on a decoy site at Rheinberg, some eighteen miles away. It was a bad night for 5 Group, which posted missing six aircraft, two-thirds of the overall casualty figure, and among them were five of the twenty Manchesters dispatched, a loss rate of 25%.

While this operation was in progress, thirty-six Hampdens and a single Manchester returned to the Artichoke garden to maintain the pressure on the U-Boot fleet based in Lorient's massive bunker system. 408 (Goose) Squadron dispatched ten Hampdens between 18.41 and 19.21, seven for Lorient with S/L Clayton the senior pilot on duty and three with the freshman crews of P/Os Vipond and Williams and Sgt Copeman to deliver nickels to the residents of Rennes in north-western France. Conditions were similar to those of the previous night and the same pinpoints were employed to establish positions for the start of the timed runs. The mines were dropped into the briefed locations from 600 to 900 feet between 21.32 and 22.22, while some eighty miles to the north-east, the crew of P/O Williams dispensed fifty-four bundles of what Harris described as toilet paper from 12,000 feet at 21.45 and Sgt Copeman and crew followed up ten minutes later with fifty bundles from 8,500 feet. They landed at Exeter and the bombers at Chivenor, while the Vipond crew found refuge at Stoke Orchard in Gloucestershire, it is believed having fulfilled their brief.

Two unnamed crews took part in a sea search for ditched crews on the morning of the 26th, but found nothing. Later, that day, instructions were received to withdraw Lancasters from operations and to restrict training flights to a fuel load not exceeding 580 gallons in inner tanks only. This resulted from an incident of wingtip rippling and loose rivets and brought an end to operations for 44 and 97 Squadrons for the remainder of the month. S/L Clayton was promoted to acting wing commander rank and would be appointed to command the squadron two days hence on the departure of W/C Timmerman. P/O Vipond and crew took off from Stoke orchard at 16.00 to return to base, and at 16.30 AE139 crashed near Abingdon, killing the pilot and two others and injuring the wireless operator. Those losing their lives had been on their maiden sortie and the survivor his tenth, and what caused the crash was not determined.

A force of 115 Wellingtons and Stirlings was assembled to return to Essen that night, while 5 Group detailed thirty Hampdens and fifteen Manchesters to conduct mining operations in the Yam, Nectarine I and Deodar gardens, respectively in Jade Bay/Weser estuary, off the southern Frisians and the Gironde estuary leading to the port of Bordeaux in south-western France. 408 (Goose) Squadron supported the Deodar and Nectarine I endeavours with four and one Hampdens respectively, which departed Balderton between 18.40 and 18.55 with S/L Price leading the former, while the freshman crews of Sgts Clothier, Johnstone and McClintock took off between 18.47 and 19.12 to deliver reading matter to the Rennes area. P/O Coulter and crew landed at Moreton-in-Marsh two hours after taking off and reported that the wireless operator had been lapsing into unconsciousness, presumably as the result of oxygen starvation. Sgt Craig and crew were the first to arrive at their destination off Terschelling under a half-moon and began their timed run from the western end of the island to plant their vegetable according to brief from 600 feet at 20.23. The nickellers spent some time searching for their target area in north-western France, and those of Sgts McClintock and Johnstone eventually identified it after pinpointing initially on Cap Frehel and heading south under bright moonlight to dispense 108 bundles each of propaganda from 9,500 and 10,000 feet at 22.06 and 22.37. Sgt Clothier and crew obtained a pinpoint on an inlet south-west of Dinard and conducted a timed run, but still failed to locate the Rennes area and headed home at 8,000 feet dropping sixty-three bundles of leaflets on the way as far as Hirel on the Brittany coast. Meanwhile, the three remaining gardeners had followed the Biscay coastline south from St-Nazaire and reached the Gironde estuary to find ten-tenths cloud at 7,000 feet but good visibility below. They pinpointed on Ile-de-Re and Ile-d'Oleron as the starting point for their timed runs and delivered their mines from 800 to 1,000 feet between 22.45 and 22.58, before returning safely to land at Chivenor.

A naval and commando raid was mounted on the evening of the 27th against the lock gates in St-Nazaire, for which bomber Command provided a force of thirty-five Whitleys and twenty-seven Wellingtons for bombing support if the weather allowed. In the event, only four aircraft were able to bomb and while this was ongoing, eighteen Hampdens from Balderton, North Luffenham and Swinderby conducted mining sorties in the Rosemary, Yam and Nectarine gardens. 408 (Goose) Squadron assigned three experienced crews to Yam and five freshmen to Nectarine I and sent them on their way from Balderton between 19.15 and 19.27 to head out over Skegness on a night of favourable conditions with minimal cloud and a half-moon to provide light. Inexplicably, Sgt Norton and crew were unable to locate Terschelling and returned their mine to store, while the crews of Sgts Gordon, Halcro and Meech and F/Sgt Dillon each established a pinpoint on the island and planted their vegetables from 600 to 800 feet between 21.36 and 21.55. They all returned safely to make their reports and the expectation was that they would be joined on the ground shortly by the crews of F/L Brown RCAF in AT176, P/O Beaver RNZAF in L4140 and P/O Fraser RCAF in AE219 on their return from the Jade Bay/Weser estuary region some 110 miles further to the east. It eventually became clear that they would not be returning home, and no trace of the aircraft and crews was ever found. It is believed that two had fallen victim to the Luftwaffe Ace, Hptm Helmut lent of II./NJG2, and one to Ofw Siegfried Ney, who also lost his life on this night. P/O Beaver had been on his thirty-first sortie, P/O Fraser his twentieth and F/L Brown his seventeenth, and they and their crews would be keenly missed by the squadron and Balderton communities.

W/C Timmerman left the squadron on the 28th on posting back to Canada to become the Director of Training at No 34 O.T.U., and he left behind him a highly efficient squadron after nine months in command.

In another foretaste of things to come, Harris launched a major assault on the historic Hansastadt (ancient free-trade city) Lübeck, situated on an island on the Baltic coast, believing that if he could provide his crews with the means to locate a target, they would hit it. Coastlines offered the most distinctive features for the purpose of identification, but Lübeck, located to the east of Kiel, also contained narrow streets and half-timbered buildings in its old town, which would aid the spread of fire. The operation, to be carried out on the night of the 28/29th, was to be conducted along the same lines as the highly successful attack on the Renault factory at the start of the month, and a force of 234 aircraft was assembled, 5 Group represented by forty-one Hampdens and twenty-one Manchesters. They crossed the North Sea in excellent visibility under bright moonlight that allowed them to map-read their way across the Schleswig-Holstein peninsula to gain the western Baltic. The target was identified easily by the coastline and the River Trave, and the attack created many fires, the glow from which remained visible for seventy miles into the homeward flight. Post-raid reconnaissance and local sources confirmed the operation to have been a major success, which destroyed almost fifteen hundred houses and seriously damaged almost two thousand more in a 190-acre area of devastation representing some 30% of the city's built-up area. It was the first major success for area bombing, and another sign of what was in store for the residents of Germany's towns and cities. There was an outcry following this unexpected attack on Lübeck, which was a city of culture and a vital port for the Red Cross. An agreement was struck that ensured its future protection from bombing, and, with a few exceptions, this was adhered to.

While the above was in progress, six 408 (Goose) Squadron Hampdens departed Balderton between 19.05 and 19.22 bound for the Nectarine I garden with freshman crews on board. They benefitted from high cloud, bright moonlight and excellent visibility, despite which, Sgt Markle and crew were unable to establish a pinpoint and brought their mine home. The others located Texel, Vlieland and Terschelling with ease and planted their vegetables from 600 to 800 feet between 21.08 and 21.47 before returning safely from uneventful sorties. On the following night, six different freshman crews took off between 19.09 and 19.18 to revisit Nectarine I and enjoyed the same favourable condition, which enable all to establish their positions and deliver their mines into the briefed locations from 600 to 900 feet between 20.58 and 21.29.

Eighteen Hampdens and eight Manchesters were made ready for further gardening operations on the 29th, all but two assigned to the Nectarine gardens, while two of the Manchesters ventured as far as the Bottle garden off Haugesund on Norway's western coast. A return to the madness of daylight "moling" cloud cover operations on the 31st involved eleven Hampdens and six Wellingtons, whose crews had been briefed to seek out railway targets in north-western Germany. They flew out with the reassuring protection of ten-tenths cloud, but this began to disperse as they approached the Frisians and some crews turned back, while others pushed on across Holland to within ten miles of the German frontier, before they, too, decided to abandon their sorties.

During the course of the month the squadron took part in sixteen operations and dispatched seventy-three sorties for the loss of five Hampdens and crews.

April 1942

The new month began for 5 Group with operations on the 1st in company with Wellingtons, although not operating together. Twenty-two Hampden crews were briefed to take part in a raid on the docks and shipping at Le Havre, while fourteen others were to carry out low-level attacks on railway targets in north-western Germany in the Meppen and Lingen region just over the frontier from Holland. 408 (Goose) Squadron briefed six crews for the former, each captained by a sergeant pilot and loaded their Hampdens with six 250-pounders each before dispatching them from Balderton between 19.22 and 19.38. Sgt Manson and crew turned back immediately because of a gyro issue, leaving the others to fly south for the Channel crossing under clear skies and in such good visibility that they were able to pick out the Seine estuary when twenty miles away. Sgt Meech and crew arrived at the French coast near Fecamp and inexplicably turned to port rather than starboard, which left them searching in the wrong area for the target until arriving over Abbeville, where they dispensed six bundles of the F13 leaflets from 11,500 feet at 21.30 and retained their bombs. The others attacked the target from 10,000 to 12,000 feet between 21.15 and 21.41, some observing bursts and others not, and all returned safely from uneventful sorties.

It turned into a disastrous night for 3 Group, whose railway targets were at Hanau and Lohr to the east of Frankfurt, from which five out of twelve 57 Squadron Wellingtons failed to return and seven of fourteen belonging to 214 Squadron. On the following night, twenty-three Hampdens were detailed for mining duties in the Gorse garden in Quiberon Bay, situated on the western coast of Brittany, north-west of St-Nazaire, while five Hampdens and four Manchesters returned to Le Havre for another tilt at the docks and shipping. The 408 (Goose) Squadron freshman crews of Sgts Johnstone and Gordon took off at 19.27 on another night of ideal bombing conditions, and delivered their attacks from 10,000 feet at 21.20 and 9,000 feet at 21.35 and resupplied the residents with toilet paper.

The first major operation of the new month was directed at Cologne on the night of the 5/6th and involved a new record force of 263 aircraft, which included a 5 Group contribution of forty-four Hampdens and eleven Manchesters, while Balderton remained inactive. The aiming point was the Klöckner-Humboldt engineering works in the Deutz district on the East Bank of the Rhine in the city centre, which manufactured aero-engines and a wide range of military vehicles. Those reaching the target area encountered bright moonlight, which penetrated the up-to-nine-tenths cloud and glinted off an S-bend in the Rhine to the south of the city centre, thereby assisting some crews to establish a position for the bombing run. Despite the advantages, however, many crews failed to identify Cologne and those that did scattered their loads right across the built-up area, destroying or seriously damaging ninety houses but nothing of industrial significance.

On the following night, Harris turned his attention back upon Essen, with the first of three raids against it in six nights, to which 5 Group contributed eighteen Hampdens and ten Manchesters. The 408 (Goose) Squadron crews of S/L Price, F/L Dowie and P/O Farrow departed Balderton between 23.31 and 23.40 and adopted the southerly route to the central Ruhr via Orfordness, Blankenberg on the Belgian coast and Nivelles, to then swing south of Bonn before heading north to the target. They encountered electrical storms and severe icing conditions over the North Sea that threatened to destroy lift and forced some crews to turn back, while those pressing on encountered up to ten-tenths cloud and industrial haze that blotted out all ground detail. Bombs were delivered on e.t.a. and on the evidence of searchlights and flak, the crews of F/L Dowie and S/L Price releasing their 1,900-pounder and two 250-pounders each from 10,000 and 14,000 feet at 03.21 and 03.30 respectively. Having run into searchlights south-east of Liege, P/O Farrow and crew turned south in a vain attempt to evade them, and on spotting a night-fighter, attempted and failed to jettison the bombs and had to bring them home. Only a third of crews reported bombing the primary target, which escaped with minor damage at a cost to the Command of five aircraft, three of them belonging to 5 Group.

Hamburg was posted as the target on the 8th, and yet another record force, this time of 272 aircraft, was made ready. 5 Group stepped up with thirty-two Hampdens and thirteen Manchesters assigned to the Blohm & Voss shipyards located to the west of the city centre, while the seven Lancasters and nine further Hampdens were to attack aiming point C, the industrial centre of the city. 408 (Goose) Squadron briefed three crews for the main event, nine for mining duties in the Rosemary garden in Heligoland Bight and the crew of Sgt Manson to deliver printed matter to the residents of the Paris area. They departed Balderton together between 20.34 and 20.55 and would reach their respective targets 440 miles apart more or less simultaneously. The Manson crew headed south and pinpointed on the Seine estuary over four-tenths cloud at 4,000 feet and followed the River to the French capital to deliver 108 bundles of the F29 leaflet from 11,000 feet at 23.35. The crews of S/L Price, F/L Dowie and P/O Farrow, meanwhile, had run into one of the towering electrical storms with icing conditions that frequently built up over the North Sea to bar the approaches to north-western Germany, and, on this night, not all who set out would reach their intended destination. Those arriving over Germany's second city pinpointed on the River Elbe through eight-tenths cloud at 10,000 feet and were largely unable to identify the briefed aiming point, settling instead for an attack on the general built-up area, the crews of S/L Price and F/L Dowie releasing their loads from 11,000 feet at 23.35 and 23.41 respectively. P/O Farrow and crew pinpointed on Sylt and carried out a timed run of 115 miles to Hamburg and dropped their 1,900-pounder and two 250-pounders on e.t.a. from 15,000 feet at 23.59. In fact, only 188 crews would report bombing somewhere in the Hamburg area on estimated positions, and the result was another poor performance, which deposited no more than the equivalent of fourteen bomb loads in the city and caused eight fires.

Of the gardeners, Sgt Gordon and crew turned back from a position twenty miles out from Skegness when their compass failed, while the others continued on in what most described as good conditions with minimal cloud and good visibility that enabled them to pinpoint on various locations including Westerhever, Amrum Island and Sankt Peter-Ording. Unaccountably, the crews of Sgts Craig and Copeman found poor visibility that prevented them from establishing their position and they brought their mines home, while the others planted theirs according to brief from 600 to 900 feet between 23.09 and 23.35.

It was back to Essen for 254 aircraft on the 10th, an operation supported by 5 Group with forty-three Hampdens, ten Manchesters and eight Lancasters, 408 (Goose) Squadron contributing just two Hampdens, while detailing thirteen of eighteen Hampdens and four Manchesters for a freshman raid on the docks and shipping at Le Havre. The latter departed Balderton first between 20.34 and 20.50, each carrying six 250-pounders, and lost the services first of Sgt Copeman and crew because of flames issuing from the exhaust, and later Sgt Meech and crew with compass trouble when fifteen miles out over the Channel. The others reached the target area to report either no cloud or amounts of cloud ranging from three to ten-tenths, but all were unanimous concerning the extreme darkness, which prevented many crews from carrying out an attack. Four of the Balderton crews took their bombs home, while the remainder delivered theirs from 10,000 to 12,000 feet between 22.28 and 22.48. Meanwhile, the crews of F/L Dowie and P/O Farrow had taken off at 21.38 bound for aiming point B at Essen and had set course via Skegness for Enkhuizen on the eastern shore of the Den Helder peninsula, before swinging round the eastern end of the Ruhr and running in on the target from east to west. On this night, they were expecting to find the clear skies forecast at briefing, but instead were confronted by a layer of eight-tenths cloud across the central Ruhr at between 5,000 and 8,000 feet. The route in was described by F/L Sandford of 44 (Rhodesia) Squadron as "hot", with scores of searchlights from all sides working in conjunction with light and heavy flak. The 408 (Goose) Squadron pair bombed from 14,400 at 00.10 and from 11,000 feet at 00.16 and reported bursts and the glow of fires beneath the cloud, but little of use to the intelligence sections at debriefing. Local sources confirmed the operation to have been another dismal failure, which destroyed only twelve houses and caused no industrial damage.

As previously mentioned, Balderton was a satellite of Syerston, and the 5 Group ORB continued to refer to 408 (Goose) Squadron as a Syerston rather than Balderton unit. On the 10th G/C Taafe relinquished his post as station commander and was succeeded by G/C Augustus "Gus" Walker, an officer of small physical stature but huge character, who had commanded 50 Squadron during the first ten months of 1941. Later in the year he would lose his lower right arm in trying to prevent a bomb load from exploding on the ground. Once recovered, he would return to duty, moving to 4 Group and continuing to rise through the ranks, his personality an inspiration to those around him wherever he served. A rare training accident occurred on the 11th during bombing practice, when AT186 crashed on the outskirts of Beeston in Nottinghamshire at 14.40 and was written off, happily without casualties among the crew of Sgt Marment RNZAF.

Orders were received across the Command on the 12th to prepare another large force to return to Essen that night, and 251 aircraft were made ready accordingly, 5 Group responding with thirty-one Hampdens and nine Manchesters, while the Lancaster element was busy training for an epic daylight raid five days hence. 408 (Goose) Squadron made ready just two Hampdens for the main event, four for mining duties in the Rosemary garden and five for Hawthorn II, respectively in the Heligoland Bight and the Waddensee off Schleswig-Holstein. The Hawthorn-bound element departed Balderton first between 21.19 and 21.24 with P/O Sanderson the only commissioned pilot on duty, and they were followed into the air by the other sections between 21.27 and 21.38. Sgt Norton was contending with misfiring engines and an inability to maintain height and eventually aborted the sortie to Essen and jettisoned the bombs. It is believed that Sgt Meech and crew carried out an attack before heading home and were last heard from in a W/T signal received at Heston at 04.22. AT120 did not return and the eventual recovery of two bodies washed ashore on east coast beaches confirmed that it had crashed in the North Sea. This was the first all-Canadian crew to be lost by 408 (Goose) Squadron, which like all Bomber Command squadrons was a polyglot of British and Dominion nationalities.

Meanwhile, after Sgt Manson and crew had turned back because of rising oil temperature, the eight remaining gardeners had reached their respective neighbouring target areas to find largely clear skies and good visibility, those in the Rosemary garden pinpointing on Sankt-Peter-Ording and

Westerhever as the starting point for their timed runs. They released the mines from 600 and 700 feet between 00.37 and 00.48, while further north, those serving the Hawthorn II garden pinpointed on Lim Fjord and Ringkøbing and planted theirs from 500 to 900 feet between 00.30 and 01.04.

An analysis of the Essen raid revealed that 173 crews claimed to have bombed in the general area of the Krupp districts but bombing photos captured many Ruhr locations, while local sources confirmed a slight improvement in the bombing, reporting some damage and a large fire in the Krupp complex and the destruction of twenty-eight dwelling units. This brought to an end a series of eight heavy raids against the city since the night of the 8/9th of March, during which 1,555 sorties had resulted in fewer than two-thirds of the crews claiming to have bombed in the target area, and just twenty-two bombing photos being plotted to within five miles of Essen. In exchange for this, sixty-four aircraft had been lost, industrial damage had been slight, and housing damage modest in the extreme.

On the following night, fifteen Hampdens and seven Manchesters were assigned to mining duties in the Rosemary and Nectarine I gardens, 408 (Goose) Squadron briefing the crews of P/Os Farrow and Coulter for the former and those of Sgts Copeman, Dillon and Fern for the latter. They departed Balderton between 21.07 and 21.20 and lost the services of P/O Farrow in the first hour after the artificial horizon failed. P/O Coulter and crew pressed on only to be defeated by a heavy sea haze that blotted out all ground features and it was a similar story for the crews of Sgts Copeman and Dillon further south. In visibility of one to two miles, the Islands of Terschelling and Ameland appeared out of the haze sufficiently for Sgt Fern and crew to establish their position and plant their vegetable from 800 feet at 23.46.

W/C Pitt Clayton's brief reign as commanding officer concluded on the 14th, but no replacement would be appointed until mid-May, leaving S/L Price to fill the breach in the meantime, as he had done recently while W/C Clayton was on sick leave. Dortmund was posted as the target for a force of 208 aircraft on the 14th, in what was by far the largest effort yet against this industrial giant situated at the eastern end of the Ruhr. 5 Group made a contribution to the operation of thirty-four Hampdens and four Manchesters, three of the former provided by 408 (Goose) Squadron, which also contributed four freshman crews to an attack on the docks and shipping at Le Havre. The latter departed Balderton first between 21.22 and 21.25, each carrying six 250-pounders, and they were followed into the air between 22.01 and 22.10 by the crews of Sgts Gordon, McClintock and Norton, each sitting on a single 2,000-pounder. The French coast was found to be clear of cloud and the visibility good enough to enable crews to pinpoint on Cap de la Heve and follow the coast south for the short distance to the target. The docks were identified easily, and the bombs dropped from 11,000 and 12,000 feet between 23.25 and 23.53.

The Ruhr-bound force had to run the gauntlet of intense searchlight and flak activity as it traversed the most heavily defended region of Germany, and under clear skies, crews were able to map-read their way by river and railway features to the aiming point. Despite the advantages, neither of the two returning 408 (Goose) Squadron crew was able to report that they had located the briefed aiming point but had bombed the general built-up area instead from 11,000 and 13,000 feet at 02.10 and 02.25, while attempting to dodge some eighty searchlights in cones. AT141 was absent from its dispersal pan on the following morning, having been shot down, it is believed, by a night-fighter. The location of the wreckage three miles south-west of Dortmund offers no clue as to whether or not the target had been attacked, and as Sgt McClintock RCAF and his crew all lost their lives, during what for three of them was their seventh sortie, we will never know. It would be established later that the bombing had been scattered over a forty-mile stretch of the region, with no significant damage to the intended target.

A reduced force of 152 aircraft was assembled for the same target twenty-four hours later, this time supported by 5 Group with nineteen Hampdens and seven Manchesters, five of the former provided by 408 (Goose) Squadron along with the crews of Sgt Manson and F/Sgt Dillon for mining duties in the Beech garden off St-Nazaire. The latter were airborne by 21.10 and were already over France by the time that the bombing element departed Balderton between 23.04 and 23.16 with S/L Price the senior pilot on duty. Clear skies and good visibility over the Biscay coast enabled the gardeners to establish their position on Yeu and Noirmoutier Islands to the south of the port and conduct a timed run to the release point, where the mines were observed from 500 and 700 feet to enter the water at 00.03 and 00.36. Meanwhile, S/L Price had turned back when south of Peterborough because of an unserviceable air speed indicator (a.s.i.), leaving the rest of the bombing brigade to contend with severe icing conditions on the southern approaches to the Ruhr, only then to run into intense searchlight and flak activity over the target, where two-tenths low cloud combined with the industrial haze to muddy the vertical visibility. Only the crews of F/L Dowie and Sgt Halcro positively identified Dortmund and bombed the built-up area from 13,000 and 12,000 feet at 03.03 and 03.19 respectively, while P/O Williams and crew believed they had found it but were uncertain and turned south to follow a river to the town of Lüdenscheid, which they bombed from 12,000 feet at 03.46. P/O Farrow and crew lost their a.s.i. to icing and attacked Bonn as a last resort target from 18,000 feet at 02.30. Despite the effort and the courage of crews, this raid was another dismal failure that scattered bombs over a wide area and caused only the slightest damage in the target city.

Minor operations occupied the night of the 16/17th, for which 5 Group contributed ten Hampdens and two Manchesters for gardening duties off the Biscay coast and five Hampdens and two Manchesters for nickelling activities over Lille in north-eastern France. Sgt Gould and crew departed Balderton at 21.31 to deliver reading matter and arrived at their destination under clear skies to dispense 108 bundles of the F29 propaganda leaflet, assisted in target identification by the poor blackout, before returning safely a tad more experienced than when they had taken off three hours and fifty minutes earlier.

At noon on the 17th, six crews each from 44 (Rhodesia) and 97 (Straits Settlement) Squadrons filed into the briefing rooms at Waddington and Woodhall Spa to be enlightened as to their immediate future. They were incredulous to learn that they were soon to embark on Operation Margin, an epic low-level deep-penetration flight to Augsburg in Bavaria, to attack the diesel engine assembly shop in the middle of a large factory complex belonging to the Maschinen Fabrik Augsburg Nürnburg Aktien Gesellschaft, otherwise known as the M.A.N. works, situated on the outskirts of the beautiful and historic city. Strategically, this particular shop was the most important part of the factory and was believed to be the bottleneck in the entire U-Boot industry at a time when the Battle of the Atlantic was the main preoccupation of both Britain and the United States. Four of the 44 (Rhodesia) squadron Lancasters were shot down over France on the way out and a fifth crashed beyond the target and two 97 (Straits Settlement) Lancasters were also lost in the target area, but some useful damage was inflicted upon the target and S/L Nettleton of 44 (Rhodesia)

Squadron was awarded the VC. Harris disliked low-level operations in heavy bombers, particularly in daylight, and the Augsburg losses cemented that opinion.

That night, according to Bomber Command War Diaries, Hamburg was selected to host a raid by a force of 173 aircraft, which included a contribution from 5 Group of five Manchesters but no Hampdens. However, 49 and 408 (Goose) Squadrons contributed five and six Hampdens respectively, those at Balderton taking to the air between 22.59 and 23.20 with F/L Dowie the senior pilot on duty and a 1,900-pounder in each bomb bay, supplemented with two 250-pounders. They navigated to the target via the Frisian chain, pinpointing on Schiermonnikoog and Amrum, and by the time that they arrived at the latter, Sgt Halcro and crew realised that they were too far behind schedule to reach the target within the bombing window and dropped their large bomb on a searchlight and flak concentration on the island from 12,000 feet at 03.51. Sgt Gordon and crew were led astray by a faulty compass and having been unable to pinpoint as planned on Heligoland, abandoned their sortie, arriving at the English coast over Flamborough Head, some seventy miles north of their intended landfall over Skegness. P/O Coulter and crew missed the Frisian Island pinpoints and ended up, they believed, over the island of Sylt off the Schleswig-Holstein coast, where they dropped their bombs from 10,000 feet onto a searchlight and flak concentration at 02.29. Those reaching Germany's second city found it under clear skies but shrouded in haze and protected by the usual intense searchlight and flak barrage from both banks of the River Elbe. The city-centre aiming point could not be identified, and the remaining three 408 (Goose) Squadron participants attacked the built-up area generally from 11,000 to 14,000 feet between 03.10 and 03.20, helping to set off seventy-five fires, thirty-three of which were classed by the city authorities as large. Even so, fewer than a third of the bomb loads had actually found the mark and local sources estimated a force of only fifty aircraft.

While the above was in progress, 5 Group sent nine aircraft to mine the waters of the Rosemary garden in the Heligoland Bight, the five representing 408 (Goose) Squadron departing Balderton between 22.51 and 23.04 with P/Os Sanderson and Taylor the commissioned pilots on duty. They found the target area to be under clear skies with visibility at four to five miles and easily located pinpoints at Westerhever, Sankt Peter-Ording and Pellworm from which to conduct timed runs at an average of 150 mph indicated air speed (i.a.s.) and plant their vegetables from 700 to 1,000 feet between 02.10 and 02.33.

Ten 408 (Goose) Squadron Hampdens were made ready on the 19th for mining duties in the Nectarine I garden off the southern Frisians as part of a 5 Group effort of twenty-five Hampdens, ten Manchesters and two Lancasters. They departed Balderton between 21.07 and 21.19 with F/L Dowie the senior pilot on duty and headed out via Mablethorpe to pinpoint on the gap between Ameland and Terschelling, where the ten-tenths cloud base was at 2,000 feet or below and the visibility poor as a result of extreme darkness and haze. The crews of Sgts Copeman, Fern and Macgregor and F/Sgt Manson were unable to establish a pinpoint and returned their mines to the station store, while the others identified Terschelling and Vlieland and delivered their mines according to brief from 700 to 1,000 feet between 22.57 and 23.36.

S/L Pim DFC was posted to 29 O.T.U. on the 22nd on the conclusion of his tour and he would be joined there by P/O Farrow. S/L Clift OBE was posted in from 455 Squadron RAAF as the new A flight commander.

The first attempt to employ Gee as a blind bombing aid took place on the night of the 22/23rd, when Cologne was the target for a 3 Group force of sixty-four Wellingtons and five Stirlings. Fewer than 20% of the bomb loads fell into the city, and some landed up to ten miles away, proving that Gee was capable of guiding a force to a general area, but lacked the precision necessary to deliver a telling blow on an urban target. While this operation was in progress, 5 Group provided a diversion by dispatching twenty-two Hampdens and a dozen Manchesters on gardening duties on both sides of the Schleswig-Holstein peninsula in Forget-me-not (Kiel Harbour), Quince (Kiel Bay), Radish (Fehmarn Belt) and Rosemary (Heligoland Bight). Those reaching the western Baltic encountered clear skies and good visibility and pinpointed on the southern tip of Denmark's Langeland Island and on the German mainland north-east of Kiel, before making their timed runs and dropping their mines into the briefed locations. 408 (Goose) Squadron assigned the crews of F/L Dowie and P/O Coulter to the Forget-me-not garden and the rest to Rosemary and sent them on their way from Balderton between 19.42 and 19.57. The Coulter crew spent so much time attempting to establish a pinpoint on the western coast of Schleswig-Holstein that they ran out of time to reach the Baltic and dropped their mine in an alternative garden, probably Hawthorn, from 800 feet at 00.14. F/L Dowie and crew found clear skies and moderate visibility, which enable them to establish their pinpoint and head in a south-westerly direction to the release point, where the mine was delivered from 1,000 feet at 23.19.

The Rosemary garden was covered by nine-tenths cloud with a base at 3,000 feet or below, and P/O Sanderson and crew were not too far distant when the starboard engine failed and the mine had to be jettisoned. It went down "live" into the alternative Hawthorn garden from 2,300 feet at 22.10, after which the Hampden limped home to a landing at Coningsby, where it joined those of the crews of Sgts Gould and Markle, who had been defeated by engine and instrument failure respectively. P/O Williams and crew were unable to identify a pinpoint and headed towards an alternative garden, only to be discouraged by the appearance of a night-fighter and jettison the mine, before joining their colleagues at Coningsby. P/O Taylor and crew also failed to fulfil their brief and landed at Driffield, leaving only the crews of F/Sgts Manson and Copeman to reported planting their vegetables into the allotted locations from 700 and 900 feet between 22.44 and 23.01. The return of Sgt Macgregor RNZAF and crew was awaited in vain, and it is believed that their AE237 was the Hampden shot down by the night-fighter of Ofw Paul Gildner of II./NJG2 to crash into the sea without survivors north-west of Ameland at 00.07. The pilot was on his fifth sortie.

In an attempt to repeat the success gained at Lübeck, the nearby Baltic coastal town of Rostock was earmarked for a series of four raids on consecutive nights from the 23/24th, with the old town and the Heinkel aircraft factory at Marienehe on its north-western outskirts the specific aiming points. A force of 161 aircraft was assembled, 143 of them assigned to the town and eighteen to the factory, and 5 Group managed to put up eleven Hampdens, six Manchesters and a single Lancaster. This would be the swansong for 49 Squadron Hampdens, but 408 (Goose) Squadron would soldier on with the aging type for the remainder of its time with 5 Group, although Balderton was not required to contribute on this night. Those reaching the target area found favourable weather conditions and good visibility, despite which, the majority of crews failed to find the mark at either aiming point and the bombing fell between two and six miles away.

The 5 Group element for round two at Rostock amounted to thirty-four aircraft, including four Lancasters from the newly-converted 207 Squadron at Bottesford, and all were assigned to the Heinkel factory, while ninety-one aircraft from the other groups focused on the old town. The thirteen 408 (Goose) Squadron participants departed Balderton between 21.13 and 21.24 with S/L Price the senior pilot on duty and S/L Pim also mentioned as taking part, although, as he had already concluded his time with the squadron, mention of him was in error. It is unlikely that S/L Clift would be thrust so soon into action, and so the identity of the second squadron leader remains unknown. Each Hampden engaged in the main event carried a bomb load of one 1,900-pounder and two 250-pounders, and they were followed into the air at 21.58 by Sgt Gould and crew, bound for Dunkerque to attack the docks and shipping with six 250-pounders. A navigational error on approach to the Danish coast left Sgt Craig and crew with no choice but to turn back, while the others pressed on, drawn on from the Baltic coast by the fires already burning many miles ahead. On arrival at the target, they found bright moonlight illuminating the Unterwarnow River, which runs south from the coast to the heart of the town and on this night provided an excellent reference for the low-level attacks. The town ahead seemed to be ablaze as they crossed the Heinkel factory, which most attacked on existing fires while trying to evade the attentions of the many searchlights co-operating with light flak. The 408 (Goose) Squadron crews bombed from 6,000 to 10,000 feet between 01.29 and 01.58, with the exception of Sgt Manson and crew, whose bombing switch failed to function. They jettisoned the bombs over the Baltic in order to preserve enough fuel to get home. According to the observations of returning crews, the Heinkel factory and adjacent aerodrome had been hit by many bombs and were left burning, and while post-raid reconnaissance revealed extensive damage within the town, the factory buildings were revealed to be still intact, demonstrating that the impressions gained by crews in the heat of battle could be somewhat unreliable. Meanwhile, Sgt Gould and crew had attacked Dunkerque docks from 10,000 feet at 00.04 and had returned safely from an uneventful sortie.

The third Rostock raid was launched on the night of the 25/26th and involved 110 aircraft assigned to the town, while eighteen from 5 Group targeted the Heinkel factory led by 106 Squadron's commanding officer, W/C Guy Gibson. Ideal weather conditions again prevailed, and post-raid reconnaissance revealed that the factory had, at last, been hit, and that the town had suffered severe damage without loss to the attackers.

On the 26th, Balderton was visited by the newly appointed A-O-C, AVM Coryton, while the business of the day, the preparation of a dozen Hampdens for the fourth and final Rostock raid to be launched that night, went on around him. A force of 106 aircraft was detailed, which included a contribution from 5 Group of nineteen Hampdens, nine Manchesters and a single Lancaster assigned to the Heinkel factory. The Balderton element took off between 21.47 and 21.58 with S/L Price the senior pilot on duty and Sgt Gould followed on later bound for mining duties in the Rosemary garden in the Heligoland Bight. They flew out over Mablethorpe, and P/O Coulter and crew were some thirty-five miles into the North Sea crossing when the starboard engine failed and forced them to turn back. Those reaching the target area found moonlight, excellent visibility, many coastal reference points and existing fires to aid target location, and another successful raid ensued, during which the 408 (Goose) Squadron crews delivered their 1,900-pounder and two 250-pounders each from 4,000 to 8,000 feet between 02.10 and 02.52. Sgt Gould and crew were first home following another uneventful mining sortie in which they had released their store under clear skies from 1,000 feet at 03.22. At debriefing, many hits were claimed on sheds and other buildings, and an analysis of the Rostock campaign revealed it to have been highly successful, destroying 1,765 buildings and seriously damaging five hundred more, which represented 60% of the town's built-up area. In his diaries, Propaganda Minister Goebbels used the phrase "Terrorangriff", terror raid, for the first time.

5 Group did not take part in a raid on Cologne by ninety-seven aircraft on the 27th, which produced outstanding results for the period, damaging to some extent nine industrial units and 1,520 houses. With the exception of 408 (Goose) and 420 (Snowy Owl) Squadrons RCAF, 5 Group had now fully converted to the Manchester and the Lancaster and the ill-fated Manchester was within two months of being consigned to non-operational duties. 408 (Goose) Squadron was called into action on the 28th as the sole 5 Group representatives in a force of eighty-eight aircraft targeting Kiel. Ten of its Hampdens were loaded with either a 1,900-pounder and two 250-pounders or 360 x 4lb incendiaries and departed Balderton between 21.53 and 22.03 with S/L Price the senior pilot on duty and lost the services of Sgt Craig and crew to starboard engine failure when a hundred miles out over the North Sea. S/L Price and crew lost their port engine as they approached the Schleswig-Holstein coast and bombed the southern end of Sylt as a last resort target from 8,000 feet at 01.26. The target area was bathed in bright moonlight from beneath a clear sky and crews were able to map-read their way to the aiming points by navigating on landmarks like the Selenter Lake. A smoke screen was successful in concealing the briefed aiming points, which were almost certainly the three shipyards, and most aimed their bombs at the general built-up area, the 408 (Goose) Squadron participants from 10,000 to 13,000 feet between 02.16 and 02.35. AE426 failed to return with the crew of Sgt Gordon RCAF, having crashed at 02.35 onto a furniture factory in Hamburg with fatal consequences for all on board. It was the pilot's eighth sortie, while the crew members had one or two more to their credit.

The month ended for 5 Group with a raid by nine 420 (Snowy Owl) Squadron Hampdens on the 29th against the Gnome & Rhóne aero engine factory at Gennevilliers in Paris. During the course of the month, the squadron took part in twenty-five bombing, mining and leafleting operations and dispatched 137 sorties for the loss of five Hampdens and four crews.

May 1942

The weather kept the Command on the ground on the night of the 1/2nd, but it had relented sufficiently on the following day for ninety-six aircraft from 3 and 5 Groups to be detailed for mining operations that night. 5 Group provided twenty-one Lancasters, eight Manchesters and twelve Hampdens for gardens in the Baltic and off the Biscay coast, and nine Manchesters and two 408 (Goose) Squadron Hampdens for nickelling duties in the Rennes area of north-western France. At Balderton, a dozen Hampdens were made ready for mining sorties in the Artichoke garden off Lorient, and they took off between 00.29 and 00.54, all but one with an NCO pilot, and they were followed into the air at 00.57 and 01.00 by the crews of P/O Parks and Sgt Maiment bound for Rennes. They crossed the Channel to make landfall on the Brittany coast and F/Sgt Dillon and crew were heading south towards the Biscay coast at Concarneau at 100 feet when the flew into high-tension cables, damaging the starboard wingtip and aileron and smashing the windscreen. The mine and wing-mounted 250-pounders were jettisoned as the Hampden turned for home trailing a ten-foot length of cable, and a safe landing was carried out at Upper Heyford.

Meanwhile, the nickellers had followed the River Vilaine to their target area, where, unaccountably, one found no cloud and the other eight-tenths and a total of 162 bundles of leaflets were dispensed from 10,000 feet at 03.45 and 03.58. The gardeners encountered clear skies but disagreed on visibility, which ranged from good in bright moonlight to poor in haze, but, with one exception, all established a pinpoint on Quiberon Point and the Ile-de-Groix, before planting their vegetables from 400 to 1,000 feet between 02.25 and 04.05. Sgt Fern and crew were thwarted by an unreliable compass and jettisoned their load after failing to confirm their position.

Hamburg was posted as the primary target for a force of eighty-one aircraft on the 3rd, the numbers somewhat reduced in the face of a forecast of poor weather conditions. 5 Group contributed just five Hampdens from 420 (Snowy Owl) Squadron RCAF, while some other elements from the group were occupied by minor endeavours elsewhere.

Orders were received on the 4th to make ready for the first of what would be a "Rostock-style" sustained assault on the important industrial southern city of Stuttgart over three consecutive nights. A force of 121 aircraft included a contribution from 5 Group of nineteen Hampdens and fourteen Lancasters, the crews of the former briefed to aim for the highly important Robert Bosch factory located in the north-western district of Feuerbach, which was engaged in the manufacture of dynamos, injection pumps and magnetos, while the Lancaster crews were briefed to attack military barracks. At Balderton, 408 (Goose) Squadron made ready a dozen Hampdens for the main event and three for mining duties in the Rosemary garden in the Heligoland Bight and sent them on their way together between 21.29 and 21.57 with S/Ls Clift and Price the senior pilots on duty, the former undertaking his first sortie since joining the squadron. P/O Taylor and crew were approaching Cambridge when overheating engines persuaded them to turn back, leaving the rest to press on to the target area, where Sgt Fern and crew described good visibility above the nine-tenths cloud at 4,000 feet, while the others reported a range of cloud conditions from nil to six-tenths, no moon but thick haze, through which some were able to identify ground features like a fork in the River Neckar. Most, however, were unable to locate the briefed aiming point and the bombs were aimed at the general built-up area from 4,000 to 10,000 feet between 01.15 and 01.36, while the crews of Sgts Oliver and Gillham attacked aerodromes at Saarbrücken and Ettlingen as last-resort targets. At debriefings, only one 5 group crew claimed to have attacked the Bosch works, while the others reported bombing fires and red flares through the cloud. Local sources confirmed that the operation had scattered bombs over a wide area and onto a decoy site at Lauffen, fifteen miles to the north of the city, which was "defended" by thirty-five searchlights and fifty flak guns. It was a clever ruse that would lure away many bomb loads during the course of the war, that might otherwise have caused damage and casualties in Stuttgart.

While the above was in progress, the crews of P/Os Beranek and Parks and Sgt Marment encountered between five and ten-tenths cloud in the Heligoland Bight region, but an adequately high cloud base and visibility that enabled them to pinpoint on Amrum Island and Westerhever, before delivering their mines according to brief from 700 feet between 00.12 and 00.19.

5 Group contributed four 97 (Straits Settlement) Squadron Lancasters to the same target on the following night, and they again bombed the town rather than the Bosch factory to which they had been assigned. Despite clear skies, ground detail was obscured by haze, and no bombs fell in the city. Sgt Wood and crew departed Balderton at 21.43 to deliver "toilet paper" to the residents of

Paris and established their position by following the course of the River Seine. From clear skies, 108 bundles of the leaflet F32 were released from 10,000 feet at 23.59 and a safe return to base completed at 02.28.

It was Stuttgart again on the 6th, for which 5 Group detailed ten 408 (Goose) Squadron Hampdens and ten Lancasters from 44 (Rhodesia) squadron in an overall force of ninety-seven aircraft. Each Hampden received a bomb load of either a 2,000 or a 1,900-pounder and departed Balderton between 21.50 and 22.01, having been preceded into the air by the crews of P/Os Parks and Beranek at 21.31 and 21.34 bound for Nantes in north-western France to attack the Loire docks and shipping with six 250-pounders each. Sgt Oliver became unwell as they passed to the west of Soham and was forced to abort the sortie, while the rest of the main element exited the English coast at Orfordness on course to traverse Belgium on their way to the German frontier south of Luxembourg. P/O Taylor and crew were unable to establish themselves at the French coast and spent an hour attempting to gain their bearings before running out of time and heading home. After an outward flight lasting almost three hours, the others reached the target area to find largely clear skies, but haze again making target identification difficult. Most picked out a built-up area on e.t.a., backed up by evidence of searchlights, flak and burning incendiaries from other aircraft, and scattered their bombs over a wide area, those from Balderton attacking from 5,000 to 9,000 feet between 01.06 and 01.30. The operation was another massively ineffective affair, which again failed to land a single bomb in Stuttgart, but did hit 150 buildings in Heilbronn, a large town situated five miles from the Lauffen decoy site and twenty miles from Stuttgart. Meanwhile, the Nantes pair had benefitted from clear skies and good visibility, which enabled them to pinpoint on the Loire and deliver their attacks from 8,000 and 12,000 feet at 01.00 and 01.10.

The night of the 7/8th was devoted to mining operations involving eighty aircraft of 3 and 5 Groups operating mostly in the Baltic, although 408 (Goose) Squadron's Sgt Wood and crew would be joining nine Manchesters from 49 and 106 squadrons and two Hampdens from 420 (Snowy Owl) Squadron in the Rosemary garden in Helgoland Bight. First, however, the crews of Sgts Copeman and Craig and F/Sgt Manson departed Balderton between 23.09 and 23.31 bound for the Carrot garden in the Little Belt, located between Jutland and Denmark's Fyn Island, and it was a further twenty minutes before the Wood crew took to the air. Sgt Craig and crew were approaching Mablethorpe when instrument failure ended their interest in proceedings and F/Sgt Manson and crew became confused by low cloud at the coast at western Jutland and decided to drop their mine in an alternative position south of Ringkobing in one of the Hawthorn gardens. Sadly, they experienced a hang-up and had to take their mine home. In contrast, the Wood crew found conditions off north-western Germany to be favourable with moderate visibility and no low cloud and a pinpoint was established on the Island of Pellworm, from where a timed run at 500 feet at 135 i.a.s. on a westerly heading culminated with the release of the mine into the briefed location at 03.50. This left the Copeman crew as the sole 408 (Goose) Squadron representatives in the Baltic, some one hundred miles to the north-east, and they found a pinpoint on Holmsland Klit, before planting their vegetable in the briefed location from 700 feet at 03.28.

The recent successes at Lübeck and Rostock may have encouraged the posting of another Baltic coast target on the 8th, this time, Warnemünde, situated on the West Bank of the estuary ten miles north of Rostock. The docks were the site of U-Boot crew training, and also supplied German forces on the Russian front, but, equally important was the Heinkel aircraft factory, the destruction of which was handed to 5 Group. An initial force of more than two hundred aircraft was detailed, to which 5 Group contributed twenty-one Lancasters, nine Manchesters and nineteen 408 (Goose) and 420 (Snowy Owl) Squadron Hampdens. An elaborate plan called for a three-phase operation, beginning at zero hour with eighteen aircraft delivering high-explosives in a five-minute slot, followed by phase two, which involved 104 aircraft attacking with general purpose (GP) bombs, and phase three, six 44 (Rhodesia) Squadron Lancasters and a dozen aircraft from other groups targeting the Heinkel factory at low level to ensure its destruction. As this was ongoing, sixty-two 1 Group Wellingtons were to drop incendiaries, while others carried out low-level attacks on searchlight and flak batteries. In the event, 193 aircraft took off, which would reduce slightly the aircraft available for each phase. Nine of the twelve-strong 408 (Goose) Squadron element received a bomb load of a 1,900-pounder, while three others assigned to searchlight suppression carried four 500 and two 250-pounders each and departed Balderton between 21.15 and 21.32 with S/L Price the senior pilot on duty. Sgt Gillman and crew turned back because of overheating engines when at the midpoint of the North Sea and Sgt Halcro and crew were approaching the west coast of Jutland when forced to abort their sortie with instrument failure.

From the eastern coast of Jutland, a veritable forest of searchlights could be seen seventy miles distant at the target, which was reached soon afterwards under clear skies and the coastline and estuary easily identified. Searchlight glare prevented many from identifying their specific aiming point and the Balderton crews mostly bombed the general target area from 3,000 to 11,500 feet between 01.26 and 01.50, some observing bursts and others not. On return, Sgt Fern and crew reported that each of their approaches to bomb had been compromised by searchlights and they eventually released their load on Barth aerodrome further to the east from 12,000 feet at 01.30, while Sgt Huband and crew attacked an aerodrome at the northern end of Ærø Island on the way home. The operation cost nineteen aircraft, 10% of the force, and 5 Group posted missing four Lancasters, three Hampdens and a Manchester, two of the Hampdens belonging to 408 (Goose) Squadron. AE288 crashed into the Waddensee off Jutland's western coast without survivors from the crew of Sgt Norton RCAF, the remains of whom eventually washed ashore for burial. It was an experienced crew the members of which had completed between seventeen and twenty-five sorties. AE279 came down somewhere in northern Germany or just off the coast and claimed the lives of Sgt Markle RCAF and his crew, three of whom were on their eleventh sortie. Bomber Command claimed a moderately successful attack, but no local report emerged to provide details.

Losses were a fact of life in Bomber Command and could not be allowed to interfere with the process of war. A team from the Committee of Adjustment would descend upon the billets of the missing men and remove all trace of them to prepare the way for the next occupants. Such was the size of a bomber squadron, and the constant turnover of arrivals and departures, that close friendships beyond one's own crew were discouraged. Perhaps it was different among officers, who were fewer, and were more frequently in each other's company in the officers' mess, but, generally, the faces of the missing soon faded from memory, and those returning within a matter of months after evading capture were often shocked to discover how few faces they recognised.

The following night brought a small-scale mining effort by 5 Group in the Baltic and Heligoland Bight, and it was for the latter that Sgt Wood and crew departed Balderton at 23.54. They pinpointed on Pellworm Island and delivered their mine into the briefed location from 600 feet at 03.10, before returning safely from an uneventful sortie.

With the advent of the four-engine heavy bomber with a greater crew complement, it became necessary to make changes to the make-up of a crew, and this took place on the 11th with the removal of second pilots, second navigators and second wireless operators to create a crew consisting of a pilot (captain), flight engineer (pilot's mate), navigator, bomb-aimer, wireless operator/gunner and mid-upper and rear gunners. The changes would not be felt at 408 (Goose) Squadron until it left 5 Group for 4 Group in the autumn.

A force of fifty aircraft sent mining in the western Baltic on the 15th included sixteen Hampdens and six Lancasters from 5 Group, thirteen of the former provided by 408 (Goose) Squadron, which departed Balderton between 22.19 and 22.42 bound for the Pumpkin garden at the northern end of The Great Belt between Denmark's Fyn and Zeeland Islands. Clear skies provided good visibility and those reaching the target area established pinpoints on Samsø Island to the north and Rosnaes to the south and Revenaes (untraced) and planted their vegetables from 500 to 800 feet between 01.38 and 02.21. P/O Walton and crew lost too much time seeking out a pinpoint for the briefed location and planted in an alternative. On the way home, they came upon a trawler or minesweeper in the Waddensee and attacked it with the two 250lb wing mounted bombs from 2,000 feet at 02.30, claiming a near miss. Sgt Gillham and crew also lost time and at 02.37 deposited their mine from 6,000 feet off Fanø Island in the Hawthorn garden off Jutland's western coast. P/O Sanderson and crew pinpointed on Blaavands Point, a little further south, and dropped their mine there from 500 feet at 03.18. AT224 was shot down by flak and crashed, it is believed on Zeeland with no survivors from the crew of F/Sgt Dillon RCAF, an American who was on his seventeenth sortie. AD803 fell victim to naval flak and crashed on Endelave Island off Jutland's eastern coast, delivering Sgt Copeland RCAF as the sole survivor into enemy hands, on what was his thirteenth sortie.

On the 18th, W/C "Jack" Twigg was appointed as the new commanding officer, and while his two predecessors had been Canadians in the RAF, he was the first RCAF officer to attain the position. Early in the month, the squadron had taken a number of Manchesters on charge with a view to converting, and S/L Price set up a Conversion Flight for the training of crews.

Mannheim was posted as the target for a force of 193 aircraft on the 19th, which included a 5 Group contribution of fifteen Hampdens, thirteen Lancasters and four Manchesters. At Balderton, a dozen Hampdens received a bomb load of four small bomb containers (SBCs) each containing ninety 4lb incendiaries and two wing-mounted 250-pounders, while another had a 1,500lb mine winched into its bomb bay for delivery to the Rosemary garden and two others 120 bundles each of leaflets for the residents of Rouen in northern France. They took off between 22.00 and 22.43 with gardeners, Sgt Marment and crew, last off the ground and no senior pilots on duty, and soon lost the services of Sgt Gillham and crew to a jammed lever as soon as the pilot tried to raise the flaps and F/Sgt Manson and crew to the failure of the rear door to close. The others flew to the French coast, those involved in the main event on course to cross into Germany south of Luxembourg. They had to run the gauntlet of masses of searchlights before finding the target area under clear skies, but the absence of a moon and the consequent extreme darkness combined with haze to blot out all ground features. Most crews identified the city by means of a Gee-fix and the River Rhine but picking out the main post office aiming point was beyond them, and irrelevant anyway for what was an area raid designed to cause maximum damage within the built-up area. The Balderton crews bombed from 8,000 to 13,800 feet between 01.17 and 01.47 and returned with reports of a city in flames, which was an opinion not supported by local reports that only around ten bomb loads had landed in the city, and this was after the force had been heard overhead for an extended period, as if searching for it.

Meanwhile, Sgt Marment and crew had found adequate conditions in their target area and pinpointed on Amrum Island before planting their vegetable into the briefed location from 700 feet at 01.24. Some 430 miles to the south-west, Sgts Wishart and Nelson had found clear skies and good visibility over northern France and had dispensed their leaflets from 7,000 and 10,000 feet at 00.02 and 00.18 respectively during uneventful sorties.

There now followed another lull in major operations as Harris prepared for his master stroke. At the time of his appointment as C-in-C, the figure of four thousand bombers had been bandied around as the number required to wrap up the war. Whilst there was not the slightest chance of procuring them, Harris, with a dark cloud still hanging over the existence of an independent bomber force, needed to ensure that those earmarked for him were not spirited away to what he considered to be less-deserving causes. The Command had not yet achieved sufficient success to silence the detractors, and the Admiralty was still calling for bomber aircraft to be diverted to the U-Boot campaign, while others demanded support for the bomber force in North Africa. Harris was in need of a major victory, and, perhaps, a dose of symbolism to make his point, and out of this was born the Thousand Plan, Operation Millennium, the launching of a thousand aircraft in one night against a major German city, for which Hamburg had been pencilled in. Harris did not have a thousand front-line aircraft and required the support of other Commands to make up the numbers. This was forthcoming from Coastal and Flying Training Commands, and in the case of the former, a letter to Harris on the 22nd promised 250 aircraft. However, following an intervention from the Admiralty, the offer was withdrawn and most of the Flying Training Command aircraft were found to be not up to the task, leaving the Millennium force well short of the magic figure. Undaunted, Harris, or more probably his able deputy, AM Sir Robert Saundby, scraped together every airframe capable of controlled flight, or something resembling it, and pulled in the screened crews from their instructional duties. He also pressed into service aircraft and crews from within the Command's own training establishment, 91 Group. Come the night, not only would the thousand mark be achieved, but would be comfortably surpassed.

During the final week of the month, the arrival on bomber stations from Yorkshire to East Anglia of a motley collection of aircraft from training units gave rise to much speculation among crews and ground staff alike, but as usual, only the NAAFI staff and the local civilians knew what was really afoot. The most pressing remaining question was the weather, and as the days ticked by inexorably towards the end of May, this was showing no signs of complying. Harris was aware of the genuine danger, that the giant force might draw attention to itself and thereby compromise security, and the point was fast approaching when the operation would have to take place or be abandoned for the time being. Harris released some of the pressure by sanctioning operations on the night of the 29/30th, for which the Gnome & Rhone aero-engine and Goodrich tyre factories at Gennevilliers in Paris were the main targets. A force of seventy-seven aircraft included a contribution from 5 Group of fourteen Lancasters and three Hampdens, two of the latter provided by 408 (Goose) Squadron and loaded with a 1,900-pounder each and two 250-pounders. The crews of W/C Twigg and P/O Williams departed Balderton at 00.03 and 00.07 and arrived in the target area to find clear skies and excellent visibility, in which the distinctive finger-shaped docks on the northern bank of the Seine stood out clearly. P/O Williams and crew bombed from 2,800 feet at 02.22 and W/C Twigg and crew four minutes later from 2,000 feet, but it proved difficult to assess the outcome. Returning crews were largely enthusiastic, while local sources reported that the only damage caused was to eighty-seven houses, in which thirty-four people were killed and 167 injured.

It was in an atmosphere of frustration and hopeful expectation, that "morning prayers" began at Harris's High Wycombe HQ on the 30th, with all eyes turned upon the civilian chief meteorological adviser, Magnus Spence. After careful deliberation, he was able to give a qualified assurance of clear skies over the Rhineland, while north-western Germany and Hamburg would be concealed under buckets of cloud. Thus, did the fickle fates decree that Cologne would bear the dubious honour of hosting the first one thousand bomber raid in history. At briefings, crews were told that the enormous force was to be pushed across the aiming point in just ninety minutes. This was unprecedented and gave rise to the question of collisions as hundreds of aircraft funnelled towards the aiming point. The answer, according to the experts, was to observe timings and flight levels, and they calculated also that just two aircraft would collide over the target. It is said that a wag in every briefing room asked, "do they know which two?"

5 Group had seventy-three Lancasters, forty-six Manchesters and thirty-four Hampdens bombed up and ready to go, and at Balderton, nineteen Hampdens with four SBCs of 4lb incendiaries and Manchester L7401 with fourteen SBCs awaited the arrival of their crews, who had been briefed to attack one of three areas spanning the city centre from north to south, in their case, aiming point Y, bordering the western and southern extremities on the West Bank. Late that evening, the first of an eventual 1,047 aircraft took off to deliver the now familiar three-wave-format attack on the Rhineland capital, the older training hacks struggling somewhat reluctantly into the air, lifted more by the enthusiasm of their crews than by the power of their engines, and some of these, unable to climb to a respectable height, would fall easy prey to the defences or simply drop from the sky through mechanical breakdown. The 408 (Goose) Squadron Hampden element took off between 22.59 and 23.27 with W/C Twigg and S/L Constance the senior pilots on duty, leaving the Manchester on the ground until 00.48, when it departed Balderton in the hands of S/L Price only to return soon afterwards because of a hydraulics issue.

They set course for Orfordness and lost the services first of W/C Twigg and crew east of Peterborough and then Sgt Wood and crew with the coast just a few miles ahead, both to an ailing starboard engine, while the rest pressed on to make landfall over the Scheldt estuary and traverse Belgium, drawn on for the last seventy miles by the glow of the already burning city. They were greeted at the target by precisely the weather conditions of clear skies and bright moonlight predicted by Magnus Spence, which enabled them to pinpoint on the River Rhine and exploit the opportunity to deliver their ordnance onto the city from 7,000 to 12,200 feet between 01.00 and 01.40. Returning crews described a city on fire from end to end and never-before-witnessed scenes, and post-raid reconnaissance confirmed that the operation had, by any standards, been an outstanding success and had destroyed more than 3,300 buildings, while inflicting serious damage to two thousand others. Although the loss of forty-one aircraft represented a new record high, the conditions had favoured both attackers and defenders alike, and in the context of the scale of success and the numbers dispatched, it could not be considered an inordinately high figure. 5

Group registered a loss of four Manchesters, one Lancaster and one Hampden, but it was the training units that sustained the greatest losses amounting to twenty-one aircraft.

During the course of the month, the squadron took part in sixteen operations and dispatched 109 sorties for the loss of four Hampdens and crews.

June 1942

While the Millennium force remained assembled, Harris wanted to exploit its potential again immediately, and was no doubt excited about the prospect of visiting upon the old enemy of Essen a similar ordeal to that just experienced by Cologne. A force of 956 aircraft was the best that could be achieved during the 1st, 5 Group managing seventy-three Lancasters, thirty-three Manchesters and twenty-six Hampdens. The 408 (Goose) Squadron ORB is confusing as eight last minute cancellations reduced the initial number of twenty Hampdens and single Manchester. The Form 541 lists ten Hampdens and one Manchester departing Balderton and Syerston respectively between 22.58 and 23.29 with W/C Twigg the senior pilot on duty and B Flight commander S/L Price at the controls of L7401, but adds that three crews bombed the primary target, the Krupp complex, and nine the general built-up area, making a total of twelve aircraft. Crews had been briefed to employ the sprawl of the Borbeck district Krupp sector as the aiming point and flew out under favourable weather conditions that promised the possibility of actually being able to identify ground detail.

They ran into five to ten-tenths cloud at 4,000 to 6,000 feet over the target, which combined with industrial haze and smoke drifting over from Cologne to muddy the vertical visibility, and bombing took place largely on TR (Gee) supported by occasional visual references on waterways. The 408 (Goose) Squadron participants delivered their attacks from 9,500 to 15,000 feet between 01.09 and 02.13 on a variety of headings ranging from north-east, through east to due west and most observed bursts and fires. Sgt Fern and crew lost a section of bomb door to flak while they were searching for the target and jettisoned their all-incendiary load ten miles west-north-west of Essen, observing the splash of fire on impact. AT191 failed to return after falling victim to the night-fighter of Lt Karl-Heinz Vollkopf of II./NJG2 and crashing into the Ijsselmeer, taking with it the experienced crew of P/O Charlton, who was on his eighteenth sortie. F/Sgt Womar DFM, a wireless operator/gunner was on his fifty-seventh sortie having served previously with 144 Squadron. S/L Price and crew returned safely in the Manchester having completed the sortie, which would prove to be the last by the type in 408 (Goose) Squadron service.

An accurate assessment of results was not possible, and crews returned with reports of many fires, some identified as dummies, but no detail and the authorities would have to wait for post-raid reconnaissance before they could assess what had happened on the ground. In the meantime, a counting of the cost revealed the loss of thirty-one aircraft, and sadly, there would be no major success to mitigate the scale of the loss, local reports confirming that only eleven houses had been destroyed in Essen, and fewer than two hundred others damaged, mostly in southern districts. A greater number of bomb loads had actually fallen on the nearby locations of Oberhausen, Duisburg and Mülheim-an-der-Ruhr.

A follow-up raid was planned for twenty-four hours later, and a much-reduced force of 197 aircraft made ready, with 5 Group providing twenty-seven Lancasters and a dozen Hampdens, six of the latter belonging to 408 (Goose) Squadron. They each received a bomb load of four SBCs of 4lb incendiaries and departed Balderton between 23.11 and 23.26 with S/L Clift and the recently promoted F/L Coulter the senior pilots on duty. They had been preceded into the air between 23.02 and 23.09 by four freshman crews bound for nickelling duties over the Rennes area and Sgt Nelson and crew on a mining sortie to the Beech garden off St-Nazaire. F/L Frow and crew of the bombing brigade lost their intercom as they crossed the Norfolk coast and turned back, leaving the others to find clear skies over the Ruhr with the usual industrial haze, but a low moon provided some illumination, and most crews would describe the visibility as good. The deployment of flares proved beneficial as they highlighted the Rhine over to the west at Duisburg, and those equipped with Gee confirmed their positions over what they believed to be the Krupp works aiming point. The Balderton crews carried out their attacks from 9,000 to 13,600 feet between 01.40 and 01.50 and four returned safely apparently confident that they had attacked Essen. Absent from debriefing was the crew of P/O Taylor RCAF, who had been outbound over the Ijsselmeer in AT154 when crossing paths with the night-fighter of Hptm Helmut Lent of II./NJG2. The pilot was on his eighth sortie, while Sgt Ronson, a wireless operator/gunner was on his twenty-fifth. Meanwhile, the leafleteers had encountered unfavourable conditions over north-western France and three had dispensed their 108 bundles each of the F22 publication over the approximate target area from 10,000 and 11,000 feet between 01.39 and 02.20, while the fourth suffered a hang-up and brought theirs home. Last home at 05.55 was the Nelson crew, who were able to report pinpointing on Noirmoutier Island to the south of the Loire estuary and planting their vegetable in the briefed location from 500 feet at 02.40.

Local sources in Essen reported just three high explosive bombs and three hundred incendiaries falling in the city to cause only minor damage. Such was the density of the Ruhr, with overlapping town and city boundaries, it was difficult not to hit something urban, but concentration was the key to success, and the scattering of bombs over a wide area was never going to achieve a knock-out blow. Harris was stubborn and would keep trying, but it would be a further nine months before the means were to hand to make a genuine impact.

For the next operation, on the 3rd, Harris turned his attention upon Bremen, which, along with Essen and Emden, would share the Command's attention for the remainder of the month. A force of 170 aircraft was made ready for the first major attack on the port-city since the previous October, for which fifteen Lancasters, nine Hampdens and six Manchesters were provided by 5 Group. During refuelling at Balderton, AT220 caught fire and was destroyed. 408 (Goose) Squadron loaded each of its seven participating Hampdens with four SBCs of 4lb incendiaries and sent them on their way from Balderton between 22.47 and 23.00 with F/L Frow the senior pilot on duty, following in the wake of Sgt Locker and crew who had taken off for nickelling duties over Rennes ten minutes earlier. F/Sgt Manson became unwell, and he and his crew dropped out shortly after crossing the Norfolk coast, leaving the rest to make landfall on the Dutch coast and approach the target from the south-east. They found clear skies and ground haze, which prevented an identification of specific aiming points, like the Deschimag shipyards along the Weser and Focke-Wulf aircraft factory in the Hemelingen district south-east of the city centre. The Balderton crews delivered their incendiaries over the general city area from 7,800 to 12,000 feet between 01.30 and 01.34, before returning safely to report a lack of confidence in the effectiveness of their efforts.

Local sources, however, told a story of heavy damage to housing in six streets and to harbour installations, and there were also hits on U-Boot construction yards and the Focke-Wulf aircraft factory, although, any loss of production was slight. The Locker crew had also encountered hazy conditions and had dispensed their leaflets on estimated position based on dead-reckoning (DR) from 10,000 feet at 02.30.

The following night was one of small-scale minor operations involving twenty aircraft attacking the docks and shipping at Dieppe, for which 5 Group provided two Lancasters and three Hampdens each from the two Canadian squadrons. The 408 (Goose) Squadron crews of F/O Leach and Sgts Kaye and Jennings departed Balderton between 23.03 and 23.07, having been preceded into the air at 22.20 by P/O Swatton and crew bound with printed matter for Rennes. *(Much of the ORB for June 1942 is unintelligible and a few of the names that cannot be deciphered may be incorrect).* The last-mentioned encountered haze up to 11,000 feet at the French coast, and unable to establish a pinpoint, abandoned the sortie. Sgt Kaye was contending with an overheating starboard engine and circled over the sea, hoping to cool it down and attain a bombing altitude of 10,000 feet, but ran out of time and went home. The conditions at Dieppe were also unhelpful, but searchlights and flares dropped by other aircraft highlighted the docks, helping F/O Leach and crew to deliver their six 250-pounders from 8,000 feet at 01.11 and the Jennings crew from 6,000 feet at 01.25.

A force of 180 aircraft was prepared for the next intended assault on Essen on the 5th, for which 5 Group put up thirteen Lancasters and eleven Hampdens, eight of the latter belonging to 408 (Goose) Squadron. They departed Balderton between 22.47 and 23.00 with no senior pilots on duty and each loaded with four SBCs of incendiaries, and soon lost the services of F/Sgt Halcro and crew to engine trouble. The others flew out over Orfordness to make landfall over the Scheldt estuary and cross northern Belgium, entering Germany to the south-west of the Ruhr, some identifying a bend in the River Ruhr to the south-east of the target, while others relied on a TR-fix, flares or evidence of searchlight and flak concentrations to establish their positions in conditions of poor vertical visibility. F/Sgt Clothier and crew experienced a generator failure, and the SBCs were jettisoned some ten miles north-west of Essen from 12,000 feet at 01.13, and on the way home they strafed an aerodrome believed to be in the Alkmaar area. The five remaining crews carried out their attacks on estimated positions from 11,000 to 14,000 feet between 01.25 and 01.40 and had little of use to pass on to the intelligence section at debriefing. Local sources again confirmed an ineffective and wasteful raid, which caused only minor damage in Essen at a cost of twelve aircraft and crews.

The first of four attacks during the month on the naval port of Emden was posted on the 6th, and a force of 233 aircraft made ready, 5 Group contributing twenty Lancasters, fifteen Hampdens and seven Manchesters. AD980 crashed in a field north-east of Balderton during an air-test for the above, and although sustaining injuries, P/O Randall and his crew survived the experience. The squadron loaded eight of its Hampdens with four SBCs of incendiaries and two wing-mounted 250-pounders and sent them on their way between 22.54 and 23.09 with F/Ls Coulter and Frow the senior pilots on duty. P/O Williams and crew turned back from The Wash because of overheating engines, and Sgt Kaye and crew followed them home after failing to establish their position after leaving the English coast. The others found the skies over the coast of north-western Germany to be clear of cloud and the visibility to be good, which enabled some to pinpoint on the distinctive shape of Dollart Bay to the south of the port, while others took advantage of the flares illuminating the docks area. The Balderton crews bombed from 8,000 to 12,000 feet between 01.15 and 01.33 and observed some bursts and fires, but it was left to photographic reconnaissance and local sources to confirm that the raid had been responsible for the destruction of some three hundred houses, with a further two hundred severely damaged, in return for the loss of nine aircraft.

The Command entered a ten-night period of gardening and minor operations thereafter, punctuated by two further attacks on Essen. 5 Group detailed nine Lancasters and two 408 (Goose) Squadron Hampdens for mining duties in the Nectarine I garden on the 7th, and three to maintain the supply of toilet paper to the residents of Northern France. Sgt Bell and crew departed Balderton first at 23.25 bound for Rennes, leaving the crews of Sgts Locker and Wishart to follow on at 00.35 and 00.51 respectively and head for the southern Frisians. Conditions at the Brittany coast were excellent and a pinpoint on Cap Frehel provided a firm reference for the rest of the outward flight, which culminated with the release of 112 bundles of three different leaflets from 10,000 feet at 02.00. The gardeners encountered seven-tenths cloud but favourable conditions, and aided by the light from flame floats, planted their vegetables from 2,000 and 3,000 feet at 02.38 and 02.42.

The first of the two Essen raids was posted on the 8th and involved a force of 170 aircraft including thirteen Lancasters from Coningsby and Scampton and nine Hampdens. 408 (Goose) Squadron made ready two of its Hampdens for the crews of P/O Williams and F/Sgt Clothier to take part in the main event and another for Sgt Kaye and crew to employ against the docks and shipping at Dieppe. They departed Balderton in a sixteen-minute slot either side of 23.00, the Kaye crew last away and first home after benefitting from favourable conditions and pinpointing of St-Aubin aerodrome as the starting point for a timed run to the target. They delivered their four 500-pounders from 10,000 feet at 01.27 heading due north and observed one burst in the docks before returning safely after four-and-a-half hours aloft. Meanwhile, 280 miles to the north-east, Essen lay under clear skies but was cloaked by extreme darkness and the usual blanket of industrial haze and few crews were able to make a positive identification. Most bombed on e.t.a. and an impression of a built-up area below, the crews of P/O Williams and F/Sgt Clothier dropping their four SBCs and two 250-pounders each from 10,000 and 12,000 feet at 01.03 and 01.08 respectively. It was another disappointing and widely scattered raid, which local sources confirmed caused only minor housing damage.

Sgt Wishart and crew set out from Balderton at 01.15 on the 12th bound for the Nectarine I garden, where they found clear skies and good visibility but were unable to release their mine. After experiencing great difficulty, they eventually persuaded it to fall away over the middle of the North Sea on the way home.

After spending four nights on the ground because of adverse weather conditions, the Command stirred itself on the 16th at Harris's behest to have another crack at Essen, for which 106 aircraft were made ready, 5 Group contributing fifteen Lancasters. All crews had been briefed to employ TR to locate the target and bomb blindly based on that, which, under the conditions of up to eight-tenths cloud on a moonless night with visibility down to three miles, was the best that could be expected. It emerged at debriefing that only sixteen crews claimed to have bombed the primary target, while fifty-six others had found alternatives, mostly the city of Bonn. This concluded a series of five raids on Essen in sixteen nights, during which 1,607 sorties had been dispatched and eighty-four aircraft lost. The city had sustained no industrial damage, and a few wrecked houses was all that Bomber Command had to show for the massive effort expended.

While the above was in progress, a dozen 408 (Goose) Squadron Hampdens departed Balderton between 22.34 and 22.58 bound for the Artichoke garden off Lorient, where they found patchy cloud with a base at 2,000 feet. Six crews experienced no difficulty in identifying suitable pinpoints on Belle Isle, Ile-de-Groix and Quiberon to name but a few and vegetables were planted from 1,500 to 2,000 feet between 01.48 and 02.27. Unaccountably, the remaining six crews were unable to establish their position and took their mines home. On the following night the mining area for fifteen Hampdens was the Beech garden off St-Nazaire, for which the five-strong 408 (Goose) Squadron element departed Balderton between 22.33 and 22.46 and arrived in the target area to find four-tenths cloud and clearly-defined pinpoints on Noirmoutier Island to the south of the estuary, Groix Island to the north and Belle Isle to the west. Vegetables were planted from 500 to 1,000 feet between 01.32 and 02.28 and safe returns completed at the end of uneventful sorties.

For the third night in a row 408 (Goose) Squadron was called upon on the 18th to provide aircraft for mining duties, once more in the Artichoke garden off Lorient, for which ten Hampdens departed Balderton between 22.26 and 22.45. As they reached the Brittany coast the cloud base dropped to 500 feet and below and recognising the futility of pressing on with little or no prospect of being able to find a pinpoint, all turned back and all but one arrived safely home. Absent was the crew of P/O Beranek RCAF, who were in AT189, which crashed with fatal consequences for the occupants in the Bayeux area, some distance to the east of the usual route. The pilot was on his ninth sortie and wireless operator/gunner on his twentieth.

Having hosted an effective attack earlier in the month, Emden became the focus for three raids in the space of four nights, beginning on the 19th, for which a force of 194 aircraft was assembled. Nine Lancasters and eleven 420 (Snowy Owl) Squadron Hampdens represented 5 Group, their crews having been briefed to switch to Osnabrück, eighty miles to the south, if the weather conditions over the coastal region became troublesome. Part of the flare force did, indeed, initiate an attack on Osnabrück by twenty-nine aircraft, while the rest of the force arrived over the German coastal region to encounter clear skies but ground haze, which prevented most from positively identifying the port. They delivered their attacks on estimated positions and 131 returning crews claimed that they had bombed the primary target, despite which, the Emden authorities reported only a handful of high-explosive bombs falling and a few hundred incendiaries.

On the following day a force of 185 aircraft was assembled to return to the port, among them twenty-four Lancasters and a dozen Hampdens provided by 5 Group, ten of the latter belonging to 408 (Goose) Squadron. Two others were made ready at Balderton for the freshman crews of F/Sgt Cornwall and Sgt Hunter, who were to deliver leaflets to the Lille region of North-eastern France. The bombers departed Balderton between 22.58 and 23.15 with S/L Clift the senior pilot on duty and each Hampden carrying four SBCs and two 250-pounders. They headed for landfall on the Dutch coast in the Alkmaar region, and it was a further hour before the nickellers took to the air and turned towards the south-east. The docks at Emden were the briefed aiming point and the town the alternative, and the entire Balderton element arrived over Jade Bay to find five-tenths cloud at around 7,000 feet and poor visibility, which forced most to establish their positions by TR-fix and brief glimpses of the coastline. Few identified the docks and delivered their attacks instead on the alternative target, the general built-up area, from 5,000 to 13,000 feet between 01.15 and 01.42, observing bursts and fires. Of the nickellers, Sgt Hunter and crew turned back with engine trouble having reached Worthy Down and the Cornwall crew fulfilled their brief under clear skies when dispensing 110 bundles of F22 leaflets from 10,000 feet at 02.45, guided by lights from the less-than-perfect blackout. Local sources in Emden confirmed that only a proportion of the force had located the target, and around a hundred houses had been damaged.

5 Group focused on mining operations on the 21st and called upon 408 (Goose) Squadron to provide a single Hampden for the Artichoke garden off Lorient and another to deliver reading matter to the residents of Rennes. The crew of F/Sgt Cornwall departed Balderton at 23.15 bound for the Biscay coast and Sgt Kemp and crew followed them at 23.38 to begin the Channel crossing at the Dorset coast. The former were south-west of Northampton when rising oil temperature in the starboard engine persuaded them to turn back, leaving the Kemp crew to continue on and make landfall on the French coast six miles west of Cap Frehel. Lights in a building in the DR position of Rennes provided a reference point and the nickels were dispensed from 10,000 feet at 02.30 before a safe return saw them land at 05.39.

A force of 227 aircraft was assembled on the 22nd to deliver the third raid of the series on Emden, for which 5 Group contributed eleven Lancasters and eight 408 (Goose) Squadron Hampdens, the latter departing Balderton shortly after 23.00 with F/L Frow the senior pilot on duty and each loaded with four SBCs of 4lb incendiaries and two 250-pounders. F/Sgt Cornwall and crew were some seventy miles out from Skegness when engine trouble ended their interest in proceedings, but the rest continued on and most established their approach to the target by identifying the coastline and confirming it via a TR-fix backed up by flak and fires. Despite largely clear skies and moonlight and only modest ground haze, it proved difficult to pinpoint on the docks and the town again became the aiming point, the Balderton crews delivering their attacks from 7,000 to 11,000 feet between 01.17 and 01.50. Some returning crews reported that they had been able to distinguish between genuine and decoy fires, but the latter succeeded in drawing off many loads, and those finding the target destroyed a modest fifty houses and damaged a hundred more.

On the 24th, 5 Group ordered four Lancasters and three 408 (Goose) Squadron Hampdens to be made ready to bomb the docks and shipping at St-Nazaire, and the crews detailed at Balderton were those of F/Sgt Cornwall, Sgt Wishart and Sgt Kemp. They took off at 23.16, 23.17 and 23.31 respectively, each sitting on six 250-pounders and the bundles of leaflets that were an integral part of every sortie. Visibility in the target area was compromised by haze, but the River Loire provided a useful reference for the Cornwall crew, who carried out their attack from 10,000 feet at 02.20, while the remaining two brought their bombs home after dispensing nickels in the target area.

The time had now arrived for the final deployment of the Thousand Force, and indeed, of the Manchester in operational service. A force of 960 aircraft was assembled on the 25th, 142 provided by 5 Group in the form of ninety-six Lancasters, twenty-six Hampdens and twenty Manchesters. It was an indication of the failure of the Manchester, that the aircraft it had been intended to replace, the Hampden, would continue to serve 5 Group in small numbers until mid-September. To the above numbers were added five aircraft from Army Co-operation Command and 102 aircraft from Coastal Command, which had been ordered by Churchill to take part, although its contribution was to be deemed a separate operation. However, the 1,067 aircraft from all sources would represent a larger combined force than that sent to Cologne at the end of May. The fourteen participating 408 (Goose) Squadron crews were briefed to aim for the Focke-Wulf aircraft factory in the Hemelingen district located on the eastern bank of the Weser to the south-east of the city centre, and each would be sitting on a bomb load of four SBCs of 4lb incendiaries and flanked by two wing-mounted 250-pounders. They departed Balderton between 22.54 and 23.15 with S/L Price the senior pilot on duty and immediately lost the services of F/Sgt Craig and crew to a seriously vibrating starboard engine. After crossing the English coast between Mablethorpe and Skegness the 5 Group element traversed the North Sea above the ten-tenths cloud that persisted all the way to the target area, and above which was an extremely bright sky, courtesy of a full moon and the Northern Lights.

A band of nine to ten-tenths cloud lay over Bremen at between 3,000 and 5,000 feet, completely obscuring ground detail, which precluded any chance of picking up the Focke-Wulf aircraft factory and positions were established by TR-fix, the glow of fires on the ground and the volume of flak coming up through the cloud. With the exception of the crews of F/Sgt Johnstone and Sgt Wood, who were unable to establish a pinpoint, the Balderton crews attacked from 5,000 to 12,000 feet between 01.38 and 02.10, and at debriefing could claim only to have bombed on estimated positions, hopefully over the city. They reported several areas of fire, but none of the 696 crews claiming to have attacked the primary target had any real clue as to the outcome and it was local sources that provided the detail. They estimated that a force of eighty aircraft had been involved and confirmed a number of hits on the Focke-Wulf aircraft factory and some shipyards, along with the destruction of 572 houses and damage to more than six thousand others, mostly in southern and eastern districts. The level of success fell well short of that achieved at Cologne, but surpassed by far the failure at Essen, albeit at a new record loss of forty-eight aircraft, which represented 5% of those dispatched. The O.T.Us of 91 Group suffered the highest casualty rate of 11.6%, largely because they were employing tired, old Whitleys, Wellingtons and Hampdens, which were not up to the task, while 5 Group lost one Lancaster and one Manchester.

The night of the 26/27th was devoted to mining operations off the Biscay coast and the Frisians and it was for the Artichoke garden that five 408 (Goose) Squadron crews were briefed and departed Balderton between 22.54 and 23.00 with P/O Leach the senior pilot on duty. F/Sgt Cornwall was taken ill and turned back after around an hour and Sgt Ross and crew followed them home after failing to establish their position at the Brittany coast. Under clear skies the others located the Ile-de-Groix as the starting point for their timed runs and delivered a single mine each from 500 and 700 feet between 01.30 and 01.48. Sgt Kemp and crew dropped their 250-pounders from 7,000 feet on what appeared to be an aerial lighthouse, while Sgt Wishart and crew found a flak ship for theirs and collected shell holes in the mainplane and bomb doors for their cheek, before landing with a punctured tyre.

408 (Goose) Squadron had completed its operational activity for the month by the time that the first of a number of follow-up operations against Bremen was mounted on the night of the 27/28th involving 144 aircraft, including twenty-four Lancasters from 5 Group. Weather conditions were very much as those of two nights earlier, with ten-tenths cloud up to around 4,000 feet and decreasing amounts thereafter as high as 15,000 feet. The sky above was as bright as day under a large moon, even though the Northern Lights, on this occasion, were masked by high cloud. Most located the target area by TR-fix, and crews could only estimate that they were over the target.

Local reports confirmed hits on the previously damaged Atlas Werke shipyard and the Korff refinery, but further details were scant and of little value. It was Bremen again on the 29th, for which a force of 253 aircraft was assembled, including sixty-four Lancasters as the 5 Group contribution. They flew out over six to ten-tenths cloud at between 3,000 and 5,000 feet with excellent visibility above and found around seven to ten-tenths cloud in layers up to 16,000 feet in the target area, with large gaps that afforded some a glimpse of the ground. They delivered their loads from 15,000 and 16,000 feet at 01.24 and 01.27 respectively, and, in keeping with other returning crews, could provide only impressions of the raid. Local reports, however, spoke of extensive damage to the Focke-Wulf factory, the A G Weser U-Boot construction yard and three other important war-industry premises, along with the local gas works and some limited destruction of housing.

During the course of the month the squadron took part in twenty-six operations and dispatched 128 Hampden sorties and two by the Manchester for the loss of five Hampdens and three crews.

July 1942

In a gentle start to the new month, four 408 (Goose) Squadron crews departed Balderton at 09.00 to conduct a sea search for downed crews but found nothing. 5 Group operated alone on the night of the 1/2nd, when sending two Lancasters each from 97 and 106 Squadrons to mine the waters of the Great Belt in the western Baltic. The campaign against Bremen continued on the 2nd, with the preparation of a force of 325 aircraft, more than half of which were Wellingtons, while 5 Group squadrons contributed fifty-three Lancasters and twenty-eight Hampdens, fifteen of the latter belonging to 408 (Goose) Squadron. They took off between 23.02 and 23.30 with W/C Twigg and F/Ls Coulter and Frow the senior pilots on duty and a load of four SBCs and two 250-pounders on board and began the North Sea crossing at Skegness. F/L Frow and crew were sixty miles out when forced by engine trouble to turn back, and F/Sgt Cornwall and crew had just flown over the Frisian Island of Vlieland when they realised that they were north of the intended track and decided also to abort their sortie. The others made landfall south of Amsterdam, shortly after which, F/Sgt Manson and crew turned back with an engine issue, leaving the remaining twelve to reach the target under favourable weather conditions with excellent visibility, no low cloud, high cirrus at around 22,000 feet and only a little haze to spoil the view below. Positions were established by TR-fix confirmed by a visual check, but searchlight glare created great difficulty for the bomb-aimers trying to identify the Focke-Wulf aircraft factory and most would settle for estimating the release point for their bombs over the general built-up area. The Balderton crews attacked from 4,000 to 12,000 feet between 01.40 and 02.13, by which time P/O Sanderson and crew had unloaded their 250-pounders from 14,000 feet on an aerodrome fifteen miles south-east of Bremen. F/Sgt Fern and crew fell behind schedule and attacked an alternative target, which they recorded as a location on the River Weser, while on the way home, F/Sgt Clothier and crew came under fire twice from a Wellington and sustained holes in the port wing and fuel tank. Local reports spoke of a thousand houses damaged, along with four small industrial premises, and three cranes and seven ships hit in the port, one of the vessels sinking and becoming a danger to navigation. The likelihood is, however, that much of the effort was wasted beyond the city's southern boundary.

The remainder of the first half of the month would be low-key, with mining operations occupying much of the night-time activity. 5 Group detailed fifty-two Lancasters and twenty-four Hampdens on the 8th to attack the Kriegsmarinewerft shipyard in Wilhelmshaven as part of an overall force of 285 aircraft. The 408 (Goose) Squadron element of fifteen each received a bomb load of one 1,900-pounder and two 250-pounders and all but one departed Balderton between 23.27 and 23.56 with S/Ls Clift and Price the senior pilots on duty, leaving a delayed F/Sgt Johnstone and crew on the ground until 00.13. It was a deficit that could not be recovered, and they ran out of time when over the town of Dornum, some twenty-five miles west-north-west of their intended destination, where they dropped their load from 12,000 feet at 02.17. P/O Parks and crew were unable to establish a pinpoint and came upon a factory about five miles west of Wilhelmshaven, upon which the 1,900-pounder was seen to burst. Those reaching the target encountered around three-tenths thin cloud at 10,000 feet and haze below, which made it almost impossible for most to identify ground detail, including the docks and shipyard aiming points, and positions were established on e.t.a. and by TR-fix, some backed up through a visual check assisted by the use of flares. The 408 (Goose) Squadron crews delivered their attacks from 8,000 to 12,000 feet between 01.40 and 02.15 and observed fires but not much in the way of detail, and while local sources confirmed some damage in Wilhelmshaven, post-raid reconnaissance revealed that much of the bombing had missed the town to the west.

On the following night, twenty-four Hampdens were detailed for mining duties in the Nectarine III garden around the Frisian Islands off Germany's north-western coast. 408 (Goose) Squadron made ready fifteen aircraft and sent them on their way from Balderton between 23.05 and 23.34 with F/Ls Coulter and Frow the senior pilots on duty. Sgt Roux and crew were forced to turn back when their port engine caught fire, leaving the others to press on and pinpoint on Baltrum, Wangerooge, Spiekeroog and Langeroog, according to the location of their individual release point, with up to ten-tenths cloud above them as they conducted their timed runs. Vegetables were planted in the briefed locations from 600 to 2,000 feet between 01.26 and 02.09 and all returned safely, the Roux crew landing at Coltishall.

On the 10th, the Canadian High Commissioner, The Honourable Vincent Massey, paid an official visit to the squadron accompanied by Mrs Massey. They arrived at 10.30 and stayed for an hour before moving on to other engagements.

At around 04.00 on the 11th, a Hampden set out from Balderton to provide a weather report for a possible "moling" operation in Area 3A, which covered the region of Germany from north of the Ruhr to the north-western coast. Waiting on the ground were five other Hampdens, which, on receiving a positive indication that sufficient cloud existed, took off between 04.31 and 04.56 with S/L Price the senior pilot on duty and headed out across the North Sea to make landfall at various points along the Dutch and German coasts. The crews of S/L Price and F/Sgts Clothier, Halcro, Huband and Johnstone ran out of cloud as they neared land and turned back, leaving P/O Sanderson and crew to press on alone protected by ten-tenths cloud with a base at 2,000 feet, into which they could disappear if threatened. The visibility was good, and they map-read to the Dortmund-Ems Canal, where they spotted a factory two miles north of Lingen, almost certainly at Holthausen, and bombed it with eight 250-pounders from 1,500 feet at 06.50 on a due north heading. Two bursts were observed before they escaped into cloud and flew home in rainstorms and turbulent air at between 3,000 and 4000 feet.

The first daylight foray deep into enemy territory by Lancasters, the previously mentioned raid on the M.A.N diesel engine factory at Augsburg in April, had cost seven of the twelve aircraft dispatched, and Harris, despite his antipathy to such operations, sanctioned a similar plan by 5 Group for an attack on the F Schichau GmbH (Ltd) and Danziger Werft Aktien Gesellschaft *(Aktien Gesellschaft or A.G. = production company in English)* U-Boot construction yards in the distant port of Danzig on the 11th. The forty-four Lancasters of 61, 83, 97, 106 and 207 Squadrons were to fly out in formation at low level, before splitting up to cross Denmark and the Baltic independently, and then climb to bombing altitude and make their own individual approaches to the target. The attack was to be carried out in the fading light, to allow a withdrawal to take place under the cover of darkness, and the 1,500-mile round-trip would be the longest yet attempted by the Command. An unanticipated band of ten-tenths ice-bearing cloud was encountered over the North Sea extending from 1,000 to 14,000 feet, and this ruined the plan as aircraft lost contact with each other, forcing the individual crews to break formation and make their way independently to the target. This would have a detrimental effect on the raid and cause some crews to abandon their sorties or arrive late, when darkness had already settled over the area to make identification a challenge. Twenty-six aircraft bombed either the ship-building wharfs or the town, and two of them were shot down by flak.

A return to mining duties for 5 Group on the 12th resulted in fifteen Lancaster and fifteen Hampden crews attending briefing to learn that they were assigned respectively to the Nectarine, Artichoke and Beech gardens, the last-mentioned off St-Nazaire the destination for six from 408 (Goose) Squadron, which departed Balderton between 23.15 and 23.21 with P/O Swatton the only commissioned pilot on duty. Sgt Ross and crew failed to establish a pinpoint on the Brittany coast in the face of five-tenths cloud and low mist and took their ordnance home, while the others pushed on to arrive in the target area and pinpoint on the Ile-de-Noirmoutier. There were varying opinions as to the state of the visibility, but agreement on the two to three-tenths cloud with a base at around 2,000 feet, and mines were released into the briefed locations from 700 to 1,000 feet between 02.12 and 02.40. On the way home they sought out targets for their wing-mounted 250-pounders and P/O Swatton and crew found a flare path, while Sgt Wishart and crew attacked a flak concentration, Sgt Allen and crew an aerodrome and Sgt Kemp and crew a ship and an aerodrome.

The first of a series of five operations over a four-week period against Duisburg was mounted on the night of the 13/14th and involved 194 aircraft, including thirteen Lancasters from the 5 Group stations of Bottesford and Coningsby. The operation failed to find the mark in adverse weather conditions consisting of electrical storms and heavy cloud, and the bombing became widely scattered and ineffective. While this operation was in progress, six 408 (Goose) Squadron Hampdens were engaged in mining activities, four in the Artichoke garden off Lorient and one each in Nectarine I, the Dutch Frisians, and Eglantine in the Elbe estuary. They had departed Balderton between 23.23 and 01.03 and all reached their respective target areas without incident, last away and first back, F/Sgt Cornwall and crew, who planted their vegetable from 700 feet at 03.04 after conducting a timed run from the eastern tip of Terschelling. Sgt Jennings and crew were operating further north and pinpointed on Langeoog and Schärhorn Islands on their way to deliver their mine in the Elbe estuary from 1,000 feet at 02.14. Conditions off Lorient were favourable with largely clear skies and good visibility and pinpoints were easily established on Belle and Groix Islands and the mines released by the crews of Sgts Kemp, Manson, Roux and

Wood from 600, 700 and 1,000 feet at 02.30 and 02.37. The Kemp crew found a flak concentration on Lannion aerodrome to bomb on the way home from 4,500 feet at 03.24, while the others found nothing suitable and either jettisoned their 250-pounders or returned them to the bomb dump.

On the 19th, the squadron was called upon once more to provide five Hampdens for a moling operation over area 3A, for which the crews of F/L Frow, P/Os Sanderson, Swatton and Williams and F/Sgt Cornwall departed Balderton between 08.04 and 08.16 after receiving a positive cloud condition report from two weather-sortie crews. Ten-tenths cloud accompanied them across the North Sea until the Frisians and the Dutch coast loomed on the horizon, at which point it dissipated and forced all to turn back, four of them to arrive at base safely. AT227 failed to return with the crew of P/O Ed Swatton, whose remains washed ashore on the Danish coast in September. It was established postwar that the Hampden had collided with the night-fighter of Uffz Brejczek of II./NJG2 some fifty miles north-west of Vlieland and all on board the Hampden had perished on what was the pilot's ninth sortie.

The main event on this night was carried out by a force of ninety-nine four-engine aircraft against the Vulkan U-Boot construction yards at Vegesack, situated on the River Weser a few miles to the north-west of Bremen city centre. 5 Group contributed twenty-eight Lancasters to the attack, and those arriving in the target area were met by up to ten-tenths cloud with tops at 10,000 to 12,000 feet and delivered their attacks on the basis of a Gee-fix (TR). They gained an impression that a lot was going on beneath the cloud, but, in reality, the raid had completely missed the target, confirming the fact that Gee was useful as a guide to navigation, but was not precise enough to employ as a blind-bombing device.

A force of 291 aircraft was assembled on the 21st for the second raid of the series on Duisburg, and this number included twenty-nine Lancasters and seventeen Hampdens representing 5 Group, six of the latter belonging to 408 (Goose) Squadron. They departed Balderton between 23.32 and 23.46 on a moonless night and lost the services of Sgt Wood and crew to an engine problem as they were passing Ely in Cambridgeshire. The others flew out over Southwold to enter Fortress Europe via the Scheldt estuary, and despite the presence of clear skies over the target, extreme darkness and the usual industrial haze took their toll on vertical visibility, the effects of which, it was hoped, would be negated by flares dropped from the leading aircraft by TR (Gee). However, these proved to be not entirely accurate, and some illuminated an area of open country on the western bank of the Rhine, which led inevitably to a scattered raid. The Balderton crews carried out their attacks from 8,000 to 11,500 feet between 01.38 and 01.55 and four returned safely to offer what little useful information they had gleaned to the intelligence section at debriefing. Absent from that process was the crew of Sgt Wishart RCAF, who along with two others, was on his eighth sortie, while wireless operator/gunner, P/O Ashton RAF, was on his twenty-second. It was learned eventually that AT139 had crashed in the Waddenzee off the Dutch coast and three bodies were recovered for burial. Local sources in Duisburg confirmed extensive damage in residential districts, with ninety-four apartment buildings destroyed and 256 seriously damaged, and there was also mention of damage to the Thyssen steel works and to two other important war-industry factories. While this operation was in progress, Sgt Page and crew took off at 02.12 for the short hop across the North Sea to the Trefoil garden off the southern tip of Texel, but turned back immediately after the starboard engine cut out. One member of the crew baled out and landed safely and was soon reunited with his crew.

Sgt Page and crew were given a second chance on the 23rd, when they and the crew of F/Sgt Cornwall set off from Balderton to plant a vegetable each in the Trefoil garden. The weather conditions were favourable and the visibility good as both crews pinpointed on the lakes to the south of Den Helder and conducted a timed run towards the west to release their stores, the Cornwall crew from 900 feet at 03.22 and the Page crew from 700 feet eight minutes later. The main event on this night involved a reduced force of 215 aircraft, including a 5 Group contribution of forty-five Lancasters, to continue the assault on Duisburg, those reaching the target encountering seven to ten-tenths cloud with tops as high as 12,000 feet in places but a large gap that afforded some crews a sight of the ground. Despite that, for many, there was little chance of locating the briefed aiming point, which was probably the Thyssen steel works, and the Gee-based (TR) flares were again scattered and largely ineffective, leaving most crews to carry out their attacks on their own TR-fix. Returning crews were confident that they had hit the city's built-up area, many claiming to have identified specific ground features, and the outcome of the raid was similar to the previous one, with residential property sustaining the bulk of the damage.

The fourth raid on Duisburg was posted on the 25th, for which the largest force yet of the series was assembled amounting to 313 aircraft, among which were 177 Wellingtons and fourteen 420 (Snowy Owl) Squadron Hampdens, with the four-engine types, including thirty-three Lancasters, making up the numbers. They ran into around seven-tenths cloud over the target, with fair visibility, which enabled a visual confirmation of the TR-based approach, but not the briefed aiming point D, and the extensive and distinctive Ruhrort inland docks complex provided a solid reference point to bomb the built-up area generally for those unable to identify the briefed aiming point. It was left to local reports to confirm further damage to residential property, but less extensive than in the two previous attacks.

A maximum effort was planned on the 26th for the annual last-week-of-July attack on Germany's second city, Hamburg, and 404 aircraft answered the call, among them seventy-seven Lancasters and thirty-three Hampdens, eighteen of the latter belonging to 408 (Goose) Squadron. They departed Balderton between 22.30 and 22.51 with F/Ls Coulter and Frow the senior pilots on duty and joined up with the other 5 Group elements as they flew out between Skegness and Mablethorpe. Once some distance out over the North Sea, they had to negotiate the frequently met conditions on this route of towering cloud, electrical storms and severe icing, but none of the Balderton crews turned back. The skies over the target were largely clear and the visibility excellent, which allowed the crews to confirm their positions by visual reference, with the docks area, the River Elbe and the Binnen and Aussen Alster Lakes standing out particularly clearly in the bright moonlight. The 408 (Goose) Squadron crews had been handed aiming point D, which was probably the shipbuilding yards to the west of the city centre but found smoke already drifting across the built-up area to obscure some ground detail. Fifteen of them delivered their 1,900-pounder and two 250-pounders each from 8,500 to 13,000 feet between 01.20 and 02.00, while unaccountably, the crews of F/L Coulter, F/Sgt Gould and Sgt Wood were unable to establish a pinpoint and jettisoned their bombs live over alternative locations.

P/O Leach and crew were some twenty miles into the return flight when attacked by a Ju88, which fired off one full burst before being driven off by return fire. Two bullets hit the wireless operator/gunner, Sgt Kelly, one in the right chest, which perforated his lung, and the other breaking his right ankle, and despite efforts by other crew members to stem the flow of blood, he succumbed to his wounds at around 03.00, still two hours from landing. P/O David Williams and crew ran into a cone of searchlights as they made their way out of the target area and noticed with alarm that they were surrounded by a forest of barrage balloons tethered at 8,000 to 9,000 feet. A flak shell exploded under the port wing, flipping the Hampden onto its back and causing an engine to cut out temporarily. Somehow, P/O Williams negotiated his way out of the balloons and flak and adopted a northerly route home, whereupon the wireless operator spotted a BF109 stalking them silhouetted against the moon. Evasive action ended with the Hampden escaping into cloud and an eventful sortie was completed when the starboard engine failed in the circuit and P/O Williams pulled off a perfect three-point landing.

Sgt Allen and crew were ensnared in sixty searchlights as they left Hamburg and spent at least ten minutes trying to extricate themselves, and having done so lost the port engine and were then set upon at the Dutch coast by a Ju88, which scored hits in the starboard wing and elevator during two attacks from astern. Sgt Allen shut down the starboard engine and glided down until the engagement ended with a well-aimed burst of fire from the Hampden's rear gunner, which sent the enemy into a dive and out of sight, prompting the belief that it had been severely damaged if not destroyed. The starboard engine was restarted, and the port engine continually primed, and it spluttered all the way home to a safe landing. Sgt Ross and crew picked up flak damage over the target and were then attacked on the way home by a BF110, which climbed to meet the Hampden, only to be thrown off as Sgt Ross turned towards it and dived. This caused the enemy to fly over the Hampden's tail without firing a shot and the gunners took advantage to shoot back, although with inconclusive results. On return, other crews reported bomb bursts and thirty to forty fires that seemed to be merging into one single conflagration and described the glow from the burning city to be still visible on the horizon for around seventy miles into the homeward journey. The effectiveness of the raid was borne out by local reports, which spoke of eight hundred fires, more than five hundred of which were classed as large, and it seems that the residential and semi-commercial districts bore the brunt of the raid. When the flames had died down and the smoke cleared, 823 houses were found to have been reduced to ruins, with five thousand others damaged to some extent. This operation brought about 408 (Goose) Squadron's one-thousandth sortie.

Another maximum effort was called for on the 28th, and a force well in excess of four hundred aircraft was assembled for the return to Hamburg that night, 256 of them provided by 3 Group and the operational training units. By take-off time the weather conditions over the 1, 4 and 5 Group stations had deteriorated and prompted the withdrawal of their contributions to the operation, and as conditions worsened over the North Sea, the O.T.U aircraft were recalled. Many of the 3 Group crews turned back also, and only sixty-eight would claim to have attacked the primary target, where fifteen large fires and forty smaller ones were reported. This modicum of success was gained at the high cost of twenty-five aircraft, 15% of those dispatched, and among them were four O.T.U Wellingtons, while a fifth, a Whitley, ditched, and its crew was picked up safely.

In accordance with standard procedure, twenty-four ATC cadets arrived at Balderton on the 29th to spend the day with the squadron and enjoy air experience flights when possible. S/L Price RCAF took off at 15.01 in AT113 for an air test with Sgt Hughes as his navigator and two cadets on board and crashed fifteen minutes later in a cornfield a mile-and-a-half south-east of the station, bursting into flames and scattering wreckage over a wide area. W/C Twigg was in the air when the news reached him and he landed immediately, transferred to a van and raced to the scene to find that nothing could be done for the occupants. One body was found twenty-five yards from the wreckage and the others in the fuselage centre section, where a fire continued to rage. Aside from the tragic loss of the two cadets, S/L Price was a mainstay of the squadron and would be missed by all at Balderton and Syerston. He had been recommended for a DFC on the 6th of June, and King George VI would confirm the award in August.

Saarbrücken had been posted as the target for that night and a force of 291 aircraft assembled, which would be the largest raid by far on this major industrial and coal-producing Saarland capital city, situated right on the frontier with France in south-western Germany. 5 Group contributed sixty-nine Lancasters and seventeen Hampdens, the crews of which had been briefed to attack aiming point C, and in the expected absence of a strong searchlight and flak defence, the intention was to attack from a lower level than customary for the period. Seventeen 408 (Goose) Squadron Hampdens received a load each of either a 1,900-pounder and two 250-pounders or two 500 and two 250-pounders and two SBCs of 4lb incendiaries and departed Balderton between 22.57 and 23.28 with W/C Twigg the senior pilot on duty. They made landfall on the French coast, before following the frontier with Belgium and entering Germany south of Luxembourg. At the target, they encountered a layer of four to ten-tenths low cloud at between 2,000 and 9,000 feet, below which the visibility was good, and this enabled crews to confirm their TR positions by visual references on ground features like the River Saar and the marshalling yards. The Balderton crews carried out their attacks largely from west to east from 4,000 to 9,500 feet between 01.54 and 02.24 and were confident that their bombs had found the mark. Only P/O Leach and crew had been unable attack the target after failing to establish a firm pinpoint on leaving the English coast and being confounded by low cloud for the rest of the way. The success of the operation was confirmed by local reports of severe damage in central and north-western districts, where almost four hundred buildings had been destroyed in return for the loss of nine aircraft.

The month ended with a major assault on the Ruhr city of Düsseldorf, for which a force of 630 aircraft was assembled, the numbers bolstered by a large contribution from the training units. 5 Group offered 113 Lancasters, the first time that the one hundred figure had been reached, and they would be accompanied by twenty-four Hampdens, thirteen of the latter provided by 408 (Goose) Squadron. Each received a bomb load of four 500 and two 250-pounders and departed Balderton between 23.39 and 00.15 with F/L Frow the senior pilot on duty and lost the services of F/Sgt Craig and crew shortly after crossing the enemy coast when the port engine streamed sparks. The others benefitted from bright moonlight, clear skies and good visibility over the southern Ruhr, which enabled the crews to confirm their TR-fixed positions visually by an S-bend in the River Rhine and they delivered their attacks from 8,000 to 13,000 feet between 02.23 and 02.44 in the face of an intense and accurate searchlight and flak defence. Sgt Marment sustained a leg wound when AE150 was hit by flak and forced down to 6,000 feet, and the two 250-pounders were jettisoned to enable him to regain sufficient height for the bombing run. The bomb doors failed to open on the first pass, possibly because the pilot's numb leg had been unable to apply sufficient pressure on the pedal, but the four 500-pounders fell away from 8,000 feet on the second run.

Having observed a large number of explosions and fires, most crews were confident in the quality of their work, some commenting on a column of black smoke rising through 10,000 feet as they turned away. More than nine hundred tons of bombs were dropped, some wasted in open country, but the remainder had been scattered across all parts of the city and the neighbouring city of Neuss on the opposite bank of the Rhine. Local sources confirmed the destruction of 453 buildings, with varying degrees of damage to fifteen thousand more, and sixty-seven large fires had to be dealt with. The success came at the cost of twenty-nine aircraft, including two Hampdens and two Lancasters from 5 Group, and the O.T.U.s were again hit disproportionately hard, losing fifteen of their number. 408 (Goose) Squadron's AE244 was shot down homebound by the night-fighter of Fw Fritz Schellwat of II./NJG1 and crashed at 03.35 two miles south of Turnhout in Belgium, killing three members of the crew and delivering the pilot, Sgt Nelson, into enemy hands.

During the course of the month the squadron took part in thirteen operations and dispatched 125 sorties for the loss of four Hampdens, three complete crews and a flight commander and one other airman.

August 1942

S/L Price was laid to rest in the RAF Cemetery Brookwood on the 1st, the service attended by the squadron commander and the bombing, navigation and signals leaders. Meanwhile at Balderton, two correspondents of the Chicago Daily News were granted permission to interview aircrews.

A gentle start to the new month saw the heavy brigade remain at home because of unfavourable weather on the first two nights, before 5 Group sent out orders to Swinderby and Woodhall Spa on the 3rd to prepare small numbers of Lancasters for mining duties in the Forget-me-not and Radish gardens, respectively Kiel Harbour and the Fehmarn Belt in the western Baltic. On the following night, 5 Group contributed a handful of Lancasters and Hampdens for mining duties around the Frisians and off the Biscay coast, 408 (Goose) Squadron making ready six Hampdens for the Artichoke garden off Lorient and sending them on their way from Balderton between 23.35 and 23.49 with P/O Parkes the only commissioned pilot on duty. He and his crew were forced to turn back with intercom failure shortly after crossing the Brittany coast, while Sgt Bell and crew were heavily engaged by flak in the same area and jettisoned their load, leaving the others to find clear skies in the target area and good visibility in which Belle and Groix Islands were easily identified. An error in manipulating the bomb switch prevented Sgt Page and crew from delivering their mine, but the crews of F/Sgts Craig and Johnstone and Sgt Wood fulfilled their brief sometime after 02.00 and the Craig crew dropped their 250-pounders on a flare path at Baden aerodrome to the south-east of Lorient.

Meanwhile, ten Lancasters from 44 (Rhodesia) and 97 (Straits Settlements) Squadrons had been briefed to join twenty-eight other aircraft in a blind attack on Essen employing Gee. Once over enemy territory, they found in their path a towering, ice-bearing front with electrical storms, which topped out at 22,000 feet and extended over the Ruhr. Some crews opted not to press on to the primary target and dropped their bombs on alternatives, and just eighteen claimed to have attacked Essen based on TR readings.

The authorities deeming it necessary to repeat the exercise twenty-four hours later, when eight Lancasters were among seventeen aircraft assigned to Essen along with eight for Bochum, the crews of which were to employ Gee to locate the target before bombing visually through gaps in the cloud. Only one Lancaster bombed the target and three Halifaxes, a Lancaster and a Wellington failed to return, 20% of those dispatched. 408 (Goose) Squadron was also active on this night, dispatching five Hampdens from Balderton between 23.45 and 23.54 to return to the Artichoke garden, and the two freshman crews of Sgts McKenzie and Greig shortly after midnight to restock toilet paper supplies in the Rennes region. The nickellers arrived first at their destination to find three-tenths cloud and favourable conditions in which to dispense their reading matter from 10,000 feet at 02.53 and 03.05. Meanwhile, Sgt Marment and crew had turned back over the Channel and F/Sgt Cornwall and crew after crossing the Brittany coast, both because of engine issues, leaving the crews of P/O Boosey and Sgts Allen and Ross to arrive in their target area, where a wedge of eight-tenths cloud between 3,000 and 5,000 feet and good visibility awaited them, enabling them to pinpoint on Vannes and the Ile-de-Quiberon, from where they conducted timed runs and planted their vegetables from 700 to 800 feet between 02.39 and 02.47.

Organisational changes were taking place at this time in 5 Group, beginning with the departure of 420 (Snowy Owl) Squadron RCAF from Waddington on the 6th on transfer to 4 Group, where it would convert to Wellingtons. This paved the way for 9 Squadron to move into Waddington on posting from 3 Group to begin conversion to the Lancaster as the replacement for 83 Squadron, which was about to leave 5 Group for pastures new.

5 Group's contribution to that night's fifth and final operation of the three-week campaign against the Ruhr industrial giant of Duisburg amounted to forty-seven Lancasters and nine 408 (Goose) Squadron Hampdens, which were part of an overall force of 216 aircraft. The Balderton armourers loaded each with a 2,000-pounder and two 250-pounders and watched them take off between 00.10 and 00.29 with P/Os Leach and Parkes the senior pilots on duty. They crossed the North Sea on course for landfall over the Scheldt estuary, where F/Sgt Gould and crew were unable to establish their position over ten-tenths cloud with a base at 3,000 feet. They dropped the two 250-pounders on a heavy gun emplacement believed to be ten miles north of Amsterdam and brought their 2,000-pounder home. Sgt Page and crew were at the Dutch coast when the starboard engine temperature insisted that they jettison their load and turn back. Sgt Bell and crew were just ten minutes from the target at 02.30 when attacked suddenly and without warning from astern by a night-fighter with four cannons in its nose. The first indication of trouble was tracer streaking past, at which point the Hampden was thrown into a steep spiral dive to starboard and had reached 6,000 feet when pulling out. Damage was extensive and was evident in every part of the aircraft and a wireless operator/gunner sustained wounds, despite which, they continued the bombing run and dropped their load.

Less distracted, the others reaching the target area confirmed the cloud conditions at zero to ten-tenths with tops at 10,000 feet and barrage balloons tethered as high as 12,000 feet. Positions had to be established by TR-fix confirmed by visual reference aided by fires, flak and flares, and the distinctive Ruhrort docks complex stood out to some. Bombs were delivered by the Balderton crews from 10,000 to 13,500 feet between 02.34 and 02.56, in a number of cases after dumping the 250-pounders to gain altitude. Ten minutes after leaving the target area at 9,000 feet, the Bell crew suffered another blow with the failure of the port engine, which threw AE366 into another spin to starboard. This was arrested at 4,000 feet and Sgt Bell managed to regain two thousand feet of altitude, but it could not be maintained, and they were down to 4,000 feet again over the sea. The constant pressure on the rudder pedal to counteract the loss of an engine exhausted Sgt Bell's leg and the navigator had to grasp the pedal with his hands to lend support for the remainder of the flight. A belly-landing at Lakenheath was carried out seventy-five yards to starboard of the flare path so as not to compromise the runway, and the Hampden came to rest in a sand dune. For his airmanship and perseverance, Sgt Bell was awarded an immediate DFM. According to local sources, eighteen buildings were destroyed in Duisburg and sixty-six seriously damaged, giving a sum total over the five raids of 212 houses destroyed, 741 seriously damaged, and significant industrial damage resulting from just one raid. In return for this modest gain, Bomber Command had lost forty-three aircraft.

A dance was held for all airmen in the Corn Exchange in Newark on the 7th in honour of the squadron's first anniversary, and a general stand-down issued in the morning allowed all air and ground crew personnel to attend the event, which should have taken place in July, but had been delayed by operational requirements. A similar event for officers was held in the Officers' Mess at Syerston on the 8th and was attended by the A-O-C, AVM Coryton.

The garrison town of Osnabrück was posted as the target on the 9th, and a force of 192 aircraft assembled accordingly, 5 Group contributing forty-two Lancasters, which found clear skies over the Münsterland region of Germany to the north of the Ruhr, but haze creating poor visibility. Most crews were unable to establish their positions by TR after it was jammed by the enemy on crossing the Dutch coast, but those reaching the target area benefitted from the flares dropped to illuminate the area, and some picked out railway lines and the River Hase. Others relied on the fires, searchlights and flak that pointed the way to the aiming point, and afterwards the glow from the burning city remaining visible for eighty to a hundred miles into the return flight, TR functioning again once the Dutch coast had been crossed homebound. Local sources confirmed an effective raid, which destroyed 206 houses and a military building, and damaged a number of industrial premises along with four thousand other buildings, mostly lightly. While this operation was in progress, the 408 (Goose) Squadron crews of Sgts McKenzie and Craig took off at 23.39 and 23.58 respectively bound for the Nectarine II garden off the central Frisians. They pinpointed on Schiermonnikoog under clear skies and in good visibility and planted their vegetables according to brief from 700 feet at 02.06.

The first of two raids on consecutive nights against the city of Mainz, situated to the south-west of Frankfurt-am-Main in southern Germany, was posted on the 11th and a force of 154 aircraft assembled, the number including a contribution from 5 Group of thirty-three Lancasters for what would be the first large-scale operation against this target. The raid was highly successful, and caused major destruction in the central districts, where many historic and cultural buildings were damaged or destroyed. In the excellent tome, Bomber Command War Diaries by Martin Middlebrook and Chris Everitt, the losses from this operation are put at six aircraft, but the actual number failing to return was fourteen, while four others were lost in crashes at home.

408 (Goose) Squadron, meanwhile, made ready nine of its Hampdens for mining duties in the Eglantine garden in the Elbe estuary and two others to take the freshman crews of Sgts McKenzie and Craig to continue their education by attacking the docks and shipping at Le Havre. The gardeners departed Balderton first between 22.29 and 22.55 with P/O Parks, Sanderson and Williams the senior pilots on duty, and they were followed into the air at 01.04 and 01.08 by the bombing duo, each with four 500 and two 250-pounders on board. The latter both reached their

destination on the Normandy coast, where, as often happened, there was disagreement as to the cloud state, the McKenzie crew reporting seven-tenths cloud with tops at 8,000 feet, through which they pinpointed on the estuary and bombed from 10,200 feet at 03.30. In contrast, the Craig crew encountered ten-tenths cloud that topped out at 13,000 feet and prevented them from identifying the target and having jettisoned the 250-pounders to gain height, took their 500-pounders home. Five hundred miles to the north-east, the gardeners experienced difficulty in identifying pinpoints in poor visibility and low cloud base and only the crews of Sgts Page and Ross and P/Os Boosey and Williams were able to plant their vegetables from 700 to 900 feet between 01.08 and 02.38 having pinpointed on Ameland, Sankt Peter Ording and Schärhorn. The Williams crew was heavily engaged by flak from Sankt Peter and nearby flak ships and dropped their 250-pounders on a concentration at the former. The others were unable to establish a pinpoint and brought their mines back to base, where F/Sgt Gould and crew reported attempting to bomb Sylt, but only one 250 pounder fell away. P/O Sanderson and crew reported what appeared to be an aircraft on a parallel course burst into flames at 500 feet and lose height rapidly until crashing into the water at 02.20. They circled the spot for twenty-five minutes to obtain a fix and spotted two small lights where the crash occurred, but no discernible signal. No Bomber Command aircraft were lost in the area and the incident remained a mystery.

The ordeal was not yet over for Mainz, which was posted as the primary target again on the following day and a force of 138 aircraft made ready, 5 Group contributing thirty-three Lancasters and ten 408 (Goose) Squadron Hampdens. The latter departed Balderton between 21.57 and 22.20 with F/Ls Coulter and Frow the senior pilots on duty and a 2,000-pounder in each bomb bay. Sgt Jennings and crew were heading south-east over Cambridgeshire when the intercom failed and ended their sortie, while F/L Frow and crew had crossed the French coast between Calais and Boulogne and were some miles inland when they ran into icing conditions that persuaded them to turn back. The others reached the target area to find eight to ten-tenths cloud between 3,000 and 12,000 feet and generally poor visibility, but some still managed to identify the aiming point visually by islands in the River Rhine north and north-west of the city centre, and by the fires already burning. The 2,000-pounders were released unopposed from 4,500 to 12,000 feet between 00.45 and 01.00 and appeared to fall into the centre of the built-up area, contributing to many fires. AE150 failed to return with the crew of F/L Coulter and no trace of aircraft or crew ever surfaced. The pilot and navigator were on their twenty-third sortie and would be missed at Balderton. Post-raid reconnaissance and local reports confirmed further heavy damage in central and industrial areas of Mainz, and the main railway station was also a casualty.

A new era for Bomber Command began on the 15th, with the formation of the Path Finder Force, and the arrival of the four founder heavy squadrons on their stations in Huntingdonshire and Cambridgeshire. 83 Squadron moved into Wyton, the Path Finder HQ, as the 5 Group representative operating Lancasters, and it would be the responsibility of 5 Group's front-line units to provide a steady supply of their most promising crews. The other founder members were 35 (Madras Presidency) Squadron, which took up residence at Graveley with Halifaxes to represent 4 Group, while 156 Squadron retained its Wellingtons for the time-being at Warboys, drawing fresh crews from 1 Group, and 3 Group would be represented by the Stirling-equipped 7 Squadron at Oakington. In addition to the above, 109 Squadron was posted to Wyton, where it would spend the next six months developing the Oboe blind-bombing device and marrying it to the Mosquito under the command of W/C Hal Bufton. The new force would occupy 3 Group stations, falling nominally under 3 Group administrative control and receiving its orders through that group, which was commanded by AVM Baldwin, whose tenure, which had lasted since just before the outbreak of war, was shortly to come to an end.

A "Path Finder Force" was the brainchild of the former 10 Squadron commanding officer, G/C Sid Bufton, Hal's brother, and now Director of Bomber Operations at the Air Ministry. He had used his best crews at 10 Squadron to find targets by the light of flares and attract other crews by firing off a coloured Verey light, and it could be said, that the concept of target-finding and marking had been born at 10 Squadron. Once at the Air Ministry, Bufton promoted his ideas with vigour and gained support among the other staff officers, culminating with the idea being put to Harris soon after his enthronement as Bomber Command C-in-C. Harris rejected the principle of establishing an elite target-finding and marking force, a view shared by the other group commanders with the exception of 4 Group's AVM Roddy Carr. However, once overruled by higher authority, Harris gave it his unstinting support, and his choice of the former 10 Squadron commanding officer, and still somewhat junior, G/C Don Bennett, as its commander was both controversial and inspired, and ruffled more than a few feathers among more senior officers. Australian, Bennett, was among the most experienced aviators in the RAF, a pilot and a Master Navigator of unparalleled experience, with many thousands of hours to his credit. He also had the recent and relevant experience as a bomber pilot through his commands of 77 and 10 Squadrons and had demonstrated his strong character when evading capture and returning from Norway after being shot down while attacking the Tirpitz in April. Despite his reserve, total lack of humour and his impatience with those whose brains operated on a lower plane than his, he would inspire in his men great affection and loyalty, along with enormous pride in being "Path Finders". He would forge the new force into a highly effective weapon, although this would not immediately be apparent.

There is some confusion surrounding 5 Group operations on the night of the 15/16th, the group ORB recording no operations because of the weather conditions, while at least five squadron ORBs revealed that their aircraft had contributed to an overall force of 131 aircraft bound for Düsseldorf. At Balderton, seven Hampdens were loaded with a 2,000-pounder and two 250-pounders each and took off between 23.53 and 00.13 with F/Ls Cardell and Gilmore the senior pilots on duty. Sgt McKenzie and crew turned back at the Dutch coast near The Hague after failing to establish a pinpoint, leaving the others to press on to the southern Ruhr to encounter six to nine-tenths cloud at 10,000 feet with poor to modest visibility, and not all were able to establish their position in relation to the briefed aiming point. Most employed a TR-fix confirmed by a visual confirmation on the River Rhine, while others simply relied on e.t.a. The Balderton crews carried out their attacks from 8,000 to 12,000 feet between 02.18 and 02.24, and at debriefing reported a number of bursts and flashes and an abiding impression of a scattered attack, which was confirmed by local reports from Düsseldorf and its neighbour across the Rhine, Neuss. F/L Cardell RCAF and crew failed to return in AE432, which went missing without trace. John Cardell was on his third sortie, while his wireless operator/gunner, Sgt Edwin Mitchell, was on his twenty-sixth.

Orders were received at five 5 Group stations on the 17th to prepare for a return to Osnabrück that night as part of a 5 Group effort of thirty-two Lancasters and ten Hampdens in an overall force of 139 aircraft. It had been intended that the Path Finder Force would make its debut on this night, but the commanding officers decided that the squadrons were not yet ready, and the operation would have to go ahead without them. 408 (Goose) Squadron made ready eight Hampdens for the main event and a singleton to take the crew of F/L Gilmore on a mining sortie to the Trefoil garden between Texel and Den Helder. The latter departed Balderton at 20.43 and returned to the circuit three hours later having been thwarted by ten-tenths cloud that prevented them from establishing a pinpoint. The bombing brigade took off between 21.42 and 21.55 with F/L Frow the senior pilot on duty, a 2,000-pounder in the bomb bay and a 250 pounder under each wing, and soon lost the services of Sgt Ross and crew to an overheating port engine. The others reached the target area, most after making a timed run from the Dümmer Sea, a large lake situated some twenty miles to the north-east. They were greeted by three to five-tenths cloud at between 11,000 and 14,000 feet with haze at 4,000 feet to compromise the vertical visibility, but some crews were able to identify the river and railway lines and bombing by the 408 (Goose) Squadron crews was carried out either on the briefed aiming point or on the built-up area generally from 8,000 to 11,000 feet between 00.15 and 00.49. Local reports confirmed a moderately destructive raid, which fell mainly into northern and north-western districts, and thereby, built on the damage inflicted eight nights earlier.

The Path Finders took to the air in anger for the first time on the 18th, when contributing thirty-one aircraft to an overall force of 118, of which twenty Lancasters and sixteen Hampdens were provided by 5 Group. They were bound for the naval and shipbuilding port of Flensburg, situated on the eastern coast of the Schleswig-Holstein peninsula close to the border with Denmark, where the U-Boot pens were the briefed aiming point. Sixteen 408 (Goose) Squadron Hampdens departed Balderton between 20.14 and 20.44 with W/C Twigg and F/Ls Frow and Gilmore the senior pilots on duty and either a 1,900 or 2,000-pounder in the bomb bay supplemented by two 250-pounders. They flew out over Skegness on course for the west coast of Jutland, before traversing the peninsula to what had been selected as a worthwhile and easy-to-locate target. Sadly, the planners had not factored in an incorrect wind forecast, which pushed the bomber stream north of the intended track and over southern Denmark, a situation that the Path Finders failed to notice. As a result, in conditions of haze and two-tenths cloud at 6,000 feet, they illuminated an area of similar coastal terrain north of where they believed themselves to be, which led to a scattering of bombs across Danish territory up to twenty-five miles north of the frontier and into the towns of Abenra and Sønderborg. The 408 (Goose) Squadron crews were unable to positively identify Flensburg and trusted that they were over its approximate location as they delivered their loads from 5,000 to 10,000 feet between 23.15 and 23.39. F/L Gilmore and crew returned with their bomb load intact after the wireless operator/gunner had lost his helmet in the slipstream while poking his head out after spotting a possible night-fighter. They must have been very close to the target at the time as they were the last to land. It was an inauspicious operational debut for the Path Finder Force, which in time, would become a highly efficient, successful and vital component in Bomber Command's armoury.

Frankfurt was selected on the 24th to host the second Path Finder-led operation, for which a force of 226 aircraft was assembled. 5 Group contributed forty-seven Lancasters, which headed out across The Wash on course for the Belgian coast and reached the target area to find five to nine-tenths cloud at between 7,000 and 9,000 feet, with ground haze adding to the difficulties experienced by the Path Finders in locating the aiming point. Opinions at debriefing would be mixed, some satisfied with the results and others not and no mention was made of the Path Finder contribution, which, at this early stage of its development was restricted to identifying and then illuminating the target. Sixteen aircraft failed to return, 7.1% of those dispatched, and among them were five Path Finders.

The third Path Finder-led operation was to be directed at the city of Kassel, the home to three Henschel aircraft and tank factories and other important war-industry concerns, as well as being the HQ for the military's Wehrkreis IX and the site of a subcamp of the Dachau concentration camp, which supplied slave labour to the factories. A force of 306 aircraft was assembled on the 27th, 5 Group detailing seventy-five Lancasters and a dozen Hampdens, the latter departing Balderton between 20.04 and 20.21 with the newly promoted F/L Williams the senior pilot on duty and each carrying two 500 and two 250-pounders and two SBCs containing ninety 4lb incendiaries. Sgt Greig and crew turned back after about an hour because of engine trouble, while the remainder arrived at the target to be greeted by minimal cloud, bright moonlight and good visibility, with only ground haze between them and the aiming point. The Path Finder flares assisted greatly in enabling the crews to pick out ground detail, like a bend in the River Fulda and lakes to the south-west, and all of the Balderton crews took advantage to deliver their ordnance from 6,000 to 9,000 feet between 23.24 and 23.42. Local sources confirmed the effectiveness of the raid, which was spread across the city and destroyed 144 buildings, while causing serious damage to more than three hundred others. Among those afflicted to some extent were all three Henschel factories and a number of military establishments, and the fire services had to deal with seventy-three large blazes. However, the success was gained at the high cost of thirty-one aircraft, twenty-one of them Wellingtons, of which fifteen belonged to 1 Group. Sgt Jennings and crew failed to return in the veteran P1244, which crashed somewhere in the Hannover defence zone on what for the pilot and navigator was their seventeenth sortie, and there were no survivors.

A force of 159 aircraft was assembled on the 28th to send to the city of Nuremberg, deep in southern Germany, which had been the scene of massive Nazi Party rallies during and after Hitler's rise to power during the thirties. The Path Finders were to employ target indicators (TIs) for the first time in adapted 250lb bomb casings. 5 Group detailed sixty-three Lancasters, while also contributing seventeen Hampdens to a simultaneous raid on Saarbrücken by a force of 113 "oddments", which included 4 Group Halifaxes and new crews from other groups, but no Path Finders. At Balderton, the 408 (Goose) Squadron aircraft were loaded with a 2,000-pounder each and sent on their way between 19.54 and 20.10 with W/C Twigg the senior pilot on duty. They made landfall on the French coast near Dunkerque and Sgt Greig and crew were following the Franco/Belgian frontier when engine trouble curtailed their sortie as they passed to the south-east of Lille. P/O Parks and crew ran into flak as they crossed the coast and were so severely delayed by evasive action that they had insufficient fuel and time to carry on. Those reaching the target area found excellent conditions in which the city and its marshalling yards and waterways stood out clearly through slight ground haze, and the Balderton crews delivered their attacks from 4,000 and 9,000 feet between 23.09 and 23.44.

It is difficult to establish at what stage of the raid that they ran into night-fighters, but AE197 crashed at Walcourt some fourteen miles south of Charleroi at 23.22, halfway through the attack on Saarbrücken more than a hundred miles away to the south-east, which suggests that W/C Twigg had turned back early. On board with him were the bombing, signals and gunnery leaders, and only the bombing and signals leaders, F/L Fisher and F/O Van den Bok survived, ultimately to evade capture. W/C Twigg was on his fifteenth sortie, while the others were on their twenty-sixth to twenty-ninth, and the loss of such enormous experience would be felt by the squadron. AE227 was also shot down by a night-fighter five miles north-east of the target and there were no survivors from the mixed RCAF and RAF crew of the just-commissioned P/O Gould RNZAF, three of whose sortie count had reached the mid-twenties. The other two casualties, AE829 and AT228, both crashed in France near Sedan and Laon respectively, the pilot, Sgt Kemp, alone prevailing from the former and falling into enemy hands, while P/O Lyons and his crew all perished in the latter. These were the Squadron's final Hampden operational losses, although one more would be written off in September.

During the course of the month, the squadron took part in fourteen operations and dispatched 108 sorties for the loss of seven Hampdens and crews.

September 1942

The 1st of September brought a new commanding officer in the imposing form of W/C "Tiny" Ferris, who, like his predecessor, was a RCAF officer. The first half of the new month would distinguish itself through an unprecedented series of effective operations, although, it would begin ignominiously for the Path Finder Force, when posting a "black" on the night of the 1/2nd by marking the wrong town. The city of Saarbrücken had been briefed out to 231 crews, of which sixty-nine represented 5 Group, sixty-two to fly Lancasters and seven in Hampdens, which had just two more weeks of front-line service ahead of them. They departed Balderton between 23.05 and 23.23 with F/L Williams the senior pilot on duty and a 2,000-pounder in each bomb bay and lost the services of F/Sgt Roux and crew to an ailing port engine halfway into the sea crossing to Dunkerque. The others reached south-western Germany to find the target under clear skies with good visibility, and established their positions by TR, confirmed by a visual identification of the River Saar and other ground features and Path Finder flares. Five of the Balderton crews bombed from 7,000 to 9,000 feet between 02.07 and 02.14, while P/O Sanderson and crew suffered the frustration of a hang-up and had to bring their load home. Most observed bursts and fires, and some crews from other squadrons reported the entire area of the northern bank of the Saar to be on fire and commented on a very large explosion occurring in the midst of the conflagration. There was no question in the minds of the crews as they retreated to the west, that this had been an outstandingly accurate attack, and some claimed to be able to see the glow of fires from up to 140 miles into the return flight. It was only later that the truth emerged, that the Path Finders had marked not Saarbrücken, but the non-industrial town of Saarlouis, situated thirteen miles to the north-west, which lay in a loop of the river similar to that at the intended target. Much to the chagrin of its inhabitants and those in surrounding communities, the main force bombing had been particularly accurate and concentrated, and heavy damage had been inflicted.

This could have been an ill-omen for the month's efforts but, in fact, the Command now embarked on the unprecedented run of effective operations mentioned above. It began at Karlsruhe on the night of the 2/3rd, a city that was home to a factory belonging to the Deutsche Waffen und Munitionsfabriken A G, better known as DWM, which manufactured all types of firearms from pistols to automatic weapons for infantry and aircraft. A force of two hundred aircraft was made ready, the 4 Group Halifax brigade having now returned to operations following intensive training to restore confidence in the type after a period of above average losses and a series of design-flaw accidents. 5 Group put up sixty Lancasters and five Hampdens, the latter departing Balderton between 22.26 and 22.42 with the newly promoted S/L Gilmore the senior pilot on duty and each crew sitting on a 2,000-pounder. The target lay some fifty miles beyond Saarbrücken, which enabled the force to adopt the same route as on the previous night, passing south of Liege in Belgium and entering Germany north of Luxembourg. S/L Gilmore's navigator had been contending with an unserviceable table which prevented him from performing his role and after ninety minutes the sortie was aborted. Sgt Ross and crew were unable to make sufficient speed to remain on schedule and they, too, called it a day within two hours. It was a three-hour outward flight for the rest of the force, which reached the target area under clear skies and found Karlsruhe basking in moonlight and naked to the eyes of the bomb-aimers high above. The autobahn and the Rhine and its docks stood out clearly as a guide to the aiming point, and bombing was carried out by the three Balderton crews from 9,000 and 9,500 feet between 02.00 and 02.20. The city appeared to be swallowed by a sea of flames, before becoming obscured by smoke, and returning crews reported as many as two hundred fires, the glow from which remained visible for a hundred miles into the homeward journey. Post-raid reconnaissance confirmed much residential and some industrial damage, and local reports mentioned seventy-three fatalities.

Scampton welcomed a new resident unit on the 4th when 57 Squadron arrived on transfer from 3 Group to begin conversion to the Lancaster. When Bremen was posted as the target for that night, 5 Group responded with a contribution of forty-six Lancasters in an overall force of 251 aircraft. Crews were told at briefing that the Path Finders would be rolling out a new three-phase technique based on illumination, visual marking and backing-up, which, if successful, would form the basis of Path Finder operations for the remainder of the war. The force was greeted in the target area by clear skies and good visibility, although ground haze and smoke created challenging conditions for target identification. The first Path Finder flares and incendiaries went down at around 01.50, after which the 5 Group element bombed the Focke-Wulf aircraft factory. Generally, crews noticed a less-intense flak defence over the city than usual, but much increased hostility as they withdrew towards the Frisian island of Norderney. Twelve aircraft failed to return from this successful operation, and debriefing reports of fires in the central districts were confirmed by a local assessment, which listed 460 dwelling houses, six large/medium industrial premises and fifteen small ones destroyed, and a further fourteen hundred buildings seriously damaged.

The next operation was to be directed at the Ruhr city of Duisburg on the night of the 6/7th for which a force of 207 aircraft was assembled, fifty-four Lancasters and four Hampdens representing 5 Group. The 5 Group and 408 (Goose) Squadron ORBs confirm that four Hampdens were involved but the squadron Form 541 lists only the crews of P/O Leach and Sgt McKenzie departing Balderton at 00.43 and 00.56, while the Form 540 records take-off beginning at 00.38. All reached the target area to find it partially concealed by cloud, below which, the usual industrial haze rendered ground detail indistinct. Positions were established by TR and confirmed as far as possible by visual reference in the light of flares, and the two 408 (Goose) Squadron crews for which we have a record delivered their 1,900-pounder each from 10,500 and 11,000 feet at 02.49 and 03.14 in the face of a searchlight and flak defence operating to its usual high standard. The Duisburg authorities reported the heaviest raid to date, which destroyed 114 buildings and seriously damaged more than three hundred others, and, while this was only fairly modest, it still represented something of a victory at this notoriously elusive target.

The squadron conducted its final mining operation with Hampdens on the 7th, when the Artichoke garden off Lorient was the destination for seven crews, which departed Balderton between 19.41 and 19.52 with S/L Gilmore the senior pilot on duty. Clear skies and good visibility afforded ideal conditions for pinpointing on Belle and Groix Islands and the mines were released from 700 to 1,500 feet between 22.39 and 23.05. The crews of Sgt Ross and F/Sgts Cornwall and Marment aimed their 250-pounders at flak ships moored off Groix Island's north-eastern coast and claimed near misses.

There had been no pattern to the choice of targets thus far in the month, southern and north-western Germany and the Ruhr all featuring during the busy first week, and Frankfurt in south-central Germany was posted as the latest target on the 8th, for which a force of 249 aircraft was assembled. 5 Group contributed sixty-two Lancasters and nine Hampdens, the latter departing Balderton between 19.57 and 20.05 with F/L Williams the senior pilot on duty and a 2,000-pounder in each bomb bay. F/Sgt Cornwall and crew dropped out immediately when the artificial horizon failed, while F/Sgt Marment and crew made it to within ten miles of the French coast before the pilot became too unwell to continue. The others reached the target area, where, according to some, the skies were clear of cloud and the visibility good, while others reported up to eight-tenths cloud at 2,000 feet and poor to moderate visibility. Another factor was the intensity of the searchlight and flak activity, which should, perhaps, have helped to guide the Path Finders to the aiming point but, surprisingly, they failed to locate the city. Path Finder flares were in evidence but scattered over a wide area, and it was clear that they were by no means certain of their position in relation to Frankfurt. Crews established their own positions by what they could glimpse on the ground and the dozens of searchlights fingering the darkness, and those from 408 (Goose) Squadron bombed the primary target from 9,000 to 11,000 feet between 23.30 and 00.01, observing fires in what appeared to be the built-up area. According to local reports, only a handful of bomb loads hit the intended target, and this halted the run of successes thus far in the month. The majority of bombs appeared to have fallen to the south-west of Frankfurt as far as Rüsselsheim, fifteen miles away, where the authorities confirmed damage to the Opel tank works and a Michelin tyre factory, which compensated in small measure for the failure to hit the primary target.

The Path Finder Force was constantly evolving in tactics and equipment and had a new weapon in its armoury for the next operation, which was to be directed against the Ruhr city of Düsseldorf on the 10th. "The Pink Pansy", which weighed in at 2,800lbs, was the latest attempt to produce a genuine target indicator and used converted 4,000lb cookie casings. A force of 479 aircraft included a contribution from the training units of 91, 92 and 93 Groups, and eighty-one Lancasters and eight Hampdens from 5 Group. The 408 (Goose) Squadron element set off from Balderton between 19.51 and 20.04 with W/C Ferris the senior pilot on duty and undertaking his first sortie since taking command. Each Hampden was carrying a 2,000-pounder, all but one of which would reach the target after F/Sgt Craig and crew had turned back because of an overheating engine with the Scheldt estuary in sight. Clear skies awaited them in the target area with the usual industrial haze muddying the vertical visibility, but fires were already burning to help them identify the target visually and pick out major features like a bend in the Rhine and the docks complex. The red flares were reported by some to be a little north of the main city area with the greens over to the west, while the white illuminators highlighted the more central districts. The 408 (Goose) Squadron crews bombed from 8,000 to 12,000 feet between 22.25 and 22.34, observing fires to develop, and they turned away believing the attack to have been successful. Returning crews made complimentary comments about the performance of the Path Finders and reported the glow of the fires to be visible from the Scheldt on the way home. Post-raid reconnaissance and local reports confirmed this operation to have been probably the most successful since Operation Millennium at the end of May. Other than the northern districts, all parts of the city and its neighbour, Neuss, had been hit, and 911 houses had been destroyed with a further fifteen hundred seriously damaged. In addition to the destruction also of eight public buildings, fifty-two industrial firms in the two cities sustained damage sufficient to cause a total shut down of production for varying periods. It had been an expensive victory for the Command, however, with thirty-three failures to return, of which sixteen were from the training units.

The last Hampden to be written off in Bomber Command service occurred as the result of a training accident on the 12th, when AE385 stalled and crashed close to the airfield, killing Sgt Frame and his passenger.

Seven 408 (Goose) Squadron crews attended briefing on the 13th to learn that Bremen was to be their destination that night, the second time during the month that the port-city had been targeted. A force of 446 aircraft was assembled, again bolstered by aircraft and crews from the training groups, and there was a contribution from 5 Group also of ninety-eight Lancasters. The Balderton element took off between 23.55 and 00.21 with no senior pilot on duty and a 2,000lb bomb load, and lost the services of Sgt Blackhall and crew to engine trouble shortly after they crossed the coast at Skegness. P/O Gamble and crew also turned back after failing to coax more than 110 i.a.s. out of AT180, leaving the rest to reach the target area and find clear skies but considerable ground haze, which made pinpointing something of a challenge. Some major ground features, like the docks, could be identified visually, otherwise it was down to flares and fires to point the way, and the 408 (Goose) Squadron participants mostly believed that they were over the built-up area as they carried out their attacks from 10,000 to 12,000 feet between 02.35 and 03.07. A number of crews were convinced that some early arrivals had bombed at Delmenhorst, a few miles to the south-west of Bremen, and the 5 Group ORB described the Path Finder performance as unhelpful. However, the success of the operation suggested otherwise and by far exceeded the destruction resulting from June's Thousand Bomber raid. A total of 848 houses was destroyed and much damage was inflicted on the city's industry, including to the Lloyd Dynamo works, where two weeks production was lost, and parts of the Focke-Wulf factory were put out of action for between two and eight days. Of the twenty-one aircraft lost, fifteen belonged to the training units.

The end of the Hampden era arrived on the following night, when the naval and shipbuilding port of Wilhelmshaven was posted as the target for 202 aircraft. Sixty-two Lancasters and four Hampdens were made ready as the 5 Group contribution, the latter, consisting of the crews of P/O Boosey, F/Sgt Craig and Sgts Page and Wood, departing Balderton for the final time in anger between 19.43 and 19.52 each with a 2,000-pounder beneath their feet. They all arrived to find clear skies over the coastal region of Jade Bay, with extreme darkness and ground haze to impede vertical visibility, but the shoreline and the docks provided an adequate pinpoint for the Path Finders to establish their position and mark accurately. Three of the Balderton crews carried out their attacks from 9,000 and 12,000 feet between 22.15 and 22.24 with light flak bursting around them at between 15,000 and 17,000 feet. It was difficult to distinguish individual bomb bursts, but the consensus was of a successful outcome and crews from other squadrons reported an enormous explosion, believed to be from an ammunition dump. It lit up the ground for five seconds and emitted flames a hundred feet into the air along with a cloud of smoke that rose to several thousand feet. On return, Sgt Page and crew reported that they had been unable to maintain speed and had attacked a flare path four miles north-east of Norden near the coast on the western side of the headland from 8,000 feet at 22.10 and caused the airfield lights to be extinguished. They were the last to land at 01.56 to bring to an end the squadron's and 5 Group's association with what had been a trusty and highly effective bomber. Local sources confirmed that this had been Wilhelmshaven's most destructive raid to date.

The run of outstandingly effective operations concluded at Essen on the 16/17th, when even this most elusive of targets suffered quite extensive damage at the hands of over three hundred aircraft, despite the fact that the bombing was scattered over a wide area of the Ruhr. If any period in Bomber Command's evolution to effectiveness could be described as the turning point, then perhaps these first sixteen nights of September was it. The development of tactics, and the emergence of the Path Finder Force from its shaky start had come together at this time, and although failures would continue to outnumber successes for some time to come, the encouraging signs were clearly evident.

On the 17th, a 408 (Goose) Squadron advance party set out from Balderton to make the ninety-mile journey to the squadron's new home at Leeming, near Northallerton in northern Yorkshire, where it would embark on a new era in a new group and with new aircraft. ATA pilots descended upon Balderton to fly the Hampdens to maintenance units and G/C "Gus" Walker, the Syerston station commander, thanked the squadron for a job well done. There was sadness at leaving Balderton but excitement at the prospect of bigger and better things at their new home. The main party arrived by rail at 13.00 on the 20th, by which time a conversion flight had been set up to begin the training of crews on the Halifax Mk V, which differed from the Mk II only in having Dowty rather than Messier undercarriage. Forty-eight aircrew personnel were detached to 1652 HCU at Marston Moor on the 23rd, while ground crews were sent to other Halifax units to begin their training. The larger crew complement of the new type demanded an increase in personnel, and these would arrive over the ensuing weeks from the OTUs.

October to December 1942

408 (Goose) Squadron's time with 4 Group would be relatively brief and a period of operational inactivity, while its crews learned the ways of the Halifax, a type with a chequered history and reputation. The type had entered service late in 1940 in the hands of 35 (Madras Presidency) Squadron and following its operational baptism in March 1941 had spent frequent periods of grounding while essential modifications were carried out. The original three-turret design, problems in marrying the Rolls Royce Merlin engine to the airframe and the addition of a plethora of fixtures and fittings had resulted in an overweight and under-performing aircraft, which was not suited to retrospective modifications. This meant that a new variant resulted from each major modification and the Mk II appeared in many different guises, including a faired-over front turret, waist gunners in place of a mid-upper and large square fins to replace the original triangular arrangement that had led to rudder-lock and a spate of fatal accidents. The crew positions would have been faintly familiar to former Hampden fliers in that the pilot sat alone on the flight deck with the flight engineer in a compartment behind, while the navigator, bomb-aimer and wireless

operator occupied a cabin beneath the pilot's feet. 408 (Goose) Squadron was one of eleven RCAF units, some newly formed, to gather on 4 Group stations in north Yorkshire and Middleton-St-George in County Durham in preparation for the official establishment on New Year's Day 1943 of 6 Group, a RCAF group financed by Canada but controlled by Harris.

The excellent news arrived on the 2nd of October that F/L Fisher and F/O Van den Bok of W/C Twigg's crew had reached Gibraltar and were on their way home, soon to visit their former colleagues. For the aircrew at Leeming, it was a time of lectures while they awaited the arrival of the first two Halifaxes on the 11th, an event which created much interest and a renewed desire to return to operations. On the following day the 408 (Goose) Squadron Conversion Flight became 1659 Canadian Conversion Unit and the first two crews were posted to it to begin training. The period from the 17th to the 29th was occupied by the receipt and modification of the next batch of Halifaxes and the continuing courses for new aircrew arrivals. On the 30, F/L Roux, the deputy A Flight commander, and F/L Powell, the navigation leader, joined the Path Finder Force with a posting to 35 (Madras Presidency) Squadron at Graveley in Cambridgeshire. The month ended at Leeming with thirteen Halifaxes on charge and seventeen crews under conversion, while the Wellingtons of 419 (Moose) Squadron, the other resident unit, flew the operational flag.

November followed a similar pattern, only with an increase in flying whenever the weather allowed a diet of cross-countries, circuits and landings and fighter affiliation and it was during the last-mentioned on the 9th that DG238 stalled and crashed at 15.30 five miles east of the 4 Group station at Croft, killing F/Sgt Bell DFM RCAF and the other four occupants. This was the first Mk V Halifax to be lost in Bomber Command service. On the following day the squadron played its first hockey match of the season and defeated 419 (Moose) Squadron four goals to two, and this was followed by a victory by default over 424 (Tiger) Squadron on the 17th and a narrow win by two goals to one over 420 (Snowy Owl) Squadron on the 24th. 419 (Moose) Squadron had now also been stood down from operations to focus on its own conversion to the Halifax. In between the hockey matches, an intensive round of day and night flying moved the squadron ever closer to the goal of resuming operations at the earliest opportunity. On the 26th, the popular Kiwi Air Officer Commanding 4 Group, AVM "Roddy" Carr, visited the squadron to interview a number of NCOs and bestow upon them a commission, while the 28th brought the fourth hockey match and the seven to nil thrashing of 425 (Allouette) Squadron. The squadron was informed on the 30th that its thirteen Mk V Halifaxes were to be exchanged for Mk IIs.

Ten Mk Vs were flown to 18 Maintenance Unit at Dumfries on the 2nd of December and over the ensuing days the remainder departed Leeming for the same destination, while Mk IIs began to trickle in. On the 9th of December, pilots S/L Newson, F/Os Gamble and Hatle, P/O Carver and Sgts Cochrane and Smith flew with 102 Squadron crews as "second dickies" on a trip to Turin. There is no mention of the fifth hockey match but the sixth on the 15th resulted in a one to nil victory over 403 Squadron RCAF, a fighter unit, and a comment in the ORB that this was the sixth straight win. This was followed up on the 19th by a five-two victory over 410 Squadron RCAF, a night-fighter unit. On the 20th, pilots S/L Newson, F/O Gamble and Sgts Blackman, Cochrane, Harty and Syrett accompanied 102 Squadron crews to Duisburg and returned safely a little more experienced that when they had taken off. The fourth wartime Christmas passed at Leeming in traditional RAF style and a show in the NAAFI in the evening produced by station staff was enjoyed by all. Flying training resumed on the 28th and continued through to New Year's Eve, 408 (Goose) Squadron's final day under the banner of 4 Group.

During the squadron's absence from the operational scene between October and December, the Command embarked on a series of major operations against Italian cities. Beginning on the 22nd of October at Genoa, the campaign lasted until the 11th of December and targeted also Milan and Turin. It coincided with the second Battle of El Alamein between the 23rd of October and 11th of November, which resulted in Montgomery's victory over Rommel, and was in support of the Allied landings in North Africa under Operation Torch. The operation against Duisburg mentioned above masked a small-scale but hugely significant undertaking by six Mosquitos of 109 Squadron, which were conducting the first live trial of "Oboe", a radar-guided bombing system that would provide Bomber Command with the accuracy over the Ruhr for which it had striven since the advent of strategic bombing. As previously mentioned, during the second half of 1942 the squadron had been dedicated to the marriage of Oboe to the Mosquito under the leadership of W/C Hal Bufton. The target for this first trial was a power station in the Dutch town of Lutterade, which was chosen as a crater-free testbed to gauge the margin of error of the device. Unfortunately, three of the Mosquitos suffered Oboe failure and went on the bomb Duisburg, while the remaining three found that their target area was pockmarked by stray bomb craters from an attack in October on Aachen. It proved impossible to identify the Oboe craters, but it was a temporary setback and further trials were launched on the last night of the year and throughout January.

W/C Nelles W. Timmerman DSO, DFC, MiD, CD.

408 Squadron Commanding Officer 24th June 1941 – 25th March 1942

408 Squadron Hampden AE280 with L – R: Sgts A W Wood, H D Murray, D L Henderson, W M Fraser.

Sgt D M Ross, Sgt K W McGrail, Sgt H E Marshall, Sgt J K Fraser 30th September 1941

408 Squadron Hampden during pre-flight engine test 13th December 1941

Members of 408 Squadron watch the testing of a "Dinghy". Below: L – R: W/C N W Timmerman, DFC, P/O T W Dench, Cpl Bangs, RAF; F/O Houston, RAF, F/L P A C Clayton, DFC, G/C R T Taaffe, S/L H Fowler, Medical Officer.

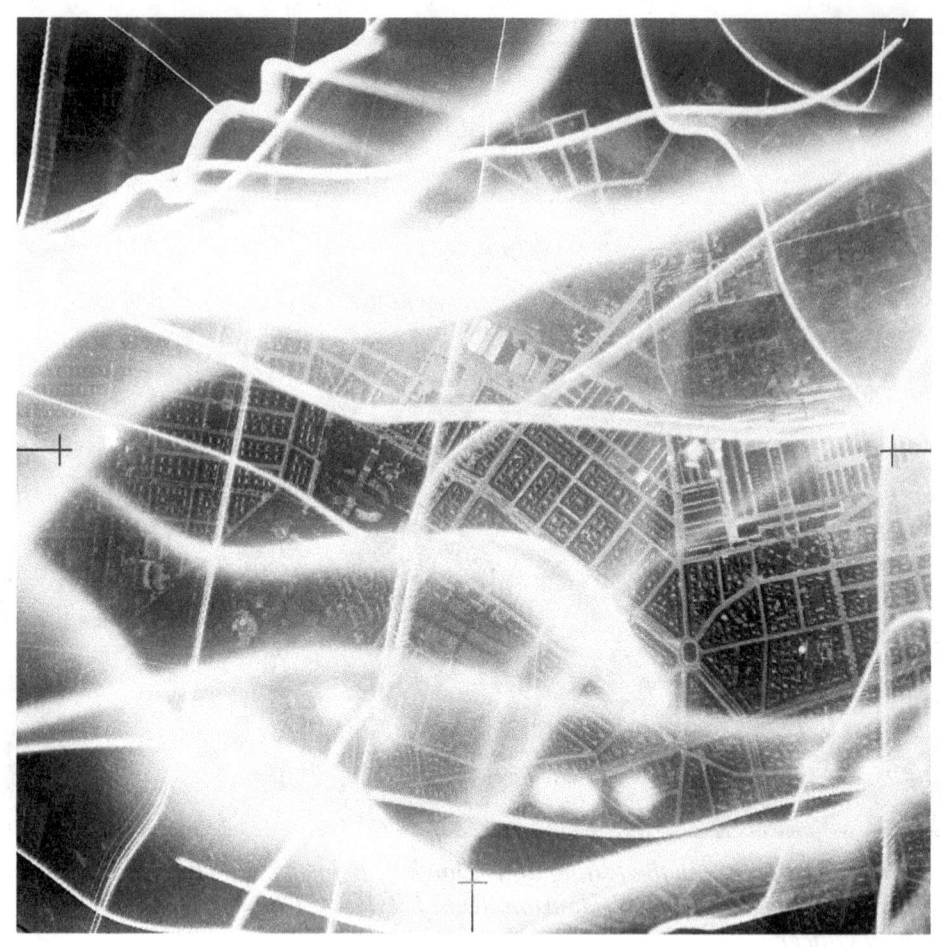

A vertical aerial photograph taken during a raid on Berlin on the night of 2/3rd September 1941. The broad wavy lines are the tracks of German searchlights and anti-aircraft fire. It shows bombs exploding in the vicinity of the central cattle-market and railway yard (middle right), east of the city centre. The broad wavy lines are the tracks of German searchlights and anti-aircraft fire can also be seen. Also illuminated by the flash-bomb in the lower half of the photograph are the Friedrichs Hain gardens and sports stadium, St Georgs Kirchhof and Balten Platz.

408 Squadron Hampdens bombing-up

Hampden Cockpit

Above W/C Timmerman and below: W/C Timmerman with Canadian and RAF air and ground crews in front of a Hampden at RAF Syerston.

A Hampden bomber is shown taking off from a Canadian Bomber Squadron somewhere in England for a trip over German occupied territory with its bomb load.

408 Squadron Hampdens

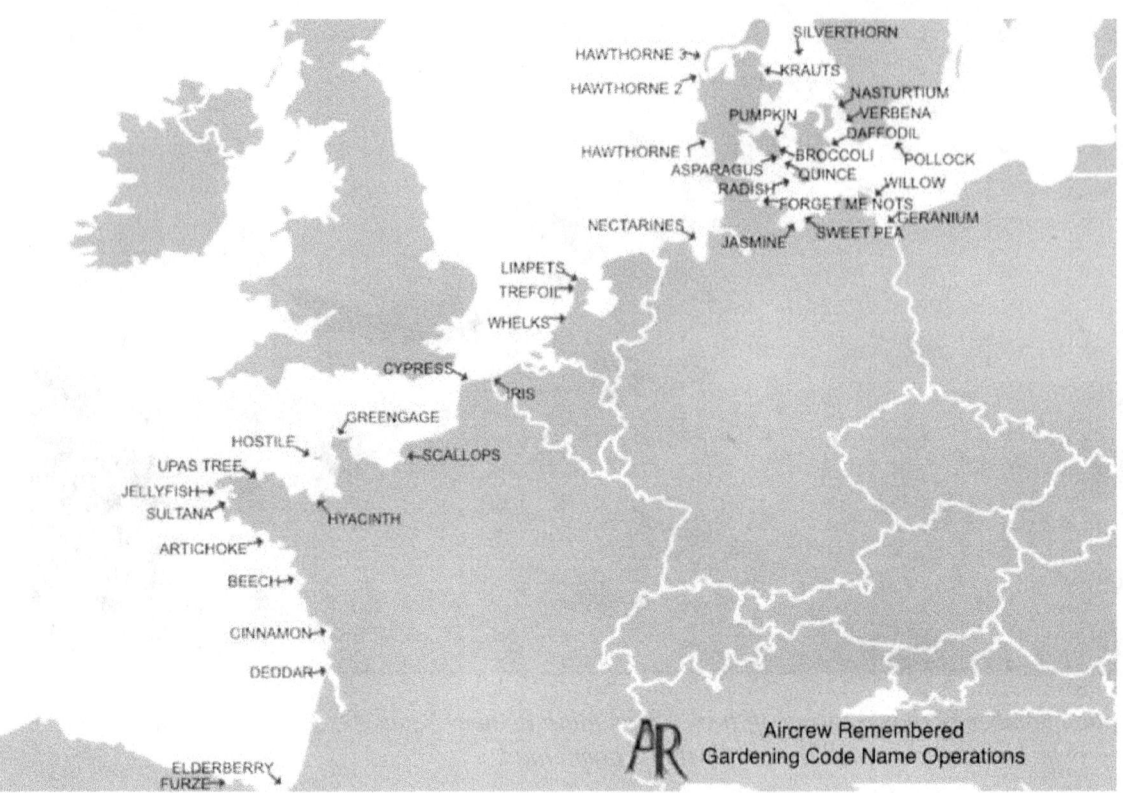
Mine Laying (Gardening) Areas (Aircrew Remembered)

King George VI speaking to S/L Pitt Clayton on the occasion of the King's first visit to 408 Squadron November 13th 1941. Escorting the King are W/C Timmerman and G/C Taafe.

408 Squadron members 1942

Lancaster DS601 September 1942 with four Hercules Engines and below: same aircraft airborne

A gunnery course at No. 2 Bombing and Gunnery School – Mossbank, Saskatchewan (donated by D A Eglison via Bomber Command Museum of Canada).

<u>General Hints for Air Gunners (Condensed)</u>

Search sky before take off and landing, your a/c is most vulnerable.

If gun fire, search for fighter; take evasive action.

Always watch your own tail.

Conserve your ammo; if you're fired upon from long range, instruct pilot to use evasive action.

Use good team work with rest of crew.

Never turn away from an attack, always towards.

If using tracer at night, remember it tends to momentarily destroy your night vision; hold your fire until necessary.

If on reconnaissance aircraft; your job is to return with information; not to seek combat with enemy aircraft.

Aim of enemy fighter is to destroy; aim of bomber air gunner is to get safely to target and back to base.

Never fire until fired upon.

All aircraft approaching are considered to be enemy until identified otherwise.

Sgts Cornwall, Dunn, Manson and Norton beside their Hampden at Balderton, January 18th 1942.

Kiel bomb damage.

Scharnhorst

Gneisenau

W/C N Timmerman hands over to the new CO W/C P Clayton 14th April 1942.

Battle damage. R-L: S/L A C P Clayton DFC, F/Sgt WL Reinhart DFM, Cpl H Kite, S/L L L B Price

The Zoo flak tower, Berlin. April 1942

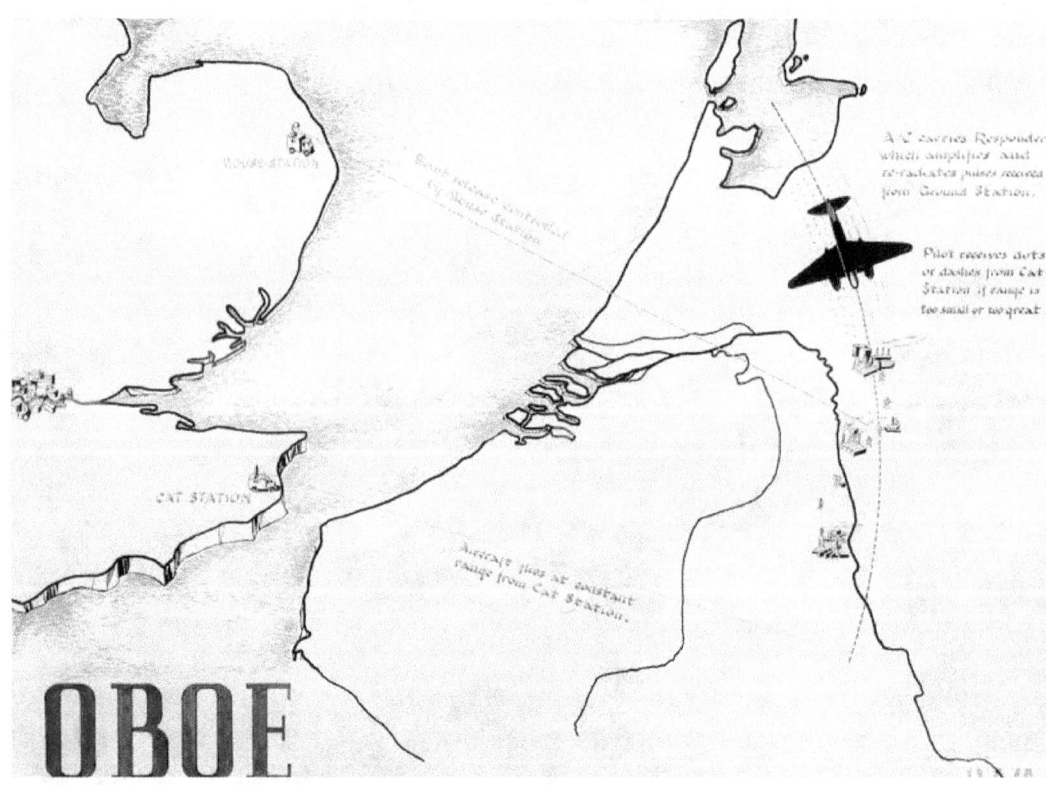
An illustration of Oboe. Two radar stations track the flight of the aircraft. The southern station is the Cat which generates pulses whose arc is defined by the distance from the station to the target. The aircraft will fly along the arc from a start point ten minutes flight from the target. As it approaches the intersect with the arc from the Mouse station the aircraft is signalled to prepare for bomb release. When the aircraft reaches the point where the two arcs intersect the Mouse station transmits the signal to release bombs.

408 Squadron Manchester.

During May/June 1942, the Squadron had one Manchester aircraft L7401 EQ-N for evaluation as a possible replacement for the Hampden. Manchester conversion flight was set up under S/L L Bryce who flew this aircraft on its two sorties with the squadron - the 1000 bomber raid on Cologne on the 30/31st May and the bombing of Essen on the 1/2nd June. The Manchester had to turn back from Cologne owing to hydraulic failure. In the raid on Essen, it dropped 126 4lb incendiaries.

Krupps Factory, Essen

ACM Sir Arthur Harris, Commander in Chief of RAF Bomber Command, seated at his desk at Bomber Command HQ, High Wycombe.

Wing Commander Jack Twigg (KIA) 408 Squadron Commanding Officer 18th May 1942 – 26th August 1942

The Flakturm IV in Hamburg, Germany. It measured 75 by 75 m, with a height of 39 m. Notice the four twin 12.8 cm Flak Zwilling 40 guns.

Canadian crews fly these Halifax bombers at a Canadian Bomber Group Station in England and Canadian ground crew keep them ready to do their job over Germany. This is "Zombie" one of the bombers of the Goose Squadron, getting a once-over before being sent out on the line for operational duty again.

Flight engineer F/L Eric Mulligan

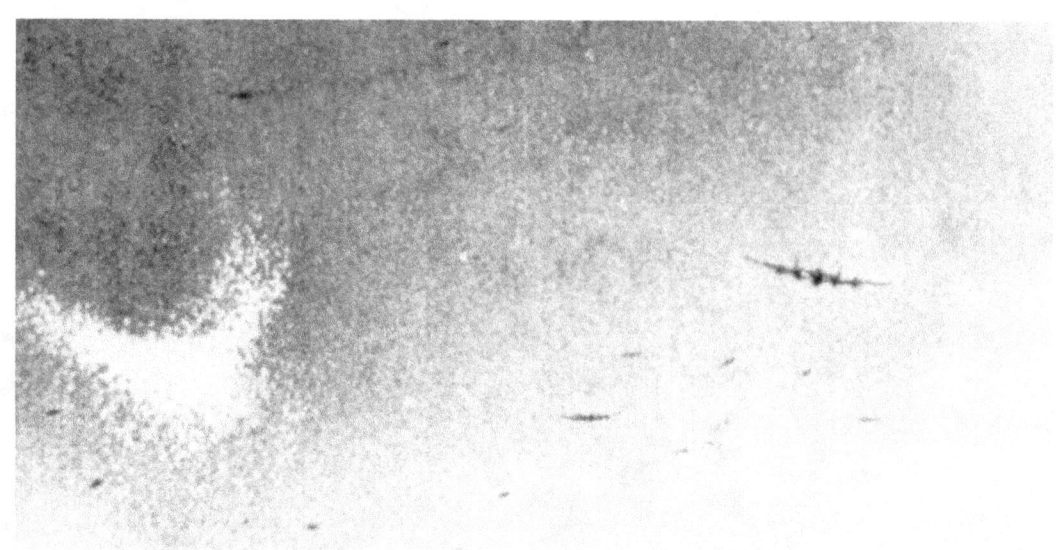

A Lancaster dropping Window (the crescent-shaped white cloud on the left of the picture)

A Lancaster (bottom left) and a Halifax (top right) fly over Essen, Germany, during a major daylight attack by 771 aircraft which inflicted heavy damage on buildings and the city's remaining industries. The Lancaster is flying over the Krupps steelworks from which clouds of smoke from exploding bombs is rising into the air.

Hamburg during Operation Gomorrah 1943

The McLeod crew from 408 Squadron standing in front of a Lancaster Mk II, coded OW-X (either DS-848 or DS-841). Second from the left is F/Sgt John Plemel RCAF (W.Op). Third from the right is F/Sgt A. Stock, RCAF (BA). The remaining members in no certain order are: W/O1 C. McLeod RCAF, (Pilot); Sgt Innes RAF (FE), WOII A. Bjarnason RCAF (Nav), Sgt L. Silver RCAF, (MUG) and F/Sgt J. Lawder RCAF, (RG).

The crew of Lancaster DS737 (below) when it crashed on Murton Common, Yorkshire. Left to right: F/Sgt J O E J Boily, F/O M E Marynowski, Sgt T L Dee, F/O R S Clark, Sgt K R Wood, Sgt L A Moran and F/Sgt L J Yeo. All, except Sgt Moran and F/Sgt Yeo, were killed on 16th December 1943 while attempting to decrease height through cloud.

408 Squadron LAC Sidney Morris poses in Lancaster DS737 'Countess'. The Lancaster lost on 16th December 1943 after a Berlin raid.

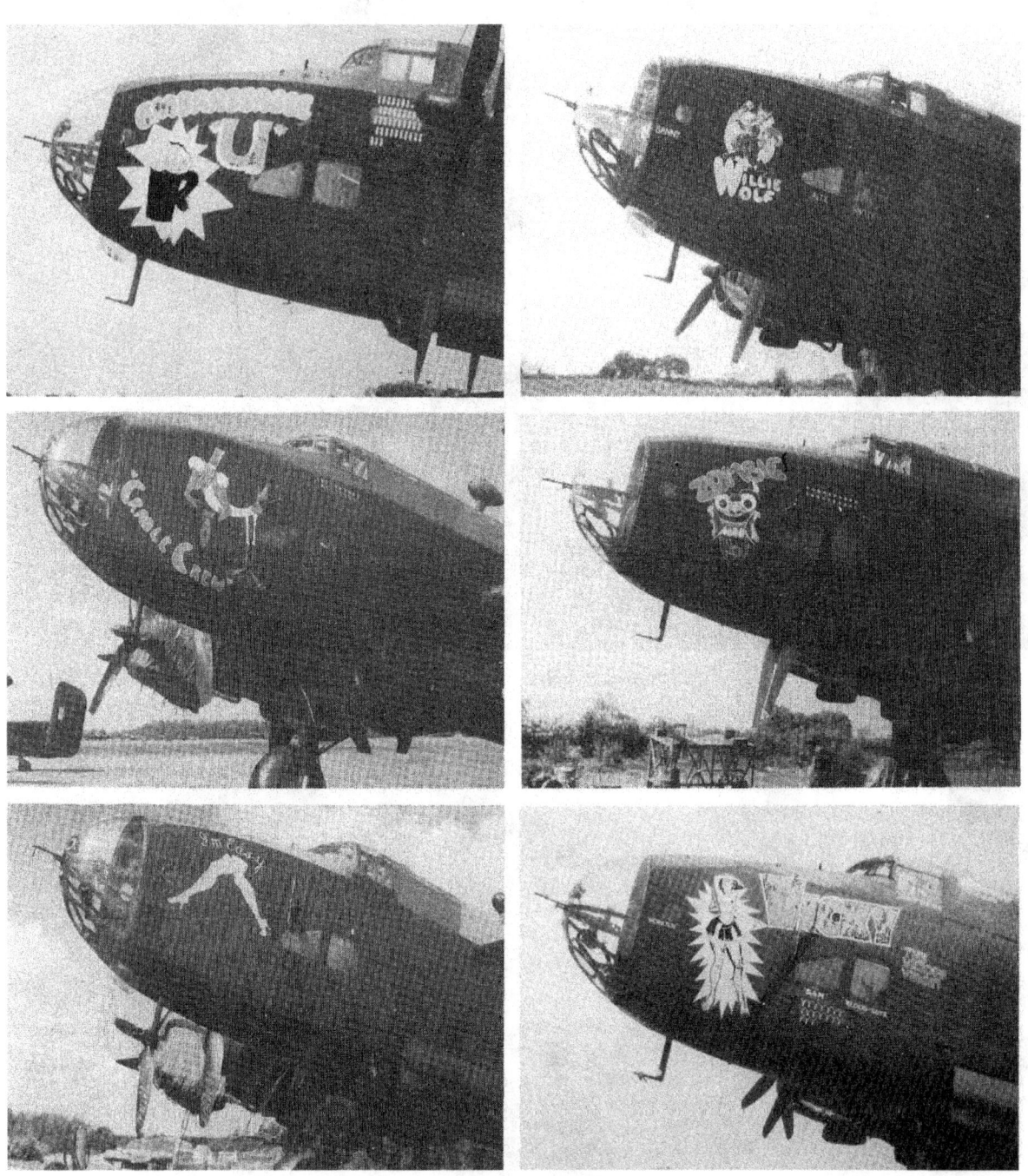

408 Squadron Nose Art
There was no common theme to 408's markings. Several like 'Willie Wolf' and 'Embraceable U' elaborated on the aircraft's code letter often adding some sort of risqué interpretation such as 'I'm Easy' and 'Vicky the Vicious Virgin'. The origins of others like 'Chesty' and 'Cradle Crew' or less easily identified.

408 Squadron Briefing

Flight engineer P/O Harry Inman with panel of a Halifax

Wing Commander D.S. Ferris DFC
408 Squadron Commanding Officer
1st September 1942 – 27th October 1943

Wing Commander Alex C. Mair DFC (KIA)
408 Squadron Commanding Officer
28th October 1943 – 26th November 1943

Wing Commander D S Jacobs 1943
408 Squadron Commanding Officer
17th November 1943 – 22nd May 1944 (KIA)

Berlin, Dönhoffplatz - Construction of splinter trenches
Soldiers are deployed in the capital of the Reich to dig splinter trenches in the public squares in an effort to protect the population against air bombing. 1943.

It was normal practise for those who stayed behind to come to the take off point to wave good luck to those departing for another night's raid.

Load of 20 bombs packed into the Lancaster's huge bomb bay.

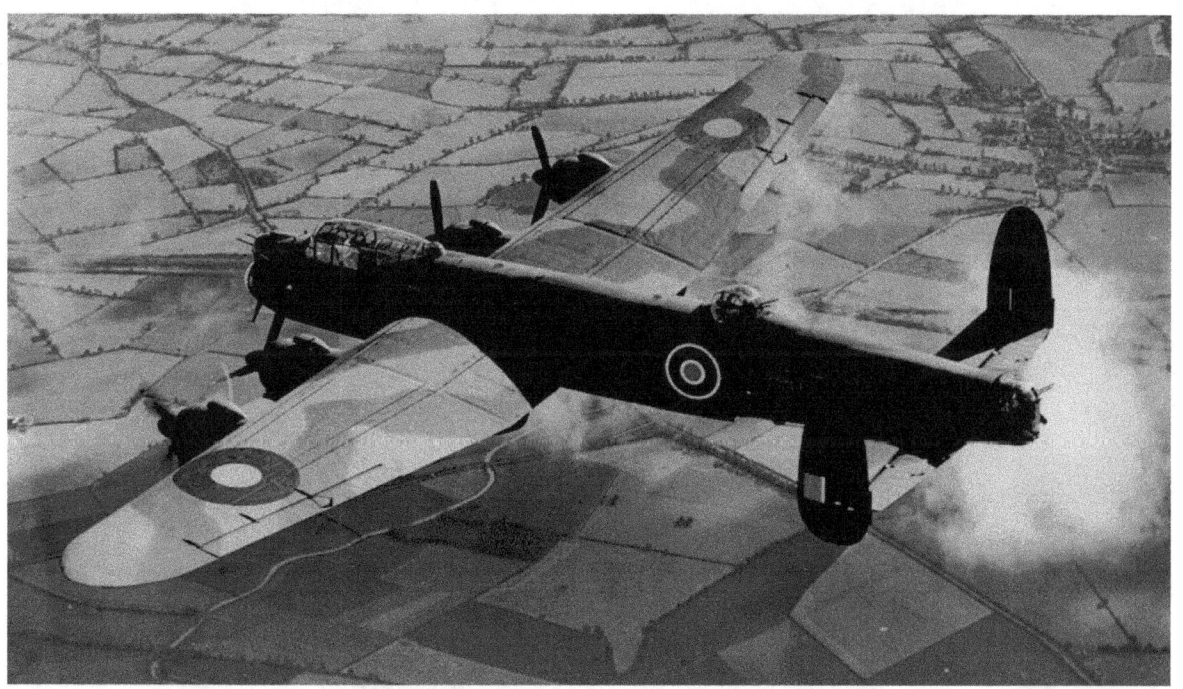

Lancaster DS704. Lost on 20/21st December 1943. Believed to have been shot down by the tail-gunner of another Lancaster and crashed in Belgium. Sgt R W Heaton and P/O A F Wright were killed, F/Sgt E A Salmon became a PoW while F Sgt D Maclachlan. P/O A G Dumbrell P/O L C Morrison and Sgt T J Reynolds evaded.

Long ammunitions belts feed the guns on a Halifax Bomber and the gunners make sure that everything is in order before they take off. Here Sgt R.T. Wiggett checks the ammunition belts with Sgt G R Butchart, wireless air gunner, examining them before taking off on a raid over Germany.

Sgt Ian MacKenzie (later P/O) KIA 15th August 1943. Shot down over Rheims, France

Halifax JB858 of 408 Squadron was shot down at Legden, Germany on 26th June 1943 during an attack on Gelsenkirchen. The rear part of the aircraft has broken off from the rest of the fuselage. With the exception of Sgt R. B. Wright who was taken prisoner, the remaining crew members were all killed: Sgt B. R. Milligan RCAF, Sgt J. F. Male RCAF, F/O F. C. Culbert, RCAF, Sgt J. H. McNess RAF, Sgt D. Aiken RCAF, Sgt J. D. B. Hunter RCAF, Sgt G. N. Acton RCAF.

Almost like a conveyor system are the ammunition belts in Britain's heavy bombers. Three of those which feed the guns of a Halifax are shown in the picture with Sgt G.R. Butchart, wireless operator/air gunner, examining them before taking off on a raid over Germany.

January 1943

As the clock ticked towards midnight on New Year's Eve the Canadian government prepared for a moment of significance. They awaited not so much the New Year but that which came with it, the birth of 6 Group, Canada's own group in RAF Bomber Command, a shining symbol of the burgeoning status of the independent Canada. There were many non-British squadrons in Bomber Command, but this was the first foreign organisation to muscle in with its own group, and while in public there was harmony between the two High Commands, in private it was a different matter. Harris was strongly opposed to the formation of a Canadian group, and while he valued Canadian airmen and welcomed their presence in the war, he found it difficult to come to terms with their lax attitude in matters of RAF etiquette and discipline. He wanted to distribute Canadians throughout the existing RAF groups, but Whitehall wanted otherwise, and Whitehall won. Harris also harboured an intense dislike for Air Marshal Edwards, the Commander-in-Chief of Canada's overseas Air Force, and for the man who would initially be the Air Officer Commanding 6 Group, AVM Brookes. Both men were British-born, and as far as Harris was concerned, neither was worthy of holding a position of authority, particularly anywhere near his Bomber Command. A Head Quarters was established in the baronial Allerton Hall, on the two-thousand-acre estate of Allerton Park, the ancestral home of Lord Mowbray, located four miles east of Knaresborough. Its dark, somewhat angular and forbidding aspect soon saw it renamed Castle Dismal by its Canadian tenants.

At 00.01 on the 1st, 6 Group officially came into being and the 4 Group stations upon which its squadrons had been lodging were officially handed over. Not all Canadian squadrons were posted immediately to join it, and it began with eight founder squadrons, 408 (Goose) and 419 (Moose) equipped with Halifaxes and 420 (Snowy Owl), 424 (Tiger), 425 (Allouette), 426 (Thunderbird), 427 (Lion) and 428 (Ghost) Squadrons with Wellingtons, of which only 408, 419 and 427 were operational. The Canadian government was demanding Lancasters, and the type would eventually become dominant in the group, but that would be by war's end. In the meantime, most of the existing Wellington units and those awaiting posting in or yet to form would eventually find themselves operating the unpopular Halifax.

There was no fanfare to herald the operational debut of the new group, in fact, it was a damp squib as the appalling weather conditions forced the cancellation of the intended maiden operation on New Year's Night. For the Command generally, a continuation of the Oboe trials would occupy the first two weeks, during which 109 Squadron marked for small forces of 1 and 5 Group Lancasters at Essen on seven occasions and Duisburg once. For the first time, the cloud cover and ever-present blanket of industrial haze would have no bearing on the outcome of the raid as reliance on e.t.a., DR and Gee was cast aside in favour of Oboe, at least, that is, at targets within the device's range. Until the advent of mobile transmitter stations late in the war, Oboe would be restricted by the curvature of the earth and the altitude at which Mosquitos could fly, but this meant that the entire Ruhr lay within range of Harris's bombers. That said, the success of a raid would still rely on the ability of the Path Finders to back up the initial Oboe markers and maintain a supply of target indicators (TIs) on the aiming point.

AVM Brookes visited Leeming on the 3rd and during a special parade held at 14.00 presented the squadron crest, before interviewing around thirty members of aircrew who had been recommended for a commission. Bad weather had prevented 6 Group from becoming operational until that night, when six 427 (Lion) Squadron Wellingtons were sent mining in one of the Nectarine gardens, three of them successfully and three not. On the 8th, the Path Finder Force was granted group status as 8 Group, and the stations it occupied were transferred from 3 Group. For the purpose of this book, the titles Path Finder and 8 Group are interchangeable.

408 (Goose) Squadron had to wait until the 9th to begin its new era as part of a 6 Group force of thirteen Halifaxes and twenty-five Wellingtons, the latter type bolstered by an element from 425 (Allouette) Squadron, which had just been declared operational. There was great excitement at the Leeming briefing at the prospect of returning to operations, for which the eight-strong 408 (Goose) Squadron element took off between 16.34 and 16.41 bound for the Nectarine II and III gardens off the central Frisians with S/L Newson the senior pilot on duty and two mines in each bomb bay. S/L Newson and crew arrived in the target area to find visibility at two miles and pinpointed on Simonszand Island to the east of Schiermonnikoog, from where they conducted a timed run for seven minutes on a north-north-easterly heading at 174 i.a.s., before releasing the mines from 700 feet at 18.58. The other crews established similar pinpoints and radiated out on their timed runs to release their mines from 500 to 1,200 feet between 18.55 and 19.08, after which they returned safely to make their reports at debriefing.

The weather persisted in unhelpful mode, and while elements of 1 and 5 Groups continued to support the Oboe trials programme over the Ruhr, 6 Group remained operationally inactive. It was boosted on the 12th by the news that 424 (Tiger) and 426 (Thunderbird) Squadrons had been declared ready to go to war. The hockey war continued on this day, when 408 (Goose) Squadron inflicted a six goal to three defeat on 419 (Moose) Squadron.

A new Air Ministry directive was issued on the 14th, which authorised the area bombing of the French ports with concrete bunkers and support facilities providing a home for U-Boots. A list was drawn up accordingly, headed by Lorient with its K1, K2 and K3 edifices on the Keroman peninsula and included Brest, St-Nazaire and La Pallice. As previously stated, the concrete structures were impervious to the bombs available to Bomber Command at the time and the purpose of this new campaign was to render the town and port uninhabitable and block or sever all road and rail communications to them.

The first of the series of nine attacks on Lorient over the ensuing four weeks took place that very night at the hands of a force of 122 aircraft, of which six Halifaxes and nine Wellingtons were provided by 6 Group, the numbers depleted by the cancellation of many because of adverse weather conditions. It was left to 408 (Goose) Squadron and 426 (Thunderbird) Squadron at Dishforth to fly the flag, for which six Halifaxes departed Leeming between 22.09 and 22.19 with S/Ls Gilmore and Newson the senior pilots on duty and thirteen SBCs of 4lb incendiaries in the bomb bays supplemented with two 1,000-pounders. S/L Gilmore lost two engines on take-off, the ORB not stating whether or not the Halifax had become airborne first, but through the skill of the pilot, destruction of the aircraft and possibly the crew was averted. The remaining five headed for the south coast to begin the Channel crossing to the St-Malo region of Brittany, and on the way lost the services of Sgt Greig and crew to the failure of the rear turret. Those arriving in the target area found up to eight-tenths cloud with tops at 16,000 feet and a base at 4,000 feet but good visibility aided by Path Finder flares. The River Scorff provided a firm pinpoint as the Leeming element bombed from 12,500 to 16,000 feet between 01.09 and 01.25, and despite accurate marking by the Path Finders, the main force bombing was scattered and destroyed a modest 120 buildings.

An overall force of 157 aircraft made up predominantly of Wellingtons, Halifaxes and Stirlings was assembled to return to Lorient on the 15th with 83 Squadron of 8 Group providing the only four Lancasters. 6 Group detailed six Halifaxes each from 408 Goose) and 419 (Moose) Squadrons and thirty-one Wellingtons, the Leeming element taking to the air between 17.08 and 17.13 with W/C Ferris and S/L Gilmore the senior pilots on duty and up to fifteen SBCs and two 1,000-pounders in the bomb bays. They began the Channel crossing near Lyme Regis and arrived in the target area to find three to five tenths cloud with tops at 7,000 feet, but otherwise excellent conditions for the attack. Bombing by the Leeming element was carried out from 12,800 and 15,000 feet between 20.02 and 20.19, and a more concentrated bombing performance was observed than that of twenty-four hours earlier. This was confirmed by post-raid reconnaissance, which revealed the destruction of more than eight hundred buildings.

Two operations were planned against the "Big City", Berlin, to be carried out on consecutive nights beginning on the 16th, for which a force of 201 aircraft was made ready. This would be the first raid on Germany's capital for fourteen months and would bring with it the first use of custom-designed target indicators (TIs). The main force was made up predominantly of 5 Group Lancasters, with others from 1 Group, while five of the eleven Halifaxes were provided by 35 (Madras Presidency) Squadron in a Path Finder element of seventeen aircraft. Those reaching the target would be sharing the airspace over it with the broadcaster, Richard Dimbleby in a 106 Squadron Lancaster captained by W/C Guy Gibson. *(Most commentators, including myself, have written that Dimbleby flew on the following night's operation, but the 106 Squadron ORB clearly shows that Gibson took part only in the first one.)* Some returning crews reported black smoke rising through 5,000 feet as they turned away, but many were unconvinced of the effectiveness of the raid, and this was borne out by local sources, which reported scattered bombing in mostly southern districts. One notable scalp was the ten-thousand-seater Deutschlandhalle, the largest covered venue in Europe, which was hosting the annual circus as the bombers approached and was efficiently emptied of people and animals with only minor injuries to a few people. Shortly afterwards, incendiaries set fire to the building and reduced it to ruins. Remarkably, only a single Lancaster failed to return from this operation, but the balance would be redressed somewhat twenty-four hours later.

170 Lancasters and seventeen Halifaxes were made ready on 1, 4, 5 and 8 Group stations on the 17th for the return to Berlin that night, while the Canadians again watched from the sidelines. The Path Finders were up to thirty-seven minutes late, and the sparse target marking was once more concentrated over the southern fringes of the city rather than over the centre. Little was seen of the results of the bombing, and local reports confirmed that the operation had not been successful, and no significant damage had occurred. The disappointment was compounded by the loss of twenty-two bombers, 11.8% of those dispatched, and many of these disappeared without trace in the Baltic or North Sea.

408 (Goose) Squadron suffered only its second defeat of the hockey season when beaten six goals to three by an all-aircrew team put out by W/C Dudley Burnside's 427 (Lion) Squadron on the 19th. It was a bitter pill to swallow but had to be put to the back of the mind when orders were received on the 21st to prepared for mining duties that night. 6 Group detailed fifteen Halifaxes and twenty-five Wellingtons in an overall mining effort in the Nectarine gardens of seventy aircraft. The five 408 (Goose) Squadron crews of F/L Black, F/O Cornwall, F/Sgts Harty and Wood and Sgt Sirett were assigned to Nectarine II off the central Frisians and departed Leeming between 17.00 and 17.06. Low cloud over the Yorkshire coast dissipated to leave clear skies in the target area illuminated by bright moonlight, and all were able to pinpoint on Simonszand as the starting point for their timed runs. The vegetables were planted in the briefed locations from 700 to 1,500 feet between 18.42 and 19.25 and all returned safely from uneventful sorties, until that is, Sgt Sirett lost first one engine on the way home and then another over base but landed without incident.

A new round of Oboe trials had begun that night at Essen and shifted to Düsseldorf on the 23rd, while the third attack on Lorient was also scheduled for the latter occasion and a force of 121 aircraft assembled, which included fifteen Halifaxes representing 6 Group. Earlier in the day, six Wellingtons from 420 (Snowy Owl) and 425 (Allouette) Squadrons had been sent "moling" in the Esens coastal region between Emden in the west and Wilhelmshaven in the east and had returned safely after successfully fulfilling their brief. The 408 (Goose) Squadron crews of F/O Hatle, F/Sgt Harty and Sgts Blackhall, Cochrane and Greig departed Leeming between 17.14 and 17.20, the Hatle and Cochrane crews sitting on seven 1,000-pounders and the others up to fifteen SBCs of incendiaries. All made it to the target area, where ahead of them, the Path Finder illuminator and marker crews had arrived to find some thin cloud at 3,000 feet but generally clear conditions and good visibility, which enabled them to carry out timed runs from Groix Island to the aiming-points A, B and Y. The Leeming crews ran in at between 14,000 and 15,500 feet, following the line of the Blavet and Scorff estuaries to reach the built-up area and delivered their payloads between 20.04 and 20.40. During the return flight, DT678 lost both starboard engines and crash-landed at Ossington in Nottinghamshire at 23.30, and while the Halifax would never fly again, Sgt Greig RAAF and his six RCAF crew mates walked away to resume their operational careers. Other returning crews reported many fires with smoke beginning to obscure ground detail and the glow from the burning port lingering on the horizon for seventy miles into the homeward flight. Bombing photos confirmed the accuracy of the raid, which had cost of a single Stirling.

On the 26th, the squadron returned to winning ways on the hockey pitch with a four to one thrashing of 420 (Snowy Owl) Squadron. That afternoon, a force of 157 aircraft, mostly Wellingtons, was assembled from 1, 3, 4 and 6 Groups for the next raid on Lorient, the fourth in the series, for which 6 Group detailed fifty-five Wellingtons, while the Halifaxes remained at home. The Path Finder element arrived at the target to find five-tenths cloud at 2,000 feet and thick haze, which made pinpointing difficult for some. Returning crews reported a number of cookie detonations in the town and the glow of fires remaining visible for thirty minutes, but it was not possible to make an accurate assessment. It did appear, however, that the searchlight and flak defence had been "beefed up" since the previous raid.

Düsseldorf was selected as the primary target on the 27th, when the Path Finders were to use ground marking for the first time, rather than skymarking. Ground markers, which were TIs fused to burst and cascade just above the ground, could be seen through thin or partial cloud and industrial haze, and were much more reliable than the previously employed parachute flares that drifted in the wind. However, skymarkers would remain an indispensable part of target marking techniques on nights of heavy cloud or to use in combination with ground markers. 6 Group was excluded from the order of battle and detailed six Wellingtons for *gardening* duties. The main weight of the Düsseldorf raid fell into the southern half of the city, where ten industrial premises were destroyed or seriously damaged along with 456 houses and nine public buildings. From this point onwards, Path Finder heavy aircraft would back-up the Mosquito-laid Oboe markers throughout a raid, to ensure that the aiming-point remained marked, and would also provide preliminary warning flares at the start of the bombing run.

It was back to Lorient for seventy-five Wellingtons and forty-one Halifaxes on the 29th, 6 Group responsible for sixty-nine aircraft, with 408 (Goose) Squadron providing ten of the Halifaxes. They departed Leeming between 16.54 and 17.05 with S/L Newson the senior pilot on duty and thirteen SBCs of incendiaries supplemented by two 1,000-pounders in each bomb bay. Shortly after crossing the French coast near Saint-Brieuc, Sgt Childers and crew lost their Gee and turned back, leaving the others to traverse the Brest peninsula and all but one to arrive in the target area and encounter ten-tenths cloud with tops in places estimated to be at 20,000 feet. F/Sgt Smith and crew had not reached the target when the fuel situation persuaded them to abandon their sortie and head for home. The others were forced to bomb on a Gee-fix from 12,000 to 15,000 feet between 20.34 and 20.45 and were unable to assess what was happening on the ground. F/Sgt Ross and crew lost an engine and some instruments on the way home but landed safely at Squires Gate at Blackpool. HR662 failed to return after crashing to the north-west of the target with fatal consequences for Southern Rhodesia-born F/O Roux and his crew, the pilot on his twenty-fourth sortie and most of his crew on their third. On the 30th, eleven 6 Group Wellingtons were sent moling over north-western Germany between Emden and Wilhelmshaven, and six turned back early because of lack of cloud cover.

During the course of its first month on Halifaxes, the squadron took part in six operations and dispatched forty sorties for the loss of two aircraft and one crew.

February 1943

It was a time of honing and refining for Bomber Command in preparation for the launching of a major campaign a month hence and February would bring an increase in operations. It opened with the posting of Cologne as the target for an experimental operation by a force of 161 aircraft on the 2nd, for which two marking methods were to be employed. Situated just to the south of the Ruhr, the Rhineland capital city was within range of Oboe Mosquitos, and these were to be supplemented by Path Finder aircraft relying on H2S, a new ground-mapping radar with a scanner housed in a cupola aft of the bomb bay, which produced images of the terrain on a cathode-ray tube. The early model required much practice by the operator to interpret what he was seeing, and the jumble of images over an urban sprawl the size of a major city like Berlin would lead to inaccurate marking, but in time, and with the advent of an improved version, H2S would become an indispensable device that would eventually become standard equipment for main force as well as Path Finder aircraft.

Leeming was not invited to take part in the night's main event and instead prepared seven Halifaxes for mining duties in company with six from 419 (Moose) Squadron in the Silverthorn IV garden in the Kattegat region of the Baltic to the south of Anholt Island. F/Sgt Wood and crew had landed away after the last operation and during transit from Syerston to Leeming, DT682 suffered an engine fire, which necessitated a crash-landing near the 5 Group station at Bottesford on the Nottinghamshire/Leicestershire border. The crew members sustained slight injury, and after an inspection the Halifax was declared to be beyond economical repair. At some point during the day the hockey team defeated 429 (Bison) Squadron five goals to three to make the play-offs.

The gardeners departed Leeming between 16.43 and 16.55 with F/L Black the senior pilot on duty and headed for landfall on the western coast of Jutland before traversing southern Denmark to access the Baltic. All reached the target area, where, as often was the case, there were diverse opinions concerning the conditions, P/O Carver and crew reporting the cloud base at sea-level, which prevented them from establishing a pinpoint, while Sgt Grant and crew described fairly good visibility but rain showers which thwarted their attempts to fulfil their brief and both crews returned with their two mines still on board. P/O Cornwall and crew found the cloud base to be at 1,000 feet and climbed to 12,000 feet to gain clear air, by which time the intercom and broken down and it was decided to abort the sortie. In contrast, the crews of F/L Black and F/Sgts Harty, Marment and Smith were able to establish pinpoints on Fornaes and Kullen Island from which to conduct a timed run and deliver their stores into the briefed locations from 900 and 1,000 feet between 19.47 and 20.25. Meanwhile at Cologne, few crews had been able to observe their own bombs burst, but many scattered fires were evident, the glow from which could be seen from a hundred miles into the return journey. Local reports confirmed bombs falling all over the city, but nowhere with concentration, and damage was, consequently, not commensurate with the size of the force and the effort expended.

Germany's second city, Hamburg, was posted as the target on the 3rd, for which a force of 263 aircraft was made ready, unusually, with Halifaxes representing the most populous type followed by Stirlings. For what was its first major bombing operation 6 Group contributed twenty-five Halifaxes and twenty-one Wellingtons, fourteen of the former belonging to 408 (Goose) Squadron, which departed Leeming between 18.00 and 18.15 with W/C Ferris and S/L Newson the senior pilots on duty. They crossed the Yorkshire coast in sight of Flamborough Head lighthouse on course either for the Dutch coast or the islands off the River Elbe estuary and to join up with the bomber stream during the passage across the North Sea. P/O Kaye and crew had their intercom fail before crossing the English coast, and W/C Ferris lost his artificial horizon at around the same time, while F/Sgt Marment and crew were some twenty-five miles out when the port-inner engine displayed signs of stress and forced them to turn back also. North-western Germany benefitted from the frequent presence of a gatekeeper in the form of massive weather fronts with towering cumulonimbus clouds that contained violent electrical storms and icing conditions. Extending to 20,000 feet and beyond and too wide to circumnavigate, this night's front persuaded many crews to turn back, most of them citing frozen guns, although in the case of Sgt Greig and crew it was their inability to climb to clear air over the Amsterdam region of Holland. Having arrived at the target the Path Finders were unable to deliver concentrated and sustained marking by H2S, and scattered red and green skymarker flares were all that the 408 (Goose) Squadron bomb-aimers had as a reference as they released their two 1,000-pounders and thirteen SBCs of 4lb incendiaries each from 9,000 to 18,500 feet between 20.58 and 21.20. No results were observed, and the impression was of an ineffective attack, which was confirmed by local reports of forty-five large fires but no concentration or significant damage, and this disappointing outcome cost the Command sixteen aircraft. DT680 was the 408 (Goose) Squadron representative among the missing after crashing in the target area, killing F/L Black RCAF and delivering his crew into enemy hands. William Black was on his eighth sortie and his crew members had completed between two and eight. The losses by type made interesting reading and would reflect the trend for the remainder of the year, with the Stirlings suffering the highest numerical and percentage casualties, followed by the Halifaxes and Wellingtons, with the Lancasters clearly at the top of the food chain.

A return to Italy was posted on the 4th with Turin the target for a force of 188 aircraft, while 128 others, mostly Wellingtons, were prepared to continue the assault on Lorient. Turin in northern Italy was home to Fiat's Lingotto and Mirafiori car plants, the Lancia motor works, the Arsenale army munitions factory, the RIV submachine gun works, the Nebioli foundry and plants belonging to the American Westinghouse company. 6 Group contributed fifteen Halifaxes to this endeavour, including ten representing 408 (Goose) Squadron, and sixty Wellingtons to the sixth raid of the series on Lorient. The Leeming element took to the air between 17.41 and 17.59 with W/C Ferris the senior pilot on duty and three 1,000-pounders and five SBCs in each bomb bay. Sgt Childers and crew had just crossed the Normandy coast when an inability to climb to the height required to traverse the Alps persuaded them to turn back and they endured a torrid time from the Portsmouth searchlight and flak batteries as they headed home. The others adopted the standard route across France and after crossing the Alps in cloud at 21,000 feet, found conditions on the Italian side much improved with clear skies and excellent visibility, which facilitated a visual confirmation of the accuracy of the Path Finder TIs. An estimated one hundred searchlights were active, and the flak defence had also been "beefed-up" but was still inaccurate and in keeping with expectations at an Italian target. *(Following a raid on a German target, a bomb symbol was painted on the forward fuselage below the glasshouse, but after a raid on an Italian target, the symbol would be an ice-cream cone.)* Red TIs were much in evidence in the city centre as the Leeming crews carried out their attacks from 15,000 to 20,000 feet between 21.40 and 22.06 and returned with enthusiastic reports of the effectiveness of their work. Local sources confirmed later that serious and widespread damage had resulted.

On the 6th, 6 Group detailed nine Halifaxes and twenty-nine Wellingtons for mining duties in the Nectarine and Trefoil gardens off the Dutch Frisians. The six-strong 408 (Goose) Squadron element departed Leeming between 17.25 and 17.30 with F/L Boosey the senior pilot on duty and the Nectarine I garden as their destination. Apart from patches of sea fog, visibility was good enough to enable most crews to pinpoint on Terschelling and five delivered their two mines each from 500 to 1,100 feet between 19.06 and 1947, while F/Sgt Grubert and crew were defeated by rain and sleet and returned their mines to the dump.

The seventh raid in the series on Lorient was posted on the 7th and was by far the largest to date, employing 323 aircraft, of which eighteen Halifaxes and fifty-one Wellingtons were provided by 6 Group. The operation was to be conducted in two waves an hour apart, and it was for the second wave that 408 (Goose) Squadron made ready eight Halifaxes and sent them on their way from Leeming between 19.00 and 19.16 with S/L Gilmore the senior pilot on duty and two 1,000-pounders and thirteen SBCs of 4lb incendiaries in each bomb bay. The first wave had arrived in the target area to find clear skies and ideal bombing conditions, which they exploited after making a visual identification of the aiming point confirmed by Path Finder TIs. As they were returning home to report an outstandingly destructive raid, they left behind them a glow in the sky visible from the English coast, which acted as a beacon for the second-phase element to home in on. They encountered heavy smoke and haze over the target, through which the 408 (Goose) Squadron crews bombed from 14,000 to 18,000 feet between 21.32 and 21.48, before heading home to report what appeared to be a devastating raid. Absent from debriefing was the crew of F/Sgt Smith RCAF in HR655, which crashed in the target area with no survivors.

Before the penultimate raid on Lorient took place, attention was switched to the important naval and shipbuilding port of Wilhelmshaven, situated on the north-western coast of Jade Bay, some sixty miles to the west of Hamburg. Renamed in 1935 from Reichsmarinewerft to the Kriegsmarinewerft, the shipyard had launched the Deutschland class "pocket battleships", Admiral Scheer and Admiral Graf Spee in 1934 and 1936, the Scharnhorst heavy cruiser in 1939 and the mighty Bismarck class Tirpitz in 1941 in addition to twenty-seven type VII U-Boots. A force of 177 aircraft was put together on the 11th from 1, 4, 5 and 8 Groups to carry out an attack, while 6 Group sent twenty-four Wellingtons to the Nectarine I and Jellyfish gardens, respectively off the Dutch Frisians and the port of Brest. Ten-tenths cloud over Wilhelmshaven with tops at around 10,000 feet dictated the use of the least reliable marking method, H2S skymarking, although on the credit side, at this more modest and compact urban target with a coastline, it was easier to interpret the images on the cathode-ray screens, and on this night great accuracy was achieved. The red and green flares were right over the aiming point as the force delivered its high explosives and incendiaries, but it was impossible to assess what was happening beneath the cloud until an enormous explosion took place, the glow from which lingered for ten minutes. Many crews commented on this at debriefings across the Command, and there must have been much speculation about the source, which turned out to be the naval ammunition depot at Mariensiel, situated to the south of the town. It blew itself into oblivion, devastating 120 acres and causing widespread damage in the dockyard and town.

On the 12th, the squadron played its final hockey match of the season, losing the play-off for the final by four goals to nil to 424 (Tiger) Squadron. The heartbreak had to be banished from the minds on the following day, when briefings took place for the penultimate raid on Lorient. It was to be the largest force to date, employing 466 aircraft and a thousand tons of bombs, 6 Group initially detailing twenty-six Halifaxes and seventy-five Wellingtons, all but five of which would take off. The 408 (Goose) Squadron element of a dozen Halifaxes departed Leeming between 17.55 and 18.06 with S/L Gilmore the senior pilot on duty and four 1,000-pounders and eleven SBCs in each bomb bay. The crews of Sgt Greig and F/Sgt Grubert turned back before reaching the Channel coast because of oxygen supply failure and an engine issue respectively, and they were followed home by the crews of Sgt Sirett and F/O Hatle, also because of engine malfunctions. As the others began the Channel crossing in the Exmouth area, some crews reported observing flares going down over the target two hundred miles away as the first wave attacked. It had been planned to station a number of Path Finder aircraft over the Ile-de-Groix, an island situated some five miles off the mouth of the estuary leading to the port and illuminate it continuously as a navigation point. The other Path Finder crews followed up over Lorient itself with flares, green TIs and 1,000-pounders in a number of passes from 11,000 to 14,000 feet between 20.35 and 20.56, paving the way for the main force element to carry out their attacks. The target was located with ease in excellent visibility under clear skies, which allowed them to make a visual identification of both aiming points, the U-Boot pens on the Keroman peninsula and the town, before smoke began to drift across the area. The 408 (Goose) Squadron crews bombed from 15,000 to 17,000 feet between 20.35 and 20.47 and all returned safely to report massive fires right across the town and the port area.

Orders were received on 1, 5 and 8 Group stations on the 14th to make ready for a return to Italy that night for a crack this time at Milan, for which a force of 142 Lancasters was assembled, while 243 Halifaxes, Stirlings and Wellingtons from 3, 4, 6 and 8 Groups were made ready to try their hand at Cologne. 6 Group provided twenty Halifaxes and thirty-five Wellingtons, nine of the former belonging to 408 (Goose) Squadron, which departed Leeming between 18.15 and 18.23 with W/C Ferris the senior pilot on duty and a bomb load each of two 1,000-pounders, eleven SBCs of 4lb and two of 30lb incendiaries. F/O Gamble and crew turned back within the hour because of electrical system failure and a jammed rear turret, and they were followed home by P/O Allen and crew who also suffered turret malfunctions, while the others pressed on to the Scheldt estuary and beyond, eyes watching out for the green route-marker flares dropped by the Path Finders some twenty miles short of the target. The Path Finders arrived in the target area to encounter ten-tenths cloud with tops at around 7,000 feet and established their positions by H2S and evidence of the accurate flak penetrating the cloud tops. They opened the attack bang on scheduled at 20.15 with red flares with green stars and 1,000-pounders and the main force followed on their heels, those from Leeming bombing from 12,000 to 18,000 feet, mostly on skymarkers. The cloud prevented an assessment of the results, and the intensity of the flak dissuaded crews from hanging around, but they observed some evidence of burgeoning fires that gave some hope of a successful raid. By the time that F/L Boosey and his mixed RAF, RCAF and RAAF crew were on final approach to Leeming they had lost the navigator's intercom connection and the rear turret had become unserviceable. To compound the problems, the port-outer engine caught fire and the port-inner lost power when the pilot tried to throttle up to regain some height, and he was able to reach 1,000 feet to enable five of the crew to bale out. The pilot crash-landed DT750 four miles north-west of Sowerby at 23.57, and he and the other occupant walked away from the wreckage, only to learn the sad news that the rear gunner, F/O Parker, an American in the RCAF, had died when his parachute failed to deploy in time. Local sources in Cologne confirmed only limited success in western districts, the failure to achieve better results, perhaps in part, caused by a bunch of red flares with green stars observed to fall ten miles to the north.

The final raid of the series on Lorient was posted on the 16th, for which another large force of 377 aircraft was assembled, of which twenty-four Halifaxes and fifty-seven Wellingtons were provided by 6 Group. The 408 (Goose) Squadron element of eleven departed Leeming between 18.25 and 18.35 with S/Ls Gilmore and Newson the senior pilots on duty and four 1,000-pounders, nine SBCs of 4lb incendiaries and two of 30lbs in each bomb bay. P/O Cornwall and crew dropped out because of oxygen system failure when some twenty miles south of Portland Bill, while the others pressed on via the Channel Islands towards the Brittany coast. They were among the earlier arrivals at the target and found clear conditions aided by an almost full moon, which enabled them to deliver their bomb loads onto the Keroman peninsula from 14,000 to 16,000 feet between 20.47 and 21.08 guided by red Path Finder TIs. The majority of the force dropped incendiaries into the town, which, after nine attacks, 1,926 sorties and four thousand tons of bombs, was now a desolate and deserted ruin.

Preparations were put in hand on the 18th to make ready 195 aircraft for the second of the month's four raids on Wilhelmshaven, for which 6 Group contributed just four Halifaxes with P/O Allen and crew alone representing 408 (Goose) Squadron. Before they departed Leeming at 18.38, seven others had taken off between 17.45 and 17.57 as part of a 6 Group contribution of fifteen Halifaxes and fifteen Wellingtons to the night's mining effort taking place from the Frisians to St-Nazaire. The 408 (Goose) Squadron crews were bound for the Nectarine II garden off the central Frisians with F/Os Harriss and Stewart the senior pilots on duty, and all arrived in the target area under clear skies and in good visibility, which enabled them to pinpoint on the western tip of Juist and conduct timed runs. The mines were released from 700 to 1,500 feet between 19.43 and 19.56 and only F/O Stewart and crew brought theirs home after three runs along Juist had failed to establish a pinpoint. Meanwhile, the Allen crew had reached the Wilhelmshaven area, which was identified visually in excellent conditions and by red TIs, which were in the bomb sight as they carried out their attack with three 1,000-pounders and SBCs of incendiaries from 18,000 at 20.47. Bombs were observed to burst and fires to spring up and returning crews were confident that an accurate and concentrated attack had taken place. However, bombing photos revealed that the operation had been a failure, after the main weight of bombs had fallen into open country to the west of the town, and this demonstrated how easy it was to be misled by what the eye saw. Local reports admitted to a number of bombs hitting the town, causing no serious damage or casualties. One of the 408 (Goose) Squadron Halifaxes involved in this night's activities was the first with the "Z" modification, a faired-over front turret and nose arrangement, which, according to the ORB, performed satisfactorily.

Twenty-four hours later a force of 338 aircraft set off to return to Wilhelmshaven, with Wellingtons and Halifaxes accounting for 230 of the number and Stirlings and Lancasters the rest. 6 Group dispatched twenty-four Halifaxes and sixty Wellingtons, a dozen of the former representing 408 (Goose) Squadron and departing Leeming between 17.55 and 18.06 with S/Ls Gilmore and Newson the senior pilots on duty. Each crew was sitting on three 1,000-pounders, eight SBCs of 4lb and four of 30lb incendiaries as they climbed out over the station and set course for the Yorkshire coast. There were no early returns and on arrival over Germany's north-western coast they again encountered excellent conditions with visibility that enabled them to identify the coastline and line themselves up on the target. The aiming point was marked by green TIs, onto which the bombs were delivered from 15,000 to 18,500 feet between 20.01 and 20.13, and the bursts and fires observed in the docks area and the town left the crews with the impression that another successful raid had taken place. However, bombing photos told a different story, and revealed that the Path Finder marking had fallen to the north of the built-up area, partly through reliance upon outdated maps, which would now need to be replaced. Of the twelve missing aircraft, five were Stirlings and represented 8.9% of those dispatched, thus confirming the type's vulnerability compared with the Lancaster and Halifax. The four missing Lancasters represented a 7.7% loss rate, while no Halifaxes failed to return, but this would prove to be a blip. During the course of the year, the food chain would become established with Lancasters firmly at the top, Halifaxes in the middle and Stirlings at the bottom, when all types operated together.

The final raid of the series on Wilhelmshaven was posted on the 24th and would involve a main force of twenty-seven Halifaxes and seventy-one Wellingtons of 6 Group with seventeen Path Finder Stirlings and Lancasters to provide the marking. The 408 (Goose) Squadron element of thirteen Halifaxes departed Leeming between 18.16 and 18.30 with S/L Gilmore the senior pilot on duty and a similar bomb load to that of the previous raid on this target. For the second raid running there were no early returns, but unlike the previous occasion, they were met by ten-tenths cloud with tops at between 8,000 and 15,000 feet and had to rely on Path Finder skymarkers released on H2S. The bombing was carried out from 14,000 to 20,000 feet between 20.33 and 20.40 with no prospect of assessing the outcome, and local sources would describe the raid as small and causing little damage in the town. On the credit side, no aircraft were lost, and the port would now be left in peace until October 1944.

A major operation against Nuremberg was posted on all but 6 Group stations across the Command on the 25th, for which a force of 337 aircraft was assembled. 6 Group, meanwhile, detailed seven Halifaxes and thirteen Wellingtons for mining duties in the Nectarine I garden, for which 408 (Goose) Squadron dispatched the crews of F/O Hatle, P/O Allen and Sgts Batchelor and Troy from Leeming between 21.20 and 21.45. The cloud base over the North Sea and Terschelling Island was at 1,500 feet with haze below, and this prevented the crews of F/O Hatle and Sgt Troy from establishing a pinpoint and they brought their mines home, while the Allen and Batchelor crews found a pinpoint on the island's south-western tip and planted their stores from 1,500 feet at 23.17 and 800 feet at 23.27 respectively. Some 370 miles to the south, the bombing brigade had to wait for the Path Finder element to turn up some sixteen to twenty minutes after the raid was due to begin and drop marker flares on the approach, from which the 5 Group crews carried out a time-and-distance run to the aiming point marked by red and green TIs. All of the indications, including what looked like an oil-depot exploding, suggested a concentrated attack, which fell predominantly in northern and western districts. This was confirmed by local reports, which mentioned damage to three hundred buildings but also revealed that bombs had fallen onto other communities and open country up to seven miles to the north.

When Cologne was posted as the target on the 26th, 6 Group responded with twenty-six Halifaxes and sixty-one Wellingtons as part of an overall force of 427 aircraft, of which 408 (Goose) Squadron was responsible for fourteen of the Halifaxes. They departed Leeming between 18.47 and 19.01 with S/Ls Gilmore and Newson the senior pilots on duty and bomb loads of three 1,000-pounders, eight SBCs of 4lb and four of 30lb incendiaries. They adopted the standard route to the target via the Scheldt estuary and only Sgt Troy and crew failed to reach it after the DR compass became unreliable and the hydraulics to the bomb doors failed. The doors were pumped down and the bomb load jettisoned over a built-up area some forty miles south-east of Cologne, where fires were started. The others reached the Cologne area to find good vertical visibility for the bomb-aimers, some of whom were able to identify the bridges over the Rhine. It seems from some comments from other squadrons that a proportion of the force bombed before the Path Finders had a chance to mark, but once the red and green TIs appeared on the ground, the 408 (Goose) Squadron crews aimed their loads at them from 15,500 to 18,500 feet between 21.13 and 21.26. S/L Gilmore's DT675 was badly damaged over the target by flak and lost its astrodome, while holes appeared in flying surfaces and the fuselage, the hydraulics feed to the wing bomb doors was cut, the rear turret doors jammed, and three engines failed. The Halifax dived from 17,000 to 4,000 feet to evade the searchlights and the order was given to prepare to abandon it, at which point the three dead engines picked up, the order was rescinded, and a safe return was made to Manston. Fires were reported in the city centre, as were decoys to the west of the city, and the glow from the burning city remained visible for up to a hundred miles. At debriefing, F/Sgt Harty and crew reported that they had begun their bombing run five minutes early and that their bomb doors had failed to open on each of two passes over the aiming point. The selector switch was left on open and the doors lowered as they crossed Holland on the way home, allowing them to bomb the aerodrome at Eindhoven from 18,000 feet at 21.49. P/O Kaye and crew bombed a built-up area from 18,000 feet at 21.15 and worked out later that it must have been Duisburg, thirty-five miles north of the intended target. Bombing photos showed fire tracks and smoke that suggested an effective raid, when, in fact, a large proportion of the effort had fallen to the south-west of the city, and perhaps only a quarter had landed in the built-up area, causing much damage to housing, minor industry and public buildings.

A large mining effort around the Frisians occupied ninety-one aircraft on the 27th, 6 Group contributing fifteen Halifaxes and nineteen Wellingtons to the Nectarine II garden, for which the 408 (Goose) Squadron element of seven departed Leeming between 17.57 and 18.13 with F/O Stewart the senior pilot on duty. They began the North Sea crossing at Bridlington and reached the target area to find clear skies and a little haze, which prevented the crews of F/O Stewart and P/O Carver from picking up a pinpoint and they returned their mines to the station store. The others pinpointed on the eastern end of Simonszand and planted their vegetables into the briefed locations from 750 to 1,400 feet between 20.05 and 20.20.

Having dealt with Lorient under the January Directive, attention now turned upon St-Nazaire, situated further south along the Biscay coast. The force of 437 aircraft assembled on the 28th included a contribution from 6 Group of twenty-two Halifaxes and fifty-three Wellingtons, ten of the former belonging to 408 (Goose) Squadron. They departed Leeming between 18.26 and 18.35 with S/L Newson the senior pilot on duty and two 1,000-pounders and mix of 4lb and 30lb incendiaries, and all reached the target area to find clear skies and good visibility with only a little ground haze to contend with. They bombed on red TIs from 11,000 to 21,000 feet between 21.24 and 21.47, and it was clear from the many explosions and at least forty fires burning in the docks that the port was undergoing an ordeal of destruction. Post-raid reconnaissance revealed that the marking had been concentrated and the bombing accurate, and local reports confirmed that 60% of the town had been destroyed.

This concluded the month's activity, during which, the squadron had taken part in sixteen operations and had dispatched 142 sorties for the loss of four Halifaxes, two crews and a rear gunner.

March 1943

March would bring with it the opening rounds of the Ruhr campaign, the first for which the Command was adequately equipped and genuinely prepared, with a predominantly four-engine bomber force at its disposal to carry an increasing weight of bombs and Oboe to provide accuracy. First, however, the crews would have to negotiate operations to Germany's capital and second cities, and it was the "Big City" itself, Berlin, that opened the month's account on the 1st. The crews learned at briefing that six Path Finder Halifaxes and ten Stirlings equipped with H2S were to drop a "landmark" yellow TI each at Butzow, situated some eighty miles north of Berlin, which were to be backed up by seven Halifaxes and sixteen Lancasters. The "special" (H2S-equipped) aircraft were then to release red warning flares twelve miles short of the target followed by red TIs on the aiming-point at the time-on-target of 22.00, which the seven Halifaxes and sixteen Lancasters would back-up with green TIs. As always, the plan was based on a forecast of favourable conditions, in the absence of which, skymarkers would substitute for TIs. A force of 302 aircraft was assembled, made up of 156 Lancasters, eighty-six Halifaxes and sixty Stirlings, 6 Group putting up twenty-one Halifaxes, of which nine represented 408 (Goose) Squadron. They departed Leeming between 18.41 and 18.49 with W/C Ferris and S/L Gilmore the senior pilots on duty, a sign of good leadership by the commanding officer to lead his men into battle on a challenging operation. Each Halifax was carrying two 1,000-pounders and seven and three SBCs respectively of 4lb and 30lb incendiaries as they climbed out over base before heading for the Yorkshire coast near Flamborough Head. S/L Gilmore and crew were a hundred miles out over the North Sea when an unserviceable rear turret ended their interest in proceedings, while P/O Kaye and crew had reached the enemy coast after contending since take-off with a failing intercom system and dropped their bombs on a searchlight and flak position on the Island of Sylt before also turning back.

At 21.15, F/O Harriss and crew expected to see the "landmark" TI to confirm their position but saw nothing and orbited for a time in the hope of receiving their guidance, until giving up and setting course for Berlin, only to run into flak in the Rostock area. By the time that they had negotiated their way through, it was already 22.10, too late to reach the target in time, and they turned for home, on the way bombing what they believed to be Kiel from 18,000 feet. Those reaching the target found it to be under clear skies with only haze to impair the vertical visibility, however, reliant upon H2S, the Path Finder navigators experienced great difficulty in establishing their positions based on the images on their cathode-ray tubes over such a massive urban sprawl, and this led to scattered marking. As a result, the main weight of the attack fell into south-western districts, where the 408 (Goose) Squadron crews bombed on red and green TIs from 14,500 to 20,000 feet between 22.03 and 22.22. Seventeen aircraft failed to return, among them the "Goose" Squadron's DT797, which was homebound when crossing paths with the night-fighter of Hptm Herbert Lutje of III./NJG1. The Halifax crashed at 00.10 some five miles east of Deventer in central Holland, killing Sgt Cochrane RCAF and all but the mid-upper gunner, who fell into enemy hands. Apart from the RAF flight engineer, it was an all-Canadian crew, who were on their ninth operation together, while the pilot was undertaking his eleventh sortie. At debriefing, some crews reported the glow of fires to be visible from two hundred miles into the return flight. A post-raid analysis based on bombing photos revealed the attack to have been spread over an area of a hundred square miles, but because of the increasing bomb tonnage now being carried, more damage was inflicted on the city than on any previous raid. 875 buildings, mostly houses, were destroyed and twenty factories seriously damaged, along with railway workshops in the Tempelhof district. It is interesting to analyse the percentage loss rate of each type on this night, as it would be an accurate indicator of their future fortunes. The statistics revealed the loss rate of Lancasters to be 4.5%, and those of the Halifaxes and Stirlings to be 7%.

On the following afternoon the crews of F/L Gamble and P/O Allen conducted a five-hour search over the North Sea for ditched crews but found nothing. Having spent five months on detachment to Coastal Command, 405 (Vancouver) Squadron began moving into Topcliffe as a three-day temporary home on the 3rd, before taking up a relatively short-term residence at Leeming three days hence as it resumed its Bomber Command career in 4 Group. A force of 417 aircraft was assembled to send against Hamburg on the 3rd, of which eighteen Halifaxes and fifty-seven Wellingtons were provided by 6 Group. The nine 408 (Goose) Squadron aircraft were each loaded with two 1,000-pounders and nine and four SBCs respectively of 4lb and 30lb incendiaries, before departing Leeming between 18.27 and 18.35 with S/L Gilmore the senior pilot on duty. Sgt Grant's gunners tested their equipment soon after crossing the Yorkshire coast and found all guns to be defective, prompting the decision to continue on in the hope that the problem could be rectified. Sadly, it could not, and they turned back from a position some one hundred miles out, leaving the others to press on to the turning point north of the target and ultimately to find Hamburg nestling under clear skies and in good visibility. Some Path Finder and main force crews had identified the primary target's Hamburg-America landing stage, the Blohm & Voss shipyards, the Binnen-Alster Lake and the main railway station and those representing 408 (Goose) Squadron carried out their attacks from 16,000 to 20,000 feet between 21.23 and 21.32, aided by the H2S-laid Path Finder TIs. On return, crews reported numerous fires in the docks area along with black smoke rising to meet them as they turned away and the glow on the horizon visible for up to eighty miles. What was not appreciated, was the fact that a proportion of the markers had fallen onto the town of Wedel, situated some thirteen miles downstream of the Elbe, and had attracted perhaps the bulk of the bombs, while those hitting the primary target had caused a hundred fires that needed to be dealt with before the fire services could go to the aid of their less illustrious neighbour. Ten aircraft failed to return, but there were no empty dispersal pans at Leeming.

The night off for most of the Command on the 4th provided the opportunity for maximum serviceability as the decks were now cleared for the opening of the Ruhr offensive, which over the ensuing months, would change the face of bombing and provide for the enemy an indication of the burgeoning power of the Command. This was a culmination of all that had gone before during three and a half years of Bomber Command operations, the backs-to-the-wall desperation of 1940, the tentative almost token offensives of 1941, the treading water and the gradual metamorphosis under Harris in 1942, when failures still outnumbered successes. It had all been leading to this night, from which point would begin the calculated and systematic dismantling of Germany's industrial and population centres. The only shining light during these dark years had been the quality and spirit of the aircrew, and this had never faltered. The new era would begin on the 5th at Essen, Harris's nemesis thus far and the home of the giant armaments-producing Krupp complex occupying the Borbeck districts, and for the first time since the war began, the Command would have at its disposal a device which would negate the industrial haze protecting this city and its neighbours. The magnificent pioneering work on Oboe by W/C Hal Bufton and his crews at 109 Squadron was about to bear fruit in spectacular fashion, and the towns and cities of Germany's arsenal would suffer destruction on an unprecedented scale.

A force of 442 aircraft included twenty Halifaxes and fifty-eight Wellingtons representing 6 Group, 408 (Goose) Squadron's ten aircraft for this momentous occasion containing the crews of S/L Newson in DT673, F/L Gamble in DT772, F/O Harriss in DT749, P/O Carver in HR654, P/O Kaye in DT679, F/Sgt Marment in DT781, Sgt Batchelor in HR658, Sgt Grant in DT790, Sgt Sirett in HR656 and Sgt Troy in DT752. The main force element was to bomb in three waves, Halifaxes first, followed by Wellingtons and Stirlings with Lancasters bringing up the rear. Six Path Finder Halifax and fifteen Lancaster crews had been briefed to drop a warning yellow TI each when fifteen miles from the target, before backing up the Oboe Mosquitos' red TIs on the aiming-point with greens, and the force was to adopt the southern route to the central Ruhr, making landfall over the Scheldt estuary. The 408 (Goose) Squadron Halifaxes each received a bomb load of three 1,000-pounder and eight and four SBCs respectively of 4lb and 30lb incendiaries before departing Leeming between 18.55 and 19.04, only to lose the services of Sgts Batchelor and Sirett and their crews over the North Sea after test-firing revealed their guns to be unserviceable. An unusually high number of early returns and the bombing of alternative targets, involving thirteen 6 Group aircraft, reduced the size of the force reaching Essen and bombing as briefed to 362 aircraft. F/O Harriss and crew lost the use of their rear turret over Holland and bombed what they believed was Leeuwarden aerodrome from 18,500 feet on the way home, despite the fact that it was well to the north of where they might expect to have been.

The main force crews employed the Path Finders' yellow route markers as the initial reference point, before exploiting the good visibility to bomb through the industrial haze onto red and green TIs, those representing 408 (Goose) Squadron from 15,000 to 20,000 feet between 21.04 and 21.15. The overwhelming impression was of a concentrated attack, which left many fires burning and a glow in the sky reported by some to be visible from the North Sea homebound. At debriefing, crews across the Command reported terrific explosions among fires, which lit up the sky, and a pall of smoke was observed hanging above the dull, red centre of the conflagration. The operation cost the Command an acceptable fourteen aircraft, while post-raid reconnaissance revealed 160 acres of devastation and damage to fifty-three buildings within the Krupp district. The success of the operation was confirmed by local reports of 3,018 houses destroyed and more than two thousand others seriously damaged, and it was a most encouraging start to what would become a five-month-long offensive.

It would be a further week before round two of the Ruhr offensive was mounted, and in the meantime, Harris turned his attention upon southern Germany, beginning with Nuremberg on the 8th. A force of 338 aircraft included nineteen Halifaxes of 6 Group, the crews of which learned at briefing that zero hour was to be 23.15 and that three Path Finder Stirlings and two Halifaxes were to drop illumination flares across the target in two sticks by H2S, to be followed by six Stirlings and three Halifaxes dropping green TIs on the aiming-point, also by H2S, and employing additional flares if necessary. The remaining Path Finder marker crews were to back up with green TIs, unless cloud negated the illuminator flares, in which case red TIs were to be dropped by the H2S-equipped aircraft and backed up by the others with greens, and all Path Finder aircraft were to deliver yellow route markers on the way in and out. The nine-strong 408 (Goose) Squadron element departed Leeming between 19.06 and 19.14 with S/Ls Gilmore and Newson the senior pilots on duty and each Halifax carrying a 1,000-pounder, one 500-pounder and seven and four SBCs respectively of 4lb and 30lb incendiaries. Those reaching the target area had followed the yellow route markers and encountered clear skies with ground haze and extreme darkness. This seemed to impede the Path Finders' ability to locate the city centre blind by H2S, and the main force crews experienced the same difficulty in identifying ground detail, allowing themselves to be guided to the aiming point by a few red and green TIs, which appeared to lack concentration and soon burned out. The 408 (Goose) Squadron crews had predominantly red TIs in the bombsights but also a few scattered greens and carried out their attacks from 14,000 to 18,000 feet between 23.24 and 23.47. The initial impression was of a scattered raid, but a greater concentration of fires developed and the glow from these was reported by some to be visible for two hundred miles into the return journey. At debriefing, 83 Squadron's S/L Cooke reported that a cookie and yellow TIs had been jettisoned east of Heilbronn, some forty miles short of the target and accurately backed-up by other Path Finders. Inevitably, this would have drawn off other bomb loads, and local sources confirmed the marking and bombing of Nuremberg to have been spread along a ten-mile stretch, half of it falling short of the city boundaries, while the rest destroyed six hundred buildings and damaged fourteen hundred others, including a number of important war-industry factories.

On the following day, preparations were put in hand to return to southern Germany to attack the city of Munich, situated deep in the Bavarian mountains of south-eastern Germany, a round-trip of more than 1,200 miles. A force of 264 aircraft included a 6 Group contribution of eighteen Halifaxes, the nine made ready by 408 (Goose) Squadron at Leeming receiving a similar load as for the previous operation. The crews learned at briefing that white TIs were to be dropped by the Path Finders as route markers to aid the main force crews, and white and green flares over the northern tip of the Ammersee, a large lake situated some twenty miles to the west-south-west of the city centre, which the 5 Group crews, in particular, would use as the starting point for their time-and-distance runs. Nine Stirlings and four Halifaxes were to ground mark by H2S with red TIs at the same time as releasing white flares, and four Lancasters were to drop flares also if required, and then join with eleven Lancasters and four Halifaxes to back up with green TIs. The 408 (Goose) Squadron element took off between 19.51 and 20.06 with S/L Newson the senior pilot on duty and lost the services of Sgt Reynolds and crew some two hours into the outward flight through a fault in the feed to the overload fuel tanks.

The others reached the target area, where clear skies and good visibility prevailed, and the Path Finder green and white TIs could be seen to have fallen within the built-up area. An enormous orange explosion occurred in a south-western district as crews were carrying out their timed runs to the aiming point from the Ammersee, and those from 408 (Goose) Squadron had the TIs in the bomb sights as they released their loads from 12,000 to 18,500 feet between 00.17 and 00.46. Another huge explosion at 00.25 lit up the sky for twenty seconds and illuminated an area of ground with a ten-mile radius, described by some as the largest they had experienced, and another particularly large one occurred at 00.43. Fires were taking hold and sending a large pall of smoke rising above the city as the bomber force withdrew to the west, and one 5 Group crew counted eighteen blazes in or close to the city centre. A post-raid analysis concluded that a strong wind had pushed the attack into the western half of the city, where 291 buildings had been destroyed and 660 severely damaged, and this was in exchange for the relatively modest failure to return of eight aircraft. The aero-engine assembly shop at the B.M.W factory was put out of action for six weeks, and many other industrial concerns also lost vital production.

The trio of operations to destinations in southern Germany concluded with the highly industrial city of Stuttgart, a major centre before the war of car production and now home to many war industry companies including Robert Bosch and I G Farben. A force of 314 aircraft was assembled on the 11th, 6 Group contributing thirty-five Halifaxes, the number bolstered by the return to the fray of 405 (Vancouver) Squadron. Briefings revealed that the Path Finders were to deliver flares and red TIs by H2S across the aiming point, and that these were to be backed up visually with green TIs. At Leeming, take-off was accomplished safely between 19.09 and 19.17 with F/L Boosey the senior pilot on duty and a load of a single 2,000-pounder, four 1,000-pounders and a 500-pounder. They crossed the English coast over Eastbourne, heading for the French coast near Dieppe, before pushing on across France to enter Germany in the Strasbourg area with Stuttgart fifty miles straight ahead. F/Sgt Blackhall's gunners tested their guns over the Channel and finding those in the rear turret to be wanting, turned back and were joined on the ground by Sgt Patry and crew who had been some two hours out when an engine issue ended their interest in proceedings. F/O Stewart RNZAF and his mixed RAF, RCAF and RNZAF crew were outbound at 20,000 feet not far from the target when an engine on the port wing failed. Unable to maintain height, they jettisoned the bomb load close to the target and turned for home and were at 8,500 feet when attacked and shot down by a BF110. The Halifax was abandoned and crashed in the Haut-Marne region of north-east-central France and F/O Stewart, who was on his eighth sortie, and two others were taken into captivity, while four were spirited away by the Resistance network to evade a similar fate.

The main force element arrived late at the target because of inaccurately forecast winds and found excellent visibility but the Path Finder TIs already burning out on the ground. This left the way clear for dummy TIs to lure the bombing away from the city centre, and in this endeavour, they were largely successful, although to the bomb-aimers high above, the green TIs appeared to be legitimate and were bombed by the 408 (Goose) Squadron crews from 12,000 to 17,000 feet between 23.00 and 23.06. On the way home over France, F/Sgt Marment and crew were attacked by a BF110, whose cannon and machine-gun fire caused the port-inner and starboard-outer engines to fail, necessitating the jettisoning of all moveable equipment to maintain height over the Channel. On final approach to Langar the port-outer engine began to surge, and the flight ended with a wheels-up landing from which the crew walked away unscathed. According to local sources, most of the effort was wasted in open country but the south-western suburbs of Vaihingen and Kaltental were hit and 118 buildings, mostly houses, were destroyed. It was a disappointing outcome, which cost eleven aircraft, five of them belonging to 6 Group and four of those were from 405 (Vancouver) Squadron, three containing eight-man crews.

Round two of the Ruhr campaign was posted on the 12th, when 457 crews learned at briefing that Essen was once more to be their destination with a time-on-target for the Path Finders of 21.15. They were to adopt the northern route to the Ruhr, and sixteen Path Finders were to ground mark the town of Dorsten with white TIs as a track guide before backing up the Mosquito-borne Oboe red TIs with greens to provide the main force crews with a solid aiming point. 6 Group detailed twenty-three Halifaxes and sixty-seven Wellingtons, of which eight of the former were provided by 408 (Goose) Squadron and took off from Leeming between 19.10 and 19.26 with W/C Ferris and S/L Gilmore the senior pilots on duty and three 1,000-pounders and mix of 4lb and 30lb incendiaries in each bomb bay. P/O Carver's escape hatch blew open and jammed, making it impossible for him and his crew to continue, and they returned to base some three hours after leaving it to be joined on the ground soon afterwards by S/L Gilmore and crew who had been let down by their intercom system.

The others reached the target to find fierce fires already burning beneath clear skies, the smoke from which combined with industrial haze to blot out ground detail. Oboe rendered this of little consequence as the red and green Path Finder TIs identified the aiming point for the 408 (Goose) Squadron crews to attack from 7,000 to 18,500 feet between 21.20 and 21.30, the low height that of Sgt Childers and crew, who were coned over the target and delivered their load as they dived from 17,500 to 1,500 feet to escape the beams. DT790 had been damaged by flak and when on final approach to land, both port engines cut, causing the Halifax to yaw violently and crash at

00.47 short of the airfield, happily without injury to F/O Hatle and his crew. At debriefings crews again expressed confidence in the quality of their work and many reported the glow from the burning city to be visible from the Dutch coast. It was clear that the bombing was accurate and mostly concentrated around the Oboe-laid TIs, and this time, the Krupp complex found itself in the centre of the area of destruction. The defences fought back to claim twenty-three bombers, in return for which, according to post-raid reconnaissance, another highly successful assault on this centre of war production had been achieved. In fact, substantially fewer buildings had been destroyed, but a greater concentration of bombs had inflicted 30% more damage on Krupp than the raid of a week earlier.

Later that morning the crews of F/L Boosey and Sgt Reynolds took off to carry out a sea search for ditched crews and returned after three hours with nothing to report. Following the commitment of eighteen Wellingtons on mining duties on the 13th, 6 Group stood down for a week during a spell of adverse weather, and during this lull on the 14th, 1659 Heavy Conversion Unit moved out of Leeming for a new home at Topcliffe, allowing 405 (Vancouver) Squadron to move in the opposite direction for what would be a brief period of residence at Leeming.

It was the 22nd before orders came through to prepare for the next assault on St-Nazaire, for which a force of 357 aircraft was assembled, including a contribution from 6 Group of thirty-eight Halifaxes, fifteen of them belonging to 408 (Goose) Squadron. Each was loaded with two 1,000-pounders and nine and four SBCs respectively of 4lb and 30lb incendiaries before departing Leeming between 18.27 and 18.47 with S/L Gilmore and F/L Gamble the senior pilots on duty. At some point, 3 Group sent out a recall signal, to which fifty-five Stirling crews responded, leaving just eight to continue on to the target. The bomber stream flew out over Portland Bill and all from 408 (Goose) Squadron reached the target area to find clear skies and moonlight that enabled the port and docks to be identified visually aided by the abundance of red and green TIs. The 408 (Goose) Squadron crews delivered their bombs from 14,500 to 18,500 feet between 21.41 and 22.00 and contributed to an accurate and concentrated attack, which left the town and port areas in flames and massively damaged.

Duisburg was selected as the host for the third operation of the Ruhr offensive, for which a force of 455 aircraft was assembled, 6 Group detailing thirty Halifaxes and eighty-six Wellingtons, although not all would take off. The crews learned at briefing that the Oboe Mosquitos were to drop warning flares five and two-and-a-half minutes before the aiming-point, and then employ the "Musical Wanganui" marking method, the code for Oboe skymarking, releasing red flares with green stars at regular intervals thereafter. Ten 408 (Goose) Squadron Halifaxes each received a bomb load of two 1,000-pounders and six and seven SBCs respectively of 4lb and 30lb incendiaries before departing Leeming between 19.03 and 19.11 with F/Ls Boosey and Gamble the senior pilots on duty. There were no early returns as they made their way to the target area, where they found ten-tenths cloud with tops at 10,000 feet and good visibility above. They were greeted by the Oboe release-point parachute flares, which were in the bomb sights as the 408 (Goose) Squadron crews dropped their loads from 15,000 to 19,500 feet between 21.46 and 22.00, and a large explosion was witnessed at 21.53. What the crews couldn't know, was that five of the Oboe Mosquitos had returned early with equipment failure and a sixth had been shot down, leaving just three to deliver what could be only sparse marking. This was insufficient and led to a scattered and ineffective attack, which, according to local reports, caused only minor damage. Fortunately, the failure cost a modest six aircraft, three of them 6 Group Wellingtons.

Orders were received on stations across the Command on the 27th to prepare for a trip to the "Big City" that night, and a force of 396 aircraft was duly assembled. At briefings, the Path Finder crews were told of their part in the plan, which required eleven Stirlings and eight Halifaxes to drop green route marker flares and yellow warning flares by H2S, before marking the aiming-point with red TIs for two Stirlings, five Halifaxes and twenty-one Lancasters to back up with green TIs. In the event of cloud blotting out the ground, skymarking would be employed. 6 Group contributed thirty-one Halifaxes, eleven of them made ready by 408 (Goose) Squadron, which each received a bomb load of two 1,000-pounders and five SBCs each of 4lb and 30lb incendiaries, before departing Leeming between 19.50 and 20.02 with no senior pilots on duty. The route took them from the Yorkshire coast across the North Sea to make landfall between the Frisian Islands of Texel and Vlieland and then on a course a little north of Hannover to a point to the south-west of the capital for the run-in to the intended city-centre aiming-point. F/Sgt Blackhall and crew were afflicted by severe icing and turned back from a position some seventy miles out over the sea, leaving the others to press on in the bosom of the bomber stream. The Path Finders were reliant upon H2S and established two areas of marking, both well short, and the main force crews had little choice but to aim for them. There was the usual discrepancy in the reported cloud state of zero to nine-tenths as the 408 (Goose) Squadron crews tracked in across yellow TIs and carried out their attacks from 14,000 to 20,000 feet between 23.00 and 23.25. From bombing altitude, the attack appeared to be effective but local reports confirmed that the main weight of bombs had fallen between seven and seventeen miles short of the target, and 25% of those hitting the city had failed to detonate. What might be considered a modest nine aircraft failed to return, among them 408 (Goose) Squadron's BB332, which had been hit by flak in the Hannover defence zone on the way to the target, and sustained damage to both port engines and a fuel tank. A course was set to Sweden, where the Halifax was crash-landed at Blindberg and Sgt Batchelor and his crew handed themselves over to the authorities to enjoy the legendary hospitality of their hosts under internment until being returned to England in April.

There would be an opportunity to rectify the failure two nights hence, but in the meantime, St-Nazaire would face its third heavy assault under the January Directive, for which a force of 323 aircraft was made ready on the 28th. 6 Group detailed fifteen Halifaxes and ninety-two Wellingtons, with just the freshman crews of Sgt Jennings and P/O Cavanaugh representing 408 (Goose) Squadron and departing Leeming at 19.29 and 19.32 respectively, each sitting on two 1,000-pounders and assortment of 4lb and 30lb incendiaries. They encountered good visibility in the target area and benefitted from red and green Oboe-laid TIs marking out the aiming point as they delivered their attacks from 16,500 and 17,000 feet at 22.19 and 22.22. Returning crews reported concentrated fires, and post-raid reconnaissance confirmed the accuracy and effectiveness of the raid.

The month's final operation was posted on the 29th, when the red tape on the briefing-room wall maps ended again at Berlin. A force of 329 aircraft was made ready, of which twenty-three Halifaxes were provided by 6 Group, ten of them representing 408 (Goose) Squadron, while 149 Wellingtons, seventy-five belonging to 6 Group, were prepared for an attack on Bochum in the central Ruhr. The plan for the main event required all Path Finder aircraft to drop yellow route markers at predetermined points, and the marker crews to illuminate the Müggelsee to the south-east of Berlin with sticks of white flares and bundles of green flares with red stars by H2S, before they and the backers-up carried out a DR run to the aiming-point to deliver red TIs. The 408 (Goose) Squadron contingent departed Leeming between 21.27 and 21.55 with S/L Newson and F/Ls Boosey and Gamble the senior pilots on duty and crossed the English coast over Flamborough Head on course for Mandø Island off Jutland's western coast. They met bad weather in the form of heavy ice-bearing cloud and static electricity extending from the North Sea to the Baltic, which forced many crews to turn for home, among them fifteen belonging to 6 Group, eighteen from 5 Group and a massive twenty-four from 4 Group. Eight of the 408 (Goose) Squadron crews turned back between 22.24 and 23.15 after jettisoning their loads and landed between 23.41 and 01.10, leaving the freshman crews of P/O Cavanaugh and Sgt Jennings in DT679 and HR654 respectively unaccounted for. It would be learned later that the former had crashed on Stapelmoor on the outskirts of the town of Leer, located on the River Ems to the south-east of Emden, without survivors, while the latter had been shot down by a night-fighter and had come down at 00.36 seven miles south-south-east of Flensburg on Germany's Baltic coast with just two survivors. The wireless operator, Sgt Cherry, was severely injured and died six hours after being admitted to hospital and the bomb-aimer was taken into captivity. Both pilots were on their third sorties and their crews on their second.

The rest of the force, meanwhile, had continued on across Jutland and traversed Kiel Bight and Mecklenburg Bay, before crossing the German coast between Wismar and Rostock on track for the "Big City", where good visibility enabled them to identify the Müggelsee to the south-east of the city as a reference point from which to run in on the aiming-point. The Path Finders were again short with their marking, and the main force arrived late after some of the markers had already burned themselves out. The bombing was carried out in the face of a heavy searchlight and flak defence and crews set off for home in the belief that the fires they had left behind, the glow from which was still visible from 150 miles away, indicated that an effective attack had been delivered. In fact, as an analysis of the operation revealed, most of the bombing had been wasted in open country to the south-east of the city, and an accurate figure for damage was not forthcoming. In return for this failure, the Command lost twenty-one aircraft, three belonging to 6 Group, in addition to which, nine 6 Group Wellingtons were missing from the Bochum raid.

During the course of the month, the squadron took part in a dozen operations and dispatched 116 sorties for the loss of six Halifaxes and five crews, one of which was on extended leave in Sweden and would return.

April 1943

April would be the least rewarding month during the Ruhr offensive, principally because of the number of operations directed at targets in regions of Germany beyond the range of Oboe. On the 2nd, orders were received to prepare for the final raids on St-Nazaire and Lorient that night, which would bring down the curtain on the January directive. Forces of fifty-five and forty-seven aircraft were made ready with four Halifaxes and five Wellingtons of 6 Group included in the former, the 408 (Goose) Squadron crews of F/Sgt Leaver and P/O Smuck departing Leeming at 19.44 and 19.46 respectively, each sitting on eight 1,000-pounders. Conditions in the target area were favourable with good visibility and a little ground haze, that facilitated a visual identification of the target aided by green Path Finder TIs. The 408 (Goose) Squadron duo delivered their attacks from 14,000 feet at 22.24 and 22.34 in the face of heavy and accurate flak and no results were observed. Both St-Nazaire and Lorient had long since been abandoned by the civilian populations and the outcome of the raids was not commented upon by local sources.

The next round of the Ruhr campaign was announced across the Command on the 3rd, when Essen was posted as the target for the third time and a force of 348 aircraft made ready. The heavy brigade consisted of 225 Lancasters and 113 Halifaxes, twenty-two of the former representing 6 Group, and this would be the first occasion on which more than two hundred Lancasters had operated against a single target. The Path Finder contribution amounted to ten Oboe Mosquitos and twenty Lancasters from 83 and 156 Squadrons, the crews of which were to identify the Krupp complex as the aiming-point, and in the event of cloud, skymark it with coloured flares, or if clear skies prevailed, ground mark with red TIs. The twelve-strong 408 (Goose) Squadron element departed Leeming between 19.44 and 19.56 with S/L Newson the senior pilot on duty and a bomb load of two 1,000-pounders and seven and six SBCs respectively of 4lb and 30lb incendiaries. They joined the bomber stream over the North Sea on their way to make landfall on the Dutch coast near Haarlem and uncomfortably close to the Amsterdam defences. Sgt Childers became unwell and was unable to continue after an hour or so, while the others pressed on to find almost clear skies over the Ruhr region and the anticipated industrial haze negated by the accuracy of the Oboe markers falling around the aiming-point.

The attack began slowly, some crews apparently confused by the employment of both sky and ground markers on a clear night, but it built to a crescendo, during which a massive explosion was observed by many crews in the centre of the bombing. The 408 (Goose) Squadron crews attacked from 15,000 to 19,000 feet between 21.55 and 22.15, aiming mostly at the TIs burning on the ground and many explosions were witnessed, with fires emitting large volumes of smoke. F/Sgt Wood RCAF and crew were unable to lower their undercarriage and DT673 was belly-landed at base at 02.07 and written off, although the crew emerged from the wreckage unscathed. Its dispersal pan would soon find another occupant, as would those of the two other 408 (Goose) Squadron absentees and two belonging to 405 (Vancouver) Squadron, and the loss to the Goose Squadron of two experienced crews would be keenly felt. HR713 disappeared without trace with the mixed RCAF, RAF and RAAF crew of F/L Gamble, while JB866 was shot down by a night-fighter and crashed in central Holland fifteen miles east of Arnhem at 22.45 with no survivors from the crew of P/O Sirett RCAF. The pilots had been on their seventeenth and tenth sorties respectively. At debriefings, many crews reported the glow from the burning city to be still visible from the Dutch coast homebound and the consensus was of a successful raid. This was confirmed by bombing photographs and local reports, which spoke of widespread destruction in central and western districts, where 635 buildings had been reduced to rubble and many more seriously damaged. The searchlight and flak defence had been intense, and it became an expensive night for the Command, which registered the loss of a dozen Halifaxes and nine Lancasters. This represented 6% of those dispatched, but it was the respective loss rates of the types that was most telling, with the Halifaxes suffering 10.62% compared with 4% for the Lancasters.

The largest non-1,000 force to date of 577 aircraft was made ready on the 4th for an attack that night on the naval and shipbuilding port of Kiel, for which 6 Group detailed twenty-three Halifaxes and 106 Wellingtons. Ten of the former belonged to 408 (Goose) Squadron, whose crews learned at briefing that the plan of attack called for a time-on-target of 23.00 and for yellow TIs to be dropped by the Path Finders as route markers, before the H2S marker crews in ten Stirlings and six Halifaxes illuminated the aiming-point with flares and marked it with red TIs. Two Stirlings, five Halifaxes and fifteen Lancasters were then to back up with green TIs, leaving two of each type to bomb with the main force. The 408 (Goose) Squadron contingent departed Leeming between 20.57 and 21.14 with W/C Ferris and S/L Gilmore the senior pilots on duty and two 1,000-pounders and eight and seven SBCs respectively of 4lb and 30lb incendiaries in each bomb bay. The headed out over Flamborough Head on course for Jutland's western coast, which might have been reached by F/Sgt Leaver and crew by the time that their DR compass failed and ended their interest in proceedings. Sgt Milligan and crew were probably even further into the outward flight when let down by the rear turret, and as they turned back towards the west the others closed on the target area, where they were guided towards the aiming point by yellow route marker flares, released by the Path Finder heavy brigade either side of 23.00. Kiel was found to be concealed beneath ten-tenths cloud with good visibility above, and the high explosives and incendiaries were released by the 408 (Goose) Squadron participants from estimated positions onto the glow of fires below the cloud from 13,000 to 18,000 feet between 23.29 and 23.35. Among twelve missing aircraft was 408 (Goose) Squadron's BB336, which was hit by flak and exploded over the sea, killing S/L Gilmore DFC RCAF and all but the rear gunner, Sgt Wiggett RCAF, who drifted on his parachute to reach land and was taken into captivity. Whether this occurred over the Waddensee or the Baltic has not been established. S/L Gilmore was on his nineteenth sortie and his crew members between their tenth and twenty-third. It was not possible to assess the outcome of the raid, and as bombing photos revealed only cloud, it was left to a post-raid analysis to conclude that decoy fires had been operating and had probably lured away a proportion of the effort, while the strong wind caused the markers to drift, leading the remainder astray and resulting in most of the bombs missing the target altogether. According to local reports, only eleven houses were destroyed, and this was a major disappointment in view of the size of the force involved.

On the 5th, 405 (Vancouver) Squadron was notified of its impending transfer to the Path Finder Force, the move to Gransden Lodge to be completed by the 19th. In the meantime, ten Halifaxes were dispatched from Leeming to undertake mining duties in the Cinnamon garden off the Biscay port of La Pallice/La Rochelle, the 408 (Goose) Squadron crews of P/O Smuck, W/O Guay, F/Sgt Leaver and Sgt Milligan taking off between 20.40 and 20.47. All arrived in the target area to pinpoint on the Ile-de-Re in favourable conditions and good visibility and planted their two vegetables each from 700 to 900 feet between 23.27 and 23.50 before returning safely to land on the 8 Group airfield at Oakington.

The Ruhr offensive continued at Duisburg on the 8th in an operation involving a mixed main force element of 379 Lancasters, Wellingtons, Halifaxes and Stirlings, while ten Oboe Mosquitos would provide the initial marking, backed up by the Path Finder heavy brigade consisting of four Stirlings, twenty Lancasters and eight Halifaxes. 6 Group contributed fifteen Halifaxes and sixty Wellingtons, just four of the former representing 408 (Goose) Squadron, which departed Leeming between 21.35 and 21.59, bearing aloft the crews of F/Sgts Blackhall and Grant and Sgts Greig and Troy and the same high explosive and incendiary bomb loads as for Kiel. They rendezvoused with the bomber stream after beginning the North Sea crossing at the Norfolk coast and had to climb through ten-tenths ice-bearing cloud before breaking into clear air at 12,000 feet. It was at this stage that Sgt Greig and crew turned back, leaving the others to make landfall at Egmond with a time-on-target set for 23.15, before which, the ten Oboe Mosquitos were to drop red warning flares and then greens with red stars and green TIs over the aiming-point. If the weather conditions permitted, one Stirling, seven Halifaxes and fourteen Lancasters would back up with red TIs, while the remaining 8 Group aircraft supported the main force. The bomber stream reached the western Ruhr to encounter ten-tenths cloud with tops in places as high as 20,500 feet, such conditions completely nullifying the Path Finders' attempts to mark either the route or the target, and the bombing had to be carried out on e.t.a., some crews embarking on a time-and-distance run from as far away as the Dutch coast as the last visual reference. The 408 (Goose) Squadron trio attacked from 20,000 feet between 23.28 and 23.53 and had nothing of value to pass on to the intelligence section at debriefing. Absent from that process were nineteen crews, in return for the loss of which, local sources confirmed a widely scattered raid that hit at least fifteen other Ruhr locations and destroyed just forty buildings in Duisburg.

Not content with the outcome, Harris ordered another raid twenty-four hours later, only this time employing a much-reduced force of 104 Lancasters and five Mosquitos. They were guided to the target by red route-marker flares and then red and green skymarkers over the aiming point, which was hidden by ten-tenths cloud with tops at 5,000 to 15,000 feet. Some crews observed a large red glow reflected in the clouds, but local sources confirmed that this was another highly scattered raid, which spread bombs over a wide area of the Ruhr and destroyed only fifty houses in Duisburg.

Frankfurt was posted as the destination on the 10th for 502 aircraft, of which the 144 Wellingtons would represent the most populous type, demonstrating that this trusty old warhorse still had an important part to play in Bomber Command operations. 6 Group provided eighty-eight of the Wellingtons along with twenty-five Halifaxes, eight of the latter belonging to 408 (Goose) Squadron and departing Leeming between 23.35 and 23.45 with F/L Boosey the senior pilot on duty and the same bomb loads as for the previous operations. The plan was standard for a target beyond the range of Oboe and required eleven Stirlings and six Halifaxes to drop yellow TIs as route markers by H2S, followed by preliminary warning flares, all of which were to be backed up by two Stirlings, ten Halifaxes and seventeen Lancasters. Cloud conditions permitting, the aiming-point was then to be marked by red TIs on H2S, and if not, by green flares with red stars and a white flare, with appropriate backing up with green TIs or coloured flares. The freshman crew of Sgt Dungey mistakenly adopted a false course for twenty-two minutes and by the time the error was realised, it was too late to make up time and the sortie was abandoned. The bomber stream adopted the usual course to this region of Germany, following the line of the Franco/Belgian frontier to cross into Germany on an east-north-easterly heading north of Saarbrücken. The H2S marker crews arrived in the target area to be confronted by ten-tenths cloud with tops at between 8,000 and 12,000 feet but found that their red TIs were visible and opted not to sky mark. This was fine in the early stages, until it became impossible to distinguish the genuine TIs from decoys, incendiaries and searchlights, and the backer-up crews experienced great difficulty in establishing an aiming-point. The 408 (Goose) Squadron crews went in at 13,000 to 18,000 feet between 02.57 and 03.11, having been guided by preliminary warning flares, and some bombed at whatever was glowing beneath the cloud or on e.t.a., without being able to assess the outcome. Bombing photos revealed nothing but cloud, and local sources confirmed that only a few bombs had fallen into the southern suburbs.

On the 13th, 208 Lancaster and three Halifax crews of 1, 5 and 8 Groups were notified of a change of scenery for their next operation, which was to be against the docks at La Spezia on Italy's northern coast some forty miles south-east of Genoa. Crews established their positions by visual reference of ground detail, such as rivers and the docks, confirmed by Path Finder flares and bombed from medium level. Three large vessels observed tied together east of the outer harbour were seen to be on fire, and the naval oil stores were targeted by some crews. By the later stages of the raid, many fires had added to the smoke obscuring the town, and a number of large explosions encouraged the crews' belief that a successful operation had taken place, which, ultimately, would be confirmed.

The busy round of non-Ruhr operations continued with the posting of Stuttgart as the target on the 14th, for which a force of 462 aircraft was made ready, 6 Group providing twenty-eight Halifaxes and eighty-five Wellingtons, ten of the former made ready by 408 (Goose) Squadron and given the standard bomb load. At briefing, the crews took in the details of the plan, which involved Path Finder aircraft dropping yellow TIs as route markers at two locations, while at the target, nine Stirlings and eight Halifaxes were to ground mark the aiming-point with red TIs on H2S, at the same time as releasing a short stick of flares. One Stirling and four Lancasters were then to identify the aiming-point visually, and mark it with green TIs for three Stirlings, six Halifaxes and eleven Lancasters to back up also with greens. This would leave three Stirlings, three Halifaxes and five Lancasters to bolster the efforts of the main force. The 408 (Goose) Squadron participants departed Leeming between 21.22 and 21.51 with S/L Newson the senior pilot on duty, but he and his crew were forced to return within two hours because of an unserviceable rear turret. An hour after they landed, P/O Smuck and crew joined them having been unable to achieve the engine performance necessary to complete the sortie. The bomber stream followed the Franco/Belgian frontier and passed beyond Luxembourg to enter Germany in the Strasbourg area before approaching the city from the north-east to find an absence of cloud. The Path Finder ground marker crews established their positions by H2S confirmed by visual reference, but as evidence of the shortcomings of H2S in its early form, they were actually short of the city centre when they delivered bundles of white flares, red TIs and 1,000-pounders between 00.47 and 00.56. The backers-up were carrying four green TIs, one of them of the long-burning variety, four 1,000-pounders and a single 500-pounder each, which they dropped between 00.50 and 01.14, also to the north-east of the planned aiming-point.

The main force crews were greeted by plentiful red and green TIs concentrated in a built-up area, and some would claim later to have picked out ground details such as marshalling yards, the railway station, the river and the Bosch factory through the copious volumes of smoke rising through 8,000 feet. This reinforced their belief that they were over the briefed aiming-point, where the TIs had mostly burned out by the time that the 408 (Goose) Squadron crews delivered their attacks on concentrations of fire from 15,000 to 19,000 feet between 01.10 and 01.31, and there was little information to glean and pass on at debriefing. On the way home over north-east-central France, F/O Sergent and crew survived an attack by a night-fighter, which was driven off by return fire, while some seventy miles closer to home, JB909 was brought down by a night-fighter to crash at 03.15 on the north-western outskirts of Reims. The pilot, P/O Mackenzie RAAF, lost his life on what was his twentieth sortie, while six of the other seven members of the experienced mixed RCAF and RAF crew fell into enemy hands and Sgt Canter, who was gaining experience as second pilot, managed to evade a similar fate. Even closer to home, BB311 fell to the guns of a night-fighter and crashed some nine miles south of St-Quentin, killing the single RAF member of the otherwise all RCAF freshman crew of P/O Usher, who were taken into captivity. It was the pilot's third sortie and the first for all but one of his crew. In all twenty-three aircraft failed to return, eight of them belonging to 6 Group. Bombing photos and post-raid reconnaissance confirmed that the Path Finders had not marked the centre of the city, and that a "creep-back" had developed, which had spread along the line of approach.

Creep-back was a feature of many large raids and was caused by crews bombing the first fires they came upon, rather than pushing through to the planned aiming-point. It could work for or against the effectiveness of an attack, and on this night worked in the Command's favour by falling across the industrial district of Bad-Canstatt, situated to the north-east of the city centre on the East Bank of the River Neckar. The bombing continued to spread further back along the line of approach onto the residential suburbs of Münster and Mühlhausen, and it was here that the majority of the 393 buildings were destroyed and more than nine hundred others severely damaged.

Two major operations were planned for the 16th, the main event employing 327 Lancasters and Halifaxes to target the Skoda armaments factory at distant Pilsen in Czechoslovakia, while a force of 271 aircraft, consisting predominantly of Wellingtons and Stirlings, created a large-scale diversion at Mannheim some 240 miles to the west. A force of 197 Lancasters and 130 Halifaxes was detailed for Pilsen, of which twenty-seven of the latter were provided by 6 Group in the absence now of 405 (Vancouver) Squadron, which had been stood down while it transferred to 8 Group. In an unnecessarily complicated plan, the Path Finders were to drop yellow route markers at the final turning point, seven miles from the target, which the main force crews were to then locate visually in the anticipated bright moonlight and bomb from as low a level as practicable. The plan briefed out to the Path Finder crews was more detailed and seems to have contained elements that were not part of the main force briefings. It called for six 35 (Madras Presidency) Squadron crews to employ H2S to drop long sticks of flares from south-west to north-east across the city and green TIs on the south-western edge of the Skoda works as a rough guide. These were to be backed up by green TIs delivered by two Halifaxes and twenty Lancasters, unless cloud conditions rendered this impossible, in which case, red TIs were to be employed by both the markers and backers-up. Two further Halifaxes and five Lancasters were to attack with the main force. It was a plan of attack that invited confusion and failure, and the outcome would question the quality of some of the briefings.

At Leeming, a dozen Halifaxes each received a bomb load of four 1,000-pounders and two SBCs each of 4lb and 30lb incendiaries, before taking off between 20.56 and 21.11 with S/L Newson the senior pilot on duty and a roundtrip of some 1,500 miles to negotiate. They headed for Dungeness on the Kent coast to make landfall on the French coast in the area of Cayeux-sur-Mer, before swinging round Amiens and tracking eastwards towards the German frontier near Saarbrücken. There were no early returns to Leeming, and on arrival in the target area crews found the forecast favourable weather conditions, with a layer of eight-tenths cloud at around 9,000 feet. The visibility beneath the cloud was good with ground features apparently standing out in bright moonlight, and the 408 (Goose) Squadron crews delivered their bomb loads onto what they believed were the factory buildings from 7,000 to 12,000 feet between 01.42 and 01.58 in the face of copious amounts of smoke and dust.

The briefings should have made clear that the bombing was to be carried out visually from below the cloud base after making a timed run from the turning-point, which had been marked by yellow TIs. Many crews reported bombing on TIs, proving that they had failed to understand and comply with the instructions at briefing and had bombed the turning point instead of the target. Some made reference to yellow and green TIs and white illuminator flares, and many described difficulties in locating and identifying the factory buildings, some after spending time searching while having to dodge searchlights and flak. The details of the crew reports across the groups demonstrated that they could not have related to the Skoda works. Post-raid reconnaissance revealed the truth, that despite the claims of returning crews, no bombs had fallen within miles of the factory and had been concentrated instead around an asylum at Dobrany, some seven miles to the south-west. This failure was compounded by the loss of thirty-six aircraft, split equally between the two types, and this represented a massive 11% of the force.

It was a sobering night for Leeming, which had four empty dispersal pans to contemplate in the cold light of dawn. JB925 crashed into a wood between Bierfeld and Nonnweiler some eighteen miles south-east of Trier close to Germany's frontier with Luxembourg and there were no survivors from the eight-man predominantly Canadian crew of F/L Hatle RCAF, who was on his fifteenth sortie. JB854 came down nine miles north-west of Bar-le-Duc in the Grande-Est region of eastern France with fatal consequences for Sgt Heming RCAF and his crew, the pilot on his second sorties and most of the others on their first. BB343 had reached the Laon area of north-eastern France on the homeward flight when crashing at Liesse, some ten miles north-east of the city, with no survivors from the crew of W/O Guay RCAF, who was on his fifteenth sortie and flying with a freshman crew. DT752 was shot down by the night-fighter of Hptm Ludwig Meister of 1./NJG4 and crashed at 04.08 at Nassogne in south-eastern Belgium, killing F/O Sergent RCAF and his mixed RCAF and RAF crew. The pilot was on his ninth sortie and his crew were only a little less experienced.

The losses from Pilsen had to be added to the eighteen aircraft also missing from the Mannheim contingent, to which 6 Group had contributed ninety Wellingtons and lost five, but, at least the destruction of 130 buildings had been achieved along with damage to some degree to three thousand others. The combined casualty figure of fifty-four aircraft represented a new record for a single night.

A return to the docks at La Spezia was notified to the Lancaster squadrons of 1, 5 and 8 Groups on the 18th, and 8 Group would also contribute five Halifaxes to the overall force of 178 aircraft. The aiming point was identified visually after a timed run from Palmaria Island to the south, and confirmed by red Path Finder TIs, on which the main force bombed from medium level, setting off fires that were becoming concentrated as they turned away and set course for home, completely satisfied with their night's work. Photographic reconnaissance revealed that the marking and bombing had fallen to the north-west of the dockyards but had caused extensive damage to the railway station and public buildings in the town centre.

On the 20th, 339 crews attended briefings to learn of their part in that night's operation to Stettin, the port city situated 650 miles from the bomber stations as the crow flies and at the midpoint of Germany's wartime Baltic coast. The force included twenty-one Halifaxes representing 6 Group, and as they were being prepared for battle, their crews were devouring the details of the route that would take the bomber stream across the North Sea to a point north of Esbjerg on the Danish coast, before traversing Jutland to then head south-east towards the target. The distance, which was similar to that for Pilsen, would keep some crews in the air for more than nine hours, and would require a small reduction in bombs among the main force element in favour of fuel. Navigation by coastline was expected to be simple in the prevailing conditions, which negated the need for route markers, and once illuminating flares had laid bare the aiming point, the marking would be by H2S-based red TIs backed up by greens. The eight-strong 408 (Goose) Squadron element departed Leeming between 21.11 and 21.18 with W/C Ferris the senior pilot on duty, and a single 1,000 and 500-pounder in each bomb bay along with four and five SBCs respectively of 4lb and 30lb incendiaries. They headed out over Flamborough Head to rendezvous over the North Sea with the rest of the bomber stream and completed the outward flight under clear skies which persisted all the way to the target, where they benefitted from bright moonlight and horizontal visibility estimated to be fifty miles. Crews were able to identify ground features as they bore down on the aiming point and the Leeming crews bombed on green TIs from 12,000 to 17,000 feet between 01.06 and 01.45. The last time was that of Sgt Greig and crew who appear to have been delayed and would land forty minutes after most of their colleagues, and even then, landed forty minutes ahead of the very last to arrive back at Leeming, Sgt Johannesson and crew after more than ten hours aloft.

There were targets, like Duisburg and later, Braunschweig, that for a period at least, seemed to enjoy something of a charmed life and managed to dodge the worst ravages of a Bomber Command attack, but Stettin was not among them, perhaps because of its location on a river near an easily identifiable coastline. On this night, the perfect conditions paved the way for the Path Finders to deliver a flawless marking performance, which was exploited by the main force crews to devastating effect. Returning crews reported fires raging across the built-up area and the glow visible on the horizon for ninety miles into the return journey. It was thirty-six hours before a reconnaissance aircraft captured photographs of the still-burning city, and these revealed an area of one hundred acres of devastation across the centre. Local reports confirmed that thirteen industrial premises and 380 houses had been destroyed, in return for which Bomber Command lost twenty-one aircraft.

Orders on the 26th signalled a return to the Ruhr and Duisburg, for which a large force of 561 aircraft was assembled, the numbers bolstered by the inclusion of 135 Wellingtons, while 215 Lancasters represented the largest contribution by type. 8 Group was boosted by the operational debut of the recently transferred 97 (Straits Settlement) Squadron and 405 (Vancouver) Squadron RCAF in a plan that called for eight Oboe Mosquitos to drop yellow route markers and red TIs on the aiming-point. The yellows were to be backed up by others of the same colour delivered by a dozen Lancasters, while three Stirlings, five 35 (Madras Presidency) Squadron Halifaxes and seven Lancasters backed up at the aiming-point with green TIs. 6 Group was responsible for twenty-four Halifaxes and sixty-five Wellingtons, four of the former belonging to 408 (Goose) Squadron and containing the crews of S/L Newson, F/O Harriss and P/Os Smuck and Stovel, each sitting on two 1,000-pounders and seven SBCs each of 4lb and 30lb incendiaries. They departed Leeming between 00.55 and 01.02, and after climbing out, set course for the Dutch coast near The Hague for the northern approach to the Ruhr, losing the services of P/O Stovel and crew to oxygen system failure within ninety minutes. The others reached the target area after approaching from the north-east to find largely clear skies and good visibility and were guided to the aiming point by red and green TIs, upon which the bombing by the Leeming element was carried out from 15,500 to 16,500 feet between 02.50 and 02.55. A large orange explosion was witnessed to the east of the aiming point at 02.34, but fires had not fully gained a hold by the time that the force withdrew, although black smoke was rising through 7,000 feet. Opinions were divided as to the degree of concentration achieved, but what was not in doubt was the failure to return of seventeen aircraft. Post-raid reconnaissance revealed that the attack had fallen short of the city centre and had been focused on the north-eastern districts under the line of approach, thus sparing Duisburg yet again from the full weight of a Bomber Command heavy raid.

The 27th was devoted to the largest mining operation of the war to date, which involved 160 aircraft targeting the waters off the Brittany and Biscay coasts and the Frisians. 6 Group detailed nineteen Halifaxes and fifteen Wellingtons, nine of the former representing 408 (Goose) Squadron and departing Leeming between 01.30 and 01.38 bearing aloft freshman crews, among which the most senior pilot was the recently arrived flight commander elect, F/L Campbell DFC, who had served with the squadron in 1941 and was already seven sorties into his second tour when posted back. They were bound for the Nectarine I garden off the southern Frisians, where low cloud and poor visibility hampered attempts to locate a pinpoint for a timed run and two crews returned their mines to the dump. Of the others, five managed to establish themselves off the western tip of Terschelling, while two others relied upon a Gee-fix to deliver their mines from 700 to 3,500 feet between 03.20 and 03.40.

The following night brought an even larger gardening effort involving 207 aircraft, of which nineteen Halifaxes and eighteen Wellingtons were provided by 6 Group, the 408 (Goose) Squadron element of eleven freshman crews departing Leeming between 20.25 and 20.52 with F/L Campbell again the most senior pilot on duty. The destination for eight of them was the Silverthorn I garden in the Kattegat off Jutland's most northerly tip, where pinpoints were obtained under largely clear skies by eight crews on Hirtshal and Skaw, while three others established positions further south on the north-western tip of Anholt Island or Lim Fjord, which put them in the Hawthorn II garden. The vegetables were planted unopposed from 650 to 1,000 feet between 23.52 and 00.32 and all returned safely, most having been aloft for seven hours. Elsewhere in the Baltic, low cloud was encountered, and flak proved to be troublesome, contributing to the loss of twenty-two aircraft, which would prove to be the largest-ever loss to result in a single night from mining. On the credit side, the 593 mines planted in enemy shipping lanes was also a record for one night and would not be surpassed.

Essen was posted as the target on the 30th as attention swung once more towards the Ruhr and would remain upon it almost exclusively now until well into July. A force of 305 aircraft included twenty 6 Group Halifaxes, six of them at Leeming receiving a bomb load of two 1,000-pounders and six and seven SBCs respectively of 4lb and 30lb incendiaries. They took off between 23.55 and 23.59 with S/L Newson and F/L Campbell the senior pilots on duty and ran into a layer of ice-bearing cloud over the North Sea, which put such a strain on the engines of F/O Harriss's DT749 that they overheated even at minus 29 degrees at 21,000 feet and the sortie had to be aborted. Most crews negotiated the weather front to reach the target to be greeted by ten-tenths cloud with tops in places as high as 21,000 feet and red and green Oboe-laid Wanganui flares (skymarkers) identifying the aiming point. Some crews carried out a time-and-distance run from green tracking markers, and most of the 408 (Goose) Squadron crews had some kind of flare in the bomb sight, or at least the glow of one, as they released their loads from an average of 19,000 feet either side of 03.00. Returning crews reported the glow of fires beneath the cloud and a number of large explosions, but it was impossible to determine whether or not concentration had been achieved, particularly as bombing photos showed only cloud. Post-raid reconnaissance and local reports confirmed a lack of concentration and the liberal distribution of bombs onto ten other Ruhr locations, particularly Bottrop to the north, but 189 buildings had been destroyed and 237 severely damaged in Essen, and importantly, Krupp sites sustained further damage.

During the course of the month, the squadron took part in thirteen operations and dispatched ninety-two sorties for the loss of ten Halifaxes and nine crews.

May 1943

May would bring a return to winning ways, with a number of outstanding successes and new records as the Ruhr offensive expanded its horizons to include targets other than Essen and Duisburg. It was, in fact, Duisburg that was posted as the target for each of the first three nights of the new month, before the operations were cancelled. The first of the "new" targets was Dortmund, which had been attacked many times before, but not on the scale that it was about to face on the 4th, when the force of 596 aircraft represented the largest non-1,000 effort to date. 6 Group made available thirty-two Halifaxes and thirty-eight Wellingtons, fourteen of the former made ready at Leeming and receiving a bomb load each of two 1,000-pounders and six and seven SBCs respectively of 4lb and 30lb incendiaries, while their crews were being informed of the plan at briefing. They learned that Oboe Mosquitos were to drop yellow track markers, before eight of them ground-marked the aiming-point with green TIs, leaving two in reserve to bomb with the main force if not required for marking duties. Twenty-two Lancasters and two Halifaxes were to back up with red TIs, and all remaining Path Finder aircraft were to bomb with the main force.

The 408 (Goose) Squadron participants took off between 21.14 and 21.49 with W/C Ferris and the newly promoted S/L Campbell the senior pilots on duty and F/L Mair, a future commanding officer of the squadron, flying as second pilot with the present one. They flew out over the Yorkshire coast to rendezvous with the bomber stream over the North Sea and lost the services of Sgt Johnson and crew after the rear gunner found the doors to his turret to be jammed, preventing him access to his parachute in an emergency. The others pushed on across Holland to enter Germany to the north of the Ruhr and make their way to the eastern end, where they found clear skies, good visibility and only industrial and smoke haze to spoil the vertical view. Yellow Path Finder tracking skymarkers were used as the starting point for a timed run to the target, while the defences responded with many searchlight cones and intense heavy flak, and much evasive action would be required after bombing to vacate the target area intact.

The initial Path Finder marking was accurately placed around the city centre, but some of the backing-up fell short and a decoy site was also successful in luring away a proportion of the bombing. The 408 (Goose) Squadron crews aimed at red or green TIs from 18,000 to 21,000 feet between 01.05 and 01.36, and while the incumbent scribe failed to record all bombing times and heights, he left us with a range of heights from 14,000 to 19,500 feet and times between 01.10 and 01.35. On return, they reported many sizeable explosions, including a particularly large on at

01.12, which may have been the one reported by a 50 Squadron crew that threw flame to a height of 2,000 feet and burned for ten seconds. They also described developing fires, the glow from which could be seen, according to some, from 150 miles into the return flight. Absent from debriefing were the crews of Sgt Johannesson RCAF and F/Sgt Blackhall RCAF in HR658 and JB898 respectively, the former disappearing without trace to become the first all-Canadian crew to be lost by the squadron. The pilot was on his sixth sortie and his crew on their second to tenth. The latter was shot down by the night-fighter of Oblt Lothar Linke of IV./NJG1 and crashed at 00.52 a dozen or so miles south-south-east of the famed "Wespennest" (Wasps' Nest) Luftwaffe fighter aerodrome at Leeuwarden in northern Holland. The pilot, an American in the RCAF, who was on his fifteenth sortie, and two others lost their lives, while the five survivors were taken into captivity. The sortie tally of the crew before this operation ranged from one to twenty-seven. Post-raid reconnaissance revealed that approximately half of the force had bombed within three miles of the aiming point and had destroyed 1,218 buildings and seriously damaged more than two thousand others. Local reports confirmed a death toll of 693 people, which was a record from a Bomber Command attack. It was not a one-sided affair, however, and the loss of thirty-one aircraft was a foretaste of what was in store for the bomber crews operating over "Happy Valley".

There would be no major operations during the ensuing week, and on the 5th, 427 (Lion) Squadron completed its move from Croft to Leeming, which it would call home for the rest of the war. When the Command as a whole was next called into action, on the 12th, it was for a major assault on Duisburg, for which a heavy force of 562 aircraft was assembled. Nine Oboe Mosquitos were to drop yellow TIs on track as a preliminary warning and red TIs on the aiming-point, which would be backed up with green TIs by five Stirlings, five Halifaxes and twenty Lancasters. 6 Group detailed twenty Halifaxes and forty Wellingtons, nine of the former belonging to 408 (Goose) Squadron, which departed Leeming between 23.33 and 23.46 with S/Ls Campbell and Newson the senior pilots on duty and the standard squadron Ruhr load in each bomb bay. After climbing out over the station, they headed for the North Sea to rendezvous with the bomber stream and make landfall on the Dutch coast in the area of Castricum-aan-Zee. Sgt Brooke and crew were some twenty-five miles out when an electrical storm upset their P4 compass and persuaded them to turn back, while S/L Newson and crew were approaching the midpoint of the North Sea crossing when oxygen system failure ended their interest in proceedings. The others were guided to the target by the yellow tracking flares and found ideal bombing conditions with no cloud and good visibility, which helped the Oboe and H2S crews to mark with great accuracy and focus.

The main force crews were able to identify ground features and exploit the opportunity to produce a display of unusually concentrated bombing, those from 408 (Goose) Squadron delivering their attacks onto red and green TIs from 12,000 to 20,000 feet between 02.10 and 02.25. Perhaps, for the first time at this target, the attack proceeded according to plan, and Duisburg finally succumbed to a devastating assault. Returning crews described a large explosion at 02.30, streets outlined by fire and a highly successful outcome, the best yet witnessed by some, and their impressions were confirmed by photo-reconnaissance, which revealed extensive damage in the city centre and the Ruhrort Rhine docks, the largest inland port in Germany. 1,596 buildings were totally destroyed and the Thyssen steelworks was hit, while dozens of barges and ships were sunk or damaged. However, many crews were absent from debriefing at stations across the Command, and it soon became clear that the success had been gained at the high cost of thirty-four aircraft. The loss rates by type again made interesting reading and confirmed the established food chain, the Lancasters sustaining a 4.2% loss, compared with 8.9% for Wellingtons, 7.1% for Stirlings and 6.3% for Halifaxes. Such was the level of destruction that Duisburg would now be left in peace for a year.

On the following night, a 5 Group force of 124 Lancasters and thirty-two Lancasters and twelve Halifaxes of 8 Group was assembled to attempt to rectify the recent failure at the Skoda armaments works at Pilsen, while a simultaneous raid was planned against the Ruhr city of Bochum, another new target for the campaign, which would involve 442 aircraft from the other groups. 6 Group contributed twenty-seven Halifaxes and thirty-four Wellingtons, eleven of the former provided by 408 (Goose) Squadron and departing Leeming between 23.40 and 23.50 with S/L Campbell the senior pilot on duty and the standard war load in each bomb bay. S/L Campbell DFC and his crew were outbound at 11,000 feet and approaching landfall over the Scheldt estuary when JB931 was shot down into the sea off Vlissingen (Flushing) by a night-fighter, killing the pilot, flight engineer and both gunners, and delivering the three surviving crew members into enemy hands. S/L Campbell was on the twelfth sortie of his second tour, while most of the crew were on the thirteenth sortie of their first and mid-upper gunner, P/O Horne RAAF, was on his twenty-sixth. At about the same location off Walcheren, F/Sgt Taylor's rear gunner reported that his turret and guns had become unserviceable, and they had no choice but to turn back.

The others continued on under clear skies and in good visibility, guided initially from forty miles away by the fires already raging, then by tracking flares and finally red and green TIs cascading over the target. They carried out their attacks from 15,000 to 19,000 feet between 02.26 and 02.40 and observed the centre of the city to be engulfed in flames with smoke spiralling up through 10,000 feet as they turned away, confident that they had dealt a telling blow. F/O Smith and crew were the last from 408 (Goose) Squadron over the target and immediately after bombing, were coned for the second time by searchlights, which necessitated violent evasive action. During the next fifteen minutes they shed all but two hundred feet of their original 18,000 feet and discovered that the mid-upper gunner had taken the decision to bale out. It is believed that decoy markers were deployed and may have lured away a proportion of the bombing, despite which, according to local sources, 394 buildings were destroyed and 716 severely damaged at a cost to the Command of twenty-four bombers. The attack at Pilsen turned into another failure to damage the Skoda works and no further attempts would be made by Bomber Command.

The above operations proved to be the last major outings for the Path Finders and main force squadrons for nine days, and it was during this lull that 617 Squadron entered bomber folklore with its epic attack on the Ruhr Dams under Operation Chastise on the night of the 16/17th, in which many Canadians took part, and some lost their lives. Earlier on the 16th, authority had been received for 426 (Thunderbird) Squadron to convert to the Hercules-powered Lancaster Mk II, while 428 (Ghost) Squadron would receive Halifaxes. The Thunderbird Wellingtons were to be passed on to a brand-new unit, 433 (Porcupine) Squadron at East Moor, and a second new unit, 434 (Bluenose) Squadron, was to be formed with Halifaxes at Tholthorpe.

By the time that the next major operation was posted on the 23rd, main force squadrons had undergone an expansion with the addition to many units of a third or C Flight, which, in most cases, would eventually be hived off to form the nucleus of a brand-new squadron. The giant force of 826 aircraft was the largest non-1,000 force to date and surpassed the previous record set three weeks earlier by a clear 230 aircraft. The number of available Lancasters had leapt by eighty-eight,

Halifaxes by forty-eight, Stirlings by forty and Wellingtons by forty-one, and their destination for the second time in the month was to be Dortmund. The Command had been restored to full health and vigour and activity on all participating stations was hectic as preparations were put in hand to resume the Ruhr offensive. The ground crews and armourers worked tirelessly, while the aircrews attended briefings to learn of their part in that night's grand plan, which called for eleven Mosquitos to drop yellow preliminary warning TIs on track, before marking the aiming-point with Oboe-laid red TIs, which eight Stirlings, eleven Halifaxes and fourteen Lancasters were to back up with green TIs. 6 Group detailed twenty-eight Halifaxes and forty-eight Wellingtons, of which a dozen of the former were made ready by 408 (Goose) Squadron and given the standard Ruhr bomb load. They departed Leeming between 22.55 and 23.13 with no senior pilots on duty and headed out over Flamborough Head to join up with the bomber stream.

Having made landfall near Castricum-aan-Zee, they adopted a south-easterly course to the eastern Ruhr, which all from the squadron reached to find clear skies but considerable industrial haze. Before the advent of Oboe, this would have rendered the attack a lottery, now, however, the thirteen Path Finder Mosquitos marked the centre of the city accurately and the Path Finder heavy brigade backed-up to maintain the aiming point with red and green TIs. These could be seen from twenty miles away on approach, as could the yellow track markers assisting the early 5 Group arrivals for their time-and-distance runs. The 408 (Goose) Squadron crews bombed largely on the clusters of red and green TIs from 16,000 to 18,000 feet between 01.11 and 01.36, observing many explosions and fires, which were merging into a large area of conflagration with thick columns of black smoke rising up through 18,000 feet as the bombers turned away. Returning crews reported fierce night-fighter activity over the target and on the way home, and this was reflected in the high casualty rate of thirty-eight aircraft, the largest loss of the campaign to date. Almost half of these were Halifaxes and eight were Lancasters, two Halifaxes and a Wellington belonging to 6 Group, and among the former was JB841, which crashed at Bergkamen, ten miles north-east of the target, killing F/O Colvin RCAF and his predominantly Canadian crew. The pilot had been on his fourth sortie, the navigator on his tenth and the rest of the crew on their second.

Later, on the 24th, 427 (Lion) squadron was officially adopted by the MGM Film Corporation and the company's photographer was on hand at Leeming to capture images of the presentation of a small bronze lion, the company's emblem. The Ruhr offensive continued with the posting of Düsseldorf as the target on the 25th, for which a force of 759 aircraft was assembled, 6 Group ultimately contributing 9 Lancasters from 408 (Goose) Squadron and forty-nine Wellingtons after adverse weather conditions prevented 419 (Moose) Squadron from getting away along with four of the intended 408 (Goose) Squadron element and two Wellingtons. Briefings had revealed the standard procedure of Mosquito-laid yellow preliminary warning TIs on track and red TIs delivered by Oboe onto the aiming-point, after which eight Stirlings, twelve Halifaxes and twenty-three Lancasters were to back these up with green TIs, leaving five Stirlings, fourteen Halifaxes and twenty-five Lancasters to bomb with the main force. The 408 (Goose) Squadron element departed Leeming between 23.33 and 23.59 with no senior pilots on duty and each Halifax carrying the standard Ruhr load, and as they arrived at the Dutch coast, some crews claimed that they were able to observe feverish activity at the target some one hundred miles and thirty minutes flying time away. Düsseldorf lay beneath two layers of thin cloud, and the generally poor visibility impacted the Path Finders' ability to back up the Mosquito-laid TIs to the extent that two red TIs were seen to be thirty miles apart. There were also decoy markers and dummy fire sites operating, which succeeded in causing confusion and prevented a concentration of bombing. The 5 Group crews carried out time-and-distant runs from yellow track markers, while those from the other groups identified the target visually and by red and green TIs. The 408 (Goose) Squadron scribe did not record all bombing times and heights and provided a selection which ranged from 17,000 to 18,500 feet between 01.44 and 02.13. Post-raid reconnaissance and local reports confirmed that the raid had failed to achieve concentration and had developed into an "old-style" scattering of bombs across a wide area, leading to the destruction in Düsseldorf of fewer than a hundred buildings. Twenty-seven aircraft failed to return, three of them 6 Group Wellingtons.

Harris was not yet done with Essen and the fifth visitation by the bomber force during the campaign was notified to stations on the 27th, for which a force of 518 aircraft was assembled, 6 Group putting up twenty-three Halifaxes and twenty-seven Wellingtons, a dozen of the former made ready at Leeming. 8 Group prepared two plans of attack, one for ground marking and an alternative for skymarking in the event of cloud cover, and in the event, the latter would be employed, involving a dozen Oboe Mosquitos to drop red flares nineteen miles short of the target and green ones ten-and-a-half miles short as a preliminary warning. Continuing on to the target, they were to sky mark the aiming-point with red flares with green stars and two white flares for the rest of 8 Group to bomb with the main force. The 408 (Goose) Squadron element became airborne between 23.10 and 23.23 again with no senior pilot on duty and all reached the target to be greeted by six to eight-tenths cloud with tops at 12,000 feet. Tracking flares guided them in with, ahead of them, Wanganui skymarkers gently descending into the cloud tops over the aiming point. The 5 Group crews carried out time-and-distance runs, while the other groups bombed on white flares and red parachute markers with green stars, those from 408 (Goose) Squadron from 15,000 to 20,000 feet between 01.19 and 01.30. Post-raid reconnaissance revealed that much of the bombing had fallen short, but 488 buildings had been destroyed, mostly in central and northern districts, and ten nearby towns reported themselves to be victims of collateral damage. Twenty-three aircraft failed to return, and the Halifaxes again represented almost half of the casualties, 6 Group losing a single Halifax and three Wellingtons. DT674 was shot down by a night-fighter in the target area killing both gunners, while F/Sgt Greig RAAF and four of his all-RCAF crew survived to be taken into captivity. The pilot was on his fifteenth sortie and the navigator on his twenty-fourth, while the rest of the crew were on their tenth, eleventh or twelfth.

A force of 719 aircraft was assembled on the 29th to pitch against another new Ruhr target, the conurbation known as Wuppertal, perched on the southern rim of the Ruhr Valley east of Düsseldorf. It consisted of the towns of Barmen and Elberfeld, which had grown wealthy on the proceeds of rich coal deposits. The aiming-point for this night's attack was to be the Barmen half at the eastern end, for which 6 Group detailed forty-four Wellingtons and thirty-nine Halifaxes, including thirteen of the latter belonging to 427 (Lion) Squadron on its return to operations following conversion. The 408 (Goose) Squadron element of twelve departed Leeming between 22.40 and 23.05 with F/L Mair the senior pilot on duty and lost the services of P/O Patry and crew early on because of port-inner engine failure and P/O Symes and crew, who were recalled for an undisclosed reason. On this occasion, the route markers were to be dropped by two 8 Group Stirlings and two Halifaxes, while ahead, the Oboe Mosquitos took care of ground marking with red TIs. These would be backed up by four Stirlings, eleven Halifaxes and twenty-three Lancasters with greens, at the same time as thirteen Stirlings, twenty Halifaxes and twenty-one Lancasters acted as fire raisers by dropping incendiaries, leaving two Stirlings, five Halifaxes and seven Lancasters to bomb with the main force.

Having negotiated the southern approach to the Ruhr, running the gauntlet of searchlights and flak in the Cologne and Düsseldorf corridor, crews were greeted by clear skies in the target area, with the usual industrial haze extending up to 10,000 feet. The yellow tracking flares clearly identified the final turning-point, and the backers-up went in at 16,000 to 18,000 feet between 01.03 and 01.51 to reinforce the red TIs with greens. Meanwhile, the thirteen fire-raisers had attacked with a 2,000-pounder and 1,164 x 4lb incendiaries each, leaving the way clear for the main force to exploit the opportunity to deliver a massive blow. The depleted 408 (Goose) Squadron element delivered their standard war loads from 14,500 to 19,500 feet between 01.00 and 01.31 and it was clear to all that something extraordinary was taking place as the built-up area beneath them became a sea of explosions and flames with smoke rising very rapidly through 15,000 feet. Post-raid reconnaissance revealed this to be the most awesomely destructive raid of the campaign thus far, which devastated by fire a thousand acres, or around 80% of the built-up area, and destroyed almost four thousand houses, five of the six largest factories and more than two hundred other industrial buildings. It would be some time before the human cost could be established, but it is now accepted that 3,400 people lost their lives during this savage Saturday night. The defenders had their say also, and fought back to claim thirty-three bombers, including two 419 (Moose) Squadron Halifaxes and four Wellingtons from 6 Group.

During the course of the month, the squadron carried out seven operations and dispatched seventy-nine sorties for the loss of five Halifaxes and crews.

June 1943

There were no major operations at the start of June because of the moon period, and although bomber stations were alerted on most of the first ten days, no operations other than gardening, actually took place. This kept the Path Finder and main force crews kicking their heels on the ground until the 11th, when Düsseldorf was briefed out to 783 crews. The plan would follow the standard pattern, in which Mosquito-borne yellow preliminary warning flares would be backed up by the other 8 Group aircraft, while the Oboe-laid red TIs on the aiming-point were backed up with greens. However, uncertainty concerning the weather conditions resulted in the Mosquitos also carrying target-marking red flares with green stars. 6 Group was responsible for fifty-one Halifaxes and forty-nine Wellingtons, 408 (Goose) Squadron providing eighteen of the former and loading each with a 2,000-pounder and usual mix of incendiaries before sending them on their way from Leeming between 22.50 and 23.21 with the recently promoted S/L Harriss and F/L Mair the senior pilots on duty. The crews of Sgts Ells and Thould turned back within ninety minutes because of engine and oxygen supply issues respectively, leaving the bomber stream to adopt the southern approach to the Ruhr via the Scheldt estuary. On the way across the North Sea they had to contend with static and lightning conditions in towering ten-tenths cloud with tops in places at 23,500 feet, which largely dissipated over land to leave just small amounts at 2,000, 5,000 and 10,000 feet over the southern Ruhr, dependent upon the time of arrival on final approach.

Those in the vanguard of the main force were drawn on by yellow tracking flares from 01.05, and red skymarkers with green stars at 01.16, while those a little further back in the bomber stream were guided to the mark by red and green skymarkers. The Paramatta marking (ground-marking TIs) did not seem to appear until these crews were turning away, but they were clearly visible to those in the rear-guard, by which time a sea of flames had spread over a massive area with columns of smoke rising through 21,000 feet. The 408 (Goose) Squadron crews delivered their attacks on red TIs from 16,000 to 20,000 feet between 01.30 and 02.04, before all but one returned safely to report a successful night's work. Absent from debriefing was the predominantly RCAF crew of P/O Grant RCAF in JB972, which was brought down by flak during the bombing run with fatal consequences for the pilot and both gunners, while the four survivors fell into enemy hands. When all aircraft had been accounted for, thirty-eight were found to be missing, a figure that equalled the heaviest loss of the offensive to date, and 6 Group had lost two Halifaxes and eight Wellingtons. Post-raid reconnaissance revealed an area of fire across central districts measuring eight by five kilometres, and local reports confirmed 8,882 individual fire incidents. More than seventy war-industry factories suffered a complete or partial loss of production, 140,000 people were bombed out of their homes and 1,292 lost their lives. Had it not been for an errant Oboe marker attracting a proportion of the bombing onto open country some fourteen miles to the north-east, the destruction would have been greater.

Bochum would face its second heavy visitation of the campaign on the 12th, and a force of 503 aircraft was made ready for the purpose, 6 Group contributing thirty-eight Halifaxes, a dozen of them provided by 408 (Goose) Squadron. Briefings revealed that two Mosquitos were to drop yellow preliminary warning TIs, before joining seven others to mark the aiming-point with red TIs, which twenty-five Lancasters would back up with greens. The 408 (Goose) Squadron crews departed Leeming between 23.20 and 23.21 with F/Ls McLernon, Mair and Thompson the senior pilots on duty and set course via Texel to pass over central Holland and enter Germany to the west of Münster, before turning south for a direct run on Bochum, situated between Essen to the west and Dortmund to the east. It is believed that night-fighters were waiting in Dutch airspace and over the frontier region, and a number of bombers fell victim at this stage of the operation, 408 (Goose) Squadron's JB790 crossing paths with the night-fighter of Hptm Egmont Prinz zur Lippe Weissenfeld of III./NJG1 when some fifty miles north of the target and fifteen minutes flying time away. The Halifax crashed at 01.22 at Sellen, two miles north-west of the town of Steinfurt, delivering F/O Large and four of his predominantly RCAF crew into enemy hands, while the bomb-aimer and RAF flight engineer lost their lives. The leading Path Finder crews encountered clear skies but eight to ten-tenths stratocumulus drifted across the city during the course of the raid with tops at 14,000 feet and obscured ground detail. The 408 (Goose) Squadron crews had red and green TIs in the bomb sights as they attacked from 17,500 to 20,000 feet between 01.38 and 01.47, and on return reported concentrated fires, the glow from which was visible for up to a hundred miles into the homeward journey. Twenty-four aircraft failed to return, at least nine of them having fallen victim to night-fighters, and just three were missing from the ranks of 6 Group. Photo-reconnaissance revealed 130 acres of devastation, backed up by local reports that 449 buildings had been destroyed and more than nine hundred severely damaged.

Following a night's rest, the Ruhr offensive continued at Oberhausen, situated between Duisburg to the west and Essen to the east and home of the Ruhr Chemie synthetic oil plant at Sterkrade-Holten on the northern outskirts. Although the town itself had not been targeted in numbers before, it had been hit by many bombs intended for its near-neighbours, and on this night would face an all-Lancaster heavy force numbering 197 aircraft. Local reports confirmed that the Wanganui flares had been right over the city centre, where 267 buildings were destroyed and 584 seriously damaged. On the 16th, 1, 5 and 8 Group stations were notified that Cologne was to be the target for that night, for which a force of 202 Lancasters and ten Halifaxes was made ready. They learned at briefings that there would be no Oboe Mosquitos on hand to mark the target, as that role was to be undertaken by the Path Finder Halifax element and six Lancasters employing H2S. The impression offered at debriefings was that a proportion of the bombing had been concentrated where intended, but that some of it had been lured away by dummy markers, and local reports suggesting that only around a hundred aircraft had been involved, tended to support this view. Residential districts bore the brunt of the raid, and 401 houses were destroyed, with 13,000 others sustaining damage to some extent, mostly lightly, while sixteen industrial premises and nine railway stations were hit, along with public and utility buildings.

In the previous October 5 Group had mounted an audacious daylight attack by more than ninety Lancasters on the Schneider armaments works at Le Creusot and its power source, the nearby Henri Paul power station at Montchanin, situated in east-central France. Labelled the French "Krupp", the company was founded by the famous family, whose name will forever be associated with the Schneider Trophy, for which Britain, France, Italy and the USA competed bi-annually in float plane speed trials between 1913 and 1931. The competition ended when Britain won the trophy outright after three straight victories, the last of which was achieved by the Supermarine S6B powered by the forerunner of the Rolls Royce Merlin engine. The attack, code-named Operation Robinson, which was believed initially to have been successful, was later shown to have caused little damage, and a new attempt to halt production of artillery pieces for use by the Germans was planned for the night of the 19/20th.

290 aircraft were made ready on 3, 4, 6 and 8 Group stations, of which forty-two Halifaxes were provided by 6 Group, thirteen of them belonging to 408 (Goose) Squadron, which were each loaded at Leeming with a single 2,000-pounder, one 1,000-pounder and eight 500-pounders. The plan called for fourteen Stirlings and ten Halifaxes to drop green flares and yellow TIs as route markers by H2S, and for four Stirlings and two Lancasters to illuminate the aiming-point blindly with long sticks of flares. These and the remaining illuminators would keep the aiming-point highlighted, while the main force went about its business, before flying on to Montchanin to repeat the process. The 408 (Goose) Squadron contingent took off between 21.40 and 22.13 with S/Ls Harriss and Newson the senior pilots on duty, and no Geese returned early during the 450-mile outward flight. Time-on-target for the leading Path Finder crews was scheduled for 01.45, and on arrival in the target area, the weather conditions were found to be excellent, enabling the crews to identify lakes and other landmarks with ease. There was no opposition, which was fortunate, as Path Finder crews would have to make up to five passes over the aiming-points, not counting dummy runs, depending upon their respective roles. The Leeming crews established their positions visually, many employing a fork in either of two lakes to the south of the town as the main reference and delivered their loads from between 6,000 to 7,500 feet between 01.54 and 02.15, some during two passes conducted from different directions. Returning crews reported explosions, fires and blue electrical flashes and the consensus was of a successful operation. However, while bombing photos revealed the attack to have fallen within three miles of the aiming-point, only about 20% of the bombs had hit the target and it was established later that drifting smoke and glare

from illumination flares had hampered target identification and that the Breuil steelworks had attracted most of the bombs in error, while the transformer station had escaped damage altogether. Just three aircraft failed to return, all Halifaxes and one of them was 408 (Goose) Squadron's JD107, which was shot down by a night-fighter to crash near Caen, killing four members of the crew and delivering P/O Symes BEM and two others into enemy hands. The cause of the failure to destroy the target was due in part to the fact that main force crews had been trained to aim at TIs from medium to high level and were unused to identifying targets visually from medium to low level.

A hectic round of four major operations to the Ruhr in the space of five nights began at Krefeld on the 21st, for which a force of 705 aircraft was assembled, 6 Group contributing forty-four Halifaxes and twenty-eight Wellingtons, thirteen of the former representing 408 (Goose) Squadron. They departed Leeming between 23.35 and 00.04 with S/L Harriss the senior pilot on duty and a 2,000-pounder and six and seven SBCs respectively of 4lb and 30lb incendiaries in each bomb bay. There were no early returns as they crossed the North Sea to make landfall over the Scheldt and skirt the Belgian/Dutch frontier and enter Germany to the west of Mönchengladbach. The target, situated a short distance to the south-west of Duisburg and on the opposite side of the River Rhine, was located in ideal conditions, with small amounts of thin cloud at between 6,000 and 10,000 feet and bright moonlight, which would benefit attacker and defender alike. The Path Finders delivered a near-perfect marking performance, red TIs falling in concentrated fashion to clearly identify the city centre aiming point for the main force crews, among which, those from 408 (Goose) Squadron that made it home, carried out their attacks from 16,000 to 20,000 feet between 01.59 and 02.08. They described a sea of red fire giving off masses of smoke, with one particular jet-black column rising through 18,000 feet as they turned away.

There was no hint of troublesome flak or night-fighters, and yet forty-four aircraft failed to return, the heaviest casualties of the campaign to date, and 35 (Madras presidency) Squadron of the Path Finder Force lost six of its nineteen Halifaxes. Many bombers were lost to the Nachtjagd on the way home over Holland and 6 Group posted missing four Halifaxes and five Wellingtons, four of the latter belonging to 429 (Bison) Squadron. It was a sombre night also for 408 (Goose) Squadron, which lost JD209 in the target area with the crew of P/O Patry RCAF, who perished alongside three others of his crew, while three survived to fall into enemy hands. BB375 had reached the Utrecht area of central Holland homebound when it was intercepted by the night-fighter of Hptm Hans-Dieter Frank of I./NJG1 and shot down to crash at 02.24 into the River Lek at Lopik, killing Sgt Reichert RCAF and four of his all-Canadian crew. Of the two survivors, navigator, P/O Russell, and gunner, Sgt Pridham, were taken into captivity, the latter having lost a leg when a cannon shell exploded, he having been ordered by his pilot to bale out. He would be repatriated in May 1944. DT772 came down at Zeist, to the east of Utrecht, and there were no survivors from the predominantly Canadian crew of Sgt Brooke RAF. The pilots respectively were on their fourteenth, fifteenth and ninth sorties. Returning crews were convinced of the success of the operation, and one crew likened it to the Wuppertal-Barmen raid. It had, indeed, been an accurate and concentrated attack, which left the entire central area in flames and destroyed more than 5,500 houses.

The medium-sized town of Mülheim-an-der-Ruhr, a close neighbour of Duisburg, Oberhausen and Essen, lies around a dozen miles to the north-east of Krefeld, and it was here that the red ribbon terminated on the target maps at briefings across the Command on the 22nd. A force of 557 aircraft was prepared, of which twenty-five Halifaxes and twenty-three Wellingtons were provided by 6 Group, eight of the former representing 408 (Goose) Squadron, each loaded with two 1,000-pounders and six and seven SBCs respectively of 4lb and 30lb incendiaries. The plan of attack called for eight Oboe Mosquitos plus two in reserve to drop yellow preliminary warning TIs on track, before marking the aiming-point with red TIs for twenty-nine Path Finder Lancasters to back up with greens. The 408 (Goose) Squadron element departed Leeming between 23.39 and 23.46 with F/L Mair the senior pilot on duty and lost the services of P/O Smith and crew to a faulty a.s.i during the climb-out and Sgt Milligan and crew after an hour when the bomb-aimer developed an ear problem.

The others made their way via the Scheldt through the Cologne corridor and arrived at the target to find small amounts of cumulostratus cloud at between 5,000 and 10,000 feet, with red and green TIs clearly visible and defining the aiming point. The 408 (Goose) Squadron crews bombed from 17,000 to 19,500 feet between 01.42 and 01.48 and witnessed the development of a concentrated area of fire, which was visible from the Dutch coast homebound. Returning crews commented on the intense searchlight and flak response and the number of night-fighters and reported that Krefeld was still burning from the night before. Local reports confirmed that the town had suffered severe damage, particularly in the northern districts, where 1,135 houses had been destroyed and more than 12,000 others damaged to some extent. The road and telephone communications to Oberhausen had been cut, preventing any passage out of the town other than on foot. In fact, some of the bombing had spilled into the eastern districts of Oberhausen, which was linked to Mülheim for air-raid purposes. It was another expensive night for the Command, however, which registered the loss of thirty-five aircraft, with the Halifaxes and Stirlings representing two-thirds of them and suffering a respective loss rate of 7.7% and 11.8%. 6 Group lost four 427 (Lion) Squadron Halifaxes and three Wellingtons.

Having destroyed the Barmen half of Wuppertal at the end of May in one of the most devastating attacks to date, it was time to visit the same catastrophe on the western half, Elberfeld, for which a force of 630 aircraft was made ready on the 24th. 6 Group supported the operation with thirty-six Halifaxes and twenty-seven Wellingtons, nine of the former provided by 408 (Goose) Squadron, and they departed Leeming between 23.00 and 23.21 with F/Ls Mair and Miles DFC the senior pilots on duty. On this occasion, six Lancasters, three Stirlings and three Halifaxes of 8 Group were to deliver the yellow route markers on H2S, while seven Oboe Mosquitos marked the aiming-point with red TIs and eighteen Lancasters, seven Halifaxes and three Stirlings backed them up with greens. They made landfall over the Scheldt estuary and ran the usual gauntlet of searchlights and flak from the Cologne and Düsseldorf defence zones, the gun battery crews aided by the formation of condensation trails at between 18,000 and 21,000 feet to advertise the presence of the bomber stream. There seemed to be fewer guns firing at them over the target, however, where small amounts of cloud with tops at 17,000 feet were insufficient to obscure the ground and the 5 Group crews carried out time-and-distant runs from yellow tracking flares until observing cascading red and green TIs. The 408 (Goose) Squadron element delivered their standard Ruhr loads from 12,000 to 19,000 feet between 01.16 and 01.33 and those arriving at the tail end of the attack, when the built-up area was well-alight, described thick columns of smoke already passing through 19,000 feet and the glow of fires visible from the Dutch coast. Post-raid reconnaissance revealed another massively concentrated and accurate attack, which had reduced to rubble an estimated 90% of Elberfeld's built-up area, including three thousand houses and 171 industrial premises. It had also severely damaged 2,500 houses and dozens of important factory buildings, and the fact that more buildings were destroyed than damaged, provided a telling commentary on the conditions on the ground. The number of fatalities stood at around eighteen hundred, and some of the survivors might have been cheered to know that thirty-four bombers, containing 240 of their tormentors, would not be returning to England that night. Three of 6 Group's four missing Halifaxes belonged to 419 (Moose) Squadron and three Wellingtons completed the group's casualty figure.

Instructions were received across the Command on the 25th to prepare for the first major attack on the Ruhr city of Gelsenkirchen since 1941, when it had been a regular destination under the Oil Directive. A force of 473 aircraft was assembled, and the crews briefed to focus on the Gelsenkirchener Bergwerke AG synthetic oil plant, known to Bomber Command as the Nordstern plant and to the Germans as Gelsenberg AG. The German synthetic oil industry relied on two main production methods, the Bergius process, which involved the hydrogenation of highly volatile bituminous coal to manufacture high-grade petroleum products like aviation fuel, and the Fischer-Tropsch process, which produced lower-grade diesel-type fuels for vehicle, Tank, U-Boot and shipping requirements, and Nordstern was of the Bergius variety. 8 Group was to provide seven Oboe Mosquitos plus two in reserve to drop route markers and skymark the aiming-point, and two others to bomb after the main force had finished, but none of its heavy aircraft was to be involved. Thirty Halifaxes and eleven Wellingtons were provided by 6 Group, eight of the former made ready by 408 (Goose) Squadron at Leeming, where they each received the standard Ruhr bomb load before taking off between 23.22 and 23.39 with F/L Miles the senior pilot on duty.

Sgt Dungey and crew were well into the North Sea crossing when their port-outer engine let them down and forced an early return, while JB858, containing the experienced crew of Sgt Milligan RCAF, crossed paths with the night-fighter of Hptm Wilhelm Dormann of III./NJG1 and came down at 01.28 at Holtwick, some thirty-five miles north of the target. The pilot was on his nineteenth sortie and the second pilot his second and only the flight engineer survived to fall into enemy hands. The others reached the target area to find ten-tenths stratus lying over the region with tops at 10,000 to 15,000 feet, which would not have been a problem for Oboe, had five of the twelve participating Mosquitos not suffered equipment failures. This caused tracking flares to be late and to drop in the wrong sequence in a somewhat scattered manner at a time when the crews were contending with an intense flak barrage. Searchlights illuminated the cloud as those from 408 (Goose) Squadron bombed on red flares with green stars from 18,000 to 20,000 feet between 01.27 and 01.41. A large explosion was witnessed at 01.43, and the glow from the target was visible from the Dutch coast, to which the returning bombers were chased by a large deployment of enemy night-fighters. Post-raid reconnaissance and local reports confirmed that the operation had failed to achieve accuracy and concentration, and in an echo of the past, bombs had been sprayed all over the Ruhr, leaving Gelsenkirchen largely untouched. Thirty aircraft were missing, three of them 6 Group Halifaxes.

On the 26th, the A Flight commander, S/L "Bill" Newson, was rewarded for his outstanding service with 408 (Goose) Squadron with a command of his own at 431 (Iroquois) Squadron stationed at Burn but shortly to move to Tholthorpe. In May 1944 he would be rested but would return to the front line in the rank of group captain in November to assume command of 405 (Vancouver) Squadron of the Path Finder Force and would survive the war.

A series of three operations against Cologne spanning the turn of the month began on the night of the 28/29th, when 608 aircraft took off in the late evening to deliver what would be the Rhineland capital's greatest ordeal of the war to date. At briefings, crews took in the details, which for those of 8 Group, involved nine Mosquitos dropping green flares as route markers sixteen miles short of the target, and then red TIs and red flares with green stars on the aiming-point, which four Stirlings, ten Halifaxes and eighteen Lancasters were to back up with green TIs. 6 Group contributed thirty Halifaxes and twenty-one Wellingtons, the 408 (Goose) Squadron element of ten departing Leeming between 23.22 and 23.44 with W/C Ferris the senior pilot on duty. For the second operation running Sgt Dungey and crew were forced to return early, this time because of an oil leak in the starboard-outer engine, leaving the others to press on to the target area, where they encountered ten-tenths cloud below them at 8,000 to 10,000 feet and good visibility above. The main force crews were unaware that five of the Oboe Mosquitos had turned back and a sixth was unable to drop its skymarkers, leaving just six to do so, and these were behind schedule by seven minutes and could manage only intermittent flares. The omens for a successful attack were not good, particularly as skymarking was the least reliable method because of drift. The 408 (Goose) Squadron crews arrived to be greeted by red and white flares and carried out their attacks from 17,000 to 20,000 feet between 02.03 and 02.12, deducing from the glow beneath the clouds and the presence of smoke rising through them that they had contributed to a successful operation. This was confirmed by post-raid reconnaissance and local reports, which provided details of forty-three industrial buildings and 6,374 others completely destroyed, and a further fifteen thousand sustaining damage to some extent. The death toll was put at 4,377, the greatest by far from a Bomber Command attack, and 230,000 others had lost their homes for varying periods. By recent standards, the figure of twenty-five missing aircraft could be considered moderate, but that was no consolation to the individual stations with an empty dispersal pan.

On the 30th, it was decided that sufficient crews of 428 (Ghost) Squadron had become proficient on Halifaxes to allow a limited return to operations.

During the course of the month 408 (Goose) Squadron participated in eight operations and dispatched ninety-one sorties for the loss of seven Halifaxes and crews.

July 1943

The first two days of the new month were beset by poor weather conditions, which kept all but a few gardeners and Mosquitos on the ground. Among the former in action on the 2nd were the freshman crews of F/Os Bennett and Whiston and Sgts Burns and Laine, who departed Leeming between 23.31 and 23.34 bound for the Nectarine I garden. They encountered eight to ten-tenths cloud in the target area with a base at 1,200 feet and relied on a Gee-fix to establish their positions, before dropping four mines each into the briefed locations, the ORB providing details of three crews' efforts from 800, 1,000 and 2,000 feet between 01.20 and 01.28.

The second attack of the current campaign against Cologne was scheduled for the night of the 3/4th, and crews were called to briefings on all operational stations during the late afternoon as a force of 653 aircraft was assembled. The Path Finder crews listened with interest as they were told that ten Mosquitos were to drop green flares four-and-a-half miles from the target as a preliminary warning, and red, green and white flares and red TIs on the aiming-point. On this night, the aiming-point was on the East Bank of the Rhine in the industrial Deutz district, where the Klöckner-Humboldt-Deutz works manufactured aero-engines and heavy and tracked vehicles for the Wehrmacht, served by the extensive Kalk and Gremberg marshalling yards. Nine Halifaxes and twenty-four Lancasters were to back up the red TIs with greens, but in the event that cloud concealed the TIs, they were to bomb on H2S with the main force, along with the remaining nine Halifaxes and seventeen Lancasters. 6 Group contributed forty-four Halifaxes, including ten from 428 (Ghost) Squadron on its debut with the type and a dozen representing 408 (Goose) Squadron, along with twenty-seven Wellingtons. At Leeming, the Goose Halifaxes each received the standard Ruhr war load and took off between 22.55 and 23.13 with S/L Harriss the senior pilot on duty, losing the services of Sgt Burns and crew to a port-inner engine issue over the North Sea. Sgt Bungey RCAF and his crew had crossed the Scheldt estuary and safely negotiated the flak hotspot at Antwerp and were heading for the German frontier near Aachen when intercepted by the night-fighter of Hptm Walter Milius of III./NJG3. JB913 soon became a lost caused and was abandoned by its experienced crew to crash at Tessenderlo, fifteen miles north-west of Hasselt. Five members of the crew were captured, while the pilot, on his twenty-first sortie, and mid-upper gunner evaded a similar fate after being spirited away by the local resistance force.

The meteorological experts had forecast nine-tenths cloud from the English coast all the way to the target, but what the leading Path Finder heavy crews actually encountered was a clear sky and red Oboe-laid TIs, which they backed up with greens. There was a certain amount of haze or perhaps, two to three-tenths cloud at 8,000 feet, but this did not interfere with the accuracy of the attack, which developed in concentrated form in the face, initially, of an intense flak defence. The leading first-phase main force crews were drawn on by green tracking flares and by the time that the raid reached its crescendo, Cologne was visible to approaching crews from a hundred miles away and it was nine-tenths smoke rather than cloud that greeted them. The 408 (Goose) Squadron participants delivered their bombs on red and green TIs from 15,000 to 20,000 feet between 01.29 and 01.44 midway through the raid, and on return described a city engulfed in flames, with smoke rising to 10,000 feet and blotting out ground detail. The glow remained on the horizon for 170 miles into the homeward flight, and at debriefings, some crews reported a large explosion to the west of the Rhine, a mile from the planned aiming point at 01.18, and also that some of the early bombing had fallen short. Some other crews also noticed a creep-back, while the overall impression was of another operation more successful than the Thousand raid against this city at the end of May 1942. Post-raid reconnaissance and local reports confirmed another stunningly accurate and concentrated attack, in which twenty industrial premises and 2,200 houses had been destroyed and 72,000 people bombed out of their homes at a cost to the Command of thirty aircraft. F/Sgt Taylor's JB796 was the second 408 (Goose) Squadron failure to return, having crashed twenty miles south-west of Amiens on the way home killing all but the mid-upper gunner, who was taken into captivity. The predominantly RCAF crew members were a third of the way into their tour, while the RAF pilot was on his thirteenth sortie.

Some crews commented on the presence of day fighters over the target, and this was clear evidence of a new tactic being employed by the Luftwaffe. The newly formed JG300 was operating for the first time, employing the Wilde Sau (Wild Boar) tactics, which was the brainchild of former bomber pilot, Major Hans-Joachim (Hajo) Herrmann. The unit had been formed in June with borrowed standard BF109 and FW190 single-engine day fighters to operate directly over a target, seeking out bombers silhouetted against the fires and TIs. On this night, the unit would claim twelve victories but would have to share them with the flak batteries, which claimed them also. Unaccustomed to being pursued by fighters over a target, it would take time for the bomber crews to work out what was happening, and until they did, friendly fire would often be blamed for damage incurred by unseen causes.

On the 5th, a comment in the ORB concerning Halifax W1165 described the former 35 (Madras Presidency) Squadron aircraft as a piece of junk that was being foisted upon 408 (Goose) Squadron by Bomber Command.

The series against Cologne would be completed on the 8th by an all-Lancaster heavy force of 282 aircraft drawn from 1, 5 and 8 Groups, with six Oboe Mosquitos to carry out the initial marking. The bombers had to fly through the tops of towering cumulonimbus as they made their way to the target, where ten-tenths cloud at around 10,000 to 15,000 feet concealed the ground from view but did not adversely affect the outcome. When the dust had settled over Cologne, the local authorities catalogued the destruction over the three raids of more than eleven thousand buildings and a death toll of almost 5,500 people, with a further 350,000 rendered homeless.

The Ruhr campaign was winding down by the time that Gelsenkirchen was posted across Lancaster and Halifax stations on the 9th as the target for that night, for which a heavy force of 408 aircraft was made ready. At briefings, the crews learned of the plan, which required seven Oboe Mosquitos to drop red flares twenty miles short of the target and green flares nine miles further on, before marking the aiming-point with white flares and reds with green stars. Ten 408 (Goose) Squadron Halifaxes were among forty-two representing 6 Group, and they departed Leeming between 22.36 and 22.59 with the newly promoted S/L Mair the senior pilot on duty and two 1,000-pounders and six SBCs each of 4lb and 30lb incendiaries in the bomb bays. As F/Sgt Grubert and crew raced down the runway in JB959 at 23.44, the a.s.i failed and the pilot attempted to abort the take-off. This resulted in a ground-loop and a written-off Halifax at the end of the runway, but no injuries were reported, and the following aircraft were able to get away. The bomber stream came together over the North Sea and made its way to the target above ten-tenths cloud, which stretched over the Ruhr at around 16,000 feet and topped out in places at 20,000 feet. The Oboe skymarkers were several minutes late, partly as a result of a 50% failure rate of the Oboe equipment, while a sixth Mosquito dropped its markers ten miles to the north.

The 408 (Goose) Squadron crews carried out their attacks mostly on red and green skymarkers or on e.t.a. from 19,000 to 20,500 feet between 01.24 and 01.40 and reported large explosions at 01.22, 01.38 and 01.41, the last one lighting up the sky like day for ten seconds. A red glow beneath the cloud suggested that an extensive fire was developing, but returning crews could offer only impressions at debriefing and none was certain as to the outcome. According to local reports, it had appeared that the attack had been meant for Bochum and Wattenscheid, which received more bombs than Gelsenkirchen, where limited damage occurred in southern districts. Seven Halifaxes and five Lancasters failed to return, among them two of the former belonging to 408 (Goose) Squadron. JB922 crashed some ten miles south of the target after bombing and F/O Mellish RCAF perished along with two members of his predominantly RCAF crew, while the four survivors were taken into captivity. The pilot had been on his seventh sortie and his crew on their fifth. It seems likely from the location of their initial burial that JD216, containing the predominantly RCAF eight-man crew of F/O Lancaster RCAF, had crashed after crossing the Dutch/German frontier and during the north to south approach to the target over the Münsterland. The pilot had been on his ninth sortie while the second pilot was on his first and the others had completed between three and twelve.

Although two more operations to the region would be launched late in the month, Harris was already planning his next attempt to shorten the war by bombing and was buoyed by the success of the spring offensive. He could look back on the past four and a half months with genuine satisfaction at the performance of his squadrons, and as a champion of technological innovation, take particular pride in the performance of Oboe, which had been the decisive factor. Although losses had been grievously high and the Ruhr's reputation as "Happy Valley" well earned, its most important towns and cities had suffered catastrophic destruction. In Britain, the aircraft factories had more than kept pace with the rate of attrition, while the training units both at home and overseas were pouring eager new crews into the fray to fill the gaps. With confidence high in the ability of his Command to destroy almost any target at will, Harris prepared for his next major campaign, the erasure from the map of a prominent German city in a short, sharp series of maximum effort raids to be launched during the final week of the month.

In the meantime, 1, 5 and 8 Groups were alerted to prepare for a trip to Italy to attack the city of Turin, for which 295 Lancasters were made ready on the 12th. They pinpointed on Lake Annecy in the foothills of the Alps before arriving in the target area to be greeted by clear skies, good visibility and defences up to their usual poor standard, characterised by ineffective searchlights and inaccurate light flak rising to 15,000 feet. The marking was punctual, accurate and concentrated, as was the bombing, and a column of black smoke was observed rising through 12,000 feet as they withdrew.

Aachen, Germany's most westerly city and an important railway hub between Germany and the occupied countries, was posted as the target on the 13th and a force of 374 aircraft made ready. This consisted largely of Halifaxes, Wellingtons and Stirlings and in the absence of a 5 Group presence, just eighteen Lancasters among the 8 Group contribution. 6 Group provided forty-eight Halifaxes and twenty-one Wellingtons, eleven of the former made ready by 408 (Goose) Squadron while their crews attended briefing to learn of the plan of attack, which called for ten Halifaxes to drop yellow TIs as route markers, and six Oboe Mosquitos to ground mark the aiming-point with red TIs, backed up with green TIs by nineteen Halifaxes. The 408 (Goose) Squadron element took off between 00.05 and 00.15 with F/L Miles the senior pilot on duty and a 2,000-pounder and six SBCs each of 4lb and 30lb incendiaries in each bomb bay. While attempting to coax sufficient height out of JB968 to continue, Sgt Harvey ran out of time to reach the target within the allotted window and turned back. A strong tail wind drove the main force crews across Holland and Belgium to the target ahead of schedule, where they were confronted with seven to nine-tenths cloud lying predominantly over the eastern half of the city with tops at around 9,000 feet. As F/O Bain and crew closed on the target, just five minutes flying time away, they were attacked by a night-fighter, which inflicted damage upon the hydraulics system and prevented the bomb doors from opening. As soon as the red TIs went down, so did much of the bombing, including that of the 408 (Goose) Squadron participants, who released their loads from 18,000 to 21,000 feet between 01.59 and 02.08, contributing to a sudden proliferation of fires. Soon afterwards, cloud slid across the area to obscure ground detail and prevent an assessment of results.

Twenty aircraft failed to return, fifteen of them Halifaxes, six of which and a Wellington belonged to 6 Group and one to 408 (Goose) Squadron. DT769 was shot down outbound by the night-fighter of Lt Rolf Bussman of I./NJG1 and crashed on Dutch soil at 01.40 a few miles inland from the Scheldt estuary, killing P/O Smuck RCAF and four of his crew and delivering the two survivors into enemy hands. It had been an experienced crew halfway through its tour of operations. Meanwhile, F/O Bain RCAF and his predominantly RAF crew were coming to terms with the fact that they could not deploy the undercarriage and were unable to carry out a belly-landing with a full bomb load on board. They had no choice but to abandon JD174 to its fate, while they drifted down on their parachutes, six of them to make a safe landing. F/O Bain sustained a broken leg, but the immediate award of a DFC no doubt eased the discomfort to a degree. At 05.50 the Halifax smacked into the side of a hill some twelve miles from Leeming and exploded on impact. It was left to local sources at Aachen to confirm the severity of the damage inflicted upon the city, which amounted to 2,927 buildings completely destroyed, with many industrial, public and cultural buildings seriously damaged.

On the 14th, aircrew demonstrated their appreciation of the work of the Leeming ground crews by hosting a party for them in the NAAFI, an occasion which served partly as a celebration of the news that the squadron would be moving to Linton-on-Ouse on the 10th of August to convert to Mk II Hercules-powered Lancasters.

Most of the main force crews enjoyed a long rest after Aachen, as Harris continued his preparations for his next campaign. Hamburg had been a regular target for the Command throughout the war to date, and had been attacked, amongst other occasions, during the final week of July in 1940, 1941 and 1942. It had been spared by the weather from hosting the first "One Thousand" bomber raid at the end of May 1942, but Harris now identified it as the ideal candidate for destruction under Operation Gomorrah, the intention of which was to cause the maximum impact to the enemy's morale in a short, sharp campaign employing ten thousand tons of bombs. Hamburg's political status was second only to Berlin's, and its value to the war effort in terms of ship and U-Boot construction and other war production was undeniable, but it suited Harris's criteria also in other respects. Its location close to a coastline aided navigation and made it accessible from the North Sea without the need to spend time over hostile territory, and its relatively short distance from the bomber stations enabled a force to approach and retreat during the few hours of darkness afforded by mid-summer. Finally, lying beyond the range of Oboe, which had proved so decisive at the Ruhr, Hamburg had the wide River Elbe to provide a solid H2S signature for the navigators high above.

There had been no operations for most squadrons for nine days, despite a number being posted, and by the time that 791 crews trooped into their respective briefing rooms on the 24th, they probably expected the day to end with yet another scrub. Instead, they were read a special message from the commander-in-chief, to announce the beginning of the Battle of Hamburg. They listened intently to the revelation that they would be aided by the first operational use of "window", aluminium-backed strips of paper of precise length, which, when released in bundles into the airstream at a predetermined point, would drift down slowly in vast clouds to swamp the enemy night-fighter, searchlight and gun-laying radar with false returns and render it blind. The device had actually been available for a year, but its use had been vetoed in case the enemy copied it for use against Britain. It was not realized that Germany had, in fact, already developed its own version called Düppel, which it had withheld for the same reason.

The plan of attack called for eleven Lancasters and nine Halifaxes to drop yellow TIs as route markers, before continuing on to mark the aiming-point with yellow TIs, and if conditions permitted, illuminator flares. The route markers were to be backed up by six Stirlings, thirteen Lancasters and nine Halifaxes, and six Lancasters and two Halifaxes were to use the yellow TIs as a guide, and with the aid of flares, mark the aiming-point with red TIs, which would be backed up with greens by the remaining marker crews. 6 Group supported the operation with fifty-one Halifaxes and twenty-one Wellingtons, fourteen of the former belonging to 408 (Goose) Squadron and departing Leeming between 22.30 and 22.54 with W/C Ferris and S/L Mair the senior pilots on duty. Each was carrying a 2,000-pounder and usual incendiary load as they climbed out and headed for the Yorkshire coast to begin the North Sea crossing, and F/Sgt Grubert and crew were two hours out when they lost their port-outer engine and had to turn back. The others pressed on and at a predetermined point over the North Sea, wireless operators began to dispense "window" through the flare chute, beginning shortly after 00.30, and the effects appeared to be immediate as few fighters rose to meet the approaching bombers. A number of aircraft were shot down over the sea during the outward flight, two of them 103 Squadron Lancasters, but these were off course and outside of the protection of the bomber stream and may well have been among those returning early with technical difficulties.

The effectiveness of "window" was made more apparent in the target area, where the crews noticed an absence of the usually efficient co-ordination between the searchlights and flak batteries and defence appeared random and sporadic. This offered the Path Finders the opportunity to mark the target by visual reference and H2S virtually unmolested, and although the red and green TIs were a little misplaced and scattered, they landed in sufficient numbers close to the city centre to provide the main force crews with ample opportunity to deliver a massive blow. It rarely happened that aircraft arrived in strict bands according to their task, and some main force crews were already over the target from the opening of the raid at 01.00. The 408 (Goose) Squadron crews carried out their attacks from 18,000 to 20,000 feet between 01.29 and 01.50 and reported violent explosions at 01.33 and 01.37, part of the city ablaze and a column of smoke rising through 20,000 feet. Post-raid reconnaissance revealed that a six-mile-long creep-back had developed, which cut a swathe of destruction from the city centre along the line of approach, out across the north-western districts and into open country, where a proportion of the bombing had been wasted. In fact, less than half of the force had bombed within three miles of the city centre during the fifty-minute-long raid, in which 2,284 tons of bombs had been delivered, despite which, the city had suffered a telling blow, and fifteen hundred of its inhabitants lay dead. For the Command it was an encouraging start to the campaign, particularly in the light of just twelve missing aircraft, for which "window" was largely responsible.

In the expectation that Hamburg would be covered by smoke, Harris switched his force on the 25th to Essen, where he could take advantage of the body blow dealt to the enemy defensive system by "window". A force of 705 aircraft was made ready and a plan prepared, which called for Halifaxes and Lancasters of 35 (Madras Presidency) and 156 Squadrons to drop preliminary yellow warning TIs on track by H2S, which would be backed up by elements of 7 and 156 Squadrons. Ahead, fourteen Oboe Mosquitos would mark the aiming-point with red TIs, which nineteen Lancasters, nine Halifaxes and five Stirlings were to back up with greens. 6 Group detailed forty-eight Halifaxes and twenty Wellingtons, fifteen of the former representing 408 (Goose) Squadron and departing Leeming between 22.22 and 22.47 with S/L Harriss the senior pilot on duty and the same bomb load as for Hamburg. There were no early returns from the Goose brigade, and they arrived in the target area to find four to five-tenths cloud to the west but clear skies over the aiming-point, with just the usual ground haze to spoil the vertical visibility. They carried out their bombing runs at 17,000 to 20,000 feet between 00.53 and 01.07 and watched a highly concentrated attack develop, which left the ground enveloped in smoke from the many fires and explosions. Returning crews reported concentrated fires around the aiming-point in a one-and-a-half-square-mile area of the city, two large, red explosions at 00.36 and 00.39 and a column of smoke rising through 20,000 feet as they withdrew to the west, the glow remaining visible from as far away as the Dutch coast. Post-raid reconnaissance confirmed the raid to be another outstanding success against this important war-materials-producing city, with more than 2,800 houses destroyed, while the complex of Krupp manufacturing sites suffered its heaviest damage of the war to date. Twenty-six aircraft failed to return, only two of which belonged to 6 Group, while a Wellington ditched, and the crew was rescued by the Cromer lifeboat.

During the course of the 27th, a force of 787 aircraft was assembled for round two of Operation Gomorrah, for which 6 Group detailed sixty-two Halifaxes and nineteen Wellingtons, fifteen of the former belonging to 408 (Goose) Squadron. The crews attended briefing to learn that yellow route markers would be dropped by H2S on the enemy coast and backed up, and that "Y" aircraft (H2S blind markers) were to deliver red TIs and a stick of flares over the aiming-point for visual markers to confirm and back up with green TIs. The 408 (Goose) Squadron element departed Leeming between 22.22 and 22.51 with F/L Stovel the senior pilot on duty and lost the services of F/O Whiston and crew early when the pilot's escape hatch blew open and could not be shut. Sgt Smith and crew followed them home after losing the use of their Gee and were unable to establish their position. Finally of the "boomerangs", Sgt Grubert was unable to fully retract the port undercarriage and the additional drag prevented the climb to operational height. A landing was made at Wittering, upon which the undercarriage leg collapsed, but both Halifax and crew would be returned to duty. The others reached the Schleswig-Holstein coast to the north of Hansastadt Hamburg, none of them having any concept of the events that were to follow their arrival.

A previously unknown and terrible phenomenon was about to present itself to the world and introduce a new word "firestorm" into the English language. A number of factors would conspire on this night to seal the fate of this great city and its hapless inhabitants in an orgy of destruction that was quite unprecedented in air warfare. An uncharacteristically hot and dry spell of weather had left the city a tinderbox, and the spark to ignite it came with the Path Finders' H2S-laid yellow and green TIs, which fell with almost total concentration some two miles to the east of the intended city-centre aiming-point and into the densely populated working-class residential districts of Hamm, Hammerbrook and Borgfeld. To compound this, the main force, which had been drawn on to the target by yellow release-point flares, bombed with rare precision and almost no creep-back and deposited much of its 2,300 tons of bombs into this relatively compact area. The 408 (Goose) Squadron crews delivered their bomb loads onto the yellow markers from 17,000 to 21,000 feet between 01.12 and 01.37 and observed many explosions and a sea of flames developing below. Those bombing towards the later stages of the raid observed a pall of smoke rising through 20,000 feet, and the glow of fires was reported to remain visible for up to two hundred miles into the return journey.

On the ground, individual fires began to join together to form one giant conflagration, which sucked in oxygen from surrounding areas at hurricane speeds to feed its voracious appetite. Trees were uprooted and flung bodily into the inferno, along with debris and people and temperatures at the seat of the flames exceeded one thousand degrees Celcius. The defences were overwhelmed and the fire service unable to pass through the rubble-strewn streets to gain access to the worst-affected areas. Even had they done so, they could not have entered the firestorm area, and only after all of the combustible material had been consumed did the flames subside. By this time, there was no-one alive to rescue and an estimated forty thousand people died on this one night alone. A mass exodus from the city, which would ultimately exceed one million people, began on the following morning and this undoubtedly saved many from the ravages of the next raid, which would come two nights hence. Seventeen aircraft failed to return, reflecting the enemy's developing response to the advantage gained by the Command through "window". No gain was ever permanent, and the balance of power would continue to shift from one side to the other for the next year. For a change, it was the Lancaster brigade that sustained the highest numerical casualties on this night, accounting for eleven of the failures to return. 408 (Goose) Squadron's DT749 was shot down by the night-fighter of Lt Sachsenberg of II./NJG3 and crashed near Neumünster some thirty-five miles to the north of the target at the start of the bombing run. F/L Stovel DFC RCAF and four others lost their lives and the three survivors soon found themselves in enemy hands. It was a highly experienced crew, and F/L Stovell DFC was on his twenty-seventh bombing sortie and forty-second in a combined Coastal Command/Bomber Command tour, while the others, with the exception of the second pilot, who was on his first, had completed between fourteen and twenty-seven.

Bomber Command's heavy brigade stayed at home on the following night, while four Mosquitos carried out a nuisance raid on Hamburg to ensure that the residents' sleep was disturbed. A force of 777 aircraft was put together to continue Hamburg's torment on the 29th, while the crews attended briefings to learn of their part in the proceedings. They were told that red TIs and flares were to be employed as route markers, before seventeen Lancasters and eight Halifaxes marked the aiming-point with yellow TIs by H2S to be backed up by thirty-four Lancasters, six Stirlings and nine Halifaxes. 6 Group detailed sixty Halifaxes and twenty-five Wellingtons, of which a dozen of the former made ready by 408 (Goose) Squadron and departed Leeming between 22.18 and 22.46 with F/Ls Miles and Smith the senior pilots on duty. After climbing out above the station they rendezvoused with the bomber stream over the North Sea and reached the target area to find clear skies and the city protected only by slight ground haze. The plan involved approaching from due north to hit the northern and north-eastern districts, which, thus far, had escaped serious damage, but the Path Finders strayed two miles to the east of the intended track and dropped their markers just to the south of the already devastated firestorm area. A four-mile creep-back rescued the situation for the Command by spreading along the line of approach into the residential districts of Wandsbek and Barmbek and parts of Uhlenhorst and Winterhude. The 408 (Goose) Squadron crews carried out their attacks from 18,000 to 20,000 feet between 01.07 and 01.20 and released their loads on yellow and green TIs, before returning home to report smoke rising through 17,000 feet and fires visible for two hundred miles into the homeward journey. It was another massive blow against this proud city, but as the defenders began to recover from the effects of "window", so the bomber losses began to creep up, and twenty-eight aircraft failed to return home on this night, just two of them from 6 Group.

Before the final round of Operation Gomorrah took place, the curtain on the Ruhr offensive was brought down finally with a raid on the town of Remscheid, situated on the southern edge of the region some six miles south of Wuppertal, where the main industries were mechanical engineering and tool-making. Up until this point, only twenty-six people had lost their lives in this town as a result of stray bombs, but it was now to face a modest force of 273 aircraft consisting of roughly equal numbers of Lancasters, Halifaxes and Stirlings with six Oboe Mosquitos to mark out the aiming-point with red TIs. After adjustments to the plan that saw the final three waves cancelled, 6 Group's original contribution was reduced to twelve Halifaxes each from the Leeming squadrons and five each from 419 (Moose) and 428 (Ghost) Squadrons at Middleton-St-George. The Geese took off between 22.00 and 22.25 with F/L Smith the senior pilot on duty and a 2,000-pounder and incendiaries in each bomb bay, and all reached the target area to find clear skies and good visibility and bombed on red TIs from 19,000 to 21,000 feet between 01.15 and 01.26, observing many bursts and a pall of smoke rising through 5,000 feet. They returned home with a red glow in the sky behind them that remained visible as they crossed the enemy coast homebound and gave promise of another Ruhr town in ruins. Fifteen aircraft failed to return, the Stirling brigade suffering 10% casualties, and a Halifax from each squadron was absent from Leeming. Sgt Chalk RAF and his predominantly RAF crew were on their fourth sortie together when JD365 was shot down to crash at Düren to the east of Aachen with fatal consequences for all but the navigator and bomb-aimer, who fell into enemy hands. It would be left to a post-war bombing survey to establish that a mere 871 tons of bombs had laid waste to around 83% of Remscheid's built-up area, destroying 107 industrial buildings and 3,117 houses. Three months war production was lost, and the town's industry never recovered fully.

During the course of the month, the squadron carried out nine operations and dispatched 105 sorties for the loss of nine Halifaxes and seven crews.

August 1943

Briefings for the final act of Operation Gomorrah took place on the 2nd, and a force of 740 aircraft was assembled, 6 Group detailing fifty-six Halifaxes and twenty Wellingtons, all but three of which would take off. 408 (Goose) Squadron briefed fifteen crews for what would prove to be their final operation on Mk II Halifaxes, setting out the intention for the Path Finders to mark the aiming-point with red TIs by H2S and for the visual markers to follow up with yellow TIs for the backers-up to reinforce with greens. They lifted off from Leeming between 22.50 and 23.01 with F/L Smith the senior pilot on duty and headed for the Yorkshire coast at Flamborough Head to begin the North Sea crossing and rendezvous with the bomber stream. The weather conditions, initially, were favourable, and it was engine issues that forced F/L Smith and crew to turn back after an hour, and they were joined on the ground by the crew of Sgt Brager, whose rear turret had become unserviceable. The rest of the bomber stream then came into contact with a towering bank of ice-bearing cumulonimbus cloud at 7 degrees east, a not unusual feature of this regular route into north-western Germany, but on this occasion, a particularly imposing one, which could not be circumnavigated and stretched upwards to 20,000 feet and beyond. Upon entering it, aircraft were thrown around by violent electrical storms and it was a hugely terrifying experience beyond anything that most crews had ever experienced, with enormous flashes of lightning, thunder, electrical discharges and instruments going haywire. Sgt Young and crew were crossing the River Weser south of Bremerhaven when ice-accretion threatened to rob them of lift and persuaded them also to abandon their sortie. Sgt Harvey was contending with control issues as he and his crew reached a point some thirty-five miles south-west of Hamburg at 19,000 feet and jettisoned their bomb load as they turned for home. Suddenly, icing caused a loss of control that threw the Halifax into a spin, and on passing through 15,000 feet the order to abandon the aircraft was issued. Only the wireless operator had time to comply before control was regained at 12,000 feet and a safe return completed. Sgt Humphrey and crew were shedding four hundred feet per minute as they struggled at the start of their bombing run and decided not to push their luck by continuing on to the aiming point.

Those battling through the conditions to reach the target area found seven to ten-tenths cloud, and while some caught a glimpse of the Elbe and isolated yellow and green Path Finder flares, which might have been jettisoned rather than placed, the majority bombed on e.t.a., those from 408 (Goose) Squadron from 19,000 to 19,500 feet between 01.52 and 02.11. F/Sgt Morrison and crew were losing height rapidly, but completed the bombing run only to suffer the frustration of frozen bomb doors refusing to open, while chunks of ice flying off the propellers bombarded the fuselage. The bombing was spread over a hundred miles of the Schleswig-Holstein peninsula, the town of Elmshorn, some fifteen miles to the north-west of Hamburg, seeming to attract the most attention and 254 houses were destroyed. Few crews had any idea of their precise location and bombed on the glow of fires beneath the cloud and the smoke rising through it. On return, they expressed themselves to be shaken by their experience and were unanimous in their conviction that the operation had been a total failure. The outcome was of little consequence in view of what had gone before, but the Command suffered the relatively heavy loss of thirty aircraft, some of them having fallen victim to the weather conditions. During the course of the four raids of Operation Gomorrah, the squadron dispatched fifty-two sorties, forty-five of which bombed as briefed and lost just one Halifax and crew. (The Battle of Hamburg. Martin Middlebrook).

Following this operation, the squadron was stood down pending its forthcoming move south to Linton-on-Ouse, one of a number of bomber stations clustered around the city of York. Situated ten miles north-west of the cathedral city, it was already home to 426 (Thunderbird) Squadron, which was well into its conversion onto the Mk II Lancaster, and would remain the residence of both squadrons for the remainder of the war. An advance party set out from Leeming on the 9th to prepare the way for the main party to follow on twenty-four hours later, but the enormity of the task facing them was not appreciated. A farewell party went ahead that night and thirty-two buses arrived at Leeming on the morning of the 10th to ferry personnel to their new home, where no preparations had been put in hand to make the accommodation and other facilities habitable. The squadron ORB was careful not to apportion blame and cited a lack of transport available to the station authorities to move in furniture and equipment. The sleeping accommodation was particularly lacking, and many would find themselves sleeping on floors on biscuit beds under dirty blankets. Aircrew were granted seven days leave to immediately ease the situation and allow cleaning and other necessary actions to take place to bring the station up to standard, and in the meantime, the first examples of the Lancaster trickled over from the 426 (Thunderbird) Squadron side of the tarmac.

While the squadron was away from the front line for most of the ensuing two months, Bomber Command remained busy and began a new campaign against targets in Italy, which was now teetering on the brink of capitulation and in prime condition for Bomber Command to help nudge it over the edge with a short offensive against its major cities. It began with the preparation of an all-Lancaster force drawn from 1, 5 and 8 Groups for an attack on Genoa, Milan and Turin on the 7th. With preparations already in hand for, perhaps, the most important operation of the war to date to be launched in ten days' time, the Turin raid was to be used to test the merits of employing a raid controller, or Master of Ceremonies, in the manner of W/C Gibson during Operation Chastise. The man selected for the job was Group Captain John Searby, currently serving as commanding officer of 83 Squadron, and before that, Gibson's successor as commanding officer of 106 Squadron. It is believed that all 197 aircraft reached their respective targets after flying out in excellent weather conditions, and although the Master Bomber experiment at Turin was not entirely successful, experience was gained which would prove useful for the forthcoming Operation Hydra.

Although Germany took a temporary back seat while the Command focused on Italy, major operations were mounted against Mannheim and Nuremberg, the former involving forty 6 Group Halifaxes and the latter forty-one. 434 (Bluenose) Squadron had been scheduled to conduct its maiden Halifax operation at Nuremberg, but the overload tanks were not installed in time and its participation was scrubbed. 6 Group contributed forty-eight Halifaxes to a raid on Milan on the 12th, allowing 434 (Bluenose) squadron to make its debut. Once the Italian campaign had been concluded on the night of the 16/17th, all eyes turned upon Peenemünde, the research and development centre for V-1 and V-2 weapons on the Island of Usedom on Germany's Baltic coast.

Since the very beginning of the war, intelligence had suggested that Germany was researching into and developing rocket technology, and although scant regard was given to the reports by some of the leading scientific experts, photographic reconnaissance had confirmed the existence of an establishment at Peenemünde at the northern tip of the island of Usedom on the Baltic coast. The activities there were monitored through Ultra intercepts and surreptitious reconnaissance flights, and the V-1, known to the photographic interpreters at Medmenham because of its wingspan as the "Peenemünde 20", was captured on a photograph. The brilliant scientist, Dr R V Jones, had been able to gain vital information concerning the V-1's range, which would ultimately be used to feed disinformation to the enemy, largely through the double agent "Zigzag", otherwise known as Eddie Chapman. Unfortunately, Churchill's chief scientific adviser, Professor Lindemann, or Lord Cherwell as he became, steadfastly refused to give credence to the existence and feasibility of rocket weapons and held stubbornly to his viewpoint even when presented with a photograph of a V-2 on a trailer, taken by a PRU Mosquito in June 1943. It required the combined urgings of Duncan Sandys and Dr Jones to persuade Churchill of the urgency to act, and Operation Hydra was planned for the first available opportunity, which occurred on the night of the 17/18th. Earlier in the day, the USAAF 8th Air Force had carried out its first deep-penetration raids into Germany to attack ball-bearing production at Schweinfurt and the Messerschmidt aircraft plant at Regensburg, and to the shock of its leaders, had learned the harsh lesson that unescorted daylight raids over Germany in 1943 were not viable. The folks at home would not be told that sixty B17s had failed to return.

A force of 596 aircraft was assembled for Peenemünde comprising 314 Lancasters, 218 Halifaxes and fifty-four Stirlings, sixty-three of the Halifaxes belonging to 6 Group. The Stirling numbers were depleted by the late return of many to their stations following diversions on return from the previous night's attack on Turin. The crews attended briefing to learn the details of the operation, which had been meticulously planned to account for the three vital components of Peenemünde, the housing estate, where the scientific and technical staff lived, the factory buildings in which the weapons were assembled and the experimental site, where testing took place. Each was assigned to a specific wave of aircraft, which would attack from medium level, with the Path Finders bearing the huge responsibility of re-directing the point of aim accordingly, for which each squadron was to provide one crew as a "shifter". That apart, once route markers had been dropped on Rügen island, the Path Finder markers and backers-up were to follow the standard routine of red, yellow and green TIs. After last minute alterations, 3 and 4 Groups were given the housing estate, 1 Group the construction sheds, and 5 and 6 Groups the experimental site, the whole operation to be overseen by a Master of Ceremonies (referred to hereafter as Master Bomber), and as previously mentioned, the officer selected for this hazardous and demanding role was G/C Searby of 83 Squadron. His role was to direct the marking and bombing by VHF and to encourage the crews to press on to the aiming-point, a task requiring him to remain in the target area and within range of the defences throughout the attack. In an attempt to protect the bombers from the attentions of enemy night-fighters for as long as possible, eight Mosquitos of 8 Group's 139 Squadron were to carry out a spoof raid on Berlin beginning at 23.00, seventy-five minutes before the opening of the main event, and would be led by the highly experienced and former 49 Squadron commander, G/C Len Slee. In the expectation of encountering drifting smoke as the last wave on target, the 5 Group crews were instructed to employ their oft-used time-and-distance approach to the aiming-point and had practiced this over a stretch of coast near the Wainfleet bombing range at the mouth of the Wash in Lincolnshire, progressively cutting the margin of error from one thousand to three hundred yards.

The various groups made their way individually to a rendezvous point some ninety minutes flying time or three hundred miles from the English coast and sixty miles from Denmark's western coast, where they formed into a stream. Darkness had fallen as they crossed the North Sea, and twenty miles short of landfall over the southern tip of Fanø island, south of Esbjerg, windowing began in order to simulate a standard raid on a northern or north-eastern city. Southern Denmark was traversed by the Lancaster brigade at 18,000 feet, twice the altitude required for the attack, but worryingly, in a band of cloudless sky under a bright moon. They adopted an east-south-easterly course and began to shed altitude gradually during the 240-mile run to the target a little over an hour away, and at the rear of the stream, the 5 Group crews focused on the island of Rügen, the ideal starting point for their timed run to Peenemünde, which lay some fifteen miles beyond to the south-east.

The initial marking of the housing estate went awry, and some target indicators fell onto the forced workers camp at Trassenheide, more than a mile south of the intended aiming point. Many of the 3 and 4 Group bombs fell here, inflicting grievous casualties on friendly foreign nationals, who were trapped inside their wooden barracks. Once rectified, however, the attack proceeded according to plan and a number of important members of the technical staff were killed. The 1 Group second-wave crews encountered strong crosswinds over the narrow section of the island where the construction sheds were located, but this phase of the operation largely achieved its aims and they were on their way home before the night-fighters arrived from Berlin, having been attracted by the glow of fires well to the north. On arrival at Rügen, the 5 Group crews began their timed run, reaching the experimental site to encounter the expected smoke and bombed on green TIs, in the case of the 49 Squadron element, from 6,500 to 8,000 feet between 00.43 and 01.04. They and the 6 Group Halifaxes and Lancasters then ran into the night-fighters, which proceeded to take a heavy toll of bombers both in the skies over the target and on the route home towards Denmark.

Twenty-nine of the forty missing aircraft came from this third wave, seventeen of them belonging to 5 Group and twelve to 6 Group, which represented a loss rate for the Canadians of 19.7%. Returning crews praised the work of the Path Finders and the Master Bomber, and post-raid reconnaissance revealed the raid to have been sufficiently effective to delay the V-2 development programme by a number of months and ultimately to force the manufacture of secret weapons underground. The flight testing of the V-2 was eventually withdrawn eastwards into Poland, beyond the range of Harris's bombers, and thus Peenemünde had been nullified as a threat at the first attempt.

Before the next campaign began, Leverkusen was posted on the 22nd as the target for a heavy force of 449 Lancasters and Halifaxes, including sixty-two of the latter provided by 6 Group, with 8 Group Oboe-Mosquito to provide the initial marking. Situated on the Rhine just a stone's throw north of Cologne, the city was home to a factory belonging to the infamous I G Farben chemicals company, which was engaged in the development and production of synthetic oil and employed slave labour at all of its factories across Germany, including 30,000 from the Auschwitz concentration camp, where it had built a plant. One of the company's subsidiaries manufactured the Zyklon B gas used during the Holocaust to murder millions of Jewish victims. 6 Group contributed sixty-two Halifaxes, and those successfully negotiating the narrow searchlight and flak corridor near Cologne to reach the target, encountered ten-tenths cloud with tops at 18,000 feet, which completely blanketed the area. Oboe-equipment failures forced most crews to bomb on e.t.a. in the absence of markers, until the glow of fires came to their aid as the raid developed and a column of smoke was observed to be rising through 12,000 feet. Local reports revealed that up to a dozen neighbouring towns had been hit, Düsseldorf suffering the destruction of 132 buildings.

Harris had long believed that the key to ultimate victory lay in the destruction of Berlin, the seat of the Nazi government and the symbol of its power. On the 23rd, orders were received on stations across the Command to prepare for a maximum effort that night against Germany's capital city, which had not been visited by the heavy brigade since the end of March. The crews, of course, could not know that this was to be the first of an eventual nineteen raids on the "Big City", in an offensive which, with an autumn break, would drag on until the following spring. It was a campaign that would test the resolve of the crews to the absolute limit, whilst also sealing the fate of the Stirlings and the Mk II and V Halifaxes as front-line bombers. There are varying opinions concerning the true start date of what became known as the Berlin offensive or the Battle of Berlin, some commentators believing these first three operations in August and September to be the start, while others point to the sixteen raids from mid-November. However, there was little doubt in

Bomber Command circles that this was it, a fact demonstrated by the comments in numerous squadron ORBs, which spoke of the "long-awaited Berlin campaign" and similar sentiments. There would be a Master Bomber on hand for this operation and the officer chosen was Canadian W/C "Johnny" Fauquier, the tough, grizzled and one-time bush pilot and frequent brawler, who was enjoying his second spell as the commanding officer of 405 (Vancouver) Squadron, once of 4 Group, but since April, proud to be the only Canadian Path Finder unit.

A force of 727 aircraft was assembled, of which sixty Halifaxes and eight 426 (Thunderbird) Squadron Lancaster IIs represented 6 Group. Those reaching the target area found clear skies and moonlight, but the Path Finders were unable to identify the aiming point in the centre of the city, a result of the inherent difficulties of interpreting the H2S images over such a massive urban sprawl and marked the southern outskirts instead. Many main force crews then cut the corner to approach the city from the south-west rather than south-east, and this would result in the wastage of many bomb loads in open country and on outlying communities. Returning crews reported large explosions and many fires, the glow from which was visible for at least 140 miles, and a pall of smoke had already risen to meet them as they turned towards the north-west. Curiously, only a few crews commented on hearing the Master Bomber and finding his instructions helpful. A new record of fifty-six aircraft failed to return, twenty-three Halifaxes, seventeen Lancasters and sixteen Stirlings, representing a percentage loss rate respectively of 9.1, 5.1 and 12.9, which perfectly reflected the food chain when all three types operated together. Berlin experienced a scattered raid, but because of the numbers attacking, extensive damage was caused, a little in or near the centre but mostly in south-western residential districts and industrialised areas a little further east. 2,611 buildings were reported to have been destroyed or seriously damaged, and the death toll of 854 people was surprisingly high, caused largely, perhaps, by a failure to heed the alarms and go to the assigned shelters.

Orders were received on the 27th to prepare for an operation that night against Nuremberg, the plan for which included an additional ten 139 Squadron Mosquitos to provide a "window" screen in advance of the bomber stream. The Oboe Mosquitos were to mark the route with red and green TIs, backed up by H2S Lancasters, but as Berlin was beyond the range of Oboe, the aiming-point was to be marked with red TIs by H2S, backed up by greens. A force of 674 aircraft lined up for take-off in mid-evening, 6 Group contributing fifty-five Halifaxes and eleven Lancasters. The Path Finders had been briefed to check their H2S equipment by dropping a 1,000-pounder on Heilbronn, and some crews complied, while others, it seems, experienced technical difficulties. The initial marking was accurate, but a creep-back developed, which the backers-up and the Master Bomber could not correct, and this resulted in many bomb loads falling into open country, while others hit Nuremberg's south-eastern and eastern districts. Crews generally gained an impression of a fairly concentrated and accurate attack, which produced many fires and reported searchlights and night-fighters to be numerous. Evidence of this came with the failure to return of thirty-three aircraft, eleven of each type, which again confirmed the vulnerability of the Stirlings and Halifaxes when operating alongside Lancasters. The loss rate on this night was 3.1% for the Lancaster, 5% for the Halifax and 10.6% for the Stirlings.

The main event on the night of the 30/31st was a two-phase attack on the twin towns of Mönchengladbach and Rheydt, the first time that either would experience a major Bomber Command assault. Situated some ten miles west of the centre of Düsseldorf in the south-western

Ruhr, they would face an initial force of 660 aircraft of four types, in what for the crews, was a short-penetration trip across the Dutch frontier and a welcome change from the recent long slogs to eastern and southern Germany. The plan called for the first wave to hit Mönchengladbach, before a two-minute pause in the bombing allowed the Path Finders to head south to mark Rheydt. 6 Group contributed fifty-four Halifaxes, thirteen Lancasters and fifteen Wellingtons, and those reaching the target area found good visibility above the seven to ten-tenths cloud at 8,000 feet, and a near-perfect display of target-marking by Oboe delivered red and green flares to draw on the main force to bomb with scarcely any creep-back. Returning crews reported many fires, the glow from which could be seen from the Dutch coast homebound, and photo-reconnaissance confirmed a highly accurate and concentrated attack, which destroyed more than 2,300 buildings in the two towns, 171 of them of an industrial nature and 869 residential properties. Twenty-five aircraft failed to return, and Halifaxes narrowly sustained the highest numerical casualties.

The month ended with preparations for the second of the Berlin operations on the night of the 31st, for which 622 aircraft were made ready, more than half of them Lancasters, eleven of them provided by 6 Group along with forty-two Halifaxes. The route on this night took the bomber stream on an east-south-easterly heading across Texel to a position between Hannover and Leipzig, before turning to pass to the south-east of Berlin and approach the city-centre aiming point on a north-westerly track. The return leg would involve a south-westerly course to a position south of Cologne for an exit over the French coast, but despite the attempts to outwit the enemy night-fighter controller, he would be able to predict to some extent where to concentrate his fighters. The Path Finders encountered five to six-tenths cloud in the target area and this combined with H2S equipment failure and a spirited night-fighter response to cause the markers to be dropped well to the south of the planned aiming point. The main force crews became involved in an extensive creep-back, which would stretch some thirty miles into open country and outlying communities. Crews observed many fires over a wide area, and it was noted by some that two groups of green TIs were ten miles apart and both attracting attention from the main force. The outcome of the raid was a major disappointment, brought about by woefully short marking and a pronounced creep-back and resulted in the destruction of just eighty-five houses, a figure in no way commensurate with the effort expended and the loss of forty-seven heavy bombers. The percentage loss rates made alarming reading at Bomber Command HQ, the Lancasters with an acceptable and sustainable 3%, the Halifaxes with 11.3% and the Stirlings with 16%.

During the course of the month the squadron participated in just one operation and dispatched eleven sorties for the loss of a single airman.

September 1943

408 (Goose) Squadron spent the entire month in intense training as it worked towards operational status on the Lancaster. Rarely was a conversion period concluded without incidents, and the squadron suffered just one, when F/Sgt Brager RCAF had to crash-land DS732 at Newton-on-Ouse, north-west of York, after suffering an engine fire on the 7th during a fighter affiliation exercise. The rear gunner, Sgt Ogston RCAF, was thrown from his turret and sustained injuries to which he succumbed.

Although 408 (Goose) squadron was absent from the operational scene, it is necessary to chart the conduct of the bombing war and 6 group's involvement to establish continuity and the situation at the time of the squadron's return to the front line. Probably as a result of the heavy losses recently incurred by the Halifaxes and Stirlings, an all-Lancaster force of 316 aircraft was assembled on the 3rd to conclude the current series of operations against the "Big City", 6 Group contributing just three from 426 (Thunderbird) Squadron. The first TIs fell right over the aiming point, before others crept back for between two and five miles along the line of approach from the west. Fortunately, the backers up maintained the marking as the main force Lancasters came in in a single wave, and, although much of the bombing fell short of the city centre, most of it landed within the city boundaries, falling principally into the largely residential districts of Tiergarten, Wedding, Moabit and Charlottenburg and the industrial Siemensstadt, where much useful damage occurred that resulted in a loss of war production. In the absence of the poorer performing Halifaxes and Stirlings, twenty-two Lancasters failed to return, almost 7% of those dispatched.

Whether by design, or as a result of the losses sustained, Berlin was now shelved for the next ten weeks, while Harris sought other suitable targets, of which there were many. He would shortly begin a four-raid series against Hannover stretching over a four-week period but first he focused on southern Germany, beginning on the 5th with the twin cities of Mannheim and Ludwigshafen, which face each other from the East and West Banks respectively of the Rhine. The plan was to exploit the creep-back phenomenon that attended most large operations, by approaching the target from the west and marking the eastern half of Mannheim, with the expectation that the bombing would spread back along the line of approach across western Mannheim and into Ludwigshafen. A force of 605 aircraft was assembled, which included fifty-two Halifaxes and eight Lancasters representing 6 Group. Black smoke was rising through 15,000 feet as the bombers withdrew to the west, and the glow from the burning cities was visible for 150 miles and more into the return journey, which thirty-four aircraft would fail to complete. Thirteen Lancasters, an equal number of Halifaxes and eight Stirlings were missing, and the percentage loss rates continued to tell the same story. Local reports confirmed that both Mannheim and Ludwigshafen had suffered catastrophic destruction, with almost two thousand fires in the latter alone, 986 of them classed as large. Mannheim's reporting system broke down completely and little detail emerged of this raid, although it would recover in time for the next assault in fewer than three weeks' time. What is known, is that the main railway station in Mannheim and three suburban stations were destroyed and the tank and military tractor factories belonging to Heinrich Lanz and Josef Vogele respectively sustained serious damage, as did the Rashig & Sulzer chemicals plant.

Munich was posted as the target on the 6th, for which 6 Group provided forty-eight Halifaxes and five Lancasters in an overall force of 257 Lancasters and 147 Halifaxes, the Stirling brigade made conspicuous by its absence. The cloud in the target area varied between five and nine-tenths, although some ground features, like the River Isar, could be identified and the red, yellow and green TIs observed. A large number of fires was observed to be grouped around the markers, but an accurate assessment was not possible, and local reports would suggest that the attack had been scattered across southern and western districts. The searchlights were ineffective because of the cloud but large numbers of night-fighters were again evident, and sixteen aircraft failed to return, thirteen of them Halifaxes, five belonging to 6 Group, and this represented a percentage loss rate of 8.8, compared with 1.2 for the Lancasters.

A series of operations against French targets began on the night of the 8/9th with the bombing of heavy gun emplacements near the small coastal resort town of Le Portel, south of Boulogne. This was the final phase of Operation Starkey, a rehearsal for invasion, which had begun on the 16th of August and which was intended to deceive the enemy into believing that the invasion was imminent. Harris was less than enthusiastic about allowing his squadrons to participate in what he considered to be "play-acting" and managed to restrict Bomber Command's involvement to token gestures as on this night, when 6 Group contributed a dozen 432 (Leaside) Squadron Wellingtons to the overall force of 257 aircraft, the majority of which were Wellingtons and Stirlings. The batteries, codenamed Religion and Andante, were to be attacked forty minutes apart, but much confusion surrounded the marking and the subsequent inaccurate bombing caused massive destruction to the town of Le Portel and many casualties. (For a detailed analysis of this operation, see the excellent book, The Starkey Sacrifice, by Michael Cumming, published by Sutton).

A raid on the Dunlop rubber factory at Montluçon in central France was posted on the 15th, for which a force of 369 aircraft was drawn from 3, 4, 6 and 8 Groups consisted of 209 Halifaxes, sixty-three belonging to 6 Group, 120 Stirlings and forty Lancasters with a token gesture of five B17s representing the USAAF. Those reaching the target encountered eight to nine-tenths cloud at 4,000 feet, which did not prevent a view of the factory and the red, green and yellow TIs marking it out. A Master Bomber in the person of W/C "Dixie" Deane of 35 (Madras Presidency) Squadron was on hand to direct the attack, and the bombing was carried out in bright moonlight. It wasn't long before black smoke was seen to rise through 10,000 feet from the developing fires, and it was clear to all that the factory complex had been severely damaged. Opposition was negligible, and just two Halifaxes and a Stirling failed to return.

On the following day, the same groups were alerted to an operation that night against the important and extensive railway yards at Modane, situated on the main line between France and Italy in the foothills of the Alps in south-eastern France. A force of 340 aircraft was assembled, which included fifty-six Halifaxes provided by 6 Group, whose crews were informed that the marking was to be dependent upon a visual reference, but in case the conditions in the target area proved to be unfavourable, red spotfires were to be dropped on Grenoble. A careful timed run from there would culminate in the delivery of red TIs on e.t.a., followed by backing-up throughout the raid with green TIs. The force crossed the Normandy coast with more than 230 miles still to negotiate and reached the target area to find between zero and two-tenths cloud at 10,000 feet with good visibility and moonlight. Zero hour was set for 00.01, but a patch of cloud right over the aiming-point delayed the start for a brief period. The target was located in a steep valley and most of those arriving early were able to identify it visually, assisted by the red TIs that formed a good concentration and were backed up by greens. Returning crews were largely confident that the target had been dealt with, but this was not borne out by post-raid reconnaissance, which revealed that the marking had missed the mark and the yards had escaped damage.

A force of 711 aircraft was assembled on the 22nd for the first of four raids over a four-week period against the ancient city of Hannover, situated in northern Germany midway between the Dutch frontier and Berlin. 6 Group contributed sixty-nine Halifaxes, six Lancasters and fifteen Wellingtons, whose crews were informed at briefings that it was home to much war industry and was also the location of seven Nazi concentration camps, although, this was probably not known at the time among the Allies. According to Martin Middlebrook and Chris Everitt in Bomber

Command War Diaries, the first two operations produced concentrated bombing but mostly outside of the target, while only the third one succeeded in causing extensive damage, which, if the figures are to be believed, seem to be massively out of proportion. The author contends that the reports of the crews after the first two operations suggest strongly that the damage to Hannover was accumulative over the first three raids and did not result from just one, as will be explained in the following narrative. The telling feature is, perhaps, that no reports came out of Hannover to corroborate the testimony of the crews on the first two raids, although post-raid reconnaissance by the RAF after the second one did show that some of the bombing had fallen into open country, and the Path Finders did admit to at least one poor performance.

The attack was scheduled to begin at 21.30 and the first red TIs were observed three minutes later, before another was seen to cascade after overshooting the aiming point by an estimated four miles. This was followed by other red TIs overshooting by one to four miles with many greens falling among them, while the yellows seemed to be undershooting the reds by two miles and were closer to the city centre aiming-point. At debriefings, some crews observed a line of fires developing from west to east, with smoke rising through 14,000 feet, while others claimed that fires ran from the aiming point in a north-north-westerly direction across the city. All were unanimous, however, that the raid had been highly successful and that the glow of fires was still visible from the Dutch coast, a distance of two hundred miles. Twenty-six aircraft failed to return, twelve of them Halifaxes, which again sustained the highest numerical losses, and this time, at 5.3%, even exceeded the Stirling's loss rate.

Let us now examine the claim that the main weight of bombs fell two to five miles south-south-east from the city centre and that the operation largely failed. Firstly, two to five miles in any city means that the bombing fell within the boundaries and, therefore, within the built-up area. Secondly, the majority of crews, if not all, reported a highly successful raid with fires right across the city, smoke rising to 14,000 feet as they left the scene and the glow visible from the Dutch coast. It is true that crews were very frequently mistaken in their belief that an attack had been successful, but the evidence on this occasion would seem to confirm their testimony. Decoy fire-sites do not produce a glow visible from a distance of two hundred miles or sufficient volumes of smoke to reach bombing height during the short duration of a raid and be dense enough to be visible at night.

On the 23rd, and for the second time in the month, Mannheim was posted as the target and would face an initial force of 628 aircraft, including sixty-one Halifaxes and five Lancasters belonging to 6 Group. Crews attended briefing to learn that Mosquitos were to drop red and green route markers, before the Path Finder blind marker crews delivered flares and red TIs over the target by H2S to guide the visual markers to the precise aiming-point. This had been placed in the less-severely afflicted northern districts, which they would mark with yellow TIs, followed by the backers-up with greens. The bomber stream crossed France and entered southern Germany to encounter largely clear skies and good visibility, at its head, the Path Finders accurately marking out the northern districts with concentrated red, green and yellow TIs, which the main force crews exploited. Later bombing spilled over into the northern fringe of Ludwigshafen and out into the nearby towns of Oppau and Frankenthal, where much damage also resulted. Returning crews reported that smoke had reached around 6,000 feet as they turned away and that the glow of fires remained visible for 150 miles into the return journey. Thirty-two crews were absent from debriefing, and this time eighteen of them were in Lancasters, compared with seven each for the Halifaxes and Stirlings, which provided a somewhat topsy-turvy and unusual loss-rate of 5.7%, 3.6% and 6% respectively. Post-raid reconnaissance and local reports revealed that 927 houses and twenty industrial premises had been destroyed in Mannheim and that the I G Farben factory in Ludwigshafen had sustained serious damage.

Hannover was posted again as the target on the 27th and a force of 678 aircraft made ready, which included a 6 Group contribution of seventy-four Halifaxes and nine Wellingtons. The crews learned at briefing that the Steinhude Lake to the north-west of the city was to be employed again by the Path Finder blind marker crews as the starting point for a timed run to the aiming point, which would be marked with yellow TIs on H2S and identified visually by the backers-up and marked with reds and greens. The Path Finders were unaware that the weather forecasts on which their performance would be based were incorrect, and the result of that would be to push the marking some five miles from the city centre towards the north. The initially adverse weather conditions improved markedly over Germany to present the crews with clear skies at the target, allowing the main force to bomb mostly on green TIs and observe many fires with smoke rising to 15,000 feet. Returning crews again reported the glow of fires to be visible from the Dutch coast, and confidence in the success of the operation was unanimous across the Command, giving lie to the claim that little damage resulted. Post-raid photos did reveal many bomb craters in open country, but the fire and smoke evidence did not support decoy fire-sites, and no local report was forthcoming to shed further light. The loss of thirty-eight aircraft was probably something of a shock, but at least common sense returned to the statistics to re-establish the status-quo after the topsy-turvy outcome of the Mannheim raid. Seventeen Halifaxes, ten Lancasters, ten Stirlings and one Wellington failed to return, giving loss-rates for the four-engine types of 9% for the Stirling, 7.3% for the Halifax and 3.2% for the Lancaster. 6 Group posted missing six Halifaxes and one Wellington, three of the former belonging to 434 (Bluenose) Squadron, which was experiencing a torrid introduction to operations.

The month ended with an operation to Bochum in the central Ruhr on the 29th, for which 6 Group contributed thirty-nine Halifaxes in an overall heavy force of 343 aircraft. The plan of attack required the Mosquito element to drop green warning flares, before Oboe-marking the aiming-point with red TIs, and in case they could not be seen through cloud, with red flares with green stars. The main force element was kept on track by two route-marker flares at 20,000 feet, and after a two-and-a-half-hour outward flight, established their positions visually in good visibility. The Path Finders marked the aiming point with green TIs and the bombing was carried out in the face of a strong searchlight and moderate flak defence. Some returning crews described the target as a mass of flames with smoke rising rapidly to meet them, while local reports confirmed the destruction of 527 houses, with 742 others seriously damaged.

October 1943

There was excitement at Linton-on-Ouse on the 1st, when 408 (Goose) Squadron was finally declared operational on Lancasters, although it would not immediately resume its place in 6 Group's front line. The start of October was a busy time for the Lancaster squadrons, which would be called upon to participate in six major operations in the first eight nights. The month's account was opened at Hagen at the eastern end of the Ruhr on the 1st, for which a moderately sized heavy force of 243 Lancasters was drawn from 1, 5 and 8 Groups. The bombers arrived in the target area to find ten-tenths cloud with tops at 8,000 feet and red and green Oboe-laid skymarkers to aim at and returning crews reported a column of black smoke rising through the clouds, some also describing a large bluish-green explosion at 21.03, the glow of fires beneath the cloud and an effective Path Finder performance. In addition to the usual housing damage, local reports confirmed the destruction of forty-six industrial firms, among them a manufacturer of accumulator batteries for U-Boots, and this would have an impact on U-Boot production.

294 crews from 1, 5 and 8 Groups were called to briefings on the 2nd to learn that Munich was to be their target for that night. The skies over the city were clear of cloud, but the marking was scattered and led to most of the early bombing falling into southern and south-eastern districts. Returning crews suggested that the raid appeared to be concentrated on the eastern side of the city, and local authorities reported that 339 buildings had been destroyed. Meanwhile, a large mining effort employing 117 aircraft involved twenty-four 6 Group Halifaxes plying their trade in a number of gardens in the Baltic, and among them were the first to represent 431 (Iroquois) Squadron following its conversion.

It was not until the 3rd that Halifaxes of 4 and 6 Groups and Stirlings of 3 Group returned to the bombing war as part of an overall force of 547 aircraft, consisting of 223 Halifaxes, 204 Lancasters, 113 Stirlings and seven Mosquitos to target the city of Kassel. 6 Group was responsible for seventy-five Halifaxes in a plan of attack that called for the Mosquitos to provide route markers and for the Path Finder H2S crews to mark the target blind with yellow TIs and flares. The visual markers were then to identify the aiming-point and mark it with red TIs for the backers-up to maintain with greens. For Kassel, the industrial city located some eighty miles to the east of the Ruhr, this night's visit would be the first of two during the month, which, forever after, would leave their mark upon it. As home among other war industry concerns to the Henschel and Fieseler aircraft factories and the Henschel tank works where the much-feared Tiger Tank was in production, it was a target that needed attention. The bombers arrived in the target area to be met by largely clear skies but thick ground haze, which should not have caused the Path Finder blind markers to overshoot the planned aiming-point, but this they did, and because the light from the flares reflected off the haze, the visual markers were unable to determine the location of the aiming-point and withheld their red TIs. The Germans were operating decoy markers, which, together with the absence of red TIs conspired to lead a quarter of the main force crews astray and waste their bombs outside of the built-up area. The main weight of the attack fell onto the western suburbs, where the Henschel and Fieseler plants were hit, but also onto woodland beyond. However, a stray bomb load fell onto one of the largest ammunition dumps in Germany, situated three miles north-east of the aiming-point at Ihringshausen, close to the suburb of Wolfsanger, and the resulting explosion at 22.06 devastated the area and attracted more bomb loads. A second explosion ten minutes after the first added to the destruction and left eighty-four buildings on the site flattened and the ground pockmarked by craters, one of which was three hundred feet in diameter. Twenty-four aircraft failed to return, fourteen Halifaxes, six Stirlings and four Lancasters, which gave a loss-rate of 6.3%, 3.2% and 2.9% respectively.

The 408 (Goose) Squadron signals leader, F/L "Paddie" Reynolds DFC DFM, was posted on the 4th on promotion to 91 Group to assume a similar role. He had been with the squadron from the start and during his term as signals leader had set a high standard, tempered by his cheery Irish manner, which would be missed. The busy schedule of operations continued that night with the posting of Frankfurt as the target for 406 aircraft, for which 6 Group detailed fifty-nine Halifaxes from its six operators of the type. The American confidence in the ability of its 8th Air Force to deliver daylight attacks on military and war production targets in Germany had been shaken by the high loss rates, which were not sustainable. Since the attack on the Modane railway yards in mid-September, a small number of 8th Air Force B17s had been flirting with night raids alongside their RAF colleagues, and this night would bring their final involvement. Crews learned at briefing that they would be following a somewhat circuitous route, which departed England over the Sussex coast and tracked across France as if heading for southern Germany, before swinging to the north-east and passing to the west of Frankfurt for the final run-in of around eighty miles. This added significantly to the mileage but avoided the flak hotspots from the Dutch coast and north of the Ruhr. Frankfurt was found to be clear of cloud, and the Path Finder crews excelled to deliver the H2S-laid markers and illuminator flares all within three miles of the aiming-point and the visual markers within a mile-and-a-half, leaving the city at the mercy of the main force, which bombed on red and green TIs. The main weight of the attack had fallen into the eastern half of the city, which, together with the docks area, became a sea of flames. A large red explosion was observed at 21.37, which threw flames up to 3,000 feet, and smoke was rising through 8,000 feet as the bombers turned away, some crews reporting the glow from the burning city to be visible for 120 miles into the homeward leg. The success was gained at the modest cost of ten aircraft, half of which were Halifaxes.

The busy first week of the month concluded with an operation against Stuttgart, for which a force of 343 Lancasters was drawn from 1, 3, 5, 6 and 8 Groups on the 7th. A new weapon in the Command's armoury was introduced for the first time in numbers on this night with the participation of a night-fighter-communications-jamming device called "Jostle" fitted in Lancasters of 1 Group's 101 Squadron. It required a specialist operator in addition to the standard crew of seven, who, though not necessarily a German speaker, could recognise the language and on hearing it, jam the signals on up to three frequencies by broadcasting engine noise over them. At 101 Squadron the device was referred to as ABC or Airborne Cigar, and once proved to be effective, ABC Lancasters would be spread through the bomber stream for all major operations, whether or not 1 Group was otherwise involved. The Lancaster would also carry a full bomb load reduced by 1,000lbs to compensate for the weight of the equipment and its operator.

Celebrations on the 408 (Goose) Squadron side of Linton-on-Ouse signalled its return to operations as the two resident units put up fourteen Lancasters each and loaded them with a 4,000lb "cookie", and four and two SBCs respectively of 4lb and 30lb incendiaries. The Geese departed Linton-on-Ouse between 20.35 and 20.59 with W/C Ferris and S/L Miles the senior pilots on duty and F/Sgt Harvey RCAF and crew last away. Nine minutes later they abandoned DS724 seven miles west-north-west of Pickering after the controls jammed and watched it crash on farmland, where the blast of the cookie fatally injured the farmer. The mid-upper gunner sustained some non-life-threatening damage on landing, while the rest of the predominantly RCAF crew arrived safely on terra firma. P/O White and crew were well into the outward leg and had penetrated some thirty-five miles into France after crossing the coast near Dieppe, when the rear turret became unserviceable and forced them to turn back. The others reached the target area, where ten-tenths cloud at 10,000 feet concealed the ground from view and the Path Finders employed H2S to establish two areas of marking, which led to bombs falling in many parts of the city from the centre to the south-west. The 408 (Goose) Squadron crews bombed from 18,000 to 20,500 feet between 00.15 and 00.49, before returning safely to report their impressions of a scattered attack, which cost a remarkably modest four aircraft. Whether or not the presence of the radio-countermeasures Lancasters was responsible for the low casualty rate could not be certain, but it was a promising start and would lead, ultimately, to the formation of a dedicated RCM force, 100 Group, in November.

The third raid of the series on Hannover was posted on the 8th, for which a force of 504 aircraft was duly assembled, 6 Group asked to provide 102 aircraft, the first time that it had breached the hundred figure. Seventy-one Halifaxes, seventeen Lancasters and fourteen Wellingtons answered the call, 408 (Goose) Squadron loading six of its aircraft with a cookie and incendiary mix and one with a single 8,000 pounder and three and two SBCs respectively of 4lb and 30lb incendiaries. A large diversionary raid was planned for Bremen to begin at 01.15, five minutes ahead of zero-hour at the main event and would involve seventeen 8 Group Halifaxes and seven Lancasters marking for a main force of ninety-five Stirlings. The 408 (Goose) Squadron element departed Linton-on-Ouse between 22.57 and 23.33 with S/L Mair the senior pilot on duty and after climbing out, set course for the northern tip of Texel to traverse northern Holland and enter Germany north of Meppen. S/L Mair's take-off had been delayed by the need to switch to a spare Lancaster and was the one with the 8,000 pounder in its belly, and by the time that they were twenty-five miles off Texel, it was clear that they would not reach the target in the allotted time and turned back. The others reached the target area to find largely clear skies and red and green TIs marking out the city-centre aiming point, inviting the bombs of the main force crews, those from 408 (Goose) Squadron delivering theirs from 18,500 to 22,000 feet between 01.32 and 01.47. Sgt Sherlock and crew found themselves south of the aiming point, and reticent to turn back into the bomber stream because of a fear of collision, withheld their bombs until approaching the town of Hamelin to the south-west of Hannover, where the bombs were seen to detonate. Having arrived in the early stages of the attack, the 408 (Goose) Squadron crews saw fires just beginning to take hold and it became clear as they retreated westwards, that the fires were developing into a serious conflagration. After bombing, F/Sgt Morrison and crew were bombarded by incendiaries falling from above and their Lancaster sustained damage of an inconsequential nature, which would be an annoyance to the ground crew.

Curiously, despite the claim by some commentators that this was the one successful raid of the series, there was no mention of the glow being visible from a considerable distance, as had been the case with the first two operations. This time a local report did emerge, which described heavy damage in all districts except for those in the west, with a large area of fire engulfing the central districts. A total of 3,932 buildings was destroyed, while thirty thousand others were damaged to some extent and the death toll amounted to 1,200 people. These statistics seem somewhat excessive for a single operation by fewer than five hundred aircraft, particularly in the absence of the kind of crew reports common to the first two raids, and this adds weight to the author's contention, that the damage was accumulative over the three operations and the damage statistics amalgamated. Twenty-seven aircraft failed to return, six of them belonging to 6 Group, but all from 408 (Goose) Squadron returned safely, mostly to land at Bury St Edmunds.

Thereafter, what was effectively a stand-down kept the Path Finder and most of the main force squadrons on the ground for a period of ten days, during which it was left to the Mosquitos of 8 Group to take the war to Germany. Linton-on-Ouse and its squadrons were honoured to receive a visit on the 15th from Her Royal Highness the Duchess of Gloucester, who inspected the WAAFs and their quarters, while the male residents were under orders to behave impeccably.

When the next major operation was posted on the 18th, it was, no doubt, an immense relief to the crews who became bored with filling their days with routine non-operational tasks. The wall map revealed Hannover as the target for the fourth and last time in this series, and the crews learned that this was to be an all-Lancaster affair involving 360 aircraft, of which twenty-six were to be provided by 6 Group. 408 (Goose) Squadron loaded thirteen of its Lancasters with a cookie each and eight and four SBCs respectively of 4lb and 30lb incendiaries and lent the crew of F/Sgt Hansen to 426 (Thunderbird) Squadron, which had a spare aircraft. The Geese departed Linton-on-Ouse between 17.17 and 17.43 with S/L Mair the senior pilot on duty and lost the services of P/O White and crew to an oxygen supply issue at the midpoint of the North Sea crossing. The others made landfall over Texel and continued on an easterly track across Holland aiming for Cloppenburg and thence Nienburg and Celle, before turning to the south-west to run in on the target close to the Misburg oil refinery. They remained unmolested by the defences until encountering a nest of night-fighters on crossing the frontier into Germany, and at least thirteen aircraft were brought down during the ensuing forty-five minutes encompassing the approach and withdrawal phases. A layer of eight to ten-tenths cloud hung over Hannover with tops at 12,000 to 15,000 feet, and these conditions made it difficult for the Path Finders to establish the aiming point. It resulted in them dropping both sky and ground markers that lacked concentration, which would lead to a scattering of the effort. The 408 (Goose) Squadron crews bombed mostly on red and green TIs or on release-point flares from 19,500 to 21,000 feet between 20.15 and 20.22, and a colossal explosion was observed at around 20.19. The strong night-fighter presence dissuaded crews from hanging around to assess the outcome further, and the impression of those returning was of a scattered attack.

F/Sgt Hansen and crew were about to cross the Danish coast homebound when it became clear that fuel was an issue. The pilot went immediately into fuel conservation mode and gradually reduced height from 20,000 to 800 feet as they closed on the Suffolk coast. However, before they reached land, two engines on the same wing cut out because of fuel starvation, and F/Sgt Hansen turned back out to sea to attempt a ditching. Despite a twelve-foot-high swell and choppy conditions, he successfully put the Halifax down on the sea some three miles off the shore and all crew members were able to board the dinghy. Fortunately, an easterly wind carried them to the beach within about ninety minutes and apart from the effects of exposure, all were in good health. It was established later that most of the bombing at Hannover had fallen into open country, a disappointment compounded by the loss of eighteen Lancasters. The four raids on Hannover had cost the Command 110 aircraft from 2,253 sorties, a loss rate of 4.9%, but much of the city now lay in ruins and would receive no further attention for a year, when the oil offensive and the close proximity of the Misburg synthetic oil plant to the east would return the region to prominence.

The first major attack of the war on the eastern city of Leipzig was planned for the 20th, for which an all-Lancaster force of 358 aircraft was assembled from 1, 5, 6 and 8 Groups, 6 Group responsible for twenty-eight from Linton-on-Ouse. 408 (Goose) Squadron loaded each of its fourteen with a cookie and six and four SBCs respectively of 4lb and 30lb incendiaries and sent them on their way between 17.22 and 17.36 with W/C Ferris and S/L Miles the senior pilots on duty. The crews of S/L Miles and F/Sgt Harvey turned back from the midpoint of the North Sea crossing when vital flying instruments failed and thereby avoided the atrocious weather conditions created by a towering front of ice-bearing cumulonimbus cloud east of Hannover that extending upwards to beyond 20,000 feet. Many crews were persuaded to turn back as engines began to falter and ice-accretion destroyed lift, and among them was the crew of P/O White, who were at 19,000 feet some twenty miles north-east of Hannover when abandoning their sortie at 20.15. The others pushed on through the front to reach the target after a three-and-a-half-hour outward flight, to then encounter seven to ten-tenths cloud with tops as high as 14,000 feet. The Path Finders had been unable in the conditions to establish and mark the aiming point, leaving crews to bomb on e.t.a., on fires glimpsed through the cloud or on scattered skymarkers, the 408 (Goose) Squadron element from 18,500 to 21,000 feet between 21.05 and 21.14. Sixteen Lancasters failed to return, and those crews that did make it home were unable to offer any useful details at debriefing.

The final major operation of the month was the second one against Kassel, for which preparations were put in hand on the 22nd. A force of 569 aircraft ultimately stood ready to take off in the early evening, 6 Group responsible for eighty-five Halifaxes and twenty-two Lancasters, the twelve representing 408 (Goose) Squadron departing Linton-on-Ouse between 17.47 and 18.05 with S/Ls Mair and Miles the senior pilots on duty and each bomb bay containing a cookie and eight and four SBCs respectively of 4lb and 30lb incendiaries. F/Sgt Lloyd and crew turned back after two hours because of unserviceable guns, just as the bomber stream was entering an electrical storm over the North Sea, which knocked out the navigational instruments of F/Sgt Young and crew and forced them to abort their sortie also. By the time that F/L Smith and crew reached the Dutch coast, they had lost too much height and were too far behind schedule to continue and became yet another "boomerang" among seventeen afflicting 6 Group. Those emerging on the other side of the front traversed Belgium in continuing unfavourable weather conditions, which miraculously improved in the target area to leave clear skies between the bombers and the target but ten-tenths cloud above them at 24,000 feet.

At the opening of the raid, the H2S "blind" markers overshot the city-centre aiming point, leaving the success of the operation reliant upon the visual marker crews' backing up, and they did not disappoint. The red and green TIs were concentrated right on the aiming point and the main force crews followed up with accurate and concentrated bombing with scarcely any creep-back. The 408 (Goose) Squadron crews carried out their attacks from 17,000 to 21,000 feet between 21.00 and 21.17 and observed the fires just beginning to take hold as they turned away. It was after the sound of their engines had receded that the fires joined together to engulf the city in what, in some areas, developed into a firestorm, though not one as fierce as that experienced in Hamburg. The massively successful operation was achieved at a high cost of forty-three bombers, twenty-five of them Halifaxes and eighteen Lancasters, and among the twelve missing 6 Group aircraft was 408 (Goose) Squadron's DS778, which crashed at 21.30 between Hannover and Osnabrück while homebound with no survivors from the predominantly RCAF crew of F/L Whiston RCAF. The pilot was on his eleventh sortie and his crew members had completed between seven and seventeen. In Kassel, the shell-shocked inhabitants emerged from their shelters to find their city devastated and unrecognizable. After 3,600 fires had been dealt with, it would be established eventually that more than 4,300 apartment blocks containing 53,000 dwelling units had been destroyed or damaged, leaving up to 120,000 people without homes and in excess of six thousand others killed. 155 industrial buildings had also been destroyed or severely damaged, along with numerous schools, hospitals, churches and public buildings.

On the 26th, W/C Ferris was posted away, having concluded a fourteen-month tour, during which he had overseen the squadron's conversion from Hampdens to Halifaxes and Halifaxes to Lancasters. He was frequently referred to in the squadron ORB as "genial" and was clearly a popular and highly respected officer, whose departure to pastures new was regretted by the squadron and station communities. He was succeeded from within on the 28th by the newly promoted W/C Mair, whose period of tenure would be brought to a premature conclusion.

During the course of the month the squadron took part in five operations and dispatched sixty sorties for the loss a single Lancaster and crew.

November 1943

November brought with it the long, dark, cloudy nights which enabled Harris to return to his main theme, the destruction of Germany's capital city. The next four months would bring the bloodiest, hardest-fought air battles between Bomber Command and the Luftwaffe Nachtjagd and test the hard-pressed crews to the limit of their endurance. In a minute to Churchill on the 3rd, Harris stated, that with the participation of the American 8th Air Force, he could "wreck Berlin from end to end". He estimated that the campaign would cost the two forces between four and five hundred aircraft, but that it would cost Germany the war. This would remove the need for the kind of bloody, expensive and protracted land campaign, which he had personally witnessed during the Great War and had prompted him to "get into the air" at the earliest opportunity. It should be remembered that this was the first time in the history of air warfare, that the means had existed to prove the theory, that an enemy could be defeated by bombing alone. It is only in the light of more recent experiences that we have learned of the need, in a conventional conflict at least, to occupy the enemy's territory to secure submission. The Americans, however, were committed to victory on land, where film cameras could capture the glory and would not accompany Harris to Berlin.

Düsseldorf was selected to open the month's operational account that very night, and no doubt, while the Prime Minister was digesting Harris's epistle, a force of 589 Lancasters and Halifaxes was being prepared for action. 6 Group's contribution to the main event amounted to ninety Halifaxes, while twenty-five Lancasters were to join thirteen other Mk IIs from 3 Group to target the Mannesmann Rohrenwerke (tubular steel works) located on the city's northern outskirts in the first large-scale live test of the G-H bombing system. The bomber stream assembled over the North Sea and approached the south-western Ruhr after flying out over Belgium and through the concentration of fifty to sixty searchlights in the Mönchengladbach-Cologne corridor, some fifteen miles from the target. Small patches of cloud below them at 12,000 feet were drifting across the target along with smoke from the early fires, despite which, the visibility remained generally good, and the Path Finders employed both sky and ground markers to good effect to identify the aiming point in the city centre. Bombing took place on red and green TIs and skymarkers, and fires were observed to be developing on both sides of the Rhine with black smoke rising through 6,000 feet as the bombers turned away. Eighteen aircraft failed to return, and unusually, eleven were

Lancasters and only seven Halifaxes. It was on this night, that 61 Squadron's F/L Bill Reid earned the award of a Victoria Cross for pressing on to bomb the target after his Lancaster, LM360, had been severely damaged and a number of his crew either killed or wounded. Post-raid reconnaissance revealed that central and southern districts had sustained widespread damage to industry and housing, but no report came out of Düsseldorf to provide detail.

Meanwhile, the thirteen 408 (Goose) Squadron Lancasters had departed Linton-on-Ouse between 17.05 and 17.29 with W/C Mair the senior pilot on duty and a cookie and eight and four SBCs respectively of 4lb and 30lb incendiaries in each bomb bay. The crews of F/L Russell, F/O Stewart and P/O Hansen turned back early because of rear turret, engine and Gee issues respectively and were among five "boomerangs", while the G-H receivers in fifteen other aircraft failed to function over the target. Conditions in the target area were favourable with largely clear skies, good visibility and just a little ground haze and the first red TIs were observed to cascade at 19.43 and green TIs were in the bomb site of W/C Mair's bomb-aimer at the point of bomb release. The 408 (Goose) Squadron crews carried out their attacks from 20,000 to 21,000 feet between 19.50 and 20.07 and observed bursts and fires in close proximity to the TIs and watched a pall of smoke form and begin to rise. The failure of the G-H equipment nullified the operation as a test and it would be the autumn of 1944 before the system was rolled out for use by 3 Group, which would employ it to excellent effect against precision targets like marshalling yards and oil refineries through to the end of the war. Two Lancasters failed to return to Linton-on-Ouse, one from each squadron, DS774 coming down off the Dutch coast with the crew of F/Sgt Young RCAF and his crew, who, with the exception of a member of the USAAF, were also RCAF. The remains of three crew members washed ashore in a dinghy on the 12th for a burial in Rotterdam, and the rest of the crew have no known graves. The pilot had been on his eleventh sortie and most of his crew had completed between seven and nine sorties, while the wireless operator, F/O Sauve RCAF, was on the tenth sortie of his second tour.

The intended formation of 433 (Porcupine) Squadron in September had been delayed because of a lack of the new Hercules-powered Halifax Mk III, which had recently entered service with 466 Squadron RAAF and had a performance to rival the Lancaster, although could never match its bomb-carrying capability. The Porcupines would receive the Mk IIIs during November and on the 12th, authority was received to re-equip 420 (Snowy Owl), 424 (Tiger) and 425 (Allouette) Squadrons with the type.

Undaunted by the American response to his invitation to join the Berlin party, Harris would return alone, and the rocky road to the Germany's capital was re-joined by an all-Lancaster heavy force of 440 aircraft on the night of the 18/19th, while a predominantly Halifax and Stirling contingent of 395 aircraft acted as a diversion by raiding the Rhine cities of Mannheim and Ludwigshafen three hundred miles to the south-west. The Berlin-bound crews would benefit from four Mosquitos dropping dummy fighter flares, while other Mosquitos carried out a spoof raid on Frankfurt to protect the Mannheim force. The two formations would cross the enemy coast simultaneously some 250 miles apart to confuse the enemy night-fighter controllers, the route chosen for the Berlin brigade taking it via the Frisian island of Texel to a point north of Hannover, and thence to the target to pass over the centre on an east-north-easterly heading. The return route would pass south of Berlin and Cologne, before crossing central Belgium to gain the English Channel via the French coast. An innovation for this operation was a shortening of the bomber stream to reduce the time over the target to sixteen minutes. When the first Thousand Bomber raid had taken place in May 1942, with an unprecedented twelve aircraft per minute crossing the aiming point, there was considered to be a high risk of collisions. The number had since been increased to sixteen per minute, with large raids lasting up to forty-five minutes, but on this night, twenty-seven aircraft per minute were to pass over the aiming point.

408 (Goose) Squadron made ready fifteen Lancaster IIs and 426 (Thunderbird) Squadron fourteen, the former departing Linton-on-Ouse between 17.23 and 17.42 with W/C Mair and S/L Smith the senior pilots on duty and a cookie and three and one SBCs respectively of 4lb and 30lb incendiaries in each bomb bay. P/O White and crew turned back within ninety minutes because of an unserviceable rear turret, leaving the others to press on over a blanket of cloud that covered the whole of northern Germany. Crews were grateful for the red spotfire route marker dropped by the Path Finders north-east of Hannover, which confirmed that they were on track. They benefitted from good horizontal visibility despite the absence of a moon, while they were denied sight of the ground by the cloud that topped out at a lowly 6,000 feet. Searchlights illuminated the cloud as the 408 (Goose) Squadron crews carried out their attacks on H2S-laid red and green skymarkers from 19,000 to 23,000 feet between 21.01 and 21.17, and all returned home with nothing useful to pass on to the intelligence section at debriefing, most considering the bombing to have been scattered and probably ineffective. Local sources confirmed that there had been no concentration of bombing and confirmed the destruction of 169 houses and a number of industrial units, with many more damaged to some extent. The diversion at Mannheim was deemed to have been successful in its purpose and caused some useful industrial damage, most seriously to the Daimler-Benz motor factory, which suffered a 90% loss of production for an unknown period. In addition to this, more than three hundred buildings were destroyed at a cost of twenty-three aircraft, while the losses from Berlin were encouragingly low at just nine.

The Lancasters stayed at home on the 19th, while 3, 4, 6 and 8 Groups combined to put 170 Halifaxes, eighty-six Stirlings and 10 Mosquitos into the air for a raid on the Ruhr city of Leverkusen. 6 Group provided sixty-six of the Halifaxes, of which seven returned early, while the rest were greeted in the target area by ten-tenths cloud and an absence of marking, which was caused by equipment failure among the Oboe Mosquitos. A few green TIs were spotted some five to ten miles to the north-west of the target during the approach, but the crews were left to establish their positions on the basis of their own H2S, which, over a region as densely built-up as the Ruhr, was a challenge. As a result, the operation was a complete failure, which sprayed bombs over twenty-seven towns in the region, mostly to the north of Leverkusen.

Harris called for a maximum effort on Berlin on the 22nd, to which 6 Group responded with the detailing of thirty Lancasters and eighty-five Halifaxes, of which all but five would join the force of 764 aircraft. The sixteen 408 (Goose) Squadron Lancasters departed Linton-on-Ouse between 17.09 and 17.51 with S/L Smith the senior pilot on duty and after climbing out, would adopt an outward route similar to that employed by the all-Lancaster force four nights earlier. This would take them from Texel to a point north-west of Hannover, where a slight dogleg to port would put them on a due-easterly heading directly to the target. Unlike the previous raid, however, rather than the circuitous return south of Cologne and out over the French coast, they would come home via a reciprocal route. This was based on a forecast of low cloud and fog over Germany, which would inhibit the night-fighter effort, while broken, medium-level cloud over Berlin would facilitate ground marking. An additional bonus was the availability to the Path Finders of five new H2S Mk III sets, while a new record of thirty-four aircraft per minute passing over the aiming point would be achieved by abandoning the long-standing practice of allocating aircraft types to specific waves. On this night, aircraft of all types would be spread through the bomber stream, and this was bad news for the Stirlings, which, by the very nature of their design, would be below the Lancaster and Halifax elements and in danger of being hit by friendly bombs.

P/O Phillips and crew turned back from a position over the North Sea when their oxygen supply system failed, leaving the others to press on and discover that the meteorological forecast had been inaccurate, and that the city was hidden under a blanket of ten-tenths cloud with tops at 12,000 to 16,000 feet. This meant that ground marking would be largely ineffective, and that the least reliable Wanganui (skymarking) method would have to be employed. Crews ran into intense predicted flak and a mass of searchlights as they began their bombing runs, and those from 408 (Goose) Squadron, all but one of which were allotted to wave 5 with only P/O Harvey and crew in wave 1, aimed at red and green TIs and release-point flares from 20,000 to 22,000 feet between 20.17 and 20.28. (The ORB for this period is almost illegible.) The glow of fires was observed beneath the clouds and a very large explosion lit up the sky at 20.10, encouraging an impression that a successful operation was being enacted, but an assessment through the clouds was impossible and it was only once post-raid reconnaissance had taken place and local reports had filtered out that the scale of success would be realised. P/O Stewart and crew endured a torrid return flight after night-fighters appeared and evasive action resulted in a terrifying high-speed stall and spin, which cost many thousands of feet of altitude. The aircraft became unstable and required delicate handling, thereafter, eventually crossing the enemy coast on DR at around 5,000 feet and the English coast at 2,500 feet. The pilot was unsure about landing safely and suggested that the crew bale out, but they preferred to remain on board and their trust in their captain proved well-founded. P/O Brager and crew notched up the squadron's 2,000th sortie and returned DS712 to its ground crew with flak holes in various places and damage to both turrets, the bomb-aimer's compartment and the hydraulics system.

The squadron adjutants' first task on stations across the Command was to inform the families of twenty-six crews that their son, husband or brother was missing as a result of air operations, and at the same time, teams from the Committee of Adjustment had to eradicate all trace of them from the billets. Personal effects were bagged up for return to the family, and the living space prepared for the next occupant, who, in all probability, would arrive later that day. Eleven Lancasters, ten Halifaxes and five Stirlings had failed to return, which amounted to a loss-rate among the types respectively of 2.3%, 4.2% and 10.0%. The Stirling losses proved to be the final straw for Harris, who had never liked the aircraft because of its short wing design, consequent low service ceiling and the configuration of its bomb bay that restricted it to small calibre bombs. Unlike the Lancaster and Halifax, it lacked development potential and was immediately withdrawn from future operations over Germany. It would still have an important role to play on secondary duties, however, bombing over occupied territory, mining, and in 1944, it would replace the Halifax to become the aircraft of choice for the two SOE squadrons, 138 and 161, at Tempsford. Many of those released from Bomber Command service would find their way to 38 Group, where they would give valuable service as transports and glider-tugs for airborne landings.

Reconnaissance photos revealed this last raid on Berlin to have been the most effective against it of the war to date and had caused a swathe of destruction from the city centre through the western residential districts of Tiergarten and Charlottenburg as far as the suburb town of Spandau. A number of firestorm areas were reported, and the catalogue of destruction included three thousand houses and twenty-three industrial premises. Many thousands more sustained varying degrees of damage, costing 175,000 people their homes and an estimated two thousand their lives, and by daylight on the 23rd, the smoke had risen to almost 19,000 feet.

A heavy force of 365 Lancasters and ten Halifaxes was made ready with some difficulty on the 23rd for a return to Berlin. Back-to-back long-range operations put a strain on those charged with the responsibility of getting the aircraft off the ground and as an example, the Ludford Magna armourers were unable to load all nineteen 101 Squadron Lancasters with the intended weight of bombs, sending each of them off 2,000lbs short. 6 Group detailed thirteen Lancasters from each of the Linton-on-Ouse squadrons, but seven would become unserviceable and just nine from 408 (Goose) Squadron took to the air between 17.08 and 17.31 with F/L Russell the senior pilot on duty and each crew sitting on a cookie and six and two SBCs respectively of 4lb and 30lb incendiaries. F/O Stewart and crew were among many afflicted by icing, which, in their case, affected elevator control and persuaded them to turn back after an hour. The bomber stream was depleted by forty-six "boomerangs", which was a further indication of the strain of back-to-back long-range operations, and another was the dumping of bombs over the North Sea by crews intending to push on to the target but wanting to gain more height. It involved largely those from 1 Group, who were shedding their cookies in protest at their A-O-C's policy of loading each Lancaster to its maximum all-up weight at the expense of altitude. The slogan "H-E-I-G-H-T spells safety" could be found on the walls of most bomber station briefing rooms at the time.

The target was reached by way of the same route adopted on the previous night and was found to be covered by ten-tenths cloud with tops at between 10,000 and 15,000 feet. Guided by the glow of fires still burning beneath the clouds from the night before, and the presence of red and green TIs, the 408 (Goose) Squadron crews bombed from 20,000 to 21,000 feet between 20.08 and 20.15 to contribute to another stunning blow. Returning crews described a column of smoke reaching 20,000 feet and the glow of fires visible again from the Hannover area some 150 miles from the target. It was on this night that fake broadcasts from England caused annoyance to the Luftwaffe night-fighter force by ordering them to land because of fog over their bases. The airwaves resounded to a comical exchange as each claimed to be the legitimate voice, but despite any disruption caused, night-fighters still played a major role in bringing-down twenty Lancasters. LL623 failed to return to Linton-on-Ouse with the crew of F/O Bell, who disappeared without trace, the pilot on his eighth sortie and his crew on their sixth. Post-raid reconnaissance and local reports confirmed that this operation had destroyed a further two thousand buildings and killed around fifteen hundred people.

While 1, 3 and 5 Groups enjoyed a night off on the 25th, 128 Halifaxes of 4 Group and eighty-eight of 6 Group acted as the main force for an operation against Frankfurt, for which forty-six 8 Group Halifaxes and Lancasters provided the marking. The blind markers established a firm H2S fix and delivered yellow TIs and red flares with green stars to coincide with the e.t.a. of the main force crews, and according to local sources a modest amount of housing damage resulted and 3,500 people were bombed out of their homes, in return for which, eleven Halifaxes and a single Lancaster failed to return.

After a three-night rest for most of the Lancaster crews, 443 of them were briefed on the 26th for a return to the "Big City" for the fourth attack since the resumption of the campaign. 6 Group contributed thirty-nine Lancaster IIs, including ten provided by 432 (Leaside) Squadron on its operational debut on the type, and fifteen belonging to 408 (Goose) Squadron. The latter departed Linton-on-Ouse between 17.11 and 17.38 with W/C Mair the senior pilot on duty and a cookie and three and one SBCs respectively of 4lb and 30lb incendiaries in each bomb bay. A diversionary raid on Stuttgart by a predominantly Halifax force included fifty-six representing 6 Group and followed the same route as those bound for Berlin, which involved an outward leg that began the Channel crossing over Beachy Head and crossed the French coast near Dieppe, before traversing France and Belgium to a point north of Frankfurt, where they diverged. An indication of the beneficial effects of the three-day lay-off was a hefty reduction in early returns compared with the previous Berlin raid. P/O Clark and crew were defeated by a malfunctioning compass and turned back from the midpoint of the Channel, while the others continued on to find Berlin under clear skies.

Despite the favourable conditions, the Path Finders overshot the city centre aiming point by six or seven miles and marked an area well to the north-west, which happened to contain many war-industry factories. The ORB is corrupted and difficult to decipher, but as far as can be determined the 408 (Goose) Squadron crews bombed on red and green TIs from 19,000 to 23,000 feet between 21.19 and 21.29 and on return spoke of a mass of fires and thick smoke rising to 15,000 feet. Night-fighters took a heavy toll of bombers during the return flight and among twenty-eight missing Lancasters was 408 (Goose) Squadron's DS723 containing W/C Mair DFC RCAF and his RAF crew, who disappeared without trace. The loss of W/C Mair on his nineteenth sortie was, in itself, a bitter blow to the squadron, but missing with him were the navigation and signals leaders, F/O North DFC and F/L Glasspool. A large number of aircraft crashed on return, and the squadron registered such an incident involving DS712, which had lost an engine during the bombing run and was shedding height to 18,000 feet, at which point the bombs were released early at 21.16 and were observed to detonate short of the TIs on the city's western edge. On the way home they were hit by flak, which wounded the rear gunner, and then the crew had to shake off the attentions of a night-fighter over the Ijsselmeer. F/Sgt Lloyd nursed the Lancaster back with a faltering engine and control difficulties to a crash-landing two miles south-east of Lincoln, and there were no further casualties. It was learned later that thirty-eight war-industry factories had been destroyed in the Siemensstadt district to the west of the city centre and many others damaged.

The Stuttgart force reached the target to find six to ten-tenths thin cloud with tops up to 12,000 feet in places, and the blind markers released red flares with green stars either side of 20.30. These tended to become swallowed up by the cloud, but the visual markers confirmed the aiming-point with red and green TIs and the main force crews, who had been assisted in reaching the target by excellent route-marking, employed their own H2S to confirm their positions if the sky and ground markers proved difficult to make out. The glow of fires beneath the cloud remained visible for some time into the return journey, suggesting a degree of success, but this was not borne out by local reports, which described a widely scattered raid and no significant damage.

These last three operations against Berlin undoubtedly represented the best phase of the entire campaign, and according to local reports, the total death toll on the ground resulting from them amounted to 4,330 people, while the destruction of 8,700 apartment buildings containing more than 104,500 flats and damage to several times that number, robbed 450,000 residents of their homes for varying lengths of time. However, Berlin was not Hamburg, where narrow streets had aided the spread of fire. Berlin was a modern city of concrete and steel with wide thoroughfares and open spaces to create natural firebreaks, and each building destroyed added to these, so that the campaign would become a bitter struggle of ever decreasing returns.

The new commanding officer was W/C Jacobs, whose first tour had been on Hampdens, and who, like his predecessor, would eventually be lost while leading his men from the front. During the course of the month, the squadron took part in five operations and dispatched sixty-eight sorties for the loss of four Lancasters and three crews.

December 1943

Berlin would continue to be the dominant theme during December, and as November had ended, so December began. A new station commander at Linton-on-Ouse, G/C Jones, took up his post on the 2nd and oversaw the preparations for that night's operation to Berlin, for which 408 (Goose) Squadron made ready fourteen Lancasters and 426 (Thunderbird) Squadron thirteen, while over at East Moor 432 (Leaside) Squadron contributed eight. They were part of a heavy force of 443 aircraft, all but fifteen of them Lancasters, after the 4 and 6 Group Halifax elements had been withdrawn because of fog over their Yorkshire stations. The 408 (Goose) Squadron contingent took off between 16.45 and 17.11 with F/L Russell the senior pilot on duty and the usual cookie and incendiary mix in each bomb bay. After climbing out, they headed for the Yorkshire coast to rendezvous over the North Sea with the rest of the force for a straight-in-straight-out route across Holland and northern Germany with no feints or diversions. First, however, the crews had to negotiate a towering front of ice-bearing cloud over the North Sea, which would contribute to a 10% rate of early returns, and it was at this stage that F/O Clark and crew turned back with a defective rear turret, one of eight 6 Group early returns or almost 23% of those dispatched.

Many of those pushing through the challenging conditions were driven south of track by variable winds, which dispersed the bomber stream. They also had to contend with large numbers of enemy night-fighters harassing them all the way to the target, after the controller had been able correctly to predict it. The Path Finders employed H2S to establish their position at Stendal, but had strayed some fifteen miles south of track and mistakenly used the town of Genthin as their reference for the run-in. The 408 (Goose) Squadron crews were spread among the three waves and found good visibility as they were guided by release-point flares to the aiming point, where they encountered a thin layer of two to three-tenths cloud at around 5,000 feet but up to nine-tenths between 10,000 and 12,000 feet, which the searchlights were able to pierce. They bombed on skymarkers and red and green TIs and where possible ground detail like burning streets, from 19,000 to 22,500 feet between 20.10 and 20.53. They reported observing scattered fires and a number of large explosions and some claimed the glow to be visible from 120 miles into the homeward leg. At debriefing, P/O Morrison and crew reported losing their intercom at the start of the bombing run and letting their load go on a searchlight and flak concentration some eight miles west of the aiming point. They would have turned back earlier because of a defective rear turret but would not risk a collision by turning across the bomber stream completely blind in cloud. Bombing photographs suggested that the raid was only partially successful, causing useful damage in industrial districts in the west and east, but scattering the main weight of bombs over the southern districts and outlying communities to the south.

Having been spared by the weather from experiencing an effective visitation from the Command in October and exploiting the enemy's expectation that Berlin would be the target again, Leipzig found itself at the end of the red tape on briefing-room wall-maps from County Durham to Cambridgeshire on the 3rd. A force of 527 aircraft was made ready, which included a 6 Group contribution of ninety-seven aircraft, nineteen of them Lancasters, the numbers somewhat depleted by the late return from diversions after the Berlin raid. The 408 (Goose) Squadron crews of S/L Smith, P/O Smith, F/O Clark and F/Sgts Burns and Sutherland departed Linton-on-Ouse between 00.25 and 00.32 and lost the services of S/L Smith and crew to starboard-inner engine failure as they made their way across the North Sea. They were among an alarming twenty 6 Group aircraft to abort their sorties the others rendezvousing with the bomber stream as it headed for Berlin as a feint, passing north of Hannover and Braunschweig with ten-tenths cloud beneath them and an hour's journey to Leipzig still ahead of them. Then, as they turned towards the south-east, the Mosquito element continued on to carry out a diversion at the capital, and despite the fact that night-fighters had already infiltrated the stream at the Dutch coast, the feint had the desired effect, and few night-fighters were encountered in the target area, where two layers of ten-tenths cloud prevailed with tops at around 7,000 and 15,000 feet. The Path Finders marked by H2S with green skymarkers, and the 408 (Goose) Squadron crews bombed on these from 21,000 to 24,000 feet between 04.04 and 04.25, observing a large explosion at 04.05 followed by others during the course of the raid. A strong glow illuminated the base of the clouds and the emergence through the cloud tops of black smoke spiralling to 19,000 feet and beyond suggested an effective raid. The glow from the burning city remained visible for 150 miles into the return journey south-east towards the French frontier, and had many aircraft not then strayed into the Frankfurt defence zone, the losses may have been fewer. In the event, twenty-four aircraft failed to return, fifteen of them Halifaxes. Local reports confirmed this as a highly successful operation, which had hit residential and industrial areas and was the most destructive raid visited upon this eastern city during the war. Sadly, for the Command, it would take its revenge in time.

Thereafter, minor operations carried the Command through to mid-month, when on the 16th, the Lancaster stations were roused and instructed to prepare 483 of the type for that night's operation to Berlin for the sixth time since the resumption of the campaign. 6 Group put up forty Lancaster IIs, seventeen of them representing 408 (Goose) Squadron, which departed Linton-on-Ouse between 16.20 and 16.51 with W/C Jacobs and S/L Miles the senior pilots on duty and each carrying the standard cookie and incendiary bomb load. They were to cross the Dutch coast in the region of Castricum-aan-Zee, and then head due east all the way to the target with no deviations. A three-quarter moon would rise during the long return leg over the Baltic and Denmark, but it was hoped that the very early take-off and the expectation of fog over enemy night-fighter stations would reduce the risk of interception. Night-fighters were sent to meet the bomber stream at the Dutch coast and claimed a number of successes, but the majority of Lancasters were unmolested and pressed on to find Berlin obscured by ten-tenths cloud with tops at around 5,000 feet. W/O Lloyd and crew were at 17,000 feet east of Hannover when losing their port-inner engine and decided to abandon their sortie and jettison the cookie to arrest the loss of altitude. The account of the rest of the flight is contradictory and the map references unreliable, but it seems that they chose to remain within the protection of the bomber stream but avoided passing over Berlin and picked up the stream again on the homeward leg.

The aiming point was identified initially by red and green skymarkers, but red and green ground markers were in the 408 (Goose) Squadron bomb sights as the bombing took place from 19,000 to 22,000 feet between 20.01 and 20.08. The return over Denmark passed largely without major incident, but the greatest difficulties awaited the 1, 6 and 8 Group crews as they arrived home to find their airfields covered by a blanket of dense fog. With little reserves of fuel, the tired crews began a frantic search to find somewhere to land, stumbling blindly through the murk to catch a glimpse of the ground. For many, this proved fatal, while others gave up any hope of landing and abandoned their aircraft. F/O Clark RCAF was descending gingerly, and all eyes were seeking a break in the visibility when DS737 smacked into high ground at Murton Common, some fifteen miles north-east of Linton-on-Ouse, killing four of the occupants on impact and injuring the pilot and two others. F/O Clark, who had been on his ninth sortie, succumbed on the 21st and found a final resting place with the two other RCAF victims in the Canadian section of the Stonefall Cemetery in Harrogate. Twenty-nine Lancasters and a mine-laying Stirling were lost and more than 150 airmen killed in these most tragic of circumstances and to this number was added the twenty-five Lancasters failing to return from the raid, among which was 408 (Goose) Squadron's LL676, which disappeared without trace with the crew of F/O Maitland DFM RCAF, who was undertaking the first sortie of his second tour, his first having been served on Hampdens with 420 (Snowy Owl) Squadron. Returning crews reported the glow of fires, while others saw nothing through the cloud and it was a local report that confirmed a moderately effective raid, which had fallen principally onto central and eastern districts, where housing suffered most.

A three-day stand-down allowed the crews to recover from the Berlin operation and it was the 20th when all stations were notified of an operation that night to Frankfurt, for which a force of 390 Lancasters and 257 Halifaxes was assembled. 6 Group made ready thirty-four Lancaster IIs and eighty-two Halifaxes, and at Linton-on-Ouse, fifteen 408 (Goose) Squadron aircraft each received the requisite amount of fuel and a bomb load of either a cookie and ten and two SBCs respectively of 4lb and 30lb incendiaries or an 8,000 pounder and two SBCs of 4lb incendiaries. They took off between 17.01 and 17.20 with S/L Smith the senior pilot on duty, and as they made their way towards Southwold and the North-Sea crossing to the Scheldt estuary, forty-four Lancasters and ten Mosquitos of 1 and 8 Groups were outbound to conduct a diversion at Mannheim, some forty miles to the south of the main event. F/L Wilton and crew had just crossed the Cambridgeshire/Norfolk county boundary when their sortie was ended by the failure of the rear turret, and 2nd Lt Humphrey and crew were a few miles out over the sea when the a.s.i failed and forced them to turn back also. The main element passed to the north of Antwerp and flew the length of Belgium to cross the German frontier north of Luxembourg.

The German night-fighter controller had picked up transmissions from the bomber stream as soon as it left the English coast and was able to track it all the way to the target and vector his fighters into position. Many combats took place during the outward flight and the diversion failed to draw fighters away from the main action. The problems continued at the primary target, where the forecast clear skies failed to materialise, and the crews were greeted by four to nine-tenths cloud at between 5,000 and 10,000 feet. This allowed some of them to pick out ground features, while others fixed their positions by H2S, if so equipped, and the main force Lancaster crews simply waited for TIs on e.t.a. The Path Finders had prepared a ground-marking plan in expectation of good vertical visibility, and dropped red, green and yellow TIs, while the Germans lit a decoy fire-site five miles to the south-east of the city. Some crews described the marking as late and erratic, and those from 408 (Goose) Squadron bombed on red and green TIs from 18,000 to 22,000 feet between 19.39 and 19.50. Most thought the attack to be scattered in the early stages, becoming more concentrated as it progressed, and many commented on the new cookies detonating with a brighter flash than the old ones. A large red explosion was observed at 19.50 and smoke was rising through the cloud tops to give the impression at least of a moderately successful raid, and at least one crew reported the glow of fires remaining visible for 150 miles into the return journey.

Any success was achieved largely as the result of the creep-back from the decoy site, which fell across the suburbs of Offenbach and Sachsenhausen, situated on the southern bank of the River Main. 466 houses were destroyed and more than nineteen hundred seriously damaged, despite which, the operation fell well short of its aims and the loss of forty-one aircraft was a high price to pay. The Halifaxes suffered heavily, losing twenty-seven of their number, a loss-rate of 10.5% compared with the Lancasters' 3.6%. It was not a night to remember for 6 Group, which registered eleven early returns and ten failures to return, among the latter two belonging to 408 (Goose) Squadron. It is believed that DS704 was the victim of "friendly fire" from another Lancaster and crashed near Tessenderlo, some fifteen miles to the north-west of Hasselt in Belgium. Two members of the crew lost their lives and the rear gunner fell into enemy hands, while P/O Morrison RAAF and three others evaded a similar fate, the wireless operator remaining with his helpers until liberated by the Americans in September 1944. They had been on their eleventh sortie together. DS758 also came down on Belgian soil with no survivors from the crew of F/O Brager RCAF, the pilot on his thirteenth sortie, while his mixed RCAF, RAF and USAAF crew had completed between ten and seventeen.

Just two more operations remained before the year ended and both were to be directed against Germany's capital city. The first was posted on the 23rd and involved an all-Lancaster heavy force drawn from 1, 3, 5 and 8 Groups with seven Halifaxes among the Path Finder element and eight Mosquitos to provide a diversion. A relatively modest sixteen Lancasters failed to return from what was at best a modestly successful raid that had been compromised by a high failure rate of Path Finder H2S sets. Local sources named the south-eastern suburbs of Köpenick and Treptow as the ones to sustain the most damage, with 287 houses and other buildings suffering complete destruction.

The fifth wartime Christmas was observed without interruption from operational considerations, and it was not until the 29th that a maximum effort was called for the next assault on Berlin. For the Lancaster operators, this would be the first of three raids on the capital in the space of five nights spanning the turn of the year, and 457 of the type were to be joined by 252 Halifaxes and three Mosquitos to form a force of 712 aircraft. 6 Group detailed forty Lancasters and eighty-nine Halifaxes, fourteen of the former belonging to 408 (Goose) Squadron, each of which received a cookie and incendiary bomb load before departing Linton-on-Ouse between 16.59 and 17.25 with W/C Jacobs the senior pilot on duty. They rendezvoused with the bomber stream as it crossed the North Sea to make landfall over the Dutch Frisian islands pointing directly for Leipzig, and having reached a point just to the north of Leipzig, swung to the north towards Berlin, while Mosquitos carried out spoof raids on Leipzig and Magdeburg. The main force element reached the target area to find ten-tenths cloud with tops at anywhere between 7,000 and 18,000 feet, and red and green Path Finder release-point flares hanging over the city. The ground marking TIs disappeared into the cloud tops and could not be seen, leaving the success of the operation in the hands of drifting skymarkers, which appeared to most to have been deployed effectively. The 408 (Goose) Squadron crews had been allotted to the first and fifth waves and delivered their bomb loads from 19,000 and 21,000 feet between 20.04 and 20.22, on return reporting a considerable red glow beneath the clouds, which remained visible for a hundred miles and gave the impression of a concentrated and successful assault. This was not entirely borne out by local reports, which revealed that the main weight of the raid had fallen onto southern and south-eastern districts and also into outlying communities to the east. 388 buildings were destroyed, although none of significance, and ten thousand people were bombed out of their homes. Eleven Lancasters and nine Halifaxes failed to return, a loss-rate of 2.4% for the former and 3.5% for the latter and there was a single empty dispersal pan at Linton-on-Ouse. DS718 crashed some ten miles west of Lingen, close to the frontier with Holland and there were no survivors from the mixed RCAF/RAF crew of F/L Wilton RCAF. The pilot was on his seventh sortie, while his crew had completed between two and sixteen.

During the course of the month, the squadron took part in five operations and dispatched sixty-five sorties for the loss of five Lancasters and crews.

It had been a testing end to a year which had brought major successes and advances in tactics, but it had also been a year of high losses, particularly among the Stirling and Halifax squadrons. While "window" had been an instant success, it had also caused the Luftwaffe to rethink and reorganise and the night-fighter force which emerged from the ruins of the old system was a leaner, more efficient and altogether more lethal beast than that of before. As far as the crews of Bomber Command were concerned, the coming year offered the same fare as the old one, which few would view with relish and the next three months would see morale at its lowest ebb as the winter campaign ground on.

408 Squadron 1943

When the skipper and his crew are satisfied that the Lancaster is ready for the bombing mission, he gives the "chocks away" sign with a semi-circular wave of both gauntleted hands. The ground crew here LAC M G Cote and LAC Bob Rushton both aero-engine mechanics attached to Goose Squadron are pulling the ropes attached to the chocks and removing them from in front of the huge wheels.

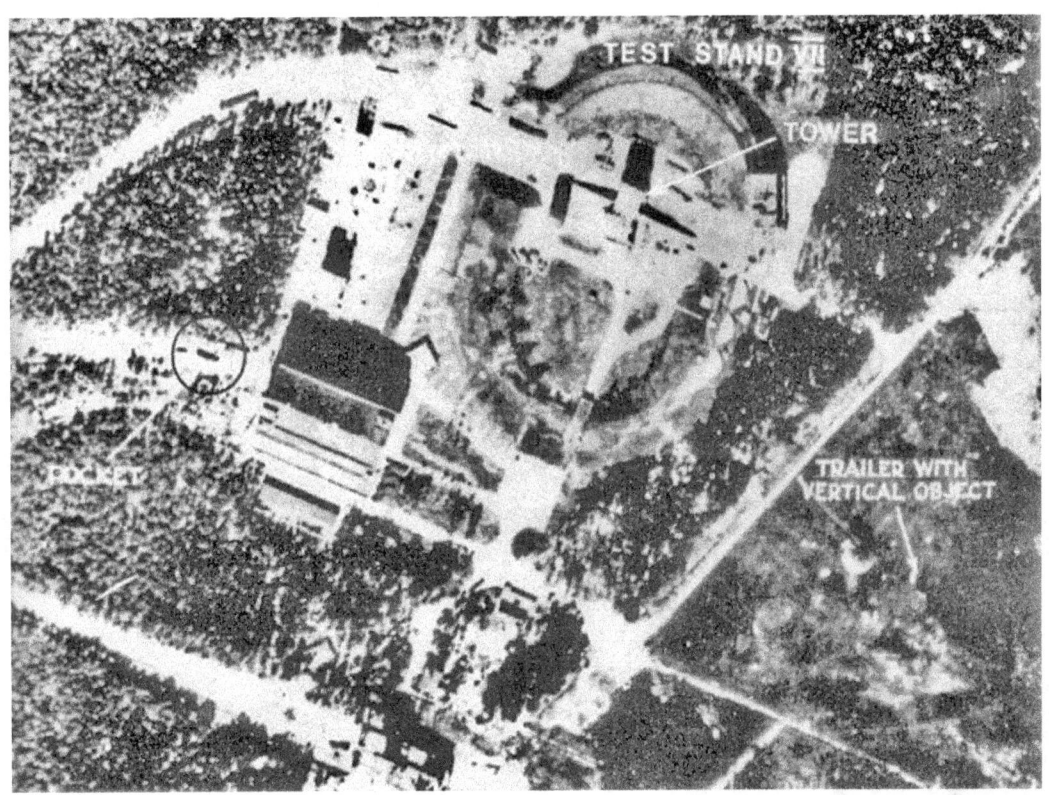

RAF reconnaissance photograph of V-2 rockets at Peenemünde Test Stands I and VII and below, post bombing.

By the end of the Battle of Berlin on 31st March 1944, the city had been visited sixteen times by 408 Squadron. Having flown on eleven of these missions, F/Sgt J D Harvey was later cited as the 408 Squadron pilot with the most trips to Berlin – and was presented with a gold wristwatch to mark the achievement.

F/Sgt John Douglas Harvey

The F/L W. Russell crew from 408 Squadron standing in front of Lancaster II DS-729 coded EQ-D. P/O W. Barrett, 2nd from the left is the Wireless Op. Crewmembers in no certain order are:
F/L W. Russell RCAF, (Pilo); P/O L James RCAF, (F/E); F/O M. Howard RCAF, (Nav);
P/O J. Moore RCAF, (BA); Sgt B. Lennox RCAF, (MUG) and F/ Sgt J. LaFlamme RCAF, RG.

Members of 408 Squadron 1944

408 Squadron Lancaster LL725 EQ-C on the ground at Linton-on-Ouse, Yorkshire. Armourers are backing a tractor and trolley loaded with a 4,000 lb HE bomb ('Cookie') and incendiaries under the open bomb bay. The aircraft was lost without trace over Hamburg on 28/29th July 1944. P/O J H A McCaffrey DFC, Sgt F Fearns, P/O's R H Mitchell and G E Cameron, W/O A F Marsden, W/OII L F Cassidy, F/Sgt A E Candline and Sgt G R Harvey are all commemorated on the Runnymede Memorial.

Wing Commander Roy A McLernon DFC
408 Squadron Commanding Officer
1st May 1944 – 13th October 1944

Wing Commander Jake F. Easton DFC
408 Squadron Commanding Officer
14th October 1944 – 15th November 1944

W/C J Easton (Left)

Presentation of DFC to W/C R A McLernon

F O J G White & crew with Lancaster DS710 EQ-A

A 408 Squadron Lancaster bears its official crest, a current record of sorties flown depicted by tiny bombs, the RCAF roundel, and the name "Miss Kingsville" in honour of the town which adopted the Squadron. In addition, it has "G for Goose". The ground crew who keep Miss Kingsville in tiptop shape are LAC Bob Ferry, in the cockpit; while below him are (reading down) left: LAC Harry Truax, LAC Harvey Harold; Sgt Jeff Godfrey. Right: LAC Keith Cinnamin; Sgt Sam McCracken and LAC Gordon Palin.

When "ops" are on, no time is wasted around the dispersal of Lancasters of the "Goose" Squadron. Here "Z - Zombie" gets bombed up for a trip to Cologne while a petrol lorry pours thousands of gallons of fuel into the tanks.

This Halifax crew was typical of most 408 Squadron crews in that it was composed of men from Canada, Britain and the United States. Clockwise from the top of the ladder are: S/L B E Harriss (Pilot), Sgt Ralph Shellington (W.Op), Sgt Bob Pridday (FE), Sgt Tommy Dimma (MUG), P/O J Bemister (Nav), Sgt Bill Willis (RG), and F/O Tom Harris (BA)

Members of the RCAF 408 'Goose' Squadron in Britain prepare for an operation.

Lancaster DS771 on an early test flight. After service with 408 Squadron, it passed to 426 Squadron with which unit it was lost with all crew on the 16th March 1944.

F/Sgt Jack J Cunningham – rear gunner in Halifax E-Easy. October 1944,

Four of the crew of Lancaster II DS-634 coded EQ-A, which crashed west of Spieka, Germany on the 29th July 1944. Of the eight crewmen, two were killed and six were taken prisoner. L-R: P/O E Goodwin (KIA), unknown but one of the remaining crew, Sgt A. Ducharme (PoW), P/O G. Boehmer (PoW). Rest of the crew: Sgt B M Hofforth (KIA), W/OII L. Phipps (PoW), Sgt L. Rourke (PoW), F/O S. Coffe (PoW). F/Sgt E Wulff (PoW)

Veterans of two complete tours of bombing operations, F/L W.S. Pullar has a chat with Sgt A W Faux the NCO in charge of his Lancaster "Our Mary". Both are members of the RCAF 408 'Goose' Squadron.

W/O Bill Wade, air gunner, and Sgt Doug Skingle, air gunner, of the P/O H. McKinley crew of 408 Squadron, exit Lancaster II DS707 EQ-C after completing their seventh operation, the day after D-Day. Just behind the bulged bomb bay doors one can see the .50 calibre barrel protruding from the mid-under gun position. This gun position was rarely seen on Lancaster IIs of 408 Squadron.

G/C G B Latimer in front of Lancaster DS707 'Our Mary II'.

Admiring the artistry of the nose art is intelligence clerk, Cpl Gordon Arscott, and seated on the four-engined bomber's nose is LAC Johnnie Linden, an aero-engine mechanic with Goose Squadron. It shows a jet-propelled goose dragging along old man 'Titus'. It was designed by the crew of T for Tommy in 408 Squadron.

There's quite a story behind "Z - Zebra" of the RCAF "Goose" Squadron, which is known to the lads who fly it as "Zombie". On a recent operational trip, one of the Lancaster's engines stopped dead and the crew had to land at an emergency airfield.

Next morning, they went to the aircraft, started the engines, and found all of them functioned perfectly.

Sgt George Oliver, the crew's rear gunner, touches up the painting.

The Franklin Crew.

Top L-R: Sgt George Oliver (RG), WOI Bergie Bergen (W.Op), F/O Claude Franklin (pilot), Sgt John Medcraft (FE).

Lower L-R: Sgt Leo Robideau (MUG), Sgt Mike Bartman (Nav) Sgt Terry Delaney (BA).

Rear-gunner Sgt George Oliver flew with 408 Squadron in Lancasters. He recalls the reason for the nose art on Lancaster LL725, "On our 8th operation to Essen, Germany on 24th March 1944, we lost an engine and had the option to dump our bomb load and return to base. The crew decided to carry on but arrived over the target late and all alone. After the release of our bomb load, 'all hell broke loose' and we were lucky to escape the intense ack-ack. On our return to base, we found out that we were posted as lost in action. After this experience we all agreed "Zombie" [return of the living dead] should become the nose art, (rather than the original Z-Zebra) and it was."

On 20th July 1944, George completed his tour of 30 operations, 22 flown in "Zombie." He flew two additional operations as the mid-under gunner with Franklin 27th May 1944 and another in Lancaster-L on 17th June 1944 with Bryson as mid-upper gunner. George says he must have come back from leave early because the money ran out and filled in for something to do. Eight days later LL725 was shot down on a raid to Hamburg, Germany, one of three Lancaster Mk. II's the squadron lost that single day.

George painted the same Lancaster nose art on to his suitcase which he donated to the Bomber Command Museum of Canada.

Lancaster EQ-E was named 'Old Faithful' and she lived up to her name. DS763 completed 35 operations with 426 Squadron and then was transferred to 408 (Goose) Squadron flying another 37 operations between 10th May to 15th August 1944. Seventy-two operations were the most completed for a Goose Squadron Lancaster Mk. II which survived the RAF air campaign in the Battle of Berlin. Though the Lancaster could absorb terrible combat damage and continue flying, it was designed with awkward escape hatches. Five of the aircrew in the front had to use the emergency escape hatch on the floor of the nose, and the last to leave was the pilot, who attempted to keep the aircraft steady for his crew. Only eleven per cent of Lancaster aircrew survived compared to twenty-nine in the Halifax bomber, and fifty per cent in the American B-17 Flying Fortress.

F/O E R Proud (2nd Pilot)   F/L E E Kearl DFC (Pilot)   P/O J F McManus (RG)
All killed together with P/O J P D Parise (Nav), P/O A Smith (BA), P/O J Adamson (W.Op/AG), P/O J A MacLean (MUG) on a Berlin operation 27th December 1944.

This Goose Squadron crew, with the exception of two members, had just completed two tours of operational flying. The five "two tour" veterans racked up 275 tours between them and to add to their record the pilot and navigator flew their first tour together. In front row at the left is F/O Larry Corbeil (BA) with the one tour Sgt Joe McCart (FE). At the back, left to right: F/L Bob Austen, F/O Sandy De Zorzi, (Nav), F/L Bob Clouthier, Pilot and F/O Bob Fitzgerald (RG). Below: F/L Clouthier and crew of 'Relic'.

A Lancaster crew enjoying a cup of coffee while awaiting their de-briefing after their return from a mission. L-R: F/Sgt C O Draper, F/O C Ridgers, F/Sgt D Mullock, F/L W Smith and F/Sgt L S Beer. All, except F/Sgt Mullock (PoW), were killed on the 26th February 1944 on an Augsburg raid. Other members of the crew lost were Sgt F Crofts and F/Sgt R E Bowler. These were an experienced crew nearing the end of their tour.

A pair of brothers serving with 408 Squadron – F/O's Jack and Harold McKinley watch as photo bombs are being winched into their Lancaster.

A bomb train with the supply of bombs on route to the Lancaster dispersals driver of the second tractor is LAC Joe Courchene of Edmonton.

F/O Brian Lanktree poses in the cockpit of his aircraft after receiving the welcome news that he has completed his tour of operations.

Sergeants Jim Harris, Joe Holland and Doug Skingle kitted up for another raid June 6th 1944.

On their way to another RCAF Halifax, 408 Squadron members Sgt Ralph Syer, rear gunner, and Sgt Walter Wilkins, flight engineer, watch a squadron mate practice bomb aiming in the nose of his Halifax.

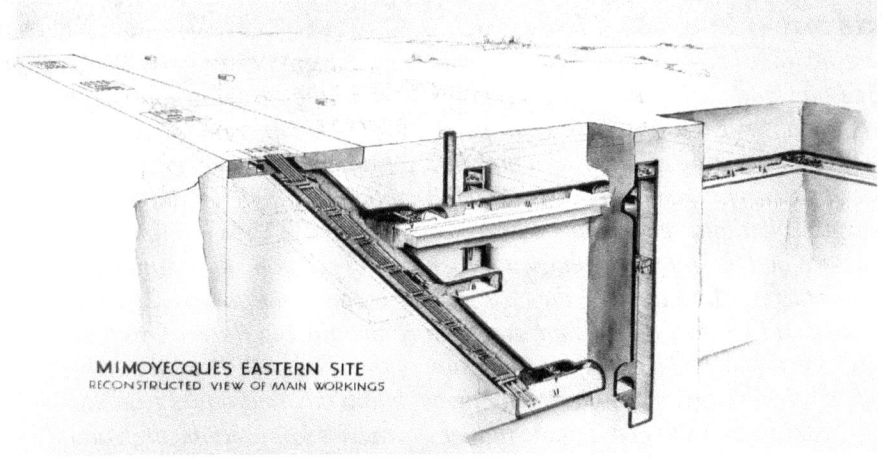

408 Squadron's target on the operation of 27th August 1944.

Standing before his smashed rear turret is 408 Squadron rear gunner F/Sgt G Pedro Lapierre. "We had just dopped our load on burning Berlin and got beyond the target area when things started to happen", said his skipper P/O W G (Bill) Phillips on their 14th trip. Said Lapierre "We gunners had our eye on an FW190 stooging along astern port quarter down about 600 yards away", said the mid upper gunner Sgt G Currie, "suddenly I saw a JU88 on the port quarter starting to dive at us from above and I warned pilot and rear gunner to prepare for action". The German night-fighter dove in directly from astern and at 200 yards let go a full charge of cannon shells and machine gun bullets right into the rear turret. Miraculously, the rear gunner escaped unscathed. "All I saw was a fighter coming in behind and I let go with my four guns before the glaring flash of his tracer blinded me." said Lapierre who was knocked out by the concussion of the shells. All Perspex in the rear turret was broken, armour plating, oxygen equipment shot away, bomb bay and doors riddled, engine cowling shot away etc. The mid upper gunner shot the fighter down as it followed through about 20 feet above his turret. "Believe me, it's terrible staring into the blazing guns of a German night-fighter", said gunner Lapierre shown here.

F/O Harry Moroz, wireless operator of 408 Squadron killed on the 22nd March 1944 when his Lancaster LL717 was believed to have been shot down by a night-fighter while on a Frankfurt raid. His crew also perished - F/Sgt J A N Pare, Sgt K L Curtis, F/Sgt G F Clough, F/O L D Proctor, Sgt A E Rickert and Sgt S E Woolhether. F/O Moroz is commemorated on the Runnymede Memorial.

Even the old stork has been enlisted for bombing the enemy as illustrated in this crest on a 'Goose' Squadron Lancaster. Wearing a messenger's cap, the bird makes sure its new arrival drops his quota of bombs on the target.

408 Squadron air and ground crew decorated 'birthday card' for Adolf Hitler. L-R: LAC Harry Elricks, F/Sgt Mike Bateman, Sgt George Oliver, Sgt Harry Russell and ACI Don Rothery. 24th April 1944.

Linton-on-Ouse 1944. L-R: F/Sgt Alex Trench (BA), F/L Allan Bryson (Pilot), Sgt Kay Moore (FE)

G/C Clare Annis and the CO discuss the raid with a crew just back from a raid. F/O's Bill Shields, Ed Bentley, W L Turner, 'Chuck' Wilson, F/L Ivan Stonelocker, F/O Don Snider and W/O Steve Evancio.

Air Gunner P/O C L Humphreys poses beside his tail turret, which is adorned with an appropriate cartoon character.

W/C (later General) Frederick Ralph Sharp CMM DFC CD
He spent over four years on instructional duties in Alberta, before being posted overseas as C.O. of. 408 Bomber Squadron, 6 Bomber Group 12th November 1944. He won a Distinguished Flying Cross on 4th May 1945 with 408 Goose Squadron and was their last wartime squadron commander.

Aircraft of 408 Squadron photographed Halifax MZ759 NP-Q of 158 Squadron on fire on the 24th March 1945.

Part of the locomotive shop of the Krupps AG works at Essen, Germany, seriously damaged by Bomber Command in 1943, and further wrecked in the daylight raid of 11th March 1945.

Nose Art "Zombie". 408 Squadron Halifax Bomber 1945. Below: A Close-up

Nuremburg 1945
Despite the catastrophic night for Bomber Command on the 31st March 1944, Nuremburg suffered severe bomb damage during the war.

W/C Sharp and F/Sgt Jim Sentis receive the Handley Page Safety Award trophy from AVM C M McEwan 22nd April 1945.

Wangerooge
One of the last great RAF raids together with RCAF against Germany. This raid was intended to knock out the coastal batteries on this Frisian island which controlled the approaches to the ports of Bremen and Wilhelmshaven.

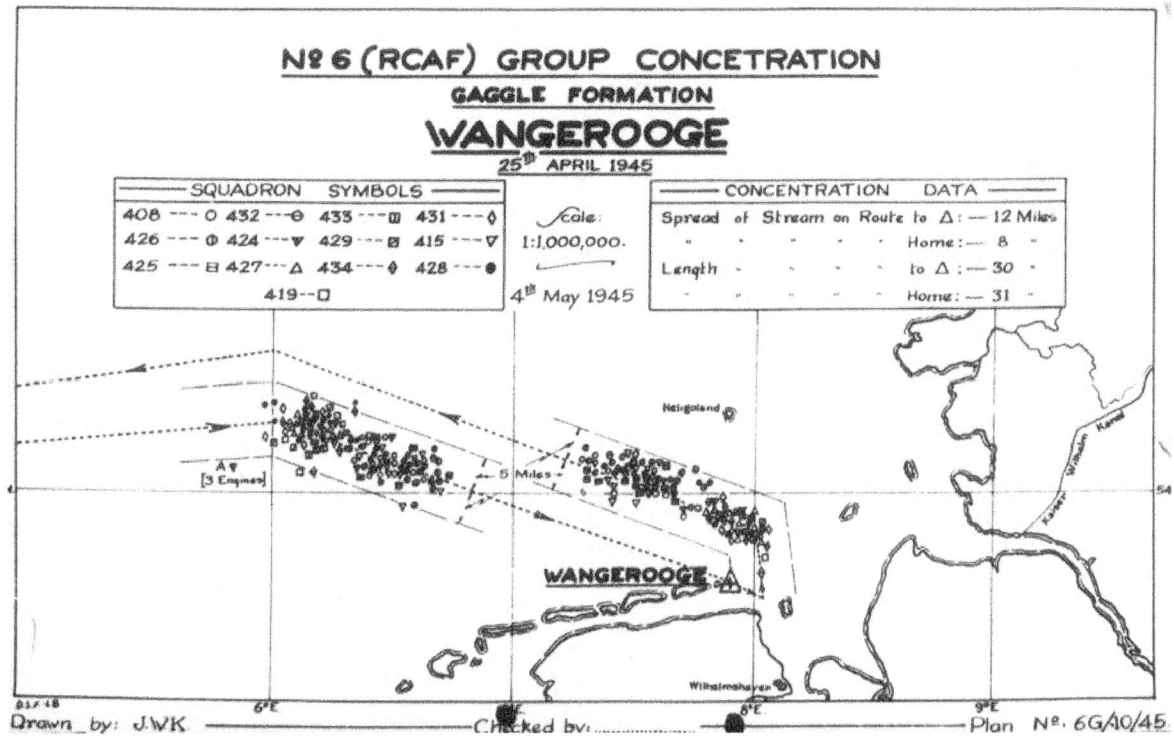

408 Squadron's last operation of the war was a joint one with other 6 Group members. Above: The gaggle sets off.

January 1944

The ORB entries at the start of the year are difficult to decipher, particularly with regard to names, and some of the times and altitudes are best guesses. The change of year was not destined to effect a change in the emphasis of operations, and this was, no doubt, a disappointment not only to the hard-pressed crews of Bomber Command but also to the beleaguered residents of Germany's capital city. Proud of their status as Berliners first and Germans second, they were a hardy breed and just like their counterparts in London during the Blitz of 1940, would bear their trials with fortitude and humour and would not buckle under the constant assault from above. "You may break our walls", proclaimed banners in the streets, "but not out hearts", and the most popular song of the day, "Nach jedem Dezember kommt immer ein Mai", "After every December there's always a May", was played endlessly over the airwaves, its sentiments hinting at a change in fortunes with the onset of spring, which was precisely how long both camps would have to wait until their wishes for a break in the campaign would be fulfilled. Harris allowed the Berliners little time to enjoy New Year, and as New Year's Day dawned, plans were already in hand to continue the onslaught. Before it ended, the first of 421 Lancasters, twenty-nine of them representing 6 Group, would be taking off and heading eastwards to arrive over the city as the clock showed 03.00 hours on the 2nd.

Take-off had actually been delayed because of doubts over the weather, and this meant that insufficient hours of daylight remained to allow the planned outward route over Denmark and the Baltic. Instead, the bomber stream would adopt the previously used almost direct route across Holland and northern Germany, but return as originally planned more circuitously, passing east of Leipzig, before racing across Germany between the Ruhr and Frankfurt and traversing Belgium to reach the Channel near the French port of Boulogne. 408 (Goose) Squadron's twelve participants were divided between the first and second waves and departed Linton-on-Ouse between 00.25 and 00.49 with F/L Burns the senior pilot on duty and each carrying the standard cookie and incendiary bomb load. The force was gradually depleted by twenty-nine early returns, one of them, that of F/O White and crew, who were unable to reach a respectable height and systematically jettisoned ordnance and equipment until the decision was taken to abort the sortie. The bomber stream had covered the four-hundred-mile leg from the Dutch coast to Berlin in under two hours without once catching a glimpse of the ground through the dense cloud, and it was no different at the target, which was completely obscured by a layer of ten-tenths cloud with tops in places as high as 19,000 feet. The Path Finders had to employ skymarking (Wanganui), which was somewhat scattered, and the 408 (Goose) Squadron crews aimed for these parachute flares from 18,000 to 21,000 feet between 03.07 and 03.20. They observed the glow of fires and smoke rising through the cloud tops and a huge explosion was witnessed at 03.07, which lit up the clouds for three seconds, but it was impossible to assess what was happening on the ground. It was established, ultimately, that the operation had been a failure, which had scattered bombs across the southern fringes of the city causing only minor damage, while the main weight of the attack had fallen beyond the city boundaries into wooded and open country. The disappointment was compounded by the loss of twenty-eight Lancasters, although none belonging to 6 Group.

During the course of the 2nd, a heavy force of 362 Lancasters and nine of the new Mk III Hercules-powered Halifaxes was made ready for a return to Berlin that night. There was snow on the ground as the crews were called to briefing, many still tired from being late to bed following the almost-eight-hour round trip the night before, and some of these were in a mutinous frame of mind at being on the order of battle again so soon. 5 Group cancelled twenty-five of its intended contribution, and six of the original thirty-four Lancasters detailed by 6 Group were also scrubbed. The ten-strong 408 (Goose) Squadron element departed Linton-on-Ouse between 23.46 and 00.30 with F/L Burns the senior pilot on duty and either a single 8,000 pounder in each bomb bay or a cookie and incendiaries. The outward route crossed the Dutch coast near Castricum and took the bomber stream to a point south-east of Bremen, followed by a dogleg to the north-west and, finally, a ninety degree change of course to the south-east in the Parchim area to leave a ninety-mile run to the target. The crews of F/L Burns and F/Os White and Stewart were among the massive sixty early returns that depleted the bomber stream, 15.7% of those dispatched, caused largely by severe icing conditions, while others abandoned their sorties because of minor problems that might have seen them carry on had they been fully rested. In the case of F/O Stewart, it was illness on his part that prevented him and his crew from continuing.

The route changes worked well to throw off the night-fighters, but they would congregate in the target area after the controller correctly identified Berlin as the target forty minutes before zero-hour. Ten-tenths cloud with tops at 16,000 feet forced the bombing to take place on the red skymarkers with green stars or on the glow of fires, the 408 (Goose) Squadron crews carrying out their attacks from 19,000 to 21,000 feet between 02.47 and 02.58. They reported smoke rising to 20,000 feet as they turned away, but it was not possible to make an accurate assessment of the outcome and the impression was of an effective attack, when, in fact, it had been another failure. Bombs had been scattered across the city and destroyed just eighty-two houses for the loss of twenty-seven Lancasters, most of which had fallen victim to night-fighters in the target area. The squadron's LL631 failed to return with the predominantly RCAF crew of F/Sgt Hilker RCAF, who were on their fourth sortie together, the pilot and mid-upper gunner losing their lives, while the five survivors were taken into captivity.

After three trips to the "Big City" in five nights, it would now be left to the Mosquitos of 8 Group's Mosquito squadrons to disrupt the resident's sleep with cookies until the final third of the month, allowing Harris to turn his attention on the 5th upon the Baltic port-city of Stettin, which had not been attacked in numbers since the previous April. A major contributor to Germany's war effort, Stettin was home among other companies to the A G Vulkan U-Boot construction yards, where the Type VII vessel was being produced, but because of bombing, only one, U901, would actually see service, while U902 was destroyed in an air attack. The shipyard made extensive use of slave workers from an attached camp, although to what extent the Allies were aware is unclear. It was to be another predominantly Lancaster affair involving 348 of the type accompanied by ten Halifaxes, 6 Group putting up thirty-five Lancaster IIs, a dozen representing 408 (Goose) Squadron. They departed Linton-on-Ouse between 00.05 and 00.30 with W/C Jacobs the senior pilot on duty and a cookie and incendiary mix in each bomb bay, and joined up with the bomber stream over the North Sea. In contrast to the high rate of early returns during the last Berlin operation, few turned back on this occasion and those that did had good reason.

The 408 (Goose) Squadron crews had been assigned to the first two waves and found themselves in thick cloud at cruising altitude, some struggling to find a clear lane even when as high as 23,000 feet, but all benefitted from a Mosquito diversion at Berlin, which kept the night-fighters off the scent. Stettin was found to be partially visible through five-tenths thin cloud with tops at around 10,000 feet, and crews were able to identify some ground features before focusing on H2S-laid flares and green TIs, which the 408 (Goose) Squadron crews bombed from 19,000 to 24,000 feet between 03.45 and 03.57. The crew captained by 2nd Lt Humphrey endured a torrid return journey after stumbling into severe icing condition on a number of occasions that cost them an engine and many thousands of feet of altitude. They had to jettison all removeable equipment to remain airborne and were last home by a considerable margin at 09.29. At debriefings, crews provided the intelligence section with accounts of a highly accurate and concentrated attack, which seemed to leave the entire city on fire. Fourteen Lancasters and two Halifaxes failed to return, in exchange for which, post-raid reconnaissance and local reports confirmed heavy damage in central and western districts, where 504 houses and twenty industrial buildings had been destroyed, a further 1,148 houses and twenty-nine industrial buildings seriously damaged and eight ships sunk in the harbour.

Following this operation, the crews of the heavy squadrons were rested until mid-month, while the Halifax units would spend three weeks in virtual hibernation apart from isolated mining forays. When briefings finally took place on the 14th, there was doubtless some relief to see the red tape on the wall maps terminate some way short of Berlin. It led, in fact, to Braunschweig (Brunswick), the historic and culturally significant city situated some thirty-five miles to the east of Hannover. It had not been attacked by the Command in numbers before, and on this night, would face a force numbering at take-off 496 Lancasters and two Halifaxes. 6 Group supported the operation with forty-six Lancasters, of which fifteen represented 408 (Goose) Squadron and departed Linton-on-Ouse between 16.47 and 17.10 with S/L Miles the senior pilot on duty and each crew sitting on a cookie, two 1,000-pounders and mix of incendiaries. After climbing out they headed towards Germany's north-western coast, where they were met by part of the enemy night-fighter response, which would harass the bomber stream all the way to the target and back. 2nd Lt Humphrey and crew were closing on the target when the navigator became unwell and was unable to continue, such incidents usually related to oxygen starvation, and they were forced to turn back. Complete cloud cover at the target, in places up to around 15,000 feet, dictated the use of red skymarkers with green stars, at which the 408 (Goose) Squadron crews aimed their cookies and incendiaries from 20,000 to 21,600 feet between 19.15 and 19.26. The enemy fighters scored consistently and accounted for the majority of the thirty-eight missing Lancasters, many of which came down around Hannover. Among them were 408 (Goose) Squadron's DS767 and LL699 with the crews of P/O Hansen RCAF and F/O Timmins RCAF respectively, and only the navigator in the latter survived to fall into enemy hands. The Hansen crew was experienced, the pilot and some of his crew on their eighteenth sortie, while F/O Timmins was on his second and operating as crew captain for the first time. The attack almost entirely missed the city, falling mostly onto outlying communities to the south and was reported locally as a light raid. This would be a continuing theme in future attacks up to the autumn, as Braunschweig enjoyed something of a charmed life, leading to a belief among the populace of the surrounding villages that they were being targeted intentionally in an attempt to drive them into the city, before a major operation destroyed it with them in it!

The Path Finders, in particular, had been taking a beating since the turn of the year, with 156 Squadron alone losing fourteen Lancasters and crews in just three operations, four and five on Berlin, and five again on Braunschweig. This was creating something of a crisis in Path Finder manpower, particularly with regard to experienced crews, and a number of sideways postings took place between the squadrons to ensure a leavening of experience in each one. One of the solutions was to take the cream of the crews emerging from the training units, rather than wait for them to gain experience at a main force squadron.

Another lull in operations kept the bomber force on the ground until the 20th, when orders were received to prepare for a maximum effort for the next round of the Berlin offensive. The Halifax squadrons, which had largely remained dormant since late December, were roused from their slumber and 264 of them joined 495 Lancasters to constitute the Path Finder and main force elements, while two small Mosquito sections were primed to carry out spoof raids on Kiel and Hannover. 6 Group weighed in with ninety-seven Halifaxes and forty-seven Lancasters, sixteen of the latter belonging to 408 (Goose) Squadron assigned to the first and fifth waves, and they departed Linton-on-Ouse between 16.25 and 17.03 with F/Ls Burns, Kearl and Laine the senior pilots on duty. It was a rare pleasure for them to be taking off in dusky daylight, and as they circled during the climb-out, they were able to observe the dozens of other aircraft rising up into the darkening skies from the neighbouring stations to join them. They turned their snouts towards the west coast of the Schleswig-Holstein peninsula at a point opposite Kiel, rendezvousing with the other groups over the North Sea and all the time shedding individual aircraft as a hefty seventy-five crews abandoned their sorties and turned back, among them seventeen of the 6 Group contingent. P/O Lloyd and crew were defeated by engine trouble within ninety minutes, leaving the others to make landfall over the Nordfriesland coast, before turning to the south-east on a more-or-less direct course for Berlin, soon to become hounded by night-fighters.

The enemy controller had fed a proportion of his resources into the bomber stream east of Hamburg, and they would remain in contact until a point between Leipzig and Hannover on the way home, and he completely ignored the two Mosquito diversions having predicted well in advance that Berlin was to be the target. The Path Finders arrived over the Müritzsee to the north of Berlin with a sixty-mile run-in to the aiming point, and they found this to be concealed beneath the same ten-tenths cloud that had accompanied them for the entire outward leg. The tops of the cloud lay beneath the bombers at up to 15,000 feet as the main force crews carried out their attacks on red skymarkers with green stars, those from 408 (Goose) Squadron from 19,000 to 22,000 feet between 19.35 and 19.57. On return, the crews commented on the lack of flak activity over Berlin and reported the glow of large fires under the cloud and smoke rising through the tops. Thirty-five aircraft failed to return, twenty-two of them Halifaxes, which represented an 8.3% casualty rate compared with 2.6% for the Lancasters. It took a little time for an assessment of the operation to be made because of continuing cloud over north-eastern Germany, by which time four further raids had been carried out. It seems from local reports that the eastern districts had received the heaviest weight of bombs in an eight-mile stretch from Weissesee in the north to Neukölln in the south, although no details of destruction emerged.

On the following day, the city of Magdeburg was posted to host its first major attack of the war. The city had, in fact, been a regular destination for small forces as far back as the summer of 1940, when the Command targeted a ship lift at the eastern end of the Mittelland Canal at its junction with the River Elbe and the important Bergius-process Braunkohle A G synthetic oil refinery (hydrogenation plant), both located in the same Rothensee district to the north of Magdeburg city centre. Situated some fifty miles from Braunschweig and slightly to the south of east, it was on an increasingly familiar route as far as the enemy night-fighter controllers were concerned, and within easy striking distance of the night-fighter assembly beacons. In an attempt to deceive the enemy, a small-scale diversion was planned at Berlin involving twenty-two Lancaster of 5 Group and twelve Mosquitos of 8 Group. 6 Group contributed eighty-nine Halifaxes and forty-five Lancasters to the main event, sixteen of the latter belonging to 408 (Goose) Squadron, which were assigned to the fifth wave and each loaded with a cookie and SBCs of incendiaries. They departed Linton-on-Ouse between 19.52 and 20.23 with S/L Miles the senior pilot on duty and lost the services of P/O Brice and crew after they lost their port-inner engine over the sea and turned back. The others flew out over the North Sea to a point some one hundred miles off the west coast of Schleswig-Holstein, before turning to the south-east to pass between Hamburg and Hannover. The enemy radar had detected H2S transmissions during night-flying tests and equipment checks and alerted the night-fighter controller to the imminent heavy raid, enabling his night-fighters to infiltrate the bomber stream even before the German coast was crossed. The recently introduced "Tame Boar" night-fighter system provided a running commentary on the bomber stream's progress, and having latched onto it the fighters could remain in contact. The final turning-point was twenty-five miles north-east of the target, and this was identified both by Path Finder markers and the bombing of twenty-seven main force aircraft. These had been driven by stronger-than-forecast winds to arrive ahead of schedule and contained crews anxious to get the job done and get out of the target area as soon as possible. They bombed using their own H2S without waiting for the TIs to go down, and together with dummy fires, would be blamed by the Path Finders as the reason for their failure to produce concentrated marking.

The conditions over Magdeburg varied according to the time of arrival, the early birds encountering seven to nine-tenths thin cloud at around 6,000 feet, while those turning up towards the end of the raid found the northern half of the city completely clear with cloud over the southern half only. The 408 (Goose) Squadron crews experienced a mixture of eight-tenths cloud and relatively clear skies, and in the face of fairly modest opposition, bombed on green TIs from 19,000 to 21,000 feet between 22.55 and 23.12, all gaining the impression that the attack was concentrated around the markers. Returning crews reported explosions and fires or their glow, and smoke beginning to rise as they turned away. A number reported a flash some twelve minutes after bombing that lit up the clouds for seven seconds, and two large explosions were witnessed at 23.15. Fires that initially seemed to be scattered, appeared to become more concentrated as the crews headed for home and the impression was of a successful operation.

While all of this was in progress, the diversionary force arrived at Berlin, some seventy miles away to the north-east, where they encountered a layer of eight to ten-tenths cloud at 10,000 feet. Bombing took place mostly from 20,000 feet and beyond either side of 23.00, and the 5 Group ORB expressed the opinion that the diversion had succeeded in the early stages in reducing the impact of the Nachtjagd, something not borne out by the figures. In the absence of post-raid reconnaissance and a local report, the outcome at Magdeburg was not confirmed and it is generally believed now that most of the bombing fell outside of the city boundaries. A record fifty-seven aircraft failed to return, thirty-five of them Halifaxes, and this provided another alarming statistic of a 15.6% loss-rate compared with 5.2% for the Lancasters. The 408 (Goose) Squadron absentee was DS790, which was attacked by a night-fighter during the outward flight and had both port engines erupt in flames. With these feathered and the bomb load jettisoned, the aircraft entered a violent spin before exploding and flinging clear P/O Mill and his second pilot and bomb-aimer as the only survivors among the eight occupants. The pilot was on his seventeenth sortie, the second pilot on his first, and most of the other crew members had completed between twelve and twenty-two sorties.

The end of the month would bring the final concerted effort to destroy Berlin and involve three trips in the space of an unprecedented four nights. This hectic round of operations began on the 27th, after five nights of rest since the bruising experience of Magdeburg and involved an all-Lancaster heavy force of 515 aircraft. 6 Group put up forty-eight Lancaster IIs, sixteen of them belonging to 408 (Goose) Squadron, which departed Linton-on-Ouse either side of 18.00 with W/C Jacobs and S/Ls Miles and Smith the senior pilots on duty. After climbing out and rendezvousing with the rest of the group, they set course on a complex route that would take the bomber stream towards the north German coast, before swinging to the south-east to enter enemy territory over the Frisians and northern Holland. Having then feinted towards central Germany, suggesting Leipzig as the target, the force was to turn north-east to a point west of Berlin, from where the final run-in would commence. The long return route passed to the west of Leipzig before turning due east to miss Frankfurt on its northern side and traverse Belgium to gain the Channel south of Boulogne. Sgt Smitton and crew turned back early because of W/T and intercom issues, leaving the others to press on towards the target, while a mining diversion off Heligoland and the dispensing of dummy fighter flares and route-markers partially succeeded in reducing the numbers of enemy night-fighters making contact. It was, therefore, a relatively intact bomber force that approached the target over ten-tenths cloud with tops at 15,000 feet, which required the Path Finders to employ sky-marking, and red Wanganui flares with green stars led the 408 (Goose) Squadron crews to the aiming point, where they bombed from 19,600 to 22,000 feet between 20.30 and 20.43. At debriefings, crews reported the glow of fires and the appearance of a successful raid, but no detailed assessment was forthcoming.

Of course, not all made it back to tell their stories at debriefing, and thirty-three Lancaster dispersal pans stood empty in dawn's early light. It was a particularly bad night for 6 Group and Linton-on-Ouse, from which seven of the group's eight missing Lancasters had taken off. 408 (Goose) Squadron had to come to terms with the loss of three eight-man crews, most of the members of which were highly experienced and would be sorely missed by the squadron and station communities. Exactly where DS710 came down is uncertain, but the remains of the crew of S/L Charles Smith DFC RCAF were interred in the Reichswald War Cemetery, where most of those lost in the Ruhr area found a final resting place. The popular flight commander was on his twenty-third sortie, and apart from his RCAF second pilot and RAF flight engineer, who were each operating for the first time, the rest of the all-RCAF crew had between eleven and twenty sorties under their belt. DS849 crashed somewhere in the Hannover defence zone with no survivors from the crew of F/L Laine DFC RCAF, who had between fourteen and twenty sorties behind them. DS709 is believed to have come down near Storkow, south-east of Berlin, almost certainly after bombing, delivering the sole survivor from the crew of F/L Kearl DFC RCAF into enemy hands during their seventeenth sortie together. As some small recompense, W/O Harvey's gunners shot down a BF110. Reports from Berlin described bombs falling over a wide area, more so in the south than the north, and damage to fifty industrial premises, a number of them engaged in important war work, while twenty thousand people were bombed out of their homes. A feature of the campaign was the number of outlying communities suffering collateral damage, and on this night sixty-one such hamlets recorded bombs falling.

The early time-on-target had allowed crews to get a full night in bed and they were, hopefully, fully rested, when news came through on the 28th that many of them would be returning to the "Big City" that night. A heavy force of 673 aircraft was assembled, of which 432 were Lancasters and 241 Halifaxes, thirty-four of the former and ninety of the latter provided by 6 Group. 408 (Goose) Squadron made ready ten Lancasters, which were assigned to the first and fifth waves and departed Linton-on-Ouse between 00.11 and 00.37 with F/L Russell the senior pilot on duty and a cookie and incendiaries in each bomb bay. They were routed out over southern Denmark before turning south-east on a direct course for the target, with an almost reciprocal return and various diversionary measures to distract the night-fighter controller. Sgt Smitton and crew were already in trouble as they crossed the English coast and lost the use of their radio receiver, but opted to continue on until the port-inner engine failed some eighty miles short of the Jutland coast and ended their interest in proceedings. W/O Harvey and crew lost their bearings and so much time attempting to get back on track that they found themselves too far behind schedule and also abandoned their sortie. They were among sixty-six crews turning back early, fourteen of them belonging to 6 Group, suggesting some adverse reaction to the back-to-back operations. Those reaching the target area encountered ten-tenths cloud and a mixture of sky and ground-marking to aim at, the 49 Squadron crews delivering their bombs on red and green release-point flares from 20,000 to 24,000 feet between 03.13 and 03.27. Some crews reported huge explosions at 03.15, 03.18 and 03.25, the second-mentioned one described by a 10 Squadron crew as lighting up the sky over a radius of fifty miles. Forty-six aircraft failed to return, twenty-six of them Halifaxes as the defenders fought back to exact another heavy toll of bombers, but all of Linton-on-Ouse's dispersal pans were occupied come the morning and it was the Leeming and Croft communities that had to deal with the trauma of heavy losses. The impression gained from returning crews at debriefing was of a concentrated and effective attack, and this was partly borne-out by local reports of heavy damage in western and southern districts, where 180,000 people were bombed out of their homes. However, as had been the pattern throughout the campaign against Berlin, seventy-seven outlying communities had also been afflicted.

After a night's rest a force of 534 aircraft was made ready on the 30th for the final operation of this concerted effort against Berlin. 6 Group offered thirty-seven Lancasters, thirteen belonging to 408 (Goose) Squadron, and ten Halifax Mk IIIs of 433 (Porcupine) Squadron. The Geese departed Linton-on-Ouse between 17.06 and 17.21 with S/L Miles the senior pilot on duty, and after climbing out, they joined with the rest of the group to follow a route similar to that adopted two nights earlier, remaining relatively free of harassment in the bomber stream. On reaching the target they were greeted by ten-tenths cloud at around 8,000 feet and the sight of Path Finder skymarking in progress and bombed on these flares from 19,000 to 23,000 feet between 20.19 and 20.31. All commented on the smoke rising through 12,000 feet and the glow of fires beneath the cloud, which, according to some, was still visible from a hundred miles into the return flight. Thirty-two Lancasters and a single Halifax failed to make it home, in return for which significant losses and according to local reports, central and south-western districts suffered heavy damage and serious areas of fire. Other parts of the city were also hit, while many bomb loads were again scattered liberally onto outlying communities, and at least a thousand people lost their lives. 112 heavy bombers and their crews had been lost to the Command as a result of these three operations, and with the introduction of the enemy's highly efficient Tame Boar night-fighter system based on running commentaries, the advantage had swung back in the defenders' favour.

Two further heavy raids would be directed at Berlin before the end of the winter offensive, one in February and the other in March, but they would be almost in isolation. There is no question that Germany's capital had been sorely afflicted by the three latest operations, but it remained a functioning city and showed no signs of imminent collapse. During the course of the month the squadron participated in nine operations and dispatched 120 sorties for the loss of seven Lancasters and their crews.

February 1944

The moon period and bad weather during the first two weeks of February allowed the crews to draw breath and the squadrons to replenish. Harris had intended to maintain the pressure on Berlin and would have launched a further attack had he not been thwarted by the conditions, and as a result, the time was filled with training and mining operations. When the Path Finder and main force squadrons next took to the air, it would be for a record-breaking effort to Berlin on the 15th, which would also be the penultimate operation of the campaign, and indeed of the war by Bomber Command's heavy brigade against Germany's capital city. The force of 891 aircraft represented the largest non-1,000 force to date, and, therefore, the greatest-ever to be sent against Berlin, and it would be the first time that more than five hundred Lancasters and three hundred Halifaxes had operated together. 432 (Leaside) Squadron was in the process of converting to the Halifax Mk III, reducing the 6 Group Lancaster strength to the two Linton-on-Ouse squadrons. They contributed thirty-two between them, the seventeen representing 408 (Goose) Squadron assigned to the first and third waves, while the bulk of the 6 Group effort was provided by 128 Halifaxes. The bomb bays of this huge armada would convey to Berlin the greatest-ever tonnage of bombs to any target to date, and 408 (Goose) Squadron's contribution would be seventeen cookies, 10,200 x 4lb and 272 x 30lbs incendiaries.

They took off between 17.20 and 17.50 with W/C Jacobs and S/L Russell the senior pilots on duty and set course for the western coast of Denmark, joining up with the bomber stream on the way, before crossing southern Jutland and entering Germany via the Baltic coast between Rostock and Stralsund on a direct heading for the target. The return route would require the bombers to pass south of Hannover and Bremen and cross Holland to the North Sea via Castricum. Extensive diversionary measures included a mining operation in Kiel Bay ahead of the arrival of the bombers, a raid on Frankfurt-an-Oder to the east of Berlin by a small force of 8 Group Lancasters, and Oboe Mosquitos attacking five night-fighter airfields in Holland. The force had been depleted by seventy-five early returns by the time the remainder homed in on the target, where ten-tenths cloud at around 10,000 feet concealed it from their view, those with H2S able to confirm their positions, while the others relied on the Path Finders' red release-point flares with green stars and red and green TIs on the ground. The 408 (Goose) Squadron crews bombed on these from 20,000 to 23,000 feet between 21.13 and 21.40, and on return reported the markers to be highly effective and well-concentrated. The burgeoning glow beneath the clouds convinced them that they had taken part in a successful operation, and this was borne out by local reports, which confirmed that the 2,642 tons of bombs had caused extensive damage in central and south-western districts but had also spilled out into surrounding communities. A thousand houses and more than five hundred temporary wooden barracks were destroyed and important war-industry factories in the

Siemensstadt district were damaged in return for the loss to the Command of forty-three aircraft, twenty-six Lancasters, (4.6%) and seventeen Halifaxes, (5.4%). Perhaps slightly disturbing was the fact that eight of the missing Halifaxes were Mk IIIs, only one fewer than the nine now obsolete Mk IIs and Vs.

Despite the recent heavy losses, when orders were received on the 19th to prepare for another major assault that night, this time on Leipzig, where four Messerschmitt aircraft factories were the principal targets, the heavy squadrons were able offer 816 aircraft, 561 Lancasters and 255 Halifaxes. 6 Group managed to assemble ninety-six Halifaxes and thirty-one Lancasters, the latter all from Linton-on-Ouse, the eighteen belonging to 408 (Goose) Squadron assigned to the first two waves. They took off between 23.38 and 00.13 with W/C Jacobs the senior pilot on duty and a cookie and incendiary mix in each bomb bay, and after climbing out over the station, they joined up with the others heading for landfall on the Dutch coast north-east of the fishing port of Harlingen. A proportion of the Luftwaffe Nachtjagd was waiting for them, and a night-fighter caught DS788 at 20,000 feet, destroying its rudders and bringing it down to crash to the south-east of Groningen with just two survivors, the RAF flight engineer, who evaded capture, and the Canadian bomb-aimer who did not. The pilot, nineteen-year-old F/O John Frampton RCAF, was on his second sortie and operating as crew captain for the first time and was one of the youngest pilots to give his life in Bomber Command. The crews of F/O White and F/Sgt Fillion turned back early because of oxygen system and starboard-outer engine failure respectively, while the bomber stream continued on to pass south of Bremen and north of Hannover on a south-easterly course, parts of it to become embroiled in a running battle with night-fighters all the way into eastern Germany. It was during this phase that 408 (Goose) Squadron's LL632 ran into trouble at 21,000 feet near the final turning point at Stendal with the target some still ninety miles ahead of them. The Lancaster was attacked from astern by a night-fighter, whose fire mortally wounded the rear gunner and probably his counterpart in the mid-upper turret and set the starboard wing ablaze. F/Sgt Greip RCAF and his four crew mates in the section forward of the main spar were able to reach the forward escape hatch and float down on their parachutes into the arms of their captors. It was their fourth sortie together.

Inaccurately forecast winds caused some aircraft to reach the target early, forcing them to orbit while they waited for the Path Finders to arrive, and the local flak batteries accounted for around twenty of these, while four others were lost through collisions. The 408 (Goose) Squadron crews arrived to find ten-tenths cloud with tops at around 10,000 feet and bombed on green Wanganui flares and red and green TIs from 20,000 to 24,000 feet between 03.59 and 04.22. It seems that there was a brief period during the attack when skymarking stopped and led to some scattering of bombs, but the marker-flares were soon replenished with the arrival of more backers-up and a considerable glow beneath the cloud remained visible for some fifty minutes into the return journey, giving the impression of a successful assault. When all of those aircraft returning home had been accounted for, there was a massive shortfall of seventy-eight, a record loss by a clear twenty-one aircraft and eighteen of the missing belonged to 6 Group. Two further 408 (Goose) Squadron failures to return were LL719 and LL720, which are believed to have come down on French and Belgian soil while homebound and produced no survivors from the freshman crews of F/O Richter RCAF and F/L Winn RCAF respectively. Forty-four Lancasters and thirty-four Halifaxes had failed to return, with a loss-rate of 7.8% and 13.3% respectively, prompting Harris to immediately withdraw the Mk II and V Halifaxes from further operations over Germany, which at a stroke, removed a proportion of 4 and 6 Group's fire-power from the front line until they could be re-equipped with the Mk III. In the meantime, the Mk II and V operators would focus their energies for the remainder of the month on gardening duties.

Despite this depletion of available numbers, a force of 598 aircraft was made ready on the 20th for an operation that night against Stuttgart, which would be the first of three against the city over a three-week period. 6 Group managed to put up forty-one Halifaxes and twenty-five Lancasters, ten of the latter representing 408 (Goose) Squadron, which were spread among the first four waves and departed Linton-on-Ouse between 23.37 and 23.50 with S/L Russell the senior pilot on duty and a standard cookie and incendiary mix in each bomb bay. The bomber stream crossed the Channel to make landfall over the French coast, from where the cloud remained at ten-tenths with tops at 8,000 feet all the way into southern Germany. A North Sea sweep and a diversionary raid on Munich two hours ahead of the main activity had caused the Luftwaffe to deploy its forces early, and this allowed the bomber stream to push on unmolested to the target. By the time it hove into view, the cloud had thinned to five to eight-tenths at around 6,000 feet and the excellent visibility enabled the crews to draw a bead on the Path Finder red and green sky-markers and similar-coloured TIs on the ground. The 408 (Goose) Squadron crews bombed from 21,000 to 25,000 feet between 04.00 and 04.10, observing many large fires, and on return there were reports that the glow from the burning city was still visible from 250 miles into the return flight. Despite some scattering of bombs, local sources described central districts and those in a quadrant from north-west to north-east suffering extensive damage, and a Bosch factory was one of the important war industry concerns to be hard-hit. In contrast to twenty-four hours earlier, a modest nine aircraft failed to return.

In an attempt to reduce the prohibitive losses of recent weeks, a new tactic was introduced for the next two operations. A force of 734 aircraft was assembled on the 24th for an operation to the centre of Germany's ball-bearing production, Schweinfurt, situated some sixty miles to the east of Frankfurt in south-central Germany. The plan called for 392 aircraft to depart their stations between 18.00 and 19.00 and to be followed into the air two hours later by 342 others in the hope of catching the night-fighters on the ground refuelling and re-arming as the second wave passed through. While this operation was in progress, extensive diversionary measures would be put in hand that involved more than three hundred other aircraft, including 179 from the training units conducting a North Sea sweep and 110 Halifaxes and Stirlings mining in northern waters. 6 Group contributed sixty-four Halifaxes, including the first Mk IIIs in the hands of 432 (Leaside) Squadron, and thirty-five Lancasters, of which seventeen were made ready by 408 (Goose) Squadron, five assigned to the first phase and a dozen to the second. The first wave participants took off between 18.22 and 18.29 with S/L Russell the senior pilot on duty, and they were followed by the second wave element between 20.06 and 20.48 led by F/L Hales. Some main force crews were to perform the role of Path Finder supporters, which required them to accompany the target-marking force across the target to beef up the numbers and prevent searchlights and flak from latching onto individual aircraft. They would retain their bombs and release them during a second pass.

The first phase bombers reached the target to find up to three-tenths cloud at 3,000 to 4,000 feet with smoke haze slightly compromising the vertical visibility and were drawn on by already established fires towards the south-western edge of the town and red TIs cascading over the aiming point as they began their bombing runs. The aiming point was clearly marked out by red and green TIs, which were in the 408 (Goose) Squadron bomb sights as the loads went down from 21,000 to 22,000 feet between 23.21 and 23.43. Other crews over the target at this time saw no cloud and described the visibility as excellent, enabling them to pick out the River Main as they ran in to bomb. Two columns of black smoke were observed to be rising through 5,000 feet as they turned away, and the consensus was of an effective, if, somewhat scattered attack.

Meanwhile, the second phase crews were well on their way and picked up the glow of fires from the earlier raid at a distance of two hundred miles. The visibility in the target area remained good, despite the rising smoke, and bombing by the 408 (Goose) Squadron crews took place out of almost cloudless skies onto red and green TIs from 21,000 to 24,500 feet between 01.07 and 01.13. All indications suggested an effective raid, but unfortunately, both phases of the operation had suffered from undershooting after some Path Finder backers-up failed to press on to the aiming point. In that regard, it was a disappointing night, but an interesting feature was the loss of 50% fewer aircraft from the second wave in comparison with the first in an overall casualty figure of thirty-three, and this suggested some merit in the tactic of dividing the force. Both of the missing 408 (Goose) Squadron Lancasters failed to return from the second phase, DS731 containing the debutant crew of F/Sgt Keiller RCAF, who were leaving the target area at 23,500 feet when attacked by a BF110. The Lancaster sustained damage to the mainplane, while the rear turret was knocked out and fuel tanks punctured, and over the ensuing thirty minutes it sank to 7,000 feet, at which point the order was given to abandon it to its fate. It crashed somewhere in the Hannover region with the remains of the mid-upper gunner still on board, possibly having been mortally wounded during the engagement, and the survivors were taken into captivity. DS844 is believed to have fallen into the Rhine with no survivors from the experienced and predominantly RAF crew of P/O Sherlock DFC, who were mostly on their twentieth sortie together.

Since the turn of the year, a wind-finder system had been in use, which employed selected crews to monitor wind speed and direction and pass their findings back to HQ, where the figures were collated and any changes from the briefed conditions re-broadcast to the bomber stream. This had been found to be extremely useful, but as would be discovered in the ensuing weeks, the system had its limitations.

The main operation on the following night was directed at the beautiful and culturally significant southern city of Augsburg, situated around thirty miles north-west of Munich. It was home to a major Maschinenfabrik Augsburg Nuremberg (M.A.N) diesel engine factory, which had been the target for an epic low-level daylight raid by a dozen Lancasters of 44 and 97 Squadrons in April 1942. On this night, 594 aircraft were divided into two waves, and among them were forty-four Halifaxes and twenty-one Lancasters of 6 Group, eleven of the latter belonging to 408 (Goose) Squadron, all assigned to the second phase. The first wave bomber stream flew out over Belgium with ten-tenths cloud beneath them, but that had dissipated by the time the target drew near, and on arrival it was possible for crews to gain a visual reference. The Path Finders' red and green TIs were in the bomb sights as the main force crews exploited the accurate and concentrated Path Finder marking and fires were beginning to take hold as they turned away.

The second phase element got away three hours after the first, the 408 (Goose) Squadron contingent departing Linton-on-Ouse between 21.00 and 21.17 with F/Ls Hales and Smith the senior pilots on duty and the usual cookie/incendiary mix in each bomb bay. They were drawn on by the glow in the sky from a hundred miles away and arrived to find visibility still good despite copious amounts of smoke rising through 20,000 feet. The 408 (Goose) Squadron crews bombed on existing fires and red and green Wanganui flares and TIs from 22,000 to 23,000 feet between 01.15 and 01.20 and contributed to the delivery by 6 Group of thirty-four tons of high explosives and seventy-nine tons of incendiaries. The loss of twenty-one aircraft seemed to confirm the benefits of splitting the forces, and this tactic would remain an important part of Bomber Command planning for the remainder of the war. It had been a devastatingly destructive operation, in which all facets of the plan had come together in near perfect harmony, spelling disaster for this lightly defended historical treasure trove. Its heart was torn out by blast and fire that destroyed almost three thousand houses along with buildings of outstanding historical significance, and centuries of irreplaceable culture was lost forever. There was also some industrial damage, and around ninety-thousand people were bombed out of their homes. Among the twenty-one missing aircraft were two belonging to 408 (Goose) Squadron, DS845 having reached the final turning point slightly ahead of schedule and orbiting to kill time, when the engines began to falter. The bombs were jettisoned and F/Sgt Fillion RCAF and crew set course for the French coast before being forced to abandon the Lancaster to its fate near Abbeville, where the pilot and four of his crew fell into enemy hands and two evaded a similar fate. It was a sad end for a Lancaster that had survived eleven trips to Berlin. DS791 came down in southern Germany, killing F/L Smith DFC RCAF and all but the rear gunner, who joined his squadron colleagues in captivity. F/L Smith was on his twenty-ninth sortie and his crew had between twenty and twenty-seven to their credit. In contrast, the Fillion crew were on just their second trip together.

During the course of the month the squadron carried out five operations and dispatched seventy-three sorties for the loss of eight Lancasters and crews, a worrying 11%.

March 1944

March would bring an end to the winter campaign, but a long and bitter month would have to be endured first before any respite came from long-range forays into Germany. The crews had enjoyed a few nights off when the second raid of the series on Stuttgart was posted on the 1st, for which a force of 557 aircraft was made ready. The number would have been larger had seventy-four Halifaxes and Lancasters of 6 Group not been withdrawn late on because of icing conditions over northern Yorkshire and County Durham, leaving just thirty Halifaxes from East Moor and Tholthorpe to take part. Those reaching the target encountered ten-tenths cloud with tops at between 10,000 and 17,000 feet and the Path Finders employed a combination of sky and ground-marking, which became scattered. The main force effort was directed between two main concentrations, largely at red skymarkers with green stars, but it was not possible to assess the accuracy of the attack, although a column of smoke had reached 25,000 feet by the end of the raid, and large fires were evident from the glow in the sky visible from up to 150 miles away. The presence of thick cloud all the way there and back made conditions difficult for enemy night-fighters, and a remarkably modest four aircraft failed to return. It was eventually established that the raid had been an outstanding success, which had caused extensive damage in central, western and northern districts, where a number of important war-industry factories, including those belonging to Bosch and Daimler-Benz, had sustained damage.

At the end of the first week, the Halifax brigade, particularly those withdrawn from operations over Germany, fired the opening salvoes of the pre-invasion campaign, the purpose of which was to dismantle by bombing thirty-seven railway centres in France, Belgium and western Germany. It began on the night of the 6/7th at Trappes marshalling yards, situated some ten miles west-south-west of Paris, for which 6 Group contributed 119 Halifaxes and 4 Group 124 with six Path Finder Mosquitos to provide the marking. The operation took place in favourable conditions and was concluded successfully without loss.

Attention on the 7th was turned upon the marshalling yards at Le Mans in north-western France, for which a force of 242 Halifaxes, fifty-six Lancasters and six Mosquitos of 3, 4, 6 and 8 Groups was made ready, 6 Group contributing 116 Halifaxes and twenty-four Lancasters. 408 (Goose) Squadron detailed ten Lancasters to be divided between the two bombing phases and loaded each with nine 1,000 and five 500-pounders before dispatching them from Linton-on-Ouse between 19.02 and 19.30 with W/C Jacobs and S/L Miles the senior pilots on duty. They began the Channel crossing at Worthing, making landfall over the Normandy beaches earmarked for the D-Day landings three months hence and reached the target after an outward flight of some two hours and forty minutes to find eight to ten-tenths cloud at between 4,000 and 8,000 feet. Four of the 408 (Goose) Squadron element failed to find any TIs and with the risk of collateral damage too great to bomb indiscriminately, they withheld their bombs in accordance with instructions and jettisoned most in the Channel on the way home, while six others bombed on the glow of red TIs from 8,000 to 13,000 feet between 21.40 and 22.08. A large white flash was observed by some crews along with a widespread red reflection, and local reports confirmed that the raid had been successful in destroying 250 wagons, cutting track and damaging locomotives and other installations, all achieved without loss.

Following the Stuttgart raid, it was a further two weeks before the main force operated again, when Stuttgart was once more the destination, but in the meantime, matters were afoot at 5 Group, and had been ever since a frustrating series of operations against flying bomb launching sites conducted by 617 Squadron since December had failed to achieve the desired results. The problem had been an inability to put markers right on the aiming point, which was vital to destroy small, precision targets, and Oboe was just not precise enough. Effective though Oboe undoubtedly was at an urban target, where a margin of error of 400 to 600 yards represented pinpoint accuracy, precision targets required more. 617 Squadron had obliterated the Oboe markers, only for bombing photos to show that the targets, situated only a matter of yards away, had remained intact. W/C Cheshire and S/L Martin experimented with a dive-bombing technique, which had proved to be successful but impracticable in a Lancaster and Cheshire had borrowed a Mosquito for further trials. These were so promising, that the 5 Group A-O-C, AVM Cochrane, authorized a number of operations by the squadron against factory targets in France, before taking the idea to Harris. Harris approved, paving the way for 5 Group to become effectively independent of the main bomber force and begin larger-scale trials.

Following six days of inactivity for most of 6 Group, 110 Halifaxes were detailed for a return to the Le Mans marshalling yards on the 13th in company with 104 representing 4 Group, while nine Oboe Mosquitos were to provide the marking at two aiming points. Their arrival in the target area was greeted by the punctual and accurate marking of the northern aiming point, which the main force element attacked from between 11,500 and 15,000 feet, most securing an aiming point photograph that revealed that the carriage and wagon repair shops and nearby armaments and traction works had been heavily bombed. The marking of the southern aiming point was some three minutes late but was equally accurate and the bombing concentrated around the TIs. The post-raid analysis determined a much more effective attack then the previous one at the cost of a single 4 Group Halifax.

A return to the marshalling yards at Amiens was ordered on the 16th and a heavy force of thirty-one 4 Group and fifty 6 Group Halifaxes and forty-one 3 Group Stirlings was assembled as the main force, while eight Oboe Mosquitos were assigned to marking duties. Within two minutes of the release of red TIs, the north-eastern aiming point was covered by bomb bursts, and while haze rendered the crews uncertain as to the effectiveness of the attack, twenty out of twenty-nine bombing photos captured the aiming point with the other nine not far off and it was clear that the target had sustained severe damage.

Now that the Mk III Halifax was becoming available in larger numbers, the Command was quickly returning to full strength, and a force of 863 aircraft was assembled to send against Stuttgart on the 15th. This number included 101 Halifaxes and twenty-nine Lancasters provided by 6 Group, thirteen of the latter belonging to 408 (Goose) Squadron, which were divided between the first and third waves and each received a bomb load of a cookie and two and one SBCs respectively of 4lb and 30lb incendiaries. They departed Linton-on-Ouse between 19.01 and 19.40 with W/C Jacobs and S/L Miles the senior pilots on duty and rendezvoused with the rest of the force as they passed over Reading on their way to the south coast. It was an elongated bomber stream that crossed the French coast at 20,000 feet over broken cloud with clear conditions above and maintained a course parallel with the frontiers of Belgium, Luxembourg and Germany as if heading for Switzerland. The German frontier was crossed between Strasbourg and Freiburg, before the force turned towards the north-east for the run-in to the target, and it was at this juncture that the night-fighters managed to infiltrate a section of the stream and score heavily. Among the victims was 408 (Goose) Squadron's LL637, which crashed at Hilsenheim on the French side of the frontier with fatal consequences for F/Sgt Lumgair RCAF and his predominantly RCAF crew, who were on their fifth sortie together.

Adverse winds were responsible for the Path Finders arriving up to six minutes late to open the attack, employing both sky and ground-markers in the face of seven to ten-tenths cloud at between 8,000 and 15,000 feet. The Wanganui flares drifted in the wind, marking an area to the north-east of the River Neckar, while the TIs landed far apart in the north and south of the city. The 408 (Goose) Squadron crews bombed on whatever markers presented themselves, mostly red TIs, from 20,000 to 23,000 feet between 23.14 and 23.32 and observed a spread of fires, including two large ones ten miles apart and smoke rising to bombing altitude. It would be established later that some of the early bombing had been accurate, but that most of the loads had undershot and fallen into open country, a disappointment compounded by the loss mostly to night-fighters of thirty-seven aircraft. LL718 was the second Goose Lancaster to fail to return and was lost without trace with the freshman crew of F/O Colville RCAF, who was on his fifth sortie.

Many operations had been mounted against Frankfurt during the preceding two years, only a small number of which had been really effective. This state of affairs was about to be rectified, however, and the first of two raids against this south-central powerhouse of industry was posted on the 18th, for which a force of 846 aircraft was made ready. 6 Group supported the operation with ninety-four Halifaxes and twenty-five Lancasters, eleven of the latter belonging to 408 (Goose) Squadron and assigned to the second, fourth and fifth bombing waves. Three of them received a bomb load of one 8,000 pounder and four SBCs of 30lb incendiaries, and the others a single 1,000-pounder and twelve and seven SBCs respectively of 4lb and 30lb incendiaries. They departed Linton-on-Ouse between 19.05 and 19.25 with no senior pilots on duty, and benefitted from favourable weather conditions as they pressed on across France to enter Germany near Strasbourg, where they encountered a layer of haze 20,000 feet thick over the target, and according to most, no more than three-tenths cloud. This allowed the Path Finders to employ the Newhaven ground marking technique (blind marking by H2S, followed by visual backing-up), which the 408 (Goose) Squadron crews exploited when carrying out their attacks on red and green TIs from 20,000 to 23,000 feet between 22.02 and 22.13. A large explosion was witnessed at 22.05, and the participants in the raid flew home confident that their efforts had been worthwhile. They had, indeed, contributed to an outstandingly successful raid, a fact confirmed by post-raid reconnaissance and local sources, the latter calculating that six thousand buildings had been destroyed or seriously damaged in predominantly eastern, central and western districts, and this was in return for the loss of twenty-two aircraft, four of which were from 6 Group. One contained the Skipton-on-Swale station commander, G/C Wray RCAF, who had been flying as second pilot in a 433 (Porcupine) Squadron Halifax and was one of six survivors to fall into enemy hands.

Frankfurt was named again on the 22nd as the target for that night, and seventy-two Halifax and twenty-seven Lancaster crews of 6 Group learned that they were to be part of another huge force of 816 aircraft. The thirteen participants from 408 (Goose) Squadron were assigned to the first, third and fifth waves and departed Linton-on-Ouse between 18.41 to 19.13 with S/L Miles the senior pilot on duty and the two bomb-load configurations employed in the previous raid. After climbing out above their stations and forming up, they adopted an unusual route for a target south of the Ruhr, crossing the enemy coast over Vlieland and Terschelling, before passing to the east of Osnabrück on a direct course due south for the target. They arrived at the target to find five to six-tenths thin, low cloud at around 4,000 feet and Paramatta marking (blind marking by H2S) in progress and focused their attention on the release-point flares and red and green TIs marking out the aiming point. Bombing was carried out by the 408 (Goose) Squadron element from 21,000 to 24,000 feet between 21.53 and 22.01, and a massive rectangular area of unbroken fire was observed across the centre of the city, the glow from which could be seen for at least a hundred miles into the return flight. Returning crews reported numerous searchlights lighting up the cloud, and moderate to intense flak that reached up to the bombers' flight level.

Local reports confirmed the enormity of the devastation, which was particularly severe in western districts and left this half of the city without electricity, gas and water for an extended period. More than nine hundred people lost their lives and a further 120,000 were bombed out of their homes at a cost to the Command of twenty-six Lancasters and seven Halifaxes, a loss-rate of 4.2% and 3.8% respectively. 408 (Goose) Squadron was represented among the missing by DS797 and LL717, the former crashing in the Grüneburgpark located to the north-west of the city centre and taking with it to their deaths the eight-man predominantly RCAF crew of F/L Fulton RCAF, who was on his eleventh sortie. Apart from the second pilot, who was on his maiden sortie, the other crew members had completed between seven and fifteen sorties. The latter Lancaster was brought down by a night-fighter to crash near Usingen, fifteen miles north of the target, almost certainly while on the bombing run. F/Sgt Pare RCAF and crew were freshmen, the pilot on his fifth sortie and the others on their second or third and there were no survivors. It was a bad night for senior officers, 207 and 7 Squadrons losing their commanding officers, while Bardney's station commander, G/C Norman Pleasance, failed to return in a 9 Squadron Lancaster. What was about to happen over the next week and a half, however, would overshadow anything that had gone before and would certainly not fall within what might be considered acceptable.

On the following night, fifty-one 6 Group Halifaxes joined others of 4 Group and Stirlings of 3 Group to form a main force of 127 heavy bombers with a dozen Oboe Mosquitos to provide the marking for an attack on the marshalling yards at Laon in north-eastern France. Despite favourable weather conditions, the Master Bomber called a halt to proceedings after seventy-two aircraft had bombed and scattered some of the effort wide of the mark.

It was more than five weeks since the main force had last visited the "Big City", and 811 aircraft were made ready on the 24th for what would be the final raid of the war upon it by RAF heavy bombers. 6 Group put up ninety-three Halifaxes and twenty-three Lancasters, eleven of the latter belonging to 408 (Goose) Squadron and each receiving a bomb load of a cookie or a 1,000-pounder supplemented by SBCs of incendiaries. They departed Linton-on-Ouse between 18.51 and 19.02 with S/Ls Miles and Russell the senior pilots on duty and a long flight ahead of them, which would take them across the North Sea to the Danish coast near Ringkøbing and then to a point on the German Baltic coast near Rostock. When north-east of Berlin they were to adopt a south-westerly course for the bombing run, and once clear of the defence zone homebound, dogleg to the west and then north-west to pass around Hannover on its southern and western sides, before heading for Holland and an exit via the Castricum coast. The extended outward leg provided a time-on-target of around 22.30, but an unexpected difficulty would be encountered, which rendered void all of the meticulous planning.

The existence of what we now know as "Jetstream" winds was unknown at the time, and the one blowing from the north with unprecedented strength on this night pushed the bomber stream south of its intended track. Navigators, who were expecting to see the northern tip of Sylt on their H2S screens, were horrified to find the southern end, which meant that they were thirty miles south of track and about to fly over Germany rather than Denmark. The previously mentioned "wind-finder" system had been set up for precisely this eventuality, but the problem on this night was that the wind-finders refused to believe what their instruments were telling them. Winds in excess of one hundred m.p.h had never been encountered before, and fearing that they would be disbelieved, many modified the figures downward. The same thing happened at raid control, where the figures were modified again, so that the information rebroadcast to the bomber stream bore no resemblance to the reality of the situation.

By the time that the majority of crews had reached Westerhever on the west coast of Schleswig-Holstein, most realized that they were some distance south of track and set course for the north to try to regain the planned route and avoid the defences that would be met if they turned east over Germany. Many commented on the inaccurate wind information received during the outward journey, which had adversely affected their progress, and S/L Russell and crew were almost four hours into the outward flight and well south of track to the south-west of Berlin when it became clear that insufficient fuel remained for them to reach the target and get home, a realisation that persuaded them to jettison the cookie and turn back. W/O Kasper and crew were only some twenty-five miles from Berlin when stumbling into the defence zone and becoming ensnared in searchlights. Peppered by light flak and unsure as to the location of the target, they too abandoned their sortie and headed home. Many of the main force crews arriving in the target area were convinced that the Path Finders were up to ten minutes late in opening the raid, which was confirmed to some by the voice of the Master Bomber exhorting them to hurry up. Crews reported a variety of cloud conditions from three to ten-tenths at between 6,000 and 15,000 feet, but most were able to pick out the red and green TIs on the ground, and if not, found red Wanganui flares with green stars to guide them to the aiming point. The 408 (Goose) Squadron crews bombed from 21,000 to 22,000 feet between 22.25 and 22.52 and observed what appeared to be a scattered attack in the early stages, until fires began to become more concentrated in three distinct areas and large explosions were witnessed at 22.42 and 22.54. The defences were very active with moderate flak bursting at up to 24,000 feet and light flak attempting to shoot out the skymarkers, but night-fighter activity was described by the 5 Group ORB as unusually quiet. There was a shock awaiting the Command as the returning aircraft landed to leave a shortfall of seventy-two, and it would be established later that two-thirds of them had fallen victim to the Ruhr flak batteries after being driven into that region's defence zone by the wind on the way home. 408 (Goose) Squadron came through unscathed, while 6 Group posted missing thirteen crews. Post-raid analysis revealed that the wind had also played havoc with the marking and bombing and had pushed the attack towards the south-western districts of the capital, where most of the damage occurred, while 126 outlying communities also received bombs. During the campaign, which had begun in August, 408 (Goose) Squadron had participated in fifteen of the nineteen Berlin raids, despatching 205 sorties for the loss of eight aircraft. This was the second highest number of sorties in 6 Group, and the equal lowest percentage loss rate, but as was found in all Lancaster squadrons, the survival rate for crewmen was low, and only five of the sixty-two men lost lived to tell the tale. (The Berlin Raids. Martin Middlebrook).

S/L Miles DFC had been given a tough operation as the twentieth and final one of his second tour, but he came through to bring an end to an outstanding career, during which he completed fifty-two sorties, thirty-two on Stirlings with 3 Group before embarking on his second tour with 408 (Goose) Squadron. While the above operation was in progress, what became known as The Great Escape was being enacted at Stalag Luft III at Sagan in Poland, during which seventy-six PoWs made a bid for freedom through a tunnel. All but three were recaptured and fifty of them were murdered on Hitler's orders.

On the 25th, the interdiction campaign continued at Aulnoye, situated on the French side of the border with Belgium on the main railway line to Mons some twelve miles to the north. A heavy force of 176 Halifaxes, Lancasters and Stirlings was to attack the marshalling yards after sixteen Oboe Mosquitos had marked it, 6 Group contributing sixty-four Halifaxes and nine Lancasters, four of the latter belonging to 408 (Goose) Squadron. The crews of F/Ls Easton and Latimer, F/O Pullar and F/Sgt Bailey departed Linton-on-Ouse between 19.13 and 19.30, each with six 1,000 and ten 500-pounders beneath their feet, the first two mentioned assigned to the first aiming point and the latter two to the second. They arrived in the target area under clear skies with a little ground haze to slightly mar the vertical visibility and benefitted from punctual and accurate marking by the Path Finder element at both aiming points. They delivered their bomb loads onto red TIs from

7,000 feet ten minutes either side of 22.00 and observed two large explosions, one at 22.03 appearing to emanate from a factory in the north-east corner of the yards.

Although Berlin had now been consigned to the past, the winter campaign still had a week to run and two more major operations for the crews to negotiate. The first of these was posted on the 26th and would bring a return to the old enemy of Essen, for which a force of 705 aircraft was made ready. 6 Group contributed eighty-four Halifaxes and twenty-one Lancasters, ten of the latter provided by 408 (Goose) Squadron, seven of which received a bomb load of a 2,000-pounder and mix of incendiaries, while three had a 8,000 pounder supplemented also by the appropriate number of SBCs. They departed Linton-on-Ouse between 19.55 and 20.19 with F/Ls Easton, Latimer and Stewart the senior pilots on duty and assigned to bomb in the first and third waves. They climbed out over the station and set course for the Dutch coast to pass north of Haarlem and Amsterdam, before swinging to the south-east on a direct run to the target. There were no early returns, and all reached the target to find it covered by eight to ten-tenths cloud with tops in places as high as 14,000 feet, but Oboe performed well and enabled the Path Finders to mark the city with red and green TIs and Wanganui flares. The 408 (Goose) Squadron crews bombed from 18,000 and 23,000 feet between 22.01 and 22.20, before returning safely, having been unable to assess the results of their efforts. The impression was of a successful raid, based on a considerable glow beneath the clouds as they withdrew, and post-raid reconnaissance soon confirmed another outstandingly destructive operation against this once elusive target, thus continuing the remarkable run of successes here since the introduction of Oboe to main force operations a year earlier. Over seventeen hundred houses were destroyed in the attack, with dozens of war industry factories sustaining serious damage, and on a night when the night-fighter controllers were caught off guard by the switch to the Ruhr, the success was gained for the modest loss of nine aircraft including one 426 (Thunderbird) Squadron Lancaster.

While the above operation was in progress, seventy Halifaxes, thirty-two Stirlings and seven Mosquitos of 3, 4, 6 and 8 Groups attended to the marshalling yards at Courtrai (Kortrijk) in Belgium. Four 6 Group squadrons provided forty-seven of the Halifaxes without loss for what was a highly destructive attack, which spread to the town and destroyed more than three hundred buildings and killed 252 people. The Germans rounded up 450 unemployed civilians and pressganged a further 1,200 into the repair of the marshalling yards, which were back in service three days later.

The Transportation Plan continued on the 29th at Vaires, located in the Ile-de-France to the east of Paris, for which a force of seventy-six Halifaxes and eight Mosquitos was assembled, forty-nine of the former provided by 6 Group and the remainder by 4 Group. The backdrop of cloud that accompanied the bombers in the early stages of the outward flight diminished to leave clear skies and bright moonlight over the Paris area, which enabled crews to identify ground features. The Oboe marking was five minutes late, which required the first wave crews to orbit, but once the red TIs marked out the aiming point in the marshalling yards, the bombing was carried out accurately from medium level. Two ammunition trains blew up, one with particular violence at 21.40, followed by a vast cloud of smoke rolling across the scene, and, according to local sources, 1,270 German troops were killed.

The period known as the Battle of Berlin, but which was better referred to as the winter campaign, was to be brought to an end on the night of the 30/31st with a standard maximum-effort raid on Nuremberg in southern Germany. The plan of operation departed from normal practice in only one important respect, and this was to prove critical. It had become standard practice for 8 Group to plan operations and to employ diversions and feints to confuse the enemy night-fighter controllers, sometimes successfully and sometimes not, but with the night-fighter force having clearly gained the upper hand with its "Tame Boar" running commentary system and its "Schräge Musik" (Jazz) upward-firing cannons, all possible means had to be adopted to protect the bomber stream. During a conference held early on the 30th, the Lancaster Group A-O-Cs expressed a preference for a 5 Group-inspired route, which would require the bomber stream to fly a long straight leg across Belgium and Germany to a point about fifty miles north of Nuremberg, from where the final run-in would commence. The Halifax A-O-Cs were less convinced of the benefits, and AVM Bennett, the Path Finder chief, was positively overcome by the potential dangers and predicted a disaster, only to be overruled. A force of 795 aircraft was made ready, of which 201 Lancasters were to be provided by 5 Group, sixteen of them representing 49 Squadron, and the crews attended briefings to be told of the route, wind conditions and the belief that a layer of cloud would conceal them from enemy night-fighters. Before take-off, a Meteorological Flight Mosquito crew radioed in to cast doubts upon the weather conditions, which they could see differed markedly from those that had been forecast. This also went unheeded, and from around 21.45 for the next hour or so, the crews took off for the rendezvous area, and headed into a conspiracy of circumstances, which would inflict upon Bomber Command its heaviest defeat of the war.

At Linton-on-Ouse, while their Lancasters were being loaded with a cookie and SBCs of incendiaries, twenty-five crews attended briefing, the twelve representing 408 (Goose) Squadron to learn that they were assigned to the first, third and fifth waves. The Lancaster Mk IIs were equipped with a ventral gun position, which was rarely manned, but on this night, P/O Harvey and crew had an additional crew member on board for that purpose, F/Sgt Burke, while a number of other crews were accompanied by a second pilot gaining experience. They took off between 21.51 and 22.23 with W/C Jacobs the senior pilot on duty and it was not long into the flight before they and the rest of the force began to notice some unusual features in the conditions, which included uncommonly bright moonlight and a crystal clarity of visibility that allowed them the rare sight of other aircraft in the stream. On most nights, crews would feel themselves to be completely alone in the sky all the way to the target, until bang on schedule, TIs would be seen to fall, and other aircraft would make their presence known by the turbulence of their slipstreams as they funnelled towards the aiming point. Once at cruising altitude on this night, however, they were alarmed to note that the forecast cloud was conspicuous by its absence, and instead lay beneath them as a white tablecloth, against which they were silhouetted like flies. Condensation trails began to form in the cold, clear air to further advertise their presence to the enemy and the Jetstream winds, which had so adversely affected the Berlin raid a week earlier, were also present, only this time blowing from the south. As then, the wind-finder system failed to cope, and this would have a serious impact on the outcome of the operation. The final insult on this sad night was the route's close proximity to two night-fighter beacons, which the enemy aircraft were orbiting while they awaited their instructions, unaware initially that they were about to have the cream of Bomber Command handed to them on a plate.

The carnage began over Charleroi in Belgium, and from there to the target, the route was signposted by the burning wreckage on the ground of eighty Bomber Command aircraft. The windfinder system broke down again, and those crews who either failed to detect the strength of the wind or simply refused to believe the evidence, were driven up to fifty miles north of their intended track, and as a result turned towards Nuremberg from a false position. This led to more than a hundred aircraft bombing at Schweinfurt in error, which combined with the massive losses sustained before the target was reached to reduce considerably the numbers arriving at the primary target. 408 (Goose) Squadron's LL633 became the raid's seventy-fifth victim when shot down during the final run-in to the target by the combined efforts of a ME210 and a FW190. It crashed at Gerolzhofen, a small town some twelve miles south-east of Schweinfurt, delivering F/O White RCAF and four others of the eight occupants into enemy hands, while the wireless operator and both gunners perished in the wreckage. The remaining 408 (Goose) Squadron crews arrived over Nuremberg to encounter eight to nine-tenths cloud with tops as high as 16,000 feet and all but one bombed on red and green TIs and skymarkers from 19,000 to 21,000 feet between 01.12 and 01.29. The above-mentioned P/O Harvey and crew failed to pick up any markers and retained their bombs to jettison them over France on the way home. Ninety-five aircraft failed to return and many others were written off in landing crashes or with battle damage too severe to repair. Fourteen 6 Group aircraft were among the missing, one of which ditched off the French coast and all but the pilot were saved. At debriefings crews described many fires, the glow from which, according to some reports, remained visible for 120 miles into the return journey, but in reality the strong wind had driven the marking beyond the city to the east, and consequently, Nuremberg had escaped serious damage.

During the course of the month, the squadron participated in eight operations and dispatched eighty-five sorties for the loss of five Lancasters and their crews.

April 1944

The winter campaign had brought the Command to its low point of the war and was the only time when the morale of the crews was in question. What now lay before the hard-pressed men of Bomber Command was in marked contrast to that which had been endured over the seemingly interminable winter months. In place of the long slog to Germany on dark, often dirty nights, shorter range hops to France and Belgium in improving weather conditions would become the order of the day. However, these operations would be equally demanding in their way, and require of the crews a greater commitment to accuracy to avoid casualties among friendly civilians. Despite this, a decree from on high insisted that such operations were worthy of counting as just one third of a sortie towards the completion of a tour, and until this flawed policy was grudgingly rescinded late in the war, a sense of injustice pervaded the crew rooms. In fact, the number of sorties to complete a tour would fluctuate up and down between this point and the end of hostilities. Despite the horrendous losses of the winter campaign, the Command was in remarkably fine fettle to face its new challenge, with 3 Group gradually converting to Lancasters and the much-improved Hercules powered Halifax IIIs and VIIs equipping 4 Group and most of 6 Group respectively. Harris was now in the enviable position of being able to achieve what had eluded his predecessor, namely, to attack multiple targets simultaneously with enough strength to be effective. Such was the hitting-power now at his disposal, that he could assign targets to individual groups, to groups in tandem or to the Command as a whole, as dictated by operational requirements. Having developed its low-level marking system with Mosquitos and demonstrated it to be highly effective against precision targets, 5 Group had now gained virtual independence from the main force and would only occasionally operate as part of it. Although invasion considerations would come first from this point on, while Harris was at the helm, his favoured policy of city-busting would never be entirely shelved.

On the 6th, P/O Harvey's previously-mentioned ventral gunner, F/Sgt Burke, disappeared while attempting to swim across the River Ouse, and his body would remain undiscovered for seventeen days.

The pre-invasion campaign got into full swing with the posting of two operations on the 9th, one against the Lille-Delivrance goods station in north-eastern France assigned to 239 aircraft from 3, 4, 6 and 8 Groups, while the marshalling yards at Villeneuve-St-Georges, on the southern outskirts of Paris, were to be targeted by 225 aircraft drawn from all groups. 6 Group supported the former with fifty-three Halifaxes and the latter with ninety-eight Halifaxes and nine Lancasters, 408 (Goose) Squadron loading seven of its own with seven 1,000 and eleven 500-pounders each. They departed Linton-on-Ouse between 21.15 and 21 23 with F/L McIver the senior pilot on duty and joined up with the bomber stream as it headed south to begin the Channel crossing at Beachy Head. They crossed the French coast near Dieppe at around 14,000 feet and map-read their way inland, locating the target visually but exploiting the accurately placed red and green Path Finder-laid TIs to deliver their hardware from 14,250 to 14,500 feet between 00.09 and 00.15 in the face of little opposition. Many bomb bursts were observed along with orange explosions, and to those high above, the raid appeared to be highly successful. In fact, many bomb loads had fallen into adjacent residential districts, where four hundred houses had been destroyed or seriously damaged and ninety-three people killed. This was far fewer than had died in the simultaneous operation at Lille, some 130 miles to the north-east, where over two thousand items of rolling stock had been destroyed and buildings and installations seriously damaged, but at a collateral cost of 456 French civilian lives. Civilian casualties would prove to be an unavoidable by-product of the campaign.

On the following day, Monday the 10th, a further five railway yards, four in France and one in Belgium, were posted as the targets for that night and assigned to individual groups. 6 Group's Lancasters were to join others from 3 and 8 Groups to form a force of 148 Lancasters and fifteen Mosquitos to attack the Laon yards, while 122 Halifaxes joined forces with ten Path Finder Mosquitos to target those at Ghent. The fourteen 408 (Goose) Squadron Lancasters each received a bomb load of ten 1,000-pounders and four 500-pounders and departed Linton-on-Ouse between 00.45 and 00.58 with W/C Jacobs and S/L Russell the senior pilots on duty. F/L McIver and crew were immediately contending with a backfiring starboard-inner engine which blew oil out over the fuselage and the decision was taken to abort the sortie, leaving the others to head south and ultimately cross the French coast under clear skies at around 14,000 feet. They identified the aiming-point by means of red and green TIs and delivered their attacks from a uniform 11,500 to 11,800 feet between 03.36 and 03.44, before returning safely from what appeared to be a successful operation. This sentiment was echoed in both the 3 and 6 Groups' ORBs, but post-raid reconnaissance revealed that this was the night's only failure, and that the yards had escaped serious damage after only one corner had been hit. Meanwhile, a hundred miles to the north, the Halifax brigade was enjoying genuine success at the Merelbeke-Melle marshalling yards on the main line to Brussels, despite having to bomb through cloud, but collateral damage destroyed 584 buildings, killed 428 Belgians and injured three hundred others.

Apart from a number of small-scale mining forays, 6 Group sat out operations during the following week, when the main activity, which took place on the 11th, was a 1, 3, 5 and 8 Group assault on Aachen, Germany's most westerly city and an important railway hub with extensive marshalling yards at the western and eastern ends. A force of 341 aircraft inflicted massive damage in central districts and Burtscheid to the east of the centre and it would prove to be the city's worst experience of the war.

On the 14th, the Command became officially subject to the orders coming from the Supreme Headquarters of the Allied Expeditionary Force (SHAEF), under General Dwight D Eisenhower, and would remain thus shackled until the Allied armies were sweeping towards the German frontier at the end of the summer. On the 18th, 83 and 97 Squadrons were loaned to 5 Group from the Path Finders, on what amounted to a permanent detachment, along with the Mosquito unit, 627 Squadron. The Lancaster units were to become the 5 Group heavy markers, while the Mosquitos would eventually take over the low-level marking role currently performed by 617 Squadron. This was a major coup for AVM Cochrane and 5 Group and a bitter blow to AVM Bennett, the Path Finder Force chief. Relations between Cochrane and Bennett had never been cordial, but this plunged them to new depths. Both were brilliant men, Bennett, an Australian, in particular, a man of the greatest intellect, who, despite his total lack of humour, commanded the deepest respect and loyalty from his men. He and Cochrane were of vastly different opinions on the subject of target marking, Bennett believing that a low-level method exposed the crews to unnecessary danger, while Cochrane insisted that the risks in a fast-flying Mosquito were negligible and would produce greater accuracy. Though 83 and 97 Squadrons were formerly of 5 Group, and, at that time, had undoubtedly considered themselves part of the elite, most of the current crop of crews, despite beginning their operational careers in 5 Group, had come to see 8 Group as the pinnacle and were upset at being removed from what they considered to be an elevated status. They were fiercely proud, once qualified, to wear the Path Finder badge and enjoyed the enhanced benefits of their status, although, happily for them, as the squadrons were only officially on loan to 5 Group, they would retain these privileges.

The 18th was to be extremely busy and involved 1,125 sorties, more than eight hundred of them directed at four marshalling yards in France, while a further 168 aircraft were to be sent mining in the Baltic. 6 Group was to provide the main force of 113 Halifaxes and twenty-five Lancasters for the yards at Noisy-le-Sec, a north-eastern suburb of Paris, for which thirty-six Lancasters and eight Mosquitos were to provide the marking. The fifteen 408 (Goose) Squadron Lancasters each received a bomb load of nine 1,000 and seven 500-pounders and departed Linton-on-Ouse between 21.00 and 21.20 with W/C Jacobs the senior pilot on duty and all assigned to the first of two waves. They all arrived at the target to find clear skies, a little haze, a negligible amount of heavy flak bursting at 16,000 to 18,000 feet and red and green TIs cascading to provide a concentrated reference for the bomb-aimers. The 408 (Goose) Squadron participants attacked from a uniform 15,000 to 15,300 feet between 23.56 and 00.03 and returned home to report a successful operation, which caused extensive damage to the track, locomotive sheds and workshops. Around a hundred delayed action bombs caused problems over the following week, despite which a through line was established to keep traffic moving, while a full repair would not be completed before the war ended.

Another busy night of operations resulted in briefings across the Command on the 20th, at which 5 Group informed crews of their part in the first operation to include the three newly transferred squadrons, which was a two-phase attack on railway yards at La Chapelle, situated just to the north of Paris. 4 Group was to provide the main force of 175 Halifaxes for an attack on railway yards at Ottignies, situated a few miles to the south-east of Brussels in Belgium, while 154 Halifaxes of 6 Group attended to a similar target at Lens in north-eastern France. This left 357 Lancasters and twenty-two Mosquitos of 1, 3, 6 and 8 Groups to conduct the night's main event against Cologne for which the Linton-on-Ouse squadrons provided twenty-two Lancasters, fifteen representing 408 (Goose) Squadron. Each was loaded with eight 1,000 and eight 500-pounders, before taking off between 23.20 and 23.48 with W/C Jacobs and S/L Russell the senior pilots on duty, each with eight crew members, including a second pilot gaining operational experience and a ventral gunner. They adopted the standard route for this target via the Scheldt estuary and were in the spearhead of the bomber stream, having been assigned to PFF support duties, which required them to beef up the PFF presence during the bombing run to prevent the defences from latching onto individual aircraft but withhold their bombs for delivery during a second pass. They had been told at briefing to cross the enemy coast at 20,000 feet, and then climb, and arrived in the target area up to twelve minutes late to find eight to ten-tenths cloud at between 5,000 and 12,000 feet and some main force bombing having already begun on e.t.a. The first red sky-markers with yellow stars appeared at 01.58, and the 408 (Goose) Squadron crews bombed between then and 02.02 from 19,000 feet as the original supporter role was abandoned. The red glow of fires was observed in the cloud, but most crews returned with low expectations of the outcome, and the consensus was of a poor performance. In fact, the operation had caused widespread destruction and damage to industrial, residential and public buildings alike, had set off 1,290 individual fires and killed 664 inhabitants.

Düsseldorf was posted as the target on the 22nd, as Harris continued to pursue his own city-busting agenda, and a force of 596 aircraft from 1, 3, 4, 6 and 8 Groups was made ready, 6 Group contributing 136 aircraft made up of 113 Halifaxes and twenty-three Lancasters, fifteen of the latter provided by 408 (Goose) Squadron. 5 Group, meanwhile, was to provide its low-level marking method with the ultimate test, a heavily defended German city, for which Braunschweig had been selected. The night's third major operation was a two-wave affair involving 181 aircraft of 3, 4, 6 and 8 Groups against the previously attacked marshalling yards at Laon in north-eastern France, for which 6 Group put up forty Halifaxes from 419 (Moose), 428 (Ghost) and 434 (Bluenose) Squadrons. The 408 (Goose) Squadron Lancasters each received a bomb load of either a 8,000 or 2,000-pounder supplemented by a mix of incendiaries and departed Linton-on-Ouse between 20.25 and 20.43 with W/C Jacobs the senior pilot on duty. His crew consisted of three flight lieutenants, four flying officers, including a second pilot, and one lonely sergeant to man the ventral gun. It was all in vain as the starboard-inner engine caught fire during the climb-out, forcing an early return and the jettisoning of the 8,000 pounder. At about the same time F/O Snider and crew abandoned their sortie in the face of a starboard-outer engine issue, leaving the others to complete the outward flight to be greeted in the target area by clear skies with condensation trails and favourable bombing conditions. The initial Oboe red spotfires appeared to fall short, but the Master Bomber guided the efforts of the crews, who bombed on green or yellow TIs from between 19,000 and 21,000 feet between 01.13 and 01.26 in accordance with his instructions. Bursts were observed along with four explosions, and crews were then harried by night-fighters as they left the target area. Among nine missing aircraft was the 635 Squadron Lancaster containing the highly decorated W/C Cousens, who had been one of the assigned Master Bombers on duty. Returning crews were confident in the effectiveness of their work, and this was confirmed by post-raid reconnaissance and local sources, which catalogued the destruction of seven large industrial buildings and damage to forty-nine others, two thousand houses destroyed or seriously damaged and around twelve hundred fatalities.

The night of the 23/24th was another occupied by minor operations, dominant among which was a mining effort by 114 aircraft in five regions of the Baltic. 6 Group detailed thirty-seven Halifaxes from the three previously mentioned squadrons still operating the Mk II/V variants and assigned them to the Sweetpea, Willow and Radish gardens.

The busy month of operations continued on the 24th with briefings for a heavy raid on Karlsruhe in southern Germany, for which a force of 637 aircraft was assembled from all but 5 Group, with 116 of the Halifaxes and twenty-one Lancasters provided by 6 Group. 5 Group, meanwhile, would be honing its low-level marking technique at a heavily defended Munich 150 miles to the south-east. The fifteen-strong 408 (Goose) Squadron element was divided between the third and fourth waves and departed Linton-on-Ouse between 21.35 and 21.57 with W/C Jacobs the senior pilot on duty and either an 8,000 or 2,000-pounder in the bomb bay supplemented by a mix of 4lb and 30lb incendiaries. On this night the squadron commander again had a second pilot and ventral gunner on board, but this time the latter was of flying officer rank in an all-officer crew of nine. P/O Prickling and crew turned back with an engine issue after around two hours, while the remainder pressed on to encounter an electrical storm between Liege and Strasbourg, which lasted for an hour and affected some H2S sets. Sixty to seventy searchlights were operating as the Karlsruhe-bound bomber stream passed close to Mannheim, and at the target, crews were greeted by moderate flak coming up through the nine to ten-tenths thin cirrus and bursting as high as 18,000 feet. The main force crews were guided to the aiming point by release point flares and TIs and the 408 (Goose) Squadron participants attacked from 18,000 to 23,000 feet between 00.40 and 01.02. Local reports confirmed that the strong winds had pushed the attack onto the northern districts of the city and beyond, and nine hundred houses had been destroyed or seriously damaged at a cost to the Command of nineteen aircraft.

Meanwhile, the three 6 Group squadrons operating the Halifax Mk II provided eighteen aircraft between them for mining duties off the northern French ports of St-Malo, Cherbourg, Le Havre and Morlaix and the around the Frisians, while at Munich, W/C Cheshire of 617 Squadron distinguished himself with a low-level pass across the city to drop red spotfires for the heavy brigade high above, and scraped the rooftops as he dodged the light flak to escape. It was this operation that sealed the award of the Victoria Cross at the end of his operational career in July after completing one hundred sorties.

On the 26th, after a night's rest, 493 crews from 1, 3, 4, 6 and 8 Groups were called to briefing to learn that Essen would be their target for that night, while 5 Group tried out its low-level marking system at Schweinfurt and other elements of 4, 6 and 8 Groups joined forces to attend to the marshalling yards at Villeneuve-St-Georges, south of Paris. 6 Group supported the Essen endeavour with ninety-three Halifaxes and twenty-four Lancasters, sixteen of the latter representing 408 (Goose) Squadron and each loaded with either the 8,000 or 2,000-pounder and incendiaries. They departed Linton-on-Ouse between 23.04 and 23.22 with W/C Jacobs and S/L Russell the senior pilots on duty, both part of a nine-man crew with a second pilot and ventral gun operator and lost the services of P/O Sutherland and crew to the failure of their port-inner engine. The others arrived in the target area to be greeted by clear skies and good visibility, which the Path Finders exploited to mark the aiming-point for the main force crews, those from 408 (Goose) Squadron delivering their attacks on red and green TIs from 20,000 to 23,000 feet between 01.31 and 01.38, and observed large, red explosions, many fires and copious amounts of black smoke. All were unanimous in their assessment that this was a highly successful raid, which cost a very modest seven aircraft. Among them was DS719, which crashed in the Oosterschelde off Beveland on the Dutch coast with no survivors from the predominantly RCAF crew of F/O Rognan RCAF, who was on his sixth sortie. The flight engineer was RAF and the navigator USAAF, and the crew members had between two and four sorties to their credit.

At the same time some 270 miles to the south-west, thirty-one Mk II and sixteen Mk III Halifaxes of 6 Group were contributing to the destruction of installations in the railway yards at Villeneuve-St-Georges, in a raid more accurate than that of the 9th and causing less collateral damage.

The 27th saw a further three operations scheduled, two against railway yards at Aulnoye in France and Montzen in Belgium, for which 6 Group detailed ninety Halifaxes and forty-six Halifaxes and eight Lancasters respectively. The Lancasters at Montzen were Mk Xs and belonged to 419 (Moose) Squadron, which was operating the type for the first time alongside its Mk II Halifaxes on their final outing with the squadron. However, the night's largest effort would target the small city of Friedrichshafen, situated on the northern shore of Lake Constance (Bodensee) on the border with Switzerland and close to the Austrian frontier for which an all-Lancaster force of 322 aircraft was assembled. The main force element was drawn from 1, 3 and 6 Groups with fifty-nine 8 Group Lancasters to provide the marking, and at briefing at Linton-on-Ouse the nineteen crews of 408 and 426 (Thunderbird) Squadrons were told of the importance of Friedrichshafen to the German war effort as a centre of war production, particularly of tank engines and gearboxes. Six of the twelve 408 (Goose) Squadron Lancasters were loaded with a cookie and 450 x 4lb incendiaries and 32 of 30lbs, and the rest with a 500-pounder and 870 x 4lbs and 80 of 30lbs and took off between 21.35 and 21.47 with S/L Russell the senior pilot on duty with a ventral gunner on board. They exited the English coast at Shoreham-on-Sea on course for the Normandy coast, and apart from ten-tenths cloud over the Channel, the outward route was completed under clear skies, and the high-level cirrus over the target was no impediment to the crews' ability to establish their positions visually on Lake Constance. Zero hour for the main force was brought forward by ten minutes to 02.05, and the Path Finders opened the attack at 02.00 with green flares and green TIs. The 408 (Goose) Squadron crews carried out their attacks from 17,000 to 20,000 feet between 02.05 and 02.18 in accordance with the instructions of the Master Bomber and observed an accurate and concentrated pattern of bombing and many explosions and fires that inspired confidence that they had contributed to an outstandingly effective attack. It was not a one-sided affair, however, and having avoided to some extent contact with night-fighters on the way to the target, the bombers sustained heavy casualties at their hands in the target area and eighteen Lancasters failed to return. A total of 1,234 tons of bombs had been dropped on Friedrichshafen and an estimated 67% of its built-up area destroyed. Several factories sustained severe damage and the tank gearbox plant was destroyed, thus dealing a severe blow to tank production.

During the course of the month the squadron took part in eight operations and dispatched 109 sorties for the loss of a single Lancaster and crew.

May 1944

With the invasion now just five weeks away, the new month would be devoted to attacks on railway targets and coastal defences. In the case of the latter, the focus would be on the Pas-de-Calais region of France, to try to reinforce the enemy's belief that the landings would take place there, and right up to D-Day itself, the coastal region between Gravelines to the east of Calais and Berck-sur-Mer to the south-west would be subjected to constant bombardment. Six targets were posted across the Command on the 1st, three of them railway installations and the others individual factories belonging to the aircraft and motor industries. 6 Group was called upon to provide eighty-nine Halifaxes and twenty-six Lancasters for an attack on marshalling yards at St-Ghislain, a Belgian town close to the frontier with France and some thirty miles to the south-east of Lille. At Linton-on-Ouse 408 (Goose) Squadron made ready a dozen Mk II Lancasters and 426 (Thunderbird) Squadron five, on the latter's final operation before swapping the type for Mk III Halifaxes, while 419 (Moose) Squadron at Middleton-St-George provided nine MK Xs. The 408 (Goose) Squadron element took off between 22.05 and 22.35 with W/C Jacobs the senior pilot on duty with a ventral gunner on board and fourteen 1,000-pounders in the bomb bay. All from the squadron arrived in the target area, where clear skies and good visibility assisted the path Finders to illuminate the general area and mark out the aiming point with red spotfires and TIs. The 408 (Goose) Squadron crews delivered their loads from 8,500 feet between 00.02 and 00.14 in accordance with instructions from the Master Bomber, whose control was appreciated by the main force participants. W/C Jacobs and crew were frustrated by the failure of the bomb sight over the target, and they returned the bulk of their load to the bomb dump. F/O Brice and crew made three runs over the target between 00.02 and 00.13, the first two unsatisfactory, and the third too late to find any TIs still burning, and they took their bombs home also. Post-raid reconnaissance revealed the operation to have achieved its aims.

There were no further operations for 6 Group for a week, while the other groups continued with attacks on railway yards, coastal batteries, Luftwaffe aerodromes and bomb dumps. 1 and 5 Groups suffered a bloody nose on the night of the 3/4th when attacking a panzer depot and training camp at Mailly-le-Camp in France. The operation was highly successful but a communications problem led to a delay in bombing and forty-two Lancasters were brought down, mostly by night-fighters.

There was excitement at Linton-on-Ouse on the 8th when, after a week of operational inactivity, railway yards at Haine-St-Pierre were posted as the target for that night for a 6 Group main force of sixty-two Halifaxes and thirteen 408 (Goose) Squadron Lancasters. The latter took off between 01.06 and 01.33 with four pilots of flight lieutenant rank leading the way and a bomb load in each aircraft of eight 1,000 and eight 500-pounders. The target was located to the north-west of Charleroi in Belgium, and the Path Finders dropped illuminating flares and red spotfires and TIs as a guide to the approaching main force element. All of the 408 (Goose) Squadron crews arrived to find clear skies, bright moonlight and good visibility and observed yellow TIs ahead cascading over the aiming point, which would be backed up by reds and greens. They carried out their attacks in accordance with the instructions of the Master Bomber from 6,900 to 9,000 feet between 03.23 and 03.27 and witnessed a large explosion at 03.26 and another as they were leaving the target area. Smoke soon obscured the ground to prevent a detailed assessment of the outcome, but post-raid reconnaissance revealed that severe damage had been inflicted upon half of the yards and on locomotive sheds.

On the following day orders were received across the Command to prepare a total of 414 aircraft for attacks on seven coastal batteries in the Pas-de-Calais region. 6 Group was handed two targets, one for fifty-two Halifaxes at Saint-Valery-en-Caux situated on the Normandy coast between Fecamp and Dieppe, and the other for forty-one Halifaxes and a dozen 408 (Goose) Squadron Lancasters at Calais. The 408 (Goose) Squadron aircraft each received a bomb load of eight 1,000 and eight 500-pounders and departed Linton-on-Ouse between 21.47 and 21.59 with F/Ls Easton, Latimer and Rader the senior pilots on duty. Conditions were again favourable with clear skies and only a little ground haze and as the main force element arrived at the starting point of the bombing run, red TIs were already cascading over the aiming point three or four minutes ahead. Bombing was carried out on the centre of a salvo of red TIs from a uniform 10,500 feet between 23.26 and 23.35 and there were reports of a little overshooting and some wasting of bombs in the sea, but the consensus was of a successful attack which left a pall of smoke spiralling skyward.

On the 10th bomber forces totalling 506 aircraft were assembled to attack railway yards at Courtrai, Dieppe, Ghent, Lens and Lille, and it was for Ghent that 6 Group detailed eighty-Halifaxes and twenty-four Lancasters, fourteen of the latter made ready by 408 (Goose) Squadron and loaded with eight 1,000 and six 500-pounders. They departed Linton-on-Ouse between 21.45 and 22.07 with F/Ls Easton, Hales, McIver, Rader, Stewart and Weis the senior pilots on duty and the recent excellent serviceability rate continued as all reached the target area, where illuminating flares and scattered green TIs were observed at 23.38. These were followed by yellow TIs, which, in the early stages of the raid, the Master Bomber instructed were to be overshot slightly, but later called for the bombing to be directed between two clusters of yellows. All but one of the 408 (Goose) Squadron crews complied from 9,200 to 9,400 feet between 23.45 and 23.51, while F/L Rader and crew suffered a complete hang-up, a problem compounded by the failure of the intercom and to pick up the master Bomber's transmissions. It proved difficult to assess the outcome, but it was discovered later that stray bombing had killed forty-eight Belgian civilians and injured a further fifty-eight.

Marshalling yards at Boulogne and Trouville in France and Hasselt and Louvain in Belgium were handed respectively to 6, 4, 1 and 3 Groups on the 11th, each with Path Finder support, while 5 Group targeted a military camp at Bourg-Leopold in northern Belgium. 6 Group detailed eighty Halifaxes and twenty-six Lancasters for Boulogne, the fifteen Mk IIs at Linton-on-Ouse each receiving a bomb load of eight 1,000 and six 500-pounders before taking off between 22.34 and 22.46 with F/Ls Frankling, Hales, Latimer and Stewart the senior pilots on duty. Inaccurately forecast winds delayed some crews, but those arriving on time were greeted by illuminating flares from 00.24 with a few green TIs and red spotfires and then yellow TIs from around 00.32. The Master Bomber's initial instruction was to bomb the red spotfires, then to overshoot the yellows by two seconds and finally to bomb the centre of all markers, and the 408 (Goose) Squadron participants complied from 10,000 to 12,000 feet between 00.32 and 00.39, before turning for home with smoke billowing up to meet them. At debriefings large explosion were reported at 00.33

and 00.39, the former accompanied by a sheet of orange flame, but it had proved difficult to assess the outcome and it emerged later that 128 civilians had been killed in adjacent residential districts.

Louvain and Hasselt were earmarked for attack again twenty-four hours later, the former by 6 Group, for which a main force of ninety-six Halifaxes and twelve 419 (Moose) Squadron Lancasters was assembled, while 408 (Goose) Squadron remained at home and would do so for the succeeding seven nights. The operation was hugely destructive but spilled into residential districts, where a further 160 people were killed.

Thereafter, minor operations held sway until the 19th, when five railway yards, two coastal batteries and a radar station were targeted by forces totalling around eight hundred aircraft. 6 Group was assigned to a coastal battery at Merville-Franceville-Plage, a location on the Normandy coast to the east of what would be the British and Canadian Sword and Juno beaches on D-Day and detailed forty-two Halifaxes and fifteen 408 (Goose) Squadron Lancasters. The latter each received a bomb load of fourteen 1,000-pounders and departed Linton-on-Ouse between 23.04 and 23.22 with W/C Jacobs the senior pilot on duty, and all reached the target area to find clear skies and some ground haze. The marking began at around 01.30, the TIs falling in a roughly triangular pattern and attracting most of the bombing, some of it from the bellies of the 408 (Goose) Squadron Lancasters from 6,900 to 7,000 feet between 01.33 and 01.38. Deep-red explosions were observed at 01.35 and 01.38, suggesting an effective attack, and post-raid reconnaissance confirmed that some bombs had fallen around the battery but no detailed assessment was possible.

For the first time in a year, Duisburg was posted as the target for a major raid on the 21st, for which a heavy force of 510 Lancasters was drawn from 1, 3, 5 and 8 Groups, supported by twenty-two Mosquitos. While this operation was in progress, seventy Lancasters and thirty-seven Halifaxes, twenty-three representing 6 Group's 428 (Ghost) and 433 (Porcupine) Squadrons, would undertake gardening duties off the Frisians and Heligoland and in the Baltic.

Just like Duisburg, Dortmund was posted on the 22nd to host its first large-scale visit from the Command for a year and would face an all-Lancaster heavy force of 361 aircraft drawn from 1, 3, 6 and 8 Groups. While this operation was in progress, 220 Lancasters of 5 Group and five from 101 Squadron were to target Braunschweig, which, thus far, had evaded severe damage at the hands of the Command. 6 Group made available twenty-seven Lancasters, fifteen of them belonging to 408 (Goose) Squadron, each of which received the standard Ruhr bomb load of a cookie and ten and eight SBCs respectively of 4lb and 30lb incendiaries. They departed Linton-on-Ouse between 22.35 and 23.03 with W/C Jacobs the senior pilot on duty and an eight-man crew that included a second pilot under training and a ventral gunner. They climbed away into heavy cloud and severe icing conditions from 4,000 feet, which would persuade a considerable number of crews to abandon their sorties before reaching enemy territory. The Geese flew out over Flamborough Head on course for the Frisian Island of Vlieland and it was when twenty miles out over the North Sea that F/O Bryson were defeated by the icing and turned back. F/Sgt Vaughan and crew were within twenty-five miles of Texel when both port engines failed and ended their interest in proceedings. Those pressing on were rewarded with improving conditions and by the time the target hove into view, the cloud had diminished to no more than two-tenths, and the attack opened punctually with red and green TIs and red flares with yellow stars.

The 408 (Goose) Squadron crews delivered their bomb loads from 20,000 to 22,000 feet between 00.46 and 00.54 and observed many fires, some with oily smoke, leading to a consensus among returning crews of an accurate and effective raid. Eighteen Lancaster failed to return, three of them from 6 Group, and the two empty dispersals at Linton-on-Ouse that should have been occupied by 408 (Goose) Squadron aircraft told their own story. LL723 was approaching the northern rim of the Ruhr with the target some fifteen miles ahead to the south-south-west when attacked and brought down by one of the night-fighters laying in wait. The Lancaster crashed at Westrup, near the small town of Haltern, and there were no survivors from the crew of W/C Jacobs DFC RCAF, who was on the eighteenth sortie of his second tour and, therefore, just two short of completing it. With him and also deep into their second tours were the navigation leader, F/L McDougall DFC & Bar RCAF, and the gunnery leader, F/L Hanson DFC RCAF. The deputy gunnery leader, F/O Philpot, was on the twenty-eighth sortie of his first tour, while in contrast, the second pilot was on his first. DS759 was shot down by a night-fighter on the way home and crashed near Sevelen, a village between the Rhine and the Dutch frontier, and there were no survivors from the predominantly RCAF crew of F/O Sherrill RCAF. The pilot was on his fifth sortie and most of his crew on their third, but the flight engineer, Sgt Nightingale RAF, was on his twenty-first. Post-raid reconnaissance revealed that the main weight of the attack had fallen onto predominantly residential districts in the south-east of the city, where six industrial premises and more than eight hundred houses had been destroyed, and almost as many seriously damaged.

While the above operation was taking place, a 6 Group main force of 112 Halifaxes with Path Finder support targeted the marshalling yards at Le Mans, causing extensive damage to it and the nearby Gnome & Rhone aero engine factory.

The main operation on the 24th involved 442 aircraft from all but 5 Group in an attack on two marshalling yards at Aachen, Aachen-West and Rothe-Erde in the east. As the most westerly city in Germany, sitting on the frontiers of both Holland and Belgium, it was a major link in the railway network that would be a route for reinforcements to the Normandy battle front. While this operation was in progress, 5 Group would be targeting war-industry factories in Holland and Belgium, and elements of 4 and 6 Groups coastal batteries between Boulogne and Trouville-sur-Mer. 6 Group detailed sixty Halifaxes and thirty Lancasters for the main event, the sixteen of the latter at Linton-on-Ouse each receiving a bomb load of eleven 1,000 and three 500-pounders before taking off between 23.47 and 00.01 with the recently promoted S/L Stewart the senior pilot on duty. They headed south to exit the English coast at Orfordness and made landfall on the French coast near Dunkerque, benefitting from favourable weather conditions all the way to the target, where the Path Finders employed the "Musical Paramatta" technique, blind marking by H2S, to establish the aiming points for the main force crews. Those representing 408 (Goose) Squadron carried out their attacks on the Aachen-West aiming point from 18,000 to 20,000 feet between 02.24 and 02.30 in the face of a heavy flak barrage and had to dodge night-fighters as they vacated the target area. Photographic reconnaissance revealed that the yards at Rothe-Erde had escaped serious damage, and a second operation was deemed necessary.

The night of the 27/28th was to be one of feverish activity, which would generate more than eleven hundred sorties, reflecting the close proximity of the invasion now just ten days away. The largest operation would bring a return to the military camp at Bourg Leopold in Belgium, the previous attack on which by 5 Group two weeks earlier had been abandoned part-way through. There was also a repeat of the Aachen attack of the 24th, which had failed to destroy the Rothe-Erde marshalling yards at the eastern end of the city. 5 Group was not involved in either of the above, and instead prepared forces of one hundred Lancasters and four Mosquitos and seventy-eight Lancasters and five Mosquitos respectively to target marshalling yards and workshops at Nantes and the aerodrome at Rennes, situated some fifty miles apart in north-western France. There would also be operations against coastal batteries, of which there were five on this night, including one at Morsalines, situated on the eastern seaboard of the Cherbourg peninsula, some ten miles north of what, during the forthcoming Operation Overlord, would be the Americans' Utah landing ground.

A force of 331 aircraft was put together for Bourg-Leopold, which contained 267 Halifaxes, fifty-six Lancasters and eight Mosquitos, 117 of the Halifaxes and thirty-two of the Lancasters representing 6 Group. 408 (Goose) Squadron loaded each of its eighteen Mk IIs with fourteen 500-pounders and sent them on their way from Linton-on-Ouse between 23.26 and 00.17 with S/L Hales the senior pilot on duty. There were no early returns, and all arrived in the target area to find clear skies and a Master Bomber was on hand to direct the marking and bombing. Red, green and yellow TIs marked out the aiming-point, and the main-force crews obliged with an accurate attack, delivered by those from 408 (Goose) Squadron from a uniform 10,000 feet between 02.10 and 02.15. One Oboe TI had landed right on the aiming-point, and post-raid reconnaissance revealed that the camp had sustained extensive damage at a cost to the Command of nine Halifaxes and one Lancaster, six of the former belonging to 6 Group.

408 (Goose) Squadron's new commanding officer was W/C Roy McLernon DFC, who was posted in from 425 (Allouette) Squadron, where he had been the commanding officer for less than two months. Prior to that he had served as a flight commander with 434 (Bluenose) Squadron and had been shot down during the opening round of the Berlin campaign on the 23/24th of August 1943. He managed to make his way to Sweden and following a respectable term of internment, returned to Bomber Command, eventually to resume his operational career. The ORB records that he arrived at Linton-on-Ouse on the morning of the 29th but was appointed to command the squadron w.e.f the 24th. It seems likely that he officially assumed command on the 24th, but was entitled to a few days leave before arriving in person.

6 Group ended the month with an operation on the 31st against a coastal signals station at Au Fevre, located on the western side of the Cherbourg peninsula, for which a force of ninety-three Halifaxes and thirty-two Lancasters was assembled. The sixteen 408 (Goose) Squadron Lancasters each received a bomb load of fourteen 1,000-pounders before departing Linton-on-Ouse between 21.47 and 22.18 with S/L Stewart the senior pilot on duty. P/O McIntyre and crew had just passed to the west of Chatteris in Cambridgeshire when thunderstorms and severe icing persuaded them to turn back, one of seven to return early. The others pressed on and were rewarded with favourable conditions in the target area, which the Path Finder element exploited to deliver the first cascading red TIs at 00.10. All but one of the 408 (Goose) Squadron crews carried out their attacks from 8,000 to 8,400 feet between 00.14 and 00.22 and only Sgt Andrews and crew were unable to release their bombs after failing to find a marker still burning at the time of their arrival at 00.25. There were some comments at debriefing about undershooting, but the bulk of the bombs fell where intended and post-raid reconnaissance revealed that four of the station's six masts had been destroyed.

Former flight commander and two-tour veteran, S/L Miles DFC, had been elevated to wing commander rank since leaving the squadron to assume command of 1659 Conversion Unit, and the good news that he was to receive a Bar to his DFC was recorded in the ORB. During the course of the month, the squadron took part in ten operations and dispatched 146 sorties for the loss of two Lancasters and crews.

June 1944

June was to be a hectic month which would make great demands on the crews, and the first week was dominated by unsettled weather, which caused concerns for the impending launch of Operation Overlord. The bombing of coastal batteries and signals stations was to be the priority during the first few days leading up to D-Day, and 6 Group briefed 117 crews on the 1st for a return to the recently attacked Au Fevre signals station, only for it and most other operations to be cancelled. Targets on the 2nd included coastal batteries at five locations, all in the deception area of the Pas-de-Calais, radar installations at two locations, Trappes marshalling yards and there would also be a number of Mosquito nuisance raids. 6 Group detailed fifty-six Halifaxes and fourteen 408 (Goose) Squadron Lancasters and briefed their crews for an attack on the coastal battery at Neufchâtel-Hardelot to the south of Boulogne. At Linton-on-Ouse the Lancasters each received a bomb load of eleven 1,000 and four 500-pounders and took off between 22.12 and 22.23 with S/L Hales the senior pilot on duty. There were no early returns as they headed south for the sea crossing, and all arrived at the French coast to find up to seven-tenths cloud with tops at 6,000 feet and plenty of gaps, through which the first cascading green TIs were observed at 00.12. Well-concentrated TIs were in the bomb sights as the 408 (Goose) Squadron crews bombed from 7,000 to 8,000 feet between 00.14 and 0018 to contribute to the 275 tons of high explosives dropped, and large explosions were witnessed at 00.15 and 00.17. Smoke was rising through 3,000 feet as they turned away confident that they had plastered the site and were unaware that the destruction of the target was merely a secondary consideration to the main aim to continue the deception concerning the true location of the forthcoming landings. It would only be on D-Day Eve that Normandy coastal batteries were targeted in earnest.

408 (Goose) Squadron was not called into action on the ensuing nights as 6 Group conducted mining operations and on the night of the 4/5th sent fifty-five Halifaxes and fourteen 419 (Moose) Squadron Lancasters to attack a coastal battery at Calais. The 5th was D-Day Eve and, during the course of the day more than a thousand aircraft were made ready for an assault on coastal defences and in support and diversionary operations. The weather had been a source of concern for the D-Day planners, and even as Operation Overlord was given the green light, massive uncertainty attended the final decision to go. Linton-on-Ouse was the scene of feverish activity as eighteen 408 (Goose) Squadron Lancasters were made ready for that night's operation, each receiving a bomb load of eleven 1,000 and four 500-pounders. At 17.00, station commander, G/C Annis, addressed all personnel over the tannoy to inform them that the entire station was confined to barracks until further notice. Crews across the Command attended evening briefings at which no direct reference was made to the invasion, but unusually, they were given strict altitudes at which to fly and were instructed not to jettison bombs over the sea. The 408 (Goose) Squadron crews learned that ten heavy gun batteries were being targeted along the Normandy coast, and that their

specific objective was at Longues-sur-Mer, which, they were not told, overlooked Gold beach, the landing ground for British forces. The squadron would share the target with seven Lancasters of 419 (Moose) squadron, while ninety-nine 6 Group Halifaxes attended to a similar target at Merville-Franceville-Plage further to the east.

The Linton-on-Ouse element had to wait until the early hours of D-Day before taking to the air between 02.12 and 02.23 with no fewer than eight crews captained by pilots of flight lieutenant rank in the absence of more senior officers. There were no early returns and as the target was approached it was observed to be covered by nine to ten-tenths cloud with tops at up to 8,000 feet. A number of green TIs could be seen ahead at 04.15, but the main marking by Oboe with red TIs backed up with greens began at 04.17. The glow through the cloud as they burned on the ground enabled the bomb-aimers to establish the location of the aiming point and the bombing was carried out from 9,000 to 10,000 feet between 04.22 and 04.27. Flashes of bomb bursts were observed but it was impossible to assess the outcome and crews were left with the thought that if the TIs had been accurate, so had been the bombing. Aircraft were taking off throughout the night, and those crews returning in dawn's early light were rewarded with a glimpse through gaps in the cloud of the greatest armada in history ploughing its way sedately across the Channel below. A total of five thousand tons of bombs was delivered during the course of these operations, and this was a record for a single night.

At 9.30 am the station commander announced over the tannoy that Allied ground forces had landed successfully to begin the liberation of France and the news was well-received by all who had played their part in whatever role they served. The ground crews had grabbed a few hours of sleep while their charges were away but returned to their workstation in time to receive the homecoming bombers and prepare them for the next operation. Later that morning the station was called to action again to prepare for the night's operational activities, while across the Channel the beachheads were being secured and at Bomber Command the raid planners were preparing to support the ground forces with attacks on nine road and railway communications centres through which the enemy could bring reinforcements. A total of 1,065 aircraft were involved and 6 Group was to support two operations, one by ninety Halifaxes and thirty-two Lancasters against a road and rail junction at Coutances, located on the western side of the Cherbourg peninsula, and the other by 115 Halifaxes at Conde-sur-Noireau fifty miles to the east. 408 (Goose) Squadron's target was described in the ORB as a bridge and a choke point, for which a record of twenty-one Lancasters was made ready, each loaded with eighteen 500-pounders. They departed Linton-on-Ouse between 21.36 and 22.07 with W/C McLernon and S/L Hales the senior pilots on duty and a ventral gunner in seven crews, and all made it across the Channel to make landfall on the Normandy coast under seven to ten-tenths cloud with a base at around 4,500 feet. The initial yellow TIs began to fall at 00.13 and were found to be a thousand yards to the north-east of the planned aiming point, but green TIs three minutes later landed on the starboard side of the bridge and attracted the bulk of the bombing, the 408 (Goose) Squadron crews attacking in accordance with instructions from the Master Bomber from 1,400 to 5,000 feet between 00.17 and 00.23. F/L Rader and crew were frustrated by a complete hang-up but managed to jettison their load "safe" on the way home. The group dropped 463 tons of high explosives, some of which fell into the town and inevitably caused civilian casualties.

On the 7th, 6 Group detailed seventy-seven Halifaxes and twenty-three Lancasters to attack marshalling yards at Achéres, to the north-west of Paris, and twenty Halifaxes for Versailles-Matelots, two of four similar targets for the night. 408 (Goose) Squadron made ready a dozen of its Lancasters, loading each with eighteen 500-pounders before sending them on their way from Linton-on-Ouse between 22.58 and 23.23 with W/C McLernon the senior pilot on duty. There were no early returns, and all reached the target area to find up to ten-tenths cloud with clear conditions below the cloud base at around 7,000 feet. Red TIs went down at 00.18 to be followed by greens, some of which became obscured by smoke, prompting the Master Bomber to issue instructions to bomb the fires if no TIs were evident. The 408 (Goose) Squadron crews attacked from 2,000 to 6,000 feet between 01.20 and 01.23 and observed four large explosions, and all but one returned, F/L Easton and crew in DS729, which had been badly shot-up by a night-fighter over the target and could not deploy flaps for landing. The Lancaster ground-looped on touchdown without injury to the crew, and although the Lancaster remained on squadron charge, it may not have returned to duty. The eight-man crew of F/L Weis RCAF failed to return in LL643 and was lost without trace on what was the pilot's thirteenth sortie, while his crew, with the exception of the rookie ventral gunner, had completed between eleven and fifteen.

Orders were received by 6 Group on the following day to prepare seventy Halifaxes and ten 408 (Goose) Squadron Lancasters for an attack on a railway station at Mayenne, a town situated to the north-east of Rennes and north-west of Le-Mans. The Linton-on-Ouse Lancasters each received a bomb load of eighteen 500-pounders and took off between 23.03 and 23.16 with S/L Hales the senior pilot on duty. All arrived at the target to find clear conditions and good visibility beneath the ten-tenths cloud base at around 6,000 feet and bombed in accordance with the instructions of the Master Bomber on green, white and yellow TIs from 4,000 to 6,000 feet between 01.46 and 01.53. A very large explosion with a vivid orange flame at 01.47 sent black smoke rising through 5,000 feet, before dust and smoke obscured the ground to render an assessment difficult. Seven crews were diverted to Nutts Corner in County Antrim, Northern Ireland on return, presumably because of poor conditions at Linton-on-Ouse. A 426 (Thunderbird) Squadron Halifax heading home to Linton-on-Ouse was the operation's only casualty after losing an engine at low level and crashing with the loss of seven lives while attempting a forced-landing at Newton-on-Ouse, some two miles south-east of the airfield.

A total of 401 aircraft from 1, 4, 6 and 8 Groups were detailed on the 9th to target airfields in the battle area at Flers, Laval, Le-Mans and Rennes, while 5 Group concentrated on a railway junction at Etampes, south of Paris. 6 Group detailed seventy-six Halifaxes and twenty-four Lancasters for Le-Mans aerodrome, which housed an important Renault factory producing vehicles and other military equipment for the Reich. 408 (Goose) Squadron made ready ten of its Lancasters, each of which the armourers loaded with eighteen 500-pounders and waved them off the end of the runway between 21.20 and 21.40 with F/Ls Easton, Frankling and Sutherland the senior pilots on duty. All arrived in the target area to encounter up to eight-tenths cloud with a base at 5,000 feet and good visibility below, aided eventually by illuminator flares after the Path Finders turned up a minute or two late. Most were able to identify the aiming point visually and were further assisted by red and yellow TIs until the reds burned out. The bombing was carried out in the face of light flak from 1,400 to 4,900 feet between 00.19 and 00.26 and was observed to fall within the confines of the target area, leaving a hangar on fire and smoke rising through 3,000 feet by the end of the attack. The force delivered 370 tons of high-explosives without loss in what appeared to be a successful operation.

Late into the evening of the 10th, DS656 burst a tyre and crashed during the take-off run for a training flight, and although the Lancaster would never fly again, the crew of W/O Harlow RCAF walked away from its wreckage.

The Base system had been established in Bomber Command in March 1943 and consisted of a main station with up to three satellites attached, each home to two Squadrons, which improved the organisation process and allowed targets to be assigned to individual bases. The system came into its own during the post-invasion period from June 1944, when campaigns against oil, communications and flying bomb sites and tactical support for the ground forces demanded that multiple targets be attacked each day and night. In 6 Group, 61 Base consisted of the stations at Topcliffe, Dalton, Dishforth and Wombleton and contained the Conversion Units responsible for the training of new crews. 62 Base encompassed the stations at Linton-on-Ouse with 408 and 426 (Thunderbird) Squadrons, East Moor with 432 (Leaside) and from July 415 (Swordfish) Squadron and Tholthorpe, home to 420 (Snowy Owl) and 425 (Allouette) Squadrons. 63 Base consisted of Middleton-St-George and Croft, where respectively 419 (Moose) and 428 (Ghost) Squadrons and 431 (Iroquois) and 434 (Bluenose) Squadrons resided.

A return to the Transportation Plan on the 10th required the groups to assemble a combined force of 432 aircraft to attack marshalling yards at Achéres, Dreux, Orléons and Versailles, 6 Group detailing a hundred Halifaxes drawn from each of the three operational bases to target Versailles-Matelots, where the locomotive sheds were an additional attraction. Little information came out of each location, but it was believed that all four sites had been hit and damaged to some extent.

408 (Goose) Squadron had been inactive for two nights when orders came through on the 12th for 62 Base to prepare sixty Halifaxes and sixteen 408 (Goose) Squadron Lancasters to join with sixteen other Lancasters from 64 Base's 419 (Moose) Squadron to attack the marshalling yards at Cambrai in north-eastern France. This was one of six similar targets for a combined force of 671 aircraft, the others assigned to Amiens/St-Roch, Amiens/Longueau, Arras, Caen and Poitiers, 6 Group also supporting the Arras raid with eighty-nine Halifaxes from 63 and 64 Bases. The 408 (Goose) Squadron Lancasters each received the standard bomb load for this type of target, eighteen 500-pounders, and departed Linton-on-Ouse between 21.35 and 22.07 with W/C McLernon and S/L Stewart the senior pilots on duty. There were no early returns as the 408 (Goose) Squadron element began the sea crossing near Orfordness and completed it with landfall between Calais and Dunkerque before arriving in the target area to be greeted by good visibility. The Path Finders dropped illumination flares and red TIs, which were bombed by a proportion of the force during the first pass until smoke and dust obscured the ground and the Master Bomber called for the rest of the force, including most of the 408 (Goose) Squadron element, to orbit, while fresh markers went down. They then delivered their attacks from 4,000 to 4,800 feet between 00.25 and 00.34 and observed many bomb bursts on the junction, but there was also a feeling that the whole affair was disorganised, and the bombing scattered and those attacking at the tail end of the raid were reduced to bombing the smoke.

Night-fighters were lurking on the route home from the target to the North Sea and took a heavy toll of 6 Group aircraft, nine from Cambrai and six from Arras, and four empty dispersal pans at Linton-on-Ouse guaranteed that a sombre atmosphere would pervade the station for the remainder of the day. Three of the missing were 408 (Goose) Squadron Lancasters, each of which contained an experienced crew, among them that of B Flight commander, S/L Stewart RCAF. DS726 crashed three miles south-south-east of Cambrai killing the pilot and five of his crew and delivering the bomb-aimer into enemy hands, while the most experienced member of the crew, ventral gunner, P/O La Pierre DFC RCAF, a veteran of thirty sorties, managed to evade a similar fate. DS688 was dispatched by a night-fighter to crash two miles north-north-west of Cambrai with fatal consequences for F/L Brice RCAF and the other seven occupants, five of whom were also members of the RCAF. F/L Brice was on his twenty-fifth sortie and his crew had between twenty-one and twenty-eight sorties to their credit. DS772 came down seven miles east-north-east of Cambrai with no survivors from the crew of F/L McIver RCAF, who was on his thirteenth sortie. With the exception of the wireless operator, F/L Pledger DFC RCAF, who was on the eleventh sortie of his second tour, his crew had completed between ten and seventeen sorties.

It was during this operation that mid-upper gunner, W/O Andrew Mynarski RCAF, of 419 (Moose) Squadron earned the posthumous award of the Victoria Cross for trying to rescue F/O Brophy RCAF, who was trapped in his rear turret as the Lancaster burned around him. Mynarski was badly burned and after strenuous vain efforts to break open the turret doors, reluctantly joined the rest of his crew in jumping from the stricken aircraft. His parachute had caught fire and continued to smoulder, causing him to land heavily with his clothing still on fire, and although he was found to be alive, he died shortly afterwards. Brophy miraculously survived the crash and was one of four from the crew to evade capture and return to England to tell the story of Mynarski's heroism.

While the above was being played out, a force of 286 Lancasters and seventeen Mosquitos of 1, 3 and 8 Groups opened a new campaign against Germany's synthetic oil industry, targeting on this night the Gelsenkirchener Bergwerke AG synthetic oil plant located in the Horst district of Gelsenkirchen in the heart of the Ruhr, and known to Bomber Command as the Nordstern plant and to the Germans as Gelsenberg AG. The operation was highly successful and landed 1,500 high explosive bombs on the plant, bringing an end to production for several weeks at a cost to the German war effort of a thousand tons of aviation fuel per day. Collateral damage to adjacent workers' housing resulted in the deaths of 250 people on top of those killed in the plant.

428 (Ghost) Squadron had been converting to Mk X Lancasters and was invited to undertake its maiden operation on the type on the 14th as part of a 6 Group main force of sixty-one Halifaxes and thirty-seven Lancasters from 62 and 64 Bases. They were assigned to attack marshalling yards at St-Pol, located some eighteen miles north-west of Arras, one of three similar targets for the night in the region. Another was at Cambrai, which, as suspected, had not been destroyed in the attack of two nights earlier and would now face a 6 Group main force of ninety-four Halifaxes from 63 and 64 Bases, while a third target at Douai was handed to 4 Group. The Path Finders would provide a Master Bomber and deputy and carry out the marking at all three locations. 408 (Goose) Squadron loaded each of its fourteen Lancasters with the usual railway-busting eighteen 500-pounders and sent them on their way from Linton-on-Ouse between 01.23 and 01.41 with S/L Hales the senior pilot on duty. They flew out over ten-tenths cloud, which began to break up as St-Pol drew near and was at seven to nine-tenths with good visibility below as the Path Finders opened

the attack with white spotfires and red TIs, backed up with greens. The 408 (Goose) Squadron crews delivered their bombs from 7,500 to 10,300 feet between 03.14 and 03 18 and the bursts from their own bombs and those from other aircraft appeared to be concentrated around the TIs. The impression was of a successful operation, but the cloud cover prevented an immediate assessment, and it would be determined later that further raids would be required.

While the above was in progress, 337 aircraft from 4, 5 and 8 Groups targeted troop and vehicle positions near Caen, while the Command's first daylight operation since the departure of 2 Group twelve months earlier was directed at the port of Le Havre, from where the enemy's fast, light marine craft were posing a threat to Allied shipping supplying the Normandy beachheads. The two-phase operation was conducted by predominantly 1 and 3 Groups with 617 Squadron representing 5 Group and took place in the evening under the umbrella of a fighter escort. The attack was highly successful, and few craft survived the onslaught.

A force of 297 aircraft from 1, 4, 5, 6 and 8 Groups was assembled on the 15th to try to do to Boulogne what had been done to Le Havre twenty-four hours earlier. It was again left to 617 Squadron to represent 5 Group, while 6 Group detailed 130 Halifaxes and thirty-two Lancasters for what the 408 (Goose) Squadron ORB celebrated as "something new", 6 Group's first genuine daylight foray, which in reality would be a twilight rather than daylight operation. 408 (Goose) Squadron loaded thirteen of its Lancasters with eleven 1,000 and four 500-pounders and dispatched them from Linton-on-Ouse between 20.45 and 21.05 with W/C McLernon the senior pilot on duty. Five to ten-tenths cloud lay over the target with tops at 11,000 feet and a base at around 3,000 feet, despite which, some crews were able to identify the breakwater and docks, but not the briefed aiming point. They were guided to the mark by red TIs, the first going down at 22.47 to be visible beneath the cloud, and the aiming point was backed up throughout the raid, during which a particularly large explosion occurred at 22.51 that was estimated to be on the south-western corner of the Bassin Loubet. The 408 (Goose) Squadron crews bombed from 10,500 to 16,800 feet between 22.34 and 22.48 and turned for home satisfied with their evening's work. The conditions hampered a detailed assessment of the outcome, but the raid was believed to be just as successful as that at Le Havre, albeit at the cost of many civilian lives as collateral bombing hit the town.

Plans were put in hand on the 16th, to launch 829 sorties that night against a number of targets, including 405 against four flying-bomb launching sites in the Pas-de-Calais/Hauts-de-France regions of north-eastern France. Just three days earlier, the first V-1 flying bombs had landed on London, and this prompted a response in the form of a second new campaign to open during the month to target this revolutionary new menace. The large concrete flying-bomb storage and launching structures were referred to in Bomber Command circles as "constructional works" and it was one at Sautricourt, situated some twenty-five miles inland to the south-east of Boulogne and north-west of Arras, that was the target for a hundred Halifaxes of 6 Group's 62 and 63 Bases, while elements of 1, 4, 5 and 8 Groups plied their trade at three other sites. Each aiming point was marked by Oboe Mosquitos and successfully bombed without loss.

While the above operations were in progress, the oil campaign continued in the hands of 321 aircraft of 1, 4, 6 and 8 Groups with an attack on the Ruhr-Chemie synthetic oil plant at Sterkrade-Holten, a district of Oberhausen in the central Ruhr. 6 Group detailed 102 Halifaxes and thirty-seven Lancasters from 62 and 64 Bases, including sixteen of the latter provided by 408 (Goose) Squadron, which departed Linton-on-Ouse between 22.55 and 23.20 with S/L Hales the senior pilot on duty and each crew sitting on a cookie and sixteen 500-pounders. F/O Clothier and crew lost their starboard-inner engine during the climb-out over the station and headed directly for the jettison area, leaving the others to head south-east towards the exit point over Felixstowe on the Essex coast. Those reaching the central Ruhr encountered ten-tenths cloud with tops at around 14,000 feet, which meant that the TIs soon disappeared from view to leave only a faint glow for the main force crews to aim at. The 408 (Goose) Squadron crews bombed on the reflection in the cloud of red and green TIs from 18,800 to 21,000 feet between 01.17 and 01.22, some observing bursts but nothing of use to pass on at debriefing. The expectation of returning crews was that the bombing had been scattered and ineffective, and it would be confirmed later that this operation had little impact on oil production. It had been an expensive endeavour for the Command, however, which registered the loss of thirty-one aircraft, twenty-two of them Halifaxes, two-thirds falling to night-fighters. It was a sobering night for 6 Group, which registered the loss of ten Halifaxes and two 419 (Moose) Squadron Lancasters, but it was a catastrophe for Croft to which eight Halifaxes, four each from 431 (Iroquois) and 434 (Bluenose) Squadrons, failed to return.

On the 17th, 317 aircraft of 1, 3, 4 and 8 Groups were assembled to attack railway targets at Aulnoye, Montdidier and St-Martin-l'Hortier, while 6 Group provided a main force of ninety Halifaxes and a dozen 408 (Goose) Squadron Lancasters from 62 and 63 Bases to attack a flying-bomb supply site at Oisemont/Neuville-au-Bois located some ten miles south of Abbeville. The 408 (Goose) Squadron Lancasters each received a bomb load of eighteen 500-pounders before departing Linton-on-Ouse between 00.55 and 01.20 with F/Ls Bryson, Easton, Latimer and Rader the senior pilots on duty. The force was depleted by just one early return and on arrival at the target was confronted by ten-tenths cloud with tops at between 5,000 and 10,000 feet, into which the Path Finder TIs disappeared to leave a glow. The 408 (Goose) Squadron participants bombed from 11,500 to 12,300 feet between 03.09 and 03.14 in accordance with the instructions of the Master Bomber and could only speculate on the outcome. The consensus was that if the Master Bomber had accurately interpreted the fall of TIs, the operation was probably successful.

Operations were posted across the groups on each day from the 18th to the 21st, only for them to be cancelled at the last minute, on one occasion when aircraft were taxiing to the runway. It was a frustrating experience for the crews, who would have sat through a briefing and followed all of the procedures necessary before a major operation, including the build-up of tension, all for nothing and usually too late to be able to use the evening for leisure pursuits.

The 21st brought the first genuine daylight operations for 6 Group, which was called upon to provide a main force of ninety-nine Halifaxes from 63 and 64 Bases for a return to the flying-bomb supply site at Oisemont. At the same time, sixty-six Halifaxes and 39 Lancasters predominantly from 62 Base were detailed to be part of an overall force of 322 aircraft drawn from 3, 6 and 8 Groups to target three previously attacked railway targets at Aulnoye, Montdidier and St-Martin l'Hortier. The last-mentioned, situated some twenty miles south-east of Dieppe, was handed to 6 Group, for which the eighteen 408 (Goose) Squadron Lancasters each received a bomb load of eighteen 500-pounders before departing Linton-on-Ouse between 17.27 and 17.41 with five crews captained by pilots of flight lieutenant rank leading the way. F/O Paulder and crew lost their starboard-outer engine during the climb-out and proceeded to the jettison area, leaving the others to form up and head south to pick up the fighter escort that would shepherd the bomber stream to the target and back. On arrival crews found up to four-tenths cloud with tops at between 3,000 and 7,000 feet and were able to identify the aiming point visually, guided by green Path Finder TIs, which in daylight, proved to be less easily picked out. A Master Bomber was on hand to direct the bombing as the 408 (Goose) Squadron crews delivered their attacks from 15,700 to 17,500 feet between 19.43 and 19.50, the last time that of F/L Franklin and crew, who released their load during a third pass across the aiming point. There were no fires to confirm the accuracy of the bombing, but two columns of black smoke were rising as the crews turned for home.

Meanwhile, only some twenty-five miles to the north-east, the raid on the Oisemont supply site was not proceeding according to plan in the face of nine to ten-tenths cloud, which forced the Master Bomber to call a halt to proceedings after only fourteen aircraft had bombed.

5 Group entered the oil campaign for the first time on this night, sending two forces to Wesseling, south of Cologne, and the Scholven-Buer plant in Gelsenkirchen, each intending to employ the highly successful low-level marking method. The Wesseling force was hacked to pieces by night-fighters outbound, losing thirty-seven Lancasters, while ten-tenths low cloud prevented the Mosquitos from marking and the main force had to rely on H2S. Similar conditions over the Ruhr led to Oboe skymarking, and neither operation was deemed initially to be successful, but postwar reports suggest some temporary loss of production at both sites.

While the whole of 6 Group remained on the ground on the 22nd, the transportation and V-Weapon campaigns continued side-by-side with attacks planned for marshalling yards in north-eastern France in the evening, but first, constructional works in the same region at Mimoyecques, Siracourt and Wizernes during the afternoon. The Mimoyecques site, located some four miles from the French coast at Wissant, was being constructed to house a V-3 super-gun, referred to by Hitler as the "London Cannon". Originally planned as one of two sites near Cap Gris Nez, each containing twenty-five barrels angled at fifty degrees and aimed at London, test failures and delays meant that a single three-barrel shaft stretching a hundred metres into the limestone hill, 103 miles from its target, was all that existed at the time. Each fifteen-metre-long smooth-bore barrel, which was designed on the multiple-charge principle to progressively boost the acceleration of the one-ton projectile as it travelled towards the muzzle, was to be capable of pounding London at the rate of hundreds per day without let-up. It was protected by a concrete slab thirty meters wide and five-and-a-half meters thick, which was correctly believed by the designers to be impregnable to conventional bombs.

Flying bomb sites and railway yards were posted as the targets for more than six hundred aircraft on the 23rd, 6 Group called upon to provide sixty-five Halifaxes and thirty-nine Lancasters predominantly from 62 Base to attack constructional works at Biennais situated some twenty miles south of Dieppe. Seventeen 408 (Goose) Squadron Lancasters had eighteen 500-pounders winched into their bomb bays and took to the air at Linton-on-Ouse between 22.51 and 23.12 with W/C McLernon the senior pilot on duty. All arrived in the target area to find eight to ten-tenths thin cloud with tops at between 3,000 and 7,000 feet, into which the cascading red TIs disappeared to leave a glow as a reference for the bomb-aimers. The 408 (Goose) Squadron element checked their positions by Gee as they ran in at a uniform 12,000 to 12,200 feet between 00.44 and 00.50 to release their bombs but were unable to assess the outcome. Some bomb bursts, fires and two large explosions were reported, and the Master Bomber expressed confidence that the 383 tons of high explosives had been effectively deployed.

A force of 739 aircraft was assembled on the 24th to send against seven flying-bomb sites that night, the target for sixty-five 6 Group Halifaxes from 62 Base and thirty-eight Lancasters from 62 and 64 Bases a constructional works at Bamieres, located twenty miles inland from Berck-sur-Mer. The sixteen 408 (Goose) Squadron Lancasters departed Linton-on-Ouse between 23.37 and 00.04 with S/L Hales the senior pilot on duty and eighteen 500-pounders in each bomb bay. P/O Bayley and crew lost their port-outer engine as they were approaching the Thames estuary and proceeded to the jettison area while the others pressed on to cross out over the Essex coast. It was a clear night with bright moonlight to aid night-fighters, but it was searchlights and flak that proved to be most troublesome to 6 Group, which would come through unscathed. The 408 (Goose) Squadron bomb-aimers focused on the red and green TIs from 13,400 to 13,800 feet between 01.46 and 01.56 and witnessed one vivid white explosion, before returning home to report what appeared to be a concentrated attack.

On the 25th, 6 Group was called upon to provide forces for flying-bomb sites at Renescure, twenty miles south of Dunkerque, Beauvoir situated at the base of the Cherbourg peninsula and Gorenflos to the east of Abbeville. In the event, adverse weather conditions forced the cancellation of the first two-mentioned, while the last-mentioned went ahead with a main force consisting of 101 Halifaxes from 63 and 64 Bases. The attack was carried out under clear skies with good visibility and appeared to be successful.

Six flying-bomb sites were posted as the destinations for 721 aircraft on the night of the 27/28th with 6 Group again assigned to Renescure and Beauvoir, only for its participation to be cancelled. A third operation involving 6 Group escaped the chop and sixty-five Halifaxes and sixteen 408 (Goose) Squadron Lancasters representing 62 Base and twenty-five Lancasters from 64 Base took off in the late evening to target a site in the Foret d'Eawy located some fifteen miles south of Dieppe. The Geese departed Linton-on-Ouse between 22.07 and 22.32 with S/L Hales the senior pilot on duty and eighteen 500-pounders in each bomb bay. The skies were largely clear with three-tenths drifting cloud and the Path Finders took advantage of the favourable conditions to deliver red TIs, which fell in a triangular pattern and attracted the bulk of the 387 tons of high explosives. The 408 (Goose) Squadron crews attacked from 13,000 to 13,600 feet between 00.27 and 00.33 and three explosions were observed, a particularly large one at 00.33.

During the course of the month the squadron took part in sixteen operations and dispatched a record 223 sorties for the loss of five Lancasters and four crews.

July 1944

The new month began as June had ended, with three flying-bomb sites providing employment for 307 Halifaxes from 4 and 6 Groups on the 1st, 6 Group putting up 101 Halifaxes from 62 and 64 Bases for an assault on the previously attacked constructional works at Biennais. All targets were cloud-covered and marked by Oboe and no assessment of results was possible. On the following day 374 Lancasters of 1, 3 and 8 Groups continued the campaign at three sites in similar weather conditions, while 6 Group remained on the ground, its intended raid on the marshalling yards at Villeneuve-St-Georges having been cancelled. That afternoon, the experienced second-tour pilot, F/O Clothier RCAF, was mentoring the recently arrived F/O Frankling RCAF on a three-engine overshoot exercise when two engines cut suddenly and DS621 had to be crash-landed at 16.00 close to the aerodrome. There were no casualties and it is possible that they were the lone occupants of the Lancaster. On the 3rd, a 6 Group attack on Biennais was postponed until the 4th, while another against Villeneuve-St-George was cancelled but would be reinstated for the 4th. A force of ninety-nine Halifaxes from 62 and 64 Bases was assembled as the main force for Biennais on the 4th, while 4 Group was active at a similar target, both operations marked by Path Finder Mosquitos under the watchful eye of a Master Bomber and Deputy.

That night, 6 Group detailed sixty-four Halifaxes and thirty-eight Lancasters from all bases to finally target the marshalling yards at Villeneuve-St-George, for which 408 (Goose) Squadron loaded sixteen of its Lancasters with eight 1,000 and eight 500-pounders and sent them on their way from Linton-on-Ouse between 22.25 and 22.39 with F/Ls Bryson and Latimer the senior pilots on duty. The nine to ten-tenths cloud that accompanied the bombers as they headed south and across the Channel had dissipated to some extent by the time that the target drew near, and it was at this stage that LL621 was attacked by a single-engine enemy fighter while flying at 12,200 feet at 00.29. The rear gunner, Sgt Stevens, was fatally wounded, while his colleague in the mid-upper turret sustained splinter wounds to his legs, prompting P/O Burnell to abandon the sortie immediately and order the bombs to be jettisoned as he set course for home. On the way they ran into a Ju88, which was ultimately shaken off through evasive action and a landing was carried out at Dunsfold at 01.55. Sgt Stevens had been on the seventeenth sortie of his first tour.

Meanwhile, the rest of the squadron, who were in the first of two waves, had arrived at the target to encounter a layer of thin cloud with tops at around 9,000 feet, through which the yards could be identified visually. Red TIs marked out the aiming point for the 408 (Goose) Squadron crews, who carried out their attacks from 6,500 to 12,300 feet between 01.13 and 01.19 in accordance with the instructions of the Master Bomber, and the impression was that the bombing was scattered. The Master Bomber was 35 (Madras Presidency) Squadron's S/L Alec Cranswick DSO, DFC, who was among the most experienced bomber pilots in the Command and had served at home and in the Middle East since 1940 and spent a brief spell with 419 (Moose) squadron at Middleton-St-George in early 1943, before being accepted to join the Path Finder Force. On this night he was reputedly on his 106th sortie and, sadly, it was to be his last as his Lancaster and that of his deputy, S/L Lambert DFC, were shot down later in the proceedings when the 408 (Goose) Squadron crews were on their way home. Both pilots were killed, and only four of the sixteen occupants of the two Lancasters survived in enemy hands, while one managed to evade a similar fate. The second wave produced a better performance, but it proved to be an expensive operation that cost nine 6 Group aircraft.

On the 5th, 6 Group launched a hundred Halifaxes from 62 and 64 Bases against the flying-bomb site at Biennais and all the indications suggested a successful outcome achieved without loss. A further fifty-nine Halifaxes were made ready on 63 Base stations to join forces with thirty-one Lancasters from 408 and 419 (Moose) squadrons to attack the flying-bomb storage site at Siracourt in the early morning of the 6th. The Geese departed Linton-on-Ouse between 05.26 and 05.53 with F/Ls Bryson, Easton and Frankling the senior pilots on duty and each bomb bay filled with two 1,000 and sixteen 500-pounders. All reached the target to find favourable conditions in which the aiming point was identified visually and confirmed by red TIs, which were bombed in accordance with instructions from the Master Bomber from 12,000 to 12,200 feet between 07.58 and 08.00. Smoke and dust soon obscured the target and the TIs, after which the bombing was conducted visually, and the impression was that the 349 tons of high explosives had been deployed effectively. This was one of five sites dedicated to V-Weapons that received attention during the day from forces with a combined total of 551 aircraft from all groups, with 617 Squadron assigned to the previously attacked V-3 super-gun at Mimoyecques. They scored direct hits with Tallboys, and provisional reconnaissance revealed four deep craters in the immediate target area, one causing a large corner of the concrete slab to collapse. The extent of the damage underground would not be apparent to the planners at Bomber Command and its full extent would be appreciated only after the liberation of the region in late August, when it was discovered that the shafts and tunnels had collapsed, and the site had been abandoned. Although Cheshire did not know it, this was to be his final operation, not only with 617 Squadron, but also of the war in Europe.

Operations for 6 Group were not over for the day, and preparations were put in hand on 62 Base stations to make ready a force of forty-eight Halifaxes and twelve 408 (Goose) Squadron Lancasters for an attack on the constructional works at Coquereaux, situated some twenty-five miles to the east-south-east of Dieppe. It would be the first time that 6 Group squadrons had participated in two operations in one day. The Geese departed Linton-on-Ouse between 18.57 and 19.14 with F/Ls Bryson and Franklin the senior pilots on duty and a bomb load in each Lancaster of eighteen 500-pounders. There were no early returns and arrival at the target was greeted by favourable conditions in which the target was identified visually, and the aiming point marked out by yellow and red TIs. The Master Bomber assessed that the yellow TIs should be ignored, and the bombing was concentrated around the red TIs, the 408 (Goose) Squadron crews delivering their loads from a uniform 12,000 feet between 21.27 and 21.30 to contribute to the 217 tons of high explosives laying waste to the site.

During the course of the 7th, 467 aircraft from 1, 4, 6 and 8 Groups were made ready to carry out the first major operation in support of the Canadian 1st and British 2nd Armies, which were trying to break out of Caen. 6 Group contributed sixty-one Halifaxes and twenty-seven Lancasters, fifteen of the latter belonging to 408 (Goose) Squadron, each of which was loaded with eleven 1,000 and four 500-pounders before departing Linton-on-Ouse between 19.41 and 20.02 with F/Ls Bryson and Franklin the senior pilots on duty. The squadron's excellent record of serviceability continued, enabling all to reach the target area, where clear conditions and good visibility aided the Master Bomber, W/C "Pat" Daniels of 35 (Madras Presidency) Squadron to establish two clearly defined aiming points. The 408 (Goose) Squadron crews bombed on red TIs from 7,500 to 8,500 feet between 22.20 and 22.27 to contribute to the 441 tons of bombs delivered by 6 Group in an overall total of 2,276 tons. At debriefings across the Command crews reported a concentrated attack, during which dust and smoke obliterated all sight of the ground but the bombing appeared to remain focused. A message from the 2nd Army awaited the returning crews, congratulating them on the accuracy of their work and thanking them for their efforts. The problem was that the original targets, German-fortified villages, had been swapped for an area of open ground north of Caen, a decision that ultimately proved to be counter-productive as the damage in Caen's northern suburbs blocked access roads instead of inflicting damage on German forces.

408 (Goose) Squadron spent the ensuing days off the order of battle and engaged in air and ground training and was not involved when 6 Group sent forty-two Halifaxes and eight Lancasters from 62 and 64 Bases to attack a flying-bomb launching site at Mont Candon, located some eight miles south-west of Dieppe. This was one of six similar targets to receive attention from a total of 347 aircraft during the course of the afternoon, but cloud at a number of sites led to scattered bombing. At 21.58 on the 10th, P/O Shaw RCAF and a five-man crew took off in LL675 for a night exercise and at around 03.00 the burning Lancaster crashed at high speed and at a flattish angle near the village of Eaton, seven miles north-north-east of Melton Mowbray in Leicestershire, leaving a 350-yard-long swathe of wreckage and no survivors.

On the 12th, 415 (Swordfish) Squadron was transferred to 6 Group from Coastal Command and received nineteen Mk III Halifaxes, mostly from 432 (Leaside) Squadron, with others from 420 (Snowy Owl) and 425 (Allouette) Squadrons, each of which had converted to the Mk VII variant. 408 (Goose) Squadron returned to the fray on this day as part of a 6 Group force of sixty-five Halifaxes and twenty-seven Lancasters predominantly from 62 Base, which were to join forces with 4 and 8 Groups to create a force of 222 aircraft. Their target was a flying-bomb storage site at Thiverny, located in the Hauts-de-France region close to the chalk caves at Creil and St-Leu-d'Esserent, some thirty miles north of Paris, which had been attacked recently at great expense by 5 Group. The fourteen 408 (Goose) Squadron Lancasters each received a load of eleven 1,000 and four 500-pounders before departing Linton-on-Ouse between 18.06 and 18.29 with S/L Hales the senior pilot on duty. All reached the target area to encounter nine to ten-tenths cloud with tops at 7,000 to 9,000 feet and established their positions by Gee as they ran in on the aiming point, some hearing the master Bomber's broadcasts and others not. They carried out their attacks from 14,000 to 15,200 feet between 20.21 and 20.24 and returned home with little of value to report at debriefing.

That night, 230 aircraft from 4, 6 and 8 Groups targeted four flying-bomb launching sites, 6 Group sending forty-two Halifaxes and eight Lancasters to Acquet, located to the north-east of Abbeville, and forty-nine Halifaxes to Brémont-les-Hauts, twenty miles south-east of Dieppe. Conditions were largely favourable and Master Bombers on hand to direct the bombing and the latter operation was particularly destructive. 63 Base was called into action on the evening of the 14th to provide a force of fifty Halifaxes to attack a flying-bomb launching site at Anderbelck (untraced). The operation took place in favourable conditions and good visibility and the target was bombed accurately in accordance with instructions from the Master Bomber.

The targets for 6 Group forces on the evening of the 15th were a flying bomb supply site at Nucourt to the north-west of Paris and a launching site at Bois-des-Jardins located south of Amiens. 62 Base provided sixty-four Halifaxes for the former, while twenty-seven Lancasters from 408 and 419 (Moose) Squadrons attended to the latter in company with elements from other groups. The fourteen 408 (Goose) Squadron participants departed Linton-on-Ouse between 22.55 and 23.10 with S/L Latimer the senior pilot on duty and eleven 1,000 and four 500-pounders in each bomb bay. All arrived in the target area, where seven to ten-tenths cloud lay in a wedge between 11,000 and 12,500 feet, effectively concealing the aiming point from view. A Master Bomber was on hand to direct the bombing towards the glow of green TIs and most of the 408 (Goose) Squadron crews aimed at this, while a few relied on Gee, and all loads went down from 12,800 to 13,700 feet between 01.00 and 01.05. Intermittent explosions were reported but a genuine assessment was not possible, and the consensus was that if the TIs had been accurate, so had been the bombing.

6 Group called 200 crews to briefings at midnight on the 17/18th to learn of their part in a tactical support operation to be carried out at dawn by a force of 942 aircraft as part of the ground forces' Operation Goodwood, which was Montgomery's plan for a decisive breakout into wider France as a prelude to the march towards the German frontier. The aiming-points were five enemy-held villages of Colombelles, Mondeville, Sannerville, Cagny and Manneville, all situated to the east of Caen and standing in the path of the advancing British 2nd Army. The target for the 6 Group element was recorded only as Caen's suburbs, for which a force of 155 Halifaxes and forty-two Lancasters departed their stations in the early hours of the 18th, the fourteen representing 408 (Goose) Squadron getting away from Linton-on-Ouse between 03.15 and 03.44, with F/Ls Bryson and Franklin the senior pilots on duty and each crew sitting on eleven 1,000 and four 500-pounders. They began the Channel crossing at Selsey Bill and by the time that they made landfall on the Normandy coast, the ten-tenths cloud had broken up to reveal the red and yellow TIs bang on the aiming points, each of which was carefully controlled by a Master Bomber because of the close proximity of Allied troops. The 6 Group crews adopted a southerly course to cross its aiming point at 7,000 to 7,500 feet, those from 408 (Goose) Squadron releasing their bombs between 05.45 and 05.56, the later arrivals complying with the instructions of the Master Bomber to overshoot the yellow TIs by three hundred yards. Within a matter of minutes, the entire site had become enveloped in smoke and dust, and returning crews were confident of a successful outcome. At debriefings, crews described a good concentration of bombing and praised the performance of the Path Finders in general and the Master Bomber in particular. Of 6,800 tons of Bombs delivered by RAF and USAAF aircraft on these targets, more than 5,000 tons were delivered by the RAF.

Many of the crews involved in the morning activity were back in the briefing room during the late afternoon to learn of their respective targets for that night. The Command would be committing almost a thousand aircraft again, principally against synthetic oil and railway objectives, but also on a variety of support and minor operations. The Wesseling synthetic oil refinery, or to give it its full title, the Union Rheinische Braunkohlen-Kraftstoff Aktien Gesellschaft, situated on the eastern bank of the Rhine south of Cologne, was to be the target for a force of 194 aircraft made up of a 6 Group main force of 112 Halifaxes and forty-two Lancasters with six ABC Lancasters from 101 Squadron, and twenty-nine Lancasters and six Mosquitos of 8 Group to provide the marking. At the same time, 153 Lancasters of 1 Group would be joined by four Lancasters and thirteen Mosquitos of 8 Group to target the Hydrierwerke-Scholven plant in the Buer district of Gelsenkirchen. The fourteen 408 (Goose) Squadron Lancasters each received a bomb load of a cookie and sixteen 500-pounders before departing Linton-on-Ouse between 22.17 and 22.39 with S/L Hales the senior pilot on duty. An apparently new tactic was adopted, perhaps to evade night-fighters, that involved the force flying out at various levels, some aircraft as low as 2,500 feet, before climbing on approach to the target. P/O Kasper and crew had just crossed into Germany east of Liege when they were coned by searchlights and jettisoned their load as they carried out evasive action. The others reached the target to find clear conditions, good visibility and a little haze and identified the target in the light of illuminating flares and the aiming point by the presence of plentiful cascading red and green TIs. The 408 (Goose) Squadron crews delivered their attacks in the face of an intense flak barrage from 12,000 to 14,200 feet between 01.10 and 01.16 in accordance with instructions from the Master Bomber, whose broadcasts were jammed on occasions but mostly were received. A series of explosions was observed, the larger ones emitting red/orange flame and large volumes of black, oily smoke, and when a storage tank erupted, the smoke was soon passing through 11,000 feet. Approximately a thousand high explosive bombs fell within the boundaries of the plant and destroyed 20% of the installations, causing a much greater loss of production. The adjacent town was also hit and 151 houses destroyed, many of them the residences of the oil plant workers.

The 20th was devoted to daylight attacks on six flying-bomb-related targets and a V-Weapons site involving a total of 369 aircraft, of which 198 were provided by 6 Group for deployment at four locations. 62 and 63 Bases made ready two forces, one consisting of fifty Halifaxes and one of forty-nine assigned respectively to sites in the Haut-de-France region at Ferme du Grand Chemin to the north-west of Paris and Ferme du Forestel, located some twenty-five miles north-east of Abbeville, while 63 and 64 Bases combined to send forty-five Halifaxes and four Lancasters on a return to the Anderbelck site. This left other elements of 62 and 64 Bases to join forces with thirty-seven Lancasters and thirteen Halifaxes for an attack on L'Hey (untraced), for which 408 (Goose) Squadron loaded thirteen Lancasters with eighteen 500-pounders. The crews had been dragged from their beds at 06.00 and during breakfast that take-off had been pushed back by an hour to 09.00. A further postponement had the crews kicking their heels until eventually boarding their aircraft at around 13.00 and departing Linton-on-Ouse between 13.31 and 13.50 with F/L Bryson, and two F/L Franklins or one Franklin and one Frankling the senior pilots on duty. *(The squadron ORB for most of 1944 is a challenge to decipher and one of the difficulties surrounds the name Franklin. Serving with the squadron at this time were F/L E M C Franklin, F/L S R Franklin and F/O G R Franklin, the two last mentioned sometimes spelled Frankling, which seems to have confused the squadron scribe and it is possible that the confusion has found its way into this narrative.)* All arrived in the target area to find clear weather and fair to good visibility with a little haze, and most were able to identify the aiming point visually and by the concentration of red and yellow TIs, which the 408 (Goose) Squadron crews bombed in accordance with the master Bomber's instructions from 14,000 to 15,000 feet between 15.29 and 15.35. Some found the Master Bomber's broadcasts to be either inaudible or indistinct, but the bombing appeared to be concentrated on the markers and the operation was deemed a success.

On the following day, the first solo flight in a Mk VII Halifax was undertaken by a B Flight crew and the rest of the flight would be fully converted within a week. Part of the training was in the use of H2S, the ground-mapping radar that had become standard equipment in all heavy bombers. The 408 (Goose) Squadron Mk II Lancasters could not have H2S installed as they had retained the ventral gun position aft of the bomb bay, in precisely the location required for the H2S scanner housing. This had put the 408 (Goose) Squadron crews at a disadvantage, as they had to rely on Gee to establish their positions in cloudy conditions, while the rest of the bomber force enjoyed the benefits of the more precise H2S.

The squadron's third consecutive loss to a non-operational incident occurred on the 23rd, when DS705 crashed at 14.45 on approach to the 61 Base station at Dalton, to which the Lancaster was being delivered as a group pool training aircraft. The crew of P/O Snider walked away, two members having sustained minor injuries, but the Lancaster was damaged beyond repair.

There were no operations for most of the Command on the 22nd, but the 23rd would be busy and generate 1,188 sorties, the bulk of which involved night-time activity. After a two-month break from city busting, Harris had sanctioned a major raid on the naval and ship-building port of Kiel, for which a force of 629 aircraft was made ready. 6 Group detailed forty-two Lancasters for the main event and one hundred Halifaxes to target a fuel storage facility at Donges, located on the northern bank of the River Loire to the east of St-Nazaire. The fourteen 408 (Goose) Squadron Lancasters each received a bomb load of eighteen 500-pounders before departing Linton-on-Ouse between 22.51 and 23.05 with S/L Hales the senior pilot on duty and were climbing out when the starboard wing leading edge opened six minutes after take-off and necessitated an emergency return to earth. F/O Brown RCAF put the Lancaster down at 23.00 on the runway at Marston Moor with the full bomb load still on board but was unable because of the weight to bring the Lancaster to a halt and it skidded off the end of the runway. The crew scrambled clear before a fire erupted to cause irreparable damage to DS692.

After climbing out, the others headed for the coast at Flamborough Head to rendezvous with the rest of the bomber stream over the North Sea and form up behind an elaborate "Mandrel" jamming screen laid on by 100 Group. A course was set for Denmark's western coast as the starting point for the crossing of Jutland, and the bomber stream's entire approach was masked by the electronic wizardry to arrive with complete surprise in Kiel airspace, rendering the enemy night-fighter controller confused and unable to bring his resources to bear. Kiel was covered by a nine to ten-tenths veil of thin cloud with tops at 5,000 feet, and a skymarking plan was put into action, which enabled the main force crews to confirm their positions by H2S, or Gee in the case of the Mk II Lancasters. The 408 (Goose) Squadron crews delivered their attacks from 19,000 to 20,500 feet between 01.20 and 01.26, aiming at the red and green "Wanganui" markers disappearing into the cloud tops, and once the glow from these had faded, the evidence of fires became the aiming point. It was not possible to determine the outcome, but the glow of fires remained visible for a hundred miles into the return journey, and the effectiveness of the raid was confirmed by local reports that conceded that this had been the town's most destructive raid of the war. All parts of the town had been hit, cutting off water supplies for three days and gas for three weeks, but the port area, where the Germania Werft and Deutsche Werke U-Boot construction yards were located, sustained the greatest damage and many delayed-action bombs continued to cause problems for some time. The benefits of RCM were evident in the modest loss of just four aircraft.

The first of three heavy raids on Stuttgart over a five-night period was posted on the 24th and a force of 614 aircraft assembled, forty of the Lancasters provided by 6 Group, ten of them belonging to 408 (Goose) Squadron. They each received a load of a cookie and three 500-pounders before departing Linton-on-Ouse between 21.32 and 21.40 with the experienced F/L Chekaluck the senior pilot on duty. When F/O Clothier and crew left the ground at 21.32 in LL722 N-Nan it was the Lancaster's forty-sixth sortie and the squadron's 3,000th. They began the Channel crossing at Selsey Bill, from which point the cloud began to disperse and the Normandy coast was crossed near Le Havre under clear skies. It was shortly after reaching the Seine estuary that F/L Chekaluck and crew lost their port-inner engine and turned back, leaving the others to press on across France to enter Germany near Strasbourg. There the cloud built up again to ten-tenths, with tops in the target area at between 4,000 and 10,000 feet, which demanded the deployment of green skymarkers with yellow stars ("Wanganui") and red and green TIs to mark out the aiming point. The 408 (Goose) Squadron crews bombed in accordance with instructions from the Master Bomber from 18,000 to 19,000 feet between 01.46 and 02.02 and were unable to assess the outcome, but the large glow of fires was reflected in the clouds and the impression gained of a successful operation at a cost of twenty-one aircraft.

While the above operation was in progress, two 6 Group elements of fifty Halifaxes each provided the main forces for operations against flying-bomb sites at Ferfay and l'Hey, located in the Hauts-de-France region in the north-east. In the event, the Master Bomber called a halt to proceedings at Ferfay after just fifteen aircraft had bombed and sent the rest home with their bombs.

On the following night, 412 Lancasters from 1, 3, 5 and 8 Groups and 138 Halifaxes of 6 Group were made ready for a return to Stuttgart, while 114 Halifaxes of 4 Group attended to the Krupp Treibstoffwerke synthetic oil plant at Wanne-Eickel, situated between Gelsenkirchen and Herne in the Ruhr. 408 (Goose) Squadron's A Flight loaded each of its seven Lancasters with a cookie and four 500-pounders and sent them on their way from Linton-on-Ouse between 21.12 and 21.20 with S/L Hales the senior pilot on duty. After climbing out they set course for Selsey Bill, where they met seven to ten-tenths cloud and followed the same route as for the previous Stuttgart raid to arrive in the target area under a cloud base at 15,000 to 17,000 feet. They carried out their attacks from 14,500 to 19,000 feet between 01.53 and 02.01, aiming at scattered red and concentrated green TIs, which covered the target area, and the glow from the resulting fires remained visible on the horizon for 150 miles into the homeward journey. Twelve aircraft failed to make it home, four of them 6 Group Halifaxes.

The final raid on Stuttgart was posted on the 28th and was to be an all-Lancaster affair involving a heavy force of 494 aircraft from 1, 3, 5 and 8 Groups. 6 Group stations had been up early to prepare for an operation against a fling-bomb store in the Foret-de-Nieppe, but postponements eventually led to the group's involvement being scrubbed and it would be left to 4 Group to carry out the attack. Later in the day orders were received for 6 Group to contribute 188 Halifaxes and forty-seven Lancasters to an overall force of 307 aircraft to target Hamburg in company with elements of 1 and 8 Groups. This operation would signal the accession to the front line of 415 (Swordfish) Squadron, which would mark its debut with fifteen Halifaxes. 408 (Goose) Squadron made ready thirteen Lancasters and six B Flight Halifax Mk VIIs for the type's maiden operation, loading the former with a cookie and four 500-pounders each and the latter with sixteen 500-pounders. They departed Linton-on-Ouse between 22.18 and 22.40 with W/C McLernon the senior pilot on duty among the Lancaster element and S/L Latimer leading the Halifaxes and flew out over nine-tenths low cloud to find the target under eight to nine-tenths thin cloud with a base at 12,000 feet. The Path Finders employed green skymarkers with yellow stars and red and green TIs, and while the former appeared to be somewhat scattered, the latter were well-grouped. The 408 (Goose) Squadron crews bombed from 17,000 to 20,400 feet between 01.10 and 01.18 and those that made it home reported inaccurate ground defences, no night-fighters and a large, orange explosion at 01.18. In fact, night-fighters had been active on the route home, and it was the Halifax brigade that attracted the bulk of their attention, eighteen of them included in the overall loss figure of twenty-three aircraft, all but one from 6 Group. The other loss was also of a Canadian Lancaster belonging to 405 (Vancouver) Squadron of the Path Finders.

It was the 408 (Goose) Squadron Lancasters that bore the brunt of the squadron's casualties, losing three of their number along with a single Halifax. It was one of the paradoxes of the period, that a squadron could operate for extended periods without a single loss, and then suddenly, suffer a hammer-blow to redress the balance. DS634 crashed at 01.30 some ten miles south-south-west of Cuxhaven killing two members of the predominantly RCAF crew of P/O Boehmer RCAF and delivering him and five others into enemy hands. Most of this highly experienced crew were on their twenty-ninth sortie. LL687 crashed at 02.00 three miles south-south-west of Bremervörde to the west of Hamburg, killing P/O Ryan RCAF and the other six members of the RCAF on board, and only the RAF flight engineer survived to be taken into captivity. All had completed between twenty and twenty-five sorties. LL725 was lost without trace with the eight-man crew of P/O McCaffrey DFC RCAF, who were similarly experienced and the single missing Halifax, NP716, came down at 01.45 west of the target near Heide, taking with it to their deaths S/L Latimer RCAF and the other six occupants. They had between nineteen and twenty-one sorties behind them.

The month ended for 6 Group with involvement in daylight attacks on enemy troop movements in the Caen area on the 30th in which 692 aircraft took part, ninety-nine of them Canadian Halifaxes.

During the course of the month the squadron took part in thirteen operations and dispatched 174 Lancaster and six Halifax sorties for the loss of seven Lancasters and a single Halifax, four complete crews and a rear gunner.

August 1944

August would bring an end to the flying bomb offensive, and also see a return to major night operations against industrial Germany. Flying bomb sites were to dominate the first half of the month, however, and sites would be targeted in daylight on each of the first six days. It began with the commitment of 777 aircraft to operations against thirteen flying bomb-related sites during the afternoon and evening of the 1st, although there were serious doubts about the weather conditions, which were poor over England. 6 Group was assigned to three targets at Ferme du Forestel, l'Hey and Acquet and handed them respectively to 62, 63 and 64 Bases. 408 (Goose) Squadron made ready eleven Lancasters and two Halifaxes, which departed Linton-on-Ouse between 15.01 and 15.22 with W/C McLernon the senior pilot on duty, the Lancasters loaded with eighteen 500-pounders and the Halifaxes sixteen. The doubts about the weather were well-founded and all three 6 Group forces were ordered by the master Bombers to abandon the operations in the face of ten-tenths low cloud. The 408 (Goose) Squadron crews were over the target at 14,000 feet when the order came through at 17.12 and all took their bombs home.

The 6 Group operation posted on the 2nd was cancelled, and 394 aircraft from other groups attended successfully to one launching and three supply sites in favourable conditions. On the following day, 1,114 aircraft were committed to attacks on flying bomb sites at Bois-de-Cassan, Forêt-de-Nieppe and Trossy-St-Maximin. The 6 Group ORB is hugely confusing for this day and identifies the target for 205 of its Halifaxes as a labour camp at Bois-d'Amont, a location close to the Swiss frontier and clearly not part of the flying-bomb offensive. It then records that fifty-one Lancasters and five Halifaxes were to attack the supply dump at Bois-de-Cassan, located in the L'Isle-Adam, a few miles to the south-west of St-Leu-d'Esserent and north of Paris, which it would share with 179 Halifaxes of 4 Group. It must be assumed that all 261 aircraft from 6 Group were, in fact, assigned to this target, the nine Goose Lancasters each receiving a bomb load of eleven 1,000 and four 500-pounders and the five Halifaxes sixteen 500-pounders. They departed Linton-on-Ouse between 11.40 and 11.55 with S/L Hales the senior pilot on duty in a Lancaster and W/C Ledoux guesting as the pilot of Halifax NP718 in order to gain operational experience before assuming command of 425 (Allouette) Squadron later in the month.

There had been no early returns by the time that they closed on the target area, where two to five-tenths cloud was encountered at 10,000 to 12,000 feet, through which the Master Bomber identified the aiming-point at 13.56. He assessed that the red and yellow TIs had slightly overshot and called upon the main force crews to bomb with a corresponding undershoot, until smoke completely enveloped the site and it became necessary to aim for the centre of that. The 408 (Goose) Squadron crews arrived early in the action and delivered their attacks in accordance with the instructions of the Master Bomber from 14,300 to 16,000 feet between 14.00 and 14.04. By time that the 4 Group crews turned up, the TIs had mostly burned out, and while a number found reds and yellows to aim at, the majority bombed visually aiming for the smoke, eventually with a two-hundred-yard overshoot. The attack appeared to be well concentrated and three large explosions suggested a successful outcome, which was largely confirmed by bombing photographs.

Despite the success of the above operation, the Bois de Cassan site was to be attacked again on the 4th by a 6 Group main force of 169 Halifaxes and forty-two Lancasters, while 8 Group attended to Trossy-St-Maximin. A further operation by 288 Lancasters of 1, 3 and 8 Groups was to be directed at oil production and storage facilities located in the Gironde estuary on the approaches to Bordeaux in south-western France. The station armourers loaded ten 1,000 and four 500-pounders into each of ten Lancasters and sixteen 500-pounders into the five Halifaxes, before sending them on their way from Linton-on-Ouse between 10.28 and 11.16 with W/C McLernon the senior pilot on duty in a Halifax and W/C Ledoux piloting another. They all arrived in the target area to find up to five-tenths broken cloud with tops at 8,000 feet and good visibility, in which they were able to identify the site visually and the aiming point by yellow TIs. The Master Bomber called for a slight overshoot, and the 408 (Goose) Squadron crews complied to deliver their bombs from 13,000 to 15,500 feet between 13.00 and 13.06. Two very large explosions were observed, and the impression gained was of a concentrated and successful attack.

The 5th dawned bright and clear, and brilliant sunshine glinted off the Perspex of the 469 Halifaxes, 257 Lancasters and sixteen Mosquitos out on their dispersal pans on airfields from County Durham to Cambridgeshire. Preparations were in hand early to assemble the fleets of 4, 5, 6 and 8 Groups, which were to be divided between the flying-bomb storage sites in the Forèt-de-Nieppe and at St-Leu-d'Esserent. The latter occupied chalk caves north of Paris, formerly used to grow mushrooms, and had been attacked twice at considerable cost by 5 Group, including 617 Squadron with Tallboys, in early July. 6 Group assembled a record force of 248 aircraft, consisting of 196 Halifaxes and fifty-two Lancasters, 408 (Goose) Squadron providing six and thirteen respectively, the Halifaxes with a bomb load of nine 1,000 and four 500-pounders and the Lancasters two extra 1,000-pounders. They departed Linton-on-Ouse between 10.35 and 11.05 with W/C Ledoux continuing his education as the senior pilot on duty. F/L Frankling was unable to retract his Lancaster's undercarriage but continue south until port-inner engine failure on approach to the Sussex coast decided the issue and he proceeded directly to the jettison area. The others arrived in the target area to find four to eight-tenths cloud with tops in places as high as 12,000 feet and good visibility below, and complied with instructions from the Master Bomber to overshoot the red and yellows TIs until they became obscured by smoke and the smoke itself became the aiming point.

The 408 (Goose) Squadron crews carried out their attacks from 15,000 to 17,500 feet between 13.14 and 13.22 and along with the rest of the force, found it difficult to assess the outcome, but the 6 Group ORB expressed confidence that the almost 1,200 tons of high explosives had had the desired effect at a cost of a single Halifax.

More than a thousand aircraft were assembled during the course of the 7th to send against five enemy strong points in support of Operation Totalize, the Allied breakout from Caen. Two of the aiming points were west of the Caen to Falaise road and three to the east, each to be attacked by roughly two hundred aircraft under the control of Master Bombers. 6 Group detailed 196 Halifaxes to attack the Totalize 2 aiming point and forty Lancasters for Totalize 5, of which 408 (Goose) Squadron contributed five Halifaxes and ten Lancasters, the former loaded with nine 1,000 and four 500-pounders and the latter with an additional two 1,000-pounders. The Halifaxes departed Linton-on-Ouse first between 20.52 and 21.10 led by W/C Ledoux, and they were followed into the air between 21.45 and 22.05 by the Lancaster element with W/C McLernon the senior pilot on duty. As P/O Barber and crew approached the target over patchy cloud with tops at 4,000 feet, they observed the first red TIs cascade ahead at 22.53 only to burn out before they started the bombing run. Fortunately, they were replaced by other reds, which the Barber crew bombed from 9,000 feet at 23.05 and were among only ninety-five to attack before the Master Bomber called a halt to proceedings after accurate and concentrated bombing obliterated the markers. He sent the rest of the force home with their bombs, and it was the weight of these that prevented F/O Jones RCAF from slowing down NP713 before the end of the runway at East Moor. The Halifax shot straight off the end of the runway and tore off its undercarriage before coming to rest in a six-foot-deep ditch, writing it off, happily without injury to the occupants.

The Lancaster element, meanwhile, enjoyed favourable conditions with around five-tenths cloud topping out at 5,000 feet, and complied with the Master Bomber's instructions to bomb red TIs, which had been guided by red star shells fired from the ground. The 408 (Goose) Squadron crews from 8,000 to 10,000 feet between 23.47 and 23.48 and observed one very large red explosion and two smaller ones. P/O Minhinnick and crew experienced an electrical failure over the target that prevented the release of their bombs, and they jettisoned them off Le Havre on the way home.

Preparation were put in hand on all 6 Group bases on the 8th to prepare 191 aircraft for an attack that evening on an oil storage dump in the Foret-de-Chantilly in the Hauts-de-France region to the north of Paris, in the same general area as the recent targets at St Leu and Creil. 408 (Goose) Squadron loaded eleven Lancasters and five Halifaxes with eighteen and sixteen 500-pounders respectively and dispatched them from Linton-on-Ouse between 18.44 and 19.00 with F/Ls Chekaluck and Frankling the senior pilots on duty. P/O Harwood and crew were heading inland from the French coast at Fecamp when the bomb sight became unserviceable and ended their interest in proceedings. The others pressed on to find favourable conditions in the target area, which enabled crews to establish their positions with ease and identify the aiming point aided by accurately placed red TIs, which began cascading at 21.08. The 408 (Goose) Squadron Lancasters bombed from 15,000 to 16,500 feet and the Halifaxes from a uniform 17,000 feet between 21.10 and 21.11 in accordance with the clear instructions of the Master Bomber and many large fires were observed to merge into one and send thick, black smoke to a height of 12,000 feet by the time the last bomber turned for home. The rear gunners reported the smoke to be visible for fifty miles into the return journey and there was confidence at debriefings that the 706 tons of high explosives had done their job.

The 9th was a busy day for all 6 Group bases as the flying bomb campaign continued at the hands of 311 aircraft from 1, 3, 6 and 8 Groups. 63 Base made ready four forces of Halifaxes, twenty-three each for Le Neuville and Prouville, twenty for Chemins-des-Bretoux and twenty-one for the Foret-du-Croc, all to the north of Paris, while 64 Base put up seventeen Lancasters and four Halifaxes for Coulon-Villers. The destination for ninety-five Halifaxes and nine Lancasters from 62 Base was Foret-de-Nieppe/Hazebrouck situated in north-eastern France close to the Belgian frontier. 408 (Goose) Squadron was responsible for all of the Lancasters and six of the Halifaxes, each of which was loaded respectively with eleven and nine 1,000 and four 500-pounders, before departing Linton-on-Ouse between 22.33 and 22.48 with S/L Hales in a Lancaster the senior pilot on duty. The target area was clear with a little ground haze and red TIs were observed to go down in the distance at 00.07, to be joined by greens and yellows by the time the aiming point drew near. Most heard the instructions of the Master Bomber to bomb the centre of the reds and yellows and the 408 (Goose) Squadron crews complied from 10,000 to 13,000 feet between 00.15 and 00.19. Though scattered at first, the attack became more concentrated as it developed and a number of explosions were witnessed, one large that set off a fire, which continued to burn as the sound of bombers receded to the north.

The targets for elements of 5, 6 and 8 Groups on the 10th were oil storage facilities, in the Gironde estuary for 5 Group and at La Pallice further north on the Biscay coast for 6 and 8 Groups. 62 Base provided forty-one Halifaxes and nine 408 (Goose) Squadron Lancasters for aiming point B and forty-one Halifaxes to join forces with nineteen Halifaxes and twenty-eight Lancasters from 64 Base for aiming point C. The 408 (Goose) Squadron Lancasters each received a bomb load of eighteen 500-pounders and the five Halifaxes fifteen, before departing Linton-on-Ouse between 19.18 and 19.52 with S/L Hales the senior pilot on duty. There were no early returns, and all reached the target to find largely clear skies with a little low cloud and ground haze, through which the TIs were clearly visible and seemed to form a triangle. The Master Bomber's initial instructions were to bomb the centre of the green TIs, with which the 408 (Goose) Squadron crews complied from 9,500 to 11,000 feet between 22.59 and 23.04. The TIs were frequently obscured by smoke or cloud, rendering it difficult to assess what was happening, and an explosion, a fire and copious amounts of brown smoke provided the best evidence that the target had been hit. The force delivered 172 tons of high explosives and the operation was concluded without loss.

On the 11th, the King and Queen and Princess Elizabeth arrived at York railway station at 10.00 and were conveyed to RAF station Linton-on-Ouse at the start of an official visit to all four Base main stations. They were greeted by the Air-Officer-Commanding the RCAF Overseas and the 6 Group A-O-C, who accompanied the royal party for an inspection of aircraft and personnel, before investitures saw a DFC each presented to W/C McLernon and S/L Hales.

The 12th was to be a busy day across the Command and activity on 62 Base stations and at 63 Base's Skipton-on-Swale began early as a force of ninety-five Halifaxes and nine 408 (Goose) Squadron Lancasters was made ready for an attack on a fuel dump in the Foret-de-Montrichard, located some fifteen miles to the east of Tours on the northern bank of the Loire. The 408 (Goose) Squadron Lancasters each received a bomb load of eighteen 500-pounders and the five Halifaxes sixteen, before departing Linton-on-Ouse between 11.08 and 11.41 with W/C McLernon the senior pilot on duty in a Halifax. They flew out over Selsey Bill and shortly afterwards, F/O Johnson and crew were forced to turn back with a dead port-inner engine, leaving the others to cross the French coast over the Normandy beaches and map-read their way inland under clear skies and in good visibility. The target was identified visually and by red and yellow TIs, the former to be ignored in accordance with the Master Bomber's instructions as they had fallen too far south of the aiming point. The 408 (Goose) Squadron participants aimed at the yellows from 15,000 to 17,000 feet between 14.00 and 14.02, contributing to the total of 343 tons of bombs that were delivered in a concentrated manner to leave fires burning and a pall of black smoke. The entire force returned home safely but not all crews to hang up their flying boots for the rest of the day as preparations were already in hand for further operations.

The main operation that night was an experiment to gauge the ability of main force crews to locate and attack an urban target on the strength of their own H2S equipment in the absence of a Path Finder element. This resulted from the huge volume of operations generated by the four concurrent campaigns, each of which called upon the finite resources of 8 Group, compelling it, in the short term at least, to spread itself more and more thinly. The conclusion of the flying-bomb campaign at the end of the month together with the end of tactical support for the ground forces would remove the pressure and the planned independence of 3 Group through the G-H bombing system from the autumn would solve the problem altogether. In the meantime, however, it was uncertain what demands might be made of the Command, and it would be useful to see what main force crews could do when left to their own devices. The target was to be Braunschweig, for which a force of 379 aircraft was assembled, forty-eight of the Halifaxes and twenty-one Lancasters provided by 6 Group from each of its bases. It was a night of heavy Bomber Command activity at numerous locations involving more than eleven hundred sorties, of which 297 were generated by 3, 4, 5 and 8 Groups in a second large operation over Germany against the Opel tank works at Rüsselsheim, two hundred miles to the south.

408 (Goose) Squadron was not involved at Braunschweig, where some of the bombing did, indeed, hit the city, but there was no concentration and many outlying towns also reported bombs falling. Twenty-seven aircraft failed to return from this operation and a further twenty from a disappointing tilt at the Opel factory, demonstrating that the Nachtjagd still had sufficient resources to effectively divide its strength and achieve success.

While the above operation was in progress, a "rush job" called upon the services of 144 crews to attack German troop concentrations and a road junction to the north of Falaise and south of Caen, which 6 Group supported with a dozen Lancasters and thirty-six Halifaxes from all bases, five Lancasters and four Halifaxes provided by 408 (Goose) Squadron and loaded respectively with eleven 1,000 and four 500-pounders and sixteen 500-pounders. They departed Linton-on-Ouse between 23.50 and 00.17 with F/Ls Chekaluck, Easton, Frankling and Reeves the senior pilots on duty and lost the services of F/O Barber and crew to a hydraulics issue that prevented the undercarriage from retracting. The others arrived at the target to find a blanket of ten-tenths stratus cloud with tops at 2,000 feet, through which red and green TIs were clearly visible, and in accordance with the Master Bomber's instructions they bombed the centre of a cluster of greens from 7,000 to 8,400 feet between 02.16 and 02.22. A large explosion was observed at 02.22 and a column of smoke had broken through the cloud tops by the end of the raid. Post-raid reconnaissance confirmed that the area around the junction had been heavily cratered and the roads leading from it were mostly blocked.

The main activity during the afternoon of the 14th involved 805 aircraft targeting seven enemy troop positions on behalf of Operation Tractable, the aim of which was to provide tactical support for Canadian divisions in the same Falaise area. 6 Group was called upon to target two aiming points, 62 Base providing eighty-five Halifaxes and seven Lancasters and 63 Base thirteen 433 (Porcupine) Squadron Halifaxes to support the attack on aiming point 23, while 63 and 64 Bases put up eighty-five Halifaxes and thirty-seven Lancasters for aiming point 28. The station's armourers loaded seven Lancasters with eleven 1,000 and four 500-pounders and five Halifaxes with two fewer 1,000-pounders, while the crews were attending briefing to learn that their target was at Bons-Tassilly, which was probably the same road junction that had been attacked during the night. They departed Linton-on-Ouse between 12.32 and 12.45 with W/C McLernon the senior pilot on duty and all reached the target to find clear skies and a Master Bomber on hand to direct proceedings. In accordance with his instructions, the bombs were dropped onto yellow TIs from 8,000 to 9,000 feet between 14.55 and 14.56 and appeared to be concentrated around the aiming point, which was becoming obscured by smoke as the force withdrew. Despite the most stringent efforts to avoid friendly fire incidents, about halfway through the sequence of attacks, some bombs did fall into a quarry occupied by Canadian troops, killing thirteen men, injuring fifty-three others and destroying a large number of vehicles.

Now that the Command's responsibilities to SHAEF were coming to an end, Harris could prepare for his new night offensive against Germany and called for operations against enemy night-fighter airfields in Holland and Belgium. In response, a list of eight such targets was drawn up for attention, those at Eindhoven, Soesterberg, Volkel, Melsbroek, St-Trond, Tirlemont-Gossancourt and Le Culot to be targeted in daylight during the course of the morning and early afternoon of the 15th, and Venlo that night, involving, in all, 1004 aircraft. 6 Group was handed Brussels/Melsbroek and Soesterberg near Utrecht in Holland, the former assigned to 101 aircraft predominantly from 62 Base and the latter to 104 aircraft from 63 and 64 Bases. 408 (Goose) Squadron made ready six Halifaxes and seven Lancasters for what would be the squadron's final outing with the latter type, which were to go on to an even more testing time in the hands of trainee crews, mostly at 1668 Conversion Unit. Some crews were reluctant to relinquish the Lancaster, but a few were close to the end of their tour anyway, and it was better for the efficiency of Linton-on-Ouse that its resident squadrons operate the same type. The Lancasters each received a bomb load of eleven 1,000 and four 500-pounders and the Halifaxes two fewer 1,000-pounders and took off between 09.51 and 10.13 with F/Ls Easton and Reeves the senior pilots on duty. Clear skies and excellent visibility greeted the bomber force, when it eventually turned up a few minutes late after encountering an unexpected head wind. The bomb-aimers mostly picked out the target visually on approach and aimed at the concentrated TIs burning on the ground in accordance with the instructions of the Master Bomber. The 408 (Goose) Squadron crews delivered their attacks from 16,000 to 20,000 feet between 12.00 and 12.06 and observed detonations on all runways and the central dispersal area, before the site disappeared beneath a cloud of dust and smoke.

The return to Germany began on the 16th, when a force of 461 Lancasters was assembled to send against the port-city of Stettin, while a mixed force of 339 Lancasters and Halifaxes with Mosquito support was assigned to Kiel. 6 Group contributed twenty-seven Lancasters from 64 Base to the former and 144 Halifaxes from all bases to the latter, nine of them belonging to 408 (Goose) Squadron. They departed Linton-on-Ouse between 21.37 and 21.48 with W/C McLernon the senior pilot on duty and a bomb load consisting of a 2,000-pounder supplemented by 4lb and 30lb incendiaries in each bomb bay. After climbing out, they headed for the Yorkshire coast at Flamborough Head to begin the North Sea crossing to Jutland's western seaboard, making landfall over Mandø Island with some forty miles of land to traverse to reach the Baltic coast. They arrived to find two layers of patchy cloud amounting to around five-tenths cover and this adversely affected the vertical visibility, and a smoke screen was also operating, but H2S was now available to all 408 (Goose) Squadron crews and they were able to establish their positions by this means. The Master Bomber's instructions were heard clearly, and red and green TIs provided a somewhat dispersed reference upon which the 408 (Goose) Squadron crews delivered their loads from 17,000 to 20,000 feet between 00.11 and 00.16. A number of fires were large enough to produce a glow that remained visible on the horizon for a hundred miles into the return flight, while photos confirmed the scattered nature of the bombing, some of which hit the town and dock yard areas, while a proportion fell between one and six miles short. Three Halifaxes and two Lancasters failed to return, two of the former belonging to 6 Group, which had contributed 390 tons of high explosives and incendiaries.

Meanwhile, the raid on Stettin destroyed fifteen hundred houses and twenty-nine industrial premises, while sinking or damaging 20,000 tons of shipping and killing 1,150 people.

It was still somewhat risky to fly over the Ruhr by daylight, and so an attack by a 4 Group main force on the Ruhr-Chemie synthetic oil refinery at Sterkrade, a northern suburb of Oberhausen, was planned for the night of the 18/19th, while a simultaneous raid by 288 aircraft would be directed at Bremen 140 miles to the north. Other operations against marshalling yards and oil storage facilities and numerous support and diversionary activities involved more than a thousand sorties in all. 6 Group offered sixty-five Halifaxes and thirty-five Lancasters from 62 and 64 Bases for Bremen and 102 Halifaxes from 62 and 63 Bases to hit the marshalling yards at Connantre in the Grand Est region to the east of Paris. 408 (Goose) Squadron loaded nine Halifaxes with sixteen 500-pounders each and sent them on their way from Linton-on-Ouse between 20.10 and 20.35 bound for Connantre with F/L Reeves the senior pilot on duty. They arrived in the target area under clear skies and in good visibility enhanced by illuminating flares and observed the red and green TIs to be clearly visible as they complied with the Master Bomber's instructions to bomb to the right of the greens. The 408 (Goose) Squadron crews delivered their attacks from 15,500 to 16,500 feet between 23.50 and 23.52 and the initially scattered bombing soon became concentrated around the aiming point, while a number of large explosions confirmed the effectiveness of the raid. 6 Group was responsible for 351 tons of high explosives and the operation was concluded without loss.

Meanwhile, a reconnaissance Mosquito over Bremen at 01.05 reported an area of intense and unbroken fire covering 4 x 1½ miles with black smoke rising through 23,000 feet. It was confirmed later that the 1,100 tons of bombs had devastated central and north-western districts, including the docks, destroying 8,635 "dwelling houses", mostly in the form of apartment blocks and too many industrial units to count, while sinking eighteen ships in the harbour.

The following week was devoted to small-scale and minor operations, allowing the heavy brigade to draw breath after a period of intense operational activity. There were no further operations for 6 Group until the 25th, when preparations were put in hand to make ready more than nine hundred aircraft to launch against three major targets, while four hundred others would be engaged in a variety of smaller endeavours. The largest operation was to be the all-Lancaster affair involving 461 aircraft from 1, 3, 6 and 8 Groups in a return to the Opel tank works at Rüsselsheim, while 334 others attended to eight coastal batteries between Brest and the islands to the south of Lorient, leaving 5 Group to focus on Darmstadt, a university city renowned as a centre of scientific research and development, and one of a few almost virgin targets considered to be worthy of attention. 6 Group assigned thirty-four Lancasters from 64 Base to the Opel works, thirty-seven Halifaxes from 62 and 63 Bases to a light coastal battery at Pointe Robert near Brest, thirty-eight from 62 Base to a heavy battery at Cornouailles, thirty-eight from 63 Base for a medium battery at Pointe-St-Matthieu, thirty-six from 63 Base for a defended position at Kerandiou (untraced), and thirty-seven from 62 Base to attack a light battery at Kervinou. 408 (Goose) Squadron loaded fifteen of its Halifaxes with nine 1,000 and four 500-pounders each while the crews underwent briefing to learn of their specific aiming point in the Brest area. They departed Linton-on-Ouse between 22.04 and 22.28 with W/C McLernon the senior pilot on duty and flew out over the Dorset coast to begin the Channel crossing to a landfall on the Brest peninsula between Lannion and Paimpol. They arrived to find clear skies and good visibility and were instructed by the Master Bomber to orbit while red, green and yellow TIs were delivered onto the aiming points. Bombing was carried out from 9,500 to 13,000 feet between 01.20 and 01.27 and fires were observed as the force withdrew to the north, most of the 408 (Goose) Squadron crews responding to a diversion signal to land at Westcott.

Still unaware that the V-3 supergun site at Mimoyecques had been destroyed by 617 Squadron Tallboys, a further attack was planned for the evening of the 27, for which 6 Group was to provide the main force of seventy-six Halifaxes and twenty-four Lancasters from 63 and 64 Bases for aiming point A and a hundred Halifaxes predominantly from 62 Base for aiming point B. 408 (Goose) Squadron made ready sixteen Halifaxes, loading each with a 2,000-pounder and thirteen 500-pounders, and sent them on their way from Linton-on-Ouse between 18.10 and 18.44 with W/C McLernon and S/L Tambling the senior pilots on duty, the latter having recently been posted in from 61 Base. Despite encountering clear skies, haze and dust and smoke from the first wave element prevented a visual identification of the aiming point and the bombing by the 408 (Goose) Squadron crews was predominantly aimed at Yellow and green TIs from 16,500 to 18,000 feet between 20.14 and 20.16 in accordance with the Master Bomber's instructions. The group dropped 374 tons of high explosives in what was a wasted effort, but at least no casualties resulted from the raid.

With the Pas-de-Calais about to fall into Allied hands, the final operations against flying bomb launching and storage sites were carried out by small forces at twelve locations by daylight on the 28th. 6 Group detailed six forces to conduct small-scale operations, 408 (Goose) Squadron contributing nine Halifaxes to an assault on the constructional works at l'Hey and five for a gun battery on the Ile-de-Cezembre located in the Channel off St-Malo on the Brittany coast. The former operation was launched first with take-off between 17.56 and 18.30 led by F/Ls Easton, Pettit and Reeves and nine 500 and seven 250-pounders in each bomb bay, the 500-pounders with a six-hour delay fuse. The second element took off between 18.47 and 19.22 with F/Ls Chekaluck and Clothier the senior pilots on duty and each crew sitting on nine 1,000 and four 500-pounders.

Clear conditions and good visibility allowed a visual identification of what remained of the constructional works after a number of previous attacks, and bombing took place in accordance with the Master Bomber's instructions on red TIs from 14,000 feet between 19.54 and 19.57. Meanwhile, a considerable distance to the south-west, similarly favourable conditions prevailed over the Brittany coastal region, allowing the crews there also to identify the target visually and bomb to the right of yellow TIs from 12,800 to 13,000 feet between 21.06 and 21.17 in accordance with instructions from the Master Bomber. F/L Chekaluck and crew were the last to bomb after being delayed by an unserviceable bomb site, but contributed to the 110 tons of high explosives, much of which was concentrated on the south-western corner of the island and caused fires.

A total of 591 Lancasters were primed for action in the Baltic region on the 29th, 189 belonging to 5 Group to attack the port of Königsberg for the second time in three nights, while 402 Lancasters of 1, 3, 6 and 8 Groups attended to the Baltic port-city of Stettin 260 miles closer to home. 6 Group contributed thirty-six Lancasters from 419 (Moose) and 428 (Ghost) Squadrons and they contributed between them 140 tons of high explosives and incendiaries in another highly destructive raid on this city.

The eradication or capture of V-1 sites may have ended, but a new campaign against V-2 rocket storage and launching sites was about to begin, and the first salvoes were fired on the 31st with raids on nine suspected locations in the Hauts-de-France region of north-eastern France by forces totalling six hundred aircraft.

The month's operations ended for 6 Group with a return to the Ile-de-Cezembre gun battery by a force of 165 Halifaxes made up of ninety from 62 Base and forty-five and thirty respectively from 63 and 64 Bases. 408 (Goose) Squadron provided fifteen of its Halifaxes, each of which received a bomb load of nine 1,000 and four 500-pounders before departing Linton-on-Ouse between 09.56 and 10.20 with W/C McLernon the senior pilot on duty. The target area was found to be cloud-covered with rain below the cloud base contributing to poor visibility and persuading some crews to orbit before beginning their bombing runs. The bombing was carried out visually from 1,200 to 2,500 feet between 12.59 and 13.07, and those catching a glimpse of the ground reported that the aiming point had been straddled.

6 Group despatched aircraft on an incredible forty-six separate operations during the course of the month, while 408 (Goose) Squadron was involved in eighteen operations that generated 248 sorties without loss.

September 1944

The destructive power of the Command was now almost beyond belief, each of its heavy bomber groups now capable of laying waste to a German town and city at one go, and from this point until the end of the war, this would be demonstrated in awesome and horrific fashion. Much of the Command's effort during the new month would be directed towards the liberation of the three French ports Le Havre, Boulogne and Calais remaining in enemy hands, but operations began for 6 Group with participation on the 3rd in attacks by 348 Lancasters, 315 Halifaxes and a dozen Mosquitos on six Luftwaffe airfields in southern Holland. 6 Group was handed Volkel, one of a number of Luftwaffe fighter aerodromes standing in the path of bombers entering Holland via the Scheldt estuary, for which 105 Halifaxes were made ready. 408 (Goose) Squadron loaded fifteen of its aircraft with nine 1,000 and four 500-pounders and dispatched them from Linton-on-Ouse between 15.20 and 14.45 with W/C McLernon the senior pilot on duty. S/L Hales and completed an outstanding tour as a flight commander and had been posted for instructor duties to 1659 Conversion Unit, leaving the way clear for the promotion of the long-serving F/L Easton as his successor, although he is recorded in the rank of flight lieutenant on this operation. They all reached the target area to encounter patchy cloud with tops at 6,000 to 8,000 feet and good visibility, in which the scattered TIs stood out clearly, but required the Master Bomber to call for an undershoot of 400 yards on the reds and 200 yards on the greens. The 408 (Goose) Squadron participants delivered their bombs from 14,000 to 15,500 feet between 17.27 and 17.36 and all returned safely after being diverted to land at the 3 Group station at Chedburgh.

A force of 348 aircraft was assembled on the 5th to carry out the first operations against enemy strong points around the port of Le Havre, when 313 Lancasters from 1, 3 and 8 Groups were accompanied by thirty Oboe Mosquitos and five Stirlings of 149 Squadron, the last of the type in service with a bomber unit three days ahead of its retirement in favour of Lancasters.

Linton-on-Ouse was not called into action on the 6th when 6 Group committed 103 Halifaxes and thirty-six Lancasters to operate as the main force for an operation against the port of Emden, which had been a regular destination in the early war years but had not been targeted since June 1942 and would not be again after this raid. The town and its environs were left burning fiercely as the bombers withdrew to leave a column of thick, black, oily smoke rising through 10,000 feet and visible for a hundred miles and more into the return flight. Elsewhere on this day, the second assault on enemy positions at Le Havre involved 311 Lancasters, three Stirlings and thirty Mosquitos.

The 8th was devoted to Le Havre, but in difficult conditions, only 109 of 333 aircraft from 1, 3 and 8 Groups were able to bomb before the Master Bombers called a halt.

On the 9th, 62 and 64 Bases combined to make ready two forces, one of fifty-three Halifaxes and the other of fifty-one for the next round of attacks at Le Havre respectively to target aiming points 8 and 9, while 126 Halifaxes of 4 Group were assigned to aiming points 7 and 10. Assigned to aiming point 8, 408 (Goose) Squadron loaded fifteen aircraft with either nine 1,000 and four 500-pounders or sixteen 500-pounders, before sending them on their way from Linton-on-Ouse between 06.08 and 06.48 with W/C McLernon the senior pilot on duty. On arrival in the target area the crews faced seven to ten-tenths cloud with tops at 12,000 to 15,000 feet and conditions sufficiently challenging to persuade the Master Bombers to call a halt to all proceedings and send the entire force home.

The weather over northern France had improved by the 10th, and a massive effort involving 992 aircraft was mounted by the Command to deal with eight enemy positions in the afternoon and evening. The aiming-points were given the names of car manufacturers, Buick 1 and 2, Alvis 1, 2, 3 and 4 and Bentley 1 and 2, and 6 Group was handed Buick I, for which 104 Halifaxes were made ready on 64 Base stations and 62 Base's East Moor. The other 62 Base stations contributed seventy-four Halifaxes for Buick 2 and would be joined by thirty Halifaxes from 63 and 64 Bases.

408 (Goose) Squadron's eighteen Halifaxes each received a bomb load of either nine 1,000 and four 500-pounders or sixteen 500-pounders and departed Linton-on-Ouse between 14.24 and 14.44 with F/Ls Brown, Clothier, Pettit, Reeves and Smart the senior pilots on duty. All made it to the other side of the Channel, where clear skies greeted their arrival, and the Master Bomber and Deputy were already assessing the situation. The aiming point was identified visually through two to five-tenths thin patchy cloud and the bombing carried out on red TIs from 7,000 to 10,000 feet between 16.30 and 16.39. One particular explosion emitted orange flame, and smoke and dust had covered the area by the time that the 6 Group element withdrew, having dropped 446 tons of high explosives.

The 11th brought the final attacks on the environs of the port and involved 218 aircraft drawn from 4, 5, 6 and 8 Groups at two aiming-points, Cadillac 1 and Cadillac 2, 63 Base contributing fifty-five Halifaxes to the latter. In the event, the Master Bomber called "time up" at 07.42 and twenty-nine crews abandoned their sorties, but the damage had been done and the goal achieved, and the German garrison surrendered to British forces later in the day. During the morning and early afternoon 379 aircraft from 3, 4, 6 and 8 Groups were prepared for operations against three Ruhr synthetic oil refineries, the Gelsenkirchener Bergwerke A G coking plant, (Nordstern), the Klöckner Werke A G at Castrop-Rauxel ten miles to the north-east and the Chemischewerke-Essener-Steinkohle A G fifteen miles further to the east at Bergkamen. It was a formidable prospect to send such a large force by daylight to one of the most heavily defended regions of the Reich, but twenty squadrons of Spitfires and three each of Mustangs and Tempests would dissuade even the most determined Luftwaffe fighters from trying to intervene. 6 Group detailed 105 Halifaxes predominantly from 62 Base with a little help from 64 Base, 408 (Goose) Squadron loading fifteen of its own with sixteen 500-pounders each before sending them on their way from Linton-on-Ouse between 15.53 and 16.17 bound for Castrop-Rauxel with S/L Tambling the senior pilot on duty. P/O Smith RCAF and his predominantly RCAF crew were outbound in NP710 when an engine failed and forced them to turn back, dumping the bomb load on the way. They requested and were granted priority landing at base, but the Halifax overshot the approach and crashed near the motor transport section at 18.24 before bursting into flames. The pilot and five members of the crew were killed, along with a MT driver, and the two survivors were severely injured, one of them succumbing on the following day. The others pressed on to reach the target area under largely clear skies and with a Master Bomber on hand to direct the bombing. His instructions were to bomb four hundred yards to starboard of the red TIs, and the 408 (Goose) Squadron crews complied from 16,500 to 20,000 feet between 18.43 and 18.47, contributing to the 354 tons of high explosives that straddled the aiming point and caused a particularly large explosion that emitted a column of thick, black smoke. NP718 picked up flak damage and diverted to the emergency landing strip at Carnaby, where P/O Wallace landed it safely.

According to Bill Chorley in Bomber Command losses for 1944 and a number of online sites, F/O Burnell RCAF was flying as second pilot to P/O Smith, and as his death was recorded on that day, appears to have been linked to the crash of NP710, whether in error or to protect his family. However, the truth is that his name does not appear on the ORB Form 541 as being on board, and he had, in fact, according to the ORB Form 540, died that morning as the result of a self-inflicted head wound.

That night, 5 Group returned to the university city of Darmstadt in southern Germany, the target for a failed operation on the night of the 25/26th of August, while the rest of the Command had been attacking the Opel tank works at Rüsselsheim. This time, the low-level marking method worked to perfection and the city centre and neighbouring districts succumbed to a firestorm in which more than twelve thousand people perished and seventy thousand were rendered homeless out of a total population of 120,000.

The oil offensive continued on the 12th with briefings on 4, 6 and 8 Group stations for raids on the Hydrierwerke refinery at Scholven-Buer to the north of Gelsenkirchen, the Krupp Treibstoffwerke at Wanne-Eickel to the east and the Hoesch-Benzin plant a dozen miles further east in the Wambel district of Dortmund. A total force of 315 Halifaxes, seventy-five Lancasters and twenty-two Mosquitos was made ready for a late morning take-off, 6 Group supporting two of the operations with 107 Halifaxes predominantly from 62 Base for Wanne-Eickel and seventy-four Halifaxes and thirty-two Lancasters from 63 and 64 Bases assigned to Dortmund. The station armourers loaded sixteen 500-pounders into each 408 (Goose) Squadron Halifax and watched them as they lifted off the end of the runway at Linton-on-Ouse between 11.26 and 11.49 bound for Wanne-Eickel with S/L Tambling the senior pilot on duty. The weather in the target area was favourable and the visibility clear enough to facilitate a visual identification of the aiming point, but main force crews were hampered by a lack of target indicators and not all were able to hear the Master Bomber. Even so, eleven of the 408 (Goose) Squadron crews delivered an attack on red TIs or the base of smoke from 16,500 to 19,500 feet between 13.58 and 14.05 in the face of an accurate and intense flak barrage that forced a number of crews to break away and seek out an alternative target. Despite the challenges the raid appeared to be concentrated around the plant and large explosions were observed at 13.59, 14.01 and 14.02 resulting in copious amounts of smoke, which combined with the output of a smoke screen to obscure the site and render an assessment impossible. F/O Snider's NP757 was among a number from the squadron to pick up flak damage and bombed a nearby village, while the crews of F/O Brown and P/O Johnson attacked Gerthe and Bochum respectively as they sought escape from the primary target. P/O Kennedy's starboard-outer engine caught fire as a result of a flak hit over the target, but the automatic extinguisher dealt with it and the crew returned safely to land on the 3 Group station at Methwold.

Meanwhile, 1, 3 and 8 Groups were busy assembling a force of 378 Lancasters and nine Mosquitos for the final major raid of the war on Frankfurt that night, while 195 Lancasters and thirteen Mosquitos of 5 Group focused on Stuttgart with a sprinkling of 101 Squadron ABC Lancasters to provide RCM cover. Both operations were massively destructive, Frankfurt's western districts sustaining particular damage, while a firestorm developed in Stuttgart's central districts, which were effectively erased from the map, and the combined cost to Bomber Command was twenty-one Lancasters, the majority from Frankfurt.

For the fifth day running, 408 (Goose) Squadron was called into action on the 13th to support an operation, this time against the city of Osnabrück, situated in the flat agricultural Münsterland between the Ruhr to the south and Bremen to the north. 62 Base made ready twenty-four Halifaxes for aiming point E, the general built-up area, and seventy-four for aiming point C, the marshalling yards in what was an important hub in the communications system linking the Ruhr with the major ports and manufacturing centres of northern Germany. 408 (Goose) Squadron made ready thirteen Halifaxes, loading five with nine 1,000 and four 500-pounders each for the marshalling yards and eight with a 2,000-pounder and eleven SBCs of Type 14 cluster bombs for the city centre and dispatched them from Linton-on-Ouse between 15.47 and 16.33 with W/C McLernon the senior pilot on duty. All reached the target area to find clear conditions and good visibility, which they exploited in accordance with instructions from the Master Bomber to deliver their bomb loads onto their respective aiming points from 16,500 to 19,500 feet between 18.30 and 18.33. A total of 374 tons of bombs was deposited within the city boundaries and many fires were evident, sending thick, brown smoke rising through 7,000 feet as the force withdrew.

A force of 490 aircraft from 1, 4, 6 and 8 Groups was assembled on the 15th to attack the port of Kiel, the 1 Group contribution provided by 101 Squadron in an RCM role, while 6 Group put up 171 Halifaxes and thirty-Lancasters. 408 (Goose) Squadron made ready seventeen Halifaxes, loading each with a 2,000-pounder and eleven SBCs of 4lb incendiaries before dispatching them from Linton-on-Ouse between 21.59 and 22.42 with F/Ls Pettit, Reeves and Smart the senior pilots on duty. Initially poor weather conditions improved during the North Sea crossing to Rømø Island and over southern Jutland, and clear skies prevailed over the Baltic coast, at which point P/O Patzer and crew were forced to turn back when their oxygen system failed. The others turned south towards the target, and most were able to pick out some ground detail, aided by illuminator flares as they began their bombing run. A smoke screen was activated to protect the important shipyards, but the red and green TIs remained visible throughout the raid and were bombed by the 408 (Goose) Squadron crews from 18,000 to 22,000 feet between 01.18 and 01.29. Fires had gained a hold by the time the force retreated to the west, and the glow remained visible on the horizon from Denmark's western coast 120 miles away.

With Operation Market Garden about to be launched on the 17th, Bomber Command provided support with attacks in the early hours by 1 Group on four aerodromes at Rheine and Hopsten, located in the Münsterland to the west of the Dortmund-Ems and Mittelland Canals close to the Dutch frontier, and Leeuwarden and Steenwijk situated in northern Holland.

Early briefings across the Command that morning prepared 762 crews for operations against enemy troop positions at seven locations around the port of Boulogne. The raids would be staggered over a four-hour period and benefit from a 6 Group contribution of sixty-nine Halifaxes and thirty-six Lancasters from 63 and 64 Bases at aiming point 1C and 105 Halifaxes predominantly from 62 Base at aiming point 4. The sequence of attacks would begin with aiming point 1A and continue with 1B, 1C, 1A again, and then 5, 3, 2 and finally 4. At Linton-on-Ouse the 408 (Goose) Squadron element of sixteen Halifaxes each received a bomb load of nine 1,000 and four 500-pounders before taking off between 10.29 and 10.49 with F/Ls Brown and Reeves the senior pilots on duty. By the time that the Path Finders for aiming point 4 arrived over the French coast, the cloud had built to eight to ten-tenths cumulus in a wedge between 4,000 and 6,000 feet, but good visibility below enabled the Master Bomber to identify the aiming point visually and direct the bombing onto the red and yellow TIs. The 408 (Goose) Squadron participants delivered their attacks from below the cloud base from 3,000 to 4,500 feet between 12.34 and 12.48 before smoke and dust overwhelmed the target area. An analysis of the entire operation confirmed that most of the aiming-points had been dealt with successfully, although some crews had been hampered by drifting smoke. A total of three thousand tons of bombs had proved sufficient to pave the way for Allied ground forces to move in shortly afterwards to accept the surrender of the German garrison, and this left only Calais of the major French ports still under enemy occupation.

The following week passed relatively quietly for 6 Group and while 62 Base remained inactive, elements mostly of 64 Base with a little 63 Base support conducted small-scale operations against coastal batteries in the Scheldt estuary. By the 20th, the time had arrived to turn attention upon Calais as the final French port still under enemy occupation and 646 crews attended briefings across the Command in the absence of 6 Group representatives. The bombing took place in favourable conditions and was accurate and concentrated but would not be followed up by further raids until the 24th, by which time a major operation had been mounted by 549 aircraft of 1, 3, 4 and 8 Groups against the Ruhr city of Neuss on the 23rd. The assault on enemy positions around Calais resumed on the 24th, when five aiming-points were briefed out to 188 crews, the attacks upon which would follow a sequence beginning at aiming point 8, and continuing through 10, 11 and 9 before ending at 12. Adverse cloud conditions in the target area dictated that bombing had to take place either visually or on Oboe skymarkers from as low as 2,000 feet, where lethal light flak accounted for seven Lancasters and a Halifax and a third of the force retained their bombs.

A further attempt was made on the following morning involving 872 aircraft, 213 Halifaxes and forty Lancasters provided by 6 Group, ninety-five Halifaxes from 62 Base assigned to aiming point 4, sixty-five from 63 Base to aiming point B and fifty-three Halifaxes and forty Lancasters predominantly from 64 Base to aiming point 5. 408 (Goose) Squadron contributed a record nineteen Halifaxes, each of which received a bomb load of nine 1,000 and four 500-pounders before departing Linton-on-Ouse between 09.30 and 09.55 with S/L Easton the senior pilot on duty. They headed south in initially favourable weather conditions, which deteriorate dramatically over the Channel and French coast to leave a blanket of low cloud with a base at 2,000 feet. Earlier, at 08.38, the master bomber for aiming point 2A had abandoned the operation and sent the crews home with their bombs, and the master Bomber at aiming point 1B followed suit at 09.02. The 62 Base element arrived at the target to find six-tenths cloud, and while some orbited for a time, others aimed their bombs at red TIs from 5,000 to 6,000 feet between 11.09 and 11.24 in accordance with the instructions of the Master Bomber. Some crews completed up to four passes over the aiming point and two crews abandoned the attempt to bomb when unable to pick out a TI. In the event, only 287 crews bombed, and further operations would be required to wrest the port from enemy hands.

Nine separate attacks were briefed out to 722 crews across the Command during the early morning of the 26th, 531 to target four coastal batteries at Cap Gris-Nez, situated some ten miles along the coast to the west of Calais, and 191 to attack enemy positions closer to the port. 6 Group supported the operation with three forces consisting of fifty-four Halifaxes from 62 Base assigned to aiming point 8, fifty-five Halifaxes predominantly also from 62 Base for aiming point 9 and twenty-four Halifaxes and thirty-one Lancasters from 64 Base for aiming point 10. 408 (Goose) Squadron made ready eighteen Halifaxes, loading each with the standard bomb load of nine 1,000 and four 500-pounders before sending them on their way from Linton-on-Ouse between 08.54 and 09.12 with F/Ls Pettit, Reeves and Smart the senior pilots on duty. They arrived at the French coast to encounter two to four-tenths drifting cloud with a base at 2,500 to 3,000 feet but excellent visibility in which to identify the aiming point, which was marked by red TIs and bombed from 6,000 to 7,500 feet between 11.00 and 11.11 in accordance with the guidance of the Master Bomber.

Returning crews were unanimous in the belief that the bombing had been concentrated and effective and the same applied to the other aiming points.

Calais was left to 341 aircraft of 1, 3, 4 and 8 Groups on the 27th, while 6 Group assembled two forces, one each to attack the Ruhröl AG synthetic oil plant in the Welheim district of Bottrop on the northern edge of the Ruhr and the Ruhr Chemie plant at Sterkrade-Holten located some six miles to the north-west on the northern outskirts of Oberhausen. The former was the target for ninety-six Halifaxes and forty-six Lancasters from 62 and 64 Bases, and the latter for 143 Halifaxes predominantly from 63 Base with 408 (Goose) Squadron adding twenty Halifaxes and 434 Squadron of 64 Base twenty-one. The 408 (Goose) Squadron aircraft received a bomb load each of sixteen 500-pounders and departed Linton-on-Ouse between 07.46 and 08.11 with S/L Easton the senior pilot on duty. F/L Reeves abandoned the sortie during the climb-out after losing his starboard-outer engine, while F/O Minhinnick and crew found themselves behind schedule as they crossed the Scheldt estuary and decided also to turn back. The others reached the target area to find nine to ten-tenths cloud with tops at 8,000 to 10,000 feet and good visibility, and as they lined themselves up for the bombing run, the Master bomber ordered them to attack the briefed alternative target of Duisburg. Two minutes later he issued another instruction to bomb red TIs at the primary target, which resulted in eleven crews continuing their runs on Duisburg, while the crews of F/Os Brown, Kennedy, Shields and P/Os Gilson, Harpwood and Johnson complied with the latter instruction. Bombing at both locations took place from 16,000 to 16,500 feet, at Bottrop between 09.56 and 10.02 and at Duisburg between 09.51 and 10.01. P/O Barber and crew were left a little confused by the Master Bombers instructions and bombed a railway junction from 13,000 feet at 10.04. It was a similar story for the Sterkrade force and although eighty-three aircraft bombed the primary target, fifty-three others attacked alternatives, mostly the approximate position of Duisburg.

The final operations to clear the enemy from the Calais area took place on the 28th, and involved 494 aircraft from 1, 3, 6 and 8 Groups, which were assigned to four positions around the port and six coastal batteries at Cap Gris-Nez. 6 Group contributed thirty-one Halifaxes and a dozen Lancasters to aiming point 7A at Cap Gris-Nez, thirty-six Halifaxes from 63 Base and eight Lancasters from 64 Base for aiming point 7B, thirty-eight Halifaxes and six Lancasters from 63 and 64 Bases for aiming point 7C, twenty-nine Halifaxes and twelve Lancasters from 62 and 64 Bases for aiming point 7D, forty Halifaxes from 62 Base for aiming point 21 and a further forty from 62 Base for aiming point 22. The nineteen 408 (Goose) Squadron Halifaxes were divided fourteen/five between aiming points 7D and 22 and received a bomb load each of nine 1,000 and four 500-pounders before departing Linton-on-Ouse between 16.30 and 17.30 with F/Ls Pettit and Reeves the senior pilots on duty. Cloud conditions during the squadron's seventy minutes' presence in the target area ranged from three to ten-tenths, topping out at up to 6,000 feet with a base at 2,000 to 4,500 feet. They complied with the Master Bombers' instructions to bomb red TIs from 7,500 to 10,000 feet between 18.00 and 19.09 and because of the twilight found it difficult to assess the outcome. Two 408 (Goose) Squadron crews abandoned their sorties over the target, one because of a hang-up and in all sixteen sorties at the 408 (Goose) Squadron aiming points were abortive. The German garrison surrendered to Canadian ground forces soon afterwards, but there was much to do to clear and repair the ports at Le Havre, Boulogne and Calais, and the port of Antwerp also needed to be liberated to speed up the supply of equipment to the front for the push into Germany.

On the 30th, 6 Group sent instructions to 62 Base to prepare 198 Halifaxes for a return to the synthetic oil refinery at Sterkrade-Holten, which had escaped serious damage in the recent attack. 408 (Goose) Squadron made ready eighteen of its own, loading each with sixteen 500-pounders before dispatching them from Linton-on-Ouse between 10.12 and 10.36 with F/Ls Minhinnick and Smart the senior pilots on duty. P/O Harlow and crew dropped out over Lincolnshire on losing their port-inner engine, while the others pressed on to reach the target and encounter eight to ten-tenths cloud with tops at up to 10,000 feet. The aiming point was marked out by red and yellow TIs, but haze proved to be an impediment to target identification and the Master Bomber called for the alternative target, the general built-up area, to be bombed. Twelve of the 408 (Goose) Squadron crews complied from 16,500 to 19,500 feet between 12.19 and 12.23, while five attacked the primary from 17,000 to 19,500 feet between 12.20 and 12.24, leaving the crews with an impression of a concentrated assault that fell within the confines of the town, caused at least three large explosions and set on fire two oil tanks that sent a column of smoke rising through 5,000 feet.

Among those screened during the month having completed their tours were pilots F/L Chekaluck, who was posted to 61 Base, and F/O Paulder, who went to 86 O.T.U. During the course of another busy month the squadron took part in thirteen operations and dispatched two hundred sorties for the loss of a single Halifax and crew in the crash at home and a pilot to suicide.

October 1944

Having now discharged his primary obligation to SHAEF, Harris would turn his attention once more fully towards industrial Germany, with a particular emphasis on oil production. He was about to launch a second Ruhr offensive and had at his disposal a massive force in which each individual group had the potential to lay waste to an entire city in one attack. The independent 5 Group had been delivering hammer blows for months and soon, in mid-month, 3 Group would be handed a measure of autonomy in the form of the G-H bombing system, which they were to employ to great effect for the remainder of the war, principally against oil and communications targets. A theme running throughout October would be a campaign against the island of Walcheren in the Scheldt estuary, where heavy gun emplacements were barring the approaches to the much-needed port of Antwerp some forty miles upstream. Attempts to bomb these positions in September had proved unsuccessful, and it was decided to flood the land, both to inundate the batteries, and to render the terrain difficult to defend when the ground forces moved in. A force of 252 Lancasters were drawn from 1, 5 and 8 Groups and made ready on the 3rd to attack the seawalls at Westkapelle, the most westerly point of the island. A breach was opened by the fifth wave, which was extended to a hundred yards by those following behind and the flood waters had reached the town by the time the last Lancasters turned for home.

It was the 4th before 6 Group was called upon to open its new month's account, and this was for a daylight operation against U-Boot pens at Bergen in Norway, one of a number of locations being employed by the Kriegsmarine, now that it had been bombed out of its bases on the French coast. Eighty-nine Halifaxes and thirty-nine Lancasters from all three Bases took off before first light, accompanied by twelve Path Finder Lancasters, and headed north over Scotland to be met in the target area by twelve "Serrate" Mosquitos from 100 Group, which were to act as the fighter escort. The operation proceeded according to plan and the pens were hit, although not structurally compromised, while three U-Boots and a number of other ships in the harbour were damaged. Tragically, collateral damage to the town killed sixty children and some adults, who were sheltering in a school basement, which took a direct hit.

Dortmund was selected to host the opening round of a new Ruhr campaign, which would prove to be even more devastating than the first between March and July of 1943, and would face a heavy force of 495 Lancasters and Halifaxes representing 3, 6 and 8 Groups with twenty-eight 8 Group Mosquitos to assist with route and target marking. 6 Group detailed a record 293 aircraft made up of 248 Halifaxes and forty-five Lancasters, of which twenty-two of the former belonged to 408 (Goose) Squadron. A simultaneous operation by 5 Group was to be directed for the final time at Bremen, which had already endured thirty-one major raids. At Linton-on-Ouse the 408 (Goose) Squadron Halifaxes each received a bomb load of thirteen 500-pounders, before taking off between 15.50 and 16.34 with S/Ls Easton and Tambling the senior pilots on duty. The 6 Group element was depleted by a modest eight early returns, while the remainder reached the target area to find clear conditions and good visibility and green TIs cascading punctually over the aiming points. A few red TIs were also visible as the squadron participants delivered their attacks from 17,000 to 20,000 feet between 20.30 and 20.35 in accordance with the instructions of the Master Bomber and in the face of searchlights in cones of up to a dozen beams and a heavy flak barrage. Several large explosions and fires sent smoke rising to meet the bombers, and as those from 6 Group headed home to diversion airfields in 3 and 8 Group territory, they were confident in the quality of their work. Local sources confirmed that industry and transportation had taken a beating and residential districts inevitably found themselves also in the firing line.

While a 5 Group force carried out a scattered attack on Wilhelmshaven on the morning of the 5th, 531 other aircraft of 1, 3 and 8 Groups were being prepared for a two-phase operation that night against Saarbrücken in south-west-central Germany, the first attack on this city since September 1942. It was in response to a request from the American Third Army, which was advancing towards the German frontier in that region. The purpose of the first phase, to be delivered by 184 Lancasters of 3 Group and a sprinkling of 101 Squadron ABC Lancasters, was to hit the marshalling yards to cut enemy rail communications, while the second phase, by 239 Lancasters of 1 Group two hours later was to be directed at the city. 8 Group's ninety-six Lancasters and twenty Mosquitos were to be divided equally between the two phases to establish and maintain the aiming-points. Following the highly destructive operation, local reports revealed that the railway lines had been cut to stop all through traffic, and 5,882 houses had been destroyed, largely in the Altstadt and Malstatt districts, but the relatively modest death toll of 344 people suggested that what was now a front-line city had been partially evacuated.

Following the failure of Operation Market Garden, the German frontier towns of Cleves (Kleve) and Emmerich were earmarked for attention by daylight on the 7th. Five miles apart and separated by the Rhine, both suffered massive damage at the hands of large forces from 1, 3, 4 and 8 Groups.

Bochum was posted as the target on the 9th, for which a force of 435 aircraft was assembled from 1, 4, 6 and 8 Groups, of which 179 Halifaxes and thirty Lancasters represented 6 Group. The 1 Group contribution was by ABC Lancasters of 101 Squadron to provide an RCM screen, while 8

Group Lancasters and Mosquitos were to take care of the marking. Fifteen 408 (Goose) Squadron Halifaxes each received a bomb load of sixteen 500-pounders before departing Linton-on-Ouse between 17.06 and 17.24 with S/L Tambling the senior pilot on duty. All reached the target to be greeted by three to nine-tenths drifting cloud, which the Path Finders attempted to counter by providing red TIs and red skymarker flares with yellow stars, either of which provided a reference, if somewhat scattered, for the main force crews to aim at, even though, there was a two-minute period during which no marking at all took place. The 408 (Goose) Squadron participants bombed from 17,500 to 20,000 feet between 20.27 and 20.35 in accordance with instructions from the Master Bomber and observed several large explosions and noted that two areas of fire developing three hundred yards apart were beginning to merge as they turned away. Night-fighters were active at the target and on the way home, despite which, only four Halifaxes and one Lancaster failed to return, the Lancaster and two Halifaxes belonging to 6 Group. Local sources confirmed a scattered attack which destroyed or seriously damaged a modest 140 houses, which represented a disappointing outcome for such a large force at this stage of the war.

Crews were roused early from their beds on 62 and 63 Base stations on the 12th to attend briefings for an operation against the Krupp Treibstoffwerke at Wanne-Eickel in the central Ruhr. A main force of 111 Halifaxes was assembled and the fifteen belonging to 408 (Goose) Squadron were each loaded with seven 1,000 and six 500-pounders before departing Linton-on-Ouse between 07.20 and 07.45 with S/L Tambling the senior pilot on duty. They picked up canals and railways on approach to the target, where they ran into two to four-tenths stratocumulus with tops at 4,000 to 7,000 feet and found that brown smoke from the early bombing was already obscuring the aiming point. The Master bomber issued instructions to bomb the blue smoke trails left by the falling TIs and then the upwind edge of the smoke, the 408 (Goose) Squadron crews complying as best they could from 17,000 to 20,000 feet between 10.17 and 10.22. Explosions and fires were observed but an accurate assessment was beyond most crews, and it was local sources that confirmed that the refinery had escaped damage, while a nearby chemicals factory had been destroyed.

The 14th was the day on which were fired the opening salvoes of Operation Hurricane, a terrifying demonstration to the enemy of the overwhelming superiority of the Allied air forces ranged against it. Bomber Command ordered a maximum effort from all but 5 Group to attack Duisburg, for which 1,013 Lancasters, Halifaxes and Mosquitos answered the call. The American 8th Air Force would also be in business on this day, targeting the Cologne area further south with 1,250 bombers escorted by 749 fighters. 6 Group dragged 218 Halifax and forty Lancaster crews from their beds at 01.00 and briefed them for what lay ahead, while out on the dispersals the aircraft had already been loaded with seven 1,000 and six 500-pounders. There were five aiming points, including the Thyssen steelworks, but those assigned to 6 Group were not recorded. The seventeen 408 (Goose) Squadron Halifaxes departed Linton-on-Ouse between 06.35 and 07.04 with S/L Tambling the senior pilot on duty and lost the services of P/O Jones and crew during the climb out when the failure of their hydraulics system left the undercarriage and flaps down. The others pressed on across the North Sea, where the giant force picked up an RAF fighter escort, before approaching the target slightly to the north of the briefed aiming point, easily identifying the city by the canals, the Rhine and the distinctive Ruhrort docks complex. The seven to ten-tenths covering of cloud with tops at 13,000 feet presented challenges for the Master Bombers, and only four of the 408 (Goose) Squadron crews bombed the briefed aiming point, leaving the rest to aim for the general built-up area. All attacks by the squadron were delivered from 17,000 to 20,000 feet between 08.46 and 08.55 in the face of heavy and medium calibre flak bursting at between 16,000 and 20,000 feet. The 6 Group ORB made reference to "scarecrow" shells, which Bomber Command encouraged the crews to believe were designed by the Germans to simulate a fully-laden bomber blowing up. At a time when the authorities were trusted to tell the truth, most crews seem to have accepted the explanation, when in reality, scarecrows did not exist and were indeed bombers rent asunder by a direct flak hit in the bomb bay. A large orange explosion was observed at 08.53 and reported by returning crews, who described a scattered raid that had been difficult to assess. 6 Group aircraft dropped 1,041.6 tons of high explosives and 137.8 tons of incendiaries in an overall total of 3,574 and 820 tons respectively.

Later in the day, W/C McLernon was posted from the squadron at the end of a successful five month tour as commanding officer and took up a new appointment as station commander at 62 Base's East Moor, home to 415 (Swordfish) and 432 (Leaside) Squadrons. He was succeeded at 408 (Goose) Squadron by S/L Easton on promotion to acting wing commander rank, two steps above his substantive rank of flight lieutenant.

A force of 1,005 aircraft was assembled to continue Duisburg's torment that night in a two-phase operation two hours apart, for which 203 Halifaxes and forty Lancasters were provided by 6 Group, seventeen of the former belonging to 408 (Goose) Squadron. Each received a bomb load of thirteen SBCs of No14 cluster bombs and departed Linton-on-Ouse between 22.23 and 22.52 as part of the first wave and bound for aiming point S with S/L Tambling the senior pilot on duty. Sixteen 6 Group aircraft returned early and among them were two from 408 (Goose) Squadron, P/O Harpwood and crew because of starboard-outer engine failure over Yorkshire and F/O Frankling and crew from within ten miles of the French coast near Cayeux-sur-Mer because of an iced-up carburettor and a runaway propeller that couldn't be feathered. Those reaching the target found three to ten-tenths cloud with tops at 8,000 to 10,000 feet and a city still burning from the morning attack and all but one carried out an attack from 19,000 to 21,000 feet between 01.39 and 01.48 on accurately placed red and green TIs. Five explosions were observed, and as the first wave element turned away, fires had taken hold and would leave a glow on the horizon visible from 180 miles into the homeward flight. The 6 Group contingent contributed 829 tons of high explosives and 124 tons of incendiaries to the eventual 4,040 and 500 tons respectively delivered on this night operation, amounting to a combined total over the two raids of 7,614 and 1,320 tons delivered by 2,018 aircraft at a cost to the Command of eighteen Lancasters and three Halifaxes.

5 Group, meanwhile, took advantage of the activity over the Ruhr to finally deliver a telling blow on the historic city of Braunschweig, wiping out the entire centre and inflicting damage on almost every district.

There was no immediate respite from operations as preparations were put in hand on the 15th to attack Wilhelmshaven that night for what would be the last of fourteen major raids on this naval and ship-building port, where the Kriegsmarine Werft had given birth to the pocket battleships, Admiral Scheer and Graf Spee, the heavy cruiser, Scharnhorst, and the mighty Bismarck class battleship, Tirpitz. Crews would have done their best to catch up on sleep as the work of the day went on around them, and some of those who had landed at dawn were up, briefed and fed in time to join others for an early evening take-off in an overall force of 506 aircraft drawn from all but 5

Group. 6 Group offered 119 Halifaxes and fifteen Lancasters drawn from all bases, 408 (Goose) Squadron providing nine of the former as part of the third wave and loading each with seven 1,000 and six 500-pounders before sending them on their way from Linton-on-Ouse between 17.12 and 17.30 with S/L Pettit the senior pilot on duty. They flew out over Flamborough Head under clear skies until the midpoint of the North-Sea crossing, when, according to some, cloud gradually built-up to ten-tenths thin stuff with a base at around 12,000 feet. Typically, there was no agreement as to the conditions, and some crews reported clear skies with haze or cirrus cloud at between 16,000 and 19,000 feet, through which the red and green TIs could be seen and their accuracy confirmed by H2S, while the 8 Group ORB recorded that it was impossible to make out ground features from above 12,000 feet. What may have been spoof green TIs were reported some five miles to the west and north-west of the target, and these attracted some bomb loads. The 408 (Goose) Squadron crews delivered their payloads on red and green TIs from 14,000 to 19,000 feet between 19.48 and 20.04 and observed little of the outcome. Three 6 Group Halifaxes failed to return and among them was 408 (Goose) Squadron's NP773, which came down somewhere in north-western Germany, delivering F/L Smart RCAF and five members of his predominantly RCAF crew into enemy hands, while the navigator was the sole fatality. The pilot was on his twelfth sortie and most of his crew on their eleventh, but the wireless operator was on his twenty-fifth. The bombing appeared to be scattered, and this was largely confirmed by local sources, which named only the Rathaus (Town Council HQ) as completely destroyed.

On the 17th, P/O Johnston and crew were undertaking a navigation exercise in NP745 when they ran into snowstorms and severe icing conditions over the Lake District, which rendered the Halifax uncontrollable and persuaded them to take to their parachutes. The Halifax crashed into a field six miles west-south-west of Penrith, while the crew landed with varying degrees of success, four finding themselves initially in Carlisle Hospital, before the two most seriously injured were transferred to the RAF Hospital at Northallerton, where the navigator succumbed on the 2nd of December.

Small-scale operations occupied the ensuing days and nights, but one of significance represented a major step forward in Bomber Command's evolution and brought with it for 3 Group a similar degree of independence to that enjoyed by 5 Group. The G-H bombing system had been under development for around two years and mirrored to an extent the American method of releasing bombs on observing the leader's fall away. While the American system was exclusively for daylight operations, the RAF system was equally effective at night, and in 3 Group hands would prove to be particularly effective against precision targets like oil refineries and railways. As one of a few relatively intact German cities, Bonn, situated some twenty miles to the south-east of Cologne, was selected as the target for the first massed live trial on the assumption that fresh damage would be easily identified to assess the performance of G-H. The operation was mounted on the morning of the 18th and was not entirely successful, but time and practice would iron out the wrinkles.

On the 19th, an all-Lancaster heavy force of 565 aircraft from 1, 3, 6 and 8 Groups assembled for a raid on Stuttgart contained just forty-two representing 6 Group, while 5 Group targeted Nuremberg with 270 aircraft. The former failed to produce concentrated bombing, but severe damage was, never-the-less, inflicted on its central and eastern districts and outlying communities. On the 21st 6 Group detailed 205 Halifaxes to join others from 4 Group to act as the main force for a major raid on Hannover, and they were in the process of taking off when the operation was cancelled. 6 Group had launched 101 aircraft, the 408 (Goose) Squadron element of thirteen between 16.00 and 16.31, when the cancellation signal came through and they were allowed to continue on before being recalled in stages to minimise the risks of landing such a large force. They had reached the Kent coast by the time they turned back either side of 18.00, each carrying a 2,000-pounder and eleven 500-pounders, and the majority of the 500-pounders ended up on the seabed.

The Hurricane force had lain dormant since Duisburg, but was roused from its slumber on the 23rd, when Essen was posted as the target that evening for a record 1,055 aircraft carrying 4,538 tons of bombs, more than 90% of which was high explosive. Once again, this massive effort would be achieved without the involvement of 5 Group, which would be enjoying a night off. 6 Group detailed 229 Halifaxes and forty-three Lancasters, of which nineteen of the former belonged to 408 (Goose) Squadron and another was borrowed from 426 (Thunderbird) Squadron to allow twenty of its crews to depart Linton-on-Ouse between 16.09 and 16.50 with S/L Pettit the senior pilot on duty and each bomb bay filled with a 2,000-pounder, six 1,000 and four 500-pounders. They climbed out into scattered cloud before heading south to exit the English coast over Hastings on course for the French coast, from where they were to thread their way between the flak hotspots of Cologne and Mönchengladbach. The cloud thickened over the Channel until the tops were at 23,000 feet, and by the time the target hove into view, the cloud had become ten-tenths up to 14,000 feet. The Path Finders had prepared a ground and skymarking plan, and after the Oboe TIs had been swallowed up by the cloud, red skymarker flares were released at 19.28 to be followed by greens three minutes later. The 408 (Goose) Squadron crews carried out their attacks on both red and green skymarkers from 17,000 to 21,000 feet between 19.29 and 19.42 and found it impossible to observe the fall of the bombs, but an intense glow on the cloud told its own story that there was still plenty of combustible material in the tortured city. Local reports from Essen confirmed the destruction of 607 buildings and a further eight hundred seriously damaged along with a death toll of 667 people.

Harris had not yet done with his old enemy, and ordered another attack, this time by daylight on the 25th, for which 771 aircraft were made ready, while 6 Group prepared a force of 199 Halifaxes to target the Meerbeck synthetic oil refinery at Moers/Homberg, or, to give it its full title, the Gewerkschaft Rheinpreussen A G plant, located on the west bank of the Rhine opposite Duisburg on the western edge of the Ruhr. The name of this target would strike fear into the hearts of 3 Group crews, who had suffered heavy casualties while attacking the plant during the summer, but it held no such terror for 6 Group crews. 408 (Goose) Squadron loaded nineteen of its Halifaxes with five 1,000 and nine 500-pounders each and dispatched them from Linton-on-Ouse between 12.51 and 13.25 with W/C Easton the senior pilot on duty. F/O Case and crew suffered hydraulics failure during the climb-out, leaving the others to continue on as part of the third wave and reach the target area to encounter ten-tenths thick cloud with tops at 7,000 to 9,000 feet, which forced the Path Finders to deploy green skymarkers. These were plentiful, but proved difficult to pick up and the master bomber eventually instructed the main force crews to bomb on DR. The 408 (Goose) Squadron crews complied from 16,000 to 19,000 feet between 15.50 and 16.01 and returned home with no clue as to the outcome, other than four pillars of greyish smoke breaking through the cloud tops as they turned away. F/O Brown arrived back over England with a dead port-outer and starboard-inner engine and when the former shed its propeller, he ordered his crew to bale out while he landed the Halifax at the 5 Group station of Woodhall Spa. The group dropped 843.7 tons of high explosives and completed the operation without loss.

Preparations for the first of a three-raid mini-campaign against Cologne were put in hand on the 28th. The last time that the Command had targeted Cologne in such a way was in June/July 1943, when three raids had been mounted over the course of ten nights, resulting in the destruction of 11,000 buildings, 5,500 fatalities and 350,000 people rendered homeless. The operation was to be conducted in two phases, with one aiming-point in the district of Müllheim, to the north-east of the city centre, and the other in Zollstock to the south-west. A force of 733 aircraft included a 6 Group contribution of 131 Halifaxes and thirty-six Lancasters for aiming point H and sixty-four Halifaxes from 63 Base for aiming point G. 408 (Goose) Squadron supported the operation with eighteen Halifaxes, each loaded with a 2,000-pounder and twelve 500-pounders, before departing Linton-on-Ouse between 12.57 and 13.45 with S/L Pettit the senior pilot on duty. They headed for Orfordness and encountered a weather front over the North Sea on their way to making landfall on the French coast in the Dunkerque region, before pressing on to the target, where varying amounts of cloud between zero and ten-tenths topped out at 8,000 to 12,000 feet dependent upon the time of arrival. The main force was greeted by an accurate flak barrage, an inadequate number of skymarkers and intermittent and sometimes indistinct instructions from the Master Bomber to bomb the general built-up area. Some of the 6 Group element identified the Knapsack power station and chemicals factory to the south-west of the city and attacked them as alternative targets, leaving a column of smoke rising through 9,000 feet as they withdrew. Some 408 (Goose) Squadron crews found relatively clear conditions in which the marshalling yards and River Rhine were identified but complied with orders and carried out their attacks from 18,000 to 21,000 feet between 16.03 and 16.11.

Fires and copious amounts of smoke followed the bombing, and a suspension bridge over the Rhine collapsed after receiving direct hits. No great concentration of marking was achieved, and returning crews reported that there were periods when no skymarkers were visible and only a few red and green TIs were spotted intermittently and were of little use. As a result, the bombing was scattered across the south-western districts of the city, where a large explosion was reported at 16.04 following a direct hit on a factory, and smoke was rising through 15,000 feet from aiming point G as the bombers turned away. Despite reservations concerning the quality of some of the bombing, both aiming-points had been devastated, local reports confirming the destruction of 2,239 blocks of flats and fifteen industrial premises, along with many other buildings of a public nature. Severe damage had also been inflicted upon power stations, transportation and railway and river docks installations.

A force of 905 aircraft was made ready for another massive assault on Cologne on the 30th, for which 6 Group detailed 204 Halifaxes and forty Lancasters, eighteen of the former representing 408 (Goose) Squadron, each loaded with a 2,000-pounder and a dozen SBCs of 4lb incendiaries. They departed Linton-on-Ouse between 17.16 and 17.49 as part of the fifth wave with W/C Easton the senior pilot on duty, and climbed away into ten-tenths cloud, which persisted for most of the outward route. They flew out over Beachy Head, shortly after which, F/L Minhinnick's port rudder disintegrated and ended the crew's interest in proceedings, leaving the others to press on to encounter a build-up of cloud with tops reaching 20,000 feet and a bright, full moon above. As the target drew near, the cloud tops lowered to 10,000 to 15,000 feet, into which the red and white marker flares delivered by nine of the Oboe Mosquitos drifted in concentrated fashion. The main force crews confirmed their accuracy by Gee and H2S before carrying out their attacks, those from 408 (Goose) Squadron delivering their bomb loads from 16,500 to 21,000 feet between 21.13 and 21.29, and although the ground was obscured, the glow in the clouds suggested a successful outcome. This was confirmed by local reports that heavy damage had occurred in south-western suburbs, where housing, communications and utilities were the principal casualties. 6 Group was responsible for 843 tons of high explosives and 135 tons of incendiaries and sustained no casualties.

A force of 493 aircraft from 1, 3, 4 and 8 Groups was made ready on the 31st to complete the series of raids on Cologne, after which local sources reported that the southern districts had received the main weight of bombs. However, the reporting system was breaking down with the result that precise details were not forthcoming, and it is likely that the city had been largely evacuated by this stage. All future operations would be directed at its numerous and extensive marshalling yards.

During the course of the month the squadron took part in eleven operations that generated 170 sorties for the loss of two Halifaxes, one crew and one additional airman.

November 1944

As worthwhile targets became more difficult to find in a country so thoroughly destroyed by bombing, smaller, seemingly irrelevant towns and cities began to find themselves in the bomb sights, particularly if they happened to lie in the path of the retreating enemy forces or on a main railway line. Oil was now the overriding priority, and November's operations began on the 1st with a daylight attack on the Rheinpreussen (Meerbeck) synthetic oil plant at Homberg by 5 Group with 8 Group Mosquitos in attendance. That night, 8 Group provided twenty-six Lancasters and twelve Mosquitos to mark for a 6 Group main force of 202 Halifaxes and forty-eight Lancasters at Oberhausen in the central Ruhr, in what was the maiden operation for ten of 431 (Iroquois) Squadron's Canadian-built Lancaster Mk Xs as the group began a gradual conversion to the type. 408 (Goose) Squadron made ready twenty-one Halifaxes, each of which received a bomb load of a 2,000-pounder, six 1,000-pounders and four of 500lbs before departing Linton-on-Ouse between 17.10 and 17.42 with S/L Pettit the senior pilot on duty. There were no early returns and on arrival in the target area they were greeted by six to ten-tenths cloud and slight to moderate heavy flak bursting in barrage form at 16,000 to 23,000 feet. Red and yellow and later green skymarkers provided a bombing reference and those from 408 (Goose) Squadron delivered their loads from 19,000 to 21,000 feet between 20.29 and 20.37, observing the glow of fires spreading and smoke rising through the cloud tops. Enemy fighters were active over the target and during the first leg of the return route and nine combats were reported, one unnamed 408 (Goose) Squadron crew claiming to have destroyed two of its four assailants. Despite the impression of a successful raid, only thirty-six houses were destroyed in Oberhausen and precisely where the bulk of the 879 tons of high explosives and 116 tons of incendiaries fell is uncertain.

Düsseldorf's turn to face the "Hurricane" force came on the 2nd, when 992 aircraft were made ready for what would prove to be the final major raid of the war on this much-bombed city, and it was one of those rare occasions when 5 Group, or the "Lincolnshire Poachers" as they were disparagingly called in 8 Group circles were invited to operate with the rest of the Command. 6 Group detailed 180 Halifaxes and forty-two Lancasters, seventeen of the former provided by 408 (Goose) Squadron and loaded with a 2,000-pounder and five and four respectively of 1,000 and 500lbs, before departing Linton-on-Ouse between 15.53 and 16.42 with F/Ls Bracken, Parkhurst and Scheelar the senior pilots on duty. They adopted the circuitous route to the southern Ruhr via Beachy Head and Cayeux-sur-Mer and arrived at the target to encounter clear skies, moonlight and only ground haze to slightly mar the vertical visibility. The moonlight nullified the glare of the searchlights ringing the city, but of greater concern was the heavy flak bursting at 17,000 to 20,000 feet as they ran across the city towards the aiming-point. The attack opened early with red flares and TIs dropped by eight Oboe Mosquitos at 19.05, which enabled the crews to identify the river, railway tracks and built-up area visually, and the heavy marker element maintained the aiming-point throughout the raid with mostly well-placed green TIs. The 408 (Goose) Squadron participants carried out their bombing runs from 18,000 to 21,000 feet between 19.20 and 19.28 and from early on it was clear that fires were gaining a hold. Smoke was rising through 10,000 feet as the last crews headed for home with the glow from the burning city remaining visible from Charleroi in Belgium, some 115 miles away. Eleven Halifaxes and four Lancasters failed to return and among them was 408 (Goose) Squadron's NP744, which came down in Allied-held Belgium killing F/O Gilson RCAF and three of his predominantly RCAF crew, the three survivors receiving treatment in a US Army field hospital. Another enemy fighter was claimed as destroyed by an unidentified 408 (Goose) Squadron crew. It was established later that the operation had been an outstanding success that destroyed five thousand houses and many important war-industry factories, 6 Group having contributed 754 and 123 tons respectively of high explosives and incendiaries.

The continuing campaign against Ruhr cities brought Bochum into the spotlight on the 4th, when a force of 749 aircraft was drawn from 1, 4, 6 and 8 Groups, while 5 Group renewed its acquaintance with the Dortmund-Ems Canal, which had been repaired following the successful breaching of its banks near Ladbergen in September. 6 Group detailed 173 Halifaxes and forty-one Lancasters, the sixteen Halifaxes representing 408 (Goose) Squadron receiving a bomb load each of a 2,000-pounder and seven and three each of 1,000 and 500-pounders. They departed Linton-on-Ouse between 17.05 and 17.24 with F/Ls Bracken, Parkhust, Reeves and Scheelar the senior pilots on duty and flew out over Orfordness, crossing the North Sea to make landfall on the Dutch coast in the vicinity of The Hague. Here they invited the attention of the local flak batteries as they passed by, before pressing on for the remaining 130 miles to the target, which they found to be under a veil of very thin cloud of up to three-tenths at 5,000 feet. Red Oboe TIs were seen to cascade at 19.26, to be followed over the ensuing minutes by greens, and the aiming-point remained well marked for the duration of the attack. The 408 (Goose) Squadron crews carried out their attacks from 13,000 to 18,500 feet between 19.35 and 19.42, witnessing a number of large explosions, one throwing flame a thousand feet into the air, while a reconnaissance Mosquito crew reported a circular patch of fire and one particularly intense conflagration visible from one hundred miles away. The success of the operation was confirmed by post-raid reconnaissance and local reports, which confirmed that the city centre and industrial districts had borne the brunt of the attack, with four thousand buildings destroyed or seriously damaged and almost a thousand people killed. However, the flak and fighter defences, the latter including jets, demonstrated that they were not yet spent, and brought down twenty-eight aircraft, twenty-three of them Halifaxes, five belonging to 6 Group. NP750 crash-landed in France without casualties, but it was learned that the rear gunner in the predominantly RCAF crew of F/O Sokoloff had baled out over Germany and had been taken into captivity.

Bochum's neighbour, Gelsenkirchen, was posted as the target for a two-phase daylight operation on the 6th, for which a force of 738 aircraft was assembled. In the past, it had been the synthetic oil plants that had drawn the bombers on, but this time, part of the force was to attack the built-up area as well as the Nordstern refinery in the Horst district. 6 Group detailed 176 Halifaxes and forty Lancasters, fourteen of the former representing 408 (Goose) Squadron and each loaded with a 2,000-pounder and seven and four respectively of 1,000 and 500-pounders, before departing Linton-on-Ouse between 12.10 and 12.23 with S/L Pettit the senior pilot on duty. They adopted a route similar to that for the previous operation and flew into cloud that increased to almost ten-tenths at the Dutch coast. Thereafter, it began to break up to six to eight-tenths at 9,000 feet until a gap appeared right over the target, which enabled the early arrivals to pick out the distinctive L-shaped docks in the Schalke-Nord district to the north-west of the aiming point. Bombing commenced a few minutes early on red and green TIs, the latter assessed by the 35 (Madras Presidency) Squadron Master Bomber, S/L Leicester, as more accurate and he directed the crews towards them at 14.01. However, it wasn't long before thick smoke spread across the area to obscure any sight of the ground, and at 14.06 he instructed the crews to focus on the built-up area generally. The 408 (Goose) Squadron crews complied by bombing either visually or on red TIs from 19,000 to 21,000 feet between 14.14 and 14.16 in the face of accurate heavy flak, which inflicted damage on a number of aircraft and was probably responsible for the failure to return of three Lancasters and two Halifaxes. Many explosions were witnessed, and the presence of a column of black, oily smoke rising through the cloud tops through 10,000 feet suggested that the Nordstern plant had been hit. The consensus among the crews at debriefing was of a concentrated attack, although it was impossible to make an accurate assessment. NP761 was the 408 (Goose) Squadron absentee, having come down in the target area and delivering the entire RCAF crew of F/O Kellond into enemy hands. The pilot was on his nineteenth sortie and most of his crew on their sixteenth. Local reports confirmed that a "catastrophe" had befallen the city, and that more than five hundred people had lost their lives.

Apart from a small-scale mining operation, 6 Group remained off operations, while other elements of the Command, particularly the G-H-equipped 3 Group, focused on oil plants in the Ruhr and communications targets. As the American First and Ninth Armies prepared to advance eastwards between Aachen and the Rhine, the three small towns of Heinsberg, Jülich and Düren located respectively in an arc from north to east of Aachen, were earmarked for destruction. A total force of 1,188 aircraft occupied the attention of armourers and ground crews across the Command, 1 and 5 Groups providing the main force of 452 Lancasters for the last-mentioned with thirty-three Lancasters and thirteen Mosquitos of 8 Group to provide the marking, while 4 and 6 Groups were to contribute 413 Halifaxes and forty-five Lancasters between them as the main force at Jülich, supported by thirty-three Lancasters and seventeen Mosquitos of 8 Group. This left Heinsberg to be the objective for a G-H raid by 182 Lancasters of 3 Group. 6 Group detailed 149 Halifaxes and all forty-five Lancasters, fourteen of the former belonging to 408 (Goose) Squadron, each loaded with a 2,000-pounder and twelve SBCs of 4lb incendiaries, which departed Linton-on-Ouse between 12.49 and 13.09 with no fewer than six pilots of flight lieutenant rank leading the way. They crossed Belgium over cloud and turned sharply to the north-east when twenty miles south of Liege for the approach past Aachen to the unsuspecting target. Four to five-tenths low cloud lay over the town, but this did not inhibit a visual identification or conceal the red TIs around the aiming-point, which the 408 (Goose) Squadron crews bombed from 15,000 to 17,000 feet between 15.41 and 15.43. The bombing was well-concentrated, and the town soon enveloped in smoke, into which the later arrivals delivered their bombs. All three operations achieved their purpose, and while reports came out of Düren and Heinsberg, there was nothing from Jülich. Düren had not been evacuated and suffered 3,127 fatalities, while Heinsberg had been all-but emptied of civilians, but almost half of the 110 who remained lost their lives.

Briefings took place on 4, 6 and 8 Group stations on the morning of the 18th to inform 479 crews of the details for an attack on the heavily-garrisoned city of Münster, situated some twenty-five miles from the north-eastern edge of the Ruhr. 6 Group contributed 156 Halifaxes and forty-four Lancasters, thirteen of the former belonging to 408 (Goose) Squadron, which departed Linton-on-Ouse between 12.22 and 12.37 with W/C Easton the senior pilot on duty. After climbing out they exited the English coast at Flamborough Head to rendezvous with the bomber stream over the North Sea and push on to the target, where three Oboe Mosquitos delivered the initial green skymarkers at 14.58 over a blanket of ten-tenths thick cloud with tops at 8,000 feet. Red skymarkers soon followed from the heavy marker element, which had established their positions on H2S and Gee. The 408 (Goose) Squadron crews carried out their attacks either visually or on green skymarkers from 16,500 to 18,000 feet between 15.00 and 15.13, and on return reported a compact bomber stream and solid concentrations of markers, but, perhaps, a scattered attack, the results of which remained hidden beneath the cloud. F/O Tunis RCAF and crew were absent from debriefing having abandoned NP770 over Belgium, and for a time the navigator, F/O Salisbury, remained unaccounted for, but was eventually found safe and well and returned home a few days after the rest of his crew. Little information came out of the city, but what emerged seemed to confirm bombs falling across the built-up area with no points of concentration.

The night of the 21/22nd would be one of large-scale activity at numerous locations involving 1,345 sorties. 1 Group assembled a main force of 238 Lancasters to attack the railway yards at Aschaffenburg, situated some twenty miles south-east of Frankfurt, and they would be supported by thirty-six Lancasters and nine Mosquitos of 8 Group. Elsewhere, 273 aircraft with a predominantly 6 Group main force were assigned to the Klöckner Werke A G synthetic oil refinery at Castrop-Rauxel in the Ruhr, while 4 Group focused on a similar target at nearby Sterkrade-Holten as part of an overall force of 270 aircraft. 5 Group would be targeting the Dortmund-Ems and Mittelland Canals further north at Ladbergen and Gravenhorst in two forces with a combined total of 260 aircraft, while small-scale and mining operations took place at a variety of other locations. 6 Group detailed 175 Halifaxes and fifty-five Lancasters, of which fifteen of the former were provided by 408 (Goose) Squadron, thirteen Mk VIIs and two of its rarely used Mk IIIs and they each received a bomb load of sixteen 500-pounders. They departed Linton-on-Ouse between 15.18 and 15.41 with S/L Pettit the senior pilot on duty and all reached the target area to find clear conditions and good visibility. The initial red TIs went down early at 18.53 and were well backed-up by reds and greens, the latter undershooting slightly to starboard, but the Master Bomber kept the raid on track and 408 (Goose) Squadron crews added their payloads from 16,500 to 19,000 feet between 18.58 and 19.06. Red, yellow and orange explosions were observed, and a mushroom of black smoke was rising through 8,000 feet as the bombers turned away, the 6 Group element having delivered 841 tons of high explosives. NP810 went down in the target area, and the fact that only the pilot, F/L Steeves RCAF and his mid-upper gunner survived, suggests that the Halifax may have exploded and thrown them clear to fall into enemy hands. The pilot was on his third sortie and most of the crew on their second, but wireless operator, W/O Wilson, was on the first sortie of his second tour.

There would be no further operations for the majority of the heavy squadrons over the ensuing six days, despite a number being announced, but then scrubbed, while 3 and 5 Groups went about their business independently. On the 26th, W/C Easton was posted out to take up an appointment at 6 Group HQ, and he was succeeded, temporarily according to the ORB, by W/C Freddie Sharp, who arrived from 62 Base with no previous operational experience to his credit, having spent the war to date as an instructor. In the event, he would remain in command through to the end of hostilities. Among the seemingly strategically insignificant urban areas to find themselves in the bomb-sights at this stage of the war was the university city of Freiburg, situated in the south-western corner of Germany with the French and Swiss frontiers to west and south. It was believed to be inhabited by German troops preparing to resist the approaching American and French forces some thirty-five miles away and found itself a target for 341 aircraft of 1 and 8 Groups on the 27th, while 290 aircraft from 1, 6 and 8 Groups targeted Neuss on the southern extremity of the Ruhr opposite Düsseldorf.

6 Group provided the main force of 173 Halifaxes and fifty-two Lancasters with a sprinkling of 101 Squadron RCM Lancasters for company, and 408 (Goose) Squadron put up fourteen Halifaxes, each to carry of bomb load of one 2,000-pounder and a dozen SBCs of 4lb incendiaries. They departed Linton-on-Ouse between 16.54 and 17.14 with the recently promoted S/L Reeves the senior pilot on duty and all reached the target area, although behind schedule courtesy of wrongly forecast winds. They encountered eight to ten-tenths cloud with tops at 5,000 feet, through which the main force bomb-aimers were able to pick out the glow of concentrated red TIs. The 408 (Goose) Squadron element delivered their attacks from 17,000 to 19,000 feet between 20.26 and 20.37 and returned confident in the effectiveness of their work. Central and eastern districts were heavily bombed, residential, commercial and industrial areas sharing in the destruction and a series of exceptionally large explosions was witnessed at one-minute intervals between 20.28 and 20.34. Meanwhile, some 230 miles to the south, 1,900 tons of bombs were falling onto Freiburg in an orgy of destruction lasting twenty-five minutes, aided by the use of mobile Oboe stations established in liberated France. Local sources would confirm the destruction of two thousand houses and severe damage to 450 others, and a death toll of more than two thousand people with a further four thousand injured and almost nine hundred registered as missing. In contrast, the Bomber Command losses amounted to a single Lancaster.

The month ended with a heavy raid on Duisburg on the 30th, for which 576 aircraft were made ready by 1, 4, 6 and 8 Groups, 6 Group providing 191 Halifaxes and fifty-two Lancasters, thirteen of the former belonging to 408 (Goose) Squadron. Each received a bomb load of sixteen 500-pounders before departing Linton-on-Ouse between 16.27 and 17.03 with S/L Reeves the senior pilot on duty. There were no early returns, and the squadron element reached the target to find similar conditions to those of two nights earlier, namely, ten-tenths cloud with tops at around 5,000 feet. The usual positional checks were carried out by Gee and H2S-fix before the 408 (Goose) Squadron crews bombed from 17,000 to 19,000 feet between 20.08 and 20.17 on red TIs visible through the cloud and red and yellow skymarkers drifting over it. They could only report bomb bursts and the glow of fires and the likelihood of a scattered attack, when in reality, it had been more destructive than the Command suspected, local reports confirming the destruction of 528 houses with serious damage to more than eight hundred others.

During the course of the month, the squadron took part in nine operations and dispatched 137 sorties for the loss of four Halifaxes and two crews.

December 1944

December would follow a similar pattern of operations, with the accent remaining on oil and communications, but with city-busting interspersed. The new month began with a heavy attack on the town of Hagen, situated on the south-eastern edge of the Ruhr, ten miles south of Dortmund. It had not been attacked by the RAF since the 1st of October 1943, when one of the many factories severely damaged was the main supplier of accumulator batteries for U-Boots, and this had led to a serious slowing of production of the vessels. Now, on the evening of the 2nd, the town faced a force of 504 heavy bombers, predominantly from 4 and 6 Groups, with Path Finder support and seven Lancasters of 101 Squadron to provide RCM cover. 6 Group contributed 151 Halifaxes and forty-eight Lancasters, thirteen of the former made ready by 408 (Goose) Squadron and each loaded with a 2,000-pounder and a dozen SBCs of cluster bombs. They departed Linton-on-Ouse between 17.29 and 17.54 with F/L Scheelar the senior pilot on duty and flew out in very unfavourable weather conditions, which included sleet and hailstorms and icing over the French coast. At the target they were met by ten-tenths thick cloud, which prevented sight of the markers, and it seems that no skymarking took place. The 408 (Goose) Squadron crews established their positions by Gee and H2S-fix on e.t.a., before bombing from 16,800 to 18,000 feet between 21.06 and 21.12 and observing many large explosions along with the glow of fires. Returning crews had nothing to offer the intelligence section at debriefing, and the assumption at high level was that the raid had been scattered. In fact, it had been hugely destructive, and had destroyed or seriously damaged 1,658 houses, ninety-two industrial buildings, some of which lost three months production, and many others of a public nature. Among the factories destroyed was the above-mentioned Akkumulatoren Fabrik A G Berlin-Hagen (AFA), which was producing accumulator batteries for the new type XXI U-Boots under construction in Hamburg.

On the 4th, a force of 535 aircraft was assembled on 1, 6 and 8 Group stations for an operation against the city of Karlsruhe in southern Germany, for which 6 Group contributed 154 Halifaxes and forty-six Lancasters, fourteen of the former provided by 408 (Goose) Squadron and each loaded with a 2,000-pounder and twelve SBCs of 4lb incendiaries. They departed Linton-on-Ouse between 16.25 and 16.46 with F/Ls Parkhurst and Scheelar the senior pilots on duty and set course via Beachy Head for the French coast near Dieppe. F/O Dunwoodie and crew were at the midpoint of the sea crossing when their radio equipment failed and forced them to turn back, while the others continued on and found the weather conditions throughout the operation to be generally favourable, with cloud building and decreasing in turns across the Channel and France. At the target the crews found nine to ten-tenths white stuff with tops at around 14,000 feet, through which, at the start of their bombing runs, a few were able to see red and green TIs through gaps, while the majority had to rely on the glow of greens and confirm their accuracy by means of H2S or Gee. It was difficult to assess what was happening because of a scarcity of red TIs, and, although the greens were plentiful, they were scattered. However, the cloud was moving eastwards, and later arrivals were able to identify the built-up area visually. The 408 (Goose) Squadron crews delivered their attacks on the evidence of TIs from 17,000 to 19,000 feet between 19.31 and 19.41 and reported fires visible from up to a hundred miles into the homeward flight. It was established ultimately, that severe damage had been inflicted upon the city, particularly in western and southern districts, at a cost of just two aircraft.

While the above was in progress, some fifty miles away to the north-east 5 Group was laying waste to the city of Heilbronn, which had the River Neckar and a north-south rail link running through it, but otherwise, had no genuine strategic importance and its populace would not have been expecting to be attacked. An estimated 82% of the city's built-up area was destroyed by what probably amounted to a firestorm and the post-war British Bombing Survey estimated 351 acres of destruction and a death toll of at least seven thousand people.

On the 5th, a force of 497 aircraft was assembled from 1, 4, 6 and 8 Groups to send against the town of Soest, situated just to the north of the Ruhr and five miles from the now famous Möhne Reservoir and its rebuilt dam. It was one of a number of important railway hubs linking the Ruhr with greater Germany, and its marshalling yards were posted as the aiming point. 6 Group detailed 152 Halifaxes and forty-three Lancasters, thirteen of the former provided by 408 (Goose) Squadron at Linton-on-Ouse, where each was loaded with eight 1,000-pounders and a single of 500lbs before taking off between 18.00 and 18.20 with F/Ls Bracken, Parkhurst, Scheelar and Smith the senior pilots on duty. All reached the target area, where some crews described clear skies and others up to five-tenths thin cloud with tops at around 10,000 feet, however, all were agreed that the conditions were favourable, and red Oboe TIs were seen to fall close to the aiming-point to the south of the marshalling yards, where they were backed up by further reds and greens. The aiming-point was maintained throughout the raid, during which the 408 (Goose) Squadron crews carried out their attacks from 17,000 to 19,000 feet between 21.24 and 21.32. Returning crews reported a concentrated attack, punctuated by large explosions, and the resultant fires could be seen for a considerable distance into the return flight. Local reports confirmed that the main weight of the attack had fallen in the northern half of the town, where the railway yards were situated, and that a thousand houses had been destroyed along with fifty-three other buildings.

Three major operations were posted on the 6th, which together with support and minor operations would generate 1,343 sorties. A force of 475 Lancasters and twelve Mosquitos of 1, 3 and 8 Groups was to target the I G Farbenindustrie A G Merseburg-Leuna synthetic oil refinery near Leipzig in eastern Germany, while 255 Lancasters and ten Mosquitos of 5 Group attended to railway yards and the town centre of Giessen in central Germany. This left 4 and 6 Groups to assemble a main force of 363 Halifaxes and forty-four Lancasters to attack railway yards at Osnabrück, north of the Ruhr, with a sprinkling of 101 Squadron ABC Lancasters to provide RCM cover and twenty-eight Lancasters and eighteen Mosquitos of 8 Group to take care of the marking. 6 Group was responsible for 155 Halifaxes and the forty-four main force Lancasters, the fifteen of the former belonging to 408 (Goose) Squadron each receiving a bomb load of sixteen 500-pounders. They departed Linton-on-Ouse between 16.08 and 17.00 with S/L Reeves the senior pilot on duty and flew out in adverse conditions of heavy cloud and electrical storms persisting all the way to the target, which they found to be covered by ten-tenths cloud with tops at around 6,000 feet and icing to prevent them from descending to a lower altitude to obtain a better view. Few could pick out the red and green TIs, and in the absence of instructions from the Master Bomber, who could do nothing in the circumstances, they bombed on H2S and Gee-fix on e.t.a., from 14,500 to 21,000 feet between 19.41 and 19.50. A large, reddish explosion was witnessed at 19.45, and there appeared to be three distinct areas of fire developing as the bombers withdrew. The raid was at best partially successful, and caused only slight damage to the railway installations, but four factories sustained damage and 203 houses were destroyed.

The following eleven days brought frustration for 6 Group, during which major operations were posted and cancelled. The group had been alerted to prepare for the last major night raid of the war on Essen on the 12th, but in the end, it went ahead without the Canadians. The group's Lancasters were called into action on the 15th, when fifty-one of them joined forces with 224 from 1 Group to form the main force for an attack on the northern half of Ludwigshafen and the nearby town of Oppau, both locations containing an important I G Farben factory, which were engaged in the production of synthetic oil and relying heavily upon slave labour.

It was on the 16th that German ground forces began a new offensive in the Ardennes, in an attempt to break through the American lines and reach the port of Antwerp in what would become known as the Battle of the Bulge. Another virgin target was the city of Ulm, situated on the Danube to the south-east of Stuttgart and west of Augsburg in southern Germany. It was similar in nature to the recently-bombed Heilbronn, and, as a result of the catastrophic raid there, the local Gauleiter had urged the women and children to evacuate the inner city urgently. Plans were put in place to begin evacuation on Monday the 18th, so that Advent could be observed on the Sunday, but something caused a change of plan, and loudspeaker vans toured the city on Sunday urging the population to leave at once. It proved to be a fortuitous move. Unlike Heilbronn, Ulm contained industry, including the important Magirus-Deutz and Kässbohrer lorry factories, and there were also military barracks and depots. A 1 Group main force of 263 Lancasters would benefit from the marking and support of fifty-four Lancasters and thirteen Mosquitos from 8 Group, which, together delivered a concentrated attack, setting off fierce fires that consumed a square kilometre of the city's built-up area. It would be established later that almost 82% of the buildings had sustained damage to some extent, including both lorry factories. There is no question that the evacuation saved many thousands of lives and restricted the civilian death toll to six hundred.

The 6 Group Halifax brigade finally shook off the cobwebs on the 17th when 190 of them were made ready alongside forty-two Lancasters to join forces with 227 Halifaxes of 4 Group as the main force for an attack on aiming points G and H in Duisburg. Fifteen 408 (Goose) Squadron crews attended briefing to learn that 6 Group had been assigned to H and that they would each be sitting on a 2,000-pounder and eleven SBCs of cluster bombs. They had to wait until the early hours of the 18th before departing Linton-on-Ouse between 02.40 and 03.28 as part of the fourth wave, with W/C Sharp leading his men into battle for the first time. There were no early returns and their arrival at the target was greeted by ten-tenths cloud with tops mostly at 6,000 to 8,000 feet, which completely obscured the ground. Two aiming-points were marked by Oboe Mosquitos, but the TIs disappeared into the cloud to leave a glow as the only reference point for bombing, and most crews confirmed their positions by H2S and Gee before releasing their loads. The 408 (Goose) Squadron crews carried out their attacks from 17,000 to 20,000 feet between 06.23 and 06.40 but saw only flashes reflected in the cloud and explosions on approach at 06.12 and 06.16. Despite doubts about the effectiveness of the bombing, 346 houses were destroyed and more than five hundred seriously damaged, and the likelihood is that industry also suffered to some extent.

A further six days of frustration kept the majority of 6 Group's Halifaxes on the ground until the 24th, while sixteen and four respectively of 425 (Allouette) and 434 (Bluenose) Squadrons joined thirty Lancaster from 419 (Moose) and 431 (Iroquois) Squadrons on the 21st for a raid in company with fifty 4 Group Halifaxes on the Nippes marshalling yards in Cologne. This was one of a number of important marshalling yards in the city and was situated to the north of the city centre west of the Rhine, while the Gremberg and Kalk yards were on the other side of the river. The first-mentioned was known to be active in supporting the transportation of men and materials to the Ardennes battle front, and although few bombs found the mark through heavy cloud on this occasion, some did hit the track and cause useful if modest damage. This would be the final Halifax operation for the Bluenoses, who were in the process of converting to Mk X Lancasters.

Christmas Eve brought operations against aerodromes at Lohausen and Mülheim, located respectively at Düsseldorf and Essen, for which 4, 6 and 8 Group provided 327 Halifaxes and Lancasters and eleven Mosquitos. 6 Group contributed 104 Halifaxes and forty-six Lancasters for the former, 408 (Goose) Squadron loading its sixteen participating Halifaxes with nine 1,000-pounders and two each of 500 lbs and 250lbs. The departed Linton-on-Ouse between 11.30 and 11.50 with S/Ls Pettit and Reeves the senior pilots on duty and lost the services of F/O Sokoloff and crew to starboard-engine failure during the climb-out and F/O Pitu to a similar cause just north of the Thames estuary. Those reaching the target were presented with clear conditions and a little haze, through which the airfield and runways were clearly visible and marked out by red TIs and bombed by the 408 (Goose) Squadron crews from 15,000 to 18,500 feet between 14.50 and 14.57 in the face of a spirited flak defence. NP781 failed to return, and it was learned shortly afterwards that F/O Dunwoodie RCAF and his mid-upper gunner had been the sole survivors and had come down in southern Holland, ultimately to evade capture.

The final wartime Christmas period was interrupted on Boxing Day for some crews across the Command by the need to deal with the now encircled remnant of German infantry in the Ardennes. For the first time since October, elements of all of the groups came together in a force of 294 aircraft to attack enemy troop positions at St-Vith, situated close to Belgium's frontier with Germany. The operation had been delayed by a period of adverse weather conditions, but those operating on this day would enjoy clear skies and good visibility in which to bring an end to the "Battle of the Bulge". 6 Group put up sixty-three Halifaxes from 63 Base, and they contributed fifty-two tons of high explosives and 122 of incendiaries.

A force of 328 aircraft was made ready on the 27th in anticipation of an early start on the 28th for an attack on railway yards at Opladen to the north of Leverkusen on the western edge of the Ruhr. 6 Group provided 112 Halifaxes and thirty-eight Lancasters, fourteen of the former made ready by 408 (Goose) Squadron and loaded with a main armament of either nine 1,000-pounders or a 2,000-pounder supplemented with 500 and 250-pounders. They departed Linton-on-Ouse between 03.08 and 03.46 with W/C Sharp the senior pilot on duty and found the target area to be covered by ten-tenths thin cloud with tops at around 10,000 feet, through which the red and green TIs were clearly visible. The marking and bombing were well-concentrated, the 408 (Goose) Squadron crews releasing their loads from 18,000 to 20,000 feet between 06.30 and 06.37 and observing a large explosion, followed by a yellow glare at 06.38. It was not possible to assess the outcome, and no information came out of the target, but the impression was of a successful raid.

The four squadrons of 6 Group's 64 Base were now Lancaster-equipped and forty-eight of them joined forces with others from 1 and 8 Groups on the 29th to form a force of 324 Lancasters and twenty-two Mosquitos to target the Hydrierwerke refinery at Scholven-Buer to the north of Gelsenkirchen. The afternoon operation was highly successful and landed three hundred high explosive bombs in the plant causing severe damage, while 3,200 other bombs fell into the surrounding built-up area, hitting residential and industrial property and surface buildings at two coal mines. Later that day, the target for a main force of 149 Halifaxes of 62 and 63 Bases was the marshalling yards at Troisdorf, located to the north-north-east of Bonn, for which 408 (Goose) Squadron loaded each of its fifteen aircraft with sixteen 500-pounders and sent them on their way from Linton-on-Ouse between 15.14 and 15.31 with F/Ls Bracken, Brown and Scheelar the senior pilots on duty. They all arrived over the Rhineland to find ten-tenths thin cloud, through which red TIs could be seen burning on the ground and most bomb-aimers employed these as the aiming point, while a few chose skymarkers as their reference. The 408 (Goose) Squadron crews carried out their attacks from 16,500 to 20,000 feet between 19.16 and 19.27 and observed a large explosion at 19.20 and numerous bursts and smoke. It was not possible to assess what was happening on the ground and it was discovered later that most of the 510 tons of high explosives had actually failed to hit the target, fortunately without loss to the attacking force.

The final operation of the year for 6 Group was another in the series against the German railway system, and this time involved an attack on Cologne's Kalk-Nord marshalling yards on the East Bank of the Rhine. 470 aircraft from 4, 6 and 8 Groups were made ready, 151 Halifaxes and forty-nine Lancasters representing 6 Group, fifteen of the former provided by 408 (Goose) Squadron, which departed Linton-on-Ouse between 17.35 and 17.57 with F/Ls Bossenberry, Bracken, Gall and Mowatt the senior pilots on duty and a 2,000-pounder and twelve SBCs of cluster bombs in each bomb bay. They all arrived at the target to find ten-tenths cloud with tops at between 7,000 and 12,000 feet and established their positions by Gee and H2s before bombing on red skymarkers with green stars or the glow of TIs from 17,000 to 20,500 feet between 21.08 and 21.13. A number of crews reported that the bombing appeared to be concentrated in two areas two miles apart, and that the glow of fires was reflected in the clouds. A series of five large, red explosions was observed at 21.06, and the overwhelming impression of returning crews was of a successful outcome. This was confirmed by a local report, which mentioned at least two ammunition trains blowing up, two passenger stations sustaining severe damage along with nearby Autobahns, and the destruction of 116 houses and three industrial premises in adjacent areas.

During the course of the month, the squadron carried out nine operations and dispatched 127 sorties for the loss of a single Halifax and crew. It had been another uncompromising year for the Goose Squadron, but losses had been remarkably low, while the serviceability rate had been excellent. The end was in sight as the scent of victory wafted in from the Continent, but much remained to be done before the proud and tenacious enemy finally laid down his arms. The defences, although stretched far beyond their capacity to defend all corners of the Reich, were still capable of inflicting grievous losses on occasions, and many more crews would be lost before the end came.

January 1945

The final year of the war began with a flourish, as the Luftwaffe launched its ill-conceived and, ultimately, ill-fated Operation Bodenplatte (Baseplate) at first light on New Year's Day. The intention to destroy the Allied air forces on the ground at the recently liberated airfields in France, Holland and Belgium was only modestly realized, and it cost the German day fighter force around 250 aircraft. Many of the pilots were killed, wounded or fell into Allied hands, and it was a setback from which the Tagjagd would never fully recover, while the Allies could make good their losses within hours from their enormous stockpiles.

6 Group was not called into action on the 1st, when the three main operations involved 5 Group at the Mittelland Canal, 3 Group at the Vohwinkel railway yards and 4 Group attacking the Hoesch benzol (coking) plant at Dortmund with a Path Finder Lancaster and Mosquito element to provide the marking. A consequence of Operation Bodenplatte was a bunch of very twitchy and trigger-happy American anti-aircraft gunners in Belgium, who shot first and asked questions later, and two 3 Group Lancasters were hit, one of them crashing with fatal consequences for the crew.

The old enemy of Nuremberg was one of two city targets posted on the 2nd and would face a main force of 445 Lancasters drawn from 1, 3 and 6 Groups with a further sixty-nine Lancasters representing 8 Group to provide the marking and bombing support. The 6 Group contribution was provided by the four 64 Base squadrons, which managed forty-four Lancasters between them. 8 Group also contributed twenty-two Lancasters to a simultaneous attack by 351 Halifaxes of 4 and 6 Groups on two I G Farben chemicals plants, one in Ludwigshafen and the other close by in Oppau. The 6 Group contribution to this operation was 156 Halifaxes, of which the sixteen belonging to 408 (Goose) Squadron were each loaded with fifteen or sixteen 500-pounders before departing Linton-on-Ouse between 14.32 and 14.53 with S/L Pettit the senior pilot on duty. Now that mobile Oboe stations had been set up on the Continent, both operations would also benefit from a Mosquito presence, seven for Nuremberg and twenty-two for Ludwigshafen. The two forces were to follow a similar route until dividing shortly before reaching Ludwigshafen, where the Nuremberg force would continue on towards the east for a further 140 miles.

They began the outward flight over six-tenths cloud, which thickened over the Channel and remained at ten-tenths until breaking up from the Franco/German frontier region at 7°East. Ludwigshafen was found to be covered by three to ten-tenths thin, low cloud, through which it was possible to distinguish ground features and, from the opening of the attack at 18.40, the red and green TIs marking out the aiming-point. Some of the marking was scattered, but a good concentration of red TIs soon built up around the aiming-point to attract the main weight of bombing, and a series of explosions between 18.47 and 18.58 culminated with one of abnormal ferocity and brilliance, which lit up the entire area. The 408 (Goose) Squadron crews delivered their bomb loads from 17,500 to 20,000 feet between 18.45 and 18.56, and as they withdrew, both of the targeted manufacturing plants were seen to be ablaze. The success of the Ludwigshafen operation was confirmed by local reports that five hundred high-explosive bombs had fallen within the confines of the two production plants, along with many thousands of incendiaries. This had put an end to all production of synthetic oil, and adjacent industrial buildings, residential property and railway installations had also been destroyed. The Nuremberg operation had also been highly successful and had devastated the city centre, particularly the eastern half, but the bombing had spread into other districts, destroying more than 4,600 dwelling units in apartment blocks.

Briefings took place on the 5th for a major assault on the city of Hannover, which was to be conducted in two phases separated by two hours. 560 Halifaxes and Lancasters were drawn from 1, 4 and 6 Groups to create the main forces, and 8 Group added ninety Lancasters, split fifty-nine and thirty-one between the first and second phases with seven Mosquitos assigned to each. 6 Group contributed 133 Halifaxes, of which fourteen were made ready by 408 (Goose) Squadron and loaded with fifteen 500-pounders each before departing Linton-on-Ouse between 16.26 and 16.50 with W/C Sharp the senior pilot on duty. They tracked across the North Sea and northern Holland to pass south of Bremen and approach the target from the north-west and found the city to be obscured by ten-tenths low cloud with tops at between 2,000 and 5,000 feet. Good H2S returns enabled the Path Finder element to establish its position over the aiming-point in the northern half of the city, and the attack opened with illuminating flares and red skymarkers with green stars at 19.13. The Master Bomber called on the main force crews to bomb the skymarkers, and in the later stages, the centre of the glow in the clouds and the smoke emerging from it. The 408 (Goose) Squadron crews delivered their attacks from 16,500 to 19,000 feet between 19.21 and 19.30 and contributed to what was clearly an accurate and concentrated attack, which left the city burning fiercely enough for the glow to remain visible for a hundred miles into the return flight. This would act as a beacon to the second force, which was some thirty minutes from the target when the Linton-on-Ouse crews arrived back in the circuit. The second phase attack by 163 Lancasters of 1 Group and fifty-seven of 6 Group added to the destruction inflicted upon Hannover, and once the fires had been extinguished and the dust had settled, the local authorities were able to assess that almost five hundred apartment blocks containing 3,600 dwelling units had been destroyed.

In return for the success, Bomber Command suffered unexpectedly high losses amounting to twenty-three Halifaxes and eight Lancasters, 6 Group registering ten failures to return, including 408 (Goose) Squadron's NR209. This Halifax crashed homebound at 19.50 near Hollenstede, a few minutes flying time from the Dutch frontier, with fatal consequences for F/L Scheelar RCAF and three of his predominantly RCAF crew, while the three survivors fell into enemy hands. This was an experienced crew, the pilot on his twenty-sixth operation, while his crew colleagues had only one or two fewer to their credit.

Briefings took place on 1, 4, 6 and 8 Group stations on the 6th for an attack on an important junction in the enemy's railway system in the town of Hanau-am-Main, situated a short distance to the east of Frankfurt. A force of 482 aircraft included a contribution from 6 Group of 146 Halifaxes and forty-three Lancasters, fourteen of the former representing 408 (Goose) Squadron, which departed Linton-on-Ouse between 14.55 and 15.35 with S/L Reeves the senior pilot on duty and a 2,000-pounder and a dozen SBCs of cluster bombs in each bomb bay. They climbed away into cloud, which diminished over the Channel, but built up again over France, and by the time that Hanau drew near, it was at ten-tenths with tops at 9,000 to 10,000 feet. The attack opened a little early with the first red TIs cascading at 18.53 and disappearing into the cloud tops, where their glow lingered until skymarkers went down five minutes later. Thereafter, apart from a short gap between 19.06 and 19.07, a steady flow of red with green star skymarkers maintained the aiming-point until 19.11, and large explosions at 19.00 and 19.04, together with a glow beneath the clouds, confirmed the effectiveness of what was happening on the ground. The 408 (Goose) Squadron crews delivered their payloads from 17,000 to 20,000 feet between 19.00 and 19.14 and reported the glow from the target to be visible from seventy-five miles away. It was not possible to assess the outcome, but a local report confirmed damage in the area of the railway junction, and also in other parts of the town resulting in the destruction of 40% of the built-up area.

Apart from isolated mining operations, 6 Group remained inactive for a week until being alerted on the 13th to an operation against Saarbrücken's marshalling yards, which had faced a 3 Group G-H raid earlier in the day. For the night attack a force of 274 aircraft from 4, 6 and 8 Groups was assembled, of which 140 of the Halifaxes were provided by 6 Group. At Linton-on-Ouse seventeen 408 (Goose) Squadron Halifaxes each received a bomb load of eight 500 and eight 250-pounders, before being sent on their way between 15.13 and 15.44 with W/C Sharp and S/L Reeves the senior pilots on duty, and when F/O Wylie and crew took off in NP743, they notched up the squadron's 4,000th sortie of the war. They crossed France without incident and arrived at the target some three hours later to find clear skies with ground mist and Oboe Mosquitos marking the aiming-points with red TIs. The heavy marker crews backed these up with greens, and the main force crews delivered their bomb loads accurately into the two aiming points within the yards, the 408 (Goose) Squadron crews from 15,000 to 19,500 feet between 19.13 and 19.19, and all returned safely to make their reports.

On the 14th, 6 group was called upon to contribute to an operation by a total Lancaster force from 1, 5, 6 and 8 Groups of 573 aircraft supported by fourteen Mosquitos, directed against the I G Farbenindustrie A G Merseburg-Leuna refinery, which lay some 250 miles from the Dutch frontier and five hundred miles from the bomber bases of eastern England. 6 Group provided fifty-three Lancasters for this operation and 136 Halifaxes to attack the marshalling yards at Grevenbroich, situated on the main rail link between Mönchengladbach to the north-west and Cologne to the south-east. At 12.45, 408 (Goose) Squadron's NP798 caught fire while being prepared to take part and exploded, by which time all personnel had vacated the area and no injuries were reported. The loading of a further seventeen Halifaxes continued into the afternoon, and each received sixteen 500-pounders before departing Linton-on-Ouse between 15.44 and 16.42 with W/C Sharp and S/L Reeves the senior pilots on duty. Conditions in the target area were favourable with a little ground haze and the bombing was aimed at red TIs surrounded by greens. The 408 (Goose) Squadron element attacked from 17,000 to 19,500 feet between 19.33 and 19.44, observing a few fires, and a large red explosion at 19.36 was followed by another two minutes later, which emitted black smoke. Post-raid reconnaissance confirmed the success of the operation, during which 6 Group dropped 354 tons of high explosives without loss.

Feverish activity across the Command on the 16th prepared more than twelve hundred aircraft for action, the majority to participate in four major operations that night, three to target oil refineries and the largest to deliver an area attack on the eastern city of Magdeburg, which also contained the Braunkohle A G Bergius process oil (hydrogenation) plant, located in the Rothensee district to the north of the city centre. The independent 3 and 5 Groups were handed the refineries at Wanne-Eickel in the Ruhr and Brüx in Czechoslovakia respectively, leaving 320 Halifaxes of 4 and 6 Groups to take care of Magdeburg and 283 Lancasters of 1 and 6 Groups to ply their trade at Zeitz-Tröglitz, the location of another Braunkohle-Benzin A G plant, situated some twenty miles south-west of Leipzig. 6 Group detailed fifty-one Lancasters for the last-mentioned and 136 Halifaxes for Magdeburg, but the take-off crash of a 426 (Thunderbird) Squadron Halifax at Linton-on-Ouse would prevent ten others from taking off. Ultimately, eleven 408 (Goose) Squadron Halifaxes got away safely between 18.14 and 19.11 with F/Ls Bracken, Gall, Mowatt and Smith the senior pilots on duty and each carrying a 2,000-pounder and either twelve 500lb cluster bombs or SBCs of 4lb incendiaries. They flew out over Flamborough Head and rendezvoused with the Path Finder element over the North Sea as they set course to enter Germany via Jade Bay, before passing to the south of Hamburg. F/O Sokoloff and crew had been airborne for ninety minutes when the failure of their port-outer engine ended their interest in proceedings, leaving the others to press on into the night and reach Magdeburg after an outward flight of almost four hours.

Those arriving in the early stages of the attack were able to pick out the River Elbe and the built-up area from clear skies and the visibility was excellent as the Path Finders marked out the aiming-point with red and green TIs, which the 408 (Goose) Squadron crews bombed from 18,000 to 20,000 feet between 21.39 and 21.47 in accordance with the instructions of the Master Bomber. The early stages of the raid fell into the southern districts, but spread gradually into other parts of the city, and by the time that the force withdrew, the built-up area was enveloped in smoke and appeared to be on fire from end to end, producing a glow that remained visible for a hundred miles into the return flight. It was not a one-sided affair, a fact made manifest by seventeen empty dispersals that should have been occupied by Halifaxes, but all of the 408 (Goose) Squadron participants returned safely, F/O Wallis and crew to claim the destruction of a Me210 on the way out. Post-raid reconnaissance confirmed the success of the operation, and Bomber Command claimed that 44% of the city's built-up area had been destroyed.

An isolated mining operation aside, 6 Group remained off the order of battle from then until the 28th, suffering the frustrations of operations posted only to be cancelled. When fifteen 408 (Goose) Squadron crews joined others from 426 (Thunderbird) Squadron in the briefing room at Linton-on-Ouse, it was to learn of that night's trip to Stuttgart by 602 aircraft divided into two forces and separated by three hours, each with its own specific target. The first phase, by 226 aircraft, was to be directed at the marshalling yards in the town of Kornwestheim, situated just beyond the northern boundary of Stuttgart, while the second phase, involving a main force of 4 and 6 Group Halifaxes would target the Hirth aero-engine factory at Zuffenhausen, fewer than two miles to the south. 6 Group put up fifty-five Lancasters for the first phase and 124 Halifaxes for the second, those belonging to 408 (Goose) Squadron each receiving a bomb load of a 2,000-pounder and cluster bombs. The Kornwestheim-bound elements got away in the late afternoon, leaving the phase 2 brigade on the ground until their departure, 408 (Goose) Squadron becoming airborne between 19.22 and 20.14 with a whole host of pilots of flight lieutenant rank leading the way and W/C Evans, the commanding officer elect of 429 (Bison) Squadron, guesting to gain operational experience. They enjoyed an uneventful outward flight across France to enter Germany north of Strasbourg and were assisted by Path Finder Mosquitos dispensing "window" ahead of the bomber stream, which, on arrival in the target area, found ten-tenths stratocumulus with tops at up to 12,000 feet and thin stratus between 15,000 and 20,000 feet.

Oboe Mosquitos delivered TIs three to four minutes late, but they disappeared into the cloud as they cascaded and were soon lost to view. Red skymarkers with green stars were plentiful but ignited far too high before drifting in the wind and becoming scattered, which resulted in a lack of concentration and the spraying of bombs across northern Stuttgart. The 408 (Goose) Squadron participants delivered their payloads from 17,500 to 20,500 feet between 23.31 and 23.41, aiming predominantly at skymarkers, and observed large explosions at 23.36 and 23.38 and the glow of fires beneath the cloud. They headed home suspecting that they had failed to deliver an effective blow on the factory and that a decoy fire site and dummy TIs fired into the air by the defenders had also attracted some bomb loads. Their suspicions were partly confirmed by local sources, which did admit to damage to the railway installations and to a number of important war industry factories including the Robert Bosch works. This would prove to be the last of fifty-three major raids on this important industrial city, which now lay largely in ruins. It was a sad end to the month for 408 (Goose) Squadron, which had to post missing two crews, one experienced and the other containing some "old hands". NP743 and NP746 both came down somewhere in southern Germany with no survivors from the predominantly RCAF crew of P/O Johnston RCAF in the former, and just one survivor from the crew of F/O Wallis RCAF in the latter. P/O Johnston was on his fifth sortie and F/O Wallis on his twenty-fourth.

F/L Minhinnick was posted to 432 (Leaside) Squadron on the 29th as a flight commander elect in the rank of acting squadron leader and would find himself in temporary command of the squadron for the whole of February. During the course of the month, 408 (Goose) Squadron undertook seven operations and dispatched 104 sorties for the loss of four Halifaxes and three crews.

February 1945

The weather at the start of February provided difficult conditions for marking and bombing, and a number of operations would struggle to achieve their aims in the face of thick, low cloud and strong winds. Three major operations were laid on for the night of the 1/2nd, the largest by 382 Lancasters and fourteen Mosquitos of 1, 6 and 8 Groups against Ludwigshafen, while thirty-five miles to the north, 340 aircraft from 4, 6 and 8 Groups attended to the city of Mainz and further north still, 5 Group's target was the marshalling yards in the town of Siegen, situated some fifty miles east of Cologne. 6 Group detailed eighty-six Halifaxes for Mainz, ten of them representing 408 (Goose) Squadron, which departed Linton-on-Ouse between 15.39 and 15.53 with W/C Sharp, W/C Evans and S/L Smith the senior pilots on duty and each Halifax carrying a 2,000-pounder and eleven or twelve 500lb cluster bombs. The outward journey across the Channel and France took place over cloud, but when the spearhead of the bomber stream arrived at the target at the end of a three-hour flight, it found gaps that enabled crews to see TIs on the ground. They had been delivered by Oboe Mosquitos at 19.24, but the cloud cover soon became complete, topping out at 6,000 feet, and the majority of the Path Finder visual centerers retained their green TIs to allow for emergency skymarking to take over from 19.28. At times, the red and green skymarkers were well grouped and sometimes sparce, but the main part of the bombing had to be directed at these after their position had been confirmed by Gee and H2S. The 408 (Goose) Squadron crews carried out their attacks from 18,000 to 20,000 feet between 19.30 and 19.41 and observed large explosions at 19.28 and 19.31 along with a compact glow of fires. H2S photos were plotted at between one-and-a-half and two miles south-east of the aiming-point, and local reports confirmed that no significant damage had been achieved.

6 Group now had six Lancaster squadrons at its disposal following the conversion of 424 (Tiger) and 433 (Porcupine) Squadrons at Skipton-on-Swale and was able to contribute sixty of the type to the attack on Ludwigshafen, which they found concealed by cloud. They had to rely on

skymarker flares, and that resulted in scattered bombing and a degree of undershooting. Small gaps in the cloud revealed incendiary fires on both sides of the Rhine, and several large explosions were observed at 19.20, 19.25, 19.36 and 19.42.

When briefings took place on the 2nd, they came with the bad news that a tour of operations for main force crews was to be increased to thirty-six sorties. On 5 Group stations in drizzly Lincolnshire, 250 crews were told further, that the night's operation was to be against Karlsruhe in southern Germany, and that this was one of three major undertakings involving a total of 1,150 aircraft. 495 Lancaster crews from 1, 3, 6 and 8 Groups were informed that Wiesbaden would be their destination and that it would the first time that this city, separated from nearby Mainz to the south by the River Rhine, had been targeted by Bomber Command. The third operation on this night would bring a return to the Ruhr for 277 Halifaxes of 4 and 6 Groups with twenty-seven 8 Group Lancasters and nineteen Mosquitos to provide the marking for an attack on the Krupp Treibstoffwerke synthetic oil plant in the Wanne-Eickel district of Herne. 6 Group detailed sixty-five Lancasters for Wiesbaden and 107 Halifaxes for the Ruhr, the fourteen of the latter belonging to 408 (Goose) Squadron each loaded with ten 500 and six 250-pounders before departing Linton-on-Ouse between 19.53 and 20.34 with W/C Evans continuing his apprenticeship as the senior pilot on duty among a host of 408 (Goose) Squadron captains of flight lieutenant rank.

F/O Baird RCAF and crew were heading south at 17,000 feet when the starboard-inner engine had to be shut down and the propeller feathered. As the Halifax began to sink, the decision was taken to restart the engine and an unsuccessful attempt was made to unfeather the propeller, at which point the engine burst into flames and the decision was taken to abandon NP757 to its fate. Three crew members sustained injury on landing, and the Halifax crashed with a full bomb load at North Witham aerodrome nine miles south-south-east of Grantham in Lincolnshire. The others reached the target area to find ten-tenths cloud with tops at between 4,000 and 8,000 feet, which prevented the visual centerers from delivering their green TIs and left the marking reliant upon red TIs dropped by the Oboe Mosquitos from around 23.10. A red glow beneath the cloud seemed too bright to be a fire and became the focus for many of the main force crews, who took it to be a red TI. The majority of 408 (Goose) Squadron crews relied on Gee to establish the aiming point and released their loads from 17,600 to 20,000 feet between 23.14 and 23.26 in the face of intense and accurate flak bursting at between 16,000 and 21,000 feet. Large explosions were noted at 23.15, 23.20 and 23.27 but an assessment proved to be impossible, and according to local sources, most of the bombs fell into open ground around a coal mine.

Three main operations were posted again on the 4th, two of them to be supported by 6 Group and 408 (Goose) Squadron. The Gutehoffnungshütte Oberhausen A G benzol plant at Osterfeld near Leipzig was the target for a main force of a hundred 6 Group Halifaxes, while 6 Group contributed seventy-one Lancasters and twenty-nine Halifaxes to a force of 238 aircraft in company with 4 and 8 Groups for an attack on the marshalling yards in the city of Bonn. The third operation by a 4 Group main force of ninety-six Halifaxes was to be directed at the Gelsenkirchener Bergwerke A G (Nordstern) coking plant in the Ruhr. At Linton-on-Ouse, the twelve-strong 408 (Goose) Squadron element assigned to Osterfeld each received a bomb load of eight 500 and eight 250-pounders, while the four bound for Bonn were loaded with a 2,000-pounder and cluster bombs. They took off in tandem, the larger element first between 17.20 and 17.44 with W/C Sharp and S/L Norris the senior pilots on duty, the latter having been posted in from 419 (Moose) Squadron as a flight commander at the end of January. They were followed into the air by the second element between 17.45 and 17.49 led by F/Ls Austin and Bossenberry.

They Bonn-bound quartet all reached the target area, where the persistently cloudy conditions concealed the aiming-point, and only two of the Oboe Mosquitos were able to deliver red TIs, which quickly disappeared into the cloud tops at around 5,000 feet and left a glow that proved insufficient for the Path Finder visual centerers to release their green TIs on. The first red and green skymarkers were seen at 20.46 and, thereafter, provided the main-force crews with a reference to bomb, those from 408 (Goose) Squadron from 18,000 to 20,000 feet between 20.48 and 20.52. Returning crews described a bright, red glow beginning to develop in intensity beneath the clouds as they turned away, and one 10 Squadron crew insisted that it remained visible for 150 miles into the return flight, while others suggested a more conservative forty to one hundred miles. What caused it remains unknown, as most of the bombing missed the target to the south or fell on the east bank of the Rhine at Beuel.

Meanwhile, all of the 408 (Goose) Squadron aircraft had arrived in eastern Germany after a four-hour outward flight, an hour of which was taken up by the climb-out. They encountered ten-tenths cloud with tops at between 6,000 and 10,000 feet and moderately good horizontal visibility and observed a few red TIs cascading ahead only to disappear quickly into the cloud and leave a glow as the only reference. Bombs were released either on this or a Gee-fix, the 408 (Goose) Squadron crews attacking from 15,500 to 19,000 feet between 21.00 and 21.11 and observing an explosion at 21.05. An impression was gained by some that fires were spreading across the target area, but an assessment was impossible and post-raid reconnaissance revealed no fresh damage to the plant, leaving as the only positive aspect the absence of bomber casualties.

The towns of Cleves and Goch are separated by around eight miles and lie east of the Reichswald and to the south of the Rhine, where the British XXX Corps was preparing to advance. 464 aircraft of 4, 6 and 8 Groups were made ready on the 7th to attack the latter, which was part of the enemy's defensive line, while a predominantly 1 Group force dealt with the former. 6 Group detailed 131 Halifaxes and sixty-nine Lancasters, sixteen of the former provided by 408 (Goose) Squadron, which departed Linton-on-Ouse between 18.40 and 19.04 with S/L Norris the senior pilot on duty and a dozen 500 and four 250-pounders in each bomb bay. The weather was good as they climbed away over northern Yorkshire and pointed their snouts towards the south on course for the exit point at Hastings on the Sussex coast and they flew under virtually cloud-free skies until a dozen miles from the target, when it began to build and was at seven to ten-tenths in a band from 5,000 to 7,000 feet when the raid began. This prompted the Master Bomber to bring the main-force crews down to below the cloud base to provide them with a view of the red and green TIs on the aiming-point and urged them continuously between 22.12 and 22.18 to bomb the centre of the mixed TIs, before switching at 22.24 to the greens. Ten of the 408 (Goose) Squadron crews complied with his instructions from 4,000 to 12,000 feet between 22.15 and 22.33, before the aiming-point became obscured by smoke, and having observed bombs to undershoot by up to two miles, the Master Bomber called a halt to proceedings after only 155 aircraft had bombed and sent the rest home. Returning crews reported one violent explosion and a burgeoning red glow beneath the cloud that suggested an effective attack, while a few claimed that they had been unable to pick up the Master Bomber's transmissions. Despite the challenges, post-raid reconnaissance revealed much damage to the town, which had been largely evacuated by the civilian population, and most of the 180 known deaths occurred among Russian, Italian and Dutch forced workers.

Oil plants dominated the night of the 8/9th, and while 475 Lancasters of 1, 5 and 8 Groups were assembled to target the Wintershall oil refinery at Politz near Stettin, a force of two hundred Halifaxes from 4 and 6 Groups were prepared as the main force for a return to the Krupp Treibstoffwerke synthetic oil plant at Wanne-Eickel in the Ruhr town of Herne. 62 Base provided all ninety-eight 6 Group Halifaxes, the thirteen belonging to 408 (Goose) Squadron each receiving a bomb load of sixteen 500-pounders before departing Linton-on-Ouse between 02.50 and 03.22 with W/C Evans the senior pilot on duty and still weeks from gaining his own command. P/O Brown and crew abandoned their sortie during the climb-out after the hydraulics feed to the undercarriage and flaps failed and believing that landing with bomb doors open was more challenging than landing with a full bomb load, chose the latter option and touched down successfully. The others arrived in the target area to find five to eight-tenths cloud with tops at 8,000 to 10,000 feet and a base at around 5,000 feet with a large gap right over the target that allowed a clear sight of the concentrated red and green TIs. Most crews confirmed their positions by Gee before bombing the red TIs, the 408 (Goose) Squadron element from 18,000 to 20,000 feet between 06.15 and 06.25 and observing what appeared to be an accurate attack that obliterated the TIs and left a reddish-yellow fire that sent a column of black smoke rising through 10,000 feet. Despite the appearances, local sources claimed that the operation was not successful and caused only minor damage to the refinery.

A lull in main force operations thereafter extended to the 13th, when two major operations were planned, the first by a force of 368 aircraft from 4, 6 and 8 Groups to target the Braunkohle-Benzin oil plant at Böhlen, situated some seven miles to the south of Leipzig. 6 Group detailed 115 Halifaxes, and while their crews were attending briefings, sixty-seven others in the six Lancaster squadrons were learning about the first round of Operation Thunderclap, the Churchill inspired offensive against Germany's eastern cities, which was devised partly to act in support of the advancing Russian ground forces, and also as a demonstration to Stalin of RAF air power, should he turn against the Allies after the war. The historic and culturally significant city of Dresden was selected to open the offensive in another two-phase affair, with a 5 Group force of 246 Lancasters and nine Mosquitos leading the way, to be followed three hours later by 529 Lancasters of 1, 3, 6 and 8 Groups. It had proved to be a successful policy thus far, with the 5 Group low-level marking system and main force attacks providing a beacon for the second force, and should it be required on this night, 8 Group would provide any necessary marking for phase two from high level.

The sixteen 408 (Goose) Squadron Halifaxes each received a bomb load of nine 500 and four 250-pounders and took off from Linton-on-Ouse between 17.40 and 18.11 with a bevy of pilots of flight lieutenant rank leading the way. F/O Hutchson and crew had reached south-eastern Belgium when an engine issue forced them to turn back, while the others pressed on to reach the target, which they found to be concealed beneath two layers of ten-tenths cloud between 4,000 and 15,000 feet. The only reference for the bomb-aimers was the glow of red and green TIs, which were believed later to have been decoys, and the 408 (Goose) Squadron bomb loads were aimed at these from 17,000 to 20,000 feet between 21.57 and 22.09. One large, dull, orange explosion lit up the clouds for five minutes, and the glow of fires lingered on the horizon for some ninety miles into the return flight, but crews were less than enthusiastic about the outcome and believed the bombing to have been widely scattered.

Meanwhile at Dresden, the 5 Group force delivered eight hundred tons of bombs in conditions of partial cloud, and as far as the crews were concerned, this was no different from any other attack, and the fires visible for more than a hundred miles into the return journey nothing out of the ordinary. By the time that the second force of 1, 3, 6 and 8 Group Lancasters arrived three hours later, the skies had cleared, and the fires created by the earlier attack provided the expected reference point. A further eighteen hundred tons of bombs rained down onto the historic and beautiful old city, setting off the same chain of events that had devastated parts of Hamburg in July 1943 and a number of other cities since. Dresden's population had been swelled by masses of refugees fleeing from the eastern front, and many were engulfed in the ensuing firestorm, which was still burning on the following morning, when three hundred American bombers carried out a separate attack under the umbrella of a fighter escort and completed the destruction. There were claims that RAF aircraft had strafed the streets and open spaces to increase the level of terror, and such accusations abound in the city to this day. In fact, American fighters were responsible, and were trying to add to the general confusion and chaos. Initial propaganda-inspired reports from the Office of the Propaganda Minister, Joseph Goebbels, falsely claimed a death toll of 250,000 people, but an accurate figure of twenty-five thousand has been settled upon since.

The destruction of Dresden is not part of the 408 (Goose) Squadron story, but its ramifications affected all who served in Bomber Command and has been used by some in this country as well as in Germany as a weapon with which to denigrate Bomber Command and Harris, and label them as war criminals. Curiously, no accusations have been levelled at the Americans. Dresden was Germany's seventh largest city and its largest remaining largely un-bombed built-up area, which, according to American sources, contained more than a hundred factories and fifty thousand workers contributing to the war effort. It was also an important railway hub, to the extent that the marshalling yards had been attacked twice in late 1944 by the USAAF. It should also be understood that Harris had no interest in attacking Dresden and had to be nagged by Chief-of-the-Air-Staff Portal to fulfil Churchill's wishes. The aircrew simply did the job asked of them, and the Dresden raid was no different from any other attack on a city. The death toll at Hamburg was much higher, and yet, there has been no similar outcry. The legacy of this operation served to deny Harris and the men under his Command their due recognition for the massive part they played in the ultimate victory, and only in recent times has a monument been erected in Green Park in London and a campaign clasp awarded, sadly, far too little and far too late for the majority. Churchill, with his eyes set on a peacetime election, betrayed Harris and the Command in a typical politically motivated U-turn, in which he accused Harris of bombing solely for the purpose of inflicting terror. In the post-war honours, Harris was the only commander in the field to be omitted.

Round two of Operation Thunderclap was planned for the following night with Chemnitz as the target for 717 aircraft drawn from 1, 3, 4, 6 and 8 Groups, which would be divided into two waves separated by three-and-a-half hours. 5 Group would also be in the area with 224 Lancasters and eight Mosquitos to target an oil refinery in the small town of Rositz, situated twenty-five miles due south of Leipzig and thirty miles north-west of Chemnitz. 6 Group detailed sixty-six Halifaxes and fifty-two Lancasters, fifteen of the former provided by 408 (Goose) Squadron and loaded with a 2,000-pounder and cluster bombs. They departed Linton-on-Ouse as part of the first wave between

16.30 and 17.29 with the usual suspects of pilots of flight lieutenant rank leading the way, and all reached the target area to find two thin layers of ten-tenths stratus cloud with tops at 10,000 and 18,000 feet. The blind illuminators opened the attack at 20.52, but, as the cloud precluded identification of the aiming-point, the Master Bomber called for skymarking from 20.59 onwards. Salvoes of green/red flares were released by seven aircraft but proved to be scattered over a wide area with no point of concentration. However, with nothing else to aim at, the main force crews were instructed to bomb on them, and the 408 (Goose) Squadron crews complied from 16,500 to 20,000 feet between 21.01 and 21.17, and widely separated fires confirmed in their eyes a lack of focus. The second wave found the same conditions as the first and delivered an attack based initially on skymarking and later on H2S and Gee. Post-raid reconnaissance confirmed that many parts of the city had been hit, but much of the effort had been wasted in open country.

The town of Wesel had the misfortune to sit on the eastern bank of the Rhine a dozen or so miles north of Duisburg, and directly in the path of advancing Allied ground forces. By the end of the war, it would claim to be the most destroyed town of its size in Germany, and its ordeal began with a raid by 3 Group on the 16th. Twenty-four hours later, 247 Halifaxes and twenty-seven Lancasters of 4 and 6 Groups were made ready to carry out the second attack with the marshalling yards as the aiming-point and twenty-four Mosquitos of 8 Group to carry out the Oboe marking. 6 Group contributed 110 Halifaxes, fifteen of them belonging to 408 (Goose) Squadron, each of which received a bomb load of a dozen 500-pounders before departing Linton-on-Ouse between 11.27 and 11.48 with S/L Norris the senior pilot on duty. All reached the target area, only for the Master Bomber to abandon the operation in the face of ten-tenths cloud layered up to 25,000 feet. Eight aircraft, including two from 6 Group, had bombed before the order was given, and most brought their entire bomb load home to diversion airfields because of fog over Yorkshire. Wesel would be attacked again on the 18th and the 19th by 3 Group using its G-H blind-bombing system and would then be left in peace for a number of weeks before its total destruction in March.

A busy night of operations involving more than twelve hundred sorties was planned for the 20th, and preparations were put in hand on 1, 3, 6 and 8 Group stations for a major assault on the southern half of Dortmund, for which a force of 514 Lancasters was assembled, eighty-four of them on 6 Group stations. Simultaneous raids on Rhenania-Ossag oil refineries in the Reisholz district to the south of Düsseldorf city centre and at Monheim, eight miles further south were to be prosecuted by a main force of 156 Halifaxes of 4 Group and 112 Halifaxes of 6 Group respectively, both with an 8 Group element to provide the marking and Master Bomber. 5 Group had become the recognised "canal-busters" and on this night targeted the Mittelland close to its junction with the Dortmund-Ems Canal at Gravenhorst. Fourteen 408 (Goose) Squadron Halifaxes were loaded with a dozen 500-pounders each and sent on their way from Linton-on-Ouse between 21.44 and 22.12 with W/C Sharp the senior pilot on duty and all reached the target area to find eight-to ten-tenths stratocumulus with tops at between 4,000 and 12,000 feet. The aiming point was marked with well-concentrated red and green TIs, which provided half of the force with a reference, while the other half focused on red skymarkers with green stars, which were maintained throughout the raid as a constant reference. The 408 (Goose) Squadron crews carried out their attacks from 14,000 to 16,000 feet between 01.40 and 02.03 and some reported widely scattered fires covering an area of some seven square miles. Others caught a glimpse of the built-up area through a gap in the cloud and observed it to be burning and sending smoke rising through 10,000 feet, reporting at debriefing that the glow remained visible for 125 miles into the homeward flight. Despite doubts about the effectiveness of the raid, all production at the Monheim site was ended and a similar result was achieved at Reisholz.

The final heavy raid of the war on the much-bombed city of Duisburg was entrusted to 362 Lancasters of 1, 6 and 8 Groups on the night of the 21/22nd, while 349 aircraft of 4, 6 and 8 Groups delivered the first and only major raid of the war by the RAF on the ancient city of Worms. Located on the western bank of the Rhine some forty miles south-west of Frankfurt, Worms was a military stronghold and was tenaciously resisting the advance of Allied ground forces into the Rhineland. 6 Group contributed eighty-five Lancasters to the Duisburg endeavour and 111 Halifaxes for Worms, fourteen of them provided by 408 (Goose) Squadron. Each was loaded with a 2,000-pounder and cluster bombs before departing Linton-on-Ouse as part of the second wave between 16.24 and 17.49 with S/L Norris the senior pilot on duty. It is believed that all Goose aircraft reached the target area to find the luxury for a change of clear skies and good visibility, in which the roads leading into the city were clearly identified. This was of interest to the crews, who had been told at briefings that the main purpose of the operation was to cut road and rail communications. The Path Finders delivered red and green TIs onto and around the planned aiming-point, the main railway station on the edge of the city centre, and the bombing by the 408 (Goose) Squadron crews took place from 16,500 to 19,000 feet between 20.31 and 20.45. More than eleven hundred tons of bombs rained down, ninety-eight tons of high explosives and 251 tons of incendiaries delivered by 6 Group, most of it accurately, although some fell into the south-western suburbs and beyond. A large explosion was witnessed at 20.34 to the south-east of the aiming-point, and the pattern of burning streets was discernible and still developing as the force turned away. The flak defence had been moderate, but it was the night-fighters that posed the greatest risk and a Path Finder Lancaster and sixteen Halifaxes failed to return home, six of the latter belonging to 6 Group. 408 (Goose) Squadron posted missing the predominantly RCAF crews of F/Ls Sanderson and Fleming in NP711 and RG477 respectively, both of which were approaching the mid-point of their tours, and the news eventually arrived via the Red Cross that the former had all perished, while the latter had survived and were in enemy hands. Post-raid reconnaissance confirmed that Worms had sustained massive damage, and a post-war survey would assess that the level of destruction amounted to an estimated 39% of its built-up area. However, this included damage caused by a raid by the American Eighth Air Force on the 18th of March.

A force of 342 aircraft from 4, 6 and 8 Groups was assembled on the morning of the 23rd to send against Essen in the early afternoon, 6 Group contributing 119 of the 297 Halifaxes, sixteen belonging to 408 (Goose) Squadron. They departed Linton-on-Ouse between 11.36 and 12.03 with S/L Smith the senior Goose pilot on duty and W/C Evans still guesting, each crew sitting on a 2,000-pounder and a dozen 500lb cluster bombs. There were no early returns and all from 408 (Goose) Squadron reached the target area to encounter ten-tenths cloud in layers between 12,000 and 18,000 feet. The Path Finders dropped green smoke-puff skymarkers, which the 408 (Goose) Squadron crews bombed from 15,000 to 17,500 feet between 15.07 and 15.12 after confirming their positions by Gee and H2S. The results could not be assessed, but local reports revealed this to have been a highly accurate attack, which delivered three hundred high-explosive bombs and eleven thousand incendiaries onto the Krupp complex, causing massive damage.

That night, 6 Group put up fifty Lancasters in a force of 360 aircraft from 1, 6 and 8 Groups, which delivered 1,825 tons of bombs from 8,000 feet onto the city of Pforzheim in a twenty-two-minute orgy of destruction that created a firestorm and left 17,000 fatalities in its wake. This was the third highest death toll to result from a single attack on a German city after Hamburg (40,000) and Dresden (25,000). It was during this operation that the final Victoria Cross was earned by a member of RAF Bomber Command. It went posthumously to the Master Bomber from 582 Squadron, Captain Ed Swales SAAF, who continued to control the attack in a Lancaster severely damaged by a night-fighter, before sacrificing his life to allow his crew to abandon the stricken aircraft.

4 and 6 Groups continued to join forces and on the 24th put together a main force of 290 Halifaxes for a daylight attack on the Chemwerke-Steinkohle oil refinery in Bergkamen, a community in the north-eastern Ruhr close to the town of Kamen. 6 Group was responsible for 110 of the Halifaxes, while 8 Group contributed twenty-six Lancasters and twenty-five Mosquitos to provide "window", marking and main force support. The 408 (Goose) Squadron element of fifteen departed Linton-on-Ouse between 12.40 and 13.15 with S/L Norris the senior pilot on duty and sixteen 500-pounders in each bomb bay and crossed the battle front over five-tenths cloud, which had thickened to ten-tenths with tops at 6,000 to 8,000 feet by the time the target was reached. As no markers were visible, the Master Bomber ordered the crews to bomb on the information provided by their navigational aids, and the 408 (Goose) Squadron crews complied from 15,000 to 17,500 feet between 16.48 and 16.50. Returning crews had nothing to offer the intelligence bods at debriefing, and it was left to local sources to confirm massive destruction in Kamen, Bergkamen and the surrounding villages, but made no mention of the refinery. Further operations would be mounted against it over the ensuing days.

8 Group joined forces with 4 and 6 Groups again on the 27th to target the city of Mainz in south-central Germany, for which a force of 311 Halifaxes, 131 Lancasters and eighteen Mosquitos was assembled. 6 Group's contribution amounted to 102 Halifaxes and eighty-five Lancasters, seventeen of the former belonging to 408 (Goose) Squadron, which departed Linton-on-Ouse between 12.31 and 13.11 with S/L Norris the senior pilot on duty and a 2,000-pounder and other unspecified hardware in each bomb bay. On the way out a formation of B17s crossed the gaggle, but it managed to maintain cohesion and reached the target after an outward flight of more than three hours to be greeted by ten-tenths cloud as anticipated, before receiving instructions from the Master Bomber to aim for the centre of the plentiful and concentrated green smoke-puff skymarkers. All but one of the 408 (Goose) Squadron crews complied from 15,000 to 18,500 feet between 16.29 and 16.32 and were rewarded with the sight of smoke spiralling up through the cloud tops at 9,000 feet as they turned away. P/O Brown and crew observed the smoke-puff markers some five hundred yards to port and an unsuccessful attempt was made to side-slip towards it, after which they found a built-up area on the way home and bombed it from 18,000 feet at 16.38. A total of 1,545 tons of bombs rained down devastation upon Mainz, seven hundred tons delivered by 6 Group, and resulted in the destruction of 5,670 buildings, wiping out the historic Altstadt and killing more than eleven hundred people.

During the course of the month the squadron took part in fourteen operations and dispatched 191 sorties for the loss of three Halifaxes and two crews.

March 1945

Just when the crews must have been thinking that bomber operations were becoming safer, March came along to prove them wrong. The new month would see the Command continue to bludgeon its way across Germany, concentrating on oil, rail and road targets, along with the few towns still boasting a built-up area. The penultimate month of the bombing war began with a daylight operation on the 1st and was the final one of the many visited upon Mannheim, for which a force of 248 Lancasters of 1 Group and seventy of 6 Group formed the main force in company with ninety 6 Group Halifaxes, while fifty-four Lancasters and sixteen Mosquitos of 8 Group took care of the target and route marking. 408 (Goose) Squadron loaded each of its thirteen Halifaxes with two 1,000-pounders and cluster bombs and sent them on their way from Linton-on-Ouse between 11.40 and 11.56 with S/L Norris the senior pilot on duty. After climbing out, they made for the Sussex coast, joining up with the rest of the force on the way, the 1 Group element forming into vics in line astern led by the Hemswell units, which were employing yellow verey lights, yellow trailing lights and light green fins to aid identification. There is no mention in the 6 Group ORB of the forming up procedure and it is assumed that they came together in a loose gaggle before beginning the Channel crossing over five-tenths cloud. They apparently maintained good formation as the cloud built to ten-tenths from the French coast, the tailwind lighter than forecast, despite which, no attempt was made to make up time. They arrived at the target some six minutes later than planned, and at 14.47 the Master Bomber was heard to ask his Deputy if he could see the main force, to which he received a negative response and ordered the marker force to orbit above the 12,000-foot cloud tops until 15.03, when he called for release-point flares. Blue smoke-puff skymarkers went down accurately and in concentration, and the main force crews were instructed to aim for the centre of these, those from 408 (Goose) Squadron complying and delivering their loads from 17,500 to 19,000 feet between 15.14 and 15.17. On return, they were unable to provide an assessment of the results and there was no post-raid reconnaissance or local report to provide clarity, but it is known that many bombs fell on neighbouring Ludwigshafen and its surrounds, where much damage occurred.

With Cologne now almost on the front line, it too was earmarked for its final attack of the war on the morning of the 2nd, for a which a two-phase operation was planned, the first by 703 aircraft from 1, 4, 6 and 8 Groups, and the second a G-H attack by 155 Lancasters of 3 Group. 6 Group contributed ninety-eight Halifaxes and eighty-four Lancasters, fifteen of the former belonging to 408 (Goose) Squadron and departing Linton-on-Ouse between 06.52 and 07.35 with W/C Evans notching up yet one more sortie and sixteen 500-pounders in each bomb bay. After climbing out, they pointed their snouts towards Beachy Head to take their place in the elongated bomber stream before beginning the Channel crossing. All reached the target to find near perfect bombing conditions with a little cloud with tops at around 6,000 feet, and a Master Bomber on hand to tell them where to bomb, although the city's landmarks, the cathedral and nearby main railway station, stood out in the sunshine almost inviting the bombs to fall. The 408 (Goose) Squadron crews delivered their attacks either visually or guided by blue and red smoke-puff TIs from 15,000 to 19,000 feet between 10.04 and 10.15, and many, for a change, were able to see the fall of their bombs. It wasn't long before a mushroom of black smoke began to conceal the ground, and those arriving later were instructed to bomb the up-wind edge of that. The main concentration of bombing was on the western side of the Rhine, and the western end of the Hohenzollern railway bridge appeared to have been demolished and had collapsed into the Rhine. Nine aircraft failed to return home, and this figure included the 408 (Goose) Squadron's RG472, which was hit by flak as it left the target, and two of the all-RCAF crew were killed at their stations. P/O Sproule RCAF and four others baled out shortly before their aircraft exploded south-east of Bonn, and all survived to fall into enemy hands. They were in the early stages of their first tour and would have been regarded still as a freshman crew. The second wave by 3 Group was ruined by the failure of a G-H station in England and had to be halted after only fifteen aircraft had bombed. It mattered little, as the once proud city fell to American forces four days later.

The Luftwaffe mounted Operation Gisella on this night, sending some two hundred intruders to catch the bombers as they prepared to land from the night's operational and training activities, and succeeded in shooting down twenty for the loss of three of their own.

Preparations for Operation Thunderclap to return to Chemnitz were put in hand on the 5th, and a force of 760 aircraft assembled from all but 5 Group, which itself would be active some thirty-five miles to the north, attacking the oil refinery at Böhlen. 6 Group made ready 101 Halifaxes and eighty-four Lancasters, sixteen of the former representing 408 (Goose) Squadron and departing Linton-on-Ouse between 16.38 and 17.25 with W/C Sharp the senior pilot on duty. Those taking off from the northerly stations of 6 Group climbed into ten-tenths cloud with severe icing conditions, which caused seven from Linton-on-Ouse and Tholthorpe to crash, while the 408 (Goose) Squadron element avoided the difficulties, and all would reach the target and return. Aside from a slight reduction over the Channel and northern France, the complete cloud cover remained in place all the way to the target area, on the way to which some ran into predicted flak around Leipzig, which had probably been stirred-up by the above-mentioned 5 Group operation. The target area was concealed beneath ten-tenths cloud with tops at up to 13,000 feet, and crews had to listened out for the Master Bomber's instructions as they lined up for the bombing-run. They observed cascading red and green skymarkers and were told at 21.50 to bomb them with a twelve-second overshoot. When the skymarkers went out at 21.55, crews were ordered to bomb the glow in the clouds, before further skymarkers appeared and the original order was repeated. The 408 (Goose) Squadron crews carried out their attacks from 15,000 to 17,500 feet between 21.44 and 22.06, but were unable to assess the outcome, reporting only a bright glow beneath the clouds that seemed to cover an area a mile wide. They turned south towards the Czechoslovakian frontier for the homeward flight across southern Germany, where some were pestered by enemy night-fighters, which were probably largely responsible for the failure to return of fourteen Lancasters and eight Halifaxes. It was established eventually that the operation had been a major success, which had destroyed by fire much of the central and southern districts of the city. It also resulted in damage to some important war-industry factories and the destruction of the Siegmar tank-engine works.

The main operation on the 7th was to be an all-Lancaster affair against the virgin target of Dessau, a city in eastern Germany between Berlin to the north-east and Leipzig to the south, for which 6 Group contributed eighty-two aircraft to an overall force of 526 drawn from 1, 3, 6 and 8 Groups. While this was in progress, 256 Halifaxes and twenty-five Lancasters of 4, 6 and 8 Groups were to target the Deutsche Erdöl oil refinery at Hemmingstedt on the western side of Schleswig-Holstein, while 5 Group went for a similar target at Harburg on the south side of the River Elbe opposite Hamburg. 6 Group detailed a hundred Halifaxes for the oil plant, of which fifteen were made ready by 408 (Goose) Squadron, each receiving a bomb load of twelve 500-pounders before departing Linton-on-Ouse between 18.27 and 18.50 with W/C Sharp and S/L Smith the senior pilots on duty. There had been no early returns by the time they reached the target area to be greeted by clear skies and ideal bombing conditions, and began their bombing runs at medium level to give themselves the best chance of achieving accuracy. The target was identified in the light of illuminator flares, which for some reason made the green and yellow TIs difficult to distinguish and the reds appeared only later. The Master Bomber's transmissions were jammed intermittently, but most picked up enough to comply with instructions to bomb on the greens and to port of the yellows, the 408 (Goose) Squadron element carrying out their attacks from 8,000 to 12,000 feet between 21.59 and 22.09. The attack seemed to be concentrated on the green TIs, and the crews returned home confident of a successful outcome, which in their minds was confirmed by two large red explosions and a pall of black smoke rising through 4,000 feet. Unaccountably, as it was revealed later, the attack had missed the target by two to three miles, but at least the other two operations did achieve their aims. Five aircraft failed to return, four Halifaxes and the 35 (Madras Presidency) Squadron Lancaster of the Master Bomber, the legendary S/L Danny Everett DFC and two Bars, who was reputedly on his ninety-eighth sortie. 408 (Goose) Squadron posted missing the all-RCAF crew of P/O Daughters in NP718, which was brought down during the bombing run by a combination of flak and a night-fighter, with fatal consequences for the pilot and three of his crew, while the three survivors fell into enemy hands.

The pace of operations refused to slacken, and what, perhaps, should have been a wind-down towards the German capitulation, became one of the most intense operational periods in the entire war. With four major operations already behind it during the first week of the month, the second week began for 6 Group with orders on the 8th to contribute eighty-five Halifaxes from 62 Base to join forces with 156 from 4 Group for an attack on the Blohm & Voss U-Boot yards in Hamburg, where the new Type XXI vessels were under construction. While this operation was in progress, 5 Group would be conducting the last major raid of the war on the already-devastated city of Kassel some 150 miles to the south. The twelve participating 408 (Goose) Squadron Halifaxes each received a bomb load of sixteen 500-pounders and departed Linton-on-Ouse between 18.05 and 18.27 with S/L Smith the senior pilot on duty. They all reached the target area to find up to nine-tenths thin, drifting low cloud with tops at 6,000 to 8,000 feet, which eventually concealed the green TIs and forced the Path Finders to dispense red and green skymarkers as an alternative. The Master Bomber directed the bombing towards the middle of three skymarkers and those from 408 (Goose) Squadron complied from 15,000 to 20,000 feet between 21.30 and 21.41, observing two very large explosions at 21.33 and 21.36, and another a minute later that lit up the area for five or six seconds. Returning crews were optimistic that the operation had been successful, but no post-raid reconnaissance took place and local reports were sparse.

An all-time record was set on the 11th, when 1,079 aircraft, the largest Bomber Command force ever to be sent to a single target, was assembled to attack Essen for the last time. 6 Group was boosted by the return to the front line of 427 (Lion) Squadron, the latest to have converted to Lancasters, leaving 62 Base as the only one fully equipped with Halifaxes, and for the first time, 6 Group Lancasters were more numerous than Halifaxes in a 102/94 split. The 408 (Goose) Squadron element of fifteen Halifaxes departed Linton-on-Ouse between 11.18 and 11.47 with W/C Sharp and S/L Norris the senior pilots on duty and sixteen 500-pounders in each bomb bay. All arrived in the central Ruhr to find the target covered by ten-tenths cloud with tops at 6,000 feet, which required the Path Finder element to employ skymarkers in the form of blue, and later red smoke puffs, and the first of these went down at 14.59, to be backed up throughout the course of the raid. The 408 (Goose) Squadron crews attacked from 12,000 to 19,000 feet between 15.11 and 15.20, contributing to the 835 tons of high explosives delivered by 6 Group in an overall weight of more than 4,600 tons dropped into the already ravaged city and former industrial powerhouse. Smoke and dust were emerging through the cloud tops in a tight spiral that had reached 10,000 feet as the last of the bombers retreated and the city would still be in a state of paralysis when the American ground forces captured it unopposed on the 10th of April.

A little over twenty-four hours later, the short-lived record was surpassed when 1,108 aircraft departed their stations in the early afternoon bound for Dortmund, 6 Group putting up ninety-nine Lancasters and ninety-three Halifaxes, fifteen of the latter representing 408 (Goose) Squadron. They each received a bomb load of sixteen 500-pounders, before taking to the air between 12.46 and 13.30 with S/Ls Norris and Smith the senior pilots on duty and arrived over the Ruhr to find it still under a blanket of ten-tenths cloud with tops at 6,000 feet, conditions for which the Path Finders had prepared a skymarking plan based on green and blue smoke puffs. The first Oboe-aimed greens appeared at 16.26 to be followed a minute later by blues from the blind primary markers, and the Master Bomber directed the main force crews to aim for the blues. It was not long before brown smoke was observed to be climbing through the clouds to 8,000 feet from the northern end of the city, and crews also reported a ring of smoke encircling the entire area so dense, that it remained visible for 120 miles into the return flight. The returning 408 (Goose) Squadron crews reported carrying out their attacks from 16,700 to 18,000 feet between 16.45 and 16.51, and in so-doing had contributed to the delivery of a new record of 4,800 tons of bombs, 830 of them by 6 Group. Photo-reconnaissance revealed that the central and southern districts of the city had received the greatest weight and had been left in chaos with all industry silenced permanently and railway tracks torn up.

Despite having been almost totally destroyed in May 1943, the Barmen half of Wuppertal, situated on the southern rim of the Ruhr, was posted on the 13th as the target for a daylight attack by 354 aircraft, which included 310 Halifaxes of 4 and 6 Groups with Lancasters and Mosquitos of 8 Group to provide the marking. 6 Group mobilised 62 Base to prepare a hundred Halifaxes, of which fifteen belonged to 408 (Goose) Squadron and departed Linton-on-Ouse between 12.26 and 12.51 with W/C Evans notching up another sortie a month ahead of his appointment as commanding officer of 429 (Bison) Squadron. There were no early returns, and all reached the target area to find seven to ten-tenths cloud in two layers with tops at between 4,000 and 12,000 feet. Positions were established by means of navigational aids before bombing took place on red and blue smoke-puff skymarkers in accordance with instructions from the Master Bomber. The 408 (Goose) Squadron crews delivered their 2,000-pounder and clusters bombs each from 18,000 to 20,000 feet between 16.04 and 16.10, and some crews reported a large red fire through gaps in the cloud, while others commented on the flash of high-explosive bomb bursts and dark-brown smoke merging with the cloud tops as they turned away. Post-raid reconnaissance revealed another devastating assault, which had hit the eastern half of the town and its surrounds and left 562 fatalities in its wake. The series of three daylight raids in three days on the Ruhr had involved 2,541 sorties, which delivered 10,650 tons of bombs, 2,014 by 6 Group, at a cost to the Command of just five aircraft.

General Patch's 7th US Army was pushing eastwards in a wide swathe between Strasbourg in the south and Koblenz in the north, and Bomber Command was tasked with bombing the towns of Zweibrücken and Homburg, some five miles apart, to help clear the path. *(There are a number of Homburgs and Hombergs in Germany, and this one should not be confused with the Moers-Homberg location near Duisburg, which was home to the frequently attacked synthetic oil refinery)*. 6 Group put up 196 aircraft to act as the main force for the former, divided equally between the two types, and 408 (Goose) Squadron's contribution amounted to fourteen Halifaxes, which each received a bomb load of fourteen 500-pounders before departing Linton-on-Ouse between 16.28 and 16.57 with S/Ls Saunders and Smith the senior pilots on duty. They reached the target area to the east of Saarbrücken to find clear skies but considerable haze and established their positions initially by means of H2S and Gee before focussing on red and green TIs in the light of illuminator flares and bombing by all but one of the 408 (Goose) Squadron element took place in accordance with the Master Bomber's instructions from 11,900 14,000 feet between 20.16 and 20.22. One crew, captained by a pilot of warrant officer rank, whose identity cannot be deciphered, could not pick out the markers and retained their bombs. The attack seemed to be concentrated in the built-up area and large explosions were observed at 20.37 and 20.41, before smoke obscured the ground to prevent further assessment. It was established later that the operation had been highly effective and had destroyed every public building and flattened or damaged 80% of the town's houses.

Benzol plants at Bottrop and Castrop-Rauxel in the Ruhr would occupy elements of 4, 6 and 8 Groups on the 15th, 6 Group detailing seventy Halifaxes for the latter, sixty from 62 Base and ten from 63 Base's 429 (Bison) Squadron, which was in the process of converting to Lancasters. 408 (Goose) Squadron's ten representatives were loaded with sixteen 500-pounders each and sent on their way from Linton-on-Ouse between 12.38 and 12.58 with S/L Saunders the senior pilot on duty. They all arrived in the target area to find no cloud but some ground haze and confirmed their positions by Gee before complying with the clear instructions from the Master Bomber and aiming at the red TIs from 17,200 to 19,000 feet between 16.00 and 16.04. Fires took hold rapidly the smoke from which intermittently obscured the TIs, and a particularly large reddish-orange explosion at 16.03 threw up a dense cloud of smoke to 14,000 feet and beyond that remained visible from 120 miles away.

While the above was in progress preparations were in hand to make ready a 4, 6 and 8 Group force of 267 Lancasters, Halifaxes and Mosquitos for an area raid on the town of Hagen, situated on the south-eastern corner of the Ruhr some eight miles south of Dortmund. 6 Group provided ninety-nine Lancasters and forty-three Halifaxes, eight of the latter belonging to 408 (Goose) Squadron and each loaded with a 2,000-pounder and cluster bombs. They had been informed at briefing of the need to disrupt railway communications to prevent the movement of troops to meet Montgomery's advance and departed Linton-on-Ouse with that thought in mind between 16.47 and 16.59 with F/Ls Finch, Heaven and Pitu the senior pilots on duty. They were greeted at the target by clear skies and industrial haze and positions were confirmed by navigational aids, while the aiming-point was illuminated with flares, before bombing took place on red and green TIs, by the 408 (Goose) Squadron element from 17,200 to 19,000 feet between 20.31 and 20.34. Fires were observed to gain hold, creating a glow on the horizon that could be seen from a hundred miles into the return flight, and such was the level of destruction in central and eastern districts, which had been ravaged by more than fourteen hundred fires, that local reports estimated eight hundred aircraft to have been involved. It was a relatively expensive night for 6 Group, which posted missing four Lancasters and a Halifax and lost two further Lancasters and a Halifax to crashes at home.

A simultaneous operation by 257 Lancasters and eight Mosquitos of 1 and 8 Groups was mounted against the Deurag-Nerag oil refinery at Misburg, on the north-eastern rim of Hannover. Except for the Channel crossing both ways, the operation benefitted from cloudless skies, and this enabled crews to identify the target visually by the light of illuminator flares. Returning crews reported a highly successful operation, characterised by many explosions and fires visible from a hundred miles into the return journey, and there was particular praise from the main force crews for the Master Bomber and the Path Finder element generally. Local sources did not confirm the success of the raid and claimed that the main weight of bombs had fallen to the south of the target. Nuremberg and Würzburg were targeted by 1 and 8 Groups and 5 Group respectively on the night of the 16/17th, when the successful assault on Nuremberg was marred by the loss of twenty-four 1 Group Lancasters, mostly to night-fighters, demonstrating that the Luftwaffe could, occasionally, still make its presence felt, despite a lack of fuel and experienced pilots. At Würzburg, a seventeen-minute orgy of destruction caused the deaths of an estimated 5,000 people.

The town of Witten is situated at the eastern end of the Ruhr and was the home, among other contributors to Germany's war effort, to the Ruhrstahl steelworks and a factory belonging to the Mannesmann company manufacturing steel pipework. Both relied heavily on forced workers, particularly, it is believed, those from France and Ukraine housed in the nearby camp in the Schalke district of Gelsenkirchen. On the 18th, 6 Group detailed eighty-four Halifaxes and 4 Group 176 to act as the main force, while 8 Group provided forty-five Lancasters and eighteen Mosquitos to take care of the illumination and marking. It was already the 19th by the time the fourteen-strong 408 (Goose) Squadron element began to depart Linton-on-Ouse at 00.15 with the long-serving F/L Sokoloff among the senior pilots on duty and a 2,000-pounder supplemented by cluster bombs in each bomb bay. They headed for the south coast to cross the Channel and approach the target area over liberated territory, finding clear skies and the Oboe Mosquito-laid red TIs right on the aiming-point and backed up throughout by further reds and greens from the heavy marker aircraft. The 408 (Goose) Squadron crews delivered their attacks from 14,000 to 16,000 feet between 04.13 and 04.20 and observed fires taking hold as they retreated. A post-raid analysis revealed that the 1,081 tons of bombs had destroyed 129 acres, or 62% of the built-up area, and that the two factories mentioned above had sustained heavy damage.

Two oil refineries were posted for attention on the 20, a 5 Group force of 224 Lancasters and eleven Mosquitos assigned to Böhlen near Leipzig, while 166 Lancasters of 1, 6 and 8 Groups targeted the Erdöl AG refinery at Hemmingstedt, which appears in the 6 Group ORB as Heide. 6 Group's 110 Lancasters attacked in ideal conditions and contributed 513 tons of high explosives to assist in putting the plant out of action for the remainder of the war.

62 Base stations were a hive of activity on the 21st as preparations were put in hand for an evening attack on marshalling yards in the town of Rheine, located west of Osnabrück some fifteen miles from the Dutch frontier. A main force of 150 Halifaxes contained ninety representing 6 Group, fifteen of them from 408 (Goose) Squadron, each of which was loaded with ten 500 and six 250-pounders before departing Linton-on-Ouse between 14.27 and 14.58 with W/C Evans guesting as the senior pilot on duty. They all arrived in the target area to find clear skies and good vertical

visibility which enabled crews to identify the target visually by the river, the shape of the built-up area and the marshalling yards. The Master Bomber was heard clearly throughout the raid and called for bomb-aimers to aim for yellow TIs, all but one of the 408 (Goose) Squadron participants complying from 10,200 to 11,500 feet between 17.30 and 17.36 and observing explosions that sent smoke rising through 3,000 feet as they turned for home. One crew, whose identity is undecipherable, was confused by the TIs and is believed to have bombed the town of Ahaus, twenty miles to the south-west of the target.

The main operation during the afternoon of the 22nd involved elements of 1, 6 and 8 Groups targeting railway yards in Hildesheim, situated some fifteen miles south-east of Hannover, in what was the first and only Bomber Command attack on it of the war. 6 Group contributed eighty-eight Lancasters to the overall force of 227 aircraft, which left the town area 70% destroyed, with the cathedral and most of the historic buildings erased and more than sixteen hundred people killed. While this operation was in progress, further south on the northern approaches to the Ruhr, the towns of Dorsten, Bocholt and Dülmen were coming under attack, the first mentioned by a main force of a hundred 6 Group Halifaxes, seventeen of them belonging to 408 (Goose) Squadron. The Geese had taken off from Linton-on-Ouse between 11.25 and 12.02 with F/Ls Finch, Pitu and Sokoloff the senior pilots on duty, each undertaking the final sortie of their first tour. They were each sitting on sixteen 500-pounders destined to be dropped on railway and canal installations and a Luftwaffe fuel dump, which on their arrival they found were marked out by yellow TIs. The first stages of the bombing soon created fires and smoke to obscure the markers, at which point the Master Bomber called for the bombing to be directed at the smoke or to be delivered on Gee and H2S. The 408 (Goose) Squadron crews complied from 16,000 to 18,000 feet between 14.32 and 14.36 and the smoke had risen to 8,000 feet by the time the force retreated to the west, remaining visible for forty miles. Celebrations attended the safe return of the now tour-expired crews, and it was the first time that three crews had been screened on the same day.

The final phase of the ground war began on the 24th with the crossing of the Rhine near Wesel and the landing of airborne troops. Bomber Command focused on the enemy's oil industry and communications on this day, sending forces of moderate size to the Ruhr locations of Gladbeck, Dortmund, Bottrop and Sterkrade. It was for the first-mentioned that 6 Group made ready a hundred Halifaxes, sixteen of them representing 408 (Goose) Squadron, which each received a bomb load of sixteen 500-pounders before departing Linton-on-Ouse between 09.02 and 09.34 with S/L Saunders the senior pilot on duty. They were part of a main force of 153 Halifaxes in company with 4 Group, while the 6 Group Lancaster element of seventy-five aircraft targeted the Mathias Stinnes benzol plant at nearby Bottrop. Conditions in the target area were favourable and the railway lines and autobahns leading into Gladbeck stood out clearly on approach. The town was to be levelled to prevent its use by retreating German forces as some of the fiercest fighting of the war took place, and red and green TIs marked out the aiming point until they were obscured by smoke, which became the new aiming point. The 408 (Goose) Squadron crews bombed from 16,200 to 18,500 feet between 13.01 and 13.04 in accordance with the instructions of the Master Bomber and contributed to the 340 tons of high explosives delivered by 6 Group that helped to leave the town in a state of devastation.

Operations on the 25th were directed at urban areas through which enemy reinforcements might pass on their way to the Rhine battle area. 4 Group detailed 131 Halifaxes to act as the main-force for an attack on the marshalling yards at Osnabrück in the Münsterland region of Germany north of the Ruhr, while 151 Halifaxes from 4 and 6 Groups were made ready for Münster, some thirty miles to the south-west, and 251 Lancasters of 1 and 6 Groups for Hannover seventy miles to the east. 8 Group would support all three undertakings, with fourteen Lancasters and ten Mosquitos at both Osnabrück and Münster and sixteen Lancasters and eight Mosquitos at Hannover. 6 Group prepared a hundred Lancasters for Hannover and ninety-nine Halifaxes for Münster, 408 (Goose) Squadron loading sixteen of its own with a 2,000-pounder each and cluster bombs before departing Linton-on-Ouse between 06.55 and 07.33 with W/C Sharp and S/L Saunders the senior pilots on duty. The gaggle was led by Tholthorpe's 420 (Snowy Owl) and 425 (Allouette) Squadrons and as a result of a heavy shift in the wind and partial failure of the leading aircrafts' navigational equipment it became spread out in length and width, which would prevent it from achieving the hoped for concentration. An additional problem was the dropping of a cluster of TIs some 3,600 yards from the aiming point at 10.16, which created confusion and attracted some bomb loads. The 408 (Goose) Squadron crews mostly delivered their attacks before that, from 17,000 to 19,000 feet between 10.06 and 10.18 and contributed to 6 Group's 826 tons of high explosives. Among three missing Halifaxes was 408 (Goose) Squadron's NP804, which was hit by flak during the bombing run and exploded some six miles south-south-west of the target, killing F/O Burrows RCAF and all but his rear gunner, who was taken into captivity. They were a freshman crew on just their fifth sortie together and all but the flight engineer were members of the RCAF.

The focus remained on this part of Germany on the 27th, as the encirclement of the Ruhr by American ground forces required just the capture of the town of Paderborn, situated some thirty-five miles due east of Hamm. An operation against it by 1 and 8 Groups was an outstanding success, confirmed by a local report, which stated that three thousand separate fires had occurred, and that the town had been virtually destroyed.

The final operation of the hugely busy penultimate month of offensive activity by the Command was to end with a 1, 6 and 8 Group raid on the Blohm & Voss U-Boot yards in the Finkenwerder district of Hamburg, where the new Type XXI vessels were being assembled. A force of 361 Lancasters and a hundred Halifaxes was made ready on the 31st, all of the latter provided by 6 Group along with an equal number of Lancasters, including the first belonging to the newly converted 429 (Bison) Squadron. The 408 (Goose) Squadron element of sixteen Halifaxes were each loaded with sixteen 500-pounders before being sent on their way from Linton-on-Ouse between 05.53 and 06.26 with S/Ls Saunders and Smith the senior pilots on duty. They climbed out through layer cloud with an intention to rendezvous with the rest of the group and form into a gaggle behind the 1 Group line-astern column. The cloud prevented this, and the force was closing on the Dutch coast at 3°East, when the cloud broke up sufficiently to allow the forming up to take place, only for it to build again from 6°East and remain at ten-tenths for the remainder of the flight to the target. When the leading aircraft of the main force were fifteen minutes out, the Master Bomber warned them to look for smoke-puff markers, and the first of these appeared at 08.43, but only in small numbers. It was a further three minutes before they became plentiful, by which time the bombing was well underway in accordance with the frequent instructions and changing aiming points coming through from the Master Bomber. It caused a degree of jostling for position over the target, but the 408 (Goose) Squadron crews found red smoke puff markers to bomb from 17,600 to 19,000 feet between 08.52 and 09.04. Most returning crews sensed that the raid had lacked a degree of concentration, but local reports spoke of widespread damage in residential and industrial areas in the south of the city and across the Elbe in Harburg, with energy supplies and communications also hard-hit.

The Luftwaffe Tagjagd intervened, and eleven aircraft were shot down, the last occasion on which the Command's losses reached double figures from a single city target. The squadron's NP806 was one of the three missing Halifaxes and fell victim to a ME262 jet fighter to crash at 08.50 nine miles south-east of the city centre. The all-RCAF crew of F/O Blyth were on their seventeenth sortie together and all survived to fall into enemy hands.

During the course of the month the squadron took part in seventeen operations, which generated 241 sorties for the loss of four Halifaxes and crews.

April 1945

The final month of the bombing war would not be particularly kind to the squadron, and would, in fact, bring four more missing aircraft and crews. On the 1st, W/C Sharp was notified that he was to receive an immediate award of the DFC, and he took some convincing that it was genuine and not an April Fool's joke. There would be a staggered start to the month for the groups, with 1 and 8 Groups first into the fray on the 3rd to target what was believed to be be a military barracks at Nordhausen, situated in the Harz Mountains between Hannover to the north-west and Leipzig to the south-east. The site was actually a pair of enormous parallel tunnels under the Kohnstein Hill, which had been developed originally by the BASF Company to mine gypsum between 1917 and 1934. Following the destruction of Peenemünde, smaller tunnels had been created as a link between them to form a horizontal ladder effect, and the site turned over to the Mittelwerk GmbH (Gesellschaft mit beschrenkter Haftung, or Limited Company) for the manufacture of V-2 rockets and other secret projects. The "barracks" were part of the Mittelwerk-Dora forced workers camp, where inmates existed under the most horrendous conditions and brutal treatment, while they were starved, worked to death or simply executed by an increasingly desperate regime seeking to change the course of the war. The operation was moderately successful and was followed up by 5 Group on the following day, when the town was also targeted.

By the time that 4 Group crews attended briefings on the 4th, they had been off the order of battle for nine days and were fully rested and replenished, while the 6 Group crews had only enjoyed a break of three days, which was perfectly acceptable to them as most aircrew loathed long layoffs. That night brought a return to the oil offensive at three sites, Leuna and Lützkendorf near Leipzig and the Rhenania plant at Harburg on the South Bank of the Elbe opposite Hamburg. *(Lützkendorf no longer exists on a map of Germany and is now known as either Mücheln or Krumpa).* 6 Group contributed 105 Lancasters to Leuna and ninety Halifaxes to the 277-strong 4 and 6 Group main force bound for Harburg, fifteen of them belonging to 408 (Goose) Squadron, which departed Linton-on-Ouse between 19.24 and 19.52 with S/L Smith the senior pilot on duty and each carrying sixteen 500-pounders. It is believed that all reached the target area, where clear skies prevailed and illuminator flares helped the identification of the aiming-point, which the Path Finders marked accurately and backed up until thick smoke obscured it from view. The Master Bomber instructed crews to bomb initially on mixed red and green TIs, then to port of the greens, and finally on the developing fires, and the 408 (Goose) Squadron crews complied from 16,900 to 19,000 feet between 22.29 and 22.35. Returning crews reported many fires and a number of large, red explosions, one particularly violent one at 22.32, which was followed by a vivid orange light and black smoke rising through 8,000 feet as they turned away. The operation cost two Path Finder Lancasters and Halifax NP712 of 408 (Goose) Squadron, from which the predominantly RCAF crew of P/O Brown escaped with their lives to fall into enemy hands. Post-raid reconnaissance confirmed that extensive damage had been inflicted on the plant.

At briefings on the 8th, it was announced that the length of a tour for a main force crew had been reduced from thirty-six to thirty-three sorties, and those with that number already under their belt, would no doubt be celebrating in the local watering holes as the following events were enacted. A force of 440 aircraft from 4, 6 and 8 Groups was assembled for a return to Hamburg that night to target again the Blohm & Voss U-Boot construction yards and naval installations and would follow on the heels of an attack just a few hours earlier by the American 8th Air Force. 6 Group contributed a hundred Lancasters and ninety Halifaxes, fifteen belonging to 408 (Goose) Squadron, which departed Linton-on-Ouse between 19.08 and 19.39 with S/L Smith the senior pilot on duty and sixteen 500-pounders beneath the feet of each crew. The various elements joined up to form the bomber stream as they traversed the North Sea on course for Schleswig-Holstein's western coast, intending to approach the target from the north. The Oboe Mosquitos delivered red TIs at 22.24, which were seen to cascade and fall through the ten-tenths, very thin 2,000 to 3,000-foot cloud tops and leave a red glow. Through a small gap in the cloud, the Master Bomber caught a momentary glimpse of red TIs on the ground and having assessed them as being on the aiming-point, ordered them to be backed up with greens before issuing instructions to the main force crews to aim for them. When these were no longer visible from 22.34, he called for skymarkers and redirected the main force accordingly. The 408 (Goose) Squadron crews complied from 16,900 to 19,000 feet between 22.32 and 22.40 and observed large explosions at 22.34 and 22.38, but not all were convinced of the effectiveness of the raid, which had suffered from a degree of undershooting. Absent from debriefing was the freshman, predominantly RCAF crew of F/O Jensen RCAF, all but one of whom had lost their lives when NP769 crashed at 22.30 near Tostedt, between Hamburg and Bremen, while homebound. Only the mid-upper gunner survived to fall into enemy hands on what had been the crew's maiden sortie together. Post-raid reconnaissance was unable to attribute damage specifically to either the RAF or American attacks, and it is likely that the principal objectives, the shipyards, escaped, while the residential district of Altona on the northern bank sustained severe damage during what was the final heavy raid of the war on Germany's second city.

W/C Evans finally took up his appointment as commanding officer of 429 (Bison) Squadron on the 9th, by which time he could claim to be a moderately experienced bomber pilot following his frequent guest appearances at Linton-on-Ouse. On the morning of the 10th, 110 Lancaster and ninety Halifax crews filed into briefing rooms on all bases to learn of their part in the tea-time attacks on marshalling yards at two locations in the Leipzig area. The Lancaster crews were assigned to Engelsdorf, located on the eastern outskirts of the city, while the target for the Halifax crews was at Mockau in the northern suburbs. Each of 408 (Goose) Squadron's seventeen Halifaxes received a bomb load of twelve 500-pounders before departing Linton-on-Ouse between 13.25 and 14.12 with W/C Sharp the senior pilot on duty and crossed the North Sea in a gaggle to make landfall to the south of Amsterdam and skirt the northern rim of the Ruhr. It was when passing north of Dortmund that F/L Godfrey and crew turned back after falling behind schedule and failing to locate the gaggle and were perhaps lucky to remain unmolested as they flew back over enemy territory in broad daylight. The others pressed on to find the target under clear skies with excellent visibility that enabled the bomb-aimers to pick out ground features, particularly the railway track and a wooded area. They bombed either visually or on yellow TIs in accordance with the instructions of the Master Bomber, those from 408 (Goose) Squadron from 16,200 to 18,200 feet between 17.59 and 18.01, and the impression was of an accurate and concentrated attack, which sent dust and smoke rising through 5,000 feet. The Lancaster attack five miles away at Englesdorf was equally effective and the 6 Group crews between them delivered a total of 670 tons of high explosives for the loss of one Lancaster and one Halifax.

The target for a 3, 6 and 8 Group force of 377 Lancasters and 105 Halifaxes on the 13th was Kiel, for which 6 Group provided all of the Halifaxes and an equal number of Lancasters, while 3 Group was responsible for 199 Lancasters. The seventeen-strong 408 (Goose) Squadron element departed Linton-on-Ouse between 19.57 and 20.42 with S/L Saunders the senior pilot on duty and sixteen 500-pounders in each bomb bay and rendezvoused with the rest of the group to form a gaggle as they traversed the North Sea to make landfall on the western coast of Schleswig-Holstein. They reached the target to find ten-tenths thin stratus cloud with tops up to 5,000 feet, and Path Finder ground marking in progress. A Master Bomber was on hand to control the bombing, and the 408 (Goose) Squadron crews complied with his instructions to deliver their bomb loads from 12,100 to 17,000 feet between 23.28 and 23.36, observing the glow of fires and two large explosions, one of them resulting from a hit on an ammunition dump at the northern end of the harbour district. Generally, however, the bombing was scattered, and focused largely on the suburb of Elmschenhagen, two miles from the harbour.

The final major attack on a German city was directed at Potsdam on the night of the 14/15th, and this would be the first incursion into the Berlin defence zone by RAF heavy bombers since March 1944. In the twelve months since then, Mosquitos of 8 Group's Light Night Striking Force (LNSF) had maintained a regular presence over the city, acting as a constant menace, dropping cookies to unsettle the populace and robbing the workers of their sleep. So fast was the "Wooden Wonder", that it was not unknown for a single aircraft to make two trips to Berlin in one night after a change of crew. The raid by five hundred Lancasters of 1, 3 and 8 Groups with Mosquito support was confirmed as a success, but some bomb loads were found to have spilled into northern and western districts of Berlin.

On the 16th, ten crews each from 408 (Goose) and 426 (Thunderbird) Squadrons were called to briefing at Linton-on-Ouse to learn that they were to attack a target at Gablingen, situated north-north-west of the city of Augsburg deep in the Bavarian countryside in southern Germany. The target was ostensibly a Luftwaffe aerodrome but was believed to be concealing a network of tunnels in which Messerschmitt had established a test facility and manufacturing plant employing slave labour from the nearby Dachau concentration camp. Four Path Finder Mosquitos were to provide the marking, while 100 Group Mosquitos conducted diversionary sorties, and a raid on marshalling yards at Schwandorf by 120 Lancasters of 6 Group some eighty miles to the north-east and another by 5 Group against marshalling yards at Pilsen would offer a further distraction for the defenders. The 408 (Goose) Squadron Halifaxes each received a bomb load of a dozen 500-pounders, before taking off between 23.21 and 23.50 with S/L Saunders the senior pilot on duty. F/L Hutcheon and crew turned back from a position fifty miles out from the Humber after losing their port-inner engine, leaving the others to continue the long outward leg that would take them over central Holland to skirt the Ruhr's eastern end before heading south to the target. They arrived under clear skies and in good visibility and identified the aiming point by green flares and concentrated red TIs, confirming their positions first by H2S. They carried out their attacks from 16,500 to 18,000 feet between 03.38 and 03.47 and contributed to forty-five tons of high explosives, the effects of which could not be assessed.

There was good news for some main force crews to celebrate on the 17th, when the length of a tour was reduced yet again to thirty sorties, releasing many to contemplate a long future. Early briefings across the Command on the 18th informed 969 crews of an assault on the coastal batteries, naval base, airfield and town on the island of Heligoland, for which 6 Group detailed 112 Halifaxes, seventeen of them representing 408 (Goose) Squadron. Each received a bomb load of nine 1,000 and four 500-pounders and departed Linton-on-Ouse between 09.47 and 10.22 with S/L Saunders and the newly promoted S/L Bossenberry the senior pilots on duty. They flew out to the target under clear skies and in good visibility, Heligoland and its smaller neighbour, Düne, appearing as two tiny dots some thirty miles off Germany's north-western coast. Three aiming-points awaited the bombers, A, B and C, and the 6 Group elements appear to have been divided between the early waves to attack aiming point A, where proceedings opened at 12.29 with red Oboe TIs backed up by the Master Bomber with yellows. The 408 (Goose) Squadron crews attacked from 17,000 to 19,000 feet between 12.29 and 12.32 and by the end of this phase of the operation, thick smoke was beginning to obscure the ground. 408 (Goose) Squadron's NP776 failed to return with the predominantly RCAF crew of F/L Cull RCAF after crashing into the sea, and only the remains of the pilot and his bomb-aimer were eventually recovered for burial. They had been on their seventh sortie together.

As the second wave approached, smoke had spread across the south-eastern corner, but the aiming-point B remained visible for long enough to be identified, and the 4 Group wave five went in while wave six orbited awaiting instructions. The crews involved in the later phases of the operation returned home to report a large column of smoke rising steadily from the south-eastern end of the island, which hid from view what photographs would reveal later to be a surface that resembled a cratered moonscape. Heligoland's ordeal was not yet over, as on the following day, it would face an attack by 617 and 9 Squadrons, the former carrying 10-ton Grand Slams and 6-ton Tallboys and the latter Tallboys. If not already totally evacuated, the island certainly was after this operation.

On the 19th 408 (Goose) Squadron was presented with the Handley Page Trophy for achieving the lowest accident rate in 6 Group for the month of March.

As the British XXX Corps moved in on the city of Bremen, Bomber Command was asked on the 22nd to attack enemy strong points in the south-eastern suburbs, where the attack was due to take place in two days' time. A main force of 691 aircraft was drawn from 1, 3 and 6 Groups, 6 Group contributing a hundred Lancasters and a hundred Halifaxes, seventeen of the latter belonging to 408 (Goose) Squadron, which loaded each with sixteen 500-pounders. They departed Linton-on-Ouse between 16.00 and 16.35 with W/C Sharp and S/L Saunders the senior pilots on duty, and on arrival at the target were confronted by cloud and could only catch a glimpse of the ground through gaps. The Path Finder visual marker crews were unable to identify the aiming-points, and the attacks on three of them were called off, which resulted in the entire 1 and 6 Group elements returning home with their bombs. 195 aircraft bombed at aiming-point F, before that, too, was abandoned.

The final operations of the bombing war were carried out on the 25th, beginning with what was, perhaps, a symbolic attack by a main force of 335 Lancasters of 1 and 5 Groups and twenty-four Lancasters and eight Mosquitos of 8 Group on Hitler's Eaglesnest retreat and the nearby SS barracks at Berchtesgaden in the Bavarian mountains. It required an early start, from around 05.00, and the vanguard of the bomber stream arrived in the target area on time to find that all was not proceeding according to plan. The deputy Master Bomber had been unable to mark the target, and, realising this, the leader of the first wave overshot the final turning point by two-and-a-half minutes, before bringing the force back in a wide orbit. This had the effect of splitting up the formation, and aircraft began approaching the aiming-point from a variety of headings. At 09.45 the Master Bomber ordered the crews to bomb visually if they could, but a minute later a red target indicator went down, which appeared to be accurate, and crews selected whatever was best for them. A concentration of bombs was seen to fall across the SS barracks, and it seems that most fell within the confines of the general target area, causing a column of smoke to rise to 10,000 feet.

That afternoon, a force of 482 aircraft was drawn from 4, 6 and 8 Groups to target coastal batteries on the Frisian Island of Wangerooge, which controlled the approaches to the ports of Wilhelmshaven and Bremen. 6 Group's contribution amounted to a hundred Lancasters and ninety-two Halifaxes, seventeen of the latter representing 408 (Goose) Squadron, each of which received a bomb load of sixteen 500-pounders before departing Linton-on-Ouse for the last time in anger between 14.30 and 15.03 with S/L Smith the senior pilot on duty and F/O Reain and crew launching the squadron's 4,610th and final sortie. They formed into a gaggle and set course over the North Sea, and it was during this stage of the operation that tragedy struck two Lancasters of 431 (Iroquois) Squadron as they collided off the Frisian Island of Norderney and crashed without survivors. Shortly afterwards a similarly tragic incident caused the loss of two 76 Squadron Halifaxes and in the target area 408 (Goose) Squadron's NP796 collided with NP820 of 426 (Thunderbird) Squadron, causing both to crash also without survivors. F/L Ely RCAF and his predominantly RCAF crew were on just their second sortie together. The rest of the force arrived at the target to find excellent conditions with, perhaps, three-tenths cloud at 3,500 feet, but not sufficient to inhibit sight of TIs clearly marking out the aiming-point. The Master Bomber instructed the force to overshoot the red TIs, before switching attention to the yellows, and once they became obscured, he focused the bombing on the edge of the smoke. The 408 (Goose) Squadron crews carried out their attacks from 10,200 to 12,000 feet between 17.16 and 17.19 in the face of a spirited flak response, and the bombing was observed to be concentrated on the marked area. When F/L Baird RCAF and crew touched down at Linton-on-Ouse in RG473 at 20.08, unknown to them, they had the honour to bring down the curtain on 408 (Goose) Squadron's offensive operations.

During the course of the month the squadron took part in eight operations and dispatched 125 sorties for the loss of four Halifaxes and crews.

May 1945

During the course of its operational career 408 (Goose) Squadron carried out the 2nd equal highest number of overall operations and suffered the 2nd highest number of aircraft operational losses in 6 Group and ended the war with the highest number of Lancaster operational losses in 6 Group. The 8th of May signalled the end of hostilities, and 408 (Goose) Squadron began to re-equip with Canadian-built Mk X Lancasters in preparation for joining the Tiger Force to be sent against Japan. By the 21st a full complement of twenty-one Lancasters was on charge, but in the event, the atomic bombs removed the need for such a force, and by then the squadron had returned to its homeland, having left the UK on the 14th of June. 408 (Goose) Squadron was the second longest serving Canadian unit in Bomber Command, and its contribution to the offensive was almost continuous from August 1941. The airmen of Canada in Bomber Command sacrificed more than 9,900 of their number on behalf of the Allied cause, and their selfless courage and dedication should forever stand as a testimony to the strength of their national character.

Roll of Honour

Sgt	Desmond George	BRADLEY	21.10.41.
P/O	George Nelson	ACTON	26.06.43.
Sgt	James Dick	ADAM	29.01.43.
P/O	John	ADAMSON	27.01.44.
P/O	David	AIKEN	26.06.43.
Sgt	William Yarr	ALDERDICE	29.04.42.
F/Sgt	Ernest Henry	ALDERSON	24.05.43.
P/O	William Bruce	ALLAN	24.12.44.
P/O	Alfred George	ALLEN	07.03.45.
P/O	Nels Peter Helin	ANDERSON	21.02.45.
Sgt	John Robinson	APPLEBY	16.01.42.
F/Sgt	Joseph Rene	ARCHAMBAULT	22.06.43.
F/Sgt	Jack Colin	ARCHER	05.05.43.
Sgt	Steve	ARCHIE	17.04.43.
P/O	Thomas Reginald	ASHTON	22.07.42.
F/Sgt	George	ASSAF	23.05.43.
P/O	John James	ASTLES	20.02.44.
F/O	Norman Godwin	BAILY	29.01.45.
W/OII	Nelson George	BAIRD	07.03.45.
Sgt	Victor Reginald	BAKER	23.01.42.
Sgt	Richard	BALL	09.03.42.
Sgt	Robert Walton	BARKER	04.04.43.
F/Sgt	John Francis	BARNES	30.03.43.
Sgt	Robert	BARNEVELD	14.07.43.
F/Sgt	Robert Lennox	BARR	22.03.44.
LAC	Gordon James	BARRABALL	11.09.44.
Sgt	William Kenneth	BARTON	29.01.43.
P/O	Louis	BASARAB	21.11.44.
Sgt	Henry George	BASTEN	25.02.44.
Sgt	Robert Nel	BEALE	27.03.42.
P/O	Gordon Findlay	BEAVER	27.03.42.
P/O	Lloyd Stuart	BEER	26.02.44.
P/O	Ronald George	BELL	09.11.42.
F/O	Douglas Mackenzie	BELL	24.11.43.
P/O	James Gordon	BENNETT	27.01.44.
P/O	Kenneth Hugh	BENNETT	20.02.44.
Sgt	Gordon N	BENNETT	20.02.44.
Sgt	Samuel Frederick	BENTLEY	27.03.42.
F/O	Lawrence John	BENVILLE	05.01.45.
P/O	Stanley Joseph	BERANEK	19.06.42.
P/O	John Albert	BERGERON	13.06.44.

Sgt	Frank	BERRY	31.07.43.
F/Sgt	Claude Andrew	BESSE	16.12.43.
Sgt	Edwin Arthur	BIGGS	30.03.43.
W/OII	Roland	BIRCHALL	17.04.43.
Sgt	Herman Albert Benjamin	BIRD	27.03.42.
P/O	George Edward	BISHEFF	22.06.43.
F/L	William Andrew	BLACK	03.02.43.
P/O	Charles Noola	BLACK	04.04.43.
P/O	Robert Orin	BLACKHALL	05.05.43.
P/O	Joseph Laurent Andre	BLAIS	29.07.44.
F/Sgt	Joseph Omer Emile Jules	BOILY	16.12.43.
F/Sgt	Joseph	BOISVERT	15.04.42.
Sgt	Ellis William	BOLT	20.02.44.
F/O	John Raymond	BONNEVILLE	20.02.44.
F/Sgt	Donald Ivan	BOWDEN	20.02.44.
F/Sgt	Ronald Edgar	BOWLER	26.02.44.
F/O	Allan Bernard	BOYD	25.04.45.
Sgt	Gilbert Davies	BOYER	03.04.43.
Sgt	Douglas Matthew	BRACKENRIDGE	07.02.43.
P/O	Robert Joseph	BRADLEY	27.01.44.
P/O	Kenneth Lloyd	BRAGER	20.12.43.
P/O	James Edwin	BRAMBLEBY	25.04.45.
P/O	Jack	BRAY	13.06.44.
Sgt	Kenneth Oliver	BRICE	03.04.43.
F/L	Francis Thomas Sargent	BRICE	13.06.44.
Sgt	Malcolm Stanley	BRIGHOUSE	29.08.42.
P/O	Rowland George	BRINKWORTH	29.01.43.
Sgt	George Douglas	BRITLAND	11.07.44.
P/O	James Graham	BROADFOOT	27.01.44.
P/O	Denis	BROOKE	22.06.43.
Sgt	Robert	BROWN	21.01.42.
F/L	William Beaumont	BROWN	27.03.42.
Sgt	Clifford	BROWN	27.03.42.
W/OII	David Lloyd George	BROWN	14.07.43.
F/O	Charles Davis	BROWN	23.05.44.
Sgt	William Robert	BRYANS	10.07.43.
P/O	Robert Clarke (Bob)	BUCKBERROUGH	11.07.44.
F/Sgt	James Arthur	BUNTING	16.01.42.
F/Sgt	Franklyn Roy	BURKE	03.04.43.
P/O	John Joseph	BURKE	06.04.44.
Sgt	Roland Henry	BURLEY	19.07.42.
P/O	Douglas Arthur	BURNELL	11.09.44.
F/O	Bernard Arthur	BURROWS	25.03.45.
Sgt	Robert George Alfred	BURT	15.03.44.
W/OII	Graham Frederick	BUTSON	27.04.44.

F/O	James Andrew	CALDWELL	28.11.41.
P/O	Jack Burton	CAMERON	14.01.44.
F/O	Gordon Everett	CAMERON	29.07.44.
W/OII	Michael Cecil	CAMERON	18.05.45.
S/L	Halan Donald Richard Leroy	CAMPBELL	14.05.43.
Sgt	Archibald Sinclair	CAMPBELL	23.05.44.
F/Sgt	Albert Edward	CANDLINE	29.07.44.
F/O	Thomas Kenneth	CANNING	27.01.44.
Sgt	Alexander Crawford	CANTLEY	17.04.43.
Sgt	Brinley George	CAPEL	14.01.44.
F/L	John Sommerville	CARDELL	16.08.42.
Sgt	Leo Augustave	CARR	14.01.44.
P/O	Lorne Francis	CASSIDY	29.07.44.
Sgt	Francis Anthony	CAVADINO	29.01.43.
F/O	Frank Napoleon Smith	CAVANAUGH	30.03.43.
Sgt	Albert Edward	CHALK	31.07.43.
F/Sgt	Christopher Norman	CHALKEN	29.08.42.
Sgt	Thomas Herbert	CHANDLER	29.01.45.
Sgt	Peter Bernard	CHAPPLE	21.01.42.
P/O	William Frederick Dixon	CHARLTON	01.06.42.
W/OII	Lionel Greer	CHASTON	28.08.42.
Sgt	Frederick John	CHERRY	30.03.43.
W/OII	Maurice Gordon	CHURCH	03.04.43.
Sgt	Leslie Alexander	CHURCHER	10.01.42.
Sgt	Sydney Frank	CLARK	28.08.42.
F/O	Russell Stanley	CLARK	21.12.43.
Sgt	Herbert Edgar	CLARK	21.11.44.
P/O	Harold William	CLARKE	21.01.42.
F/O	Anthony Arthur	CLIFFORD	18.05.45.
F/Sgt	Roger Victor	CLITHEROE	05.05.43.
P/O	George Frederick	CLOUGH	22.03.44.
W/OII	Arnold Wallace	COCHRANE	02.03.43.
P/O	Thomas Donald	COCHRANE	20.12.43.
Sgt	Frank Robert	COCKS	17.04.43.
P/O	Clarence Leonard	COFIELD	25.03.45.
P/O	Leslie John	COLLINSON	29.01.45.
F/O	Alexander Colborne	COLVILLE	16.03.44.
F/O	James Mackenzie	COLVIN	24.05.43.
W/OII	Joseph Napoleon Pascal Eugene	COMEAU	28.05.43.
Sgt	Edward Victor	CONWELL	19.06.42.
Sgt	Edwin Arthur	CORDEROY	22.04.42.
F/L	James Stewart	COULTER	12.08.42.
Sgt	John Joseph	COURTNEY	15.04.43.
F/Sgt	William Harris	COWMAN	07.02.43.
Sgt	John	CRAMMOND	31.07.43.

Sgt	Roland	CRAWLEY	28.11.41.
P/O	Cyril	CRESSWELL	16.05.42.
P/O	Fred	CROFTS	26.02.44.
F/O	Eric	CROUCH	10.07.43.
F/L	Gordon	CROUCHER	29.07.44.
Sgt	Douglas	CRUICKSHANK	15.03.44.
F/O	Frederick Campbell	CULBERT	26.06.43.
F/L	Albert James	CULL	18.04.45.
P/O	Henry Norman	CUNLIFFE	25.02.44.
P/O	Harry Joseph	CUNNINGHAM	23.05.44.
F/O	John Charles	CUNNINGHAM	09.04.45.
P/O	Gordon	CURRIE	21.01.44.
P/O	Kenneth Lawrence	CURTIS	22.03.44.
F/Sgt	Victor Charles	DADSON	25.01.42.
P/O	Jack Stanley	DAFOE	09.05.42.
F/O	James Boustead	DALLYN	23.05.44.
P/O	John	DALY	05.01.45.
P/O	Gerald Roch	D'AMOUR	24.12.44.
F/L	John Baillie	DARROCH	05.04.43.
F/Sgt	John Haliburton	DAUGHNEY	22.04.42.
P/O	George David	DAUGHTERS	07.03.45.
Sgt	John Joseph	DAVENPORT	13.04.42.
Sgt	Harold	DAVENPORT	30.03.43.
Sgt	Harold	DAVIES	25.01.42.
Sgt	Dennis Vivian	DAVIES	16.03.44.
P/O	Stanley	DAWSON	14.01.44.
Sgt	Timothy I'Anson	DEE	16.12.43.
F/Sgt	Garry	DEIGHTON	14.01.44.
P/O	James	DENHOLM	20.06.43.
F/Sgt	Raymond James	DILLON	16.05.42.
W/OI	John	DINGWALL	29.07.44.
P/O	John Peter	DOCKERILL	22.06.43.
F/Sgt	Robert Spencer	DOHERTY	22.07.42.
P/O	William Lawrence	DORAN	15.03.44.
F/O	Angus Ward	DOUGLAS	27.11.43.
Sgt	Eldore	DRAMNITZKI	20.02.44.
P/O	Clarence Oscar	DRAPER	26.02.44.
F/Sgt	Raymond Wesley	DREYER	16.05.42.
F/O	Andre Joseph Julien Christain	DULAIT	13.06.44.
P/O	Robert Allison	DUNCAN	09.04.45.
F/Sgt	Charles Douglas	DUNN	27.03.42.
P/O	Alan Howard	DURNIN	29.07.44.
P/O	James Allan	EARLE	14.01.44.
Sgt	Reginald Grenville	EAVES	21.01.42.
F/O	Peter Leslie	EDWARDS	03.06.42.

Rank	Name	Surname	Date
Sgt	Robert George	EDWARDS	31.07.43.
Sgt	Cameron William	ELLARD	05.05.43.
Sgt	Albert Edward	ELLIOTT	21.01.44.
F/L	Arthur Blevyn	ELY	25.04.45.
Sgt	Armour John	EMERSON	25.02.44.
Sgt	Kenneth Edward	EMMONS	05.05.43.
Sgt	Bert Henry	FEARN	29.12.43.
Sgt	Francis	FEARNS	29.07.44.
F/O	David Arthur	FEHRMAN	18.05.45.
P/O	Geoffrey	FIELDING	27.11.43.
Sgt	Harrold Walter	FILL	17.04.43.
F/Sgt	Clarence Henry	FINKBEINER	09.05.42.
P/O	Grant Alexander	FLETCHER	03.04.43.
F/Sgt	Derek Noel	FLITTON	08.06.44.
Sgt	John	FOGGON	14.07.43.
Sgt	Kenneth	FORSTER	21.12.43.
F/O	Arthur Baker	FOSTER	04.07.43.
W/OII	Albert Edward	FOWELL	12.06.43.
Sgt	George Murray	FRAME	12.09.42.
F/O	John Albert	FRAMPTON	20.02.44.
P/O	William MacMillan	FRASER	27.03.42.
P/O	Clarence William	FRAUTS	27.01.44.
F/O	John Ernest	FREEMAN	02.12.44.
F/L	Walter Louis	FRIKER	24.12.44.
F/O	Lloyd William	FRIZZELL	21.11.44.
F/L	Warren Thompson	FULTON	22.03.44.
W/OII	Joseph Alphonse Paul Henri	GABOURY	22.03.44.
F/L	Robert Hodgson Perry	GAMBLE	04.04.43.
Sgt	Douglas Dean	GARDNER	09.11.42.
Sgt	Donald Frederick	GARGRAVE	17.04.43.
P/O	Leslie Lewis	GARNER	29.08.42.
F/Sgt	Wallace Mallory	GARTSIDE	12.08.42.
Sgt	Cyril Charles	GIBSON	15.12.41.
W/OII	John William	GIBSON	17.04.43.
Sgt	Anthony Patrick	GIELTY	17.04.43.
F/O	Ted Charles	GIERULSKI	16.12.43.
F/Sgt	Joseph Emery Romeo	GIGUERE	07.02.43.
Sgt	James Harry	GILBERT	27.04.44.
Sgt	Arthur Ernest Fuce	GILES	09.11.42.
S/L	Edward Gerard	GILMORE	05.04.43.
F/O	William James	GILMORE	21.02.45.
F/O	Vernon Beverley	GILSON	02.11.44.
F/Sgt	William George	GITTINGS	12.08.42.
Sgt	Gordon Arthur	GLANVILLE	10.01.42.
F/L	Sidney Arthur Henry	GLASSPOOL	27.11.43.

F/O	Albert	GLENDENNING	13.06.44.
P/O	William Harvey	GOODWIN	13.06.44.
P/O	Ernest Albert	GOODWIN	29.07.44.
F/Sgt	Richard Lawrence	GORDON	29.04.42.
F/O	William Herbert	GOULD	29.08.42.
F/O	William Angus	GRANT	05.05.43.
P/O	Arthur Gordon	GRANT	12.06.43.
F/O	Jack Gillard	GRAY	13.06.44.
P/O	Douglas Thomas	GREATREX	27.04.44.
Sgt	Herbert	GREGSON	28.08.42.
W/OII	Ivor Charles	GRICE	02.03.43.
F/O	Quinten Thomas Russell	GRIERSON	29.07.44.
Sgt	Francis George	GRIEVE	11.07.44.
P/O	Raymond William	GRIGGS	08.06.44.
W/O	Joseph Jacques Alfred	GUAY	17.04.43.
F/O	Jerry Taylor	GUTHRIE	29.07.44.
Sgt	Donald	HADDOCK	19.06.42.
F/Sgt	Francis Eldon	HAGEL	15.04.42.
F/Sgt	Lloyd George	HAINES	17.04.43.
P/O	Maxwell Palmer	HALL	05.04.43.
F/Sgt	Clarence Julius	HALVORSON	18.05.45.
Sgt	Ramsay	HAMILTON	25.03.45.
F/O	Charles Armand Georges	HANCHAR	13.06.44.
P/O	Lloyd Leonard Hans	HANSEN	14.01.44.
F/L	James Robert	HANSON	23.05.44.
Sgt	Lloyd George	HANTON	24.11.43.
Sgt	Lynn	HARDING	11.12.41.
Sgt	Thomas William	HARRIS	30.03.43.
Sgt	John McLaren	HARRISON	14.05.43.
Sgt	Edwin Alfred	HARRY	28.11.41.
Sgt	George Richard	HARVEY	29.07.44.
F/L	Clifford Oscar	HATLE	17.04.43.
Sgt	Edward	HAVILLE	19.07.42.
Sgt	Albert James	HAWKINS	04.04.43.
Sgt	Kenneth William	HAYNES	05.04.43.
Sgt	Roy William	HEATON	20.12.43.
F/Sgt	Leslie Claude	HELLEKSON	18.05.45.
Sgt	Cecil Davis	HEMING	17.04.43.
F/Sgt	George Chetwynd	HEMING	17.04.43.
F/Sgt	Donald Louden	HENDERSON	10.01.42.
P/O	Maxwell	HENDERSON	23.05.44.
P/O	Robert Elliot	HENDRY	27.04.44.
P/O	Frank	HENRY	29.01.45.
F/Sgt	Granite William	HERRINGTON	30.03.43.
F/Sgt	Reginald McLeod	HICKS	04.07.43.

Rank	Name	Surname	Date
W/OII	James Herbert	HIGGINS	02.03.43.
F/Sgt	Donald Ernest	HILKER	03.01.44.
Sgt	Geoffrey Maxted	HILL	17.04.43.
F/O	Farley Cecil	HILL	18.04.45.
P/O	Tom William	HILLIARD	03.11.43.
F/O	James Gordon	HILLMAN	25.02.44.
Sgt	Thomas	HINDLE	29.04.42.
F/Sgt	Reuben Oliver	HISCOCK	24.11.43.
P/O	Mervyn Eugene	HODGINS	25.02.44.
F/O	Robert Cyril	HODGSON	12.08.42.
P/O	Arthur Coles Kitchener	HODSON	16.03.44.
Sgt	Bernard Mathew	HOFFORTH	29.07.44.
F/O	Laurence Henry	HOLMES	17.04.43.
Sgt	Raymond Henry	HOLTHAM	30.03.43.
Sgt	John	HOOPER	24.05.43.
P/O	Albert Elliott	HORNE	14.05.43.
P/O	Douglas Carter	HORNER	20.06.43.
P/O	Brooks Earl	HOUSE	29.01.45.
F/O	George Marshall	HOUSTON	11.09.44.
P/O	Vernon Earl	HOVEY	25.04.45.
Sgt	Robert Frederick	HOWELL	27.03.42.
Sgt	Brinley	HOWELLS	15.12.41.
P/O	Frank Henry	HOYLE	29.12.43.
Sgt	Robert Henry	HUDSON	15.03.44.
Sgt	Idris	HUGHES	29.07.42.
Sgt	Cyril Armstrong	HUGHES	20.02.44.
F/O	Peter Malcolm	HUGHES	23.05.44.
Sgt	James	HUGHES	25.04.45.
P/O	Herbert	HUGILL	08.06.44.
P/O	William Francis	HULL	11.12.41.
P/O	John Douglas Bruce	HUNTER	26.06.43.
P/O	John Alexander Kay	IMRIE	29.07.44.
P/O	Alan Clifford	INESON	02.11.44.
P/O	John Alexander	INVERARITY	08.06.44.
Sgt	Peter Frederick	ISAAC	28.12.41.
P/O	Ross Banting	JACKSON	22.10.43.
W/C	David Sinclair	JACOBS	23.05.44.
Sgt	Samuel	JAMIESON	11.12.41.
W/OII	Donal Leslie	JARRETT	04.04.43.
Sgt	Clifford Stanley	JEFFERIES	09.05.42.
W/OII	Alger	JENKINS	27.03.42.
F/Sgt	Athol Herbert	JENNINGS	29.08.42.
Sgt	Gordon	JENNINGS	30.03.43.
F/O	Arne Paul	JENSEN	09.04.45.
Sgt	Harry Leonard	JEWELL	16.08.42.

F/Sgt	Gudmundur Arnpor	JOHANNESSON	05.05.43.
F/O	Crawford Lee	JOHNSTON	29.01.45.
Sgt	John	JOHNSTONE	15.04.42.
Sgt	Maurice	JONES	16.01.42.
F/Sgt	Howard Dennis	JONES	21.01.44.
P/O	Alfred Ernest	JONES	27.01.44.
Sgt	Stanley Johannes	JORGENSEN	17.04.43.
Sgt	Michael Yorke Zisslin	KALMS	16.03.44.
P/O	Peter	KALYTA	23.05.44.
Sgt	William George	KAPUSCINSKI	17.04.43.
F/L	Eldon Eastham	KEARL	27.01.44.
F/O	David Garfield	KELLAR	24.12.44.
P/O	Norman	KELLNER	22.06.43.
W/OII	Lloyd Franklin	KELLY	27.07.42.
P/O	Albert Edward	KELLY	04.07.43.
Sgt	Ralph Gordon	KELLY	20.02.44.
Sgt	Edwin	KENT	20.12.43.
F/Sgt	William George	KEOGH	12.09.42.
F/O	John Nicholas	KERRY	11.09.44.
P/O	Walter	KERSLAKE	22.10.43.
Sgt	Edgar John Jex	KILLHAM	09.05.42.
F/O	Francis Joseph	KING	22.03.44.
Sgt	Charles Frederick	KIRSCH	27.11.43.
F/Sgt	Walter Anthony	KOPACZ	30.03.43.
F/Sgt	William	KWASNEY	17.04.43.
F/O	John Irvin	LABOW	31.03.44.
F/L	Sven Roy Walfrid	LAINE	27.01.44.
F/O	Hector Beattie	LANCASTER	10.07.43.
Sgt	Harold	LANDING	29.12.43.
F/Sgt	James Murray Reginald	LANG	12.06.43.
F/Sgt	George Malcolm	LANTZ	13.04.42.
S/L	Gerald Bennett	LATIMER	29.07.44.
F/O	William Robert	LAY	25.03.45.
F/Sgt	Joseph Renee Alexis	LE BLANC	28.07.43.
P/O	Donald Alfred Parsons	LE DREW	22.03.44.
P/O	Frank George	LEAHY	31.03.44.
F/O	James Richard	LEAMAN	20.02.44.
F/O	Frank Taylor	LEITHEAD	05.01.45.
Sgt	Thomas	LEITH-ROSS	13.06.43.
W/OII	Albert Bennett	LEWIS	22.06.43.
Sgt	Ronald Stanley Victor	LEWIS-STANIFORD	30.03.43.
F/O	Thomas Bruce	LITTLE	29.01.45.
P/O	Texas Roy	LIVERMORE	24.05.43.
F/Sgt	Clarence Franklin	LLOYD	01.08.42.
W/OII	William Herbert	LOUGH	07.02.43.

Rank	Name	Surname	Date
P/O	Ralph William	LOWREY	08.06.44.
P/O	Norman Andrew	LUMGAIR	15.03.44.
F/O	Leon George	LYONS	29.08.42.
P/O	Adam	MABON	13.06.44.
Sgt	Frederick	MacDONALD	02.03.43.
F/Sgt	Irving	MacDONALD	17.04.43.
F/Sgt	James Clarence	MacDONALD	22.06.43.
Sgt	Joseph Mannix	MacDONALD	10.07.43.
F/Sgt	Colin Murray	MacDONALD	03.11.43.
Sgt	Allan James	MacGREGOR	22.04.42.
Sgt	Harry George	MACHELL	17.04.43.
P/O	Roy Alderson	MacKAY	27.01.44.
P/O	Ian Cumming	MacKENZIE	15.04.43.
F/Sgt	Fernand Fagan	MacKINNON	09.03.42.
P/O	John Angus	MacLEAN	28.01.44.
W/OII	Hugh	MacLENNAN	14.01.44.
Sgt	Michael	MAHER	16.12.43.
W/C	Alexander Campbell	MAIR	27.11.43.
F/L	Ian	MAITLAND	28.08.42.
F/L	William John	MAITLAND	16.12.43.
F/O	Thomas Ernest	MAJOR	21.12.43.
F/Sgt	John Frederick	MALE	26.06.43.
F/O	Gordon Ewart	MALLORY	13.06.44.
F/O	John Phillip	MARCHANT	25.03.45.
Sgt	Douglas Victor	MARKALL	09.11.41.
F/Sgt	Jack Wellington	MARKLE	09.05.42.
Sgt	Alfred	MARLAND	02.06.42.
Sgt	Douglas	MARSDEN	25.01.42.
P/O	Arthur Frank	MARSDEN	29.07.44.
F/Sgt	Hudson Eric	MARSHALL	28.11.41.
F/O	Michael Edmund	MARYNOWSKI	16.12.43.
Sgt	Richard William	MASON	17.04.43.
F/O	Philip Malcolm	MATTHEWS	09.11.42.
P/O	Leonard Henry	MATTHEWS	27.11.43.
Sgt	Thomas Irving	MAY	22.01.42.
F/Sgt	Thomas Dunwoody	MAYNE	22.10.43.
F/O	John Dugald	McBRIDE	03.04.43.
P/O	Dennis Albert	McCABE	29.12.43.
P/O	John Harold Alexander	McCAFFREY	29.07.44.
F/Sgt	Archibald	McCLINTOCK	15.04.42.
F/Sgt	John Henry Colin	McCLUNG	10.07.43.
F/Sgt	Ian Fowler Stewart	McCOLL	09.11.42.
P/O	Kenneth Septimus	McCOLL	04.04.43.
P/O	Roy Ernest	McCOMB	22.10.43.
LAC	Andrew Lloyd	McCONNELL	02.09.42.

Rank	Name	Surname	Date
W/OII	Harry Kenneth	McCREERY	02.03.43.
WO/II	Max Albert	McCURDY	20.12.43.
F/O	Howard William	McDONALD	28.07.43.
F/O	Martin John	McDONALD	13.06.44.
F/L	George Horne	McDOUGAL	28.07.43.
F/L	Thom Ross	McDOUGALL	23.05.44.
F/O	Clarence Francis	McDOUGALL	29.07.44.
F/L	Henry Carbee	McIVER	13.06.44.
P/O	Kenneth Bruce	McIVOR	18.05.45.
F/Sgt	Douglas George	McKAY	14.07.43.
Sgt	Orville Wilbert	McKENZIE	02.06.42.
F/O	Norman Colin	McKILLOP	12.09.44.
F/Sgt	George Percy	McLEAN	27.03.42.
Sgt	Gordon Mitchell	McLEAN	22.06.43.
P/O	John Francis	McMANUS	27.01.44.
P/O	Rupert George	McMANUS	07.03.45.
Sgt	Alexander Teryl	McMILLAN	21.10.41.
P/O	John Henry	McNESS	26.06.43.
F/Sgt	Leslie Arthur	McQUESTION	20.12.43.
Sgt	George Alfred	MEDD	26.03.42.
F/Sgt	William Ian	MEECH	13.04.42.
F/O	Thomas Roland	MELLISH	10.07.43.
F/Sgt	Malcolm Roy Edgar	METCALFE	05.05.43.
F/O	Francis Lloyd	MILBURN	13.06.43.
Sgt	Douglas John	MILBURN	11.09.44.
F/Sgt	Charles Percy	MILLER	03.11.43.
F/O	Donald Mitchell	MILLER	18.04.45.
F/Sgt	William Francis	MILLERD	16.05.42.
P/O	Bruce Ryerson	MILLIGAN	26.06.43.
Sgt	Edwin	MITCHELL	16.08.42.
P/O	Rex Harris	MITCHELL	29.07.44.
P/O	Joseph Earl	MONAHAN	22.06.43.
F/O	Lancelot Eric	MORGAN	23.05.44.
F/O	Hryhory	MOROZ	22.03.44.
Sgt	William Douglas	MORRIS	09.03.42.
P/O	Jack Clarence	MORTLEY	29.01.45.
Sgt	Hubert James	MOULAND	03.01.44.
Sgt	Thomas Charles Robert	MURLIS	29.08.42.
W/O	Harry Frederick	MURPHY	13.06.44.
P/O	Philip	MYERSON	29.01.45.
W/OII	Donat Cyprien Romain	NAULT	05.05.43.
Sgt	Henry Arthur	NIGHTINGALE	23.05.44.
F/O	Wilfred Ronald Eli	NORTH	27.11.43.
Sgt	Douglas Frederick William	NORTON	09.11.41.
F/Sgt	James Shield	NORTON	09.05.42.

F/Sgt	Reginald Sydney	NURSE	25.02.44.
Sgt	Wiliam	OATES	15.12.41.
F/O	John Anthony	O'BRIEN	29.01.45.
P/O	Robert Duncan	OCHSNER	13.06.44.
F/O	Thomas Harold	O'CONNELL	17.04.43.
F/Sgt	Robert Wilson	OGSTON	07.09.43.
Sgt	Sydney Frederick	OSMOND	17.04.43.
F/Sgt	Potter George	OYLER	05.04.43.
Sgt	Bernard William	PALASTANGA	07.11.41.
Sgt	William Dudley	PALMER	16.05.42.
P/O	Joseph Alphonse Normand	PARE	22.03.44.
P/O	Jospeh Paul David	PARISE	27.01.44.
F/O	James Courtland	PARKER	14.02.43.
P/O	Elbert Frank	PARKER	28.07.43.
P/O	George	PARKER	15.03.44.
P/O	Joseph Gaudias Albert	PATRY	22.06.43.
P/O	Alvin Alston	PATTON	31.03.44.
P/O	James Gordon	PAXTON	02.03.45.
F/O	Edwin	PAYLING	29.01.43.
P/O	Harold	PEARCE	19.07.42.
P/O	Keith Thomas	PELLETT	29.08.42.
F/Sgt	Roland	PETTITT	16.12.43.
Sgt	Henri	PHALEMPIN	26.03.42.
F/O	William George	PHILPOT	23.05.44.
F/O	Robert Alexander	PILDREM	29.12.43.
F/Sgt	Francois Rolland	PILON	17.04.43.
W/OI	Asa Nelson	PIXLEY	18.04.45.
F/Sgt	John Beverley	PLEASENCE	22.07.42.
F/L	Thomas Oswald	PLEDGER	13.06.44.
Sgt	William	PLUNKETT	20.02.44.
W/OI	John Milton	POTTER	27.04.44.
F/Sgt	William Ronald	PRENTICE	10.07.43.
S/L	Lyall Basil Burman	PRICE	29.07.42.
Sgt	Harold	PRICE	01.08.42.
F/L	Thomas Findlay	PRIEST	10.01.42.
F/O	Leonard Douglas	PROCTOR	22.03.44.
F/O	Elmer Reginald	PROUD	27.01.44.
F/O	Peter Reginald	QUANCE	20.06.43.
P/O	Thomas Phillip	QUINN	29.01.45.
F/O	Robert Alfred	QUINNEY	24.11.43.
W/OII	William Edward	RABAN	29.12.43.
Sgt	Percy Albert George	RAGG	22.10.41.
P/O	Charles	RANKIN	21.01.44.
F/O	Edmund Rothell	RAY	04.04.43.
F/O	Louis Joseph	REAUME	02.11.44.

Rank	Name	Surname	Date
Sgt	William Lewis	REED	31.07.43.
F/O	Walter William	REHKOPF	23.05.44.
P/O	Clifford Clarence	REICHERT	22.06.43.
F/O	Gilmour Murray	REID	21.01.44.
F/O	William Van Fossen	REID	16.03.44.
W/OII	Henry	RICHMOND	17.04.43.
F/O	Gordon William McKay	RICHTER	20.02.44.
P/O	Arthur Edward	RICKERT	22.03.44.
F/O	Cyril Frederick	RIDGERS	26.02.44.
Sgt	Thomas	RILEY	04.07.43.
P/O	Sherman Lewis	ROACH	20.02.44.
F/Sgt	Norman William	ROBERTS	30.03.43.
Sgt	Charles William George	ROBERTS	20.02.44.
Sgt	Evan Bertram Te Makahi	ROBERTSON	09.11.41.
Sgt	John James	ROBERTSON	16.12.43.
F/O	Everett Raymond	ROGNAN	27.04.44.
F/O	Robert Harold	ROLPH	08.06.44.
F/Sgt	James Arthur Easterbrooks	ROMAS	29.04.42.
Sgt	Ewart Gladstone	RONSON	03.06.42.
Sgt	Joseph	ROSTRON	29.01.43.
F/O	Theunis Christoffel	ROUX	29.01.43.
F/O	Adelbert Bateman	ROWLEY	21.11.44.
Sgt	Desmond	RUDGE	22.06.43.
Sgt	Donald Mac	RUSSELL	13.06.44.
P/O	Albert Leroy	RUTTER	25.04.45.
F/O	Donal Thomas	RYAN	29.07.44.
Sgt	Reginald James Peter	SALT	07.02.43.
F/L	Max	SAMUELS	20.06.43.
F/L	Donald McWilliam	SANDERSON	21.02.45.
P/O	Cyril Ian Andrew	SANDLAND	02.06.42.
W/OII	Joseph Evans	SAUNDERS	16.12.43.
F/O	James Earl	SAUVE	03.11.43.
F/Sgt	Joseph Fisher	SAYERS	07.02.43.
P/O	Andrew Franklin	SCANES	22.10.43.
F/L	Andew Frank	SCHEELAR	05.01.45.
F/Sgt	George Henry	SCOTT	27.01.44.
P/O	William	SEARLE	22.06.43.
F/Sgt	Cecil Lester	SEBELIUS	22.06.43.
F/O	Joseph Raymond Louis	SERGENT	17.04.43.
Sgt	Michael David	SHAKESPEARE	22.06.43.
F/O	Frederick Weber	SHANTZ	25.03.45.
P/O	Ernest Anson	SHAW	11.07.44.
Sgt	Ronald George Barclay	SHEA	24.11.43.
P/O	Harry	SHERLOCK	25.02.44.
P/O	Donald Edison	SHERMAN	21.02.45.

Rank	Name	Surname	Date
F/O	Thomas Russell	SHERRILL	23.05.44.
F/O	Moody Albert	SIDDONS	16.03.44.
P/O	Robert Lloyd	SIEWERT	29.01.45.
F/O	Dennis MacDonald	SIM	27.01.44.
F/Sgt	Marcel Stanley	SINCLAIR	08.05.42.
P/O	Ebenezer Alfred	SIRETT	03.04.43.
Sgt	Frederick George	SKEET	20.02.44.
F/Sgt	David	SLOBOTSKY	24.05.43.
F/Sgt	Albert Alexander	SMITH	16.05.42.
Sgt	Norman William	SMITH	16.05.42.
W/OII	Dean William	SMITH	07.02.43.
F/Sgt	James William Taylor Mason	SMITH	05.04.43.
Sgt	Robert Clifford	SMITH	03.11.43.
F/Sgt	Harold	SMITH	24.11.43.
Sgt	Bernard	SMITH	20.12.43.
F/Sgt	Alfred	SMITH	27.01.44.
S/L	Charles Woodward	SMITH	27.01.44.
P/O	Kenneth	SMITH	20.02.44.
F/L	William Robert	SMITH	26.02.44.
Sgt	Francis Ernest Albert	SMITH	16.03.44.
Sgt	James Murdoch	SMITH	22.03.44.
F/O	Grant Lyman	SMITH	11.07.44.
P/O	Ronald Ward	SMITH	11.09.44.
F/O	Reginald Bertram	SMITH	21.02.45.
F/O	Alan Osborn	SMUCK	14.07.43.
F/Sgt	Julien Louis	SOOS	23.05.43.
Sgt	Morley Frederick Roy	SORTON	27.01.44.
P/O	Charles Corey Van Dusen	SPENCER	14.01.44.
Sgt	Alfred Edward Charles	SQUIRE	19.06.42.
P/O	George Lawson	STANIAR	16.08.42.
F/O	James Kent	STANLEY	25.04.45.
Sgt	Robert Arthur	STANSFIELD	21.10.41.
Sgt	Edward James	STANSFIELD	28.08.42.
F/O	Donald Anderson	STAPLES	02.11.44.
F/Sgt	John James	STEFANCHUK	10.07.43.
Sgt	Eric William	STERLING	15.12.41.
P/O	William Richard	STEVENS	05.07.44.
S/L	William Benjamin	STEWART	13.06.44.
P/O	Lloyd Albert	STINSON	14.05.43.
F/O	Charles Theodore	STOREY	11.09.44.
F/L	Clifford Campbell	STOVEL	28.07.43.
P/O	John	STREET	02.03.45.
Sgt	Herbert Frederick	STROUD	09.05.42.
Sgt	James William	STURGESS	10.07.43.
F/Sgt	Charles Andrew Levern	SUTHERBY	29.08.42.

Rank	Name	Surname	Date
P/O	Albert James	SUTTON	05.05.43.
P/O	Edward William	SWATTON	19.07.42.
Sgt	Ernest Edward	SYKES	18.04.45.
F/O	Harold Edward	TANNER	30.03.43.
Sgt	Anthony William	TATTERSFIELD	14.01.44.
P/O	Kenneth Henry	TAYLOR	03.06.42.
P/O	Jeffrey Charles May	TAYLOR	04.07.43.
P/O	William	TAYLOR	15.03.44.
F/O	Arthur McLellan	TAYLOR	09.04.45.
F/O	John Dargavel	TESKEY	27.01.44.
F/Sgt	Desmond William	THANE	28.12.41.
F/Sgt	Ralph Lloyd	THOMPSON	15.12.41.
Sgt	Charles Herbert	THOMPSON	28.08.42.
Sgt	Frederick	THOMPSON	24.05.43.
Sgt	Gilbert Frank Allerton	THOMPSON	22.03.44.
P/O	Richard Andrew	THORNTON	22.10.43.
Sgt	Arthur	THORP	09.04.45.
F/O	Wilbert Harry	TIMMINS	14.01.44.
Sgt	Kenneth Witty	TINDALL	20.02.44.
F/Sgt	Francis Albert	TITCOMB	22.10.41.
F/Sgt	Duncan Luin	TODD	11.12.41.
F/Sgt	John William	TODD	28.08.42.
P/O	Elvin George	TODD	13.06.44.
Sgt	John Charles	TOMLIN	15.12.41.
P/O	Donald Clifford	TONKIN	24.12.44.
Sgt	Arthur Frederick	TRAWFORD	27.03.42.
P/O	Harold Edmund	TRUSCOTT	29.07.44.
F/Sgt	Albert Andrew	TSCHANTRE	17.04.43.
W/C	John Despard	TWIGG	28.08.42.
F/O	Harry	URETZKY	24.05.43.
P/O	Norman	VARLEY	13.06.44.
Sgt	John Leslie	VAUGHAN	15.12.41.
F/Sgt	Joseph Vincent John Raymond	VEYS	28.05.43.
P/O	Dalton Eastman	VIPOND	26.03.42.
P/O	Reginald Herbert	WADE	20.02.44.
P/O	William Wallace	WAGNER	21.02.45.
F/Sgt	Ronald Roderick	WALKER	22.10.41.
Sgt	Walter	WALKER	25.02.44.
P/O	James Dickson	WALKER	09.04.45.
F/O	Richard MacMillan	WALLIS	29.01.45.
Sgt	Richard	WALMSLEY	22.03.44.
F/Sgt	William Duncan	WALSH	22.06.43.
Sgt	Arthur Raymond	WARNICK	04.07.43.
Sgt	Herbert Cheval Archer	WARR	01.08.42.
F/O	Walter Simeon	WAYCHUK	11.07.44.

Rank	Name	Surname	Date
F/L	Joseph William	WEIS	08.06.44.
F/Sgt	Ross	WEISS	02.03.43.
F/Sgt	Robert Thomas James	WELCH	23.12.43.
Sgt	Richard Strickland	WESTROPE	29.07.44.
F/L	Arthur James	WHISTON	22.10.43.
P/O	Charles Henry	WHITE	18.04.45.
P/O	Robert Daniel	WHITSON	29.07.44.
F/Sgt	Gordon John	WILKIE	13.04.42.
Sgt	Wilfred Roy	WILLIAMS	15.12.41.
Sgt	Douglas Theodore	WILLIAMS	28.12.41.
F/Sgt	Ronald George	WILLIAMS	24.11.43.
F/Sgt	Arthur Raymond	WILLIAMS	14.01.44.
P/O	Roland Wesley	WILLIAMS	18.04.45.
P/O	John Cayley	WILSON	09.11.41.
F/Sgt	Robert Edwin	WILSON	22.04.42.
F/O	Hugh Ross	WILSON	27.01.44.
P/O	Harry William	WILSON	13.06.44.
P/O	Edmund Kenneth	WILSON	21.11.44.
Sgt	James	WILSON	21.02.45.
F/L	Walter Torrance	WILTON	29.12.43.
F/L	Elmer Stanley	WINN	20.02.44.
Sgt	Ronald Harry	WINTER	17.04.43.
Sgt	Murray Lyle	WIPER	14.01.44.
Sgt	Robert	WISHART	22.07.42.
F/O	John Joseph	WOLFE	15.10.44.
F/Sgt	Frederick John Ernest	WOMAR	02.06.42.
Sgt	Kenneth Roy	WOOD	16.12.43.
P/O	Hugh Raymond	WOOD	18.04.45.
P/O	Spencer Elwood	WOOLHETHER	22.03.44.
Sgt	Albert Barclay	WRIGHT	25.01.42.
P/O	Allan French	WRIGHT	20.12.43.
P/O	David Leonard	WRIGHT	27.01.44.
F/O	John Harker	WYATT	13.06.44.
W/OII	Robert Allen	YOUNG	03.11.43.
P/O	Joseph Philip	YOUNG	23.05.44.
F/Sgt	Demetre	ZALESCHUK	17.04.43.

408 (Goose) Squadron

MOTTO **FOR FREEDOM** Code **EQ**

STATIONS

LINDHOLME	24.06.41. to 20.07.41.
SYERSTON	20.07.41. to 09.12.41.
BALDERTON	09.12.41. to 17.09.42.
NORTH LUFFENHAM (Detachment)	25.01.42. to 17.03.42.
LEEMING	17.09.42. to 27.08.43.
LINTON-ON-OUSE	10.08.43. to 13.06.45.

GROUPS

5 GROUP	24.06.41. to 13.09.42.
4 GROUP	13.09.42. to 01.01.43
6 GROUP	01.01.43.

COMMANDING OFFICERS

WING COMMANDER N W TIMMERMAN DSO DFC	24.06.41. to 28.03.42.
WING COMMANDER A C P CLAYTON DFC*	28.03.42. to 14.04.42.
WING COMMANDER J D TWIGG	18.05.42. to 28.08.42.
WING COMMANDER W D S FERRIS DFC	01.09.42. to 26.10.43.
WING COMMANDER A C MAIR DFC	28.10.43. to 26.11.43.
WING COMMANDER D S JACOBS DFC	27.11.43. to 22.05.44.
WING COMMANDER A R McLERNON DFC	24.05.44. to 14.10.44.
WING COMMANDER J F EASTON DFC	14.10.44. to 26.11.44.
WING COMMANDER F R SHARP DFC	26.11.44. to 05.09.45.

AIRCRAFT

HAMPDEN	06.41. to 09.42.
HALIFAX V	10.42. to 12.42.
HALIFAX II	12.42. to 08.43.
LANCASTER II	08.43. to 08.44.
HALIFAX III	07.44. to 02.45.
HALIFAX VII	07.44. to 05.45.

OPERATIONAL RECORD

OPERATIONS	SORTIES	AIRCRAFT LOSSES	% LOSSES
457	4453	129	2.9

CATEGORY OF OPERATIONS

BOMBING	MINING	LEAFLET	RECONNAISSANCE
343	67	15	2

5 GROUP

OPERATIONS	SORTIES	AIRCRAFT LOSSES	% LOSSES
191	1234	35	2.8

CATEGORY OF OPERATIONS

BOMBING	MINING	LEAFLET	RECONNAISSANCE
118	56	15	2

6 GROUP

OPERATIONS	SORTIES	AIRCRAFT LOSSES	% LOSSES
266	3219	94	2.9

CATEGORY OF OPERATIONS

BOMBING	MINING
255	11

HAMPDENS

OPERATIONS	SORTIES	AIRCRAFT LOSSES	% LOSSES
190	1233	35	2.8

CATEGORY OF OPERATIONS

BOMBING	MINING	LEAFLET	RECONNAISSANCE
117	56	15	2

MANCHESTERS

OPERATIONS	SORTIES	AIRCRAFT LOSSES	% LOSSES
1	1	0	0.0

CATEGORY OF OPERATIONS

BOMBING
1

HALIFAXES

OPERATIONS	SORTIES	AIRCRAFT LOSSES	% LOSSES
166	2009	53	3.8

CATEGORY OF OPERATIONS

BOMBING	MINING
155	11

LANCASTERS

OPERATIONS	SORTIES	AIRCRAFT LOSSES	% LOSSES
100	1210	41	3.4

ALL BOMBING

Aircraft Histories

HAMPDEN.   **To October 1942.**

L4042 EQ-J	From 106 Squadron. To 1401 Flight.
L4086	From 420 (Snowy Owl) Squadron RCAF. Converted for use as torpedo bomber.
L4140 EQ-B-	From 16 Operational Training Unit. FTR from mining sortie 27/28.3.42.
L4204	From 185 Squadron. To 14 Operational Training Unit.
P1165 EQ-B	FTR Hüls 28/29.12.41.
P1166	From 144 Squadron. Converted for use as torpedo bomber.
P1212 EQ-T	Crashed on approach to Coningsby on return from Bremen 20/21.10.41.
P1218 EQ-Q	FTR Mannheim 22/23.10.41.
P1244 EQ-Y	From 455 Squadron RAAF. FTR Kassel 27/28.8.42.
P1314	From 420 (Snowy Owl) Squadron RCAF. Converted for use as torpedo bomber. To 1402 Flight.
P2064 EQ-A	From 14 Operational Training Unit. Converted for use as torpedo bomber. To 415 (Swordfish) Squadron RCAF.
P2073	From 106 Squadron. Converted for use as torpedo bomber. To 5 Operational Training Unit.
P5321	From 44 (Rhodesia) Squadron. To 14 Operational Training Unit.
P5334	From 7 Aircraft Assembly Unit. To 1406 Flight.
P5392 EQ-W	From 7 Aircraft Assembly Unit. Crashed in Hampshire on return from Cherbourg 15.12.41.
X2989	From 61 Squadron. To 14 Operational Training Unit.
X3051 EQ-U	From 144 Squadron. FTR Bremen 21/22.1.42.
X3140 EQ-B	From 61 Squadron. Converted for use as torpedo bomber. To 455 Squadron RAAF.
AD754 EQ-Y	To 144 Squadron and back via 61 Squadron. Converted for use as torpedo bomber. To 32 Operational Training Unit.
AD758	From 44 (Rhodesia) Squadron. To 14 Operational Training Unit.
AD782 EQ-A	From 14 Operational Training Unit. Crashed soon after take-off from Balderton for Brest 25.1.42.
AD803 EQ-L	From 106 Squadron. FTR from mining sortie 15/16.5.42.
AD829 EQ-E	From 455 Squadron RAAF. FTR Saarbrücken 28/29.8.42.
AD842 EQ-O	From 49 Squadron. Crashed soon after take-off from North Luffenham when bound for a mining sortie 9.3.42.
AD853	From 420 (Snowy Owl) Squadron RCAF. To 1 Air Armament School.
AD857	From 106 Squadron. To 7 Ferry Pilots School.
AD870 EQ-X	From 83 Squadron. Converted for use as torpedo bomber.
AD960	From 420 (Snowy Owl) Squadron RCAF. To 1402 Flight.
AD963	From 61 Squadron. Converted for use as torpedo bomber. To 489 Squadron RNZAF.
AD968	From 49 Squadron. Struck off Charge 3.2.44.

AD972	To 5 Group Training Flight.
AD980 EQ-Y	Crashed near Balderton during air-test 6.6.42.
AD982	From 44 (Rhodesia) Squadron. Converted for use as torpedo bomber. To Aeroplane &Armaments Experimental Establishment.
AD987	From 25 Operational Training Unit. Converted for use as torpedo bomber. To 144 Squadron.
AE139	From 25 Operational Training Unit. Crashed in Berkshire during transit 26.3.42.
AE148 EQ-B-	From 16 Operational Training Unit. FTR from mining sortie 11/12.12.41.
AE150 EQ-M	From 25 Operational Training Unit. FTR Mainz 12/13.8.42.
AE186	From 106 Squadron. To 14 Operational Training Unit.
AE190	From 25 Operational Training Unit. To 14 Operational Training Unit.
AE192	From 44 (Rhodesia) Squadron. To 14 Operational Training Unit.
AE196	To 44 (Rhodesia) Squadron.
AE197	FTR Saarbrücken 28/29.8.42.
AE219 EQ-R	From 61 Squadron. FTR from mining sortie 27/28.3.42.
AE227 EQ-D	From 49 Squadron. FTR Saarbrücken 28/29.8.42.
AE237 EQ-X	From 83 Squadron. FTR from mining sortie 22/23.4.42.
AE244 EQ-P	FTR Düsseldorf 31.7/1.8.42.
AE245	Converted for use as torpedo bomber. To 5 Operational Training Unit.
AE258	From 420 (Snowy Owl) Squadron RCAF. Converted for use as torpedo bomber. To 1 Air Armaments School.
AE264	From 455 Squadron RAAF. To 1404 Flight.
AE267	To 420 (Snowy Owl) Squadron RCAF.
AE286 EQ-T	From 61 Squadron. FTR Wilhelmshaven 10/11.1.42.
AE287	Converted for use as torpedo bomber. To 455 Squadron RAAF.
AE288 EQ-H	From 61 Squadron. FTR Warnemünde 8/9.5.42.
AE293	From 106 Squadron. Converted for use as torpedo bomber. To 455 Squadron RAAF.
AE295	From 5 Group Training Flight. To 14 Operational Training Unit.
AE297 EQ-F	From 207 Squadron. FTR Warnemünde 8/9.5.42.
AE360	Converted for use as torpedo bomber. To 415 (Swordfish) Squadron RCAF.
AE361	Converted for use as torpedo bomber. To Torpedo Development Unit.
AE366 EQ-U	From 420 (Snowy Owl) Squadron RCAF. Crash-landed at Lakenheath on return from Duisburg 7.8.42. To 5 Operational Training Unit.
AE372	From 49 Squadron. Converted for use as torpedo bomber. To 415 (Snowy Owl) Squadron RCAF.
AE373	From 50 Squadron. Converted for use as torpedo bomber. To Naval Air Fighting Development Unit.
AE375	From 50 Squadron. Converted for use as torpedo bomber. To 415 (Swordfish) Squadron RCAF.
AE378	From 420 (Snowy Owl) Squadron RCAF. Converted for use as torpedo bomber. To 455 Squadron RAAF.
AE385	From 420 (Snowy Owl) Squadron RCAF. Crashed at Balderton during training 12.9.42.

AE393 EQ-G	From 420 (Snowy Owl) Squadron RCAF. Crashed in Yorkshire on return from Hamburg 16.1.42.
AE418	Converted for use as torpedo bomber. To 415 (Swordfish) Squadron RCAF.
AE426	From 106 Squadron. FTR Kiel 28/29.4.42.
AE432 EQ-S	FTR Düsseldorf 15/16.8.42.
AE433 EQ-D	FTR Essen 8/9.11.41.
AE436 EQ-C	Converted for use as torpedo bomber. To 144 Squadron.
AE437 EQ-U	FTR Düsseldorf 27/28.11.41.
AE438 EQ-N	FTR Ostend 9/10.11.41.
AE439	To Aeroplane & Armaments Experimental Establishment.
AT113 EQ-A	From 455 Squadron RAAF. Crashed near Balderton during air-test 29.7.42.
AT120	FTR Essen 12/13.4.42.
AT133 EQ-X	FTR Cherbourg 14/15.12.41.
AT138	Converted for use as torpedo bomber. To 144 Squadron.
AT139 EQ-A-	From 50 Squadron. FTR Duisburg 21/22.7.42.
AT141	From 106 Squadron. FTR Dortmund 14/15.4.42.
AT143	From 144 Squadron. Crashed on landing at Booker on return from Saarbrücken 28/29.8.42.
AT154 EQ-B	FTR Essen 2/3.6.42.
AT176 EQ-A	FTR from mining sortie 27/28.3.42.
AT178	From 49 Squadron. To 1404 Flight.
AT179	From 49 Squadron. Converted for use as torpedo bomber. To 455 Squadron RAAF.
AT180 EQ-B	From 49 Squadron. To 1404 Flight.
AT182 EQ-G	From 455 Squadron RAAF. To 1404 Flight
AT186	Crashed in Nottinghamshire while training 11.4.42.
AT189 EQ-G	From 455 Squadron RAAF. FTR from mining sortie 18/19.6.42.
AT191 EQ-A	From 49 Squadron. FTR Essen 1/2.6.42.
AT220 EQ-G	Destroyed by fire at Balderton 3.6.42.
AT224 EQ-A	FTR from mining sortie 15/16.5.42.
AT225	From 420 Squadron. To 1404 Flight.
AT227 EQ-L	From 49 Squadron. FTR from Anti-shipping operation 19.7.42.
AT228 EQ-U	From 420 (Snowy Owl) Squadron RCAF. FTR Saarbrücken 28/29.8.42.

MANCHESTER. **May 1942.**

L7401 EQ-A Bar/N	To 44 (Rhodesia) Squadron.
L7415	Training only. To 44 (Rhodesia) Squadron.
R5776	From 1654 Conversion Unit. Training only. To 1654 Conversion Unit.
R5835	From 50 Squadron. Training only. To 1654 Conversion Unit.

HALIFAX II   **From October 1942 to August 1943.**

L9524	From 1659 Conversion Unit. Conversion Flight only. Became ground instruction machine.
L9532	From 102 (Ceylon) Squadron. Conversion Flight only. To 1659 Conversion Unit.
R9363	From 405 Conversion Flight. Conversion Flight only. To 1659 Conversion Unit.
R9382	From 76 Conversion Flight. Conversion Flight only. To 1659 Conversion Unit.
BB311 EQ-L	FTR Stuttgart 14/15.4.43.
BB332 EQ-H	FTR Berlin 27/28.3.43.
BB336 EQ-O	FTR Kiel 4/5.4.43.
BB343 EQ-X	FTR Pilsen 16/17.4.43.
BB375 EQ-T	FTR Krefeld 21/22.6.43.
DG231	To 1663 Conversion Unit.
DG233	To 1659 Conversion Unit and back. To 518 Squadron.
DG234	To 1659 Conversion Unit.
DG235	To 1659 Conversion Unit and back. To Rolls Royce.
DG236	To 1663 Conversion Unit.
DG237	To 518 Squadron.
DG238	Crashed near Croft during fighter affiliation exercise 9.11.42.
DG239	To 1659 Conversion Unit.
DG240	To 518 Squadron.
DG241	To 1668 Conversion Unit.
DG242	Struck off Charge 28.4.45.
DG243	To 1668 Conversion Unit.
DG246	To 1663 Conversion Unit.
DG247	To 1664 Conversion Unit.
DG248	To 1663 Conversion Unit.
DG249	To Rotol.
DG253	To 138 Squadron.
DG227	To 1663 Conversion Unit.
DT546	From 10 Squadron. To 1659 Conversion Unit.
DT673 EQ-G/A	Crash-landed at Leeming on return from Essen 4.4.43.
DT674 EQ-A	FTR Essen 27/28.5.43.
DT675	To 1656 Conversion Unit.
DT676 EQ-B	To 1659 Conversion Unit.
DT677 EQ-P	To 1659 Conversion Unit.
DT678 EQ-C	Crash-landed in Nottinghamshire on return from Lorient 23.1.43.
DT679 EQ-Q	FTR Berlin 29/30.3.43.
DT680 EQ-D	FTR Hamburg 3/4.2.43.
DT682 EQ-F	Crashed in Nottinghamshire soon after take-off during transit 2.2.43.
DT749 EQ-C	FTR Hamburg 27/28.7.43.
DT750 EQ-U	Crashed in Yorkshire on return from Cologne 14.2.43.
DT752 EQ-W	FTR Pilsen 16/17.4.43.

DT769 EQ-J		FTR Aachen 13/14.7.43.
DT772 EQ-F/E		From 405 (Vancouver) Squadron RCAF. FTR Krefeld 21/22.6.43.
DT781 EQ-D		To 1668 Conversion Unit.
DT790 EQ-S		Crashed near Leeming on return from Essen 13.3.43.
DT797 EQ-H		FTR Berlin 1/2.3.43.
HR654 EQ-R		FTR Berlin 29/30.3.43.
HR655 EQ-S		FTR Lorient 7/8.2.43.
HR656 EQ-T		FTR Stuttgart 11/12.3.43.
HR657		To 78 Squadron.
HR658 EQ-V		FTR Dortmund 4/5.5.43.
HR659		To 78 Squadron.
HR662 EQ-H		FTR Lorient 29/30.1.43.
HR664		To 78 Squadron.
HR713 EQ-F		FTR Essen 3/4.4.43.
JB790 EQ-V		FTR Bochum 12/13.6.43.
JB796 EQ-C		FTR Cologne 3/4.7.43.
JB841 EQ-K		FTR Dortmund 23/24.5.43.
JB854 EQ-D		FTR Pilsen 16/17.4.43.
JB858 EQ-S		FTR Gelsenkirchen 25/26.6.43.
JB866 EQ-T		FTR Essen 3/4.4.43.
JB893 EQ-U		From 405 (Vancouver) Squadron RCAF. To 429 (Bison) Squadron RCAF.
JB898 EQ-Q		FTR Dortmund 4/5.5.43.
JB909 EQ-G		FTR Stuttgart 14/15.4.43.
JB913 EQ-F		FTR Cologne 3/4.7.43.
JB922 EQ-H		FTR Gelsenkirchen 9/10.7.43.
JB925 EQ-R		FTR Pilsen 16/17.4.43.
JB931 EQ-O		FTR Bochum 13/14.5.43.
JB959 EQ-L		Crashed on take-off from Leeming when bound for Gelsenkirchen 9.7.43.
JB967 EQ-X		To 429 (Bison) Squadron RCAF.
JB968 EQ-R		To 429 (Bison) Squadron RCAF.
JB969 EQ-D		To 429 (Bison) Squadron RCAF.
JB971 EQ-W		To 429 (Bison) Squadron RCAF.
JB972 EQ-Q		FTR Düsseldorf 11/12.6.43.
JD107 EQ-Y		FTR Le Creusot 19/20.6.43.
JD164 EQ-K		To 429 (Bison) Squadron RCAF.
JD174 EQ-A		Abandoned near Leeming following early return from Aachen 14.7.43.
JD209 EQ-B		FTR Krefeld 21/22.6.43.
JD216 EQ-P		FTR Gelsenkirchen 9/10.7.43.
JD268 EQ-V		To 429 (Bison) Squadron RCAF.
JD271 EQ-B		To 429 (Bison) Squadron RCAF.
JD274 EQ-Q		To 429 (Bison) Squadron RCAF.
JD275		To 429 (Bison) Squadron RCAF.
JD278 EQ-O		To 429 (Bison) Squadron RCAF.
JD317 EQ-C		To 429 (Bison) Squadron RCAF.
JD318 EQ-F		To 429 (Bison) Squadron RCAF.

JD323 EQ-S	To 429 (Bison) Squadron RCAF.	
JD326 EQ-P	To 429 (Bison) Squadron RCAF.	
JD327 EQ-H	To 429 (Bison) Squadron RCAF.	
JD332 EQ-E	To 429 (Bison) Squadron RCAF.	
JD333 EQ-G	To 429 (Bison) Squadron RCAF.	
JD361 EQ-Y	To 429 (Bison) Squadron RCAF.	
JD363 EQ-A	To 429 (Bison) Squadron RCAF.	
JD365 EQ-J	FTR Remscheid 30/31.7.43.	
JD372 EQ-E	To 429 (Bison) Squadron RCAF.	
JD374 EQ-M	To 429 (Bison) Squadron RCAF.	
JD384	To 429 (Bison) Squadron RCAF.	
JD386	To 429 (Bison) Squadron RCAF.	
JD411	To 429 (Bison) Squadron RCAF.	
JD412	To 102 (Ceylon) Squadron.	
JD419	To 1659 Conversion Unit.	

LANCASTER II. **From August 1943 to July 1944.**

DS601	From 1679 Conversion Unit. To 1668 Conversion Unit.
DS614 EQ-U	From 115 Squadron via 1678 and 1668 Conversion Units.
DS621 EQ-O	From 426 (Thunderbird) Squadron RCAF via 1666 Conversion Unit. Force-landed in Yorkshire while training 2.7.44.
DS626	From 426 (Thunderbird) Squadron RCAF. To 1668 Conversion Unit.
DS631 EQ-D/I	From 115 Squadron via 1668 Conversion Unit. To 1668 Conversion Unit.
DS632 EQ-I/O	
DS634 EQ-A	From 426 (Thunderbird) Squadron RCAF. FTR Hamburg 28/29.7.44.
DS651 EQ-I/Q	From 426 (Thunderbird) Squadron RCAF via 1679 Conversion Unit.
DS656	From 426 (Thunderbird) Squadron RCAF. Crashed on take-off at Linton-on-Ouse while training 10.6.44.
DS657 EQ-L	From 426 (Thunderbird) Squadron RCAF via 1679 Conversion Unit. To 1668 Conversion Unit.
DS688 EQ-R	From 426 (Thunderbird) Squadron RCAF via 1679 and 1666 Conversion Units. FTR Cambrai 12/13.6.44.
DS692 EQ-S	From 426 (Thunderbird) Squadron RCAF. Crashed on landing at Marston Moor following early return from Kiel 23/24.7.44.
DS704 EQ-W	FTR Frankfurt 20/21.12.43.
DS705 EQ-K	Crashed on approach to Dalton while training 23.7.43.
DS707 EQ-C/D/M	From 426 (Thunderbird) Squadron RCAF. To 1668 Conversion Unit.
DS708 EQ-A	From 426 (Thunderbird) Squadron RCAF. To Short Bros.
DS709 EQ-K/P	From 426 (Thunderbird) Squadron RCAF. FTR Berlin 27/28.1.44.
DS710 EQ-H/A	From 426 (Thunderbird) Squadron RCAF. FTR Berlin 27/28.1.44.
DS712 EQ-G	Crash-landed near Lincoln on return from Berlin 27.11.43.
DS718 EQ-R	From 426 (Thunderbird) Squadron RCAF. FTR Berlin 29/30.12.43.
DS719 EQ-U	From 426 (Thunderbird) Squadron RCAF. FTR Essen 26/27.4.44.
DS723 EQ-B/D	FTR Berlin 26/27.11.43.
DS724 EQ-C/X	Abandoned soon after take-off when bound for Stuttgart 7.10.43.

DS725 EQ-B	To 115 Squadron.	
DS726 EQ-E/T/Y	From 426 (Thunderbird) Squadron RCAF. FTR Cambrai 12/13.6.44.	
DS727 EQ-A/O/X	From 426 (Thunderbird) Squadron RCAF. To 1668 Conversion Unit.	
DS729 EQ-D/H	From 426 (Thunderbird) Squadron RCAF. Struck off Charge 29.3.45.	
DS730 EQ-K/V	To 1679 and 1666 Conversion Units and back. To 1668 Conversion Unit.	
DS731 EQ-U/O	FTR Schweinfurt 24/25.2.44.	
DS732 EQ-F	Crash-landed in Yorkshire during fighter affiliation exercise 7.9.43.	
DS737 EQ-C	Crashed in Yorkshire on return from Berlin 16.12.43.	
DS739	To 432 (Leaside) Squadron RCAF via 1679 Conversion Unit.	
DS758 EQ-H	FTR Frankfurt 20/21.12.43.	
DS759 EQ-A	From 426 (Thunderbird) Squadron RCAF. FTR Dortmund 22/23.5.44.	
DS761 EQ-J/S/V	From 115 Squadron. To 46 Maintenance Unit.	
DS763 EQ-E	From 426 (Thunderbird) Squadron RCAF. To 1668 Conversion Unit.	
DS767 EQ-Q	FTR Brunswick 14/15.1.44.	
DS768 EQ-J	Written off in landing accident in Worcestershire on return from Coutances 6/7.6.44.	
DS769 EQ-J	To 115 Squadron.	
DS770 EQ-F	To 426 (Thunderbird) Squadron RCAF.	
DS771	To 426 (Thunderbird) Squadron RCAF.	
DS772 EQ-T	To 426 (Thunderbird) Squadron RCAF and back. FTR Cambrai 12/13.6.44.	
DS774 EQ-F	FTR Düsseldorf 3/4.11.43.	
DS775	To 426 (Thunderbird) Squadron RCAF.	
DS776	To 426 (Thunderbird) Squadron RCAF.	
DS778 EQ-U	FTR Kassel 22/23.10.43.	
DS788 EQ-C	From 432 (Leaside) Squadron RCAF. FTR Leipzig 19/20.2.44.	
DS790 EQ-B	FTR Magdeburg 21/22.1.44.	
DS791 EQ-F	FTR Augsburg 25/26.2.44.	
DS797 EQ-H/M	FTR Frankfurt 22/23.3.44.	
DS830 EQ-H/W	From 426 (Thunderbird) Squadron RCAF. To 1668 Conversion Unit.	
DS838 EQ-A/I	From 426 (Thunderbird) Squadron RCAF. To 1668 Conversion Unit.	
DS841 EQ-Q/X	From 426 (Thunderbird) Squadron RCAF. To 1668 Conversion Unit.	
DS844 EQ-X	From 432 (Leaside) Squadron RCAF. FTR Schweinfurt 24/25.2.44.	
DS845 EQ-V/T	Flew 11 Berlin operations. FTR Augsburg 25/26.2.44.	
DS846	To 426 (Thunderbird) Squadron RCAF.	
DS848 EQ-D/X	From 426 (Thunderbird) Squadron RCAF. To 1668 Conversion Unit.	
DS849 EQ-X	FTR Berlin 27/28.1.44.	
LL617 EQ-F/P	From 426 (Thunderbird) Squadron RCAF. To 1668 Conversion Unit.	
LL621 EQ-Y	From 426 (Thunderbird) Squadron RCAF. To 1668 Conversion Unit.	
LL623 EQ-J/U	FTR Berlin 23/24.11.43.	
LL631 EQ-G	FTR Berlin 2/3.1.44.	
LL632 EQ-G	From 432 (Leaside) Squadron RCAF. FTR Leipzig 19/20.2.44.	
LL633 EQ-L	FTR Nuremberg 30/31.3.44.	
LL634 EQ-F	From 426 (Thunderbird) Squadron RCAF. To 1668 Conversion Unit.	
LL636 EQ-G	Destroyed on the ground at Bottesford 6.1.45.	
LL637 EQ-P	From 432 (Leaside) Squadron RCAF. FTR Stuttgart 15/16.3.44.	

LL642 EQ-B		To 1668 Conversion Unit.
LL643 EQ-Q		FTR Acheres 7/8.6.44.
LL675 EQ-K/M/T		From 426 (Thunderbird) Squadron RCAF. Crashed in Leicestershire while training 11.7.44.
LL676 EQ-E		FTR Berlin 16/17.12.43.
LL687 EQ-M/H		From 115 Squadron via 426 (Thunderbird) Squadron RCAF. FTR Hamburg 28/29.7.44.
LL699 EQ-C		FTR Braunschweig 14/15.1.44.
LL700 EQ-J/R/X		From 426 (Thunderbird) Squadron RCAF. To 1668 Conversion Unit.
LL717 EQ-F/W		FTR Frankfurt 22/23.3.44.
LL718 EQ-E		From 432 (Leaside) Squadron RCAF. FTR Stuttgart 15/16.3.44.
LL719 EQ-V		From 432 (Leaside) Squadron RCAF. FTR Leipzig 19/20.2.44.
LL720 EQ-R		FTR Leipzig 19/20.2.44.
LL722 EQ-N		To 1668 Conversion Unit.
LL723 EQ-H		From 432 (Leaside) Squadron RCAF. FTR Dortmund 22/23.5.44.
LL724		From 432 (Leaside) Squadron RCAF. FTR Magdeburg 21/22.1.44.
LL725 EQ-Z/C		From 432 (Leaside) Squadron RCAF. FTR Hamburg 28/29.7.44.

HALIFAX III-VII   **From July 1944 to May 1945.**

LK201		From 426 (Thunderbird) Squadron RCAF.
LW207		From 426 (Thunderbird) Squadron RCAF.
MZ421 EQ-N		From 434 (Blue Nose) Squadron RCAF. To 425 (Allouette) Squadron RCAF.
MZ435		From 434 (Blue Nose) Squadron RCAF. Returned to 434 (Blue Nose) Squadron RCAF
MZ495 EQ-V		From 434 (Blue Nose) Squadron RCAF. To 425 (Allouette) Squadron RCAF.
MZ904 EQ-G		From 427 (Lion) Squadron RCAF. To 431 (Iroquois) Squadron RCAF.
MZ907 EQ-D		From 429 (Bison) Squadron RCAF. To 434 (Blue Nose) Squadron RCAF.
MZ908 EQ-M		From 429 (Bison) Squadron RCAF. To 434 (Blue Nose) Squadron RCAF.
NP685		From 426 (Thunderbird) Squadron RCAF.
NP710 EQ-S		From 432 (Leaside) Squadron RCAF. Crashed on landing at Linton-on-Ouse following early return from Castrop-Rauxel 11.9.44.
NP711 EQ-O		From 426 (Thunderbird) Squadron RCAF. FTR Worms 21/22.2.45.
NP712 EQ-R/N		From 432 (Leaside) Squadron RCAF. FTR Harburg 4/5.4.45.
NP713 EQ-X		From 426 (Thunderbird) Squadron RCAF. Crashed on landing at East Moor on return from Foret de Chantilly 7/8.8.44.
NP714 EQ-V		From 426 (Thunderbird) Squadron RCAF.
NP716 EQ-P		From 432 (Leaside) Squadron RCAF. FTR Hamburg 28/29.7.44.
NP717 EQ-W		From 426 (Thunderbird) Squadron RCAF.
NP718 EQ-Z/B		From 432 (Leaside) Squadron RCAF. FTR Hemmingstedt 7/8.3.45.
NP737		From 624 Squadron.
NP740		From 426 (Thunderbird) Squadron RCAF.
NP742 EQ-U		
NP743 EQ-K		FTR Stuttgart 28/29.1.45.

NP744 EQ-X	FTR Düsseldorf 2/3.11.44.
NP745 EQ-H	Abandoned over Cumberland while training 17.10.44.
NP746 EQ-E	FTR Stuttgart 28/29.1.45.
NP747 EQ-N	
NP749 EQ-Y	
NP750 EQ-F	FTR Bochum 4/5.11.44.
NP751 EQ-L	
NP754 EQ-P	To 415 (Swordfish) Squadron RCAF.
NP756 EQ-T	
NP757 EQ-B	Abandoned over Lincolnshire while bound for Wanne-Eickel 2.2.45.
NP761 EQ-A	FTR Gelsenkirchen 6.11.44.
NP768 EQ-Q	To 426 (Thunderbird) Squadron RCAF.
NP769 EQ-D	FTR Hamburg 8/9.4.45.
NP770 EQ-G	FTR Münster 18.11.44.
NP771 EQ-S	To 426 (Thunderbird) Squadron RCAF.
NP772 EQ-Q	
NP773 EQ-M	FTR Wilhelmshaven 15/16.10.44.
NP775	To 426 (Thunderbird) Squadron RCAF.
NP776 EQ-R	FTR Heligoland 18.4.45.
NP777 EQ-S	
NP780 EQ-N	
NP781 EQ-U	FTR Düsseldorf airfield (Lohausen) 24.12.44.
NP796 EQ-M	Collided with NP820 of 426 (Thunderbird) Squadron RCAF and FTR Wangerooge 25.4.45.
NP798 EQ-J	Caught fire and blew up at Linton-on-Ouse while being prepared for operations 14.1.45.
NP804 EQ-K	From 432 (Leaside) Squadron RCAF. FTR Münster 25.3.45.
NP806 EQ-Q	FTR Hamburg 31.3.45.
NP807 EQ-E	From 432 (Leaside) Squadron RCAF.
NP809 EQ-G	
NP810 EQ-H	From 426 (Thunderbird) Squadron RCAF. FTR Castrop-Rauxel 21/22.11.44.
NP811	From 426 (Thunderbird) Squadron RCAF. Returned to 426 (Thunderbird) Squadron RCAF.
NP813	From 426 (Thunderbird) Squadron RCAF.
NP814	From 426 (Thunderbird) Squadron RCAF.
NP819	To 426 (Thunderbird) Squadron RCAF.
NP820	To 426 (Thunderbird) Squadron RCAF.
NR116 EQ-L	From 426 (Thunderbird) Squadron RCAF. To 425 (Allouette) Squadron RCAF.
NR124 EQ-H	From 434 (Blue Nose) Squadron RCAF. To 415 (Swordfish) Squadron RCAF.
NR126 EQ-Z	From 434 (Blue Nose) Squadron RCAF. To 420 (Snowy Owl) Squadron RCAF.
NR199 EQ-F	From 434 (Blue Nose) Squadron RCAF. To 420 (Snowy Owl) Squadron RCAF and back. To 415 (Swordfish) Squadron RCAF.

NR209 EQ-A		From 425 (Allouette) Squadron RCAF. To 425 (Allouette) Squadron RCAF and back. FTR Hanover 5/6.1.45.
PN208		To 432 (Leaside) Squadron RCAF.
PN223 EQ-X		
PN225 EQ-J		
PN227 EQ-B		From 426 (Thunderbird) Squadron RCAF.
PN230 EQ-V		
PN232 EQ-O		
PN234		
PN240		To 415 (Swordfish) Squadron RCAF.
RG450		To 432 (Leaside) Squadron RCAF.
RG453 EQ-Z		From 426 (Thunderbird) Squadron RCAF.
RG472 EQ-T		FTR Cologne 2.3.45.
RG473 EQ-H		
RG474 EQ-L		
RG477 EQ-N		FTR Worms 21/22.2.45.

HEAVIEST SINGLE LOSS.

28/29.08.42. Saarbrücken.	4 Hampdens FTR.
16/17.04.43. Pilsen.	4 Halifaxes FTR.
19/20.02.44. Leipzig.	4 Lancasters FTR.
28/29.07.44. Hamburg.	3 Lancasters 1 Halifax FTR.

www.ingramcontent.com/pod-product-compliance
Lightning Source LLC
Chambersburg PA
CBHW080238170426
43192CB00014BA/2479